**Ordnanc**

CW00449045

ROAD ATLAS
Britain

Contents

1999 edition published by

Ordnance Survey and Philip's
Romsey Road — an imprint of Octopus
Maybush — Publishing Group Ltd
Southampton — 2–4 Heron Quays
SO16 4GU — London E14 4JP
www.ordsvy.gov.uk — www.philips-maps.co.uk

First edition 1999
First impression 1999

3 miles to 1 inch mapping; route planning map; M25
and routes into London and Central London map
© Crown Copyright 1999. Town plans; London urban
area; Scenic areas, cycling, walking map; Boundary
information map © Crown Copyright 1999 and
© George Philip Ltd 1999

Ordnance Survey is a registered trade mark and the
OS Symbol a trade mark of Ordnance Survey, the
national mapping agency of Great Britain.

The mapping between pages 2 and 177 (inclusive) in
this atlas is derived from the Ordnance Survey
1:250000 digital database.

The map detail is believed to be accurate at the date
of publication. However, the publishers cannot accept
responsibility for errors or omissions. The
representation in this atlas of a road is no evidence of
the existence of a right of way. Boundary information
on inside back cover as revised to 12.5.99 by
Ordnance Survey.

A catalogue record for this atlas is available from the
British Library.

ISBN 0 540 07814 X

Printed and bound in Spain

Inside front cover: **Legend to 3-mile mapping**

II **Route planning**
Restricted motorway junctions

VIII **Distances chart**

1 **Key to 3-mile map pages**
2 **Ordnance Survey 3 miles to 1 inch maps**

178 **London**
178 *London urban area*
182 *Central London*

186 **Town plans**
186 *Aberdeen, Bath, Birmingham*
187 *Blackpool, Bournemouth,*
Bradford, Brighton
188 *Bristol, Cambridge, Canterbury*
189 *Cardiff, Cheltenham, Chester*
190 *Coventry, Croydon, Derby, Dundee*
191 *Durham, Edinburgh, Exeter*
192 *Glasgow, Gloucester, Hull*
193 *Leeds, Liverpool*
194 *Leicester, Manchester, Middlesbrough*
195 *Milton Keynes, Newcastle, Oxford*
196 *Norwich, Nottingham*
197 *Peterborough, Plymouth,*
Portsmouth, Reading
198 *Salisbury, Sheffield, Shrewsbury*
199 *Southampton, Stratford, Swansea, York*

200 **Index**
230 **English Heritage and National Trust properties**

231 **Boundary information**
232 **Scenic areas, cycling, walking**

Inside back cover: **M25 and routes into London**

Ordnance Survey

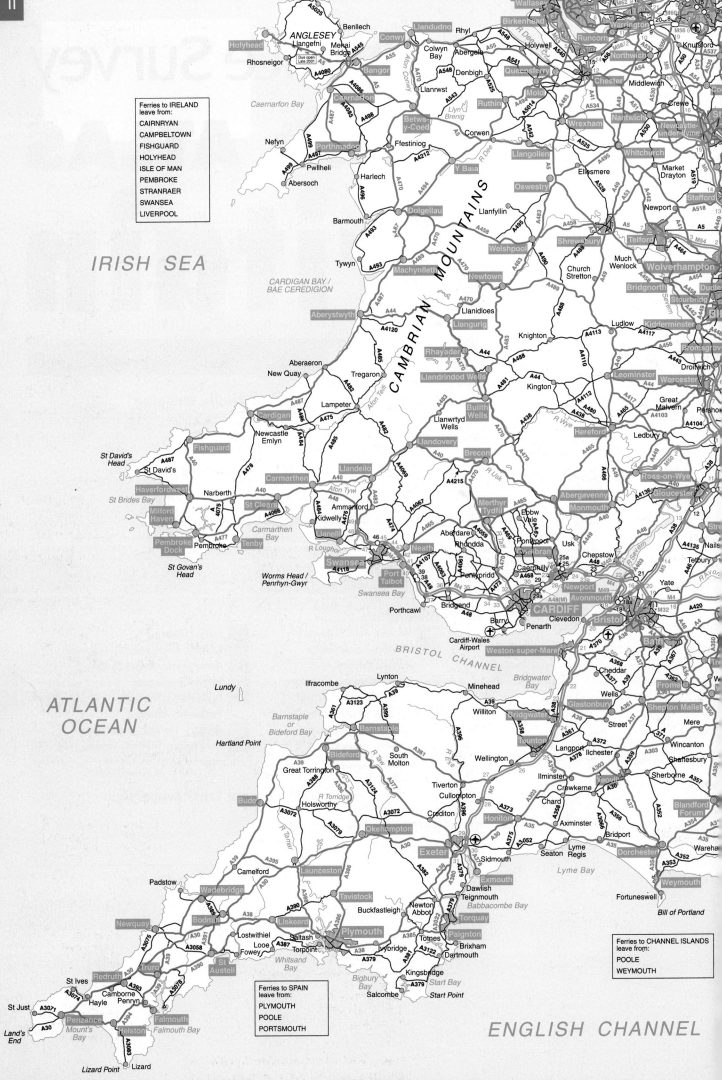

IRISH SEA

ATLANTIC OCEAN

ENGLISH CHANNEL

BRISTOL CHANNEL

CARDIGAN BAY / BAE CEREDIGION

Ferries to IRELAND leave from:
CAIRNRYAN
CAMPBELTOWN
FISHGUARD
HOLYHEAD
ISLE OF MAN
PEMBROKE
STRANRAER
SWANSEA
LIVERPOOL

Ferries to CHANNEL ISLANDS leave from:
POOLE
WEYMOUTH

Ferries to SPAIN leave from:
PLYMOUTH
POOLE
PORTSMOUTH

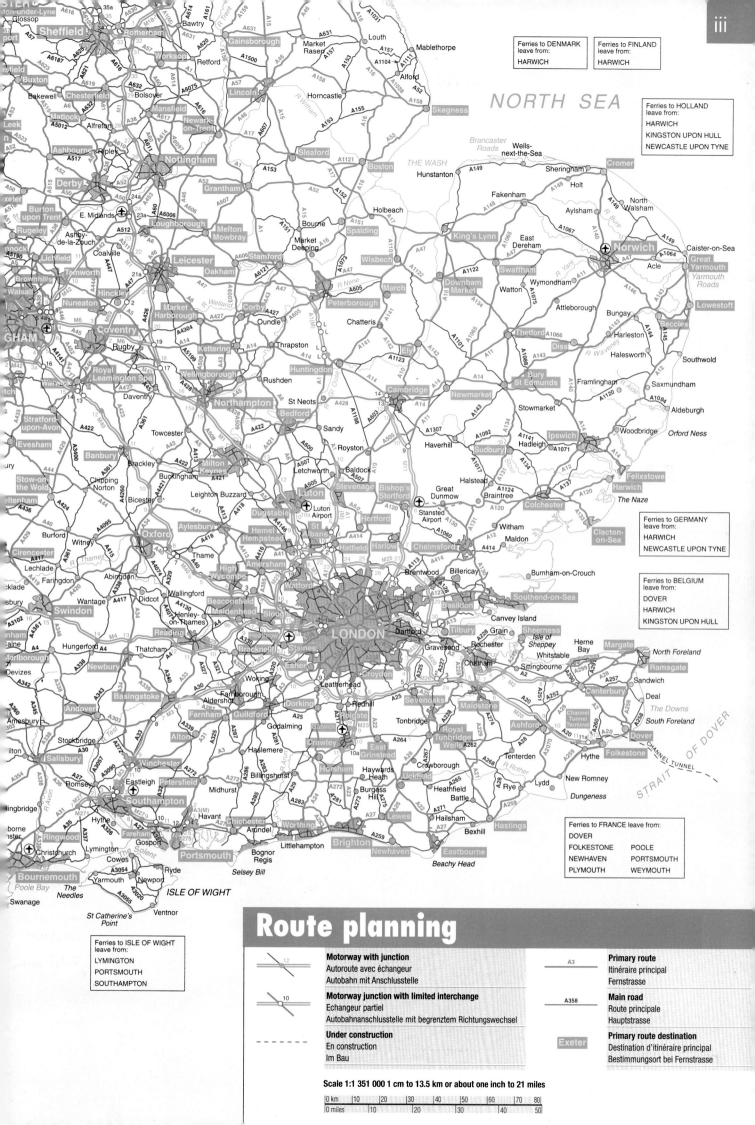

Route planning

	12	**Motorway with junction**	Autoroute avec échangeur	Autobahn mit Anschlusstelle
	10	**Motorway junction with limited interchange**	Echangeur partiel	Autobahnanschlusstelle mit begrenztem Richtungswechsel
		Under construction	En construction	Im Bau

A3	**Primary route**	Itinéraire principal	Fernstrasse
A358	**Main road**	Route principale	Hauptstrasse
Exeter	**Primary route destination**	Destination d'itinéraire principal	Bestimmungsort bei Fernstrasse

Scale 1:1 351 000 1 cm to 13.5 km or about one inch to 21 miles

0 km 10 20 30 40 50 60 70 80
0 miles 10 20 30 40 50

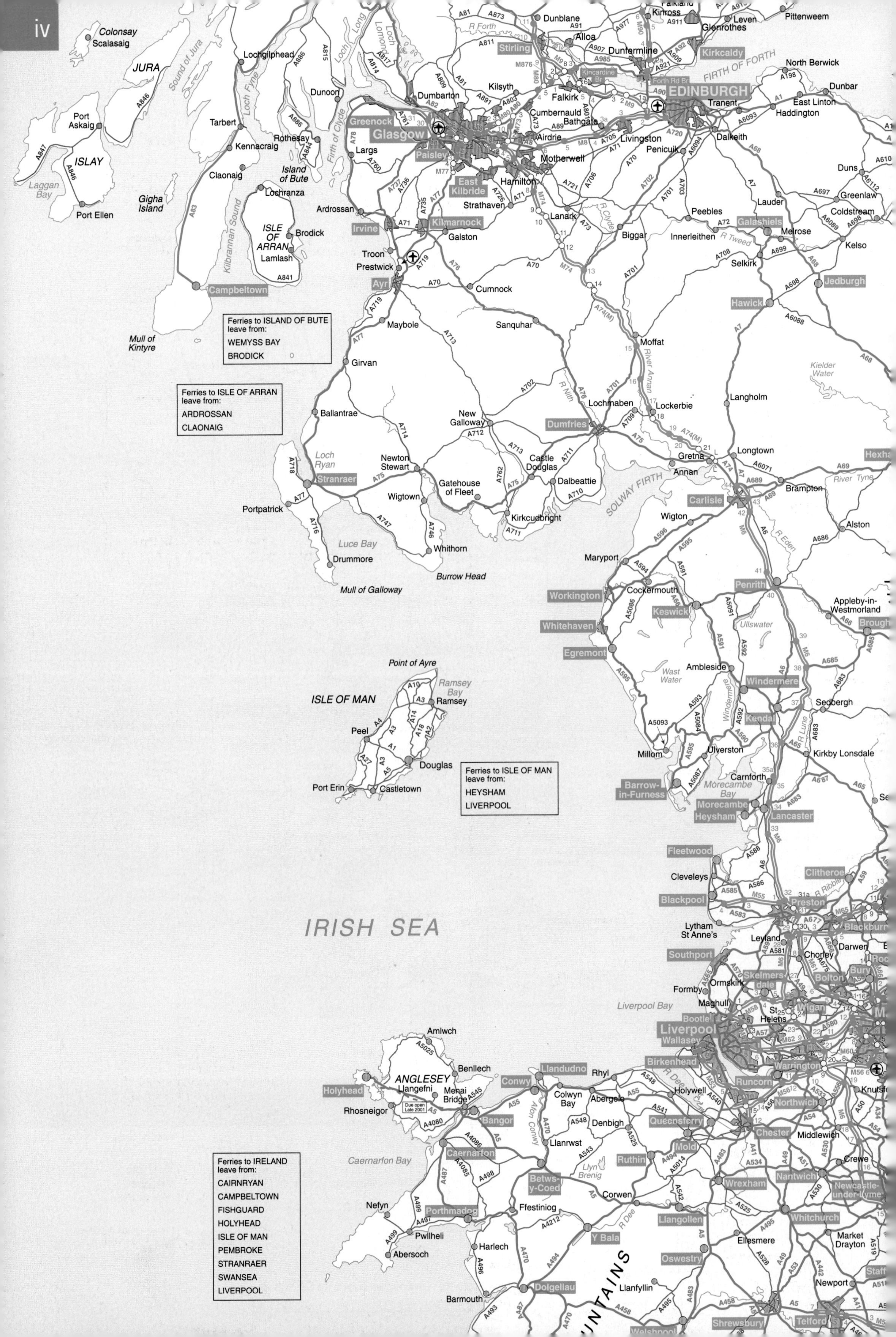
Ferries to ISLAND OF BUTE
leave from:
WEMYSS BAY
BRODICK
Ferries to ISLE OF ARRAN
leave from:
ARDROSSAN
CLAONAIG
Ferries to ISLE OF MAN
leave from:
HEYSHAM
LIVERPOOL
Ferries to IRELAND
leave from:
CAIRNRYAN
CAMPBELTOWN
FISHGUARD
HOLYHEAD
ISLE OF MAN
PEMBROKE
STRANRAER
SWANSEA
LIVERPOOL
IRISH SEA
Colonsay
Scalasaig
JURA
Sound of Jura
Port Askaig
ISLAY
Laggan Bay
Port Ellen
Lochgilphead
Tarbert
Loch Fyne
Kennacraig
Claonaig
Gigha Island
Kilbrannan Sound
Campbeltown
Mull of Kintyre
Dunoon
Rothesay
Island of Bute
Lochranza
ISLE OF ARRAN
Brodick
Lamlash
Firth of Clyde
Loch Long
Loch Lomond
Greenock
Glasgow
Paisley
Largs
Ardrossan
Irvine
Kilmarnock
Troon
Prestwick
Ayr
Maybole
Girvan
Ballantrae
Loch Ryan
Stranraer
Portpatrick
Luce Bay
Drummore
Mull of Galloway
Burrow Head
Whithorn
Wigtown
Newton Stewart
Gatehouse of Fleet
Kirkcudbright
Castle Douglas
Dalbeattie
New Galloway
Cumnock
Sanquhar
Galston
Dumbarton
Kilsyth
Stirling
Dunblane
Alloa
Dunfermline
Kinross
Glenrothes
Leven
Kirkcaldy
Pittenweem
FIRTH OF FORTH
North Berwick
Dunbar
EDINBURGH
Tranent
East Linton
Haddington
Dalkeith
Falkirk
Cumbernauld
Bathgate
Airdrie
Livingston
Penicuik
Motherwell
Hamilton
East Kilbride
Strathaven
Lanark
Biggar
Peebles
Innerleithen
Galashiels
Melrose
Lauder
Duns
Greenlaw
Coldstream
Kelso
Selkirk
Jedburgh
Hawick
Moffat
Kielder Water
Langholm
Lockerbie
Lochmaben
Dumfries
Gretna
Annan
Longtown
SOLWAY FIRTH
Carlisle
Brampton
Alston
Wigton
Maryport
Workington
Cockermouth
Whitehaven
Keswick
Penrith
Egremont
Appleby-in-Westmorland
Ullswater
Wast Water
Ambleside
Windermere
Kendal
Sedbergh
Millom
Ulverston
Barrow-in-Furness
Carnforth
Kirkby Lonsdale
Morecambe Bay
Morecambe
Heysham
Lancaster
Fleetwood
Cleveleys
Blackpool
Clitheroe
Preston
Lytham St Anne's
Leyland
Blackburn
Darwen
Chorley
Southport
Ormskirk
Skelmersdale
Bolton
Bury
Formby
Maghull
Wigan
St Helens
Liverpool Bay
Bootle
Liverpool
Wallasey
Birkenhead
Warrington
Runcorn
Northwich
Knutsford
Middlewich
Chester
Crewe
Nantwich
Whitchurch
Market Drayton
Newcastle-under-Lyme
Wrexham
Ellesmere
Oswestry
Shrewsbury
Telford
Newport
Point of Ayre
ISLE OF MAN
Ramsey Bay
Ramsey
Peel
Douglas
Port Erin
Castletown
Amlwch
ANGLESEY
Benllech
Holyhead
Llangefni
Menai Bridge
Rhosneigor
Due open Late 2001
Bangor
Caernarfon
Caernarfon Bay
Llandudno
Conwy
Colwyn Bay
Rhyl
Abergele
Holywell
Denbigh
Llanrwst
Ruthin
Mold
Queensferry
Betws-y-Coed
Llyn Brenig
Corwen
Llangollen
Ffestiniog
Porthmadog
Nefyn
Pwllheli
Abersoch
Harlech
Y Bala
Barmouth
Dolgellau
Llanfyllin
Welshpool
MOUNTAINS

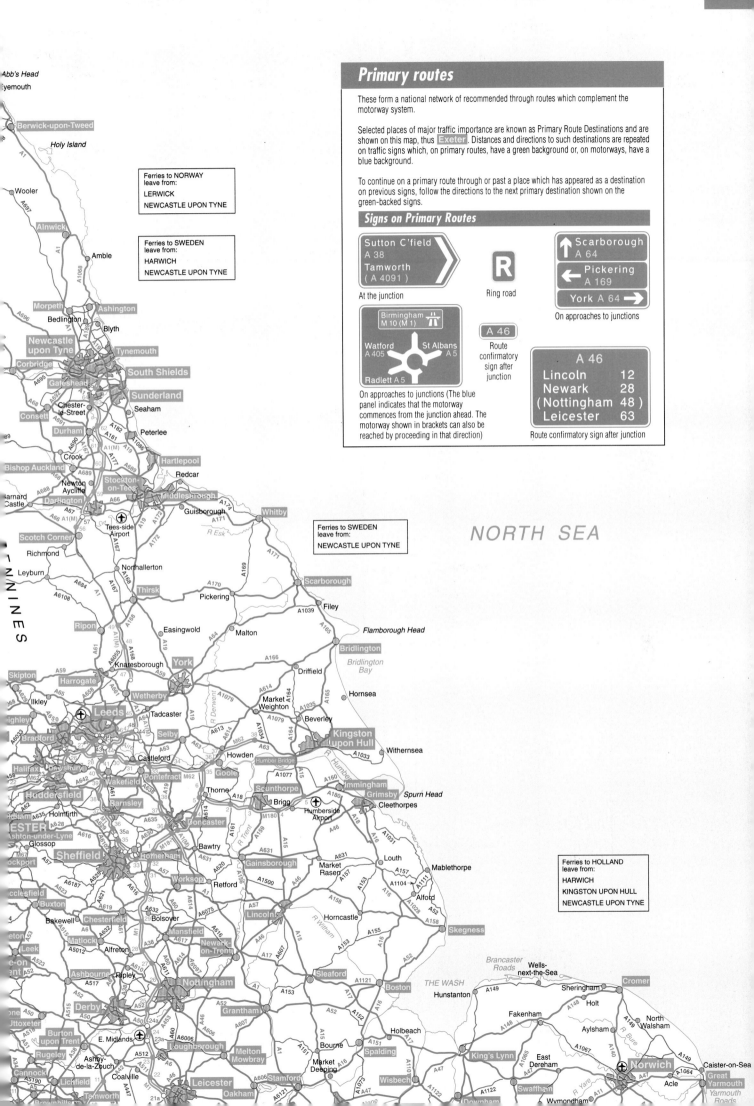

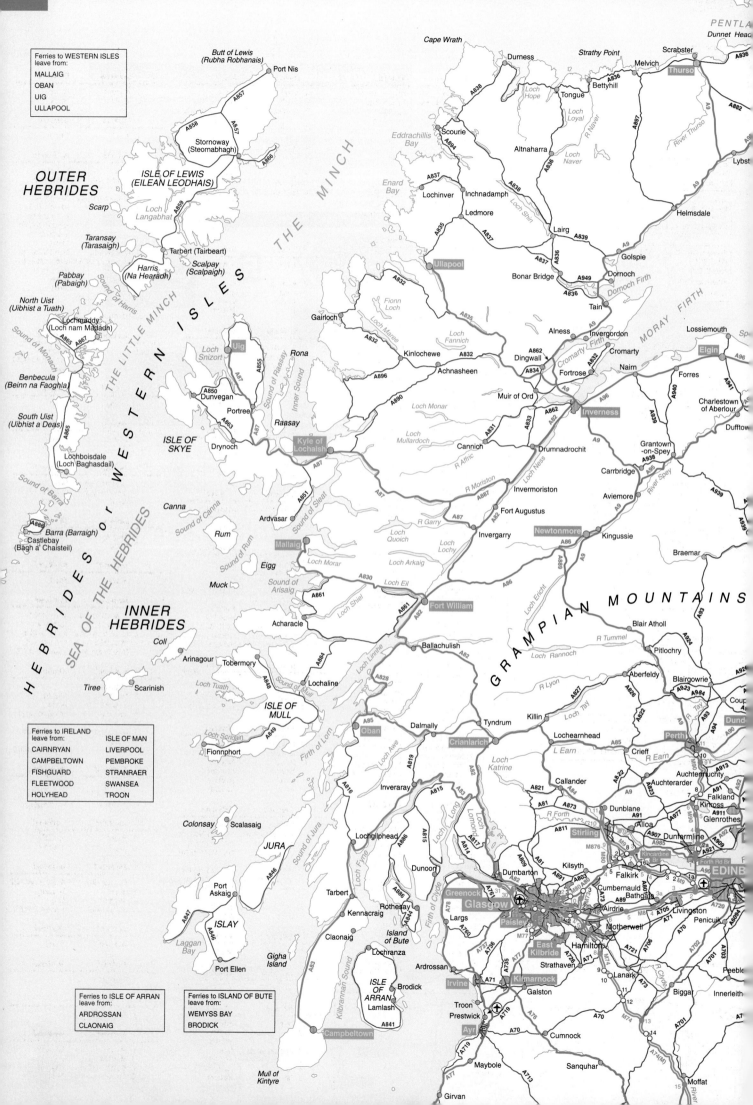

Ferries to WESTERN ISLES
leave from:

MALLAIG
OBAN
UIG
ULLAPOOL

Ferries to IRELAND
leave from:

CAIRNRYAN
CAMPBELTOWN
FISHGUARD
FLEETWOOD
HOLYHEAD

ISLE OF MAN

LIVERPOOL
PEMBROKE
STRANRAER
SWANSEA
TROON

Ferries to ISLE OF ARRAN
leave from:

ARDROSSAN
CLAONAIG

Ferries to ISLAND OF BUTE
leave from:

WEMYSS BAY
BRODICK

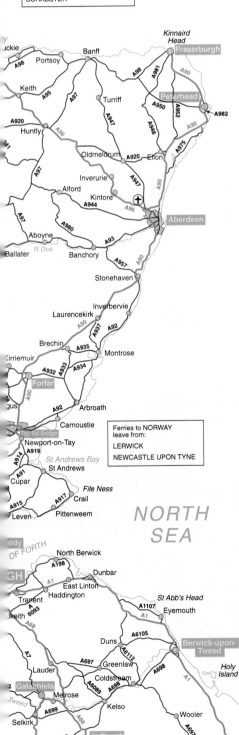

South Ronaldsay
FIRTH
Duncansby Head
John o' Groats
Sinclair's Bay
Wick

Ferries to FAROE ISLANDS leave from:
LERWICK (Shetland Islands)

Ferries to SHETLAND ISLANDS leave from:
Stromness (Orkney Islands)

Ferries to ORKNEY ISLANDS leave from:
ABERDEEN
INVERGORDON
SCRABSTER

Kinnaird Head
Fraserburgh
Banff
Portsoy
Keith
Turriff
Peterhead
Huntly
Oldmeldrum
Elfon
Inverurie
Alford
Kintore
Aboyne
Aberdeen
Ballater
R Dee
Banchory
Stonehaven
Inverbervie
Laurencekirk
Brechin
Montrose
Kirriemuir
Forfar
Arbroath
Carnoustie
Newport-on-Tay
Tay Rd Bridge
St Andrews Bay
St Andrews
Cupar
Fife Ness
Crail
Pittenweem
Leven

Ferries to NORWAY leave from:
LERWICK
NEWCASTLE UPON TYNE

NORTH SEA

OF FORTH
North Berwick
Dunbar
East Linton
Haddington
Tranent
St Abb's Head
Eyemouth
Duns
Berwick-upon-Tweed
Greenlaw
Lauder
Coldstream
Holy Island
Galashiels
Melrose
Kelso
Selkirk
Wooler
Jedburgh
Hawick
Alnwick
Amble

Restricted motorway junctions

A1(M)	Southbound	Northbound
65	No exit to A1	No access from A1
57	No exit to A66(M)	No access from A66(M)
L	No access	No exit; no access
L	No exit	
L	No access	No exit to A14
L	No access	No exit
5	No exit; no access	No exit
3	No access	
2	No exit	

A3(M)	Southbound	Northbound
4	Junction with unclassified road; no exit	Junction with unclassified road; no access

A38(M)	Southbound	Northbound
L	No access	No exit

A40(M)	Southbound	Northbound
L	No access	No exit

A48(M)	Eastbound	Westbound
29a	No exit	No access

A74(M)	Southbound	Northbound
14 (North)	No access	No access; no exit
14 (South)	No access; no exit	
18	No exit	No access
21	No access	No access
L		No access
L	No exit	No access

A102(M)	Southbound	Northbound
L	No access	No exit

M1	Southbound	Northbound
35a	No exit	No access
34 (North)	No exit	No exit
34 (South)	No exit	No access
23a	No exit to A453	No access from A453
21a	No exit	No access
19	No access from A14	No exit to A14
17	No exit	No access
7	No access	No exit
6a	No access from M25	No exit to M25
4	No access	No exit
2	No access	No exit

M3	Eastbound	Westbound
8	No exit; access from A303 only	Exit to A303 only; no access
10	No access	No exit
14	No exit	No access

M4	Eastbound	Westbound
46	No exit	No access
39	No access; no exit	No exit
38		No access
29	No exit	No access from A48(M)
25a	No exit	No access
23	No access; exit to M48 eastbound	No exit; access from M48 westbound
21	No exit; access from M48 eastbound	No access; exit to M48 westbound
2	No exit to or access from A4 westbound	No exit to or access from A4 eastbound
1	No exit to A4 westbound	No access from A4 eastbound

M5	Southbound	Northbound
10	No access	No exit
11a	No exit to A417 westbound	No access from A417 eastbound
12	No exit	No access
18	No exit	No access
18a	No exit to M49	No access from M49

M6	Southbound	Northbound
30	No access	No exit
25	No access	No access
24	No access	No exit
20		No exit
31a	No exit	No access
10a	No exit	No access
5	No exit	No access
4a	No access; exit to M42 only	No exit; access from M42 southbound only

M8	Eastbound	Westbound
28a	No exit	No access
28	No exit	No access
25	No access from A739 northbound	No access from A739 northbound
23	No exit	No access
22	No exit	No access
21	No access	No exit
20	No exit	No access
18		No access
16	No exit	No exit
14	No access	No exit
9	No exit	No exit
8		No access from A8 eastbound, A89 eastbound or M73 southbound

M9	Eastbound	Westbound
8	No exit	No access from M876 northbound
6	No access	No exit
3	No exit	No access
2	No access	No exit
1a	No exit	No access

M11	Southbound	Northbound
14	No access from A1307 or A45 eastbound	No exit to A1307 or A45 westbound
13	No exit	No access
9	No access	No access
5	No exit	No access
4	No exit to A1400	No access from A1400

M20	Eastbound	Westbound
2 (North)	No access	
2 (South)		No exit
3	No exit	
11a	No exit	No exit

M23	Southbound	Northbound
7	No access from A23 northbound	No exit to A23 southbound
10a	No access	No exit

M25	Clockwise	Anticlockwise
5	No exit to A21 from M26 and no access to M26 from M25	No access to M26 from A21
9 (Central)	No access; no exit	No access; no exit
9 (North)	No access; no exit	
19	No access	No exit
21	No exit to M1 southbound; no access from M1 northbound	No exit to M1 southbound; no access from M1 northbound

M27	Eastbound	Westbound
4 (West)	No access	No exit
4 (East)	No exit	No access
10	No exit	No access
12	No access to M27	No exit from M27

M40	Eastbound	Westbound
16	No access	No exit
14	No access	No exit
13	No exit	No access
L	No exit	No access
7	No exit	No access
3	No exit	No access

M42	Southbound	Northbound
1	No access	No exit
7	Access from M6 only; no exit	Exit to M6 West only; exit to and access from unclassified road only
7a	Exit to and access from unclassified road only	Exit to M6 East only; exit to and access from unclassified road only
8	Exit to M6 only; no access	Exit to M6 only; no access

M45	Eastbound	Westbound
L	No access	No exit

M53	Southbound	Northbound
11	No access	No exit

M56	Eastbound	Westbound
15	No exit	No access
9		No access to M6 southbound
8	No access; no exit	No exit
7		No access
4	No exit	No access
2	No exit	No access

M57	Southbound	Northbound
3	No access	No exit
5	No access	No exit

M58	Eastbound	Westbound
1	No exit	No access

M60	Clockwise	Anticlockwise
2	No exit	No access
3	No exit to A34 northbound	No exit to A34 northbound
4	No access from M56	No exit to M56
5		No exit to A5103 northbound; no access from A5103 northbound
7		No access
14	No exit to A580 clockwise; no access from A580	No exit to A580; no access from A580 anticlockwise
16	No access	No exit
25	No access	No exit
26	No access; no exit to A560	
27		No exit

M61	Southbound	Northbound
3		No access
2		No access from A580 eastbound

M62	Eastbound	Westbound
23	No access	No exit

M65	Eastbound	Westbound
9	No access	No exit
11	No exit	No access

M66	Southbound	Northbound
L	Access from A56 southbound only	Exit to A56 northbound only
1	No exit	No access

M67	Eastbound	Westbound
1	No access	No exit
2	No exit	No access

M69	Southbound	Northbound
2	No access	No exit

M73	Southbound	Northbound
3	No access from A80 northbound	No exit to A80 southbound
2	No access from A89; no exit to M8 (Junction 8) or A89	No exit to A89; no access from M8 (Junction 8) or A89

M74	Southbound	Northbound
2	No access	
3	No exit	No access
7	No access	No exit
9	No access	No exit; no access
10	No exit	
11	No access from B7078	No exit to B7078
12	No exit	No access from A70

M77	Southbound	Northbound
4	No access	No exit
L	No exit to A77 northbound	No access from A77 southbound

M80	Southbound	Northbound
3	No exit	No access
5	No exit	No access

M90	Southbound	Northbound
10	No exit to A912	No access from A912
8	No exit	No access
7	No access	No exit
2a	No exit to A92	No access from A92

M180	Eastbound	Westbound
1	No access	No exit

M876	Eastbound	Westbound
2	No access	No exit

M606	Northbound	
L	No access	

M621	Eastbound	Westbound
L	No exit	No access
4	No access	
5	No exit	No access
6	No access	No exit

Distances chart

Distances are shown in miles and, in *italics,* kilometres.
For example, the distance between Southampton and York is
258 miles or *415* kilometres.

	Southampton		
Stranraer	445 *716*		
Swansea	417 *671*	161 *259*	
York	272 *438*	222 *357*	258 *415*

The towns in this chart are shown in **bold** type on the key
map (opposite).

London (column head)

Aberdeen — 517 / *832*

Aberystwyth — 445 211 / *716 340*

Ayr — 317 183 394 / *510 295 634*

Berwick-upon-Tweed — 134 311 182 352 / *216 501 293 567*

Birmingham — 274 289 114 420 117 / *441 465 183 676 188*

Blackpool — 123 181 180 153 308 234 / *198 291 290 246 496 364*

Bournemouth — 270 147 412 436 207 564 107 / *435 237 663 702 333 908 172*

Braemar — 524 281 385 148 143 405 59 482 / *843 452 620 238 230 652 95 776*

Brighton — 534 92 286 163 409 446 253 573 52 / *859 148 460 262 658 718 407 922 84*

Bristol — 147 477 82 204 81 362 370 125 493 122 / *237 768 132 328 130 583 595 201 793 196*

Cambridge — 169 116 438 154 208 100 306 307 214 471 54 / *272 187 705 248 335 161 493 575 344 758 87*

Cardiff — 190 45 182 483 117 209 103 368 382 105 505 157 / *306 72 293 778 188 336 166 592 615 169 813 253*

Carlisle — 289 264 277 370 196 343 87 196 87 93 224 221 301 / *465 425 446 596 316 552 140 315 140 150 360 356 484*

Doncaster — 142 209 116 175 236 310 235 94 94 184 235 176 344 171 / *229 336 187 282 380 499 378 151 151 296 378 283 554 275*

Dover — 242 389 238 125 202 82 553 174 312 194 424 478 292 588 71 / *390 626 383 201 325 132 890 280 502 312 683 769 478 947 114*

Dundee — 523 275 152 441 406 430 517 52 495 239 349 113 117 376 67 448 / *842 443 245 710 654 692 834 84 797 385 562 182 188 605 108 721*

Edinburgh — 56 462 219 96 385 345 373 456 91 439 183 292 57 73 320 125 390 / *90 744 352 154 620 555 600 734 146 707 295 470 92 117 515 201 628*

Exeter — 450 518 248 251 353 121 249 76 184 201 82 495 157 428 446 201 569 181 / *724 834 399 404 568 195 401 122 296 885 132 454 253 689 718 323 916 291*

Fishguard — 230 399 460 331 247 297 112 270 154 291 493 222 209 170 371 373 56 504 260 / *370 642 740 533 398 478 180 435 248 468 794 357 336 273 597 600 90 811 418*

Fort William — 486 560 144 127 596 357 206 485 479 486 575 125 539 296 392 190 133 430 149 510 / *782 901 232 204 959 575 332 781 771 782 926 201 867 476 631 306 214 692 240 821*

Glasgow — 101 376 449 44 83 488 249 96 385 372 373 468 110 439 183 292 101 33 320 145 397 / *163 605 723 71 134 786 401 154 620 599 600 753 177 707 295 470 163 53 515 233 639*

Gloucester — 346 454 153 111 349 410 191 150 247 56 123 35 159 443 99 174 56 318 330 102 468 109 / *557 731 246 179 562 660 307 241 398 90 198 56 256 713 159 280 90 512 531 164 753 175*

Great Yarmouth — 225 419 527 366 335 386 484 185 167 320 284 82 275 480 477 240 252 180 345 402 294 517 128 / *362 674 848 589 539 621 779 298 269 515 457 132 443 290 768 386 406 290 555 647 473 832 206*

Harwich — 82 196 432 543 337 279 413 469 125 194 336 246 67 217 128 504 187 275 167 372 425 281 535 76 / *132 316 695 874 542 449 665 755 201 312 541 396 108 349 206 811 301 443 269 599 684 452 861 122*

Holyhead — 349 334 191 330 438 167 282 333 394 360 181 231 270 206 334 426 288 141 148 331 305 111 439 269 / *562 538 307 531 705 269 454 536 634 580 291 372 348 435 332 538 686 463 227 238 501 491 179 707 433*

Inverness — 474 569 553 504 166 66 542 618 158 132 622 383 262 549 505 539 617 75 597 348 458 215 199 486 105 550 / *763 916 890 811 267 106 872 995 254 212 1001 617 422 884 813 867 993 121 961 560 737 346 320 782 169 885*

John o' Groats — 129 603 693 677 628 295 195 671 744 285 259 747 507 391 680 630 668 741 202 724 478 574 342 328 601 232 663 / *208 970 1116 1090 1011 475 314 1080 1197 459 417 1201 816 629 1094 1014 1075 1193 325 1165 769 924 550 528 967 373 1067*

Kingston upon Hull — 518 394 231 196 169 198 254 369 280 309 234 295 256 47 158 244 139 233 245 327 264 127 134 185 251 223 364 184 / *834 634 372 316 333 272 409 594 451 497 377 475 412 76 254 393 224 375 394 526 425 204 216 298 404 359 586 296*

Kyle of Lochalsh — 445 189 84 514 611 602 528 179 79 567 628 216 186 671 432 275 564 555 552 651 159 618 372 471 263 212 499 189 586 / *716 304 135 827 983 969 850 288 127 913 1011 348 299 1080 695 443 908 893 888 1048 256 995 599 758 423 341 803 304 943*

Land's End — 763 421 868 741 405 390 446 235 573 686 353 123 374 200 308 665 205 405 281 552 290 313 692 297 / *1228 678 1397 1193 652 628 718 378 922 1104 568 198 924 1033 613 602 768 394 602 322 496 1070 330 652 452 888 917 504 1114 478*

Leeds — 405 394 55 487 360 176 223 196 174 215 329 237 270 202 258 260 29 119 232 145 194 260 293 255 72 113 156 212 169 327 189 / *652 634 283 359 315 280 346 530 381 435 325 415 418 192 373 233 312 419 472 410 116 182 251 341 272 526 304*

Leicester — 95 320 500 102 588 461 190 147 140 85 314 422 209 196 295 349 185 74 352 299 153 414 97 / *153 515 805 164 947 742 306 237 225 137 505 679 336 315 476 562 298 119 332 248 109 193 267 626 254 225 63 406 481 246 666 156*

Lincoln — 51 68 371 476 44 554 427 216 155 128 159 291 399 272 247 258 314 202 39 191 208 85 183 197 357 209 128 90 224 274 199 383 131 / *82 109 597 766 71 892 687 348 249 206 256 468 642 438 398 415 505 325 63 307 335 137 295 317 575 336 206 145 360 441 320 616 211*

Liverpool — 129 130 75 361 407 130 511 382 102 265 240 140 216 329 160 237 216 286 299 86 120 165 194 161 272 318 234 49 219 213 104 341 202 / *208 209 121 581 655 209 822 615 164 427 386 225 348 530 257 381 348 460 481 138 193 272 312 259 438 512 377 79 150 352 343 167 549 325*

Manchester — 35 84 92 40 361 406 95 500 373 124 228 212 124 228 212 197 236 215 285 276 61 119 183 165 161 257 318 212 40 80 196 212 129 340 185 / *56 135 148 64 581 654 153 805 600 200 367 341 203 346 530 317 323 197 236 215 285 276 61 119 183 165 161 257 315 341 208 547 298*

Newcastle upon Tyne — 132 168 159 187 92 498 318 132 395 268 272 308 281 266 148 253 329 364 110 166 358 114 57 325 241 299 352 201 347 129 207 64 149 257 235 378 / *212 270 256 301 148 802 512 212 636 431 438 496 452 428 238 407 529 586 177 267 576 183 92 523 388 481 567 323 558 208 333 103 240 414 378 460*

Norwich — 264 185 220 105 119 76 421 582 149 654 529 311 73 20 204 385 94 549 121 117 585 148 477 468 62 252 175 457 214 232 166 328 382 276 496 114 / *425 298 354 169 192 283 678 937 240 1053 852 501 117 32 328 620 811 552 466 589 679 280 237 465 422 100 406 282 735 344 373 267 528 615 444 798 183*

Nottingham — 130 157 73 98 35 25 70 345 479 90 557 430 185 150 153 110 293 401 220 221 262 328 205 43 194 172 83 145 193 353 183 111 50 221 274 164 393 122 / *209 253 118 158 56 40 113 555 771 145 896 692 298 241 246 177 472 646 354 356 422 528 330 69 312 277 134 233 311 568 295 179 80 356 441 264 633 196*

Oban — 390 492 233 307 308 387 419 307 665 128 346 244 117 427 524 515 441 92 49 481 549 123 530 285 384 180 94 412 178 499 465 123 530 285 384 180 94 412 178 / *628 792 375 494 496 623 674 494 1070 206 557 393 188 687 843 829 710 148 79 774 884 108 188 942 557 303 768 753 748 910 227 853 459 618 290 151 663 286 803*

Oxford — 462 109 145 260 144 172 127 73 168 274 550 192 656 532 238 145 200 52 356 472 205 156 372 433 141 145 260 108 82 74 108 465 90 187 64 324 353 154 483 57 / *744 175 233 418 232 277 221 117 270 441 885 309 1056 856 383 233 322 84 573 760 330 251 599 697 227 233 418 174 134 119 174 749 145 301 103 521 568 248 777 92*

Plymouth — 199 587 267 343 410 283 283 293 242 316 89 674 355 790 664 328 309 365 157 495 595 264 46 496 532 399 167 293 122 224 587 128 328 203 474 492 237 615 218 / *320 945 430 552 660 455 455 472 389 509 143 1085 571 1271 1069 528 497 588 253 797 958 425 74 798 888 483 478 642 269 472 196 361 945 206 528 327 763 792 382 990 351*

Portsmouth — 176 77 545 191 207 162 257 259 633 269 737 613 311 166 221 119 448 555 251 135 453 514 130 234 348 142 144 97 48 547 52 264 141 401 430 222 560 70 / *283 124 877 307 333 542 380 409 323 261 414 417 1019 1186 987 501 267 192 721 893 404 217 729 827 209 376 560 229 232 156 77 881 84 425 692 357 901 113*

Sheffield — 230 283 135 339 37 146 125 38 72 46 62 33 361 427 65 520 393 168 187 166 248 348 215 237 235 291 245 18 152 194 120 161 226 320 216 86 76 190 245 159 360 159 / *370 455 217 546 60 235 201 61 116 74 100 53 581 687 105 837 632 270 301 267 203 399 560 346 381 378 468 394 29 245 312 193 259 364 515 348 138 122 306 394 256 579 256*

Shrewsbury — 82 207 225 106 364 93 205 283 283 111 93 214 135 105 488 726 169 567 413 140 235 77 272 382 145 179 221 288 251 109 176 181 159 103 226 311 185 98 45 265 269 77 399 160 / *132 333 362 171 586 150 330 323 111 93 214 135 175 283 785 1169 272 912 665 225 378 124 438 615 233 288 441 463 404 175 283 256 166 364 597 298 158 72 426 433 124 642 258*

Southampton — 185 199 21 151 64 530 176 206 324 221 239 204 137 232 228 618 256 723 598 293 164 220 105 433 551 233 105 438 500 143 209 324 121 148 76 61 532 31 251 128 388 417 201 547 77 / *298 320 34 243 103 853 283 332 521 356 385 328 220 373 367 995 412 1164 963 472 264 354 169 697 871 375 169 705 805 230 336 521 195 238 122 98 856 50 404 206 624 671 323 880 124*

Stranraer — 445 277 263 461 500 379 148 290 403 158 220 221 298 330 220 585 263 379 475 144 285 343 84 195 392 454 241 731 200 269 190 414 163 410 390 610 608 765 312 715 303 478 274 521 228 402 / *716 446 423 742 805 610 238 467 649 254 354 356 480 531 354 942 423 417 610 422 544 660 686 422 135 314 631 ... 200 269 190 414 163 410 390 610 608 765 312 715 303 478 274 521 367 647*

Swansea — 417 118 117 482 518 388 194 341 506 192 301 342 81 187 195 233 177 248 285 594 264 696 572 184 267 323 89 409 496 67 161 412 473 274 232 309 41 227 85 222 505 167 216 119 383 379 73 507 194 / *671 259 190 349 293 332 227 815 309 485 159 485 169 294 64 99 75 108 24 411 407 ... 296 428 530 143 658 798 108 259 663 761 441 373 497 66 365 137 357 813 269 348 192 616 610 117 816 312*

York — 272 222 258 133 52 278 333 181 190 77 181 84 64 99 75 108 24 411 407 77 181 84 64 99 75 108 330 261 287 194 250 282 34 121 244 165 222 275 285 269 96 130 148 214 195 313 209 / *438 357 415 214 84 448 536 291 497 124 291 135 103 159 121 174 39 661 407 ... 60 771 566 328 367 323 304 489 402 454 55 195 393 266 357 443 459 433 154 209 238 344 314 513 333*

Key to 3-mile map pages

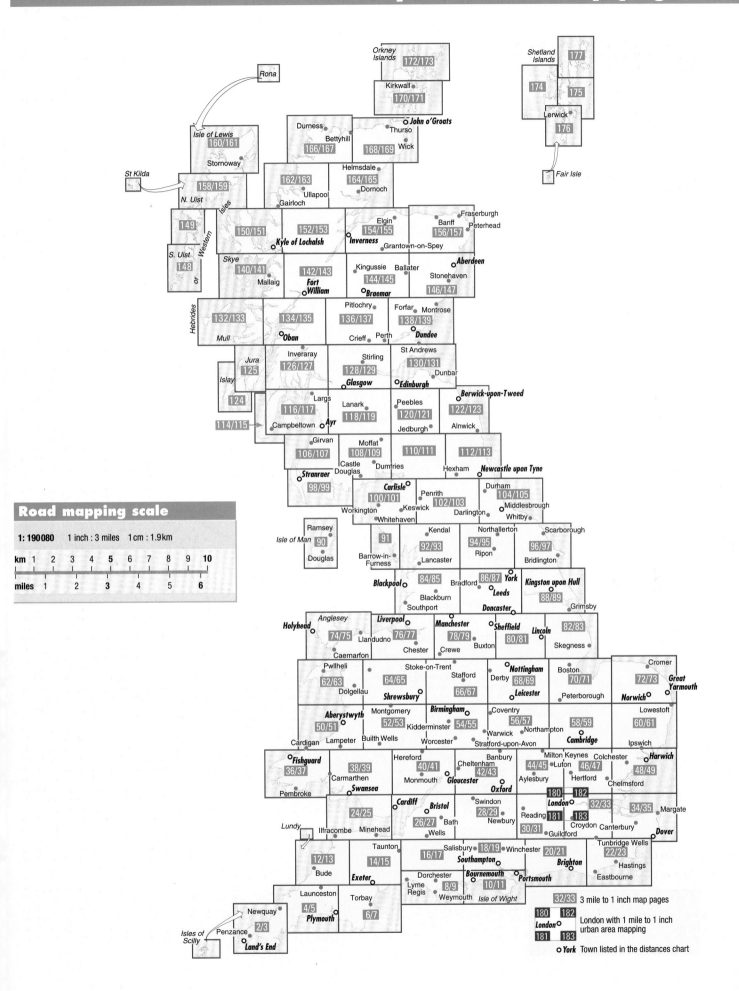

Rona

Orkney Islands 172/173

Kirkwall 170/171

Shetland Islands 177

174 175

Lerwick 176

Fair Isle

Durness
Bettyhill
166/167

Thurso
John o'Groats
168/169
Wick

Isle of Lewis 160/161

Stornoway

St Kilda

158/159

N. Uist

Helmsdale 164/165
Dornoch

162/163
Ullapool
Gairloch

Fraserburgh
Banff Peterhead
156/157

149

Isles

S. Uist 148

150/151

Skye 140/141

Western

or

Hebrides

Kyle of Lochalsh 152/153

Elgin 154/155
Inverness
Grantown-on-Spey

Kingussie Ballater
144/145

Aberdeen
Stonehaven
146/147

Mallaig

142/143
Fort William
Braemar

132/133

134/135

Mull

Oban

Pitlochry 136/137

Crieff Perth

Forfar Montrose
138/139
Dundee

Islay

Jura 125

124

Inveraray 126/127

St Andrews
Stirling 130/131
128/129
Dunbar

Glasgow Edinburgh

Largs
116/117
Campbeltown Ayr

114/115

Lanark 118/119

Peebles
120/121
Jedburgh

Berwick-upon-Tweed
122/123
Alnwick

Girvan 106/107

Castle Douglas

Stranraer 98/99

Moffat 108/109
Dumfries

110/111

Hexham

112/113

Newcastle upon Tyne

Road mapping scale

1: 190 080   1 inch : 3 miles   1 cm : 1.9km

km	1	2	3	4	5	6	7	8	9	10

miles	1	2	3	4	5	6

Carlisle 100/101

Penrith
Keswick 102/103
Workington
Whitehaven

Durham 104/105
Middlesbrough
Darlington Whitby

Ramsey
Isle of Man 90
Douglas

91

Kendal
92/93
Lancaster

Barrow-in-Furness

Northallerton
94/95
Ripon

Scarborough
96/97
Bridlington

Blackpool 84/85
Blackburn
Southport

Bradford
86/87 York
Leeds
Doncaster

Kingston upon Hull
88/89
Grimsby

Holyhead

Anglesey
74/75
Llandudno
Caernarfon

Liverpool
76/77
Chester

Manchester
78/79
Crewe Buxton

Sheffield
80/81

Lincoln
82/83
Skegness

Pwllheli
62/63
Dolgellau

Stoke-on-Trent
64/65
Stafford
66/67
Shrewsbury

Derby Nottingham
68/69
Leicester

Boston
70/71
Peterborough

Cromer
72/73 Great Yarmouth
Norwich

Lowestoft
60/61

Aberystwyth
50/51

Montgomery
52/53
Kidderminster

Birmingham
Worcester 54/55

Coventry
56/57
Warwick Northampton
Stratford-upon-Avon

Cambridge 58/59

Ipswich

Cardigan Lampeter Builth Wells

Harwich

Fishguard 36/37
Carmarthen
Swansea 38/39
Pembroke

Hereford
40/41
Monmouth

Cheltenham
42/43
Gloucester

Banbury

Oxford

Milton Keynes Colchester
44/45 Luton 46/47
Aylesbury Hertford

48/49
Chelmsford

Lundy

Ilfracombe Minehead
24/25 Cardiff Bristol

26/27 Bath
Wells

Swindon
28/29
Newbury

London
180 182
181 183
Reading 30/31 Croydon
Guildford

32/33

34/35 Margate

Canterbury Dover

Taunton
16/17
14/15
12/13
Bude

Salisbury
18/19
Southampton

Winchester
20/21

Tunbridge Wells
22/23
Hastings
Eastbourne

Brighton

Exeter
Launceston
Torbay

Dorchester
8/9
Lyme Regis Weymouth

Bournemouth
10/11
Portsmouth
Isle of Wight

Newquay
Penzance 2/3
Isles of Scilly

4/5
6/7
Plymouth
Land's End

32/33   3 mile to 1 inch map pages

180 182   London with 1 mile to 1 inch
London
181 183   urban area mapping

○ York   Town listed in the distances chart

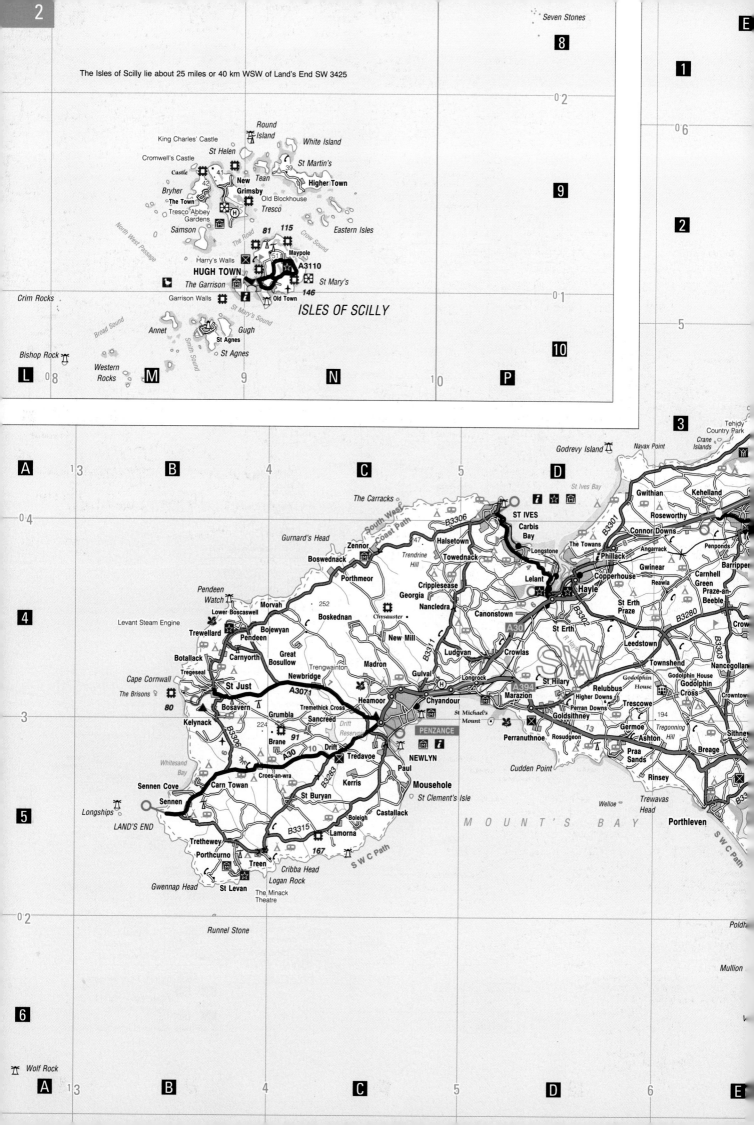

Seven Stones

8

1

The Isles of Scilly lie about 25 miles or 40 km WSW of Land's End SW 3425

Round
Island

White Island

King Charles' Castle

St Helen

Cromwell's Castle

St Martin's

Castle 41
42

New
Grimsby

Tean 39

Higher Town

Bryher

Old Blockhouse

The Town

Tresco

Tresco Abbey
Gardens

Samson

Eastern Isles

North West Passage

The Road

81 115

Crow Sound

9

2

Harry's Walls

Maypole

HUGH TOWN

51

A3110

The Garrison

St Mary's

Crim Rocks

Garrison Walls

Old Town

146

St Mary's Sound

ISLES OF SCILLY

0.1

5

Broad Sound

Annet

Gugh

St Agnes

Smith Sound

St Agnes

10

Bishop Rock

Western
Rocks

L 0.8

M

N

P

0.9

0.10

3

Tehidy
Country Park

Godrevy Island

Navax Point

Crane
Islands

The Carracks

St Ives Bay

Gwithian

Kehelland

South West Coast Path

B3306

ST IVES

Roseworthy

A 0.3

B

C

D

Carbis
Bay

Connor Downs

Gurnard's Head

Zennor

Halstown

47

Longstone

The Towans

Angarrack

Penponds

0.4

Boswednack

Trendrine
Hill

Towednack

Lelant

Phillack

Barripper

Porthmeor

Cripplesease

Copperhouse

Gwinear

Reawla

Carnhell
Green

Pendeen
Watch

Morvah

252

Boskednan

Georgia

Nancledra

Hayle

Praze-an-
Beeble

Lower Boscaswell

Chysauster

Canonstown

St Erth
Praze

B3280

Levant Steam Engine

Trewellard

Bojewyan

New Mill

B3311

A30

St Erth

Leedstown

B3303

Crow

4

Pendeen

Ludgvan

Crowlas

4

Botallack

Carnyorth

Great
Bosullow

Madron

Trengwainton

Gulval

Longrock

St Hilary

SW

Townshend

Nancegollan

Cape Cornwall

Tregeseal

Newbridge

Heamoor

Chyandour

A394

Relubbus

Higher Downs

Godolphin House

Godolphin

The Brisons

St Just

A3071

PENZANCE

St Michael's
Mount

Marazion

Perran Downs

Trescowe

Crowntown

80

Bosavern

Tremethick Cross

Goldsithney

194

3

Kelynack

Grumbla

Sancreed

Drift
Reservoir

NEWLYN

Perranuthnoe

Rosudgeon

Germoe

Ashton

Tregonning
Hill

Sithney

3

B3306

224

91

Brane

A30

10

Drift

Paul

Praa
Sands

Breage

B33

Whitesand
Bay

Croes-an-wra

Tredavoe

Mousehole

Cudden Point

Rinsey

Sennen Cove

Carn Towan

B3283

Kerris

St Clement's Isle

Welloe

Trewavas
Head

Longships

Sennen

St Buryan

Boleigh

Castallack

MOUNT'S BAY

Porthleven

5

LAND'S END

B3315

Lamorna

167

SWC Path

5

Trethewey

Porthcurno

Treen

Cribba Head
Logan Rock

Gwennap Head

St Levan

The Minack
Theatre

0.2

Runnel Stone

Poldh

Mullion

6

Wolf Rock

A 13

B

4

C

5

D

6

E

Alphington
A30
9
Shillingford
St George
31
Kennford
Kenn
Powderham
Powderham
Castle
Kenton
Starcross
Cockwood
Ashcombe
250
Idon
lvedere
Ideford
Luton
B3192
Little
Haldon
Bishopsteignton
A381
247
Combeinteignhead
therton
Haccombe
Plant World
Gardens
Coffinswell
Daccombe
Maidencombe
Barton
A379
rphay
ckington
A3022
Torre
Abbey
Aquarium

TOPSHAM
Exminster
M5
F
Topsham
Exminster
Canal
R. EXE
Powderham
Castle
Starcross
Cockwood
Dawlish
Warren
DAWLISH
Holcombe
TEIGNMOUTH
R. TEIGN
Shaldon
Stokeinteignhead
BABBACOMBE
BAY
S W C Path
Babbacombe
TORQUAY
Hope's Nose

Clyst St George
8
A3052
Woodbury
Salterton
Woodbury
15
G
Ebford
Exton
B3179
B3180
Black Hill
Lympstone
A-La-Ronde
28
B3178
EXMOUTH
Knowle
Littleham
BUDLEIGH
SALTERTON
Nature Reserve Visitor Centre

Hawkerland
176
Colaton
Raleigh
Hayes
Barton
Yettington
East
Budleigh
Bicton Park
Garden
Otterton
Watermill &
Craft Centre

Newton
Poppleford
Pinn
SIDMOUTH
H
Salcombe
Regis
177
Branscombe
Donkey
Sanctuary
25
Vicarage
J
B3174
Seaton
Bay
South West Coast Path
Beer Head

8
2
3
7
4
6
5
6
4
7

TORBAY
PAIGNTON
Paignton Zoo
TOR BAY
Goodrington
mpton
Marina
Berry Head
Berry Head Country Park
Churston Ferrers
BRIXHAM
9
Sharkham Point
Hillhead
A379
B3205
Kingswear
Scabbacombe Head
Ferry
Castle
Coleton Fishacre
House & Garden
Mew Stone
Dartmouth Castle

E N G L I S H   C H A N N E L

9
F
30
G
1
H
32
J

WEYMOUTH to	🚢
Guernsey	2 hrs
Jersey	4 hrs
St Malo	4 hrs
(summer only)	

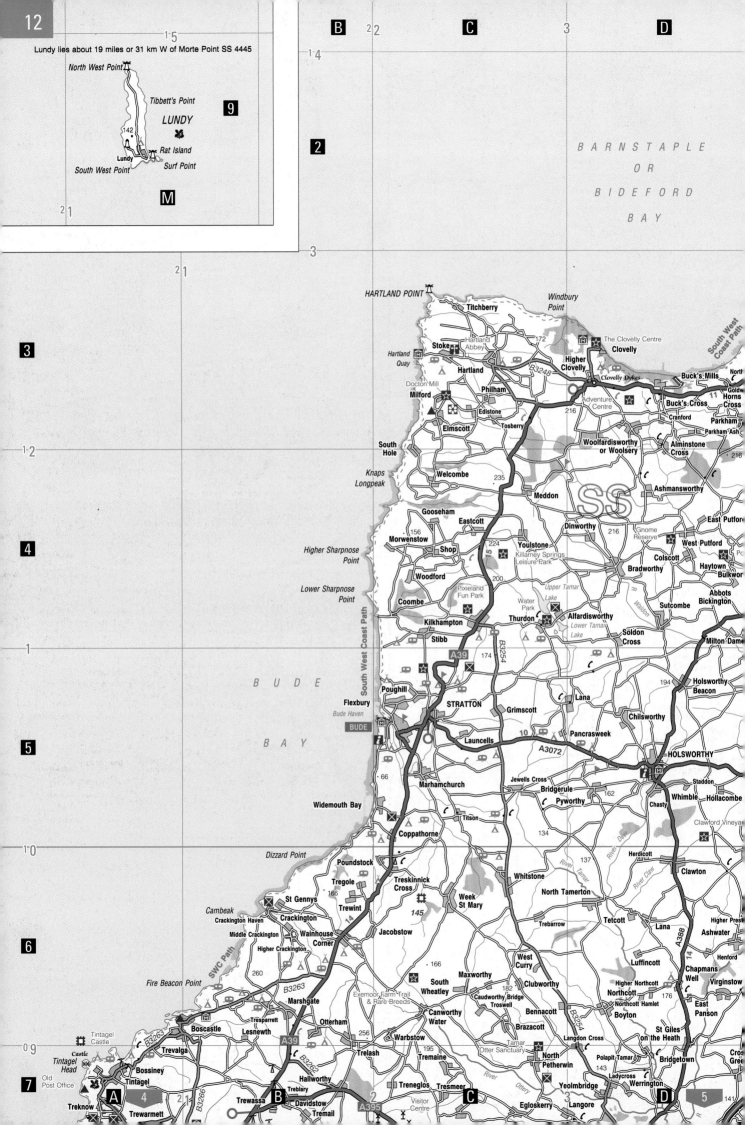

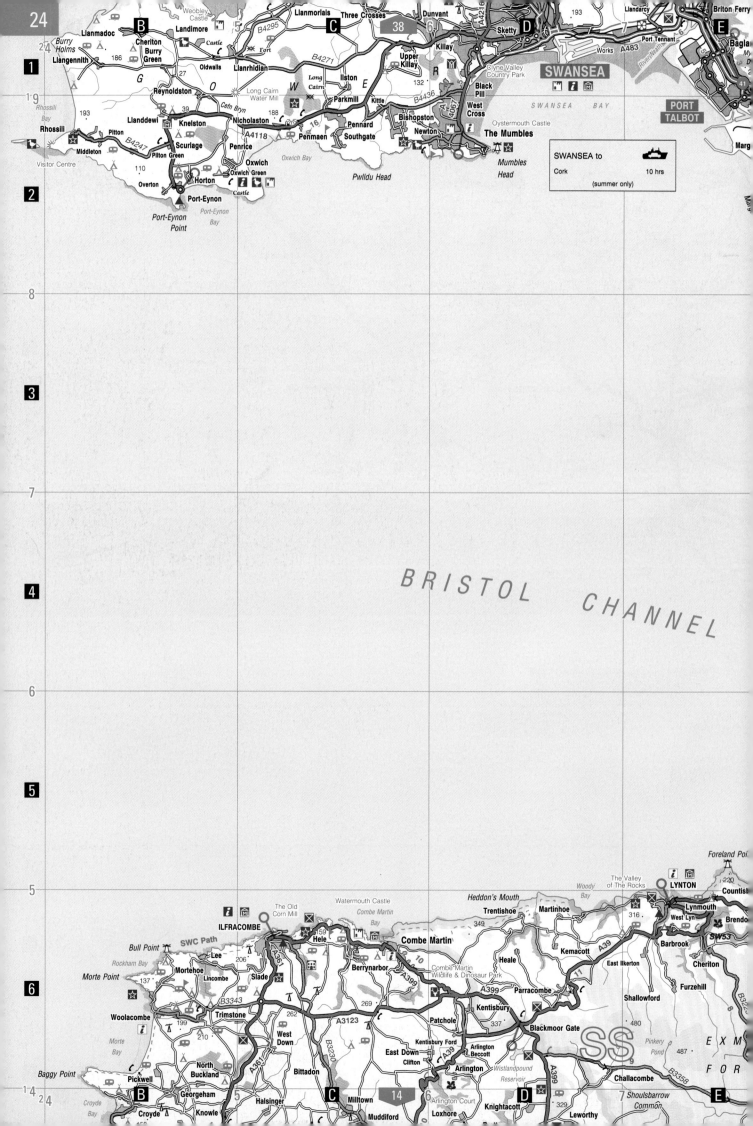

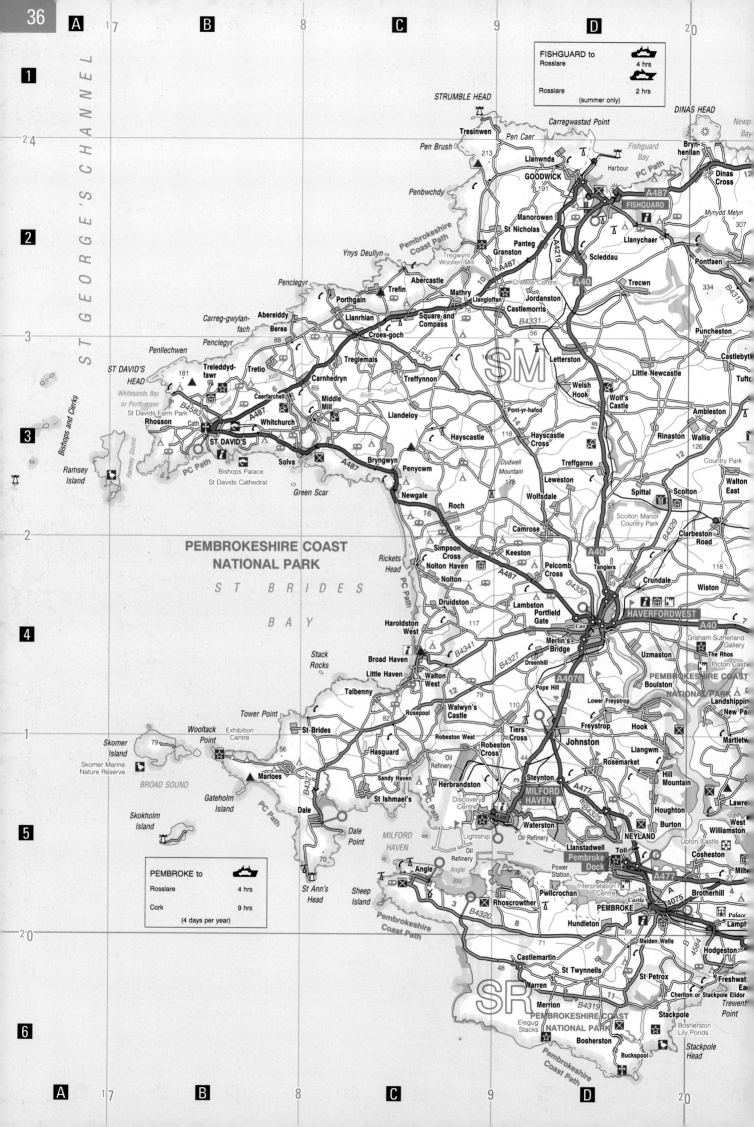

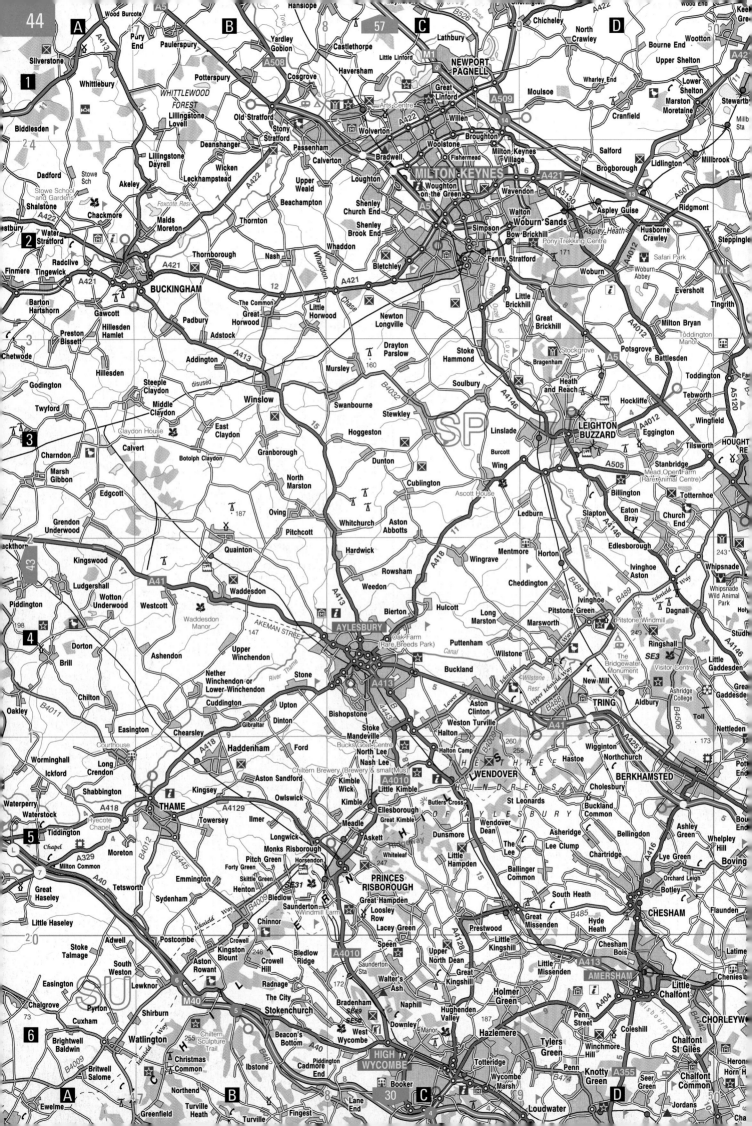

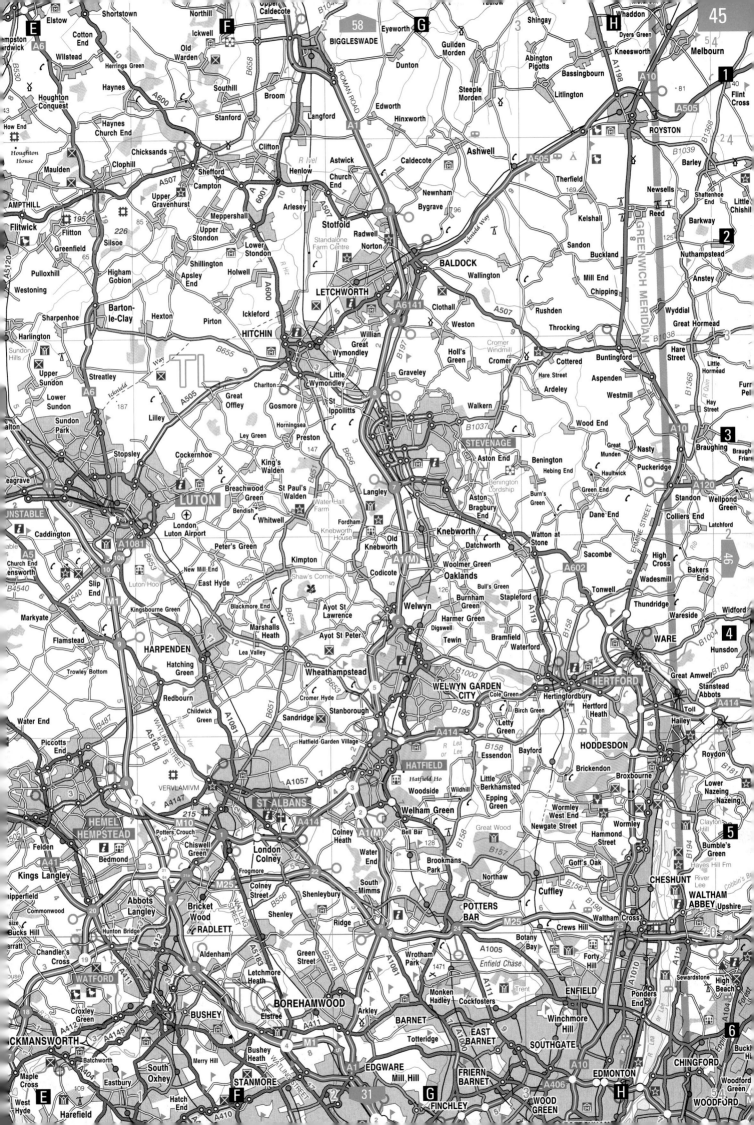

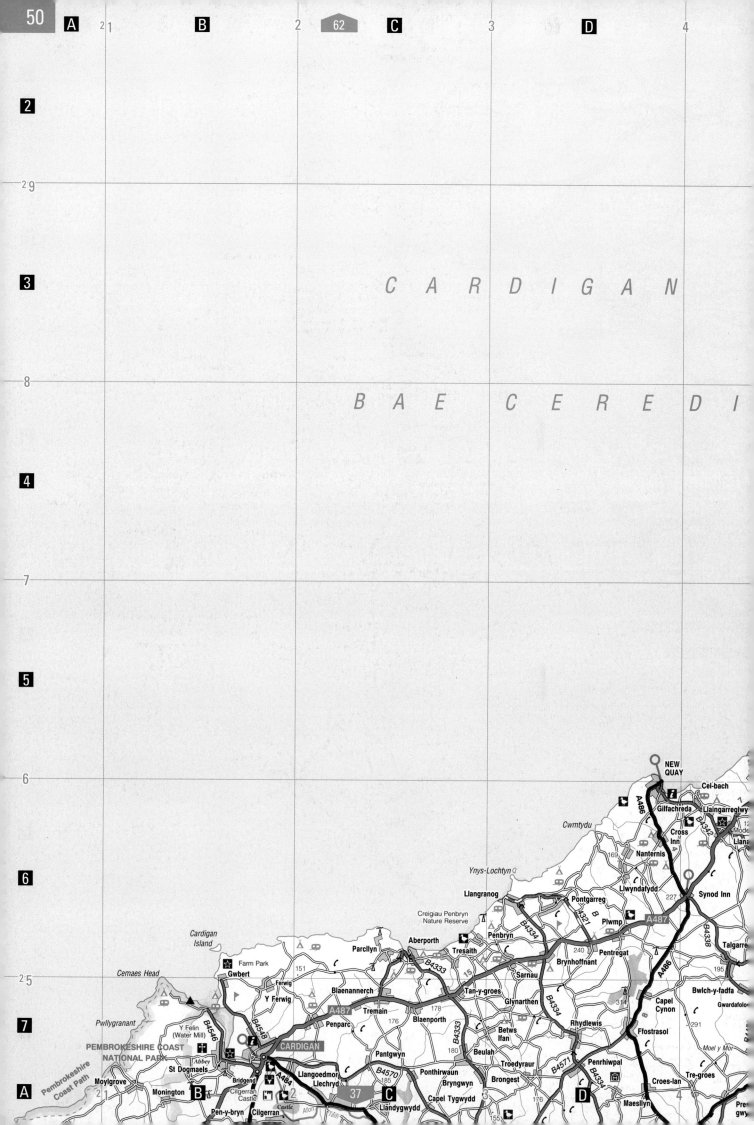

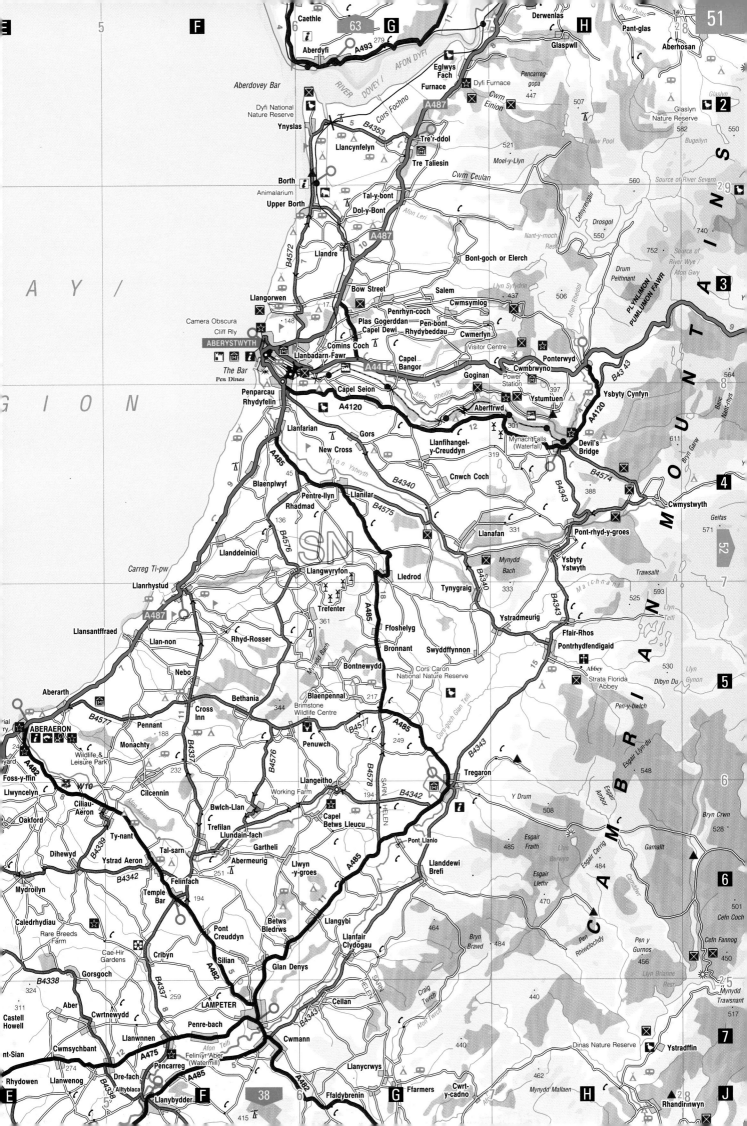

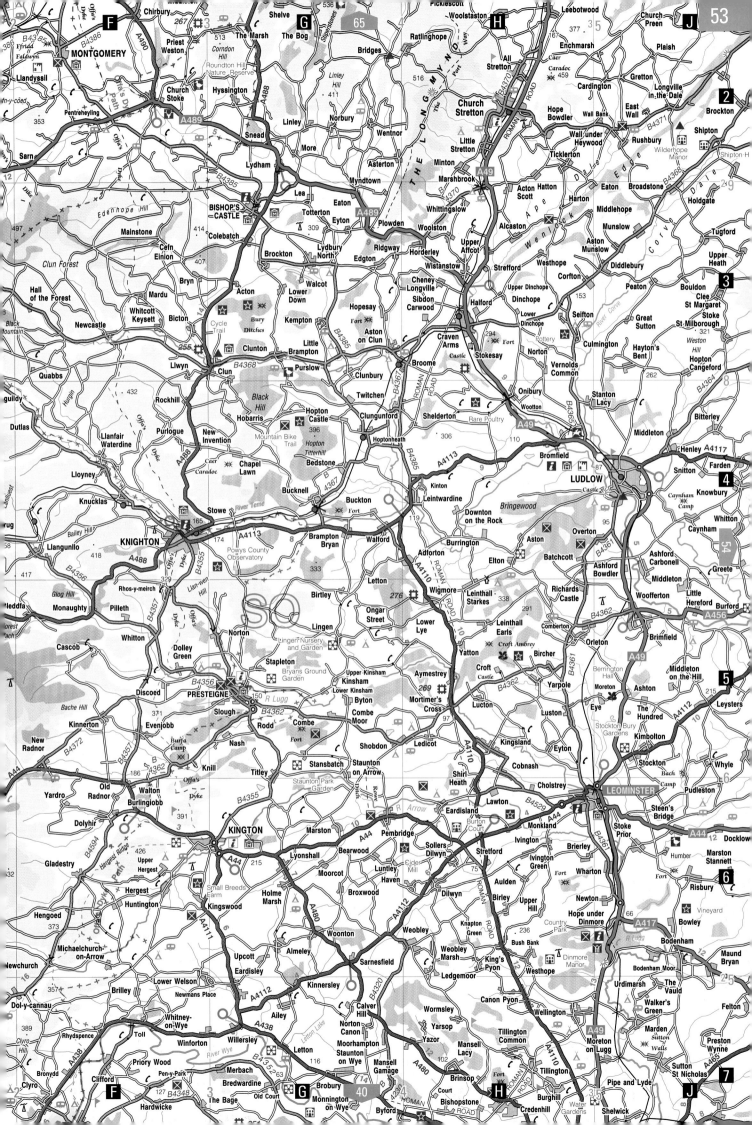

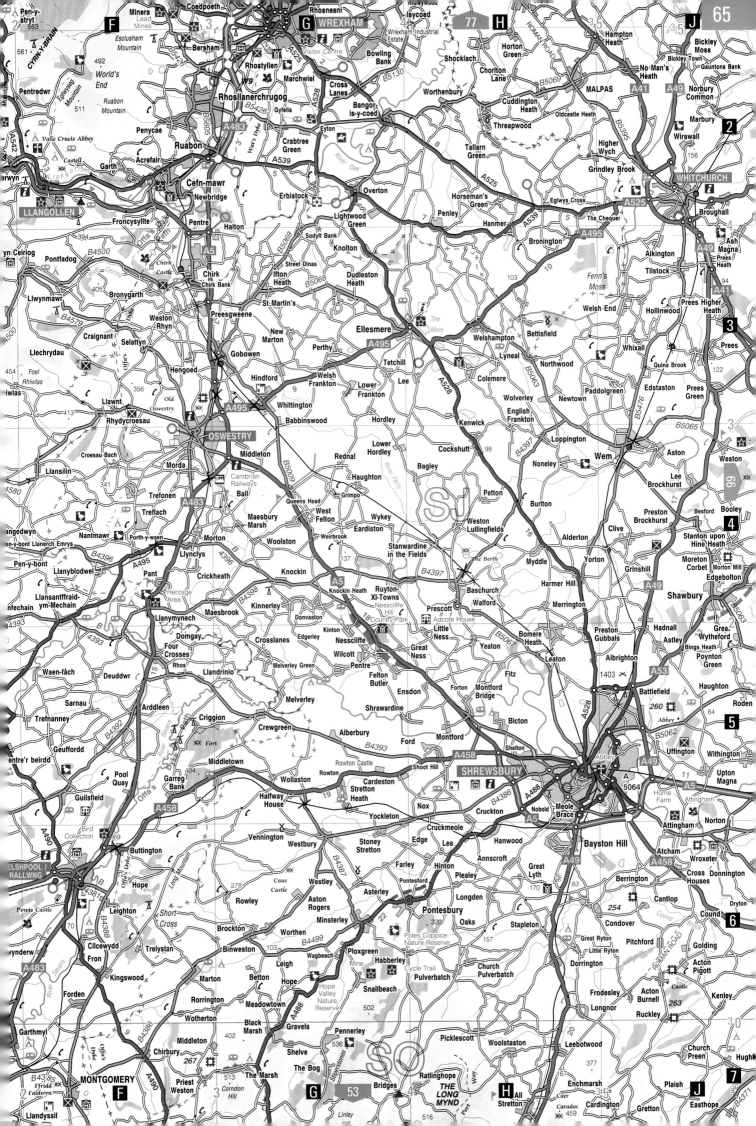

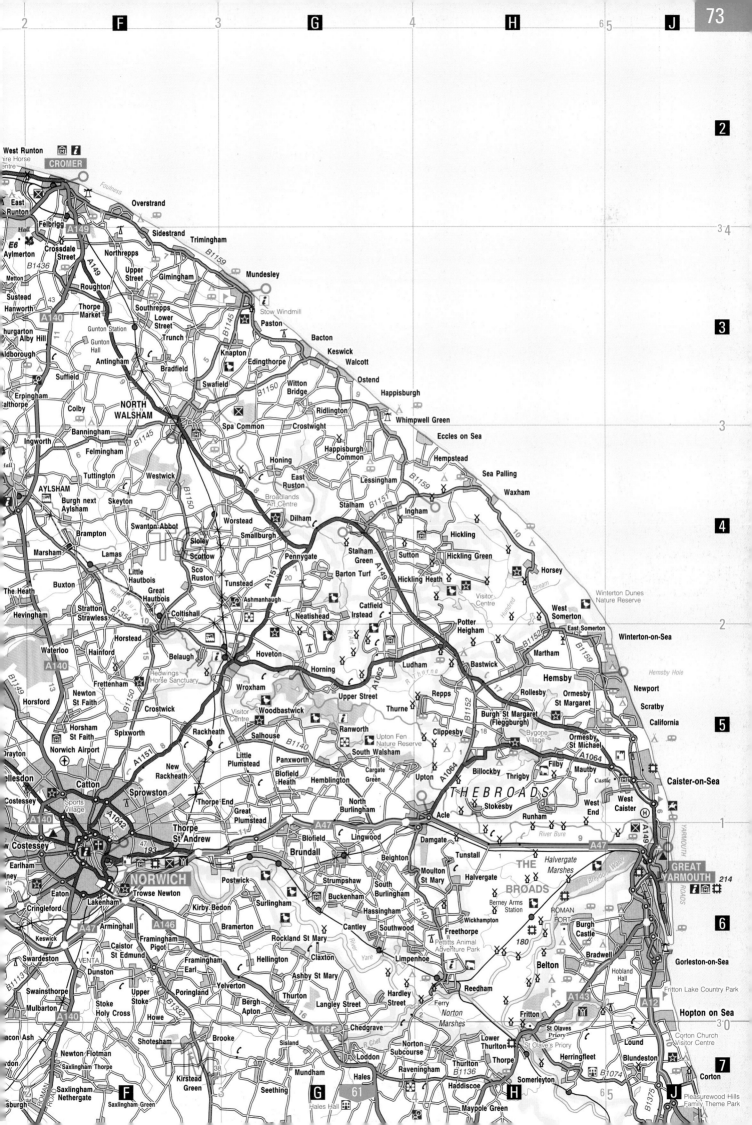

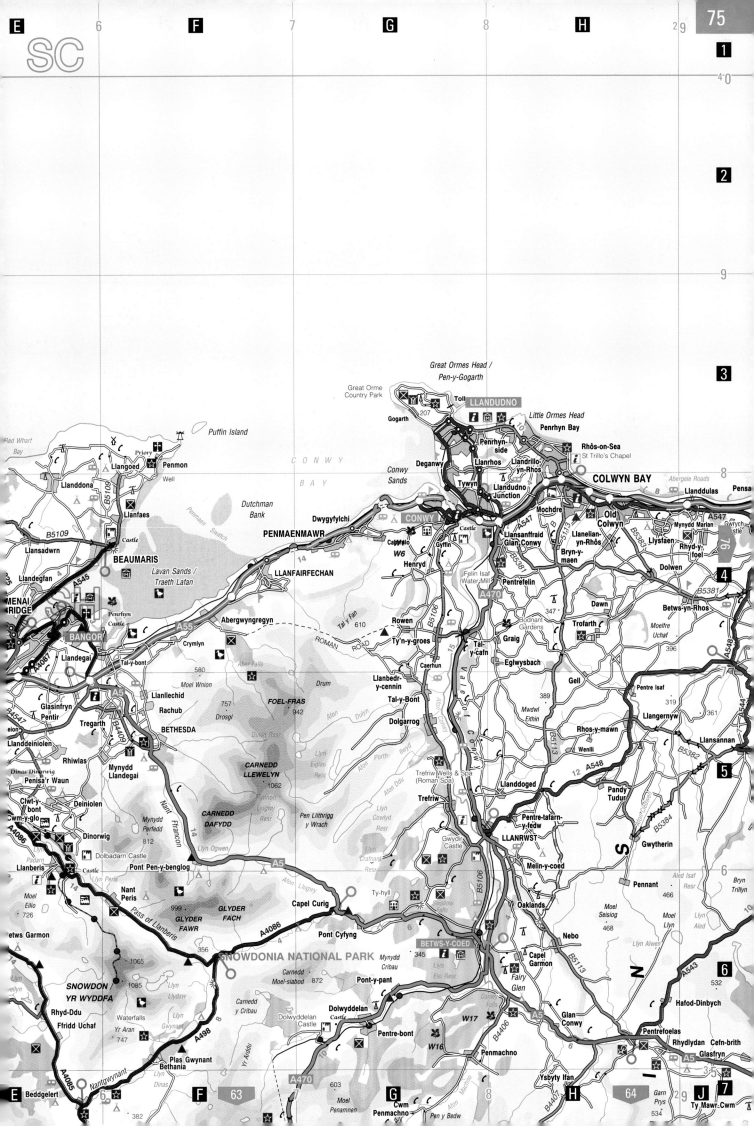

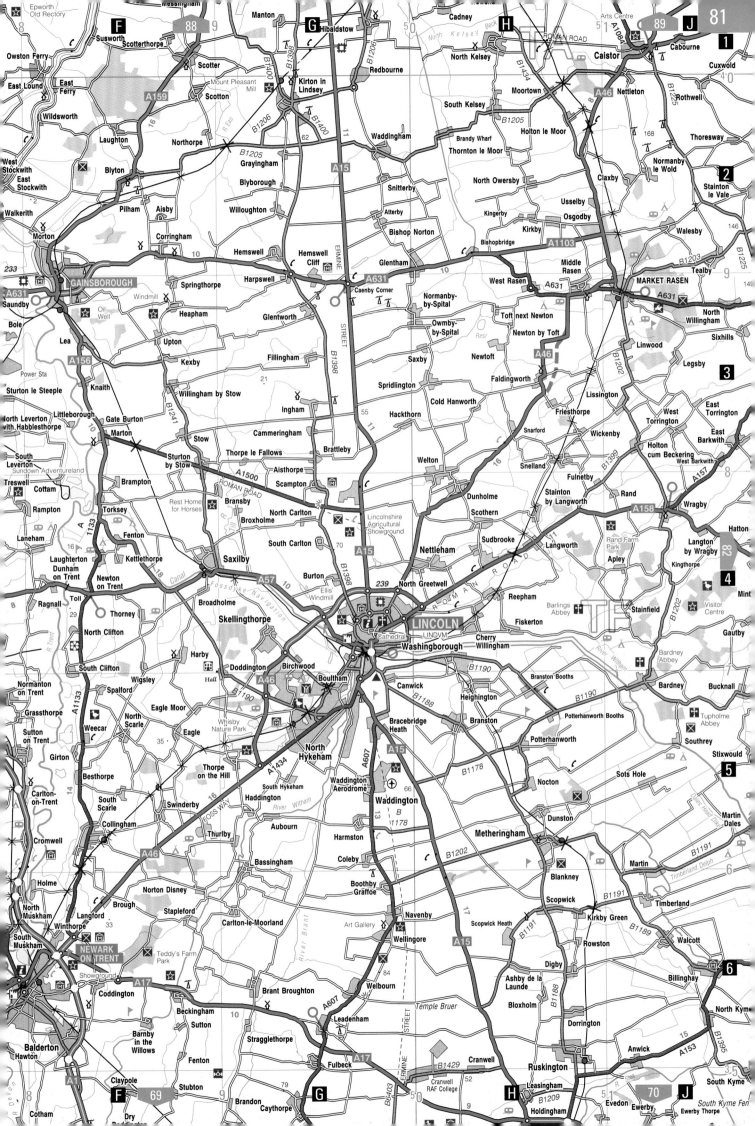

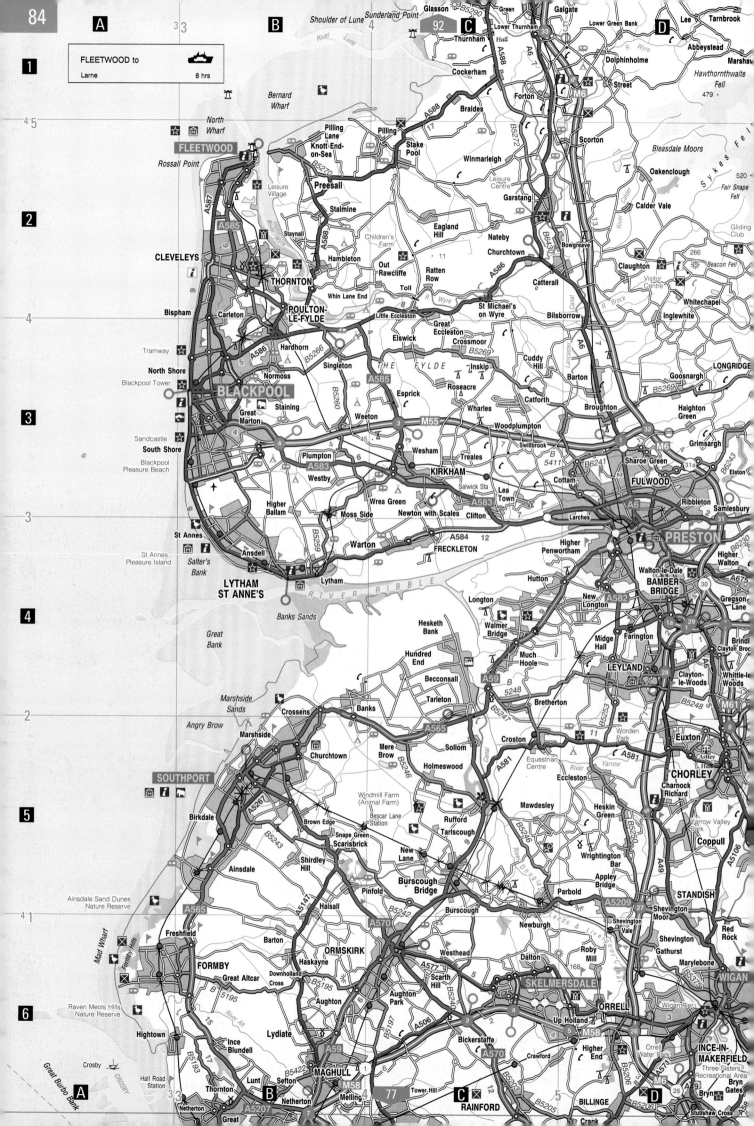

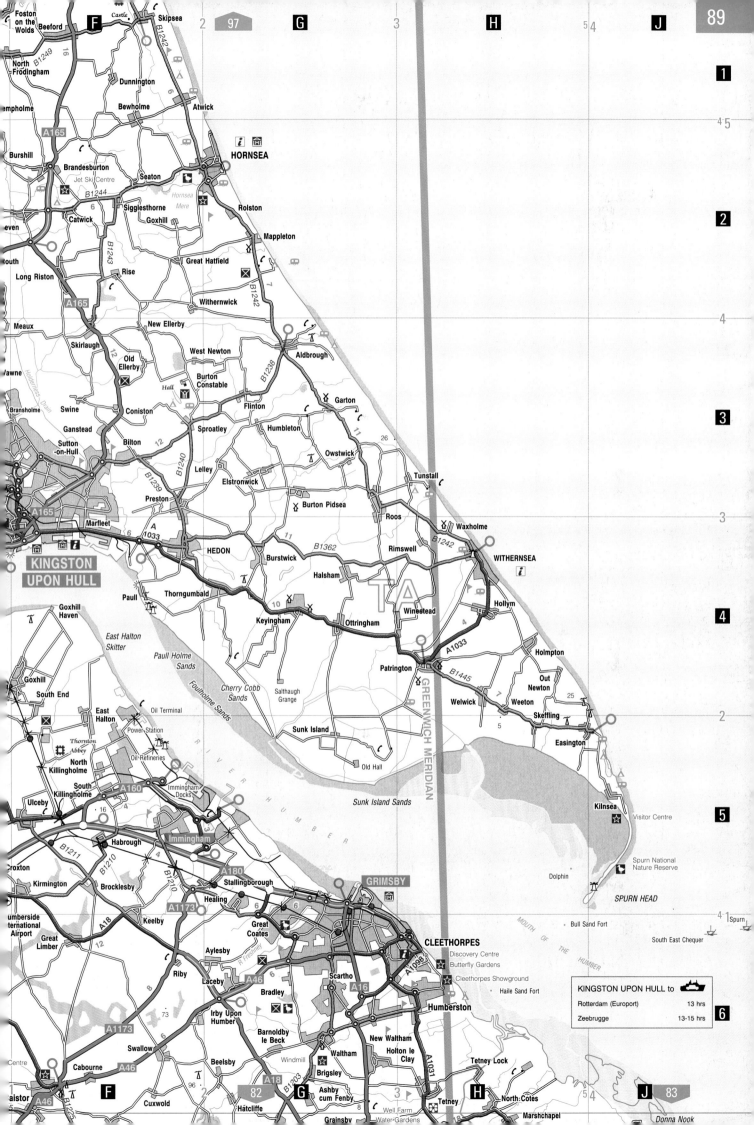

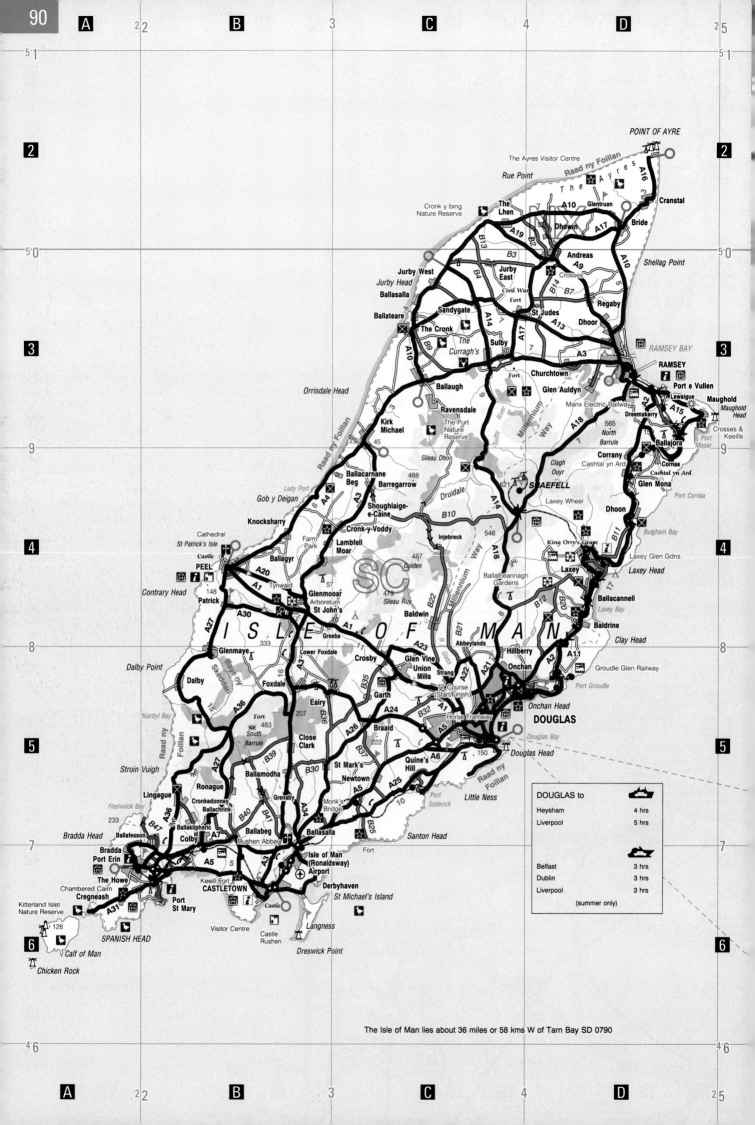

POINT OF AYRE

The Ayres Visitor Centre

The Ayres

Rue Point

Cronk y bing
Nature Reserve

Glentruan

Cranstal

The
Lhen

Dhowin

Bride

A16

A10

A17

A19

B2

B13

B3

Shellag Point

Jurby West

Jurby Head

Jurby East

Andreas

A9

Crosses

A10

Ballasalla

Ballateare

Sandygate

Civil War
Fort

St Judes

B4

B14

B7

Regaby

RAMSEY BAY

The Cronk

The
Curragh's

Sulby

A14

A17

B9

Dhoor

A13

RAMSEY

Orrisdale Head

Churchtown

Fort

A3

Port e Vullen

Ballaugh

Glen Auldyn

Manx Electric Railway

Lewaigue

Maughold

Maughold
Head

Ravensdale

River Sulby

A18

Dreemskerry

A15

Crosses &
Keeills

The Purt
Nature
Reserve

Ballajora

Cornaa

Kirk
Michael

Slieau Dhoo

565
North
Barrule

Cashtal yn Ard

Port Mooar

45

Corrany

Cashtal yn Ard

Port Cornaa

Ballacarnane
Beg

Barregarrow

488

Druidale

621

Clagh
Ouyr

Glen Mona

Gob y Deigan

Lady Port

Shoughlaige-
e-Caine

SNAEFELL

Laxey Wheel

Dhoon

Knocksharry

B10

A14

Cronk-y-Voddy

Injebreck

King Orry's Grave

Bulgham Bay

Cathedral

St Patrick's Isle

Farm
Park

Lambfell
Moar

546

Ballaheannagh
Gardens

Laxey

Laxey Glen Gdns

Laxey Head

Castle

PEEL

Ballagyr

487
Colden

SC

A18

B22

B11

Ballacannell

Laxey Bay

Contrary Head

Patrick

A20

Glenmooar

Tynwald

57

Arboretum

Slieau Ruy

479

Millennium Way

B20

Baldrine

148

A1

St John's

Greeba

Baldwin

Clay Head

A30

ISLE

Greeba

OF

Abbeylands

MAN

Groudle Glen Railway

333

11

A23

B21

A21

Glenmaye

Crosby

Hillberry

A2

A11

Dalby Point

Lower Foxdale

Glen Vine
Union
Mills

Onchan

Port Groudle

Dalby

16

A3

B35

Strang

A22

Onchan Head

Foxdale

Garth

TT Course
(Start/Finish)

DOUGLAS

Eairy

207

B36

A24

B32

A1

Horse Tramway

Fort

483
South
Barrule

Braaid

A5

Douglas Bay

Raad ny
Foillan

Close
Clark

B39

222

B37

A6

150

Douglas Head

Ronague

B30

St Mark's

Quine's
Hill

Lingague

Cronkedonney

Newtown

Little Ness

Ballachrink

A25

A5

Fleshwick Bay

Ballamodha

Grenaby

Monk's
Bridge

Port
Soderick

233

B40

B41

A34

10

Bradda Head

Ballakilpheric

Colby

Ballabeg

B25

Ballafesson

A7

Rushen Abbey

Ballasalla

Santon Head

Bradda
Port Erin

Fort

The Howe

A5

5

A3

Isle of Man
(Ronaldsway)
Airport

Chambered Cairn

Cregneash

Keeill Fort

CASTLETOWN

Derbyhaven

Kitterland Islet
Nature Reserve

A31

Port St Mary

St Michael's Island

128

Visitor Centre

Castle

Langness

SPANISH HEAD

Castle
Rushen

Calf of Man

Dreswick Point

Chicken Rock

The Isle of Man lies about 36 miles or 58 kms W of Tarn Bay SD 0790

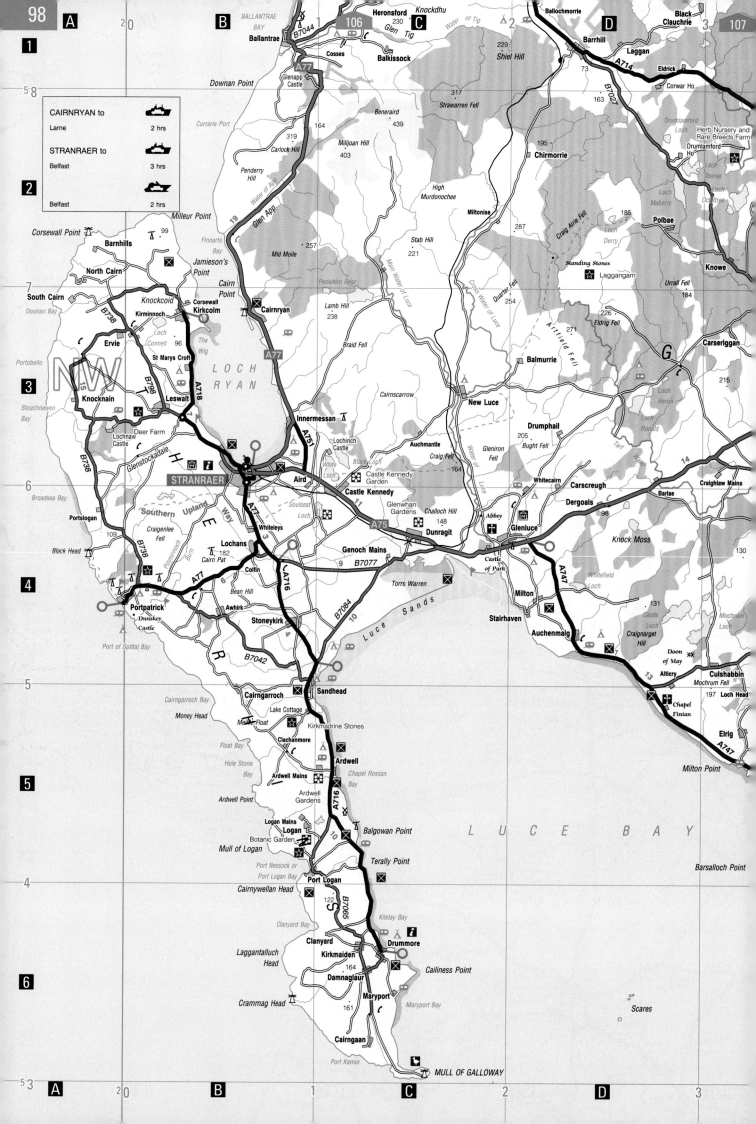

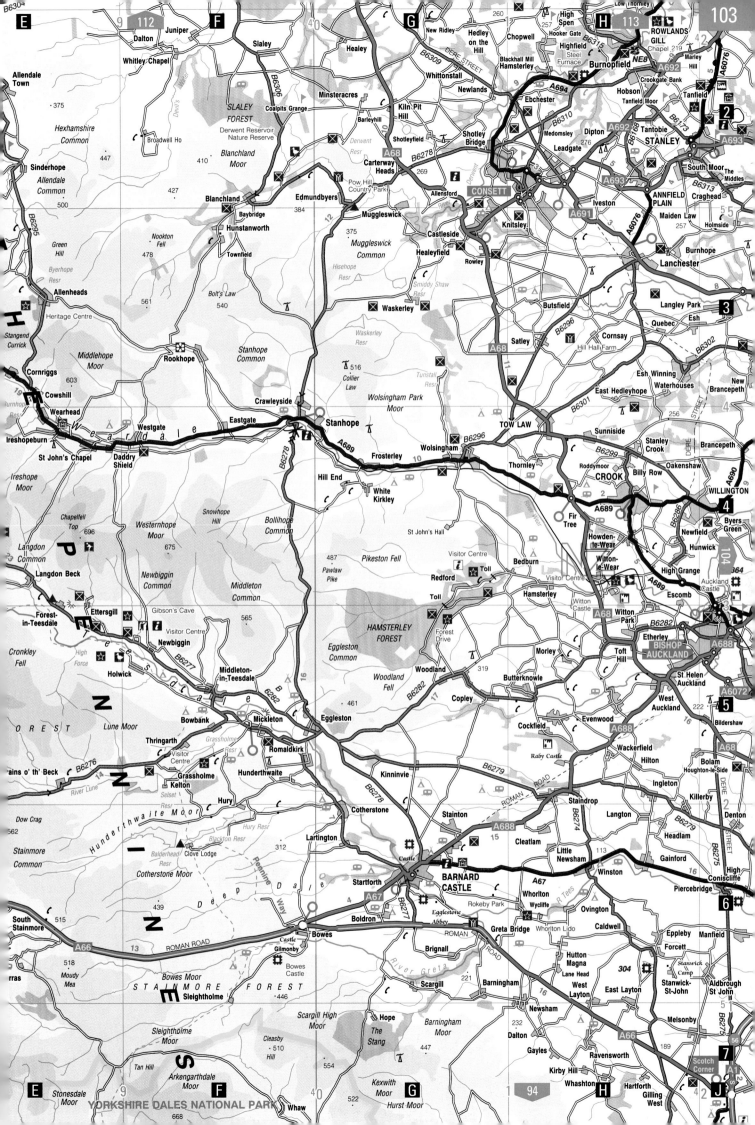

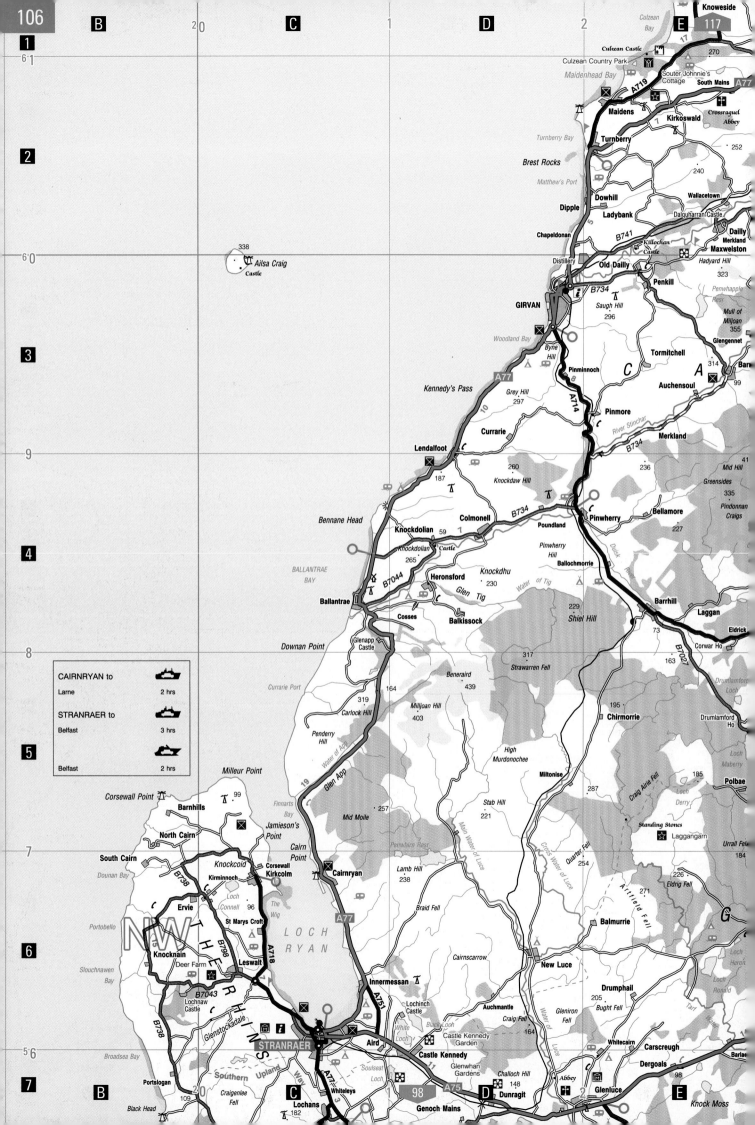

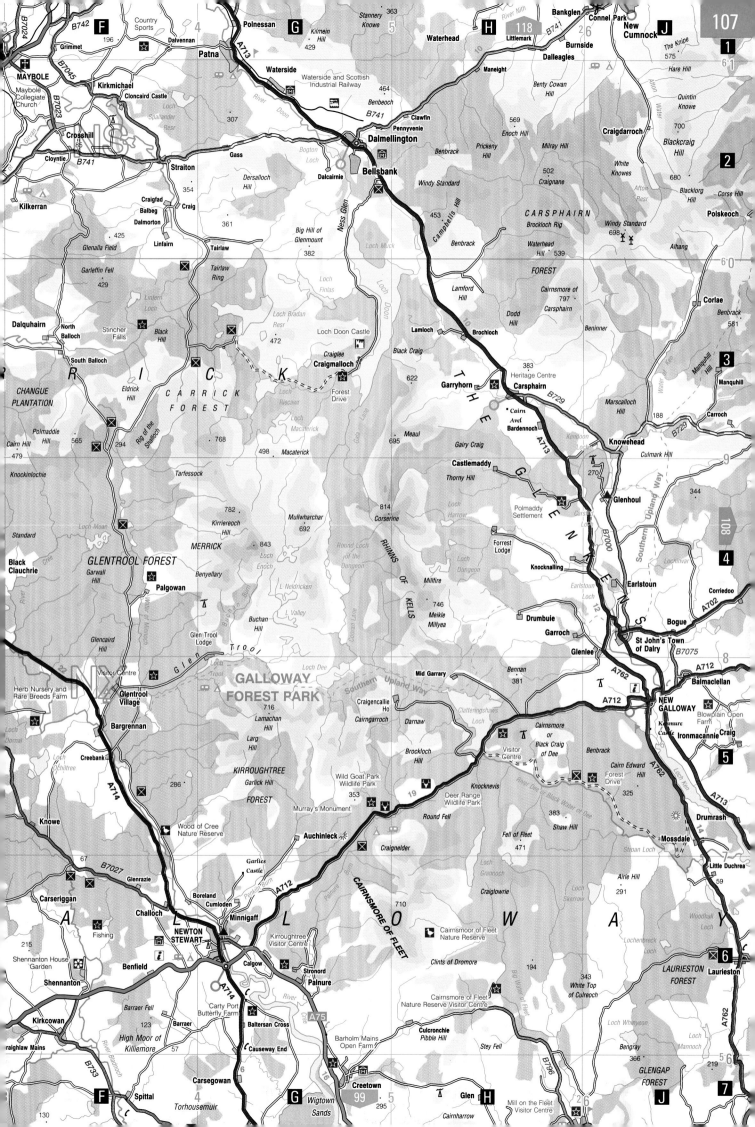

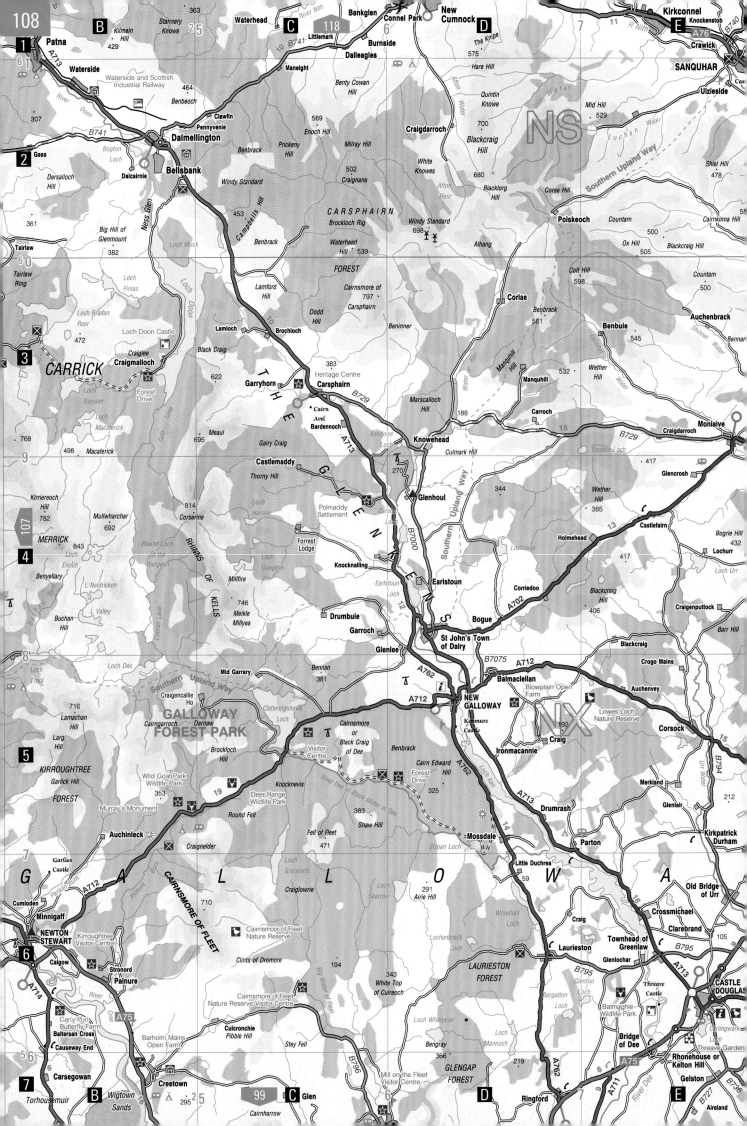

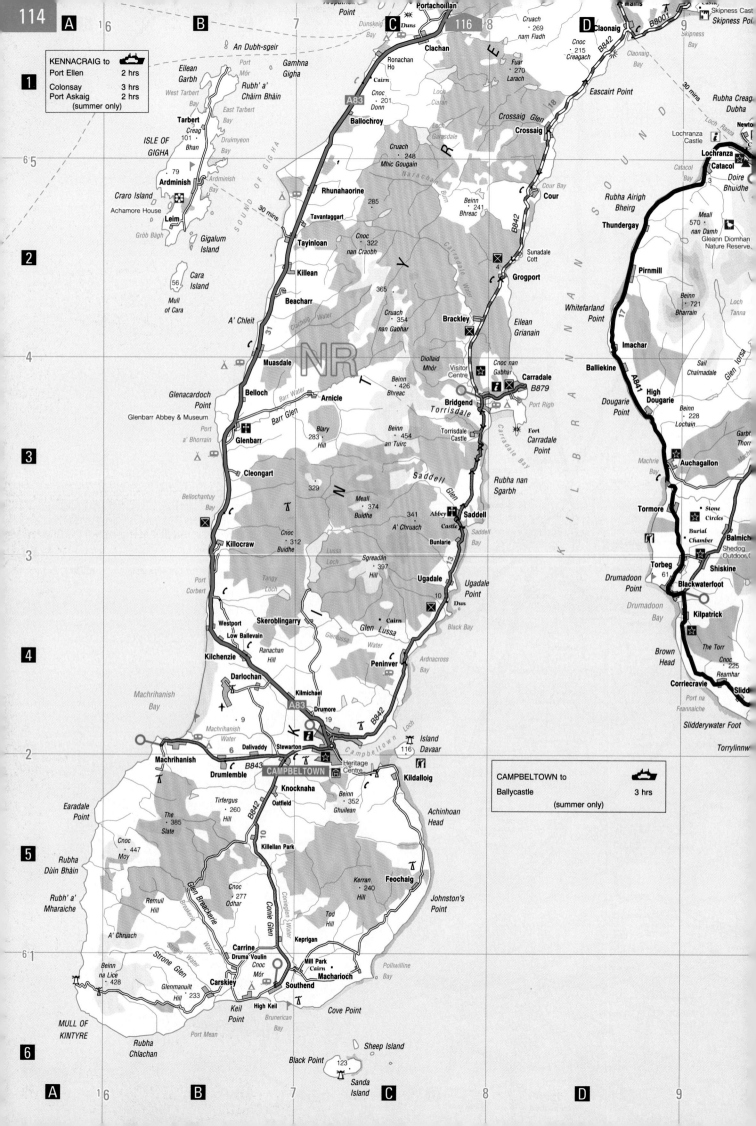

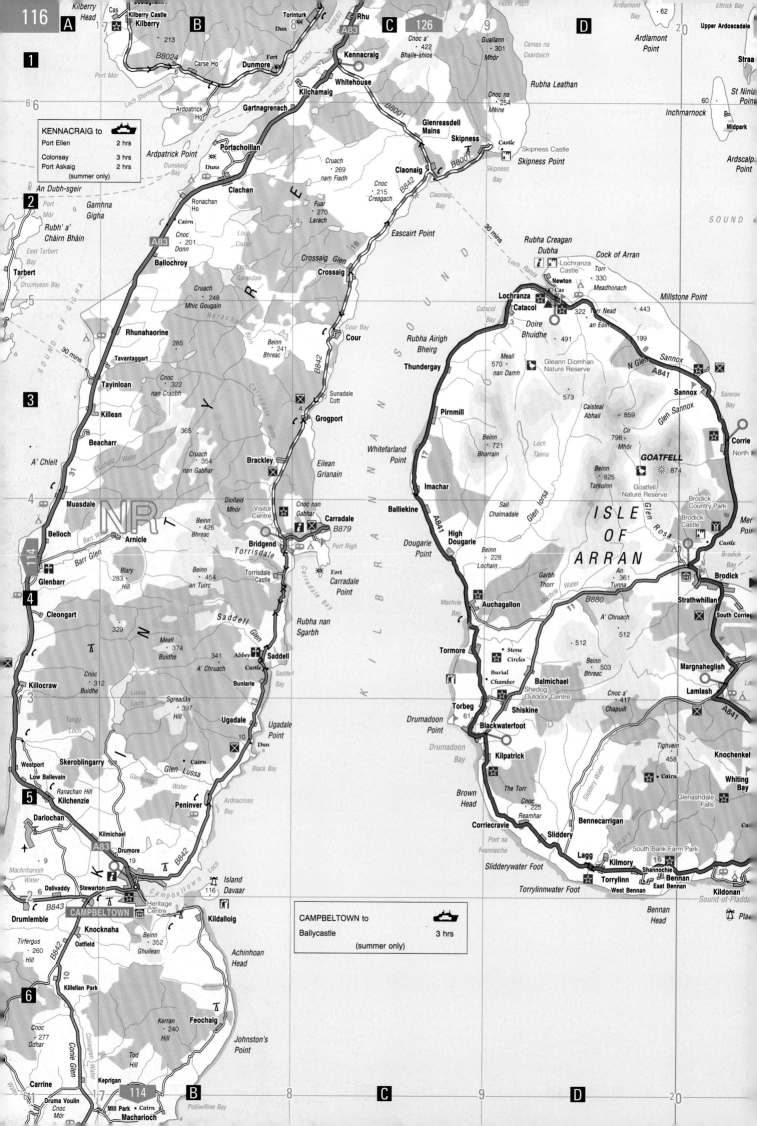

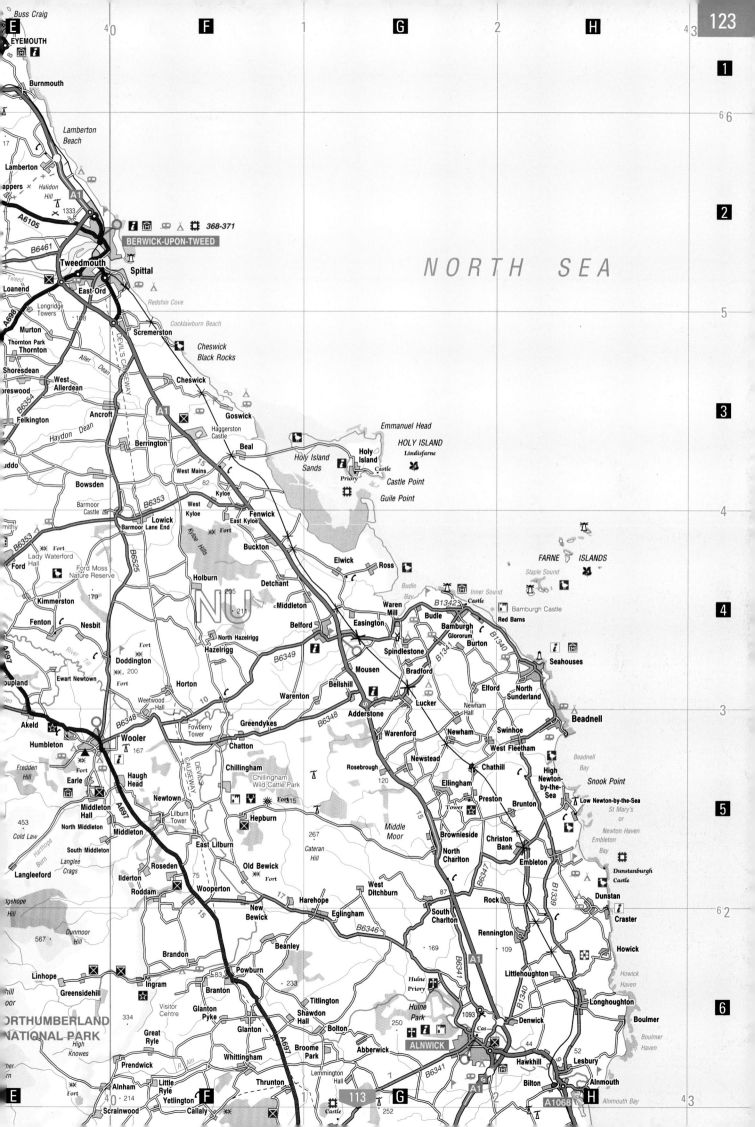

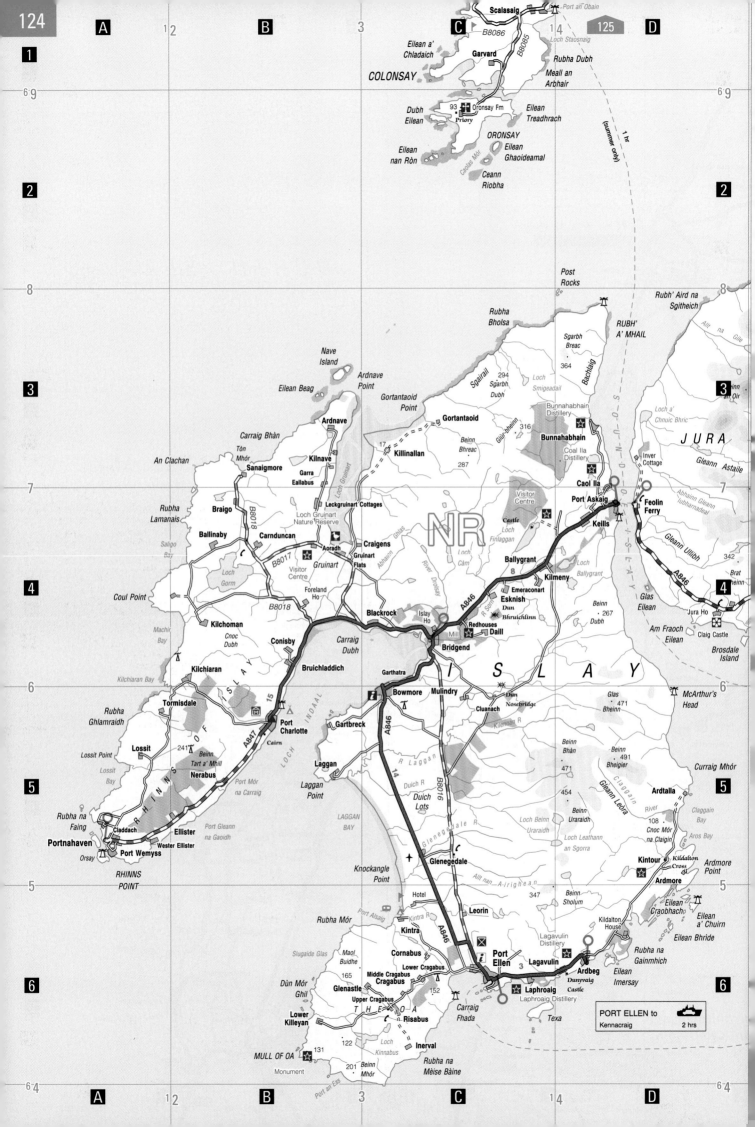

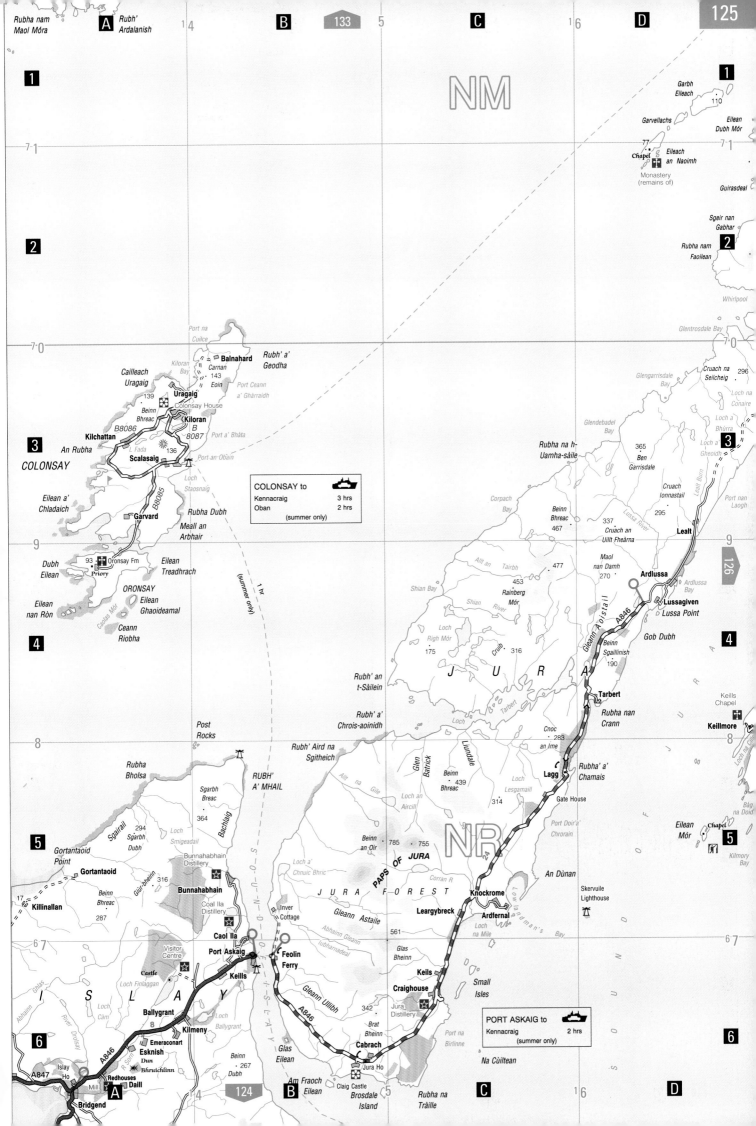

Rubha nam Maol Móra · **A** · Rubh' Ardalanish · 14 · **B** · 5 · **C** · 16 · **D**

1

NM

Garbh Eileach · 110

Garvellachs · 77 · Eilean Dubh Mór

+ Chapel · Eileach an Naoimh

Monastery (remains of) · Guirasdeal

2

Sgeir nan Gabhar

Rubha nam Faoilean

Whirlpool

Glentrosdale Bay

Port na Cuilce

3

Cailleach Uragaig · Kiloran Bay · **Balnahard** · Rubh' a' Geodha · Carnan 143 Eoin · Port Ceann a' Ghàrraidh

Beinn Bhreac 139 · **Uragaig** · Colonsay House · Port a' Bhàta

Kilchattan · B8086 · **Kiloran** · B 8087 · Port an-Obàin

COLONSAY · An Rubha · **Scalasaig** · L Fada · 136 · Loch Staosnaig

Eilean a' Chladaich · B8085 · **Garvard** · Rubha Dubh · Meall an Arbhair

9

Dubh Eilean · 93 · Oronsay Fm · Eilean Treadhrach

Priory · ORONSAY · Eilean Ghaoideamal

Eilean nan Ròn · Caolas Mór · Ceann Rìobha

1 hr (summer only)

Glengarrisdale Bay · Cruach na Seilcheig · 296

Glendebadel Bay · Loch na Conaire

Rubha na h-Uamha-sàile · 365 · Ben Garrisdale · Cruach Ionnastail · 295 · Loch a' Bhùrra · Loch a' Gheoidh

Corpach Bay · Beinn Bhreac 467 · 337 · Cruach an Uillt Fheàrna · Port nan Laogh

Lealt

Allt an Tairbh · Lussa River · 477 · Maol nan Damh 270 · **Ardlussa** · Ardlussa Bay · Lussagiven

Shian Bay · 453 · Rainberg Mór · A846 · **Lussagiven** · Lussa Point

Shian River · Gleann Aoistail · Beinn Sgaillinish 190 · Gob Dubh

COLONSAY to 🚢
Kennacraig ... 3 hrs
Oban ... 2 hrs
(summer only)

4

Loch Righ Mór · 175 · Cruib · 316 · **JURA**

Keills Chapel

Rubh' an t-Sàilein · Loch Tarbert · **Tarbert** · Rubha nan Crann · + Keillmore

8

Post Rocks

Rubh' Aird na Sgitheich · Rubh' a' Chrois-aoinidh · Allt na Gile · Glen Batrick · Liundale · Cnoc an Ime 283 · **Lagg** · Rubha' a' Chamais

RUBH' A' MHAIL

Rubha Bholsa · Sgarbh Breac · Beinn Bhreac 439 · Loch Lesgamaill · 314 · Gate House · Port Doir'a' Chroráin · Eilean Mór · + Chapel

5

Sgairail · Sgarbh Dubh 294 · 364 · Bachlaig · Loch Smigeadail · Bunnahabhain Distillery

Gortantaoid Point · **Gortantaoid** · Gùr-bheinn 316 · Beinn an Òir 785 · 755 · PAPS OF JURA · Loch a' Chnuic Bhric · Corran R · 561 · NR

Bàg na Doid

Killinallan · 17 · **Killinallan** · Beinn Bhreac 287 · **Bunnahabhain** · Coal Ila Distillery · **JURA** FOREST · Gleann Astaile · Abhainn Gleann Iubharnadeal · Port na Mìle · An Dùnan

Kilmory Bay

Knockrome · Skervuile Lighthouse

Leargybreck · **Ardfernal** · Loch na Mìle

67

Visitor Centre · **Port Askaig** · Inver Cottage · **Feolin Ferry** · Glas Bheinn · **Keils** · Small Isles

Castle · **Caol Ila** · **Craighouse** · Jura Distillery

ISLAY · **Keills** · Loch Finlaggan · Jura Distillery

6

River Drolsay · A846 · **Ballygrant** · Loch Cam · **Kilmeny** · Loch Ballygrant · Gleann Ullibh · A846 · 342 · Brat Bheinn

Abhainn · Islay Ho · **Esknish** · Dun · Beinn 267 Dubh · Glas Eilean · **Cabrach** · Jura Ho · Port na Birlinne · Na Cùiltean

A847 · **Redhouses** · Mill · **Daill** · Bhruichlinn · Am Fraoch Eilean · Claig Castle

Bridgend · Brosdale Island · Rubha na Tràille

PORT ASKAIG to 🚢
Kennacraig ... 2 hrs
(summer only)

Rubha nam Maol Móra · **A** · 14 · **B** · 124 · 5 · **C** · 16 · **D**

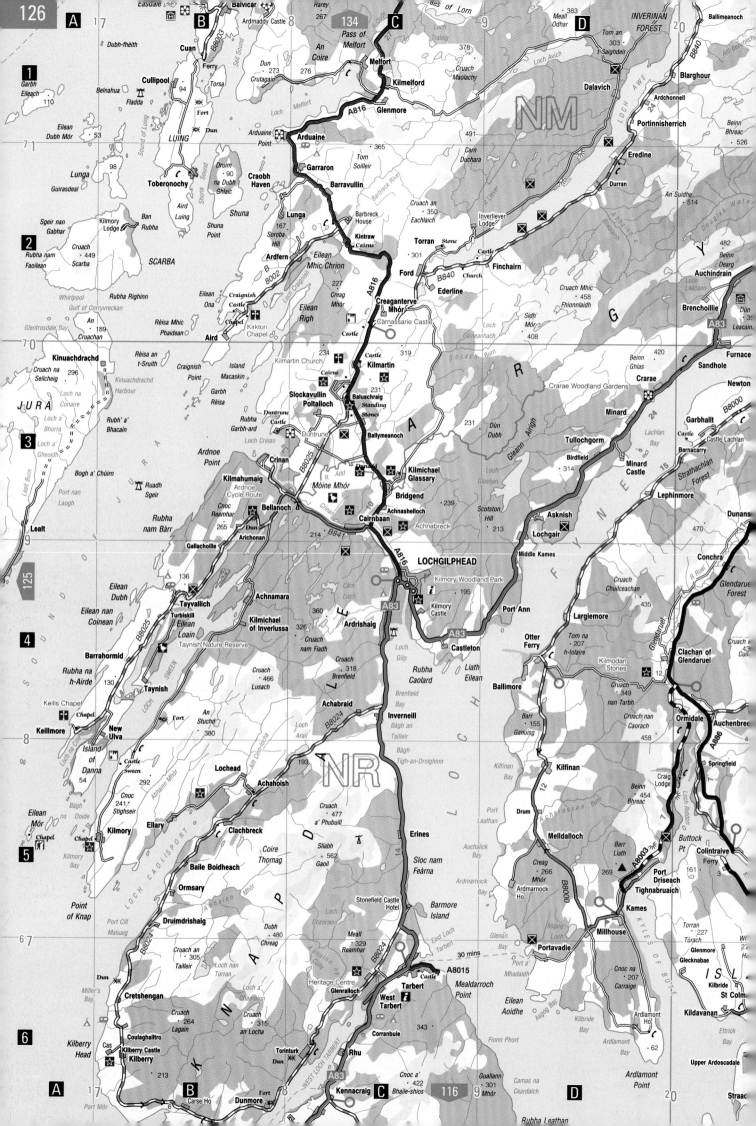

INNER HEBRIDES

COLL

Eag na Maoile

Rubha Mór
Sòrisdale
Bousd
B8072

Rubh' a'
Bhinnein

Cliad Bay
Gallanach
Arnabost

Rubha Hogh
Grishipoll
Clabhach
Ballyhaugh
B8071

Ben
104
Hogh
Hogh Bay

Loch
Cliad
Bagh
Feisdlum

Arinagour

Rubha a'
Ghraineig
Totronald
Acha
Arileod
B8070
Uig
Friesland
Eilean
Ornsay

Port Mine
Feall Bay
Breachacha
Castle

Loch
Eatharna

Port na
h-Eathar

Calgary Point
Crossapol
Bay
Rubha
Fàsachd

Gunna
Port a'
Mhurain
Soa
Breachacha

Caolas Ban

Urvaig

Dun Mór
Vaul
Bay
Vaul
Salum
Caolas
Rubha Dubh

B 8069
Ruaig

1 hr

Hough
Skerries

Rubha
Port Bhiosd
Clachan Mór
Balephetrish
Bay
Cornaigbeg
Rubha
Nead a' Gheòidh

Rubha
Chráiginis
Hough
Bay
Balevullin
119
Kilmoluaig
B8068
Kenovay
B8068
5
Gott Bay
Soa
Rubha na
Sean Charraigen

Kilkenneth
B8068
3
Scarinish
B8065

Sandaig
Moss
Heanish
Middleton
B8065
Heylipol
Baugh
TIREE
Port Mór
Crossapol
Rubha
Tràigh an Dùin
Port Bharrapol
Barrapol
2
3
HYNISH
BAY

Treshnish

Balephuil
Balemartine
Mannal
B8067
141
B8068

Rinn
Thorbhais
Balephuil
Bay
Carnan
Mór
Hynish

Bac Mór or
Dutchman's Cap
Bac Beag

Réidh
Eilean

IONA

Stac an Aoineidh

Eilean na h-
Aon Chaorach

Greave
Soa
Island

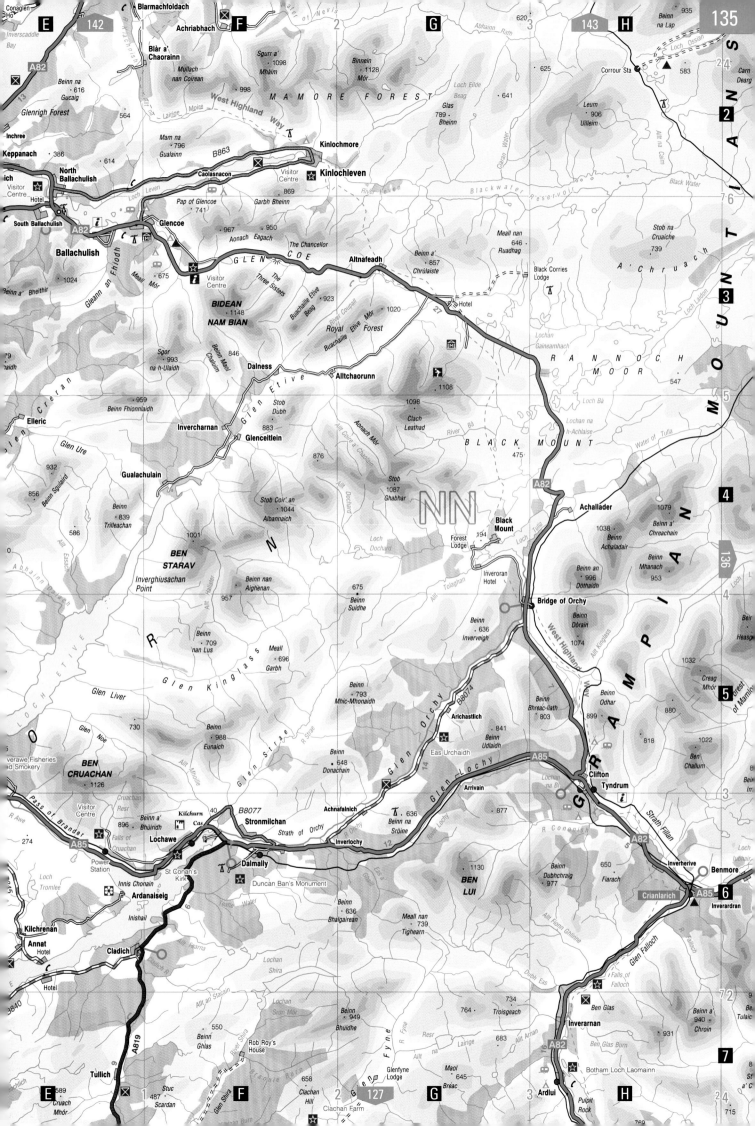

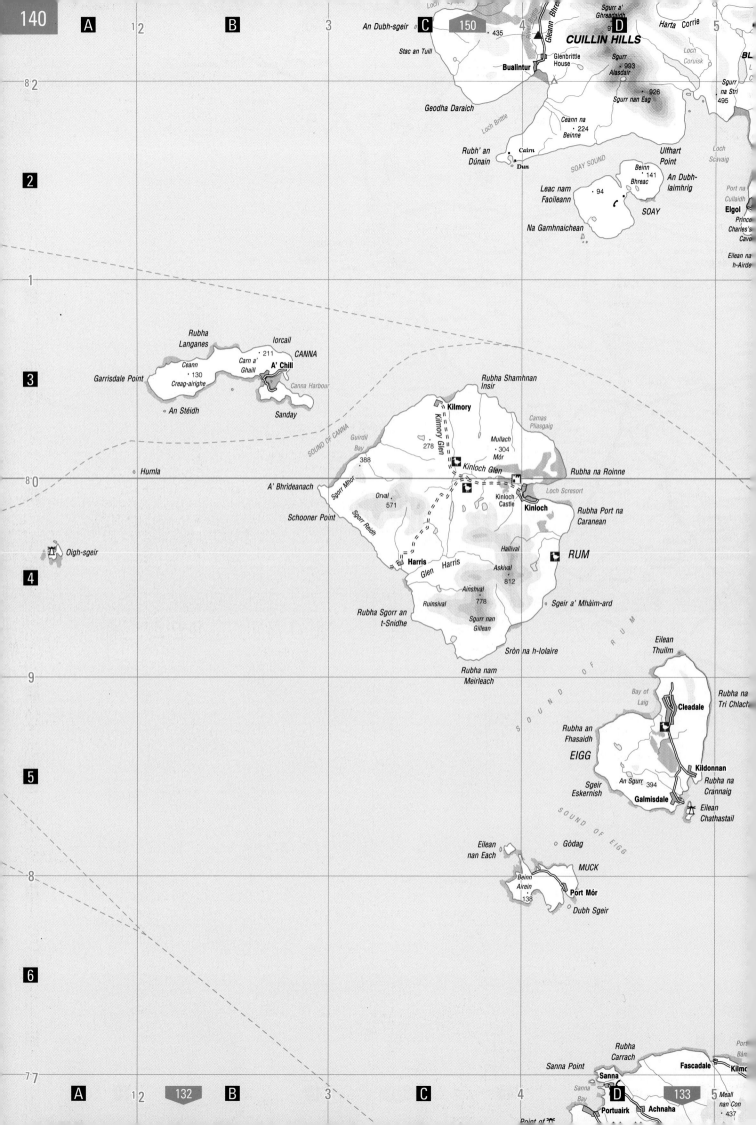

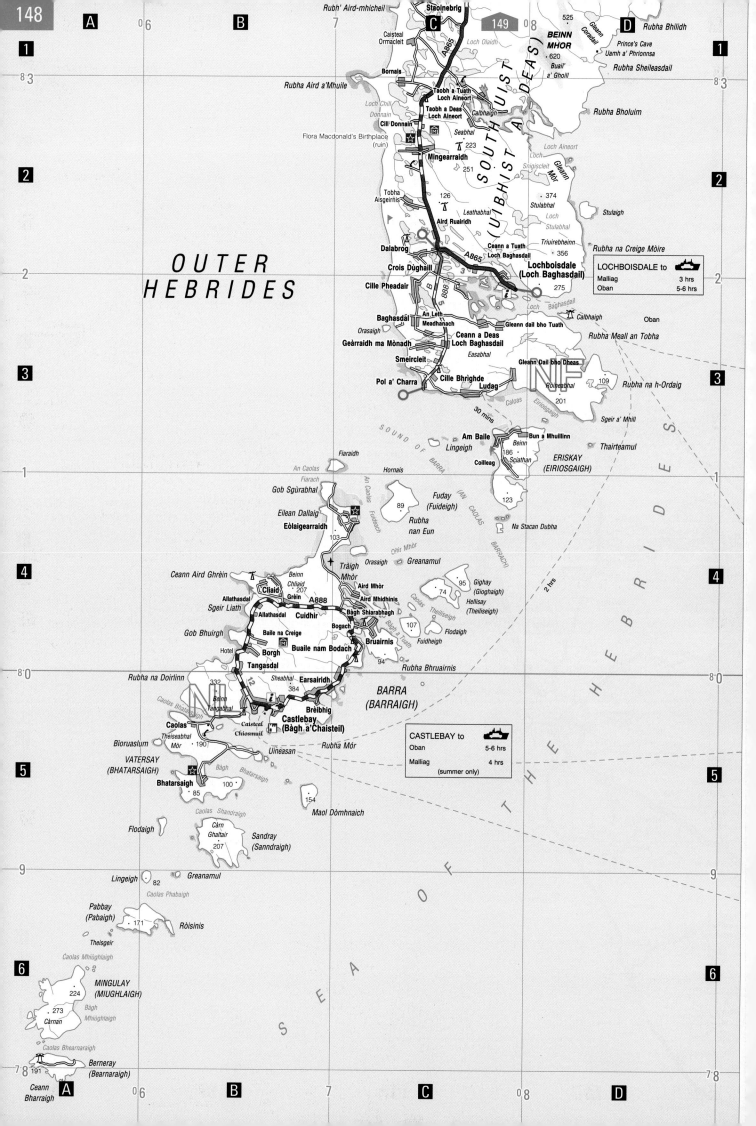

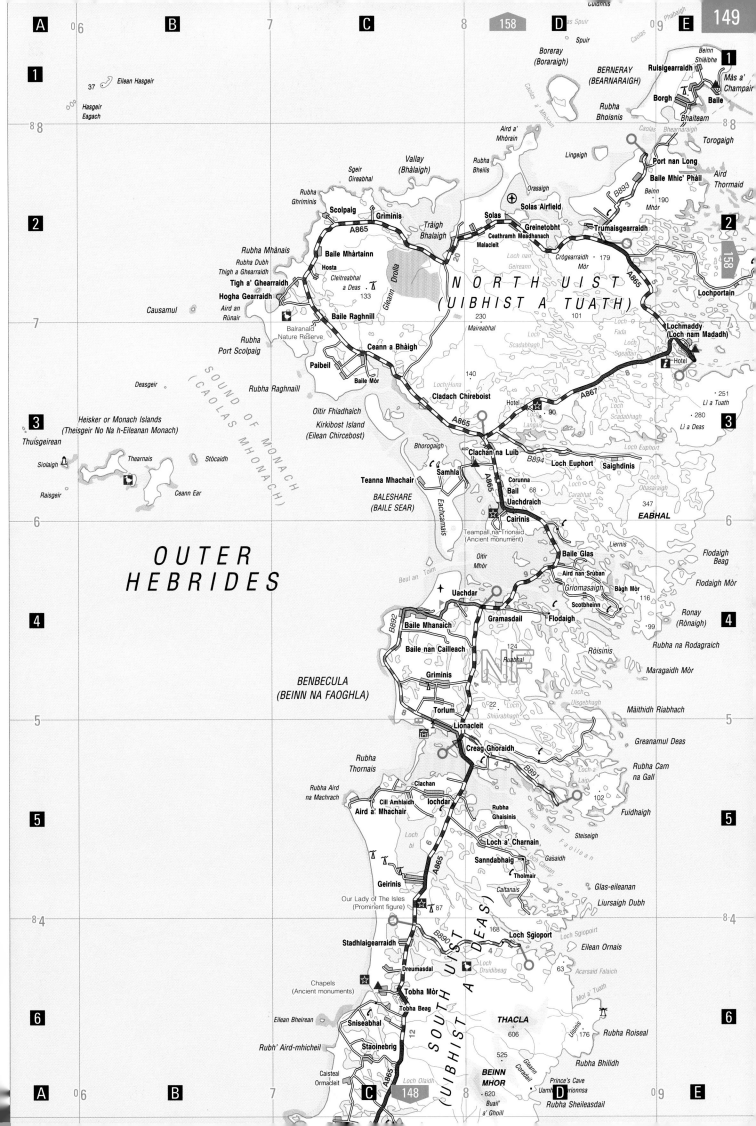

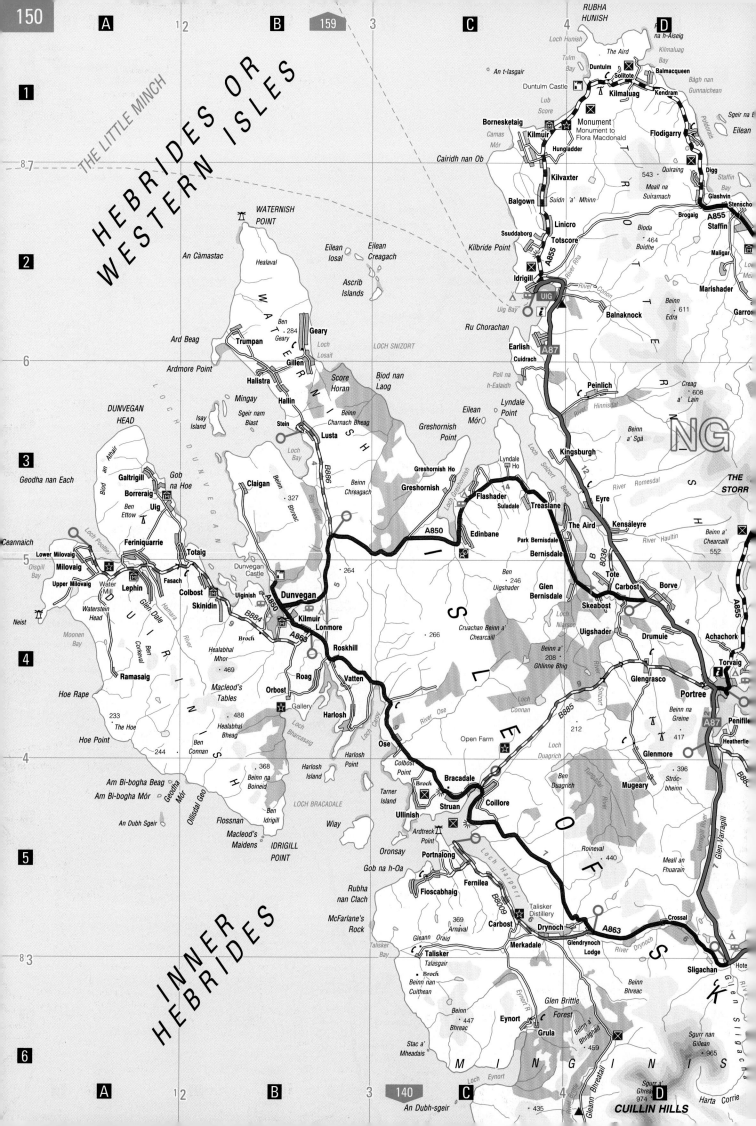

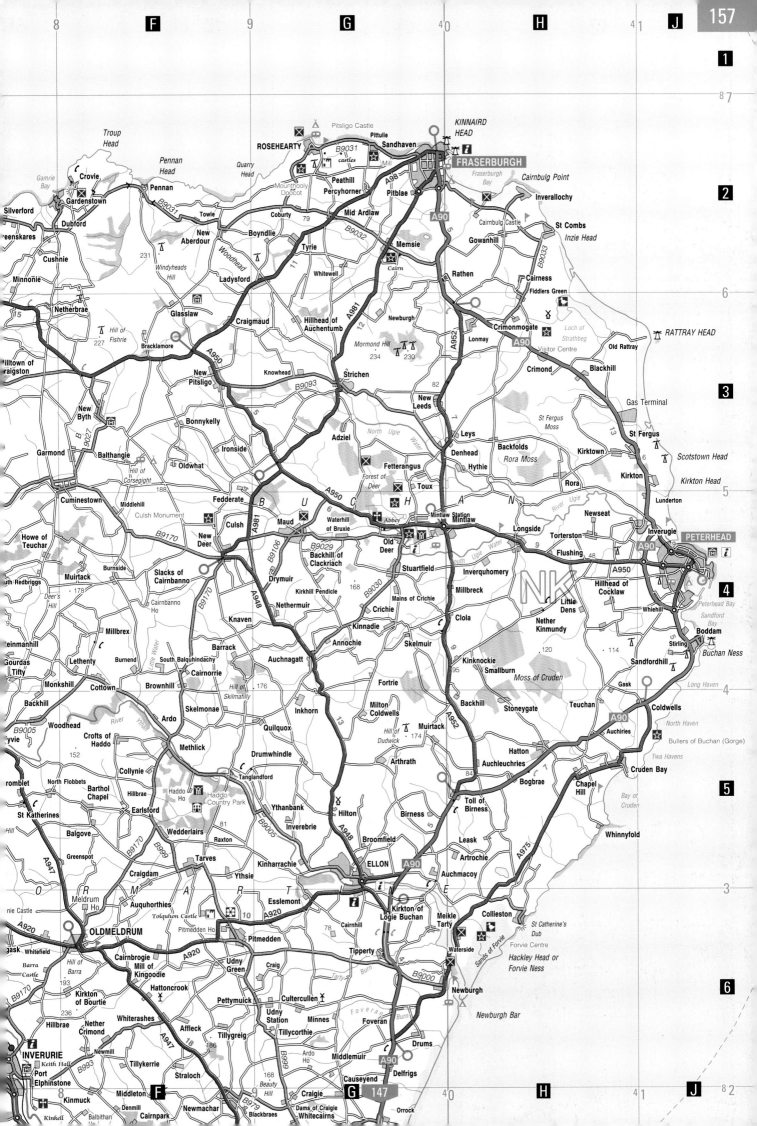

ST KILDA OR HIRTA
(HIORT)

Soay
(Soaigh)   378

376   St Kilda
Dun

Boreray
(Boraraigh)   384

8

9

L   M

St Kilda lies about 41 miles or 68 km WNW of Rubha Ghriminis NF 7276

Leibhinis

HEBRIDES
OUTER
NA

SCARP   308
Sròn
Romul   303
Taran Mòr

Mànais
Rubha Huisinis   HUISINIS
Gobhaig   489
Huiseabhal Mòr
Leòsabhal   412
Horsanais
Rubha Leacach   ABHAINN SUID
Gloraig Tharansaigh   12
Airde Mòr

Rubha nan Totag
Camus an t-Saoidhein

TARANSAY
(TARASAIGH)   267
Ben
Raah

Gàisgeir   32

Aird
Mhanais   99
SOUND OF TARA
(CAOLAS THAR

Rubha
Sgeirigin

Rubha Romaigidh   HORGABOS
158
Cleit
Niosabois
Na Buirg

Rubha Màs
a' Chnuic

Toe head
(Gob an Tobha)
Copaigh   Sgeir
Liath   Sgarasta Mhor
Sgarasta Bheag   398
Bleabhal

Ceapabhal   368
SOUTH HARRI
(CEANN A TUATH NA
Rubh' an
Teampuill   Loch Langabhat

81   Siolaigh   Taobh Tuath   281
Gràebhal
Siolaigh Bheag   Taigh a' Chaolais   Loch
Steisebhal

Caolas Shiolaigh   Rubha
Bhreinis   196
Beinn a'
Chàrnain   Rubh' a' Bhaile
Fo Thuath   A859
A859

PABBAY
(PABAIGH)   Ensay
(Easaigh)   49   Leverburgh
(An t-Ob)   459
Roineabhal

Cuidhnis   Caolas Phabaigh   Cairminis
Eilean
Chairminis

Caolas Spuir   1 hr   Killegray
(Ceileagraigh)   45   SRANNDA

Spuir   Beinn
Shlèibhe   Langaigh   Roghadal
Bhala

Boreray
(Boraraigh)   Ruisigearraidh   Màs a
Champair   SOUND OF NA HARRISH

BERNERAY
(BEARNARAIGH)   86   Baile   Grodhaigh   Gilsaigh
Borgh   Sgeir a'
Bhaiteam   Chàil   Lingeigh
Rubha
Bhoisnis   Sgeir a'   Sgarabhaigh

Caolas a' Mhòrain   Caolas   Torogaigh   Seòlait Mhic
Bhearnaraigh   Neacail   Sursaigh   Opasaigh

Aird a'   Port nan Long   Aird
Mhòrain   Thormaid
Lingeigh
Rubha   Baile Mhic' Phàil   Taghaigh   Thernatraigh
Valley   Bheilis   Beinn   190
(Bhàlaigh)   B893   Mhòr

Sgeir   Orasaigh   Loch
Oireabhal   Solas Airfield   Amhlasaraigh

Rubha   Solas   Crògearraidh   Gròdaigh
Ghriminis   Greinetobht   na Thobha
SCOLPAIG   Ceathramh Meadhanach   Trumaisgearraidh   154   Rubha
Rubha Mhànais   GRIMINIS   Malacleit   Crògearraidh   Lochportain   an Dùine
A865   Tràigh   Mòr   179
Rubha Dubh   Bhalaigh   Loch nan
Thigh a Ghearraidh   Baile Mhàrtainn   Geireann   A865
Hosta   NF   NORTH UIST   Loch
TIGH A' GHEARRAIDH   Cleitreabhal   (UIBHIST A TUATH)   Fada
a Deas   133   Loch
Hogha Gearraidh   230   101   Sgealtair   Lochmaddy
Aird an   Baile Raghnill   Maireabhal   154   (Loch nam Madadh)   Rubha an Fhigheadair
Rùnair   Loch   Hotel   Rubha nam Plèac
Balranald   Scadabhagh   Loch   Loch Maddy
Rubha   Nature Reserve   Maddy   (Loch nam Madadh)
Port Scolpaig   Ceann a Bhàigh   Madadh Gruamach
Paibeil   Loch   251
Baile Mòr   Huna   Lì a Tuath
Rubha Raghnaill   140   Hotel   280
Cladach Chireboist   Loch   90   Lì a Deas
Oitir Fhiadhaich   A867
Kirkibost Island   Loch   An t-Aigeach
(Eilean Chircebost)   Langais
Bhorogaigh   Loch
SOUND OF MONACH   Clachan na Luib   Scadabhagh   Loch Euphort   Rubha Mhic
(CAOLAS MHONACH)   B894   Gille-mhicheil
Samhla   Loch Euphort   Saighdinis   Eigneig Mhòr
Teanna Mhachair   Corunna   68   Loch
BALESHARE   Bail'   Carabhat   Obasaraigh
(BAILE SEAR)   Uachdraich   347   Eigneig Bheag
Cairinis   EABHAL

149

A865

149

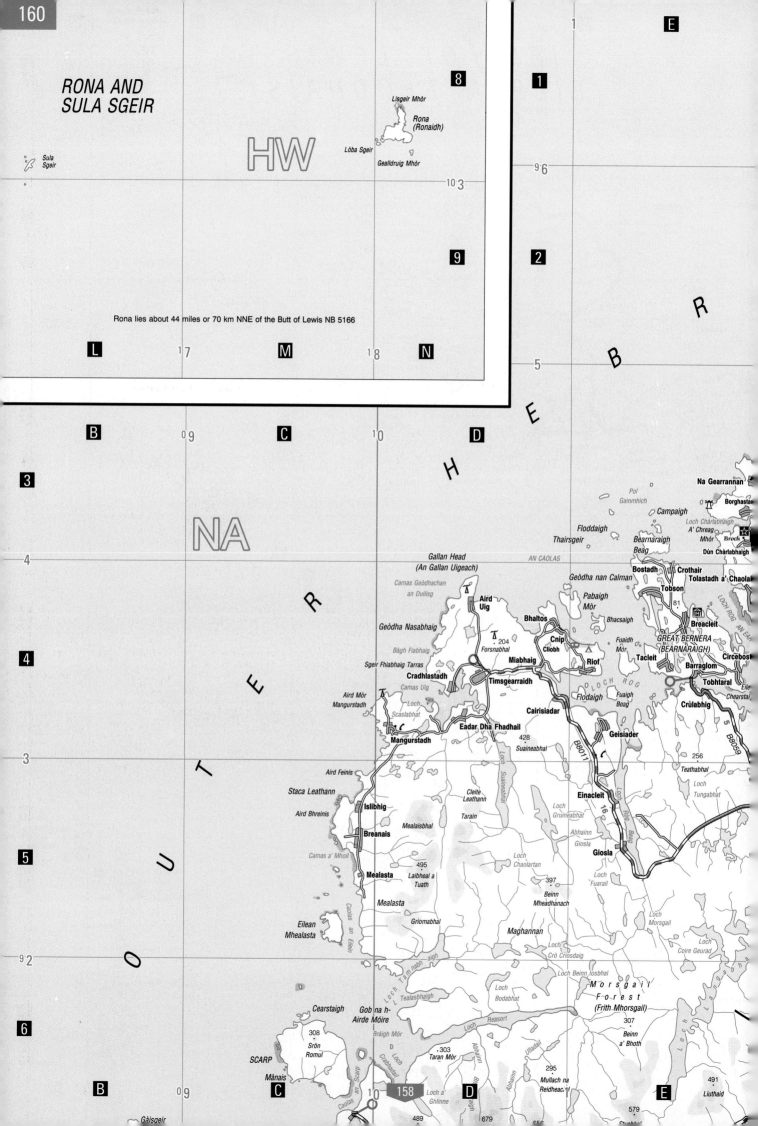

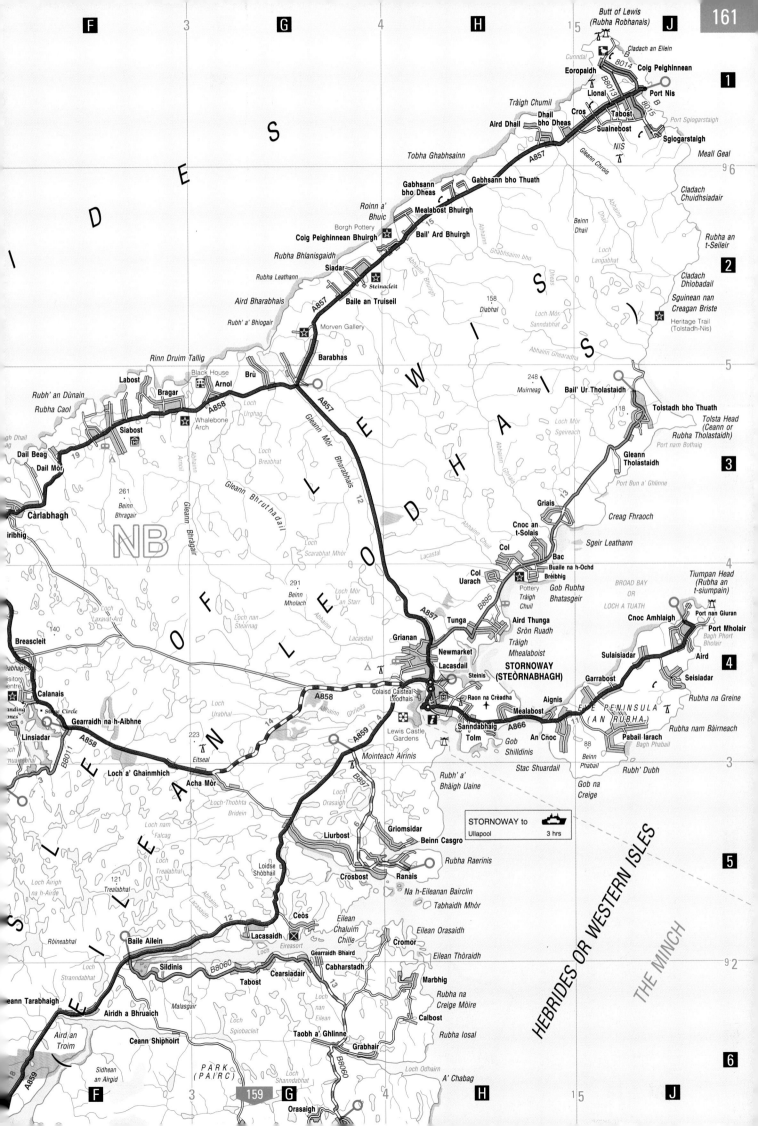

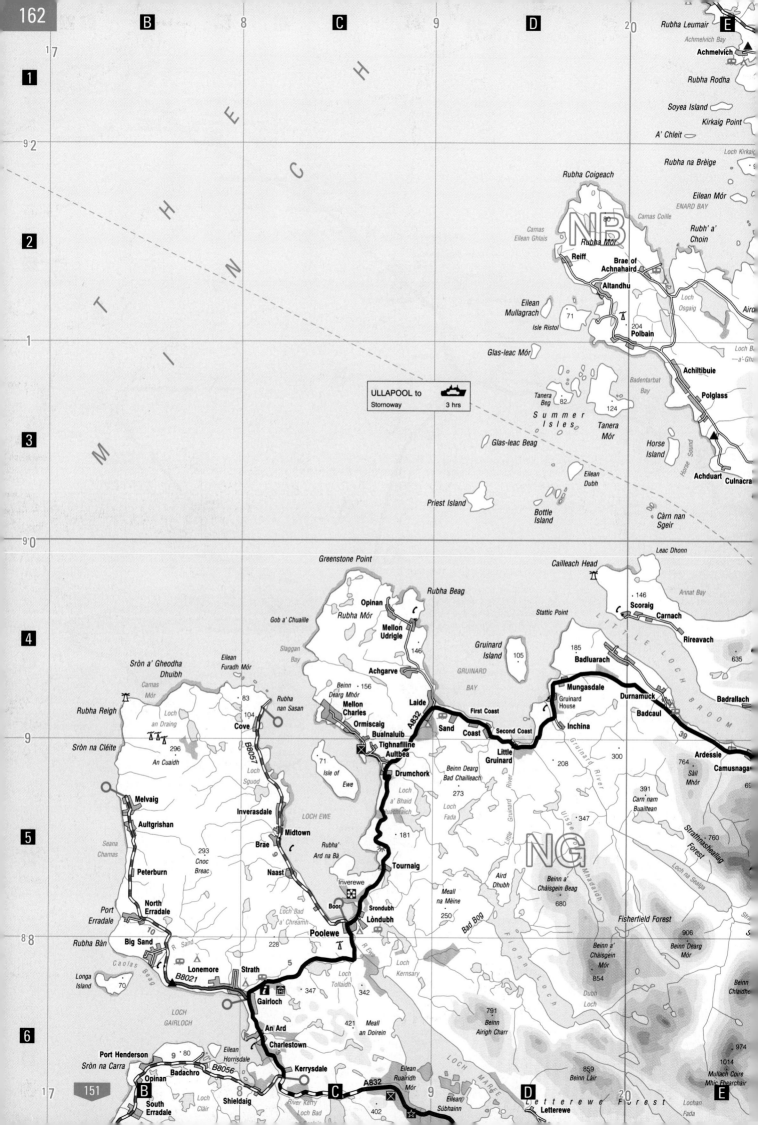

B   8   C   9   D   20   E

17

1

92

2

NB

1

3

ULLAPOOL to
Stornoway   3 hrs

90

4

NG

9

5

88

6

17   151

B   8   C   9   D   20   E

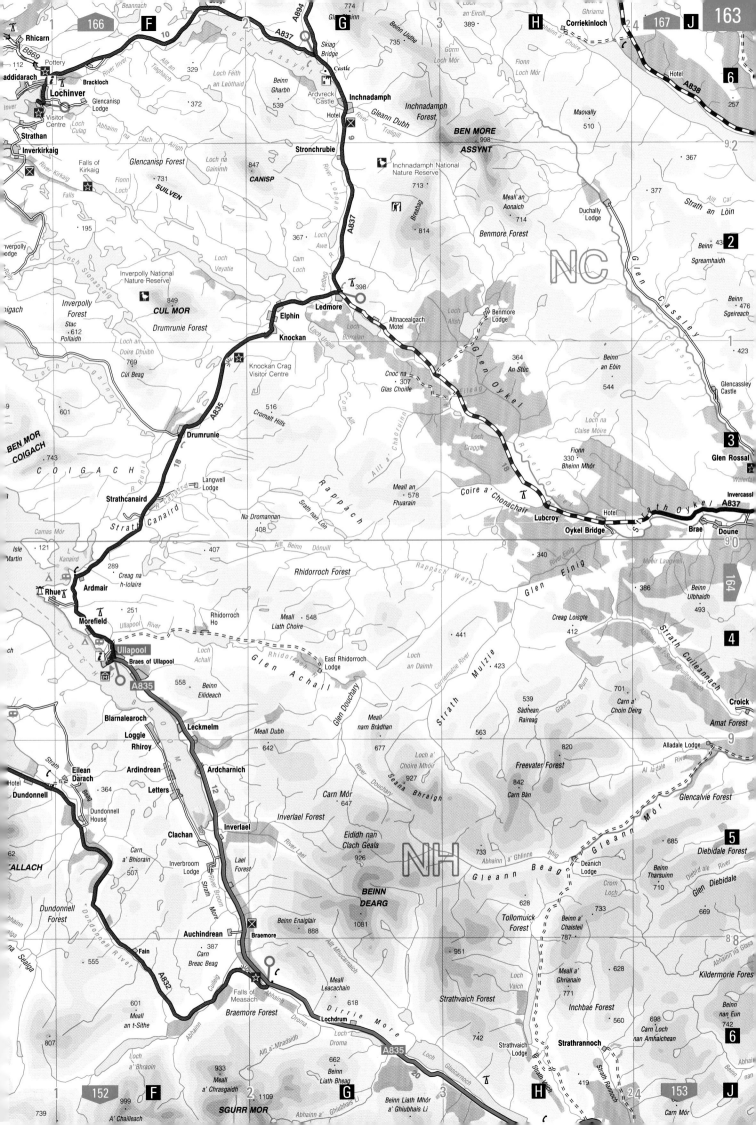

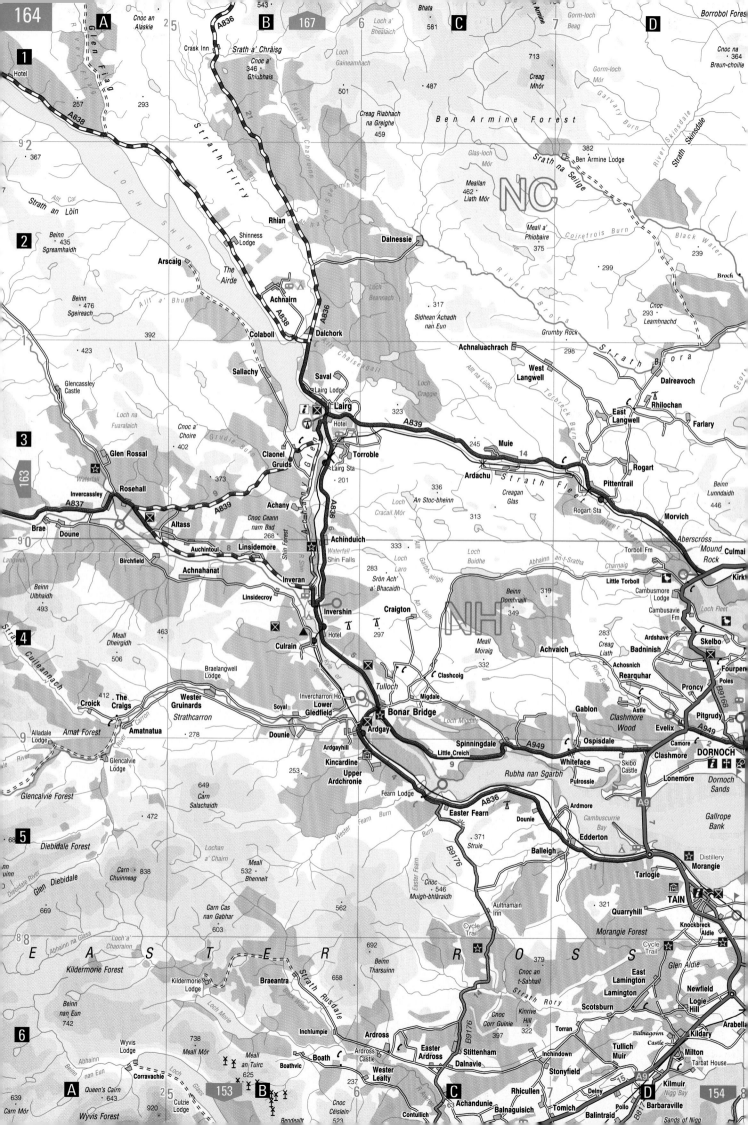

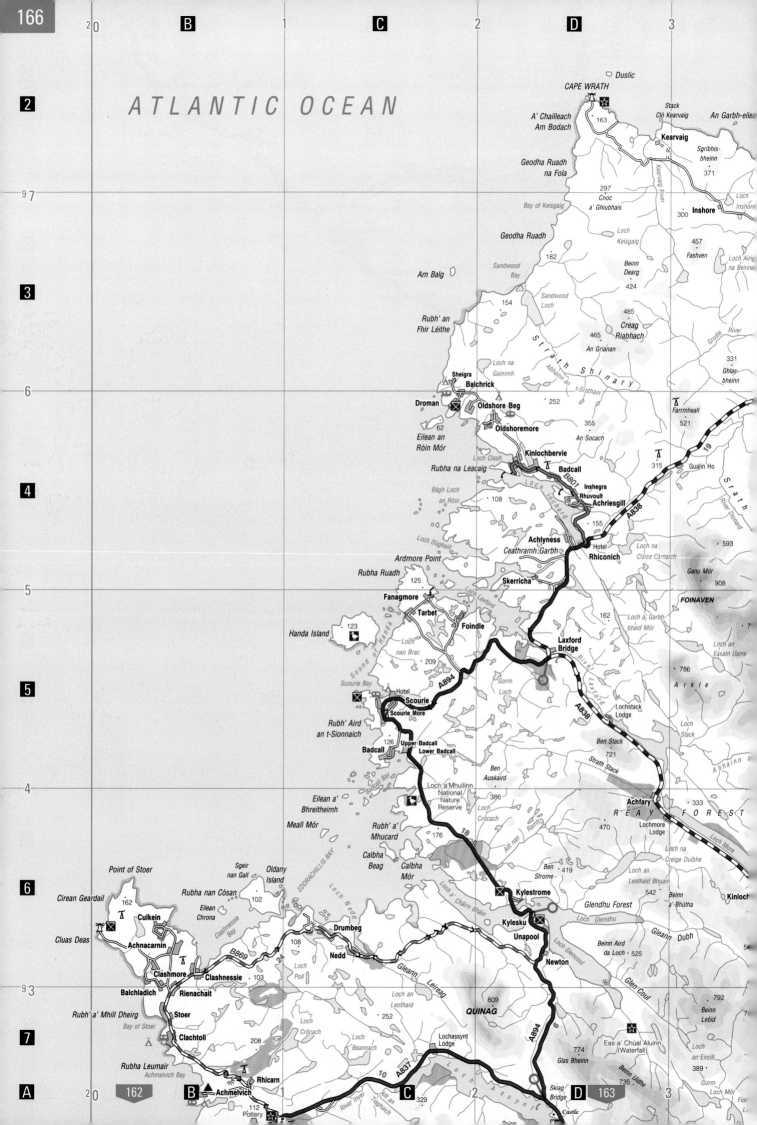

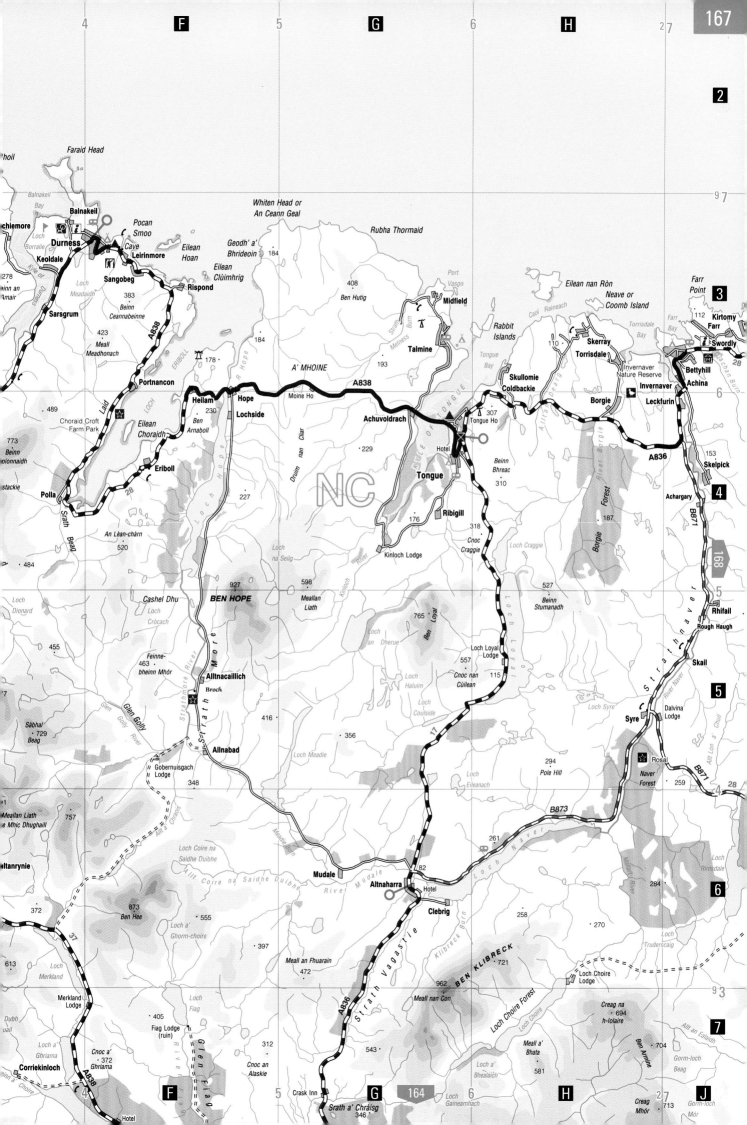

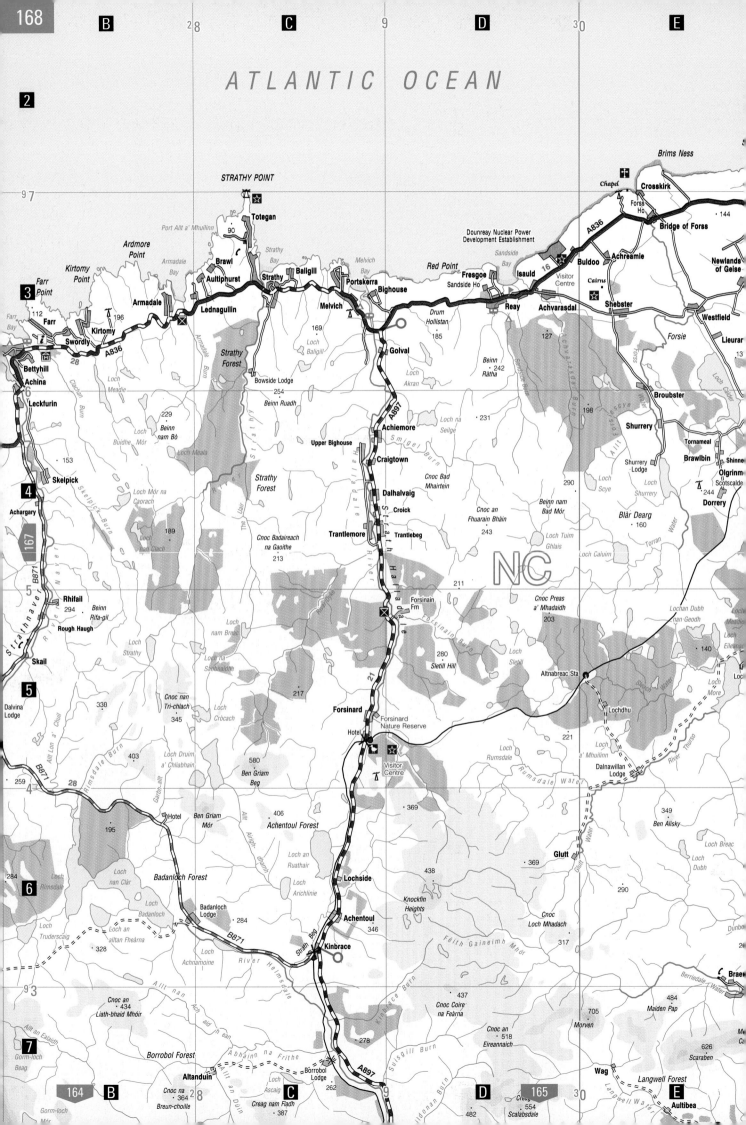

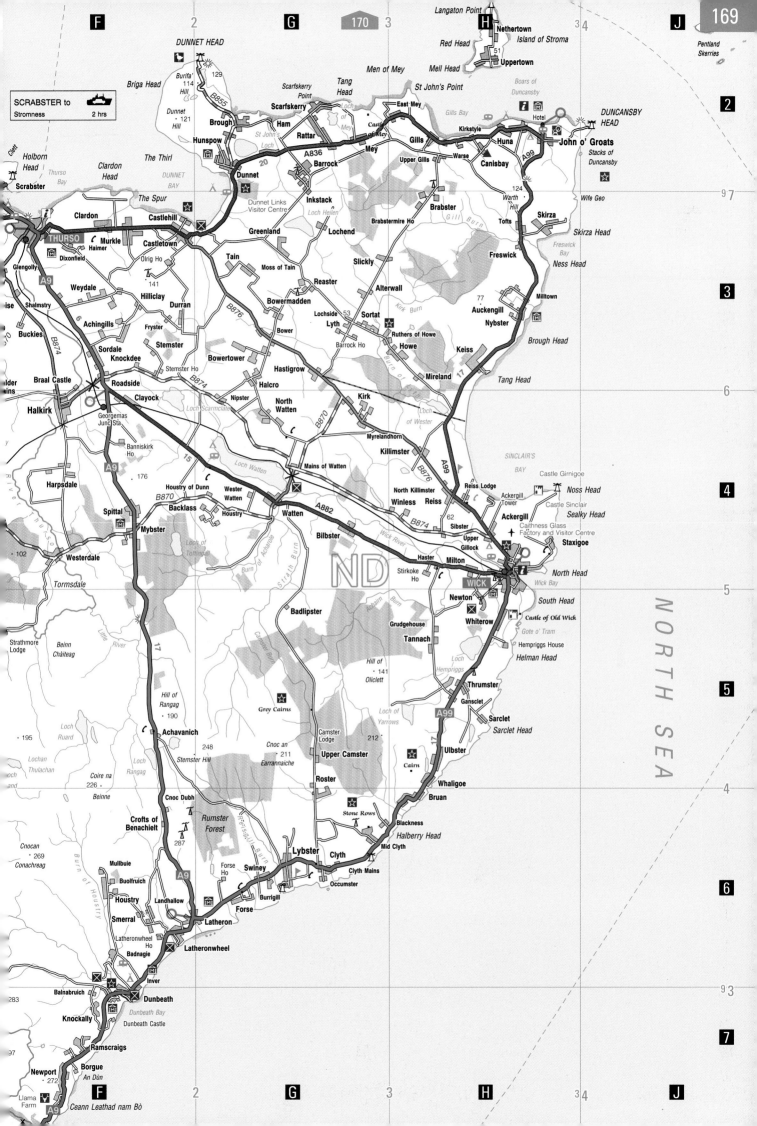

172

BROUGH HEAD

Settlement

Palace
Feavall
Abune-the-Hill
The Barony
Birsay
Birsay Bay
Kitchener
Memorial
Brockan
Marwick Head
Marwick
Boardhouse
Twatt
Kirbuster

Mar Wick
The Loons
Nature Reserve
Greeny
Beaquoy
Quoyscottie

Outshore Point
Vestra
Field
Isbister
Northdyke
Quoyloo
Sandwick
Kierfiold
Ho
Swartland
Dounby
Mirbister

Point of Howana Geo

Bay of Skaill
Hole o' Row
Skaill
Skara
Brae
Row Head
Loch of
Skaill
Aith
Hestwall
Voy
Broch
Cauldrus
Yesnaby
B9056

Neban Point
Arion
Hill of
Miffia
158
Quholm

Neblonga
Black
Craig
Outertown
STROMNESS
Bridge
of Waithe
Cairn

Breck Ness

Point of Oxan
Graemsay

STROMNESS to
Aberdeen .... 8-14 hrs
Lerwick .... 8 hrs
Scrabster .... 2 hrs

30 mins
Breckan
62

Bay of the Tongue
Kame of Hoy
Geo of Hellia
Murra
St John's Head
Cuilags
433
Linksness
Hoy
Quoyness
The Sow
481
Ward
Hill
B9047
Bring Head
Old Man of Hoy
North Hoy
Nature Reserve
Moor
Fea
Dwarfie Stane
Scad Head
RORA HEAD
304
Moorfea
Rackwick
South Burn
Rack Wick

Lyrie Geo
Withi
Gill
360
H O Y
ND
Sneuk Head
Genie
Fea
233
Lyness

Little Rack Wick
Heldale
Water
154
Rinnigill

Little Ayre
B9047
Melsetter
199
The
Berry
Hurliness
Ha Wick
Brims
Grassy Cletts
Tor Ness
Brims
Ness

DUNNET HEAD

Briga Head
Burifa'
Hill
114
129
B855

Costa
Head
A966
Skea
Whitaloo Point
10
3
A966
Monastery
Broch
Cairn

Costa
Burgar
Eynhallow
Loch of
Swannay

Aiker
Ness
Broch
Stenso
159
Redland
Evie
Loch of
Hundland
Mid
Hill
Birsay Moors
Nature Reserve
B9057
Click Mill
Kame of
Corrigall
176
221
Milldoe
HY
Tingw

Corston
Corrigal
Settiscarth
Hackl
Harray
Brough
Ward of
Redland
Breck of
Cruan
Isbister
Netherbrough
Bimbister

B9057
A986
Cairn
Maes Howe
Finstown
A965
4
N
Bay of
Da
Stone
Circles
Heddle
Grimbister
7
Cairn
Hotel
Sultigeo
Nisthouse
STENNESS
Clouston
Stenness
Ireland
Ward
Hill
269
Keelylang
Hill
Loch of
Kirbister
Hall of Clestrain
Kirbister
Hobbister
Clestrain
Orphir
Orphir
A964
19
Petertown
Crya
Swanbister
Ho
Church
Houton
Ve Ness
Waukmill Bay

Houton
Head
Midland Ness
Cava
Barrel of Butter
S C A P A
Bring Head
BRING DEEPS
1 hr
Green
Head
Rysa Little
Calf of Flotta
18
Fara
43
Roan
Head
Mill Bay
Oil
Terminal
Pegal Burn
Gutter Sound
Weddel Sound
B
9045
36
Whome
B9046
FLOTTA
Crockness
Swarth
Sound
of
Hoxa
He
Wyng
Hackness
Longhope
57
Cantick Head
SOUTH WALLS
Swithia
Melsetter
North Bay
Auth Hope
Longhope
Garth Head
Mishister Geo
Kirk Hope
Brims
The
North Hea
P E N T L A N D
Swona
The Tails
of the Tarf
F I R T

Langaton Point
Netherton
Red Head
Island of Stroma
Mell Head
St John's Point
Uppertown
169
Men of Mey
Boars of
Duncansby
51

ORKNEY

ISLANDS

KIRKWALL to
Invergordon   9 hrs

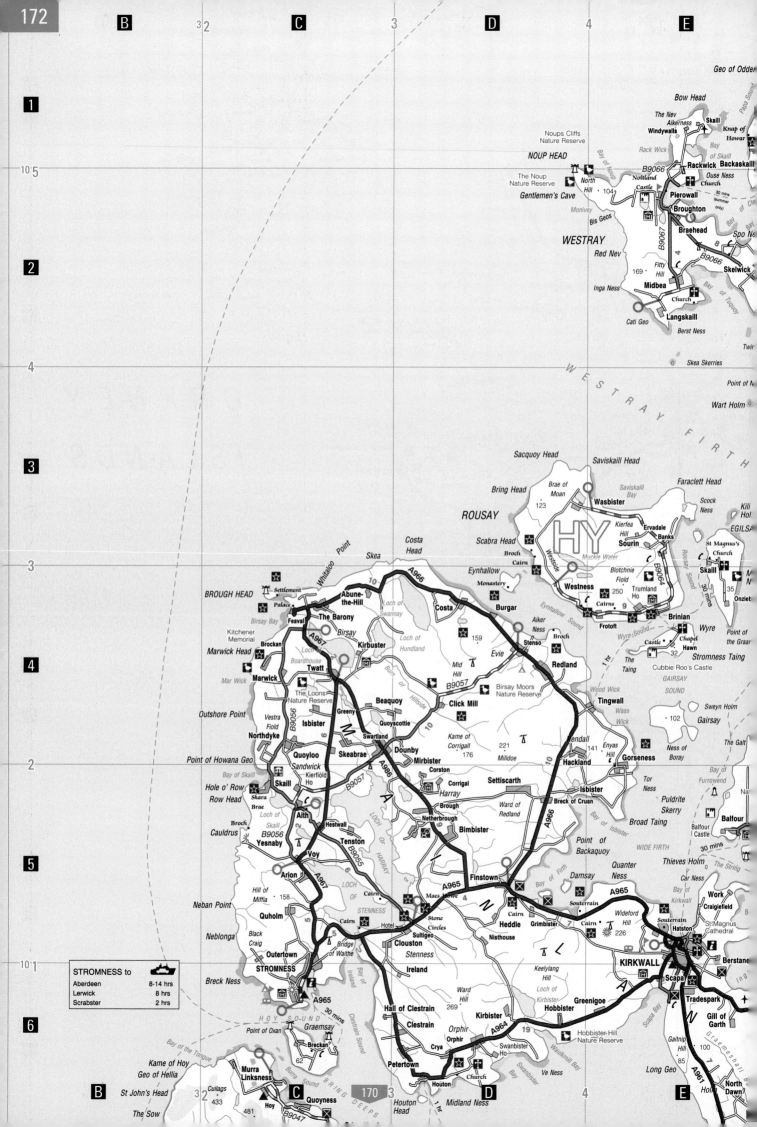

ORKNEY ISLANDS

SHETLAND
ISLANDS

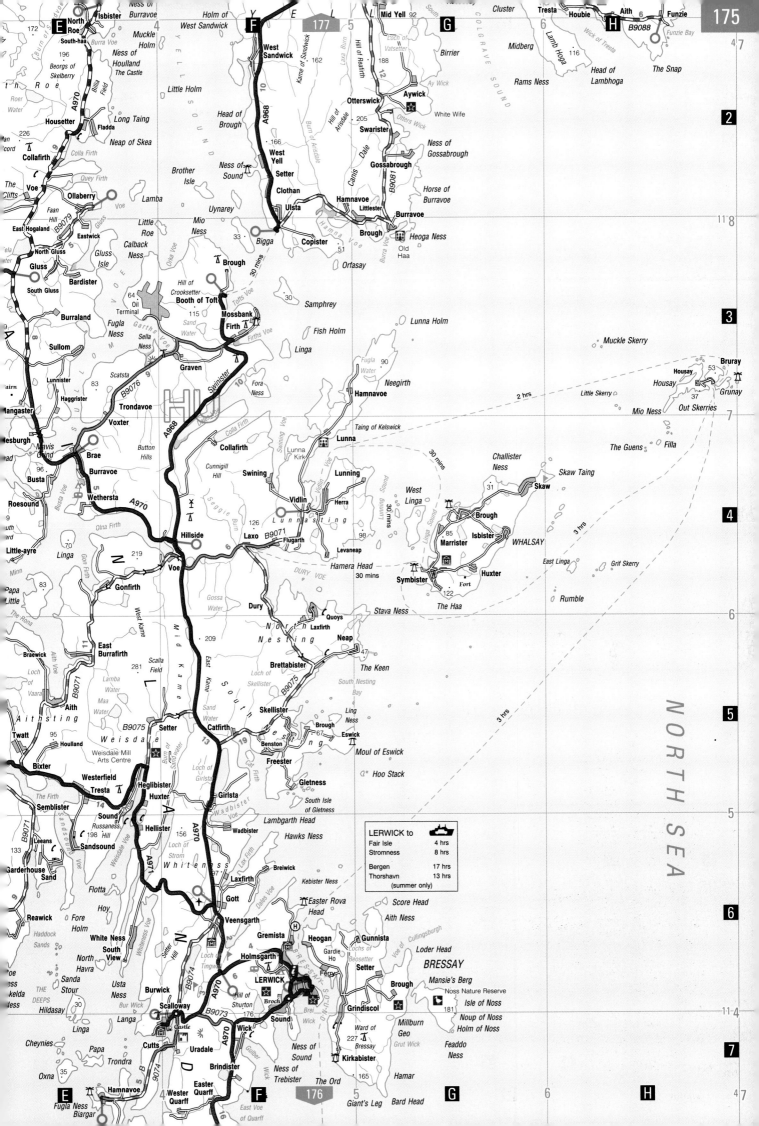

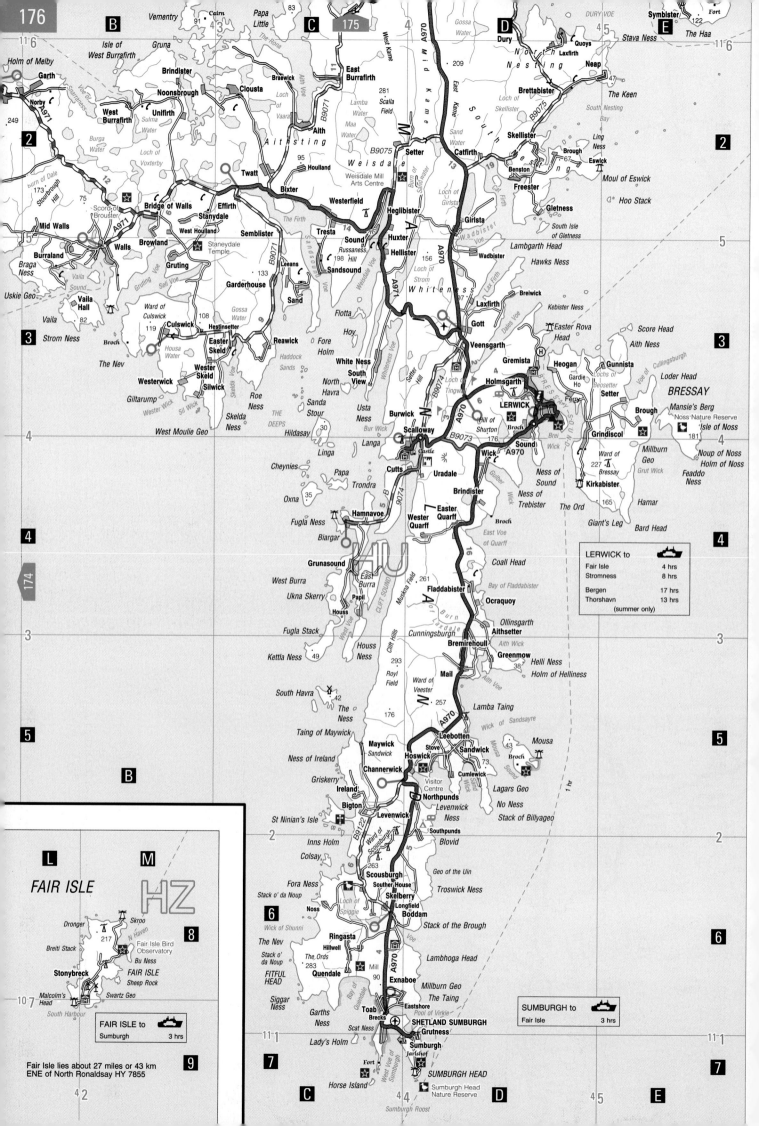

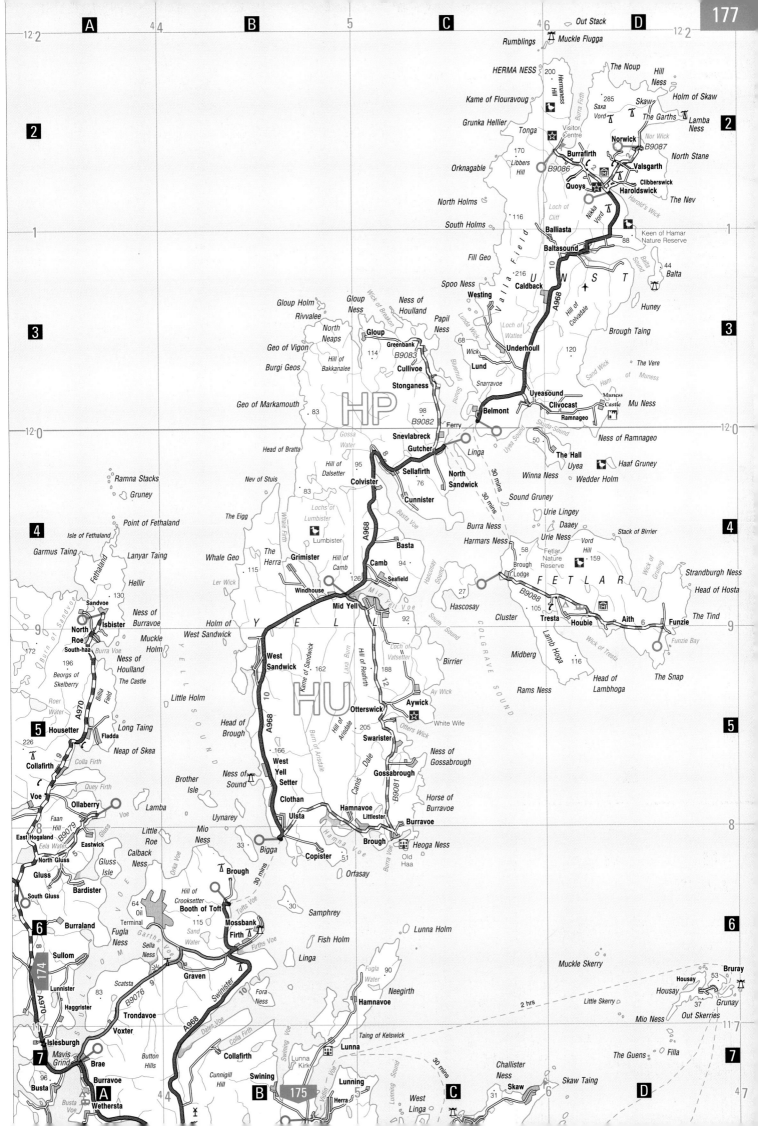

London area

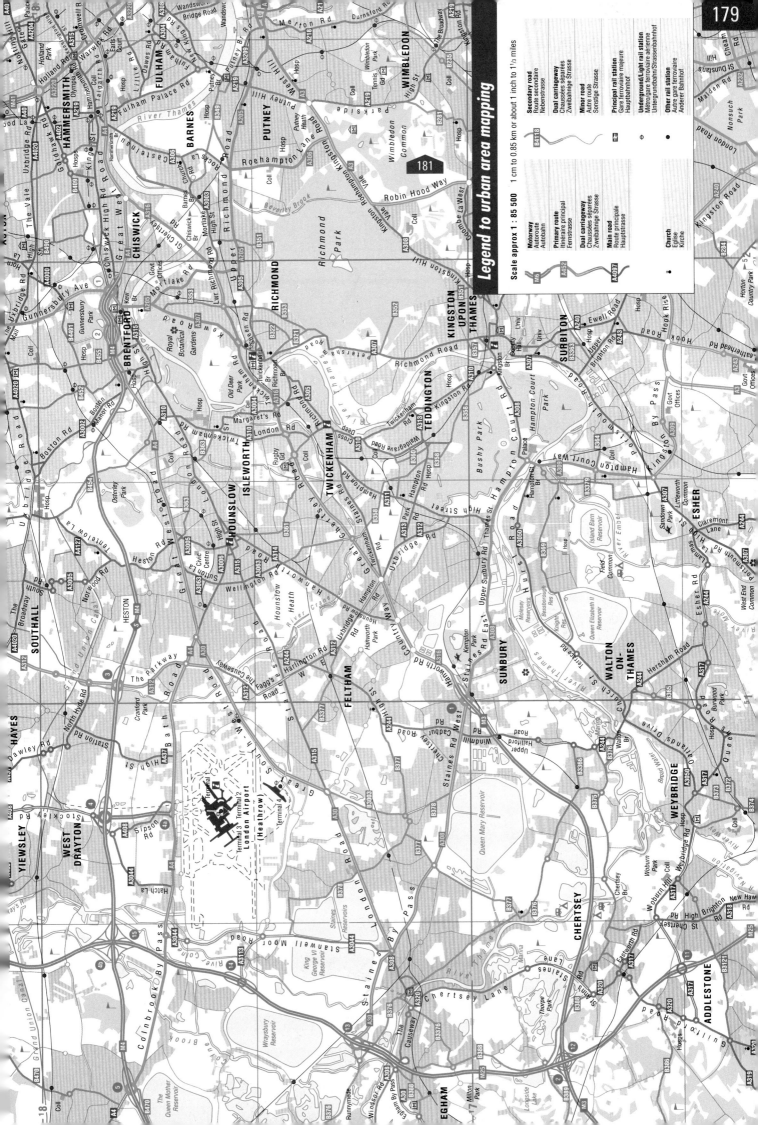

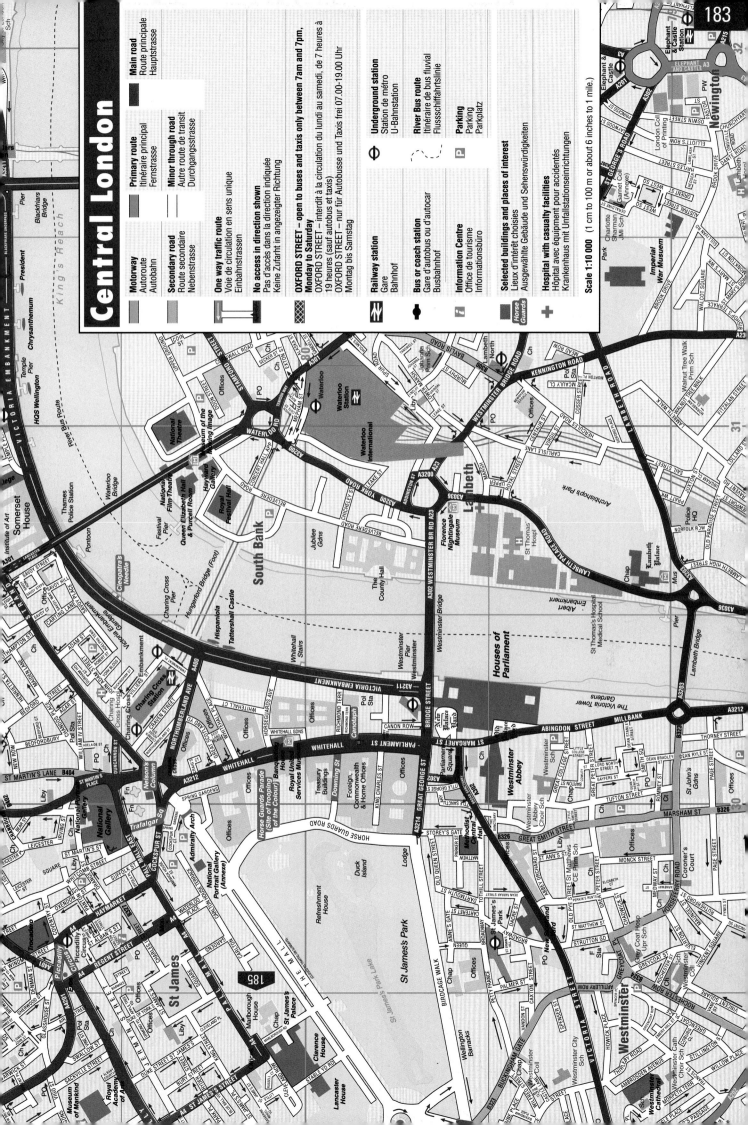

Central London

Scale 1:10 000   (1 cm to 100 m or about 6 inches to 1 mile.)

Motorway
Autoroute
Autobahn

Primary route
Itinéraire principal
Fernstrasse

Main road
Route principale
Hauptstrasse

Secondary road
Route secondaire
Nebenstrasse

Minor through road
Autre route de transit
Durchgangsstrasse

One way traffic route
Voie de circulation en sens unique
Einbahnstrassen

No access in direction shown
Pas d'accès dans la direction indiquée
Keine Zufahrt in angezeigter Richtung

**OXFORD STREET – open to buses and taxis only between 7am and 7pm,
Monday to Saturday**
OXFORD STREET – interdit à la circulation du lundi au samedi, de 7 heures à
19 heures (sauf autobus et taxis)
OXFORD STREET – nur für Autobusse und Taxis frei 07.00-19.00 Uhr
Montag bis Samstag

Railway station
Gare
Bahnhof

Bus or coach station
Gare d'autobus ou d'autocar
Busbahnhof

Information Centre
Office de tourisme
Informationsbüro

Selected buildings and places of interest
Lieux d'intérêt choisies
Ausgewählte Gebäude und Sehenswürdigkeiten

Hospital with casualty facilities
Hôpital avec équipement pour accidentés
Krankenhaus mit Unfallstationseinrichtungen

Underground station
Station de métro
U-Bahnstation

River Bus route
Itinéraire de bus fluvial
Flussschiffahrtslinie

Parking
Parking
Parkplatz

Aberdeen

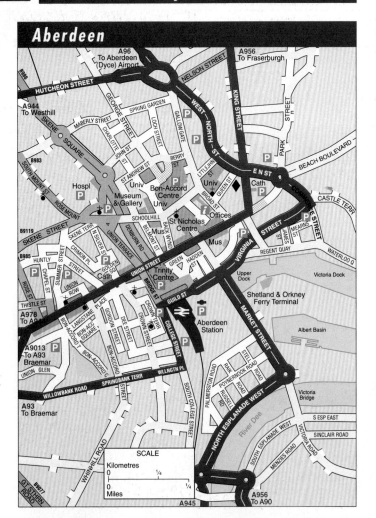

Bath

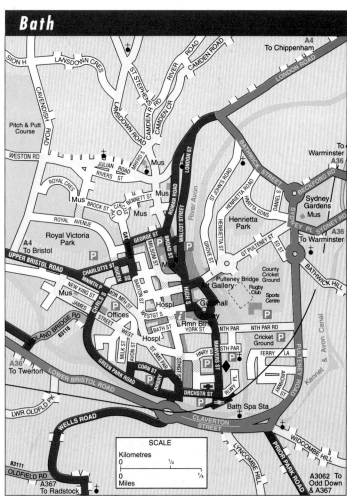

Birmingham

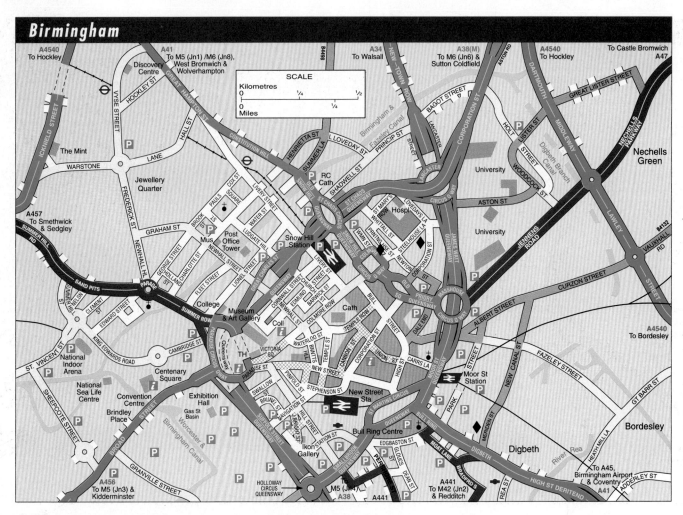

Town plans

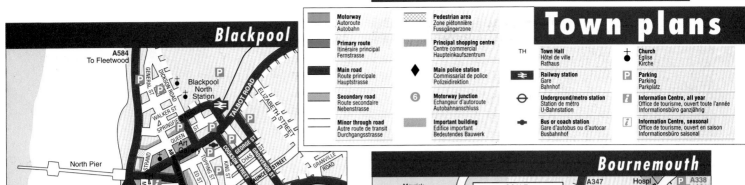

Motorway / Autoroute / Autobahn	Pedestrian area / Zone piétonnière / Fussgängerzone	TH Town Hall / Hôtel de ville / Rathaus	Church / Église / Kirche
Primary route / Itinéraire principal / Fernstrasse	Principal shopping centre / Centre commercial / Haupteinkaufszentrum	Railway station / Gare / Bahnhof	P Parking / Parking / Parkplatz
Main road / Route principale / Hauptstrasse	Main police station / Commissariat de police / Polizeidirektion	Underground/metro station / Station de métro / U-Bahnstation	i Information Centre, all year / Office de tourisme, ouvert toute l'année / Informationsbüro ganzjährig
Secondary road / Route secondaire / Nebenstrasse	Motorway junction / Échangeur d'autoroute / Autobahnanschluss	Bus or coach station / Gare d'autobus ou d'autocar / Busbahnhof	i Information Centre, seasonal / Office de tourisme, ouvert en saison / Informationsbüro saisonal
Minor through road / Autre route de transit / Durchgangsstrasse	Important building / Edifice important / Bedeutendes Bauwerk		

Blackpool

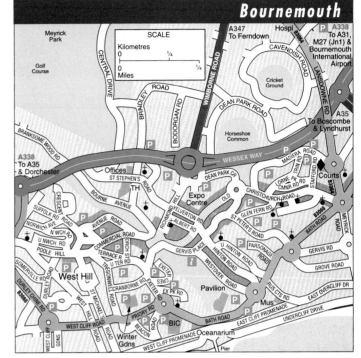

Bournemouth

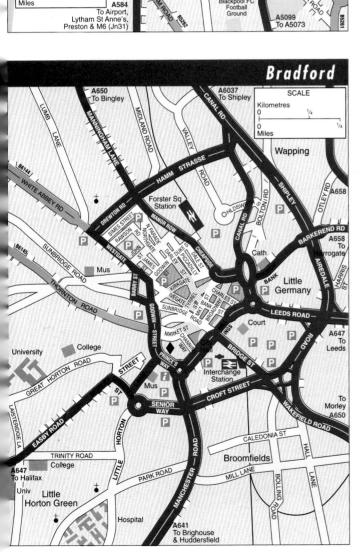

Bradford

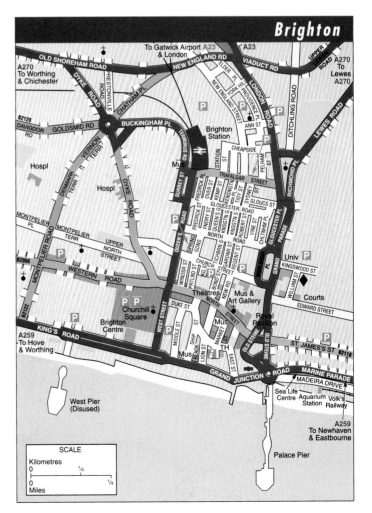

Brighton

Cambridge

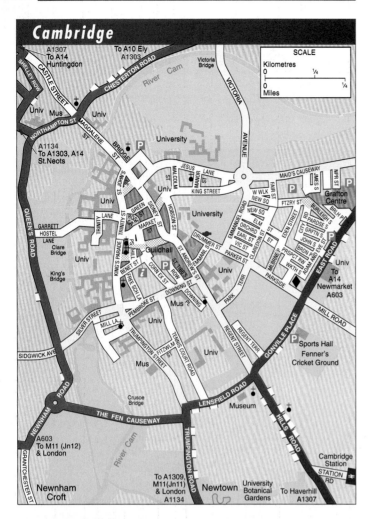

Canterbury

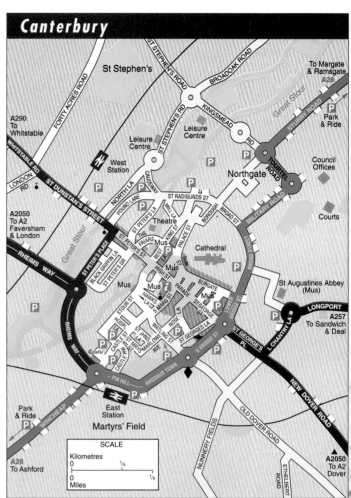

Bristol

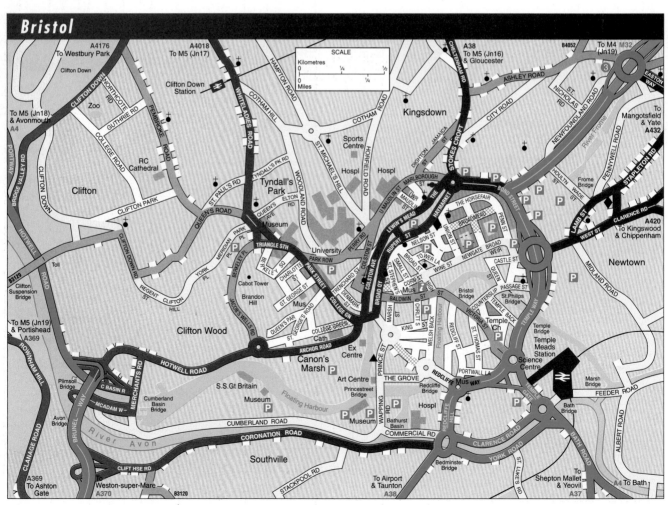

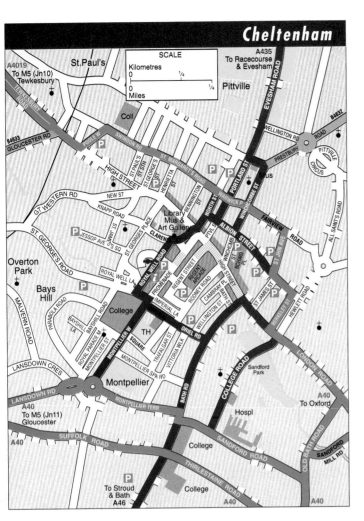

Cheltenham

SCALE
Kilometres
0 ¼
0 ¼
Miles

St.Paul's
A4019
To M5 (Jn10)
Tewkesbury
Pittville
A435
To Racecourse
& Evesham
Coll
Mus
Library
Mus &
Art Gallery
Overton
Park
Bays
Hill
College
TH
Montpellier
A40
To M5 (Jn11)
Gloucester
SUFFOLK ROAD
A40
College
Hospl
College
To Stroud
& Bath
A46
A40
Sandford
Park
To Oxford
A40

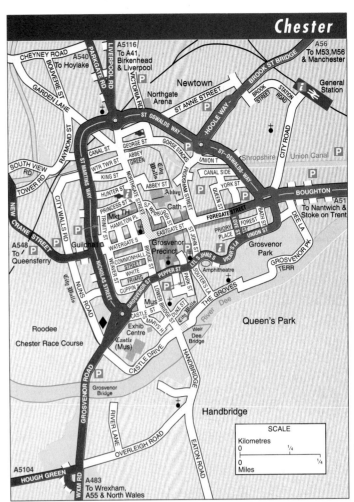

Chester

CHEYNEY ROAD
A5116
To A41,
Birkenhead
& Liverpool
A56
To M53,M56
& Manchester
Newtown
Northgate
Arena
General
Station
ST OSWALDS WAY
Shropshire
City
Walls
Abbey
BOUGHTON
A51
To Nantwich &
Stoke on Trent
Mkt
TH
Cath
Guildhall
A548
To
Queensferry
Grosvenor
Precinct
Grosvenor
Park
Grosvenor
Park
Mus
Amphitheatre
Roodee
Chester Race Course
Castle
(Mus)
Exhib
Centre
Weir
Dee
Bridge
River Dee
Queen's Park
Grosvenor
Bridge
Handbridge
A5104
HOUGH GREEN
A483
To Wrexham,
A55 & North Wales

SCALE
Kilometres
0 ¼
0 ¼
Miles

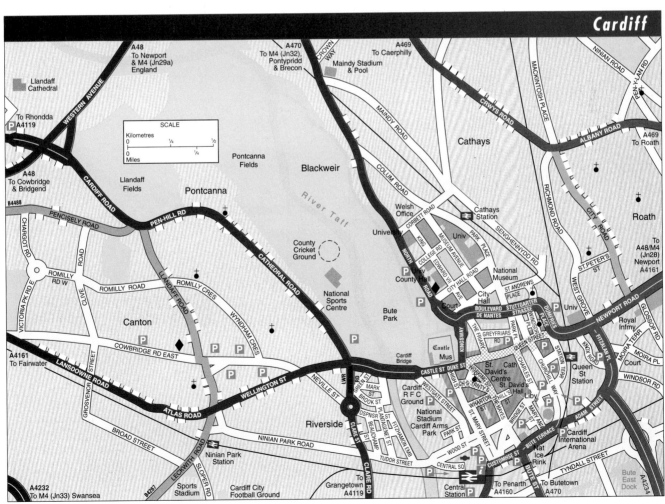

Cardiff

SCALE
Kilometres
0 ¼ ½
0 ¼
Miles

Llandaff
Cathedral
A48
To Newport
& M4 (Jn29a)
England
A470
To M4 (Jn32),
Pontypridd
& Brecon
A469
To Caerphilly
Maindy Stadium
& Pool
To Rhondda
A4119
WESTERN AVENUE
Pontcanna
Fields
Blackweir
Cathays
A469
To Roath
A48
To Cowbridge
& Bridgend
Llandaff
Fields
Pontcanna
ALBANY ROAD
PEN-HILL RD
River Taff
Welsh
Office
Roath
County
Cricket
Ground
University
To
A48/M4
(Jn28)
Newport
A4161
Canton
ROMILLY ROAD
National
Sports
Centre
Univ
County Hall
National
Museum
City
Hall
Univ
A4161
To Fairwater
LANSDOWNE ROAD
COWBRIDGE RD EAST
Bute
Park
Cardiff
Bridge
Castle
Mus
St.
David's
Centre
St David's
Hall
Liby
Royal
Infmy
ATLAS ROAD
WELLINGTON STREET
Riverside
Cardiff
RFC
Ground
National
Stadium
Cardiff Arms
Park
Queen
St Station
Ninian Park
Station
Nat
Ice
Rink
Cardiff
International
Arena
Bute
East
Dock
A4232
To M4 (Jn33) Swansea
Sports
Stadium
Cardiff City
Football Ground
NINIAN PARK ROAD
To Grangetown
A4119
Central
Station
To Penarth
A4160
To Butetown
A470
A4234

Coventry

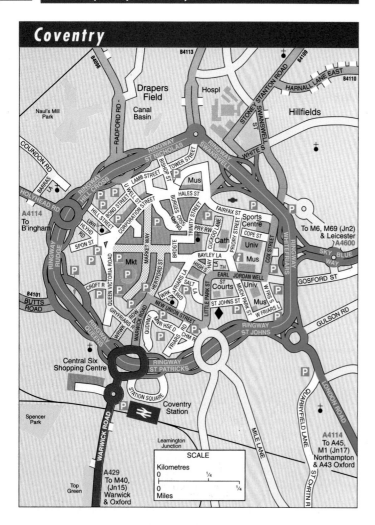

Croydon

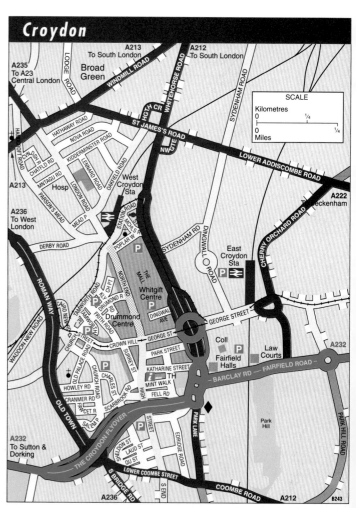

Derby

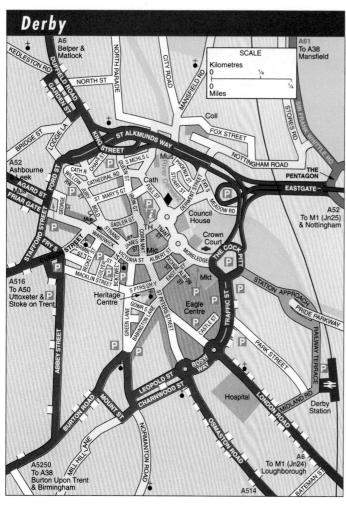

Dundee

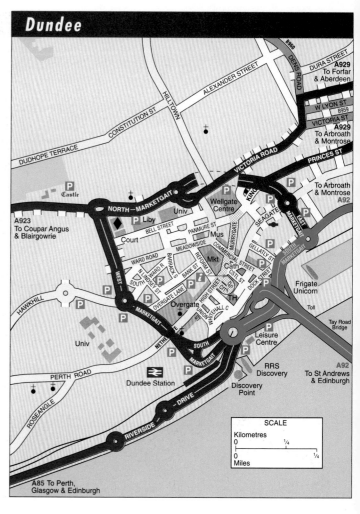

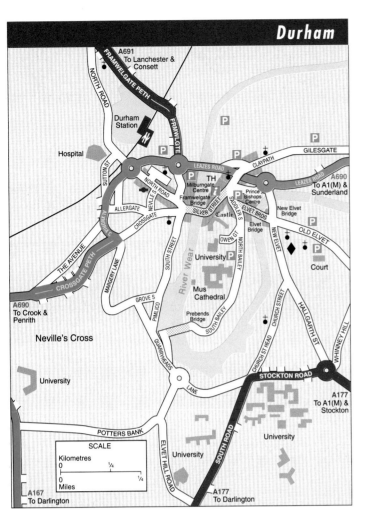

Durham

A691 To Lanchester & Consett
FRAMWLGATE PETH
NORTH ROAD
Durham Station
Hospital
FRAMWLGTE
LEAZES ROAD
GILESGATE
CLAYPATH
TH
Milburngate Centre
Framwelgate Bridge
Prince Bishops Centre
New Elvet Bridge
Elvet Brdg
Elvet Bridge
OLD ELVET
SUTTON ST
NORTH ROAD
NEVILLE S
ALLERGATE
CROSSGATE
SILVER STREET
SADDLER S
Castle
OWEN
NORTH BAILEY
NEW ELVET
Court
THE AVENUE
CROSSGATE PETH
MARGERY LANE
SOUTH STREET
PIMLICO
GROVE S
University
Mus
Cathedral
Prebends Bridge
SOUTH BAILEY
CHURCH STREET HEAD
CHURCH STREET
HALLGARTH ST
WHINNEY HILL
A690 To Crook & Penrith
Neville's Cross
QUARRYHEADS
University
LANE
STOCKTON ROAD
A177 To A1(M) & Stockton
POTTERS BANK
University
University
ELVET HILL ROAD
SOUTH ROAD
A167 To Darlington
A177 To Darlington
River Wear
LEAZES ROAD
A690 To A1(M) & Sunderland

SCALE
Kilometres 0 — ¼
Miles 0 — ¼

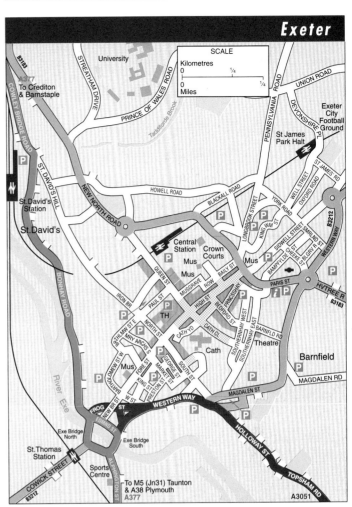

Exeter

B3183
University
A377 To Crediton & Barnstaple
COWLEY BRIDGE ROAD
STREATHAM DRIVE
PRINCE OF WALES ROAD
Taddiforde Brook
PENNSYLVANIA ROAD
UNION ROAD
DEVONSHIRE PL
Exeter City Football Ground
St James Park Halt
ST JAMES' RD
OXFORD ROAD
HOWELL ROAD
BLACKALL ROAD
WELL STREET
YORK ROAD
NEW NORTH ROAD
ST DAVID'S HILL
St.David's Station
St.David's
LONGBROOK STREET
KING WM ST
SIDWELL STREET
CLIFTON ST
ELGIN V.
WESTERN WAY
B3212
Central Station
Mus
Crown Courts
Mus
BAMPFYLDE ST
CHEEKE ST
Mus
QUEEN ST
PARIS ST
P
HVTREE R
B3183
IRON BR
PAUL ST
MUSGRAVE ROW
HIGH ST
BEDFORD ST
PRINCESSHAY
SOUTHERNHAY WEST
SOUTHERNHAY EAST
BARNFLD RD
Cath
Theatre
Barnfield
BONHAY ROAD
BARTHLMW ST E
MRY ARCHS
NORTH ST
CATH YD
CATH CL
MAGDALEN RD
TH
Mus
BARTHLMW ST W
FORE ST
GEORGE ST
MARKET ST
SOUTH ST
GANDY STREET
KING ST
PRESTON ST
Mus
W ST
River Exe
MAGDALEN ST
FROG ST
NEW BR ST
EDMUND ST
WESTERN WAY
HOLLOWAY ST
TOPSHAM RD
Exe Bridge North
Exe Bridge South
St.Thomas Station
ALPHINGTON ST
COWICK STREET
B3212
Sports Centre
To M5 (Jn31) Taunton & A38 Plymouth
A377
A3051

SCALE
Kilometres 0 — ¼
Miles 0 — ¼

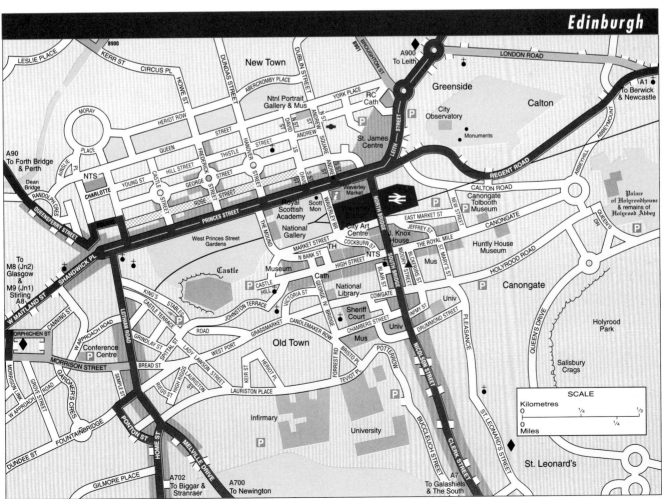

Edinburgh

B900
LESLIE PLACE
KERR ST
CIRCUS PL
DUNDAS STREET
DUBLIN STREET
New Town
BROUGHTON ST
B801
A900 To Leith
LONDON ROAD
HOWE ST
ABERCROMBY PLACE
York Place
RC Cath
Greenside
Calton
A1 To Berwick & Newcastle
Ntnl Portrait Gallery & Mus
HERIOT ROW
MORAY
PLACE
QUEEN STREET
N ST DAVID ST
ANDREW SQUARE
ST ANDREW
City Observatory
Monuments
A90 To Forth Bridge & Perth
AINSLIE PL
FREDERICK STREET
THISTLE STREET
HANOVER STREET
St. James Centre
LEITH STREET
REGENT ROAD
NTS
Dean Bridge
RANDOLPH
CHARLOTTE
YOUNG ST
HILL STREET
GEORGE STREET
ROSE STREET
Waverley Market
CALTON ROAD
Canongate Tolbooth Museum
CANONGATE
Palace of Holyroodhouse & remains of Holyrood Abbey
QUEENSBERRY STREET
ST DAVID ST
Royal Scottish Academy
Scott Mon
WAVERLEY BR
Waverley Station
NEW STREET
EAST MARKET ST
JEFFREY ST
THE ROYAL MILE
ST MARY'S ST
Huntly House Museum
HOLYROOD ROAD
PRINCES STREET
West Princes Street Gardens
National Gallery
THE MOUND
City Art Centre
NORTH BRIDGE
SOUTH BRIDGE
J. Knox House
Mus
ABBEYHILL
ABBEYMOUNT
QUEEN'S DR
To M8 (Jn2) Glasgow & M9 (Jn1) Stirling A8
SHANDWICK PL
MARKET STREET
COCKBURN ST
TH
NTS
HIGH STREET
BLACKFRIARS ST
Canongate
W MAITLAND ST
MORPHICHEN ST
Castle
Museum
Cath
National Library
COWGATE
BLAIR ST
NIDDRY ST
Univ
Holyrood Park
CANNING ST
KING'S STABLES
CASTLE TERRACE
Castle Hill
VICTORIA ST
GEORGE IV BRIDGE
Sheriff Court
INFMY ST
QUEEN'S DRIVE
LOTHIAN ROAD
JOHNSTON TERRACE
CANDLEMAKER ROW
CHAMBERS STREET
DRUMMOND STREET
Univ
Mus
Salisbury Crags
Conference Centre
GRINDLAY ST
SPITTAL ST
GRASSMARKET
ROAD
WEST PORT
LADY LAWSON STREET
Old Town
FORREST RD
BRISTO PL
POTTERROW
PLEASANCE
MORRISON STREET
BREAD ST
HIGH RIGGS
LAURISTON STREET
KEIR ST
HERIOT PL
TEVIOT PL
NICOLSON STREET
GARDNER'S CRES
GROVE STREET
SEMPLE ST
RIEGO ST
LAURISTON PLACE
Infirmary
BUCCLEUCH STREET
W APPROACH
FOUNTAINBRIDGE
HOME ST
MELVILLE DRIVE
University
CLERK STREET
ST LEONARD'S STREET
St. Leonard's
DUNDEE ST
GILMORE PLACE
PONTON ST
A702 To Biggar & Stranraer
A700 To Newington
A7 To Galashiels & The South
MORRISON LINK

SCALE
Kilometres 0 — ¼ — ½
Miles 0 — ¼

Gloucester

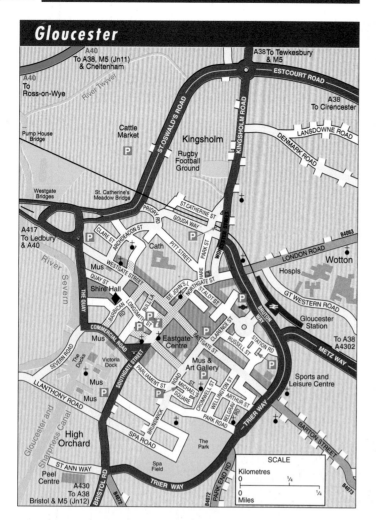

Hull

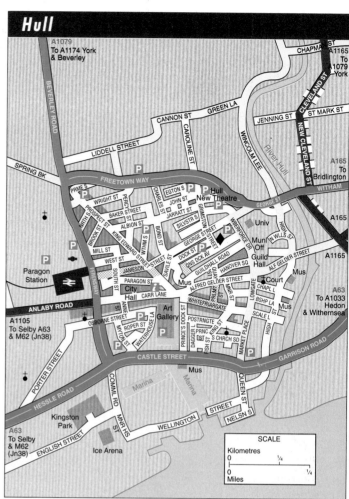

Glasgow

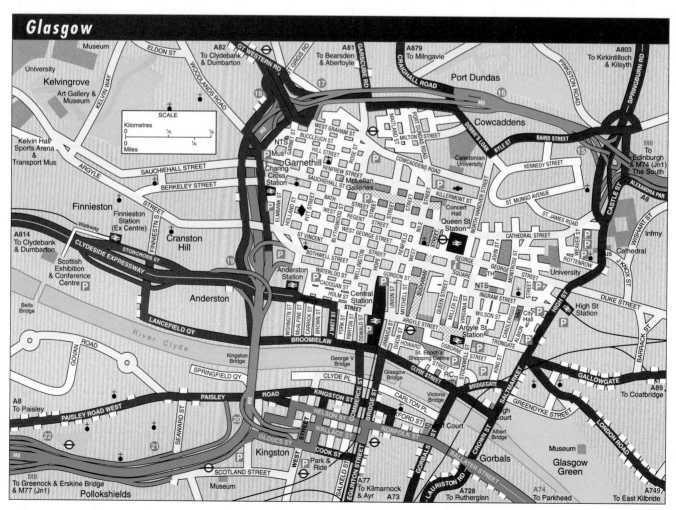

Leeds

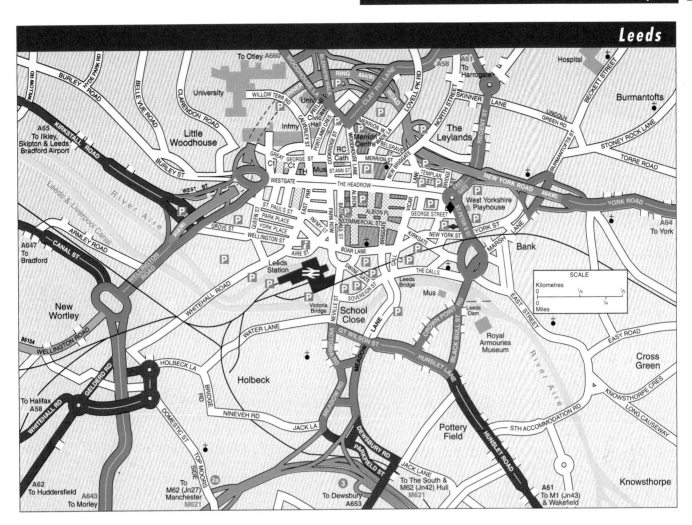

Liverpool

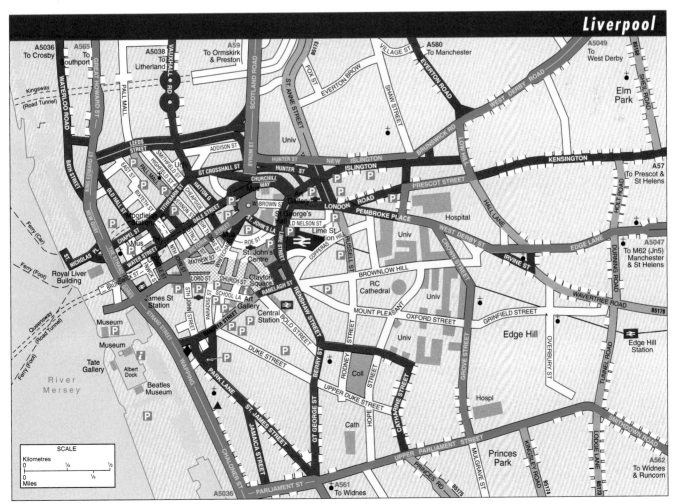

Leicester

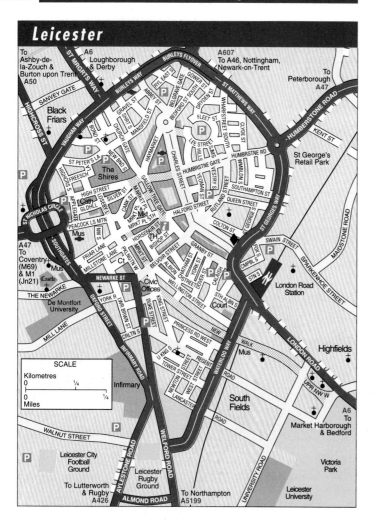

Middlesbrough

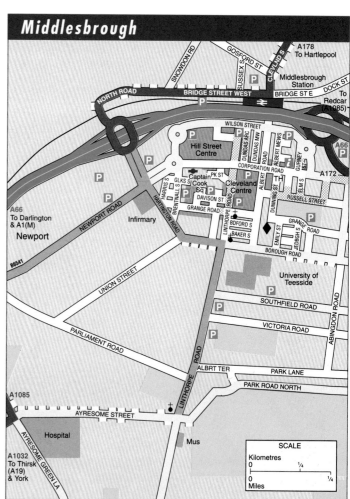

Manchester

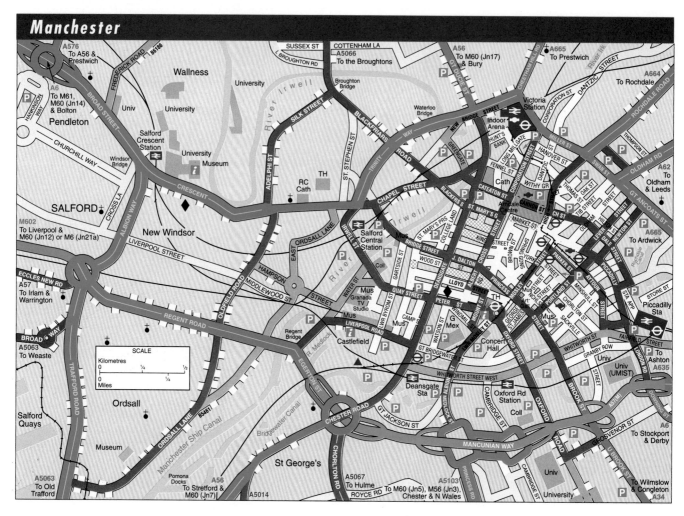

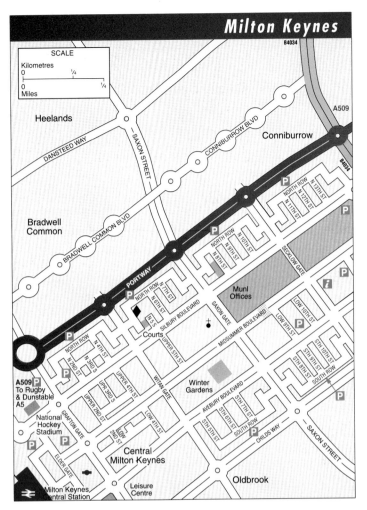

Milton Keynes

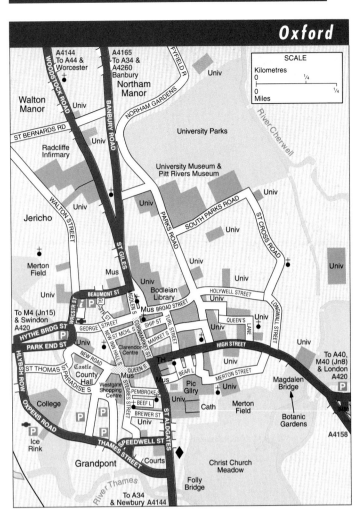

Oxford

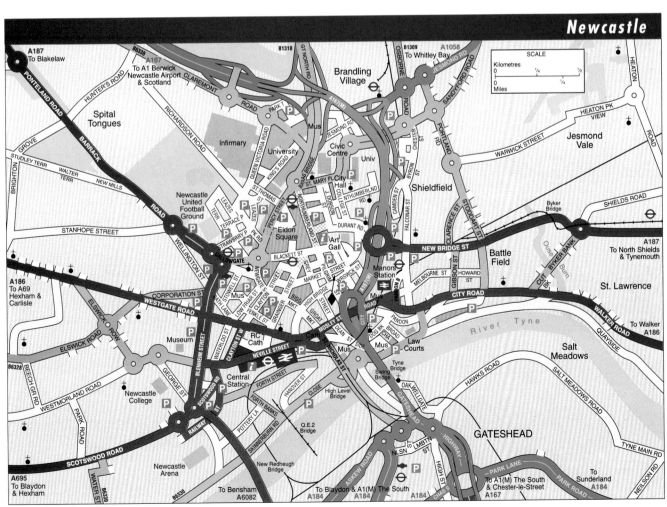

Newcastle

Norwich

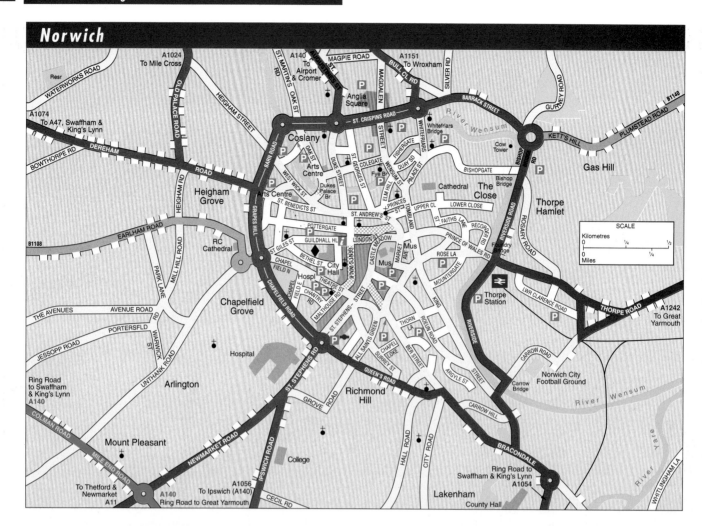

Nottingham

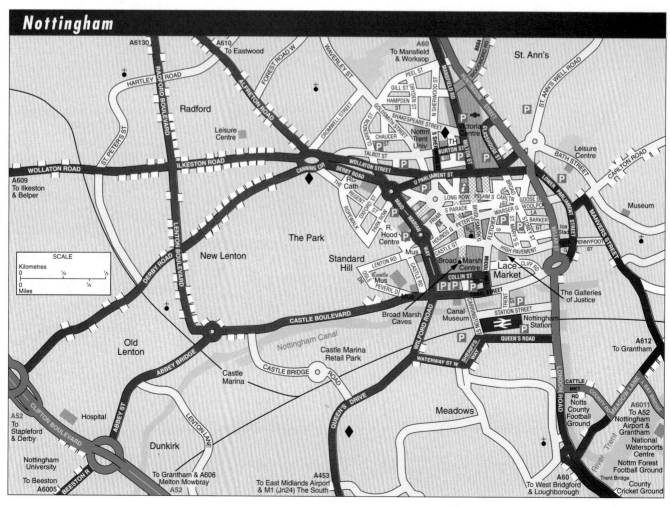

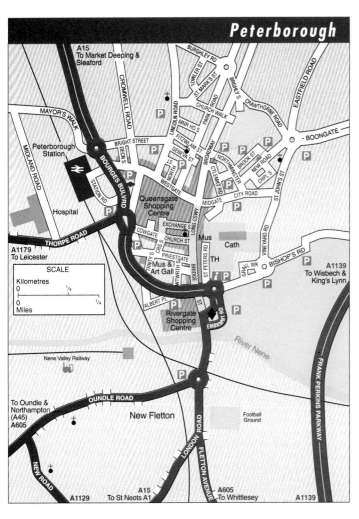

Peterborough

A15 To Market Deeping & Sleaford
BURGHLEY RD
TOWLER ST
ST MARK'S ST
CHURCH WALK
EASTFIELD ROAD
CROMWELL ROAD
MAYOR'S WALK
BRIGHT STREET
LINCOLN ROAD
MNR HO S
FITZWLAM ST
GENEVA ST
BROADWAY
NORTHMINSTER
PARK ROAD
CRAWTHORNE ROAD
BOONGATE
Peterborough Station
DECN'S
BOURGES BULVRD
STATION RD
WESTGATE
MIDLAND ROAD
Hospital
THORPE ROAD
Queensgate Shopping Centre
EXCHANGE
COWGATE
CHURCH ST
PRIESTGATE
Mus
Cath
A1179 To Leicester
Mus & Art Gall
TH
BRIDGE ST
ST PETERS RD
GR JL WK
BISHOP'S RD
A1139 To Wisbech & King's Lynn
SCALE
Kilometres
0   ¼
0   ¼
Miles
ALBERT PL
EMBKMNT
Rivergate Shopping Centre
River Nene
Nene Valley Railway
LONDON ROAD
FLETTON AVENUE
FRANK PERKINS PARKWAY
To Oundle & Northampton (A45) A605
OUNDLE ROAD
New Fletton
Football Ground
NEW ROAD
A1129
A15 To St Neots A1
A605 To Whittlesey
A1139

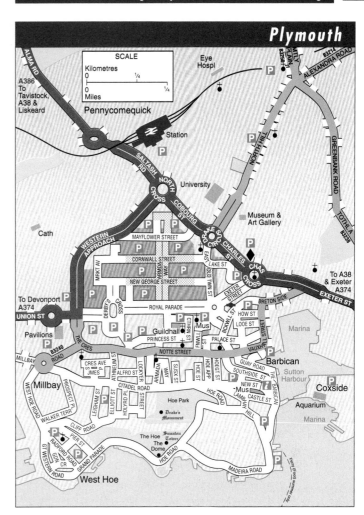

Plymouth

ALMA RD
A386 To Tavistock, A38 & Liskeard
Pennycomequick
SALTASH RD
NORTH CROSS
Station
University
NORTH HILL
Eye Hospl
ALEXANDRA ROAD
GREENBANK ROAD
TOTH'A
SCALE
Kilometres
0   ¼
0   ¼
Miles
Cath
WESTERN APPROACH
MAYFLOWER STREET
COBOURG
CORNWALL STREET
NEW GEORGE STREET
MRKT AV
ARMADA WAY
PARADE
CHARLES ST
CHAS CROSS
Museum & Art Gallery
EAST ST OLD TWN ST
LAKE ST
EXETER STREET
To Devonport A374
DERBY'S
ROYAL PARADE
Mus
BRETON SIDE
To A38 & Exeter A374
EXETER ST
UNION ST
Pavilions
THE CRES
Guildhall
PRINCESS ST
CTHRN ST
TWN
PALACE ST
LOOE ST
HOW ST
BOXLL ST
VAUXHALL STREET
Marina
B3240
MILLBAY ROAD
CRES AVE
JMES
ATHENM ST
LOCKYER ST
ALFRD ST
SUSX ST
HOE ST
HOE APP
SOUTHSIDE ST
QUAY ROAD
Barbican
Sutton Harbour
Coxside
West Hoe Road
WEST HOE ROAD
PROSPECT PL
LEIGHAM ST
WALKER TERR
ELLIOTT ST
HOLYRD PL
CITADEL ROAD
CITADEL STREET
Hoe Park
HOE ST
HOE APP
NEW ST
LAMBY
CASTLE ST
Mus
THE BARBICAN
Aquarium
Marina
Millbay
CLIFF ROAD
RADFORD ROAD
GT WESTERN ROAD
GDN CR
PIER ST
Drake's Monument
GRAND PARADE
The Hoe
The Dome
Smeaton Tower
HOE ROAD
MADEIRA ROAD
West Hoe

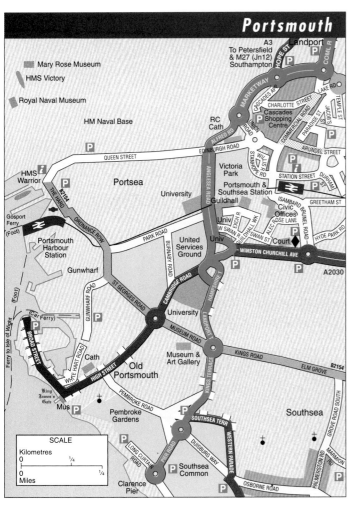

Portsmouth

Mary Rose Museum
HMS Victory
Royal Naval Museum
HM Naval Base
A3 To Petersfield & M27 (Jn12) Southampton
Landport
HOPE ST
COML R
MARKETWAY
CASCADES AP
CHARLOTTE STREET
Cascades Shopping Centre
COMMERCIAL ROAD
LAKE RD
TEMPLE ST
JACOBS ST
PARADISE ST
RC Cath
QUEEN STREET
ALFRED RD
EDINBURGH ROAD
UNION
Victoria Park
ARUNDEL STREET
STANHOPE RD
STATION STREET
DURHAM ST
GREETHAM ST
HMS Warrior
Portsea
University
Portsmouth & Southsea Station
Guildhall
ANGLESEA RD
W SWAN ST
EXCH R
GUILDHALL WK
ALEC ROSE LANE
ISAMBARD BRUNEL ROAD
Civic Offices
HYDE PARK RD
Gosport Ferry (Foot)
THE HARD
ORDNANCE ROW
PARK ROAD
BURNABY ROAD
Univ
Univ
Court
Portsmouth Harbour Station
Gunwharf
ST GEORGES ROAD
GUNWHARF ROAD
United Services Ground
WINSTON CHURCHILL AVE
A2030
Ferry to Isle of Wight (Foot)
CAMBRIDGE ROAD
HAMPSHIRE
LANDPORT
University
MUSEUM ROAD
Cath
WHITE HART ROAD
HIGH STREET
BROAD STREET
Old Portsmouth
Museum & Art Gallery
KINGS ROAD
ELM GROVE
B2154
King James's Gate
Mus
PEMBROKE ROAD
Pembroke Gardens
JESSIE TERRACE
WESTERN PARADE
Southsea
SCALE
Kilometres
0   ¼
0   ¼
Miles
LONG CURTAIN ROAD
SOUTHSEA TERR
DUISBURG WAY
Clarence Pier
Southsea Common
OSBORNE ROAD
WESTERN PARADE
MARMION RD
GROVE ROAD SOUTH
PALMERSTON RD

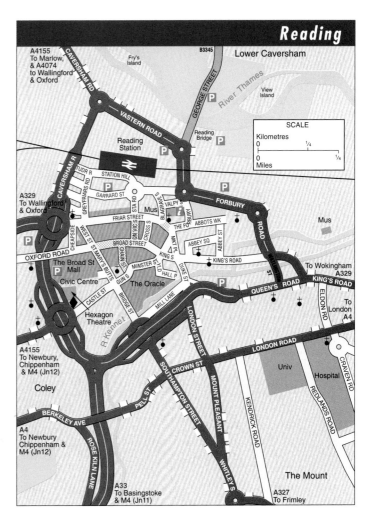

Reading

A4155 To Marlow, & A4074 to Wallingford & Oxford
CAVERSHAM RD
Fry's Island
B3345
Lower Caversham
GEORGE STREET
River Thames
View Island
VASTERN ROAD
Reading Station
Reading Bridge
SCALE
Kilometres
0   ¼
0   ¼
Miles
CAVERSHAM R
STATION HILL
TUDR RD
GREYFRIARS RD
STATION RD
GARRARD ST
FORBURY
FRIAR STREET
VALPY ST
THE FORBURY
Mus
BLAGRAVE ST
ABBOTS WK
FORBURY ROAD
Mus
A329 To Wallingford & Oxford
WEST ST
CROSS S
MKT PL
ABBEY SQ
ABBEY ST
KING'S ROAD
To Wokingham A329
OXFORD ROAD
CHEAPSIDE
ST MARY'S BUTTS
BROAD STREET
KING S
MINSTER ST
DUKE ST
KING'S ROAD
ELDON RD
The Broad St Mall
Civic Centre
The Oracle
GUN S
HALL
CASTLE ST
BRIDGE ST
MILL LANE
QUEEN'S ROAD
To London A4
Hexagon Theatre
R Kennet
A4155 To Newbury, Chippenham & M4 (Jn12)
LONDON STREET
SOUTHAMPTON STREET
CROWN ST
MOUNT PLEASANT
LONDON ROAD
Univ
Hospital
CRAVEN RD
REDLANDS ROAD
KENDRICK ROAD
Coley
PELL ST
BERKELEY AVE
A4 To Newbury Chippenham & M4 (Jn12)
ROSE KILN LANE
WHITLEY S
A33 To Basingstoke & M4 (Jn11)
The Mount
A327 To Frimley

Salisbury

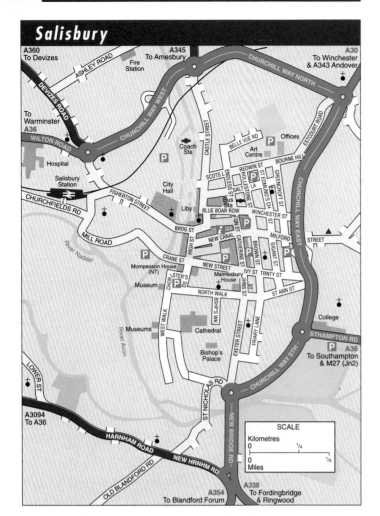

Shrewsbury

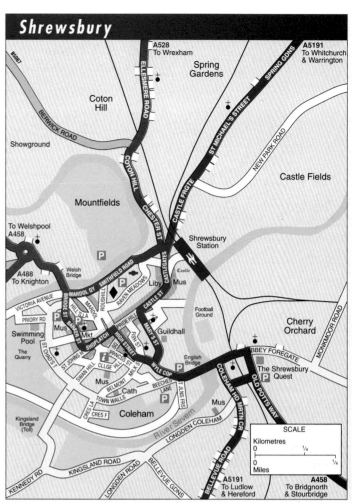

Sheffield

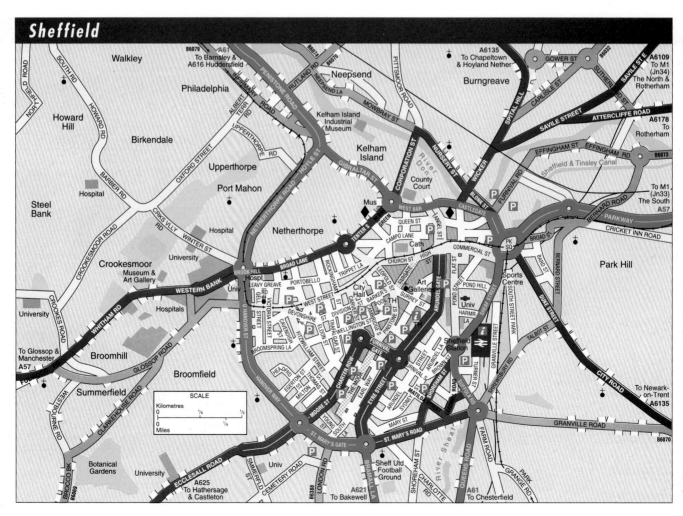

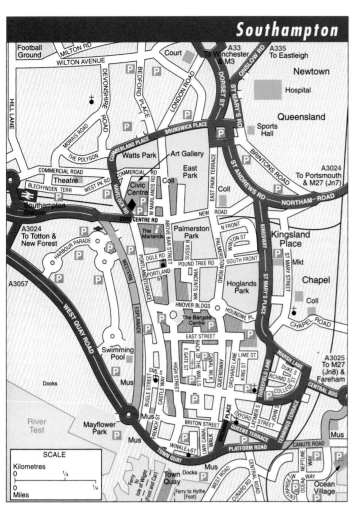

Southampton

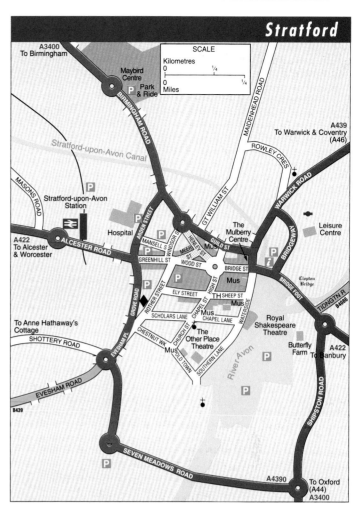

Stratford

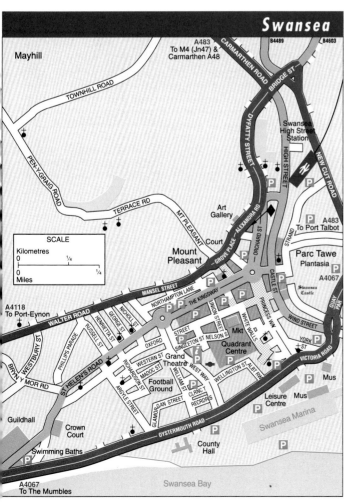

Swansea

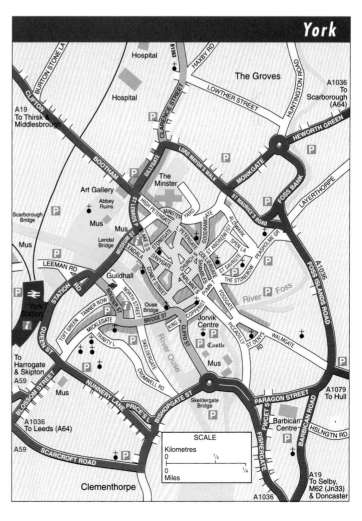

York

Index

County and new Unitary Authority names showing abbreviations used in this index

England *County & Unitary Authorities*

Name	Abbr.
Bath & North East Somerset	Bth
Bedfordshire	Beds
Blackburn with Darwen	Bburn & Da
Blackpool	Bpool
Bournemouth	Bourne
Bracknell Forest	B For
Brighton & Hove	Bri & Ho
Buckinghamshire	Bucks
Cambridgeshire	Cambs
Cheshire	Ches
City of Bristol	C of Bris
City of Derby	C of Derb
City of Kingston-upon-Hull	K-upon-H
City of Leicester	C of Leic
City of Nottingham	C of Notts
City of Peterborough	C of Peter
City of Plymouth	C of Ply
City of Portsmouth	C of Port
City of Southampton	C of Soton
City of Stoke-on-Trent	C of Stoke
Cornwall	Corn
County of Herefordshire	Co of H
Cumbria	Cumbr
Darlington	Darl
Derbyshire	Derby
Devon	Devon
Dorset	Dorset
Durham	Durham
East Riding of Yorkshire (eg8)	E Yorks
East Sussex	E Susx
Essex	Essex
Gloucestershire	Glos
Greater London	G Lon
Greater Manchester	G Man
Halton	Halt
Hampshire	Hants
Hartlepool	Hartp
Hertfordshire	Herts
Isle of Wight	I of W
Kent	Kent
Lancashire	Lancs
Leicestershire	Leic
Lincolnshire	Lincs
Luton	Luton
Medway	Med
Merseyside	Mers
Middlesbrough	Midlb
Milton Keynes	Mil Key
Norfolk	Norf
Northamptonshire	Northnts
North East Lincolnshire	NE Linc
North Lincolnshire	N Linc
Northumberland	Northum
North Somerset	N Som
North Yorkshire	N Yorks
Nottinghamshire	Notts
Oxfordshire	Oxon
Poole	Poole
Reading	Rding
Redcar and Cleveland	Red & Clev
Rutland	Rut
Shropshire	Shrops
Slough	Slou
Somerset	Somer
Southend-on-Sea	S-on-Sea
South Gloucestershire	S Glos
South Yorkshire	S Yorks
Staffordshire	Staffs
Stockton-on-Tees	Stock on T
Suffolk	Suff
Surrey	Surrey
Swindon	Swin
Telford and Wrekin	Tel & Wrek
Thurrock	Thurk
Tyne and Wear	T & W
Warrington	Warr
Warwickshire	Warw
West Berkshire	W Berks
West Midlands	W Mids
West Sussex	W Susx
West Yorkshire	W Yorks
Wiltshire	Wilts
Windsor and Maidenhead	W&M
Wokingham	Wokham
Worcestershire County	Worces
York	Yk

Wales *Unitary Authorities*

Name	Abbr.
Blaenau Gwent	Blae Gw
Bridgend	Brig
Caerphilly	Caer
Cardiff	Card
Carmarthenshire	Carm
Ceredigion	Cered
Conwy	Conwy
Denbighshire	Denb
Flintshire	Flint
Gwynedd	Gwyn
Isle of Anglesey	I of Angl
Merthyr Tydfil	Merth Tyd
Monmouthshire	Monm
Neath Port Talbot	Nth Pt Talb
Newport	Newp
Pembrokeshire	Pemb
Powys	Powys
Rhondda,Cynon, Taff	Rho,Cyn,Taf
Swansea	Swan
Torfaen	Torf
The Vale of Glamorgan	V of Glam
Wrexham	Wrex

Scotland *Unitary Authorities*

Name	Abbr.
Aberdeenshire	Aberd
Angus	Ang
Argyll and Bute	Arg & Bt
City of Aberdeen	C of Aber
City of Dundee	C of Dun
City of Edinburgh	C of Edin
City of Glasgow	C of Glas
Clackmannanshire	Clakm
Dumfries and Galloway	D & G
East Ayrshire	E Ayr
East Dunbartonshire	E Dunb
East Lothian	E Loth
East Renfrewshire	E Renf
Falkirk	Falk
Fife	Fife
Highland	Highl
Inverclyde	Inver
Midlothian	Midlo
Moray	Mor
North Ayrshire	N Ayr
North Lanarkshire	N Lanak
Perth and Kinross	Pth & Kin
Renfrewshire	Renf
Scottish Borders	Scot Bord
South Ayrshire	S Ayr
South Lanarkshire	S Lanak
Stirling	Stir
West Dunbartonshire	W Dunb
West Lothian	W Loth

Scotland *Unitary Island Areas*

Name	Abbr.
Orkney	Orkney
Shetland	Shetld
Na h-Eileanan an Iar	Na Eilean

Other Areas

Name	Abbr.
Isle of Man	I of M
Isles of Scilly	I Scilly

Unitary authorities have not been listed individually within the following areas:
Greater London
Greater Manchester
Merseyside
Tyne & Wear
West Midlands
West Yorkshire
South Yorkshire

How to use this Index

For each entry the Atlas page number is listed and an alpha-numeric map reference is given for the grid square in which the named area appears. Some entries have additional information.
For example:

Aisby, Lincs DN21 .... 81 F2
1   2   3   4 5

1 The place name. Town names are shown in CAPITALS
2 The abbreviated County or Unitary Authority name, only shown where place names are duplicated
3 The Postcode area, only shown with duplicated places located within the same County or Unitary Authority
4 The Atlas page number
5 The alpha-numeric map reference

If you want to give a National Grid Reference to a place or feature all the information you need is contained on the Atlas map pages. Grid lines appear at 10 kilometre (km) intervals and each carries a reference number (eg8) in blue. Those 10 km grid lines which fall at the top and bottom and outside edges of each Atlas map page carry an additional smaller reference number(eg51).
This smaller number is the reference of the preceding 100 km grid line.

All 100 km grid lines appear in dark blue and carry a two-figure reference number (eg50) in blue. The reference letters of the relevant 100 km grid square (eg SK, TF etc) are also printed in blue on every Atlas map page spread.

Thus Aisby on page 81 of this Atlas has a National Grid Reference accurate to the nearest 10 km of SK89 where:

SK are the reference letters of the 100 km grid in which Aisby lies

8 and 9 are the references for the grid lines running north/south and east/west respectively and which intersect to form the south west corner of the 10 km grid square in which Aisby falls.

Aisby can be pinpointed more precisely by breaking the 10 km grid square into 10 sub squares of 1 km x 1 km and constructing a four-figure reference SK 8792. The second and fourth figures in the number identify within the 10 km grid square SK89 the imaginary 1 km grid line intervals running north/south and east/west respectively and which intersect to form the south west corner of the 1 km grid square in which the centre of Aisby lies. The numbering sequence runs east and north from the south west corner of the country.

A leaflet on the National Grid reference system is available from
Sales Information,
Ordnance Survey,
Romsey Road, Southampton.
SO16 4GU.
Tel 08456 05 05 05
Fax 023 80 792615
E-mail custinfo@ordsvy.gov.uk

A

Place	Pg	Ref
A' Chill	140	B3
Ab Kettleby	69	F4
Abbas Combe	17	F3
Abberley	54	C5
Abberton, Essex	48	D4
Abberton, Worces	55	E6
Abberwick	123	G6
Abbess Roding	47	F4
Abbey	15	H4
Abbey Dore	40	C2
Abbey Hulton	66	E2
Abbey St Bathans	122	C1
Abbey Town	101	F2
Abbey Village	85	E4
Abbey-cwm-hir	52	D4
Abbeylands	90	C5
Abbeystead	92	D6
Abbot's Salford	55	F6
Abbotrule	121	F6
Abbots Bickington	12	D4
Abbots Bromley	67	F4
Abbots Langley	45	E5
Abbots Leigh	27	E3
Abbots Morton	55	F6
Abbots Ripton	58	C4
Abbotsbury	8	D5
Abbotsford	120	E4
Abbotsham	13	E3
Abbotskerswell	6	E4
Abbotsley	58	C6
Abbotswood	18	E3
Abbotts Ann	29	F6
Abdon	54	A3
Aber	51	E7
Aber Village	39	J3
Aber-banc	37	H1
Aber-Cywarch	64	B5
Aber-Giar	38	C1
Aber-nant	39	H5
ABERAERON	51	E5
Aberaman	39	H5
Aberangell	64	B6
Aberargie	138	A7
Aberarth	51	E5
Aberbargoed	39	J5
Aberbeeg	40	B5
Abercanaid	39	H5
ABERCARN	40	B6
Abercastle	36	C2
Abercegir	63	J6
Aberchalder	143	F3
ABERCHIRDER	156	D3
Abercraf	39	F4
Abercrombie	130	E2
Abercwmboi	39	H5
Abercych	37	G1
Abercynafon	39	H4
ABERCYNON	39	H6
Aberdalgie	137	H6
ABERDARE	39	H5
Aberdaron	62	B4
ABERDEEN	147	G3
Aberdeen (Dyce) Airport	147	F2
Aberdour	130	A4
Aberdulais	38	E6
Aberdyfi	51	G2
Aberedw	52	D7
Abereiddy	36	B2
Abererch	62	D3
ABERFELDY	137	F4
Aberffraw	74	C5
Aberffrwd	51	G4
Aberford	87	F3
Aberfoyle	128	C2
ABERGAVENNY	40	B4
ABERGELE	76	B4
Abergorlech	38	C2
Abergwesyn	52	B6
Abergwili	38	B3
Abergwydol	63	H6
Abergwynant	63	G5
Abergwynfi	39	F6
Abergwyngregyn	75	F4
Abergynolwyn	63	G6
Aberhosan	63	J7
Aberkenfig	25	F2
Aberlady	130	D5
Aberlemno	139	E3
Aberllefenni	63	H6
Abermeurig	51	F6
Abermule	52	E2
Abernaint	64	E4
Abernant	37	H3
Abernethy	138	A7
Abernyte	138	B5
Aberporth	50	C4
Abersky	153	H6
Abersoch	62	C4
ABERSYCHAN	40	B4
Aberthin	25	H3
ABERTILLERY	40	B5
Abertridwr, Caer	25	J2
Abertridwr, Powys	64	D5
Abertysswg	39	J5
Aberuthven	137	G7
Aberyscir	39	G3
ABERYSTWYTH	51	F3
Abhainn Suidhe	158	C2
ABINGDON	43	G6
Abinger Common	31	F6
Abinger Hammer	31	E6
Abington	119	G5
Abington Pigotts	46	D1
Abingworth	20	E4
Abington	42	D5
Abney	79	F4
Aboyne	146	C4
ABRAM	85	E6
Abriachan	153	H5
Abridge	47	E6
Abronhill	128	E5
Abson	27	G3
Abthorpe	56	E7
Abune-the-Hill	172	C4
Aby	83	G4
Acaster Malbis	87	G2
Acaster Selby	87	G2
ACCRINGTON	85	F4
Ach' an Todhair	142	C6
Acha	132	D3
Acha Mòr	161	G5
Achabraid	126	C4
Achachork	150	D4
Achahoish	126	B5
Achallader	135	H4
Achanalt	153	E2
Achandunie	154	A1
Achany	164	B3
Achaphubuil	142	C6
Acharacle	134	A2
Achargary	167	J4
Acharn, Highl	134	B3
Acharn, Pth & Kin	136	E4
Achath	146	E2
Achavanich	169	F5
Achduart	162	E3
Achentoul	168	C6
Achfary	166	D6
Achgarve	162	C4
Achiemore, Highl IV27	167	E3
Achiemore, Highl KW13	168	C4
Achiltibuie	162	E3
Achina	167	J3
Achindown	154	C4
Achinduich	164	B4
Achinduin	134	C5
Achingills	169	F3
Achintee	152	B4
Achintraid	151	H5
Achleck	133	G4
Achleek	134	B3
Achluachrach	143	E5
Achlyness	166	D4
Achmelvich	162	E1
Achmore, Highl	151	H5
Achmore, Stir	136	C5
Achnaba	134	D5
Achnabat	153	H5
Achnacarnin	166	B6
Achnacarry	142	D5
Achnacloich, Arg & Bt	134	D5
Achnacloich, Highl	141	E3
Achnaconeran	143	G2
Achnacreebeag	134	D5
Achnacroish	134	C4
Achnadrish	133	G3
Achnafalnich	135	G6
Achnagarron	154	A1
Achnaha	133	G2
Achnahanat	164	B4
Achnahannet	154	D6
Achnairn	164	B2
Achnaluachrach	164	C3
Achnamara	126	B4
Achnasaul	142	D5
Achnasheen	152	D2
Achnashelloch	126	C3
Achosnich, Highl IV25	164	D4
Achosnich, Highl PH36	133	F3
Achreamie	168	E3
Achriabhach	135	F2
Achriesgill	166	D4
Achrimsdale	165	F3
Achurch	57	J3
Achuvoldrach	167	G4
Achvaich	164	D4
Achvarasdal	168	D3
Ackergill	169	H4
Acklam, Midlb	104	D6
Acklam, N Yorks	96	C5
Ackleton	66	C7
Acklington	113	G2
Ackton	87	F4
Ackworth Moor Top	87	F5
Acle	73	H5
Acock's Green	55	G3
Acol	35	G4
Acomb	112	D6
Aconbury	40	E2
Acre	85	F4
Acrefair	65	F2
Acton, Ches	77	J6
ACTON, G Lon	31	G2
Acton, Shrops	53	G3
Acton, Suff	60	B7
Acton Beauchamp	54	B6
Acton Bridge	77	H4
Acton Burnell	65	H4
Acton Green	54	B6
Acton Pigott	65	J6
Acton Round	54	B2
Acton Scott	53	H3
Acton Trussell	67	E5
Acton Turville	27	H2
Adamhill	118	B4
Adamthwaite	93	F2
Adbaston	66	C4
Adber	16	E3
Adderbury	43	G2
Adderley	66	B3
Adderstone	123	G4
Addiewell	119	G1
Addingham	86	B2
Addington, Bucks	44	B3
Addington, G Lon	32	D4
Addington, Kent	33	G5
ADDLESTONE	31	E4
Addlethorpe	83	H5
Adeney	66	C5
Adfa	64	D6
Adforton	53	H4
Adisham	35	F5
Adlestrop	42	E3
Adlingfleet	88	C4
Adlington, Ches	78	D3
Adlington, Lancs	85	E5
Admaston, Staffs	67	F4
Admaston, Tel & Wrek	66	B5
Admington	55	H7
Adsborough	16	B2
Adstock	44	B2
Adstone	56	D6
Adversane	20	D3
Advie	155	F5
Adwalton	86	D3
Adwell	44	A6
ADWICK LE STREET	87	G6
Adwick upon Dearne	80	B1
Adziel	157	G3
Ae	109	G4
Affleck	157	F6
Affpuddle	9	G4
Afon-wen	76	D4
Aggborough	54	C4
Aglionby	101	J2
Aignis	161	H4
Aike	88	E2
Aikers	171	E5
Aiketgate	102	A3
Aikton	101	G2
Ailey	53	G7
Ailsworth	70	B7
Aingers Green	48	E3
Ainsdale	84	B5
Ainstable	102	B3
Ainsworth	85	F5
Ainthorpe	105	G7
Aintree	77	F2
Aird, Arg & Bt	126	B2
Aird, D & G	98	B3
Aird, Na Eilean	161	J4
Aird a' Mhachair	159	F1
Aird a' Mhulaidh	159	F1
Aird Asaig	159	F2
Aird Dhail	161	H1
Aird Mhidhinis	148	C4
Aird Mhighe, Na Eilean HS3 3EL	159	F3
Aird Mhighe, Na Eilean HS3 3JQ	159	E4
Aird Mhòr	148	C4
Aird nan Sròban	149	D4
Aird of Sleat	141	E3
Aird Ruairidh	148	C2
Aird Thunga	161	H4
Aird Uig	160	D4
Airdrie Mill	154	D4
AIRDRIE	128	E6
Airidriehill	128	E6
Aireland	100	B2
Airidh a Bhruaich	161	F6
Airmyn	88	B4
Airntully	137	H5
Airor	141	G3
Airth	129	F4
Airton	93	H6
Airyhassen	99	E5
Aisby, Lincs DN21	81	F2
Aisby, Lincs NG32	69	J3
Aisgernis	148	D3
Aislaby, N Yorks YO18	96	C3
Aislaby, N Yorks YO21	105	H7
Aislaby, Stock on T	104	D6
Aisthorpe	81	G4
Aith, Orkney KW16	172	C5
Aith, Orkney KW17	173	G4
Aith, Shetld ZE2 9DJ	177	D4
Aith, Shetld ZE2 9NB	175	E5
Aithsetter	176	D4
Aitnoch	154	D5
Akeld	123	E5
Akeley	44	B2
Akenham	60	E7
Albaston	5	H3
Alberbury	65	G5
Albourne	21	F4
Albrighton, Shrops SY4	65	H5
Albrighton, Shrops WV7	66	D6
Alburgh	61	F3
Albury, Herts	47	E3
Albury, Surrey	31	E6
Albury End	46	E3
Alby Hill	73	E3
Alcaig	153	H3
Alcaston	53	H3
Alcester	55	F6
Alciston	22	B5
Alcombe	25	G6
Alconbury	58	B4
Alconbury Weston	58	B4
Aldborough, N Yorks	95	F5
Aldborough, Norf	73	E3
Aldbourne	28	E3
Aldbrough	89	G3
Aldbrough St John	103	J6
Aldbury	44	D3
Aldclune	137	G2
ALDEBURGH	61	H6
Aldeby	61	H2
Aldenham	45	F6
Alder Forest	78	B1
Alderbury	18	C3
Alderford	72	E5
Alderholt	18	C4
Alderley	27	G1
ALDERLEY EDGE	78	C4
Aldermaston	29	H4
Aldermaston Soke	29	J4
Aldermaston Wharf	29	J4
Alderminster	55	H7
Aldersey Green	77	G6
ALDERSHOT	30	C5
Alderton, Glos	42	C2
Alderton, Northnts	57	F7
Alderton, Shrops	65	H4
Alderton, Suff	49	G1
Alderton, Wilts	27	H2
Alderwasley	79	H6
Aldfield	94	D5
Aldford	77	G6
Aldham, Essex	48	C3
Aldham, Suff	60	D7
Aldie	164	D5
Aldingbourne	20	C5
Aldingham	92	A4
Aldington, Kent	23	G2
Aldington, Worces	42	C1
Aldington Frith	23	G2
Aldochlay	127	H3
Aldreth	59	E4
ALDRIDGE	67	F6
Aldringham	61	H5
Aldsworth	42	D4
Aldunie	155	H6
Aldwark, Derby	79	G6
Aldwark, N Yorks	95	F5
Aldwick	20	C6
Aldwincle	57	J3
ALEXANDRIA	127	H4
Alfardisworthy	12	C4
Alfington	15	H6
Alfold	20	D2
Alfold Crossways	20	D2
Alford, Aberd	146	C2
ALFORD, Lincs	83	G4
Alford, Somer	16	E2

ALFRETON Badsworth 201

ALFRETON 80 B6
Alfrick 54 C6
Alfriston 22 B5
Algarkirk 70 C3
Alhampton 16 E2
Alkborough 88 C4
Alkerton 43 F1
Alkham 35 F6
Alkington 65 J3
Alkmonton 67 G3
All Cannings 28 C4
All Saints South Elmham 61 G3
All Stretton 53 H2
Allaleigh 6 E5
Allanaquoich 145 F4
Allandale 129 E5
Allangrange Mains 153 J3
Allanton, N Lanak 119 F2
Allanton, Scot Bord 122 D2
Allardice 147 F6
Allathasdal, Na Eilean HS9 5XT 148 B4
Allathasdal, Na Eilean HS9 5XT 148 B4
Allen's Green 47 E4
Allendale Town 103 E2
Allenheads 103 E3
Allensford 103 G2
Allensmore 40 D2
Aller 16 C3
Allerby 101 E4
Allerford, Devon 5 H2
Allerford, Somer TA24 25 G6
Allerford, Somer TA4 15 H3
Allerston 96 D3
Allerthorpe 88 B2
Allerton 77 G3
Allerton Bywater 87 F4
Allesley 55 H3
Allestree 68 B3
Allexton 69 G6
Allgreave 78 D5
Allhallows 34 B3
Allhallows-on-Sea 34 B3
Alligin Shuas 151 H3
Allimore Green 66 D5
Allington, Lincs 69 G2
Allington, Wilts SN10 28 C4
Allington, Wilts SP4 18 D2
Allithwaite 92 B4
Allnabad 167 F5
ALLOA 129 F3
Allonby 101 E3
Allostock 78 B4
Alloway 117 H6
Allscot 54 C2
Allt-nan-Sugh 152 B6
Alltchaorunn 135 F3
Alltforgan 64 C4
Alltmawr 52 D7
Alltnacaillich 167 F5
Alltsigh 143 G2
Alltwalis 38 B2
Alltwen 38 E5
Alltyblaca 38 C1
Allwood Green 60 D4
Almeley 53 G6
Almer 9 H4
Almington 66 C3
Alminstone Cross 12 D3
Almondbank 137 H6
Almondbury 86 C5
Almondsbury 27 F2
Alne 95 F5
Alne End 55 G6
ALNESS 154 A2
Alnham 123 E6
Alnmouth 113 G1
ALNWICK 123 G6
Alphamstone 48 B2
Alpheton 60 B6
Alphington 15 F7
Alport 79 G5
Alpraham 77 H6
Alresford 48 D3
Alrewas 67 G5
ALSAGER 78 B6
Alsagers Bank 66 D2
Alsop en le Dale 79 F6
Alston 102 D3
Alstone, Glos 42 B2
Alstone, Somer 26 C6
Alstonefield 79 F6
Alswear 14 D3
Altandhu 162 D2
Altanduin 168 C7
Altarnun 5 F2
Altass 164 B3
Alterwall 169 G3
Altgaltraig 126 E5
Altham 85 F3
Althorne 48 C6
Althorpe 88 C6
Alticry 98 D4
Altnafeadh 135 G3
Altnaharra 167 G6
Altofts 87 E4
Alton, Derby 79 H5
ALTON, Hants 19 J2
Alton, Staffs 67 F2
Alton Barnes 28 D4
Alton Pancras 9 F3
Alton Priors 28 D4
Alton Towers 67 F2
Altonside 155 G3
ALTRINCHAM 78 B3
Altrua 142 E5
ALVA 129 F3
Alvanley 77 G4
Alvaston 68 B3
Alvechurch 55 F4
Alvecote 67 H6
Alvediston 17 H3
Alveley 54 C3
Alverdiscott 13 F3
Alverstoke 11 H4
Alverstone 11 G5
Alverton 69 F2
Alves 155 F2
Alvescot 42 E5
Alveston, S Glos 27 F2
Alveston, Warw 55 H6
Alvie 144 C3
Alvingham 83 F2
Alvington 41 F5
Alwalton 58 B2
Alweston 17 E4
Alwinton 112 D2
ALYTH 138 B4
Am Baile 148 C3
Amatnatua 164 A4
Amber Hill 70 C2
Ambergate 79 H6
Amberley, Glos 41 H5
Amberley, W Susx 20 D4
AMBLE 113 G2
Amblecote 54 D3
AMBLESIDE 92 B1
Ambleston 36 E3
Ambrismore 117 E2
Ambrosden 43 J4
Amcotts 88 C5
Amerton 16 E2
AMERSHAM 44 D6
Amesbury 28 D6
Amington 67 H6
Amisfield 109 H4
AMLWCH 74 D2
Amlwch Port 74 D2
AMMANFORD 38 D4
Amotherby 96 C4
Ampfield 19 E3
Ampleforth 95 G4
Ampney Crucis 42 C5
Ampney St Mary 42 C5
Ampney St Peter 42 C5
Amport 29 E6
AMPTHILL 45 E2
Ampton 60 B4
Amroth 37 F5
Amulree 137 G5
An Ard 162 C6
An Cnoc 161 H4
An Leth Meadhanach 148 C3
Anaheilt 134 C2
Anancaun 152 C2
Ancaster 69 H2
Anchor 52 E3
Ancroft 123 F3
Ancrum 121 F5
Ancton 20 C5
Anderby 83 H4
Anderby Creek 83 H4
Anderson 9 G4
Anderton 77 J4
ANDOVER 29 F6
Andover Down 29 F6
Andoversford 42 C4
Andreas 90 D3
Angarrack 2 D4
Angersleigh 15 H4
Angerton 101 G2
Angle 36 C5
Angmering 20 D5
Angram, N Yorks DL11 93 G2
Angram, N Yorks YO23 87 G2
Anie 128 C1
Ankerville 165 E6
Anlaby 88 E4
Anmer 71 H4
Anna Valley 29 F6
ANNAN 110 A6
Annaside 91 B3
Annat, Arg & Bt 135 E6
Annat, Highl 152 A3
Annbank 117 J5
Annesley 80 C6
Annesley Woodhouse 80 B6
ANNFIELD PLAIN 103 H2
Annochie 157 G4
Annscroft 65 H6
Ansdell 84 B4
Ansford 17 E2
Ansley 55 J2
Anslow 67 H4
Anslow Gate 67 G4
Anstey, Herts 46 E2
Anstey, Leic 68 D6
Anston 80 C3
ANSTRUTHER 131 E2
ANSTRUTHER EASTER 131 E2
ANSTRUTHER WESTER 131 E2
Ansty, Dorset 9 F3
Ansty, W Susx 21 F3
Ansty, Warw 56 B3
Ansty, Wilts 17 H3
Ansty Cross 9 F3
Anthill Common 19 H4
Anthorn 101 F2
Antingham 73 F3
Anton's Gowt 70 C2
Antony 5 H5
Antrobus 77 J4
Anwick 82 D6
Anwoth 99 G4
Aoradh 124 B4
Apethorpe 57 J2
Apley 82 D4
Apperknowle 79 H4
Apperley 41 H3
Appersett 93 G2
Appin 134 D4
Appleby 88 D5
Appleby Magna 68 B5
Appleby Parva 68 B6
APPLEBY- IN-WESTMORLAND 102 C5
Applecross 151 G4
Appledore, Devon EX16 15 G4
Appledore, Devon EX39 13 E2
Appledore, Kent 23 F3
Appleford 43 H6
Appleshaw 29 F6
Applethwaite 101 G5
Appleton 43 G5
Appleton Roebuck 87 G2
Appleton Thorn 77 J3
Appleton Wiske 95 E1
Appleton-le-Moors 96 C3
Appleton-le-Street 96 C4
Appletreehall 120 E6
Appletreewick 94 B5
Appley 15 G3
Appley Bridge 84 D5
Apse Heath 11 G5
Apsley End 45 F2
Apuldram 20 B5
Aquhythie 146 E2
Arabella 164 E6
Arbirlot 139 F4
Arboll 165 E5
Arborfield 30 B4
Arborfield Cross 30 B4
Arborfield Garrison 30 B4
ARBROATH 139 F4
Arbuthnott 147 E6
Archiestown 155 G4
Arclid Green 78 B5
Ard-dhubh 151 G4
Ardachu 164 C3
Ardalanish 133 F7
Ardanaiseig 135 E6
Ardaneaskan 151 H5
Ardarroch 151 H5
Ardbeg, Arg & Bt PA23 127 F4
Ardbeg, Arg & Bt PA42 124 D6
Ardcharnich 163 F5
Ardchiavaig 133 F7
Ardchonnell 126 D1
Ardchuilk 153 E5
Ardchullarie More 128 C1
Ardchyle 136 C6
Ardclach 154 D4
Arddleen 65 F5
Ardechive 142 D4
Ardeley 46 D3
Ardelve 151 H6
Arden 127 H4
Ardens Grafton 55 G6
Ardentinny 127 F4
Ardeonaig 136 D5
Ardersier 154 B3
Ardery 134 B2
Ardessie 162 E5
Ardfern 126 C2
Ardfernal 125 C5
Ardgartan 127 G2
Ardgay 164 B4
Ardgayhill 164 B4
Ardgowan 127 G5
Ardgye 155 F2
Ardheslaig 151 G3
Ardiecow 156 C2
Ardindrean 163 F5
Ardingly 21 G3
Ardington 29 G2
Ardlair 156 C6
Ardleigh 48 D3
Ardler 138 B4
Ardley 43 H3
Ardlui 135 H7
Ardlussa 125 D4
Ardmair 163 F4
Ardmaleish 127 E6
Ardmay 127 G2
Ardminish 114 B2
Ardmolich 141 G6
Ardmore, Arg & Bt G82 127 H5
Ardmore, Arg & Bt PA42 124 D5
Ardmore, Highl 164 D5
Ardnacross 133 H4
Ardnadam 127 F4
Ardnagowan 127 E2
Ardnagrask 153 H4
Ardnarff 152 A5
Ardnastang 134 C2
Ardnave 124 B3
Ardno 127 F2
Ardo 157 F5
Ardoch, D & G 109 F2
Ardoch, Pth & Kin 137 H5
Ardochrig 118 D3
Ardoyne 156 D6
Ardpeaton 127 G4
Ardrishaig 126 C4
Ardross 164 C6
ARDROSSAN 117 G3
Ardshave 164 D4
Ardshealach 134 A2
Ardsley 87 E6
Ardslignish 133 H2
Ardtalla 124 D5
Ardtalnaig 136 E5
Ardtaraig 127 E4
Ardtoe 141 F6
Ardtornish 134 B4
Ardtrostan 136 D6
Arduaine 126 B1
Ardullie 153 H2
Ardvasar 141 F3
Ardvorlich 136 D6
Ardwell 98 C5
Ardwell Mains 98 C5
Areley Kings 54 D4
Arford 20 B2
Argoed 40 A6
Argos Hill 22 B3
Arichastlich 135 G5
Arichonan 126 B3
Aridhglas 133 F6
Arieniskill 141 G5
Arileod 132 D3
Arinacrinachd 151 G3
Arinagour 132 E3
Arion 170 C3
Arisaig 141 F5
Arkendale 95 E5
Arkesden 47 E2
Arkholme 92 D4
Arkley 45 G6
Arksey 87 G6
Arkwright Town 80 B4
Arlary 129 J2
Arlecdon 100 E6
Arlesey 45 F2
Arleston 66 B5
Arley, Ches 78 A3
Arley, Warw 55 H2
Arlingham 41 G4
Arlington, Devon 24 D6
Arlington, E Susx 22 B5
Arlington, Glos 42 D5
Arlington Beccott 24 D6
Armadale, Highl 168 B3
ARMADALE, W Loth 129 G6
Armathwaite 102 B3
Arminghall 73 F6
Armitage 67 F5
Armscote 42 E1
Armston 58 A3
Armthorpe 87 H6
Arnabost 132 E3
Arncliffe 93 H4
Arncott 43 J4
Arncroach 130 E2
Arne 9 H5
Arnesby 56 E2
Arngask 129 J1
Arnicle 116 B4
Arnisdale 141 H2
Arnish 151 E4
Arniston 120 C1
Arnol 161 G3
ARNOLD 68 D2
Arnprior 128 D3
Arnside 92 C4
Aros Mains 133 H4
Arpafeelie 153 J3
Arrad Foot 92 B3
Arram 88 E2
Arrathorne 94 D2
Arreton 11 G5
Arrington 58 D7
Arrivain 135 G5
Arrochar 127 G2
Arrow 55 F6
Arscaig 164 B2
Artafallie 153 J4
Arthington 86 D2
Arthingworth 57 F3
Arthog 63 G5
Arthrath 157 G5
Arthurstone 138 B4
Artrochie 157 H5
ARUNDEL 20 D5
Aryhoulan 134 E2
Asby 100 E5
Ascog 117 F1
Ascot 30 D4
Ascott 43 F2
Ascott-under-Wychwood 43 F4
Ascreavie 138 C3
Asenby 95 F4
Asfordby 69 F5
Asfordby Hill 69 F5
Asgarby, Lincs NG34 70 B2
Asgarby, Lincs PE23 83 F5
Ash, Kent CT3 35 F5
Ash, Kent TN15 33 F4
Ash, Somer 16 C3
Ash, Surrey 30 C6
Ash Barton 13 F5
Ash Magna 66 A3
Ash Mill 14 D3
Ash Priors 15 H3
Ash Street 60 D7
Ash Thomas 15 G4
Ashampstead 29 H3
Ashbocking 61 E6
ASHBOURNE 67 G2
Ashbrittle 15 G3
ASHBURTON 6 D3
Ashbury, Devon 13 F6
Ashbury, Oxon 28 E2
Ashby 88 C6
Ashby by Partney 83 G5
Ashby cum Fenby 83 E1
Ashby de la Launde 82 C6
Ashby Folville 69 F5
Ashby Magna 56 D2
Ashby Parva 56 D3
Ashby Puerorum 83 F4
Ashby St Ledgers 56 D5
Ashby St Mary 73 G6
ASHBY-DE-LA-ZOUCH 68 B5
Ashchurch 42 B2
Ashcombe 7 F3
Ashcott 16 C2
Ashdon 47 F1
Ashe 29 H6
Asheldham 48 C5
Ashen 47 H1
Ashendon 44 B4
Asheridge 44 D5
Ashfield, Carm 38 D3
Ashfield, Stir 128 E2
Ashfield cum Thorpe 61 F5
Ashfield Green 61 F4
Ashford, Devon EX31 13 F2
Ashford, Devon TQ7B 6 C6
Ashford, Hants 18 C4
ASHFORD, Kent 34 D6
ASHFORD, Surrey 31 E3
Ashford Bowdler 53 J4
Ashford Carbonell 53 J4
Ashford Hill 29 H4
Ashford in the Water 79 F5
Ashgill 118 E3
Ashill, Devon 15 G4
Ashill, Norf 72 B6
Ashill, Somer 16 B4
Ashingdon 34 B1
ASHINGTON, Northum 113 G4
Ashington, Somer 16 D3
Ashington, W Susx 21 E4
Ashkirk 120 D5
Ashleworth 41 H3
Ashley, Cambs 59 G5
Ashley, Ches 78 B3
Ashley, Devon 14 C4
Ashley, Glos 42 B6
Ashley, Hants 19 E2
Ashley, Northnts 57 F2
Ashley, Staffs 66 C3
Ashley, Wilts 27 H4
Ashley Green 44 D5
Ashley Heath, Dorset 18 C5
Ashley Heath, Staffs 66 C3
Ashmanhaugh 73 G4
Ashmansworth 29 G5
Ashmansworthy 12 D4
Ashmore 17 H4
Ashmore Green 29 H4
Ashmore Park 67 E6
Ashorne 56 B6
Ashover 79 H5
Ashow 56 B4
Ashperton 41 F1
Ashprington 6 E5
Ashreigney 13 G4
Ashtead 31 F5
Ashton, C of Peter 70 B6
Ashton, Ches 77 H5
Ashton, Co of H 53 J5
Ashton, Corn 2 E5
Ashton, Northnts NN7 57 F7
Ashton, Northnts PE8 57 J3
Ashton Common 27 H5
Ashton Keynes 42 C6
Ashton under Hill 42 B2
Ashton upon Mersey 78 B2
ASHTON-IN-MAKERFIELD 77 H2
ASHTON-UNDER-LYNE 78 D2
Ashurst, Hants 18 E4
Ashurst, Kent 22 B2
Ashurst, W Susx 21 E4
Ashurst Wood 21 H2
Ashwater 12 D6
Ashwell, Herts 46 C2
Ashwell, Rut 69 G5
Ashwellthorpe 72 E7
Ashwick 27 F6
Ashwicken 71 H5
Ashybank 121 E6
Askam in Furness 91 D4
Askern 87 G5
Askerswell 8 D4
Askett 44 C5
Askham, Cumbr 102 B5
Askham, Notts 80 E4
Askham Bryan 87 G2
Askham Richard 87 G2
Asknish 126 D3
Askrigg 93 H2
Askwith 86 C2
Aslackby 70 A3
Aslacton 60 E2
Aslockton 69 F3
Asloun 146 C2
Aspall 60 E5
Aspatria 101 F3
Aspenden 46 D3
Aspley Guise 44 D2
Aspull 85 E6
Assater 174 D3
Asselby 88 B4
Asserby 83 G4
Assington 48 C2
Astbury 78 C5
Astcote 56 E6
Asterby 83 E4
Asterley 65 G6
Asterton 53 G2
Asthall 43 E4
Asthall Leigh 43 F4
Astle 164 D4
Astley, Shrops 65 J5
Astley, Warw 56 B3
Astley, Worces 54 C5
Astley Abbotts 54 C2
Astley Cross 54 D5
Astley Green 78 B2
Aston, Ches CW5 66 B2
Aston, Ches WA7 77 H4
Aston, Co of H 53 H4
Aston, Derby 79 F3
Aston, Herts 46 C3
Aston, Oxon 43 F5
Aston, S Yorks 80 B3
Aston, Shrops 65 J4
Aston, Staffs 66 C2
Aston, Tel & Wrek 66 B6
Aston, W Mids 55 F3
Aston, Wokham 30 B2
Aston Abbotts 44 C3
Aston Botterell 54 B3
Aston Cantlow 55 G6
Aston Clinton 44 C4
Aston Crews 41 F3
Aston End 46 C3
Aston Eyre 54 B2
Aston Fields 55 E5
Aston Flamville 56 C2
Aston Ingham 41 F3
Aston juxta Mondrum 77 J6
Aston le Walls 56 C6
Aston Magna 42 D2
Aston Munslow 53 J3
Aston on Clun 53 G3
Aston Rogers 65 G6
Aston Rowant 44 B6
Aston Sandford 44 B5
Aston Somerville 42 C2
Aston Subedge 42 D1
Aston Tirrold 29 H2
Aston Upthorpe 29 H2
Aston-By-Stone 66 E3
Aston-on-Trent 68 C4
Astwick 45 G2
Astwood 57 H7
Astwood Bank 55 F5
Aswarby 70 A3
Aswardby 83 F4
Atch Lench 55 F6
Atcham 65 J6
Athelington 61 F4
Athelney 16 B3
Athelstaneford 130 E5
Atherington 13 F3
ATHERSTONE 67 J7
Atherstone on Stour 55 H6
ATHERTON 85 E6
Athron Hall 129 H2
Atlow 67 H2
Attadale 152 B5
Attenborough 68 D3
Atterby 81 G2
Attingham 65 J6
ATTLEBOROUGH, Norf 60 D2
Attleborough, Warw 56 B2
Attlebridge 72 E5
Atwick 89 F1
Atworth 27 H4
Aubourn 81 G5
Auchagallon 116 C4
Auchallater 145 F5
Aucharnie 156 D4
Auchattie 146 D4
Auchavan 145 F7
Auchbreck 155 G6
Auchenblae 146 E6
Auchenbrack 108 E3
Auchenbreck 126 E4
Auchencairn, D & G DG1 109 G4
Auchencairn, D & G DG7 100 B2
Auchencarroch 127 J4
Auchencrow 122 D1
Auchendinny 120 B1
Auchengray 119 G2
Auchengruith 109 F2
Auchenhalrig 155 H2
Auchenheath 119 F3
Auchenhessnane 109 F3
Auchenmalg 98 D4
Auchensoul 106 E3
Auchentiber 117 H3
Auchenvennel 127 G4
Auchenvey 108 E5
Auchgourish 144 D2
Auchindrain 126 E2
Auchindrean 163 F5
Auchininna 156 D4
Auchinleck, D & G 107 G5
Auchinleck, E Ayr 118 C5
Auchinloch 128 D5
Auchinroath 155 G3
Auchintoul, Aberd 146 C2
Auchintoul, Highl 164 B4
Auchiries 157 H5
Auchlean 144 C4
Auchlee 147 F4
Auchleuchries 157 H5
Auchleven 156 D6
Auchlochan 119 F4
Auchlossan 146 C3
Auchlunies 147 F4
Auchlunkart 155 H4
Auchlyne 136 C6
Auchmacoy 157 G5
Auchmair 155 H6
Auchmantle 98 C3
Auchmillan 118 C5
Auchmithie 139 F4
Auchmuirbridge 130 B2
Auchmull 146 C6
Auchnabony 100 B3
Auchnacree 138 D2
Auchnafree 137 F5
Auchnagallin 155 E5
Auchnagatt 157 G4
Aucholzie 145 H4
Auchronie 146 B5
AUCHTERARDER 129 G1
Auchteraw 143 F3
Auchterderran 130 B3
Auchterhouse 138 C5
AUCHTERMUCHTY 130 B1
Auchterneed 153 G3
Auchtertool 130 B3
Auchtertyre, Ang 138 B4
Auchtertyre, Highl 151 H6
Auchtertyre, Mor 155 F3
Auchtubh 136 C6
Auckengill 169 H3
Auckley 80 D1
Audenshaw 78 D2
Audlem 66 B2
Audley 78 C6
Auds 156 D2
Aughton, E Yorks 87 J3
Aughton, Lancs L39 84 B6
Aughton, Lancs LA2 92 D5
Aughton, S Yorks 80 B3
Aughton, Wilts 28 E5
Aughton Park 84 C6
Auldearn 154 D3
Aulden 53 H6
Auldgirth 109 G4
Auldhame 131 E4
Auldhouse 118 D2
Ault a' Chruinn 142 B1
Ault-na-goire 153 H6
Aultanrynie 167 E6
Aultbea 162 C5
Aultdearg 153 E2
Aultgrishan 162 B5
Aultibea 165 G1
Aultiphurst 168 C3
Aultmore 156 B3
Aulton 156 D6
Aultvoulin 141 G3
Aundorach 144 D2
Aunsby 69 J3
Auquhorthies 157 F6
Aust 27 E2
Austerfield 80 D2
Austrey 67 H6
Austwick 93 F5
Authorpe 83 G3
Authorpe Row 83 H4
Avebury 28 D4
Avebury Trusloe 28 C4
Aveley 33 F2
Avening 41 H6
Averham 80 E6
Aveton Gifford 6 C6
Avielochan 144 D2
Aviemore 144 C2
Avington, Hants 19 G2
Avington, W Berks 29 F4
Avoch 154 A3
Avon 10 C4
Avon Dassett 56 C7
Avonbridge 129 G5
Avonmouth 26 E3
Avonwick 6 D5
Awbridge 18 E3
Awhirk 98 B4
Awkley 27 E2
Awliscombe 15 H5
Awre 41 G5
Awsworth 68 C2
Axbridge 26 D5
Axford, Hants 29 J6
Axford, Wilts 28 E3
AXMINSTER 8 B4
Axmouth 8 A4
Aydon 112 E6
Aylburton 41 F5
Ayle 102 D3
Aylesbeare 15 G6
AYLESBURY 44 C4
Aylesby 89 G6
Aylesford 33 H5
Aylesham 35 F5
Aylestone 68 D6
Aylmerton 73 E3
AYLSHAM 73 E4
Aylton 41 F2
Aymestrey 53 H5
Aynho 43 H2
Ayot St Lawrence 45 F4
Ayot St Peter 45 G4
AYR 117 H5
Aysgarth 94 B3
Ayside 92 B3
Ayston 69 G6
Aythorpe Roding 47 F4
Ayton, N Yorks 97 E3
Ayton, Scot Bord 122 E1
Aywick 177 C5
Azerley 94 D4

B

Babbacombe 7 F4
Babbinswood 65 G3
Babcary 16 D3
Babel 39 F2
Babell 76 D4
Babeny 6 C3
Babraham 59 F6
Babworth 80 D3
Bac 161 H3
Back of Keppoch 141 F5
Backaland 173 F3
Backaskaill 172 E1
Backbarrow 92 B3
Backburn, Aberd AB39 147 F4
Backburn, Aberd AB54 156 C5
Backfolds 157 H3
Backford 77 G4
Backhill, Aberd AB42 157 H5
Backhill, Aberd AB53 157 E5
Backhill of Clackriach 157 G4
Backhill of Trustach 146 D4
Backies 165 E3
Backlass 169 G4
Backmuir of New Gilston 130 D2
Backwell 26 D4
Backworth 113 G5
Bacon End 47 G4
Baconsthorpe 72 E3
Bacton, Co of H 40 C2
Bacton, Norf 73 G3
Bacton, Suff 60 D5
Bacton Green 60 D5
BACUP 85 G4
Badachro 162 B6
Badavanich 152 D3
Badbury 28 D2
Badby 56 D6
Badcall, Highl IV274RQ 166 D4
Badcall, Highl IV274TH 166 C5
Badcaul 162 E4
Baddeley Green 78 D6
Baddesley Ensor 67 H7
Baddidarach 163 E1
Baddoch 145 F5
Badenscoth 156 E5
Badenyon 145 H2
Badger 66 C7
Badgers Mount 33 E4
Badgeworth 41 J4
Badgworth 26 C5
Badicaul 151 G6
Badingham 61 G5
Badlesmere 34 D5
Badlipster 169 G5
Badluarach 162 D4
Badminton 27 H2
Badnagie 169 F6
Badninish 164 D4
Badrallach 162 E4
Badsey 42 C1
Badshot Lea 30 C6
Badsworth 87 F5

Place	Page	Grid
Badwell Ash	60	C5
Bag Enderby	83	F4
Bagby	95	F3
Bagendon	42	C5
Baggrow	101	F3
Bàgh Mòr	149	D4
Bàgh Shiarabhagh	148	C4
Baghasdal	148	C3
Bagillt	76	E4
Baginton	56	B4
Baglan	24	E1
Bagley	65	H4
Bagnall	78	D6
Bagnor	29	G4
Bagpath	41	H5
Bagshot, Surrey	30	D4
Bagshot, Wilts	29	F4
Bagstone	27	F2
Bagthorpe, Norf	71	H3
Bagthorpe, Notts	80	B6
Bagworth	68	C6
Bagwyllydiart	40	D3
Bail Uachdraich	149	D3
Bail' Ard Bhuirgh	161	H2
Bail' Ur Tholastaidh	161	J3
BAILDON	86	C3
Baile	158	D4
Baile Ailein	161	F5
Baile an Truiseil	161	G2
Baile Boidheach	126	B5
Baile Glas	149	D4
Baile Mhanaich	149	C4
Baile Mhàrtainn	158	B5
Baile Mhic' Phàil	158	C5
Baile Mòr	149	C3
Baile Mór	133	E6
Baile na Creige	148	B4
Baile nan Cailleach	149	C4
Baile Raghnill	149	C2
Bailebeag	143	H2
Bailiesward	156	B5
Baillieston	128	D6
Bainbridge	93	H2
Bainshole	156	D5
Bainton, C of Peter	70	A6
Bainton, E Yorks	88	D1
Bainton, Oxon	43	H3
Bairnkine	121	F6
Baker Street	33	G2
Bakers End	46	D4
BAKEWELL	79	G5
Balachuirn	151	E4
Balbeg, Highl IV63 6TL	153	G5
Balbeg, Highl IV63 6XQ	153	G6
Balbeg, S Ayr	107	F2
Balbeggie	138	A6
Balbithan	147	E2
Balblair, Highl IV4	153	H4
Balblair, Highl IV7	154	B2
Balcherry	165	E5
Balchers	156	E3
Balchladich	166	B6
Balchraggan	153	H4
Balchrick	166	C4
Balcombe	21	G2
Balcomie	131	F2
Balcurvie	130	C2
Baldersby	95	E4
Balderston	85	E3
Balderton	81	F6
Baldhu	3	F3
Baldinnie	130	D1
BALDOCK	46	C2
Baldovie	138	D5
Baldrine	90	D4
Baldslow	22	D4
Baldwin	90	C4
Baldwin's Gate	66	C2
Baldwinholme	101	H2
Bale	72	D3
Balemartine	132	B4
Balephuil	132	B4
Balerno	129	J6
Balevullin	132	B4
Balfarg	130	B2
Balfield	139	E2
Balfour	172	E5
Balfron	128	C4
Balgaveny	156	D4
Balgavies	139	E3
Balgedie	130	A2
Balgonar	129	H3
Balgove	157	F5
Balgowan, Highl	143	J4
Balgowan, Pth & Kin	137	G6
Balgown	150	C2
Balgrochan	128	D5
Balgy	151	H3
Balhaldie	129	F2
Balhalgardy	156	E6
Balhary	138	B4
Balhelvie	138	C6
Baligill	168	C3
Baligrundle	134	C4
Balintore, Ang	138	B3
Balintore, Highl	165	E6
Balintraid	154	B1
Balkeerie	138	C4
Balkholme	88	B4
Balkissock	106	D4
Ball	65	G4
Ball Hill	29	G4
Ballabeg	90	B5
Ballacannell	90	D4
Ballacarnane Beg	90	C4
Ballachlaggan	145	G4
Ballachrink	90	B5
Ballachulish	135	E3
Ballafesson	90	B5
Ballagyr	90	B4
Ballajora	90	D3
Ballakilpheric	90	B5
Ballamodha	90	B5
Ballantrae	106	C4
Ballasalla, I of M IM9	90	B6
Ballasalla, I of M IM7	90	C3
Ballateare	90	C3
BALLATER	145	H4
Ballaugh	90	C3
Ballechin	137	G3
Balleigh	164	D5
Ballencreiff	130	D5
Balliasta	177	D3
Ballidon	79	G6
Balliekine	116	C4
Balliemore, Arg & Bt PA23	127	E4
Balliemore, Arg & Bt PA34	134	C6
Ballimeanoch	134	E7
Ballimore, Arg & Bt	126	D4
Ballimore, Stir	136	C7
Ballinaby	124	B4
Ballindean	138	B6
Ballingdon	48	B1
Ballinger Common	44	D5
Ballingham	41	E2
Ballingry	130	A3

Ballinlick	137	G4
Ballinluig	137	G3
Ballintuim	137	J3
Balloch, Ang	138	C3
Balloch, Highl	154	B4
Balloch, N Lanak	128	E5
Balloch, W Dunb	127	H4
Ballochan	146	C4
Ballochford	155	H5
Ballochmorrie	106	E4
Ballochroy	116	B2
Ballochyle	127	F4
Ballogie	146	C4
Balls Cross	20	C3
Ballygown	133	G4
Ballygrant	125	A6
Ballyhaugh	132	D3
Ballymeanoch	126	C3
Balmacara	151	H6
Balmacara Square	151	H6
Balmaclellan	108	D5
Balmacneil	137	G3
Balmacqueen	159	J5
Balmae	99	H5
Balmaha	128	B3
Balmalcolm	130	C2
Balmeanach, Highl IV40	151	E4
Balmeanach, Highl IV51	151	E5
Balmedie	147	G2
Balmerlawn	10	E3
Balmichael	116	D4
Balmore, E Dunb	128	D5
Balmore, Highl IV12	154	C4
Balmore, Highl IV4	153	F5
Balmore, Pth & Kin	136	E3
Balmullo	138	D6
Balmungie	154	B3
Balmurrie	98	D3
Balnabruich	169	F7
Balnacoil	165	E2
Balnacra	152	B4
Balnafoich	154	A5
Balnagall	165	E5
Balnaguard	137	G3
Balnaguisich	154	A1
Balnahard, Arg & Bt PA61	125	B3
Balnahard, Arg & Bt PA68	133	G5
Balnain	153	G5
Balnakeil	167	E3
Balnaknock	150	D2
Balnamoon	137	G3
Balnamoan	139	E2
Balnapaling	154	B2
Balnaut	145	G4
Balne	87	G5
Balnespick	144	C3
Balquhidder	136	C6
Balsall Common	55	H4
Balscote	43	F1
Balsham	59	F6
Baltasound	177	D3
Balterley	78	B6
Baltersan Cross	99	F3
Balthangie	157	F3
Baltonsborough	16	D2
Baluachraig	126	C3
Balvaird	153	H3
Balvarran	137	H2
Balvicar	134	B7
Balvraid	154	C5
BAMBER BRIDGE	84	D4
Bamber's Green	47	F3
Bamburgh	123	G4
Bamff	138	B3
Bamford	79	G3
Bampton, Cumbr	102	B6
Bampton, Devon	15	F3
Bampton, Oxon	43	F5
Banavie	142	D6
BANBURY	43	G1
Banchor	154	D4
BANCHORY	146	E4
Banchory- Devenick	147	G3
Bancyfelin	37	H4
Bancyffordd	37	J2
BANFF	156	D2
BANGOR	75	E4
Bangor-is-y-coed	65	G2
Banham	60	D3
Bank	18	D5
Bank Newton	85	H1
Bank Street	54	B5
Bankend	109	H6
Bankfoot	137	H5
Bankglen	118	D6
Bankhead, Aberd	146	D3
Bankhead, C of Aber	147	F3
Banknock	128	E5
Banks, Cumbr	111	E6
Banks, Lancs	84	B4
Banks, Orkney KW172PR	172	E3
Banks, Orkney KW172RW	171	E6
Bankshill	110	A4
Banningham	73	F4
Bannister Green	47	G3
Bannockburn	129	F3
BANSTEAD	32	C5
Bantham	6	C6
Banton	128	E5
Banwell	26	C5
Bapchild	34	C4
Bapton	17	H2
Bar Hill	58	D5
Barabhas	161	G3
Baramore	141	F6
Barassie	117	H4
Baravullin	134	C5
Barbaraville	154	B1
Barber Booth	79	F3
Barbon	93	E3
Barbridge	77	J6
Barbrook	24	E6
Barby	56	D4
Barcaldine	134	D4
Barcheston	42	E2
Barcombe	21	H4
Barcombe Cross	21	H4
Barden	94	C2
Bardennoch	108	C3
Bardfield End Green	47	G2
Bardfield Saling	47	G3
Bardister	175	E3
Bardney	82	D5
Bardon	68	C5
Bardon Mill	111	G6
Bardowie	128	C5
Bardrainney	127	H5
Bardsea	92	B4
Bardsey	87	E2
Bardsley	85	H4
Bardwell	60	C4
Barford, Norf	72	E6
Barford, Warw	55	H5
Barford St John	43	G3
Barford St Martin	18	B2

Barford St Michael	43	G2
Barfrestone	35	F5
Bargeddie	128	E6
BARGOED	39	J6
Bargrennan	107	F5
Barham, Cambs	58	B4
Barham, Kent	35	F5
Barham, Suff	60	E6
Barholm	70	A5
Barkby	68	E5
Barkestone-le-Vale	69	F3
Barkham	30	B4
BARKING, G Lon	33	E2
Barking, Suff	60	D6
Barkingside	33	E1
Barkisland	86	B5
Barkston	69	H2
Barkston Ash	87	F3
Barkway	46	C2
Barlae	98	D3
Barlaston	66	D3
Barlavington	20	C4
Barlborough	80	B4
Barlby	87	H3
Barlestone	68	C6
Barley, Herts	46	D2
Barley, Lancs	85	G2
Barleyhill	103	G2
Barleythorpe	69	G6
Barling	34	C2
Barlow, Derby	79	H4
Barlow, N Yorks	87	H4
Barlow, T & W	113	F6
Barmby Moor	88	B2
Barmby on the Marsh	87	H4
Barmer	72	B3
Barmoor Lane End	123	F4
BARMOUTH	63	G5
Barmpton	104	C6
Barmston	97	G6
Barnacarry	126	E3
Barnack	70	A6
Barnacle	56	B3
BARNARD CASTLE	103	G6
Barnard Gate	43	G4
Barnardiston	59	H7
Barnburgh	87	F6
Barnby	61	H3
Barnby Dun	87	H6
Barnby in the Willows	81	F6
Barnby Moor	80	D3
Barndennoch	109	F4
BARNES	31	G3
BARNET	46	C6
Barnetby le Wold	88	E6
Barney	72	C3
Barnham, Suff	60	B4
Barnham, W Susx	20	C5
Barnham Broom	72	D6
Barnhead	139	F3
Barnhill, Mor	155	F3
Barnhill, Northum	112	E4
Barnhills	106	B5
Barningham, Durham	103	G6
Barningham, Suff	60	C4
Barnoldby le Beck	89	G6
BARNOLDSWICK	85	G2
Barns Green	21	E3
Barnsley, Glos	42	C5
BARNSLEY, S Yorks	86	E6
BARNSTAPLE	13	F2
Barnston, Essex	47	G4
Barnston, Mers	76	E3
Barnstone	69	F3
Barnt Green	55	F4
Barnton	77	J4
Barnwell	57	J3
Barnwood	41	H4
Barr	106	E3
Barrachan	99	E5
Barrack	157	F4
Barraer	99	E3
Barraglom	160	E4
Barrahormid	126	B4
Barran	134	C6
Barrapol	132	B4
Barras, Aberd	147	F5
Barras, Cumbr	103	E6
Barrasford	112	D5
Barravullin	126	C2
Barregarrow	90	C4
BARRHEAD	118	C2
Barrhill	106	E4
Barrington, Cambs	58	D7
Barrington, Somer	16	B4
Barripper	2	E4
Barrmill	117	H2
Barrock	169	G2
Barrow, Lancs	85	F3
Barrow, Rut	69	G5
Barrow, Shrops	65	B6
Barrow, Suff	59	H5
Barrow Burn	122	D6
Barrow Gurney	27	E4
Barrow Street	17	G2
Barrow upon Humber	88	E4
Barrow upon Soar	68	D5
Barrow upon Trent	68	B3
BARROW-IN-FURNESS	91	D4
Barroway Drove	71	H6
Barrowby	69	H3
Barrowden	69	H6
BARROWFORD	85	G3
Barry, Ang	139	E5
BARRY, V of Glam	25	J4
Barry Island	25	J4
Barsby	69	E5
Barsham	61	G3
Barston	55	H4
Bartestree	41	E1
Barthol Chapel	157	F5
Barthomley	78	B6
Bartley	18	E4
Bartlow	59	F7
Barton, Cambs	58	E6
Barton, Ches	77	G6
Barton, Glos	42	D3
Barton, Lancs L39	84	B6
Barton, Lancs PR3	84	D3
Barton, N Yorks	104	B7
Barton, Tbay	7	F4
Barton, Warw	55	G6
Barton Bendish	71	H6
Barton Hartshorn	43	J2
Barton in Fabis	68	D3
Barton in the Beans	68	B6
Barton Mills	59	H4
Barton Moss	78	B2
Barton on Sea	10	D4
Barton Seagrave	57	G4
Barton St David	16	D2
Barton Stacey	29	G6
Barton Turf	73	G4
Barton- le-Clay	45	E2
Barton-le-Street	96	C5
Barton-le-Willows	96	C5

Barton-on-the-Heath	42	E2
Barton-under-Needwood	67	G5
BARTON-UPON-HUMBER	88	E4
Barway	59	F4
Barwell	56	C2
Barwick	16	D4
Barwick in Elmet	87	E3
Baschurch	65	H4
Bascote	56	C5
Bascote Heath	56	B5
Basford Green	78	D6
Bashall Eaves	85	E2
Bashall Town	85	F2
Bashley	10	D4
BASILDON	33	H2
BASINGSTOKE	29	J5
Baslow	79	G4
Bason Bridge	26	C6
Bassaleg	26	B2
Bassenthwaite	101	G4
Bassett	19	F4
Bassingbourn	46	D1
Bassingfield	68	E3
Bassingham	81	G5
Bassingthorpe	69	H4
Basta	177	C4
Bastle	111	G3
Baston	70	B5
Bastwick	73	H5
Batchcott	53	H4
Batchworth	45	E6
Batcombe, Dorset	8	E3
Batcombe, Somer	17	E2
Bate Heath	78	A4
BATH	27	G4
Bathampton	27	G4
Bathealton	15	G3
Batheaston	27	G4
Bathford	27	G4
BATHGATE	129	G6
Bathley	81	F5
Bathpool, Corn	5	F3
Bathpool, Somer	16	A3
BATLEY	86	D4
Batsford	42	D2
Batt's Corner	30	C6
Battersby	105	E7
BATTERSEA	32	C3
Battisborough Cross	6	C6
Battisford	60	D6
Battisford Tye	60	D6
BATTLE, E Susx	22	D4
Battle, Powys	39	H2
Battlefield	65	J5
Battlesbridge	47	H6
Battlesden	44	D3
Battleton	15	F3
Battramsley	10	E4
Bauds of Cullen	156	B2
Baugh	132	C4
Baughton	41	H1
Baughurst	29	H4
Baulking	29	F1
Baumber	82	E4
Baunton	42	C5
Baverstock	18	B2
Bawburgh	72	E6
Bawdeswell	72	D4
Bawdrip	16	B2
Bawdsey	49	G1
Bawsey	71	G5
Bawtry	80	D2
Baxenden	85	F4
Baxterley	55	H2
Baybridge	103	F2
Baycliff	92	A4
Baydon	29	E3
Bayford, Herts	46	D5
Bayford, Somer	17	F3
Bayles	102	D3
Baylham	60	E6
Baynard's Green	43	H3
Baysham	41	E3
Bayston Hill	65	H6
Baythorne End	47	H1
Bayton	54	B4
Bayworth	43	H5
Beachampton	44	B2
Beachamwell	71	H6
Beachans	155	E4
Beacharr	116	A3
Beachley	27	E1
Beacon	15	H5
Beacon End	48	C3
Beacon's Bottom	44	B6
BEACONSFIELD	30	D1
Beacrabhaic	159	F3
Beadlam	96	B3
Beadnell	123	H5
Beaford	13	F4
Beal, N Yorks	87	G4
Beal, Northum	123	F4
Beamhurst	67	F3
Beaminster	8	C3
Beamish	104	B2
Beamsley	86	B1
Bean	33	F3
Beanacre	28	B4
Beanley	123	F6
Beaquoy	172	C4
Beare Green	31	F6
Bearley	55	G5
Bearpark	104	B3
Bearsbridge	102	D2
BEARSDEN	128	C5
Bearsted	33	H5
Bearwood of Poole	53	G6
Bearwood, Poole	10	B4
Beattock	109	H2
Beauchamp Roding	47	F5
Beauchief	79	H3
Beaufort	40	A4
Beaulieu	11	E3
Beauly	153	H4
BEAUMARIS	75	F4
Beaumont, Cumbr	110	C7
Beaumont, Essex	49	E3
Beaumont Leys	68	D6
Beausale	55	H4
Beauvale	80	B6
Beaworthy	13	E6
Beazley End	47	H3
BEBINGTON	77	F3
Bebside	113	G4
BECCLES	61	H3
Becconsall	84	C4
Beck Foot	93	E2
Beck Hole	96	D1
Beck Row	59	G4
Beck Side	91	D3
Beckbury	66	C6
BECKENHAM	32	D4
Beckermet	100	E7
Beckermonds	93	G3
Beckfoot, Cumbr CA19	91	G1
Beckfoot, Cumbr CA5	101	E4

Beckford	42	B2
Beckhampton	28	C4
Beckingham, Lincs	81	F6
Beckingham, Notts	80	E3
Beckington	27	H5
Beckley, E Susx	22	E3
Beckley, Oxon	43	H4
Beckton	33	E2
Beckwithshaw	86	D1
Becontree	33	E2
Bedale	94	D3
Bedburn	103	H4
Bedchester	17	G4
Beddau	25	H2
Beddgelert	63	F2
Beddingham	21	H5
Beddington	32	D4
BEDFORD	57	J7
Bedhampton	19	J5
Bedingfield	60	E5
Bedlar's Green	47	F3
BEDLINGTON	113	G4
Bedlinog	39	H5
Bedmond	45	E5
Bednall	67	E5
Bedrule	121	F6
Bedstone	53	G4
BEDWAS	26	A2
BEDWORTH	56	B3
Beeby	68	E6
Beech, Hants	19	H2
Beech, Staffs	66	D3
Beechingstoke	28	C5
Beedon	29	G3
Beeford	97	G6
Beeley	79	G5
Beelsby	82	E1
Beenham	29	H4
Beer	15	J7
Beer Crocombe	16	B3
Beer Hackett	16	E4
Beesands	6	E6
Beesby	83	G3
Beeson	6	E6
Beeston, Beds	58	B7
Beeston, Ches	77	H6
Beeston, Norf	72	C5
BEESTON, Notts	68	D3
Beeston, W Yorks	86	D3
Beeston Regis	72	E2
Beeswing	109	F6
Beetham	92	C4
Beetley	72	C5
Began	26	B2
Begbroke	43	G4
Begdale	71	E6
Begelly	37	F5
Beggar Hill	47	G5
Beguildy	53	E4
Beighton, Norf	73	G6
Beighton, S Yorks	80	B3
Beinn Casgro	161	H5
Beith	117	H2
Bekesbourne	35	E5
Belaugh	73	F5
Belbroughton	54	E4
Belchamp Otten	48	B1
Belchamp St Paul	47	H1
Belchamp Walter	48	B1
Belchford	83	E4
Belford	123	G4
Belhelvie	147	G2
Belhinnie	156	B6
Bell Bar	46	C5
Bell Busk	93	H6
Bell End	55	E4
Bellabeg	145	H2
Bellamore	106	E4
Bellanoch	126	C3
Bellasize	88	B3
Bellaty	138	B3
Belleau	83	G4
Belleheiglash	155	F5
Bellerby	94	C2
Bellever	6	C3
Bellfield	119	F4
Belliehill	139	E2
Bellingdon	44	D5
Bellingham	112	C4
Belloch	114	B3
Bells Yew Green	22	C2
Bellshill, N Lanak	118	E1
Bellshill, Northum	123	G4
Bellsmyre	127	J5
Bellspool	119	J4
Bellsquarry	129	H6
Belluton	27	F4
Belmaduthy	154	A3
Belmesthorpe	69	J5
Belmont, Bburn & Da	85	E5
Belmont, Shetld	177	C3
Belnacraig	145	H2
Belowda	4	C3
BELPER	68	B2
Belper Lane End	79	H7
Belsay	113	F5
Belses	121	E5
Belsford	6	D5
Belsize	45	E5
Belstead	48	E1
Belston	117	H5
Belstone	13	G6
Belsyde	129	G5
Belthorn	85	F4
Beltinge	35	E4
Beltoft	88	C6
Belton, Leic	68	C5
Belton, Lincs	69	H3
Belton, N Linc	88	B6
Belton, Norf	73	H6
Belton-in-Rutland	69	G6
Beltring	33	G6
Belvedere	33	E3
Belvoir	69	G3
Bembridge	11	H5
Bemersyde	121	E4
Bempton	97	G4
Benacre	61	J3
Benbuie	108	E3
Benderloch	134	D5
Benenden	34	B3
Benfield	99	E3
Benholm	147	F7
Beningbrough	95	G6
Benington, Herts	46	C3
Benington, Lincs	70	D2
Benllech	74	E3
Benmore, Arg & Bt	127	F4
Benmore, Stir	136	B6
Bennacott	12	C6
Bennan	116	D5
Benniworth	82	E3

Benover	33	H6
Benson	29	J1
Benston, Lincs	175	F5
Benstonhall	173	F3
Bent	146	D6
Benthall	66	B6
Bentham	42	B4
Benthoul	147	E3
Bentley, E Yorks	88	E3
Bentley, Hants	30	B6
BENTLEY, S Yorks	87	G6
Bentley, Suff	48	E2
Bentley, Warw	55	H2
Bentley Heath	55	G4
Benton	14	C2
Bentpath	110	C3
Bentworth	19	H1
Benvie	138	C5
Benwick	58	D2
Beoley	55	F5
Beoraidbeg	141	H6
Bepton	20	B4
Berden	47	E3
Bere Alston	5	H4
Bere Ferrers	5	H4
Bere Regis	9	G4
Berea	36	B3
Berepper	3	E5
Bergh Apton	73	G6
Berinsfield	43	H6
Berkeley	41	F6
Berkhamstead	44	E5
BERKHAMSTED	44	D5
Berkley	27	H6
Berkswell	55	H4
BERMONDSEY	32	D3
Bernera	141	H1
Berners Roding	47	G5
Bernice	127	F3
Bernisdale	150	D4
Berrick Salome	43	J6
Berriedale	165	H1
Berrier	101	H5
Berriew	64	E6
Berrington, Northum	123	F3
Berrington, Shrops	65	J6
Berrow, Somer	26	C5
Berrow, Worces	41	G2
Berrow Green	54	C6
Berry Hill	41	E4
Berry Pomeroy	6	E4
Berryfield	28	B4
Berryhillock	156	C2
Berrynarbor	24	C6
Bersham	65	G2
Berstane	171	E3
Bersted	20	C5
Berwick	22	B5
Berwick Bassett	28	C3
Berwick Hill	113	F5
Berwick St James	18	B2
Berwick St John	17	H3
Berwick St Leonard	17	H2
BERWICK-UPON-TWEED	123	E2
Berwyn	65	E2
Besford, Shrops	65	J4
Besford, Worces	42	B1
Besford Court	42	B1
Bessacarr	80	D1
Bessels Leigh	43	G5
Bessingham	72	E3
Best Beech Hill	22	C2
Besthorpe, Norf	60	D2
Besthorpe, Notts	81	F5
Bestwood Village	68	D2
Beswick	88	E2
Betchworth	31	G6
Bethania, Cered	51	F5
Bethania, Gwyn	75	F6
Bethel, Gwyn	74	E5
Bethel, I of Angl	74	C4
Bethersden	23	F1
BETHESDA, Gwyn	75	F5
Bethesda, Pemb	37	F4
Bethlehem	38	D3
BETHNAL GREEN	32	D2
Betley	66	C2
Betsham	33	G3
Betteshanger	35	G5
Bettiscombe	8	B3
Bettisfield	65	H3
Betton, Shrops SY5	65	G6
Betton, Shrops TF9	66	B3
Bettws, Brig	25	G2
Bettws, Monm	40	B4
Bettws, Newp	26	B1
Bettws Cedewain	52	E2
Bettws Gwerfil Goch	64	D2
Bettws Newydd	40	C5
Bettyhill	167	J3
Betws	38	D4
Betws Bledrws	51	F5
Betws Garmon	75	E6
Betws Ifan	50	D7
BETWS-Y-COED	75	G6
Betws-yn-Rhos	75	J4
Beulah, Cered	50	C7
Beulah, Powys	52	C6
Bevendean	21	G5
Bevercotes	80	D4
BEVERLEY	88	E3
Beverston	41	H6
Bevington	41	F6
Bewaldeth	101	G4
Bewcastle	111	E5
BEWDLEY	54	C4
Bewerley	94	C5
Bewholme	89	F2
BEXHILL	22	D5
BEXLEY	33	E3
Bexleyheath	33	E3
Bexwell	71	G6
Beyton	60	C5
Bhaltos	160	D4
Bhatarsaigh	148	B5
Bibury	42	D5
BICESTER	43	H3
Bickenhall	16	A4
Bickenhill	55	G3
Bicker	70	C3
Bickerstaffe	84	C6
Bickerton, Ches	77	H6
Bickerton, N Yorks	87	F1
Bickham Bridge	6	D5
Bickington, Devon EX31	13	F2
Bickington, Devon TQ12	6	D3
Bickleigh, Devon EX5	15	F5
Bickleigh, Devon PL6	6	B4
Bickleton	13	F2
Bickley	33	E4
Bickley Moss	65	J2
Bickley Town	65	J2
Bicknacre	47	H5
Bicknoller	15	H2
Bicknor	34	B5
Bickton	18	C4

Bicton, Shrops SY3 65 H5
Bicton, Shrops SY7 53 F3
Bidborough 33 F6
Biddenden 22 E2
Biddenham 57 J6
Biddestone 27 H3
Biddisham 26 C5
Biddlesden 43 J1
Biddlestone 112 D2
BIDDULPH 78 C6
Biddulph Moor 78 D6
BIDEFORD 13 E3
Bidford-on-Avon 55 G6
Bielby 88 B2
Bieldside 147 F3
Bierley 11 G6
Bierton 44 C4
Big Balcraig 99 E5
Big Sand 162 B6
Bigbury 6 C6
Bigbury-on-Sea 6 C6
Bigby 88 E6
Biggar, Cumbr 91 C5
BIGGAR, S Lanak 119 H4
Biggin, Derby DE6 67 H2
Biggin, Derby SK17 79 F6
Biggin, N Yorks 87 G3
Biggin Hill 32 E5
Biggin Hill Airport 32 E4
Biggings 174 C4
Biggins 93 E4
BIGGLESWADE 45 F1
Bighouse 168 C3
Bighton 19 H2
Biglands 110 D6
Bignor 20 C4
Bigods 47 G3
Bigrigg 100 E6
Bigton 176 C5
Bilberry 4 D5
Bilborough 68 D2
Bilbrook, Somer 25 H6
Bilbrook, Staffs 66 D6
Bilbrough 87 G2
Bilbster 169 G4
Bildershaw 103 J5
Bildeston 60 C7
BILLERICAY 47 G6
Billesdon 69 F6
Billesley 55 G6
Billing 57 F5
Billingborough 70 B3
BILLINGE 77 H1
Billingford, Norf IP21 60 E4
Billingford, Norf NR20 72 D4
BILLINGHAM 104 D5
Billinghay 82 D6
Billingley 87 F6
BILLINGSHURST 20 D3
Billingsley 54 C3
Billington, Beds 44 D3
Billington, Lancs 85 F3
Billockby 73 H5
Billsmoor Park 112 D3
Billy Row 103 H4
Bilsborrow 84 D3
Bilsby 83 G4
Bilsington 23 G2
Bilsthorpe 80 D5
Bilston, Midlo 130 B6
BILSTON, W Mids 55 E2
Bilstone 68 B6
Bilting 34 D6
Bilton, E Yorks 89 F3
Bilton, N Yorks 87 F2
Bilton, Northum 123 H6
Bilton, Warw 56 C4
Bilton in Ainsty 87 F1
Bimbister 170 D3
Binbrook 82 E2
Bincombe 9 E5
Bindal 165 F5
Binegar 27 F6
Binfield 30 C3
Binfield Heath 30 B3
Bingfield 112 D5
Bingham 69 F3
Bingham's Melcombe 9 F3
BINGLEY 86 C3
Bings Heath 65 J5
Binham 72 C3
Binley, Hants 29 G5
Binley, W Mids 56 B4
Binley Woods 56 B4
Binniehill 129 F5
Binstead 11 G4
Binsted 30 B6
Binton 55 G6
Bintree 72 D4
Binweston 65 F6
Birch, Essex 48 C4
Birch, G Man 85 G6
Birch Green, Essex 48 C4
Birch Green, Herts 46 C4
Birch Vale 78 E3
Bircham Newton 71 H3
Bircham Tofts 71 H3
Birchanger 47 F3
Bircher 53 H5
Birchfield, Highl IV24 164 A4
Birchfield, Highl PH25 144 D1
Birchgrove 38 E6
Birchington 35 F4
Birchley Heath 55 H2
Birchover 79 G5
Birchwood 81 G5
Bircotes 80 D2
Birdbrook 47 H1
Birdfield 126 D3
Birdham 20 B5
Birdholme 79 H5
Birdingbury 56 C5
Birdlip 42 B4
Birdsall 96 D5
Birdsgreen 54 C3
Birdsmoorgate 8 B3
Birdston 128 D5
Birdwell 79 H1
Birdwood 41 G4
Birgham 122 C4
Birkby 94 E1
Birkdale 84 B5
BIRKENHEAD 77 F3
Birkenhills 156 H4
Birkenshaw, N Lanak 118 D1
Birkenshaw, W Yorks 86 D4
Birkhall 145 H4
Birkhill, Ang 138 C5
Birkhill, D & G 120 B6
Birkholme 69 H4
Birkin 87 G4
Birley 53 H6
Birling, Kent 33 G4
Birling, Northum 113 G2
Birling Gap 22 B6
Birlingham 42 B1
BIRMINGHAM 55 F3

Birmingham International Airport 55 G3
Birnam 137 H4
Birness 157 G5
Birse 146 C4
Birsemore 146 C4
Birstall 68 D6
Birstall Smithies 86 D4
Birstwith 94 D6
Birtley, Co of H 53 G5
Birtley, Northum 112 C5
Birtley, T & W 104 B2
Birts Street 41 G2
Bisbrooke 69 G7
Bisham 30 C2
Bishampton 55 E6
BISHOP AUCKLAND 104 B5
Bishop Burton 88 D3
Bishop Middleham 104 C4
Bishop Monkton 94 E5
Bishop Norton 81 G2
Bishop Sutton 27 E5
Bishop Thornton 94 D5
Bishop Wilton 96 C6
BISHOP'S CASTLE 53 G3
Bishop's Caundle 17 E4
Bishop's Cleeve 42 B3
Bishop's Frome 54 B7
Bishop's Green 47 G4
Bishop's Itchington 56 B6
Bishop's Nympton 14 D3
Bishop's Offley 66 C4
Bishop's Sutton 19 H2
Bishop's Tachbrook 56 B5
Bishop's Tawton 13 F2
Bishop's Waltham 19 G4
Bishop's Wood 66 D6
Bishopbridge 82 C2
Bishopbriggs 128 D6
Bishops Cannings 28 C4
Bishops Lydeard 15 H3
Bishopsbourne 35 E5
Bishopsteignton 7 F3
Bishopstoke 19 F4
Bishopston 24 C2
Bishopstone, Bucks 44 C4
Bishopstone, Co of H 40 D1
Bishopstone, E Susx 21 H5
Bishopstone, Swin 28 E2
Bishopstone, Wilts 18 B3
Bishopstrow 27 H6
Bishopswood 16 A4
Bishopsworth 27 E4
Bishopthorpe 87 G2
Bishopton, Darl 104 C5
Bishopton, Renf 128 B5
Bishton 26 C2
Bisley, Glos 41 J5
Bisley, Surrey 30 D5
Bispham 84 B3
Bissoe 3 F3
Bisterne 10 C3
Bisterne Close 10 C3
Bitchfield 69 H4
Bittadon 24 C6
Bittaford 6 C5
Bittering 72 C5
Bitterley 54 A4
Bitterne 19 F4
Bitteswell 56 D3
Bitton 27 F4
Bix 30 B2
Bixter 175 E5
Blaby 56 D2
Black Bourton 43 E5
Black Callerton 113 F6
Black Clauchrie 107 E4
Black Crofts 134 D5
Black Dog 14 E5
Black Heddon 113 E5
Black Marsh 65 G7
Black Mount 135 G4
Black Notley 47 H3
Black Pill 24 D1
Black Torrington 13 E5
Blackacre 109 H3
Blackadder 122 D2
Blackawton 6 E5
Blackborough 15 G5
Blackborough End 71 G5
Blackboys 22 B3
Blackbraes, Aberd 147 F2
Blackbraes, Falk 129 G5
Blackbrook, Derby 68 B2
Blackbrook, Staffs 66 C3
Blackburn, Aberd 147 F2
BLACKBURN, Bburn & Da 85 E4
Blackburn, W Loth 129 G6
Blackcastle 154 C4
Blackchambers 147 E2
Blackcraig 108 E4
Blackdams 146 E3
Blackden Heath 78 B4
Blackdog 147 G2
Blackdown, Dorset 8 B3
Blackdown, Warw 47 F3
Blackfield 11 F3
Blackford, Cumbr 110 C6
Blackford, Pth & Kin 129 F2
Blackford, Somer BA22 17 E3
Blackford, Somer BS28 26 D6
Blackfordby 68 B5
Blackgang 11 F6
Blackhall 146 D4
Blackhall Colliery 104 D4
Blackhall Mill 103 H2
Blackhall Rocks 104 D4
Blackham 22 A2
Blackhaugh 120 D4
Blackheath, Essex 48 D3
Blackheath, G Lon 32 C3
BLACKHEATH, W Mids 55 E3
Blackhill 157 H3
Blackjack 70 C3
Blackland 28 C4
Blackley 85 G6
Blacklunans 138 A2
Blackmill 25 H2
Blackmoor, Hants 20 A2
Blackmoor, N Som 26 D5
Blackmoor, Somer 15 H4
Blackmoor Gate 24 D6
Blackmore 47 G5
Blackmore End, Essex 47 H2
Blackmore End, Herts 45 F4
Blackness, Aberd 146 D4
Blackness, Falk 129 H5
Blackness, Highl 169 G6
Blacknest 30 B6
Blacko 85 G2
BLACKPOOL 84 B3
Blackpool Gate 110 E5
Blackridge 129 F6
Blackrock, Arg & Bt 125 A6
Blackrock, Monm 40 B4

Blackrod 85 E5
Blackshaw 109 H6
Blackshaw Head 85 H4
Blackshaw Moor 78 E6
Blackstone 21 F4
Blackthorn 43 J4
Blackthorpe 60 C5
Blacktoft 88 C4
Blacktop 147 F3
Blackwall Tunnel 32 D2
Blackwater, Corn 3 F3
Blackwater, Hants 30 C5
Blackwater, I of W 11 G5
Blackwaterfoot 116 C5
Blackwell, Derby DE55 80 B6
Blackwell, Derby SK17 79 F4
Blackwell, Warw 42 E1
Blackwell, Worces 55 E4
BLACKWOOD, Caer 40 A6
Blackwood, S Lanak 119 E3
Blackwood Hill 78 D6
Blacon 77 F5
Bladbean 35 E6
Bladnoch 99 F4
Bladon 43 G4
Blaen-y-coed 37 H3
Blaenannerch 50 C7
BLAENAU FFESTINIOG 63 G2
BLAENAVON 40 B5
Blaendyryn 39 G2
Blaenffos 37 F2
Blaengarw 39 G6
Blaengwrach 39 F5
Blaengwynfi 39 F6
Blaenpennal 51 G5
Blaenplwyf 51 F4
Blaenporth 50 C7
Blaenrhondda 39 G6
Blaenwaun 37 G3
Blagdon, N Som 26 E5
Blagdon, Tbay 6 E4
Blagdon Hill 15 J4
Blaich 142 C6
BLAINA 40 B5
Blair Atholl 137 F2
Blair Drummond 128 E3
Blairdaff 146 D2
Blairglas 127 H4
BLAIRGOWRIE 138 A4
Blairhall 129 H4
Blairhoyle 128 D2
Blairingone 129 G3
Blairlogie 129 F3
Blairmore 127 F4
Blairnamarrow 145 G2
Blairpark 117 G2
Blairquhomrie 128 B4
Blairskaith 128 C5
Blairvadach 127 G4
Blairydryne 146 E4
Blaisdon 41 G4
Blakebrook 54 D4
Blakedown 54 D4
Blakelaw 122 C4
Blakemere 40 C1
Blakeney, Glos 41 F5
Blakeney, Norf 72 D2
Blakenhall, Ches 66 C2
Blakenhall, W Mids 66 E7
Blakeshall 54 D3
Blakesley 56 E6
Blanchland 103 F2
Bland Hill 86 D1
Blandford Camp 17 H5
BLANDFORD FORUM 17 G5
Blandford St Mary 17 G5
Blanefield 128 C5
Blankney 82 C5
Blantyre 118 D2
Blar a' Chaorainn 135 F2
Blarghour 126 D1
Blarmachfoldach 142 C7
Blarnalearoch 163 F4
Blashford 18 C5
Blaston 57 G2
Blatherwycke 57 H2
Blawith 92 A3
Blaxhall 61 G6
Blaxton 80 D1
BLAYDON 113 F6
Bleadon 26 C5
Bleak Hey Nook 86 B6
Blean 34 E4
Bleasby 69 F2
Bleatarn 102 D6
Blebocraigs 138 D7
Bleddfa 53 F5
Bledington 42 E3
Bledlow 44 B5
Bledlow Ridge 44 B6
Blencarn 102 C4
Blencogo 101 F3
Blencow 101 J4
Blendworth 19 J4
Blennerhasset 101 F3
Bletchingdon 43 G4
Bletchingley 32 D5
Bletchley, Mil Key 44 C2
Bletchley, Shrops 66 B3
Bletherston 37 E3
Bletsoe 57 J6
Blewbury 29 H2
Blickling 72 E4
Blidworth 80 C6
Blindburn 122 D6
Blindcrake 101 F4
Blindley Heath 32 D6
Blinkbonny 154 D3
Blisland 4 E3
Bliss Gate 54 C4
Blissford 18 C4
Blisworth 57 F6
Blithbury 67 F4
Blo' Norton 60 D4
Blockley 42 D2
Blofield 73 G6
Blofield Heath 73 G5
Blore 79 F7
Blounts Green 67 F3
Bloxham 43 G2
Bloxholm 82 C6
BLOXWICH 67 E6
Bloxworth 9 G4
Blubberhouses 94 C6
Blue Anchor 25 H6
Blue Bell Hill 33 H4
Blundellsands 77 F1
Blundeston 73 J7
Blunham 58 B6
Blunsdon St Andrew 28 C2
Bluntisham 58 D4
Blunts 5 G4
Blyborough 81 G2
Blyford 61 H4
Blymhill 66 D6

BLYTH, Northum 113 H4
Blyth, Notts 80 D3
Blyth Bridge 119 J3
Blythburgh 61 H4
Blythe 121 E3
Blythe Bridge 67 E2
Blyton 81 F2
BO'NESS 129 G4
Boarhills 131 E1
Boarhunt 19 H5
Boars Hill 43 G5
Boarshead 22 B2
Boarstall 43 J4
Boasley Cross 13 F6
Boat of Garten 144 D2
Boath 164 B6
Boathvic 164 B6
Bobbing 34 B4
Bobbington 54 D2
Bobbingworth 47 F5
Bocaddon 5 E5
Bochastle 128 D2
Bockhampton 9 F4
Bocking 47 H3
Bocking Churchstreet 47 H3
Boconnoc 5 E4
Boddam, Aberd 157 J4
Boddam, Shetld 176 C6
Boddington 41 H3
Bodedern 74 C3
Bodelwyddan 76 B4
Bodenham, Co of H 53 J6
Bodenham, Wilts 18 C3
Bodenham Moor 53 J6
Bodermid 62 B4
Bodewryd 74 C2
Bodfari 76 C4
Bodffordd 74 D4
Bodham 72 E2
Bodiam 22 D3
Bodicote 43 G2
Bodieve 4 C3
Bodinnick 5 E5
Bodior 74 B4
Bodle Street Green 22 C4
Bodney 72 B6
Bodorgan 74 C5
Bodsham 34 E6
Boduan 62 D3
Bogach 148 C4
Bogallan 154 A3
Bogbrae 157 H5
Bogend 117 H4
Boghead, Aberd 146 D4
Boghead, S Lanak 118 E3
Bogmoor 155 H2
Bogniebrae 156 C4
BOGNOR REGIS 20 C5
Bograxie 146 E2
Bogrie 109 F4
Bogside 119 F2
Bogton 156 D3
Bogue 108 D4
Bohenie 143 E5
Bohetherick 5 H4
Bohortha 3 G4
Bohuntine 143 E5
Bojewyan 2 B4
Bolam 103 J5
Bold Heath 77 H3
BOLDON 113 H6
Boldon Colliery 113 H6
Boldre 10 E4
Boldron 103 G6
Bole 81 E3
Bolehill 79 G6
Boleigh 2 C5
Boleside 120 D4
Bolham 15 F4
Bolham Water 15 H4
Bolingey 3 F2
Bollington 78 D4
Bolney 21 F3
Bolnhurst 58 A6
Bolshan 139 F3
BOLSOVER 80 B4
Bolsterstone 79 G2
Bolstone 41 E2
Boltby 95 F3
Bolton, Cumbr 102 C5
Bolton, E Loth 130 E5
Bolton, E Yorks 88 B1
BOLTON, G Man 85 F6
Bolton, Northum 123 G6
Bolton Abbey 86 B1
Bolton Bridge 86 B1
Bolton Low Houses 101 G3
Bolton Lees 34 D6
Bolton Percy 87 G2
Bolton-by-Bowland 85 F2
Bolton-le-Sands 92 C5
Bolton-on-Swale 94 D2
Boltonfellend 110 D6
Boltongate 101 G3
Bolventor 5 E3
Bombie 100 B2
Bomere Heath 65 H5
Bonar Bridge 164 C4
Bonawe 134 E5
Boncath 37 G2
Bonchester Bridge 121 E6
Bondleigh 14 C5
Bonehill 67 G6
Bonhill 127 H5
Boningale 66 D6
Bonjedward 121 F5
Bonkle 119 F2
Bonnington, C of Edin 129 J6
Bonnington, Kent 23 G2
Bonnybank 130 C2
Bonnybridge 129 F4
Bonnykelly 157 F3
BONNYRIGG AND LASSWADE 130 C6
Bonnyton, Aberd 156 D5
Bonnyton, Ang DD10 139 F3
Bonnyton, Ang DD3 138 C5
Bonnyton Smiddy 139 E5
Bonsall 79 G6
Bont 40 C4
Bont Dolgadfan 64 B6
Bont-goch or Elerch 51 G3
Bont-newydd 76 C4
Bontddu 63 G5
Bontnewydd, Cered 51 G5
Bontnewydd, Gwyn 74 D5
Bontuchel 76 C6
Bonvilston 25 H3
Booley 66 A4
Boor 162 C5
Boosbeck 105 F6
Boot 91 C1
Booth of Toft 175 F3

Booth Wood 86 B5
Boothby Graffoe 81 G6
Boothby Pagnell 69 H3
Boothstown 78 B1
Bootle, Cumbr 91 C3
BOOTLE, Mers 77 F2
Booton 72 E4
Boquhan 128 C4
Boraston 54 B3
Borden 34 B4
Bordley 93 H5
BORDON 20 A2
Bordon Camp 20 A2
Boreham, Essex 47 H5
Boreham, Wilts 27 H6
Boreham Street 22 C4
BOREHAMWOOD 45 E4
Boreland, D & G DG11 110 A3
Boreland, D & G DG8 99 E3
Boreland, Stir 136 C5
Borgh, Na Eilean HS6 158 E3
Borgh, Na Eilean HS9 148 B4
Borghastan 160 E3
Borgie 167 H4
Borgue, D & G 99 H5
Borgue, Highl 169 F7
Borley 48 B7
Borley Green 60 C5
Bornais 148 B3
Bornesketaig 150 C1
Borness 99 H5
Borough Green 33 G5
Boroughbridge 95 E5
Borras Head 77 F6
Borreraig 150 A3
Borrowash 68 C3
Borrowby, N Yorks TS13 105 G6
Borrowby, N Yorks YO7 95 F3
Borrowfield 147 F4
Borth 51 G3
Borth-y-Gest 63 F3
Borthwick 120 C2
Borthwickbrae 120 D6
Borthwickshiels 120 D6
Borve 150 D4
Borwick 92 D4
Bosavern 2 B4
Bosbury 41 F1
Boscastle 12 B6
Boscombe, Bourne 10 C4
Boscombe, Wilts 18 C2
Bosham 20 B5
Bosham Hoe 20 B5
Bosherston 36 D6
Boskednan 2 C4
Bosley 78 D5
Bossall 96 C5
Bossiney 12 A7
Bossingham 34 E6
Bossington 25 F6
Bostadh 160 E4
Bostock Green 78 A5
BOSTON 70 D2
Boston Spa 87 F2
Boswednack 2 C4
Boswinger 4 C6
Botallack 2 B4
Botany Bay 46 C6
Botcheston 68 C6
Botesdale 60 D4
Bothal 113 G4
Bothamsall 80 D4
Bothel 101 F4
Bothenhampton 8 C4
Bothwell 118 E2
Botley, Bucks 44 D5
Botley, Hants 19 G4
Botley, Oxon 43 G5
Botloes Green 41 G3
Botolph Claydon 44 B3
Botolphs 21 E5
Bottacks 153 G2
Bottesford, Leic 69 G3
Bottesford, N Linc 88 C6
Bottisham 59 F5
Bottom Boat 87 E4
Bottomcraig 138 C6
Botton 96 B1
Botton Head 93 E5
Botusfleming 5 H4
Botwnnog 62 C3
Bough Beech 33 E6
Boughrood 39 J2
Boughspring 41 E6
Boughton, Norf 71 G6
Boughton, Northnts 57 F5
Boughton, Notts 80 D5
Boughton Aluph 34 D6
Boughton Lees 34 D6
Boughton Malherbe 34 B6
Boughton Monchelsea 33 H5
Boughton Street 34 D5
Boulby 105 G6
Bouldon 53 J3
Boulmer 123 H6
Boulston 36 D4
Boultenstone 146 B2
Boultham 81 G5
Bourn 58 D6
BOURNE 70 A4
Bourne End, Beds 44 D1
Bourne End, Bucks 30 C2
Bourne End, Herts 44 E5
BOURNEMOUTH 10 B4
Bournemouth International Airport 10 C4
Bournes Green 42 B5
Bournheath 55 E4
Bournmoor 104 C2
Bournville 55 F3
Bourton, Dorset 17 F2
Bourton, N Som 26 C4
Bourton, Oxon 28 E2
Bourton, Shrops 54 A2
Bourton on Dunsmore 56 C4
Bourton-on-the-Hill 42 D2
Bourton-on-the-Water 42 D3
Bousd 132 E2
Bouth 92 A3
Boveney 30 D3
Boverton 25 G4
Bovey Tracey 6 E3
Bovingdon 44 E5
Bovington Camp 9 G5
Bow, Devon 14 D5
Bow, G Lon 32 D2
Bow Brickhill 44 D2
Bow of Fife 130 C1
Bow Street 51 G3
Bowbank 103 F5
Bowburn 104 C4
Bowcombe 11 F5
Bowd 15 H6
Bowden, Devon 6 E6
Bowden, Scot Bord 121 E4
Bowden Hill 28 B4

Bowderdale 93 E1
Bowdon 78 B3
Bower, Highl 169 G3
Bower, Northum 111 G4
Bowerchalke 18 B3
Bowerhill 28 B4
Bowermadden 169 G3
Bowers Gifford 33 H2
Bowershall 129 H3
Bowertower 169 G3
Bowes 103 F6
Bowgreave 84 C2
Bowhill 120 D5
Bowland 120 D3
Bowland Bridge 92 C3
Bowley 53 J6
Bowlhead Green 20 C2
Bowling 128 B5
Bowling Bank 65 G2
Bowling Green 54 D6
Bowmanstead 92 B2
Bowmore 124 C5
Bowness-on- Solway 110 B6
BOWNESS-ON-WINDERMERE 92 C2
Bowsden 123 E3
Bowthorpe 72 E6
Box, Glos 41 H5
Box, Wilts 27 H4
Box End 57 J7
Box Hill 27 H4
Boxbush 41 G4
Boxford, Suff 48 C1
Boxford, W Berks 29 G3
Boxgrove 20 C5
Boxley 33 H5
Boxted, Essex 48 D2
Boxted, Suff 60 B6
Boxworth 58 D5
Boylestone 67 G3
Boyndie 156 D2
Boyndlie 157 G2
Boynton 97 G5
Boysack 139 F4
Boyton, Corn 12 D6
Boyton, Suff 61 G7
Boyton, Wilts 17 H2
Boyton Cross 47 G5
Bozeat 57 H6
Braaid 90 C5
Braal Castle 169 F3
Brabling Green 61 F5
Brabourne 34 E6
Brabourne Lees 23 G1
Brabster 169 H3
Brabstermire Ho 169 H3
Bracadale 150 C5
Braceborough 70 A5
Bracebridge Heath 81 G5
Braceby 69 J3
Bracewell 85 G2
Brackenfield 79 H6
Brackenmore 157 F3
Bracketter 142 D5
Brackley, Arg & Bt 116 B3
Brackley, Highl 154 C3
BRACKLEY, Northnts 43 H2
Brackloch 163 F1
BRACKNELL 30 C4
Braco 129 F2
Bracobrae 156 C3
Bracon Ash 73 E7
Bracora 141 G4
Bracorina 141 G4
Bradbourne 79 G6
Bradbury 104 C5
Bradda 90 A6
Bradden 56 E7
Braddock 5 E4
Bradenham, Bucks 44 C6
Bradenham, Norf 72 C6
Bradenstoke 28 C3
Bradfield, Essex 48 E2
Bradfield, Norf 73 F3
Bradfield, W Berks 29 J3
Bradfield Combust 60 B6
Bradfield Green 78 A6
Bradfield Heath 48 E3
Bradfield St Clare 60 C6
Bradfield St George 60 C6
Bradford, Devon 13 E5
Bradford, Northum 123 G4
BRADFORD, W Yorks 86 C3
Bradford Abbas 16 D4
Bradford Leigh 27 H4
BRADFORD PEVERELL 9 E4
BRADFORD- ON-AVON 27 H4
Bradford-on-Tone 15 H3
Brading 11 H5
Bradley, Derby 67 H2
Bradley, Hants 29 J6
Bradley, NE Linc 89 G6
Bradley, Staffs 66 D5
Bradley, Wrex 77 F6
Bradley Green 55 E5
Bradley in the Moors 67 F2
Bradmore 68 D3
Bradninch 15 G5
Bradnop 78 E6
Bradpole 8 C4
Bradshaw 85 F5
Bradstone 5 G2
Bradwall Green 78 B5
Bradwell, Derby 79 F3
Bradwell, Essex 48 B3
Bradwell, Mil Key 44 C2
Bradwell, Norf 73 J6
Bradwell Grove 42 E5
Bradwell Waterside 48 C5
Bradwell-on-Sea 48 D5
Bradworthy 12 D4
Brae, Highl IV22 162 C5
Brae, Highl IV27 163 J3
Brae, Highl IV7 154 A2
Brae, Shetld 175 E4
Brae of Achnahaird 162 E2
Braeantra 164 B6
Braedownie 145 G6
Braefield 153 G5
Braegrum 137 H6
Braehead, Ang 139 F3
Braehead, D & G 99 F4
Braehead, Orkney KW172DA 172 E2
Braehead, Orkney KW172SD 173 F3
Braehead, S Lanak ML110LE 119 F4
Braehead, S Lanak ML118EY 119 G2
Braehoulland 174 D3
Braemar 145 F4
Braemore, Highl IV23 163 F6
Braemore, Highl KW6 168 E6
Braes of Enzie 156 A3
Braes of Ullapool 163 F4
Braeside 127 G5
Braeswick 173 G3
Braeval 128 C2
Braewick 175 E5
Brafferton, Darl 104 B5

Brafferton, N Yorks 95 F4
Brafield-on-the-Green 57 G6
Bragar 161 F3
Bragbury End 46 C3
Bragenham 44 D3
Bragleenmore 134 D6
Braides 84 C1
Braidley 94 B3
Braidwood 119 F3
Braigo 124 B4
Brailsford 67 H2
BRAINTREE 47 H3
Braiseworth 60 E4
Braishfield 18 E3
Braithwaite, Cumbr 101 G5
Braithwaite, S Yorks 87 H5
Braithwell 80 C2
Bramber 21 E4
Brambridge 19 F3
Bramcote, Notts 68 D3
Bramcote, Warw 56 C3
Bramdean 19 H3
Bramerton 73 F6
Bramfield, Herts 46 C4
Bramfield, Suff 61 G4
Bramford 60 E7
BRAMHALL 78 C3
Bramham 87 F2
Bramhope 86 D2
Bramley, Hants 29 J5
Bramley, S Yorks 80 B2
Bramley, Surrey 30 E6
Bramley Green 30 A5
Bramling 35 F5
Brampford Speke 15 F6
Brampton, Cambs 58 C4
Brampton, Cumbr CA16 102 C5
Brampton, Cumbr CA8 110 E6
Brampton, Lincs 81 F4
Brampton, Norf 73 F4
Brampton, S Yorks 80 B1
Brampton, Suff 61 H3
Brampton Abbotts 41 F3
Brampton Ash 57 F3
Brampton Bryan 53 G4
Brampton en le Morthen 80 B3
Bramshall 67 F3
Bramshaw 18 D4
Bramshill 30 B4
Bramshott 20 B2
Bran End 47 G3
Branault 141 E7
Brancaster 71 H2
Brancaster Staithe 71 H2
Brancepeth 104 B4
Branchill 155 E3
Brand Green 41 G3
Brandesburton 89 F2
Brandeston 61 F4
Brandis Corner 13 E5
Brandiston 72 E4
BRANDON, Durham 104 B4
Brandon, Lincs 69 H2
Brandon, Northum 123 F6
Brandon, Suff 59 H3
Brandon, Warw 56 C4
Brandon Bank 59 G3
Brandon Creek 59 G2
Brandon Parva 72 D6
Brandsby 95 G4
Brandy Wharf 82 C2
Brane 2 C5
Branksome 10 B4
Branksome Park 10 B5
Bransby 81 F4
Branscombe 15 H7
Bransford 54 C6
Bransgore 10 C4
Bransholme 89 E3
Branston, Leic 69 G4
Branston, Lincs 82 C5
Branston, Staffs 67 H4
Branston Booths 82 C5
Branstone 11 G5
Brant Broughton 81 G6
Brantham 48 E2
Branthwaite, Cumbr CA14 100 E5
Branthwaite, Cumbr CA7 101 G4
Brantingham 88 D4
Branton, Northum 123 F6
Branton, S Yorks 80 D1
Branxholme 120 D6
Branxton 122 D4
Brassington 79 G6
Brasted 33 E5
Brasted Chart 33 E5
Brathens 146 D4
Bratoft 83 G5
Brattleby 81 G3
Bratton 28 B5
Bratton Clovelly 13 E6
Bratton Fleming 14 C2
Bratton Seymour 17 E3
Braughing 46 D3
Braughing Friars 46 E3
Braunston 56 D5
Braunston-in-Rutland 69 G6
Braunstone Town 68 D6
Braunton 13 E2
Brawby 96 C4
Brawl 168 C3
Brawlbin 168 E4
Bray 30 D3
Bray Shop 5 G3
Braybrooke 57 F3
Brayford 14 C2
Braystones 91 B1
Brayton 87 H3
Brazacott 12 C6
Brea 109 F5
Breach 35 E6
Breachwood Green 45 F3
Breacleit 160 E4
Breadsall 68 B2
Breadstone 41 G5
Breage 2 E5
Breakachy 153 G4
Breakish 151 F6
Bream 41 F5
Breamore 18 C4
Brean 26 B5
Breanais 160 C5
Brearton 94 E5
Breascleit 161 F4
Breaston 68 C3
Brechfa 38 C3
BRECHIN 139 E2
Breck of Cruan 172 D5
Breckan 170 C4
Breckles 60 C2
Breckrey 151 E2
Brecks 176 C3
BRECON 39 H3
Bredbury 78 D2
Brede 22 E4
Bredenbury 54 B6

Bredfield 61 F6
Bredgar 34 B4
Bredhurst 33 H4
Bredicot 54 E6
Bredon 42 B2
Bredon's Norton 42 B2
Bredons Hardwick 42 B2
Bredwardine 40 C1
Breedon on the Hill 68 C4
Bréibhig, Na Eilean HS2 161 H4
Bréibhig, Na Eilean HS9 148 B5
Breich 119 G1
Breighton 87 J3
Breinton 176 D3
Bremhill 28 B3
Bremirehoull 176 D5
Brenchley 33 G6
Brenchoillie 126 E2
Brendon 24 E6
Brent Eleigh 60 C7
Brent Knoll 26 C5
Brent Pelham 47 E2
BRENTFORD 31 F3
BRENTWOOD 47 F6
Brenzett 23 G3
Brereton 67 F5
Brereton Green 78 B5
Brereton Heath 78 C5
Bressingham 60 D3
Bretby 67 H4
Bretford 56 C4
Bretforton 42 C1
Bretherdale Head 92 D1
Bretherton 84 C4
Brettabister 175 F5
Brettenham, Norf 60 C3
Brettenham, Suff 60 C6
Bretton 77 F5
Brewham 17 F2
Brewlands Bridge 138 A2
Brewood 66 D6
Briantspuddle 9 G4
Brickendon 46 D5
Bricket Wood 45 F5
Brickhampton 42 B1
Bride 90 D2
Bridekirk 101 F4
Bridell 37 F1
Bridestowe 13 F7
Brideswell 156 C5
Bridford 6 E3
Bridge 35 E5
Bridge End, Lincs 70 B3
Bridge End, Northum 112 D6
Bridge Green 47 E2
Bridge Hewick 94 E4
Bridge of Alford 146 C2
BRIDGE OF ALLAN 155 F5
Bridge of Avon 155 F5
Bridge of Balgie 136 C4
Bridge of Brown 155 F6
Bridge of Cally 137 J3
Bridge of Canny 146 D4
Bridge of Craigisla 138 B3
Bridge of Dee 108 E6
Bridge of Don 147 G2
Bridge of Dun 139 F3
Bridge of Dye 146 D5
Bridge of Earn 137 J7
Bridge of Ericht 136 C3
Bridge of Feugh 146 E4
Bridge of Forss 168 E3
Bridge of Gairn 145 H4
Bridge of Gaur 136 C3
Bridge of Muchalls 147 F4
Bridge of Muick 145 H4
Bridge of Oich 143 F3
Bridge of Orchy 135 G5
Bridge of Tilt 137 F2
Bridge of Walls 174 F1
Bridge of Weir 127 H6
Bridge Reeve 14 C4
Bridge Sollers 40 D1
Bridge Street 60 B7
Bridge Trafford 77 G4
Bridge Yate 27 F3
Bridgefoot, Ang 138 C5
Bridgefoot, Cumbr 100 E5
Bridgehampton 16 D3
Bridgehaugh 155 H5
Bridgemary 11 G3
Bridgend, Aberd AB33 146 C2
Bridgend, Aberd AB54 156 C5
Bridgend, Ang 139 E2
Bridgend, Arg & Bt PA28 116 B4
Bridgend, Arg & Bt PA31 126 C3
Bridgend, Arg & Bt PA44 125 A6
BRIDGEND, Brig 25 G2
Bridgend, Cered 50 B7
Bridgend, Cumbr 101 H6
Bridgend, Fife 130 C1
Bridgend, Glos 41 H5
Bridgend, Mor 155 H5
Bridgend, N Lanak 128 D5
Bridgend, W Loth 129 H5
Bridgend of Lintrathen 138 B3
Bridgerule 4 D5
Bridges, Corn 4 D5
Bridges, Shrops 53 G2
Bridgetown, Corn 12 D7
Bridgetown, Somer 15 F2
Bridgham 60 C3
BRIDGNORTH 54 C2
Bridgtown 67 E6
BRIDGWATER 16 A2
BRIDLINGTON 97 E3
BRIDPORT 8 C4
Bridstow 41 E3
BRIERFIELD 85 G3
Brierley, Co of H 53 H6
Brierley, Glos 41 F4
Brierley, S Yorks 87 F5
BRIERLEY HILL 54 E3
Brierton 104 D5
Brig o' Turk 128 C2
Brigdefoot 146 B3
BRIGG 88 E6
Brigham, Cumbr 101 E4
Brigham, E Yorks 88 E1
Brighouse, D & G 99 H5
Brighouse, W Yorks 86 C4
Brighstone 11 F5
Brightgate 79 G6
Brighthampton 43 F5
Brightling 22 C3
BRIGHTLINGSEA 48 D4
BRIGHTON, Bri & Ho 21 G5
Brighton, Corn 4 C5
Brightons 129 G5
Brightwalton 29 G3
Brightwell 49 F1
Brightwell Baldwin 44 A6
Brightwell-cum-Sotwell 29 H1
Brignall 103 G6
Brigsley 83 E1
Brigsteer 92 C3

Brigstock 57 H3
Brill 44 A4
Brilley 53 F7
Brimfield 53 J5
Brimington 80 B4
Brimley 6 E3
Brimpsfield 42 A4
Brimpton 29 H4
Brimpton Common 29 H4
Brims 170 C6
Brimscombe 41 H5
Brimstage 77 F3
Brind 88 B3
Brindister, Shetld ZE2 9EX 176 D4
Brindister, Shetld ZE2 9NT 174 D5
Brindle 84 E4
Brindley 77 H6
Brindley Ford 78 C6
Brineton 66 D5
Bringhurst 57 G2
Brington 58 A4
Brinian 172 E4
Briningham 72 D3
Brinkhill 83 F4
Brinkley 59 G6
Brinklow 56 C4
Brinkworth 28 C2
Brinmore 154 A6
Brinscall 85 E4
Brinsley 68 C2
Brinsop 40 D1
Brinsworth 80 B3
Brinton 72 D3
Brisco 101 J2
Brisley 72 C4
Brislington 27 F3
BRISTOL 27 E3
Bristol Airport 26 E4
Briston 72 D3
Britannia 85 G4
Britford 18 C3
Brithdir 63 H5
Briton Ferry 38 E6
Britwell Salome 44 A6
BRIXHAM 7 F5
Brixton, Devon 6 B5
BRIXTON, G Lon 32 D3
Brixton Deverill 17 G2
Brixworth 57 F4
Brize Norton 43 F5
Brize Norton Airfield 43 E5
Broad Blunsdon 28 D1
Broad Campden 42 D2
Broad Chalke 18 B3
Broad Green, Cambs 59 G6
Broad Green, Essex 48 B3
Broad Green, Worces 54 C6
Broad Haven 36 C4
Broad Heath 54 B5
Broad Hill 59 F4
Broad Hinton 28 D3
Broad Laying 29 G4
Broad Marston 55 G7
Broad Oak, Carm 38 C3
Broad Oak, Co of H 40 D3
Broad Oak, Cumbr 91 C2
Broad Oak, Dorset 17 F4
Broad Oak, E Susx TN21 22 C3
Broad Oak, E Susx TN31 22 E4
Broad Oak, Kent 34 E4
Broad Street 34 B5
Broad Street Green 48 B5
Broad Town 28 C3
Broad's Green 47 G4
Broadbottom 78 D2
Broadbridge 20 B5
Broadbridge Heath 21 E2
Broadclyst 15 F6
Broadfield 21 F2
Broadford 151 E6
Broadhaugh 110 D2
Broadheath 78 B3
Broadhembury 15 H5
Broadhempston 6 E4
Broadholme 81 F4
Broadlay 37 H5
Broadley, Lancs 85 G5
Broadley, Mor 156 A2
Broadley Common 46 E5
Broadmayne 9 F5
Broadmeadows 120 D4
Broadmere 29 J6
Broadmoor 37 E5
Broadoak 8 C4
BROADSTAIRS 35 G4
Broadstone, Poole 10 B4
Broadstone, Shrops 53 J3
Broadstreet Common 26 C2
Broadwas 54 C6
Broadwater 21 E5
Broadway, Carm SA17 37 H5
Broadway, Carm SA33 37 G5
Broadway, Somer 16 B4
Broadway, Suff 61 G4
Broadway, Worces 42 C2
Broadwell, Glos GL16 41 E4
Broadwell, Glos GL56 42 E3
Broadwell, Oxon 42 E5
Broadwell, Warw 56 C5
Broadwey 9 E5
Broadwindsor 8 C3
Broadwoodkelly 13 G5
Broadwoodwidger 13 E7
Broardford Bridge 20 D3
Broardland Row 22 E4
Brobury 40 C1
Brochel 151 E4
Brochloch 107 H3
Brochroy 134 E5
Brock Hill 47 H6
Brockan 172 C4
Brockbridge 19 H4
Brockdish 61 F4
Brockenhurst 10 D3
Brocketsbrae 119 F3
Brockford Street 60 E5
Brockhall 56 E5
Brockham 31 F6
Brockhampton, Co of H 41 E2
Brockhampton, Glos 42 C3
Brockholes 86 C5
Brockholes 89 F5
Brockley Green 60 B6
Brockton, Shrops SY5 65 G6
Brockton, Shrops SY? 53 G3
Brockton, Shrops TF11 66 C6
Brockton, Shrops TF13 54 A2
Brockweir 41 E5
Brockworth 41 H4
Brocton 67 E5
Brodick 116 E4
Brodsworth 87 G6
Brogaig 150 D2
Brogborough 44 D2
Broken Cross, Ches CW9 78 A4

Broken Cross, Ches SK11 78 C4
Brokenborough 28 B2
Bromborough 77 F3
Brome 60 E4
Brome Street 60 E4
Bromeswell 61 G6
Bromfield, Cumbr 101 F3
Bromfield, Shrops 53 H4
Bromham, Beds 57 J6
Bromham, Wilts 28 B4
BROMLEY 32 E4
Bromley Common 32 E4
Bromley Green 23 F2
Brompton, Med 33 H4
Brompton, N Yorks DL6 95 E2
Brompton, N Yorks YO13 97 E3
Brompton Ralph 15 G2
Brompton Regis 15 F2
Brompton-on-Swale 94 D2
Bromsash 41 F3
BROMSGROVE 55 E4
Bromyard 54 B6
Bromyard Downs 54 B6
Bronaber 63 H3
Brongest 50 D7
Bronington 65 H3
Bronllys 39 J2
Bronnant 51 E5
Bronwydd Arms 38 B3
Bronydd 53 F7
Bronygarth 65 F3
Brook, Carm 37 G5
Brook, Hants SO20 18 E3
Brook, Hants SO43 18 D4
Brook, I of W 11 E5
Brook, Kent 34 D6
Brook, Surrey 20 C2
Brook Street, Essex 47 F6
Brook Street, W Susx 21 G3
Brooke, Norf 73 F7
Brooke, Rut 69 G6
Brookfield 127 J6
Brookhouse, Ches 78 D4
Brookhouse, Lancs 92 D5
Brookhouse Green 78 C5
Brookland 23 F3
Brooklands 109 F5
Brookmans Park 46 C5
Brooks 64 E7
Brooks Green 21 E3
Brooksthorpe 41 H4
Brookville 59 H2
Brookwood 30 D5
Broom, Beds 45 F1
Broom, Warw 55 F6
Broom, Wick 10 B3
Broom of Dalreoch 137 H7
Broombrae 146 C2
Broome, Norf 61 G2
Broome, Shrops 53 H3
Broome, Worces 54 E4
Broome Park 123 G6
Broomedge 78 B3
Broomer's Corner 21 E3
Broomfield, Aberd 157 G5
Broomfield, Essex 47 H4
Broomfield, Kent CT6 35 E4
Broomfield, Kent ME17 34 B5
Broomfield, Somer 15 J2
Broomfleet 88 C4
Broomhill 113 G2
Brooms Green 41 G2
Broroa ... Broseley 66 B6
Brotherhill 36 E5
Brothertoft 70 C2
Brotherton 87 F4
BROTTON 105 F6
Broubster 168 E3
Broughdarg 137 G6
Brough, Cumbr 102 D6
Brough, Derby 79 F3
Brough, E Yorks 88 D4
Brough, Highl 169 G2
Brough, Notts 81 F6
Brough, Orkney 172 D5
Brough, Shetld ZE2 9AL 175 G4
Brough, Shetld ZE2 9AY 177 C6
Brough, Shetld ZE2 9ES 175 G4
Brough, Shetld ZE2 9PS 175 F4
Brough, Shetld ZE2 9QT 175 F3
Brough Sowerby 102 D6
Broughall 66 A2
Broughton, Cambs 58 C4
Broughton, Flint 77 F5
Broughton, G Man 78 C1
Broughton, Hants 18 E2
Broughton, Lancs 84 D3
Broughton, Mil Key 44 C2
Broughton, N Linc 88 D6
Broughton, N Yorks BD23 85 H1
Broughton, N Yorks YO17 96 C4
Broughton, Northnts 57 G4
Broughton, Orkney 172 E2
Broughton, Oxon 43 G2
Broughton, Scot Bord 119 J4
Broughton, V of Glam 25 G3
Broughton Astley 56 D2
Broughton Beck 92 A3
Broughton Gifford 27 H4
Broughton Hackett 54 E6
Broughton in Furness 91 D3
Broughton Mills 91 D2
Broughton Moor 100 E4
Broughton Poggs 42 E5
Broughtown 173 G2
Brow Top 92 D5
Browland 174 D5
Brown Candover 19 G2
Brown Edge, Lancs 84 B5
Brown Edge, Staffs 78 D6
Brownber 19 H4
Brownhill, Aberd AB41 157 F4
Brownhill, Aberd AB53 156 D4
Brownhill, Bburn & Da 85 E3
Brownhills, Fife 139 E7
BROWNHILLS, W Mids 67 F6
Brownieside 123 G5
Browninghill Green 29 H5
Brownlow Heath 78 C5
Brownmuir 146 E6
Brownston 6 C5
Brownsburn 128 C6
Broxa 97 E2
Broxbourne 46 D5
Broxburn, E Loth 131 F5
Broxburn, W Loth 129 H5
Broxholme 81 G4
Broxted 47 F3
Broxton 77 G6
Broxwood 53 G6
Broyle Side 21 H4
Brù 161 G3
Bruachmary 154 C4
Brùairnis 148 C4
Bruan 169 H6

Bruera 77 G5
Bruern Abbey 42 E3
Bruichladdich 124 B4
Bruisyard 61 G5
Brumby 88 C6
Brund 79 F5
Brundall 73 G6
Brundish 61 F5
Brundish Street 61 F4
Brunery 142 B6
Brunthwaite 86 C2
Brunton, Fife 138 C6
Brunton, Northum 123 H5
Brunton, Wilts 28 E5
Brushford, Devon 14 C5
Brushford, Somer 15 F3
Bruton 17 E2
Brydekirk 110 A5
Brymbo 77 E6
Brympton 17 G5
Bryn, Carm 38 C5
Bryn, Ches 77 J4
Bryn, G Man 77 H1
Bryn, Nth Pt Talb 25 F1
Bryn, Shrops 53 F3
Bryn Du 74 C4
Bryn Gates 77 H1
Bryn Glas 63 G3
Bryn Golau 25 H2
Bryn Rhyd-yr-Arian 76 B5
Bryn Saith Marchog 76 C6
Bryn-coch 38 E5
Bryn-henllan 36 E2
Bryn-y-maen 75 H4
Brynamman 38 E4
Brynberian 37 F2
Bryncae 25 G2
Bryncethin 25 G2
Bryncir 63 E2
Bryncroes 62 C3
Bryncrug 63 G6
Bryneglwys 64 E2
Brynford 76 D4
Bryngwran 74 C4
Bryngwyn, Cered 50 C7
Bryngwyn, Monm 40 C5
Bryngwyn, Pemb 36 C3
Bryngwyn, Powys 53 F7
Brynhoffnant 50 B6
Brynithel 40 B5
BRYNMAWR 40 A4
Brynmenyn 25 G2
Brynna 25 G2
Brynnau Gwynion 25 G2
Brynrefail 74 D3
Brynsadler 25 H2
Brynsiencyn 74 D4
Brynteg, I of Angl 74 D3
Brynteg, Wrex 77 F6
Buaile na h-Ochd 161 H4
Buaile nam Bodach 148 C4
Bualintur 140 D1
Bualnaluib 162 C5
Bubbenhall 56 B4
Bubwith 87 J3
Buccleuch 120 C6
Buchanan Smithy 128 B4
Buchanty 137 G6
Buchley 128 C3
Buck's Cross 12 D3
Buck's Mills 12 D3
Buckabank 101 H3
Buckden, Cambs 58 B5
Buckden, N Yorks 93 H4
Buckenham 73 G6
Buckerell 15 H5
Buckfast 6 D4
BUCKFASTLEIGH 6 D4
BUCKHAVEN 130 C3
Buckholm 120 D4
Buckhorn Weston 17 F3
Buckhurst Hill 46 E6
BUCKIE 156 B2
Buckies 169 F3
BUCKINGHAM 44 A2
Buckland, Bucks 44 C4
Buckland, Devon 6 C6
Buckland, Glos 42 C2
Buckland, Herts 46 D3
Buckland, Kent 35 G6
Buckland, Oxon 43 F6
Buckland, Surrey 31 G5
Buckland Brewer 13 D3
Buckland Common 44 D5
Buckland Dinham 27 G5
Buckland Filleigh 13 E5
Buckland in the Moor 6 D3
Buckland Monochorum 5 H4
Buckland Newton 17 E5
Buckland St Mary 16 A4
Bucklebury 29 H3
Bucklerheads 138 D5
Bucklers Hard 11 F4
Bucklesham 49 F1
BUCKLEY 76 E5
Bucklow Hill 78 B3
Buckminster 69 G4
Bucknall, C of Stoke 66 E2
Bucknall, Lincs 82 D5
Bucknell, Oxon 43 H3
Bucknell, Shrops 53 G4
Bucks Green 20 D2
Bucks Hill 45 E5
Bucks Horn Oak 30 C6
Buckspool 36 D6
Buckton, Co of H 53 G4
Buckton, Northum 123 H4
Budbrooke 55 H5
Budby 80 D4
BUDE 12 C5
Budlake 15 F6
Budle 123 G4
BUDLEIGH SALTERTON 7 G2
Budock Water 3 F4
Buerton 65 B2
Bugbrooke 56 E6
Buglawton 78 C5
Bugle 4 D5
Bugthorpe 96 C2
Buildwas 66 B6
Builth Road 52 D6
BUILTH WELLS 52 D6
Buldoo 168 D3
Bulford 28 D6
Bulford Camp 28 D6
Bulkeley 77 H6
Bulkington, Warw 56 B3
Bulkington, Wilts 28 B5
Bulkworthy 12 D4
Bull's Green 46 C4
Bullbridge 79 H6
Bulley 41 G4
Bullwood 127 F5
Bulmer, Essex 48 B1

Bulmer, N Yorks 96 C5
Bulmer Tye 48 B2
Bulphan 33 G2
Bulverhythe 22 C5
Bulwark 88 C6
Bulwell 68 D2
Bulwick 57 H2
Bumble's Green 46 E5
Bun a Mhuillinn 148 C3
Bun Abhainn Eadarra 159 F2
Bun Loyne 142 E3
Bunacaimb 141 F5
Bunarkaig 142 D5
Bunbury 77 H6
Bundalloch 152 A6
Bunessan 133 F6
BUNGAY 61 G3
Bunker's Hill 83 E6
Bunlarie 116 B4
Bunloit 153 H6
Bunnahabhain 125 B5
Bunny 68 D4
Buntait 153 G5
Buntingford 46 D3
Bunwell 60 E2
Buolfruich 169 F6
Burbage, Derby 79 E4
Burbage, Leic 56 C2
Burbage, Wilts 28 E4
Burchett's Green 30 C2
Burcombe 18 B2
Burcot 43 H6
Burcott 44 C3
Burdale 96 D5
Burdrop 43 F2
Bures 48 C2
Bures Green 48 C2
BURFORD, Oxon 42 E4
Burford, Shrops 54 A5
Burg 133 C4
Burgar 172 D4
Burgate 60 D4
BURGESS HILL 21 G4
Burgh, Arg & Bt 133 G6
Burgh, Suff 61 F6
Burgh by Sands 110 C7
Burgh Castle 73 H6
Burgh Heath 32 C5
Burgh le Marsh 83 G5
Burgh next Aylsham 73 F4
Burgh on Bain 82 E3
Burgh St Margaret (Fleggburgh) 73 H5
Burgh St Peter 61 H2
Burghclere 29 G4
BURGHEAD 155 F2
Burghfield 30 A4
Burghfield Common 30 A4
Burghfield Hill 30 A4
Burghill 40 D1
Burghwallis 87 G5
Burham 33 H4
Buriton 19 J3
Burland 77 J6
Burlawn 4 C3
Burlescombe 15 G4
Burleston 9 F4
Burley, Hants 10 D3
Burley, Rut 69 G5
Burley Gate 54 A7
Burley in Wharfedale 86 C2
Burley Street 18 D3
Burleydam 66 B2
Burlingjobb 53 F6
Burlow 22 B4
Burlton 65 H4
Burmarsh 23 H2
Burmington 42 E2
Burn 87 G4
Burn of Aultmore 156 H2
Burn of Cambus 128 E2
Burn's Green 46 D3
Burnage 78 C2
Burnaston 67 H3
Burnend 157 F4
Burneside 92 D2
Burness 173 G2
Burneston 94 E3
Burnett 27 F4
Burnfoot, Pth & Kin 129 G2
Burnfoot, Scot Bord TD9 7LZ 120 C6
Burnfoot, Scot Bord TD9 8PL 120 B6
Burnham, Bucks 30 D2
Burnham, N Linc 88 E5
Burnham Beeches 30 D2
Burnham Deepdale 71 J2
Burnham Green 46 C4
Burnham Market 72 B2
Burnham Norton 72 B2
Burnham Overy Staithe 72 B2
Burnham Overy Town 72 B2
Burnham Thorpe 72 B2
BURNHAM-ON-CROUCH 48 C6
BURNHAM-ON-SEA 26 C6
Burnhead 109 F3
Burnhervie 146 E2
Burnhill Green 66 C6
Burnhope 110 D3
Burnhouse 117 H2
Burniston 97 F2
BURNLEY 85 G3
Burnmouth 123 E1
Burnopfield 110 D2
Burnsall 94 B5
Burnside, Aberd 157 F4
Burnside, Ang DD8 2RX 138 E3
Burnside, Ang DD8 3UA 138 D3
Burnside, E Ayr 118 C6
Burnside, Pth & Kin 129 J2
Burnside, Shetld 174 D3
Burnside, W Loth 129 H5
Burnside of Duntrune 138 D5
Burnswark 110 A5
Burnt Yates 94 D5
Burntcliff Top 78 D5
Burntcommon 30 E5
BURNTISLAND 130 B4
Burnton 118 B6
Burntwood 67 F6
Burpham, Surrey 30 E5
Burpham, W Susx 20 D5
Burradon, Northum 112 D2
Burradon, T & W 113 G5
Burrafirth 177 D2
Burraland, Shetld ZE2 9PD 174 D3
Burraland, Shetld ZE2 9RF 175 E3
Burras 3 E4
Burravoe, Shetld ZE2 9AY 177 C5
Burravoe, Shetld ZE2 9QY 175 E4
Burray Village 171 E5
Burrelton 138 A5
Burridge 19 G4
Burrigill 169 G6
Burrill 94 D3
Burringham 88 C6
Burrington, Co of H 53 H4

205
Burrington, Devon
Charlton, W Susx

Burrington, Devon 13 G4
Burrington, N Som 26 D5
Burrough Green 59 G6
Burrough on the Hill 69 F5
Burrowbridge 16 B3
Burrowhill 30 D4
Burry Green 24 B1
BURRY PORT 38 B5
Burscough 84 C5
Burscough Bridge 84 C5
Bursea 88 C3
Burshill 89 E2
Bursledon 19 F5
Burslem 66 D2
Burstall 48 D1
Burstallhill 60 D7
Burstock 8 C3
Burston, Norf 60 E3
Burston, Staffs 67 E3
Burstow 32 D6
Burstwick 89 G4
Burtersett 93 G3
Burthorpe 59 H5
Burtle 26 C6
Burton, Ches CW6 77 H5
Burton, Ches L64 77 F4
Burton, Dorset BH23 10 C4
Burton, Dorset DT2 9 E4
Burton, Lincs 81 G4
Burton, Northum 123 G4
Burton, Pemb 36 D5
Burton, Somer 26 A6
Burton, Wilts 27 H3
Burton, Wrex 77 F6
Burton Agnes 97 G5
Burton Bradstock 8 C5
Burton Constable 89 F3
Burton Fleming 97 F4
Burton Green, Warw 55 H4
Burton Green, Wrex 77 F6
Burton Hastings 56 C2
Burton in Lonsdale 93 E4
Burton Joyce 68 E2
BURTON LATIMER 57 H4
Burton Lazars 69 F5
Burton Leonard 94 E5
Burton on the Wolds 68 D4
Burton Overy 68 E7
Burton Pedwardine 70 B2
Burton Pidsea 89 G3
Burton Salmon 87 F4
Burton upon Stather 88 C5
BURTON UPON TRENT 67 H4
Burton-in-Kendal 92 D4
Burton-le-Coggles 69 H4
Burtonwood 77 H2
Burwardsley 77 H6
Burwarton 54 B3
Burwash 22 C3
Burwash Common 22 C3
Burwash Weald 22 C3
Burwell, Cambs 59 F5
Burwell, Lincs 83 F4
Burwen 74 D2
Burwick, Orkney 171 E6
Burwick, Shetld 176 C3
Bury, Cambs 58 C3
BURY, G Man 85 G5
Bury, Somer 15 F3
Bury, W Susx 20 D4
Bury Green 47 E3
BURY ST EDMUNDS 60 B5
Burythorpe 96 C5
Busbridge 30 D6
Busby, E Renf 118 C2
Busby, Pth & Kin 137 H6
Buscot 42 E6
Bush Bank 53 H6
Bush Crathie 145 G4
Bush Green 61 F3
Bushbury 66 E6
BUSHEY 45 F6
Bushey Heath 45 F6
Bushley 41 H2
Bushton 28 C3
Busta 175 E4
Butchers Cross 22 B3
Butcombe 26 E4
Butleigh 16 D2
Butleigh Wootton 16 D2
Butlers Cross 44 C5
Butlers Marston 56 B7
Butley 61 G6
Butsfield 103 H3
Butt Green 78 A6
Butt's Green 18 E3
Butterburn 111 F5
Buttercrambe 96 C6
Butterknowle 103 H5
Butterleigh 15 F5
Buttermere, Cumbr 101 F6
Buttermere, Wilts 29 F4
Buttershaw 86 C4
Butterstone 137 H4
Butterton 79 E6
Butterwick, Lincs 70 D2
Butterwick, N Linc 88 C6
Butterwick, N Yorks YO176PS 96 C4
Butterwick, N Yorks YO178HF 97 E4
Buttington 65 F6
Buttonoak 54 C4
Buxhall 60 D6
Buxted 21 H3
BUXTON, Derby 79 E4
Buxton, Norf 73 F4
Bwlch 39 J3
Bwlch-derwin 63 E2
Bwlch-Llan 51 F6
Bwlch-y- sarnau 52 D4
Bwlch-y-cibau 64 E5
Bwlch-y-fadfa 50 E7
Bwlch-y-ffridd 52 D2
Bwlchgwyn 76 E6
Bwlchnewydd 37 H3
Bwlchtocyn 62 D4
Bwlchyddar 64 E4
Bwlchygroes 37 G2
Byers Green 104 B4
Byfield 56 D6
Byfleet 31 E4
Byford 40 C1
Bygrave 46 C2
Byker 113 G6
Bylane End 5 F5
Bylchau 76 B5
Byley 78 B5
Byrness 111 G2
Bythorn 58 A4
Byton 53 G5
Byworth 20 C3

C

Cabharstadh 161 G6
Cabourne 89 F6
Cabrach, Arg & Bt 125 B6
Cabrach, Mor 156 A6
Cacrabank 120 C6
Cadboll 165 E6
Cadbury 15 F5
Cadbury Barton 14 C4
Cadder 128 D5
Caddington 45 E4
Caddonfoot 120 D4
Cade Street 22 C3
Cadeby, Leic 68 C6
Cadeby, S Yorks 80 C1
Cadeleigh 15 F5
Cadgwith 3 F6
Cadham 130 B2
Cadishead 78 B2
Cadle 38 D6
Cadley 28 E4
Cadmore End 30 B1
Cadnam 18 D4
Cadney 88 E6
Cadole 76 E5
Caeathro 74 D5
Caehopkin 39 F4
Caenby Corner 81 G3
Caer Llan 40 D5
Caer-Lan 39 F4
Caerau, Brig 39 F6
Caerau, Card 25 J3
Caerdeon 63 G5
Caerfarchell 36 B3
Caergeiliog 74 C4
Caergwrle 77 F6
Caerhun 75 G4
CAERLEON 26 C1
CAERNARFON 74 D5
CAERPHILLY 26 A2
Caersws 52 D2
Caerwent 26 D1
Caerwys 76 D4
Caethle 63 G7
Caim 133 H2
Caio 38 D2
Cairinis 149 D3
Cairisiadar 160 D4
Cairminis 158 E4
Cairnargat 156 B5
Cairnbaan 126 C3
Cairnborrow 156 B4
Cairnbrogie 157 F6
Cairncross, Ang 146 B6
Cairncross, Scot Bord 131 H6
Cairndow 127 F1
Cairness 157 H2
Cairneyhill 129 H4
Cairngaan 98 C6
Cairngarroch 98 B5
Cairnhill, Aberd AB41 157 G6
Cairnhill, Aberd AB52 156 D5
Cairnie 156 B4
Cairnorrie 157 F4
Cairnpark 147 F2
Cairnryan 98 B3
Caister-on-Sea 73 J5
Caistor 82 D1
Caistor St Edmund 73 F6
Caistron 112 D2
Calanais 161 F4
Calbost 161 H6
Calbourne 11 F5
Calcot, Glos 42 C4
Calcot, W Berks 30 A3
Caldarvan 128 B4
Caldback 177 D3
Caldbeck 101 H4
Caldbergh 94 B3
Caldecote, Cambs CB3 58 D6
Caldecote, Cambs PE7 58 B3
Caldecote, Herts 46 C2
Caldecote, Warw 56 B2
Caldecott, Northnts 57 H5
Caldecott, Rut 57 G2
Calder Bridge 91 B1
Calder Mains 169 E4
Calder Vale 84 D2
Calderbank 118 E1
Calderbrook 85 H5
Caldercruix 129 F6
Caldermill 118 D3
Caldhame 138 D4
Caldicot 26 D2
Caldwell, Derby 67 H5
Caldwell, N Yorks 103 H6
Caldy 76 E3
Calerdhydiau 51 E6
Calf Heath 66 E6
Calfsound 173 F3
Calgary 133 F3
Calgow 99 F3
Califer 155 E3
California, Falk 129 G5
California, Norf 73 J5
Calke 68 B4
Callakille 151 F3
Callaly 112 E2
CALLANDER 128 D2
Callestick 3 F2
Calligarry 141 F3
Callington 5 G4
Callow 40 D2
Callow End 54 D7
Callow Hill, Wilts 28 C2
Callow Hill, Worces 54 C4
Callow Marsh 54 B7
Calmore 18 E4
Calmsden 42 C5
CALNE 28 B3
Calow 79 J4
Calshot 11 F3
Calstock 5 H4
Calstone Wellington 28 C4
Calthorpe 73 E3
Calthwaite 102 A3
Calton, N Yorks 93 H6
Calton, Staffs 79 F6
Calveley 77 H6
Calver 79 G4
Calver Hill 53 G7
Calverhall 66 B3
Calverleigh 15 F4
Calverley 86 D3
Calvert 44 A3
Calverton, Mil Key 44 B2
Calverton, Notts 68 E2
Calvine 137 F2
Calvo 101 F2
Cam 41 G6
Camas-luinie 152 B6
Camasnacroise 134 C3
Camastianavaig 151 E5
Camault Muir 153 H4
Camb 177 C4
Camber 23 F4
CAMBERLEY 30 C4
CAMBERWELL 32 D3
Camblesforth 87 H4
Cambo 112 E4
Cambois 113 H4
CAMBORNE 2 E3
CAMBRIDGE, Cambs 59 E6
Cambridge, Glos 41 G5
Cambridge Airport 59 E6
Cambus 129 F3
Cambusbarron 128 E3
Cambuskenneth 129 F3
Cambuslang 118 D2
CAMDEN TOWN 32 C2
Camelford 4 E2
Camelon 129 F4
Camelsdale 20 B2
Camer 33 G4
Camerory 155 E5
Camers Green 41 G2
Camerton, Bth 27 F5
Camerton, Cumbr 100 E4
Camghouran 136 C3
Cammachmore 147 G4
Cammeringham 81 G3
Camore 164 D4
Campbelton 117 F2
CAMPBELTOWN 116 B5
Campmuir 138 B5
Camps End 47 G1
Camps Heath 61 J2
Campsall 87 G5
Campsey Ash 61 G6
Campton 45 F2
Camptown 121 F6
Camrose 36 D3
Camserney 137 F4
Camus Croise 141 F2
Camusnagaul, Highl IV23 162 E5
Camusnagaul, Highl PH33 142 C6
Camusteel 151 G4
Camusterrach 151 G4
Camusvrachan 136 D4
Canada 18 D4
Canal Foot 92 B4
Candacraig 145 H4
Candlesby 83 G5
Candy Mill 119 H3
Cane End 30 A3
Canewdon 48 C6
Canford Magna 10 B4
Canisbay 169 H2
Cann 17 G3
Cann Common 17 G3
Cannards Grave 27 F6
Cannich 153 F5
Cannington 16 A2
CANNOCK 67 E5
Cannock Wood 67 F5
Canon Bridge 40 D1
Canon Frome 41 F1
Canon Pyon 53 H7
Canonbie 110 C5
Canons Ashby 56 D6
Canonstown 2 D4
CANTERBURY 34 E5
Cantley, Norf 73 G6
Cantley, S Yorks 87 H6
Cantlop 65 J6
Canton 26 A3
Cantraybruich 154 B4
Cantraydoune 154 B4
Cantraywood 154 B4
Cantsfield 93 E4
CANVEY ISLAND 33 H2
Canwick 81 G5
Canworthy Water 12 C6
Caol 142 D6
Caol Ila 125 B5
Caolas, Arg & Bt 132 C4
Caolas, Na Eilean 148 B5
Caolas Scalpaigh 159 G3
Caolas Stocinis 159 F3
Caolasnacon 135 F2
Capel, Kent 33 G6
Capel, Surrey 31 F6
Capel Bangor 51 G3
Capel Betws Lleucu 51 G6
Capel Carmel 62 B4
Capel Coch 74 D3
Capel Curig 75 G6
Capel Cynon 50 D7
Capel Dewi, Carm 38 B3
Capel Dewi, Cered SA44 38 B1
Capel Dewi, Cered SY23 51 G3
Capel Garmon 75 H6
Capel Gwyn, Carm 38 B3
Capel Gwyn, I of Angl 74 C4
Capel Gwynfe 38 E3
Capel Hendre 38 C4
Capel Isaac 38 C3
Capel Iwan 37 G2
Capel Llanilltterne 25 H2
Capel Parc 74 D3
Capel Seion 51 G4
Capel St Andrew 61 G7
Capel St Mary 48 D2
Capel Tygwydd 37 G1
Capel Uchaf 74 D7
Capel-le- Ferne 23 J2
Capel-y-ffin 40 B2
Capelulo 75 G4
Capenhurst 77 F4
Capernwray 92 D4
Capheaton 112 E4
Cappercleuch 120 B5
Capstone 33 H4
Capton 6 E5
Caputh 137 H5
Car Colston 69 F2
Carbellow 118 D5
Carbis Bay 2 D4
Carbost, Highl IV47 150 C5
Carbost, Highl IV51 150 D4
Carbrooke 72 C6
Carburton 80 D4
Carcary 139 F3
Carclew 3 F4
Carco 118 E6
Carcroft 87 G6
Cardenden 130 B3
Cardeston 65 G5
CARDIFF 26 B3
Cardiff International Airport 25 H4
CARDIGAN 50 B7
Cardington, Beds 58 A7
Cardington, Shrops 53 J2
Cardinham 4 E4
Cardow 155 F4
Cardrona 120 C4
Cardrona Ho 120 C4
Cardross, Arg & Bt 127 H5
Cardross, Stir 128 D3
Cardurnock 110 A7
Careby 69 J5
Careston 139 E2
Careston Castle 139 E3
Carew 37 E5
Carew Cheriton 37 E5
Carew Newton 37 E5
Carey 41 E2
Carfrae 131 E6
Cargate Green 73 G5
Cargenbridge 109 G5
Cargill 138 A5
Cargo 110 C7
Cargreen 5 H4
Carham 122 D4
Carhampton 25 H6
Carharrack 3 F3
Carie, Pth & Kin PH15 136 D5
Carie, Pth & Kin PH17 136 D3
Carines 3 F2
Carisbrooke 11 F5
Cark 92 B4
Carkeel 5 H4
Càrlabhagh 161 F3
Carland Cross 3 G2
Carlby 69 J5
Carlecotes 86 C6
Carleton, Cumbr 101 J2
Carleton, Lancs 84 B2
Carleton Forehoe 72 D6
Carleton in Craven 85 H2
Carleton Rode 60 E2
Carlin How 105 G6
Carlingcott 27 F5
CARLISLE 101 J2
Carloggas 3 G1
Carlops 119 J2
Carlton, Beds 57 H6
Carlton, Cambs 59 G6
Carlton, Leic 68 C6
Carlton, N Yorks DL8 94 B3
Carlton, N Yorks DN14 87 H4
Carlton, N Yorks YO62 95 H3
CARLTON, Notts 68 E2
Carlton, S Yorks 87 E5
Carlton, Stock on T 104 C5
Carlton, Suff 61 G5
Carlton, W Yorks 86 E4
Carlton Colville 61 J3
Carlton Curlieu 69 E7
Carlton Husthwaite 95 F4
Carlton in Cleveland 95 G1
Carlton in Lindrick 80 C3
Carlton Miniott 95 E3
Carlton Scroop 69 H2
Carlton-le-Moorland 81 G6
Carlton-on-Trent 81 E5
Carluke 119 F2
Carmacoup 119 E5
CARMARTHEN 37 J3
Carmel, Carm 38 C4
Carmel, Flint 76 D4
Carmel, Gwyn 74 D6
Carmel, I of Angl 74 C3
Carmichael 119 G4
Carmont 147 F5
Carmunnock 118 D2
Carmyle 118 D1
Carmyllie 139 E4
Carn Brea Village 3 E3
Carn Towan 2 B5
Carn-gorm 152 B6
Carnaby 97 G5
Carnach, Highl IV23 162 E4
Carnach, Highl IV40 152 C6
Carnach, Na Eilean 159 G3
Carnbee 130 E2
Carnbo 129 H2
Carnbroe 118 E1
Carnduncan 124 B4
Carne 4 C7
Carnell 118 B4
CARNFORTH 92 C4
Carnhedryn 36 C3
Carnhell Green 2 E4
Carnie 147 F3
Carno 52 C2
Carnoch, Highl IV4 153 F5
Carnoch, Highl IV6 152 E3
Carnock 129 H4
Carnon Downs 3 F3
Carnousie 156 D3
CARNOUSTIE 139 E5
Carnwath 119 G3
Carnyorth 2 B4
Carperby 94 B3
Carpley Green 93 H3
Carr Shield 102 E3
Carr Vale 80 B4
Carradale 116 C4
Carragraich 159 F3
Carrbridge 154 D6
Carreglefn 74 C3
Carrick 138 D6
Carrick Castle 127 F3
Carriden 129 H4
Carrine 114 B6
Carrington, G Man 78 B2
Carrington, Lincs 83 F6
Carrington, Midlo 120 C1
Carroch 108 D3
Carrog 64 E2
Carron, Falk 129 F4
Carron, Mor 155 G4
Carron Bridge 128 E4
Carronbridge 109 F3
Carrot 138 D4
Carrutherstown 109 J5
Carruthmuir 127 H6
Carrville 104 C3
Carsaig 133 H6
Carscreugh 98 D4
Carse Gray 138 D3
Carsegowan 99 F4
Carseriggan 98 E3
Carsethorn 109 G7
CARSHALTON 32 C4
Carsington 79 G6
Carskiey 114 B6
Carsluith 99 F4
Carsphairn 108 C3
Carstairs 119 G3
Carstairs Junction 119 G3
Carswell Marsh 43 F6
Carter's Clay 18 E3
CARTERTON 43 E5
Carterway Heads 103 G2
Carthew 4 D5
Carthorpe 94 E3
Cartington 112 E2
Cartland 119 F3
Cartmel 92 B4
Cartmel Fell 92 C3
Carway 38 B5
Cascob 53 F5
Cashlie 136 B4
Cashmoor 17 H4
Cassington 43 G4
Cassop 104 C4
Castallack 2 C5
Castell Howell 51 E7
Castell-y-bwch 26 B1
Castellau 25 H2
Casterton 93 E4
Castle Acre 72 B5
Castle Ashby 57 G6
Castle Bolton 94 B2
Castle Bromwich 55 G3
Castle Bytham 69 H5
Castle Caereinion 64 E6
Castle Camps 47 G1
Castle Carrock 102 B2
Castle Cary 17 E2
Castle Combe 27 H3
Castle Donington 68 C4
CASTLE DOUGLAS 108 E6
Castle Eaton 42 D6
Castle Eden 104 D4
Castle Frome 54 B7
Castle Gresley 67 H5
Castle Hedingham 47 H2
Castle Hill 60 E7
Castle Kennedy 98 C4
Castle O'er 110 B3
Castle Rising 71 G4
Castlebay (Bàgh a'Chaisteil) 148 B5
Castlebythe 36 E3
Castlecary 128 E5
Castlecraig, Highl 154 C2
Castlecraig, Scot Bord 119 J3
Castlefairn 108 E4
CASTLEFORD 87 F4
Castlehill 169 F3
Castlemaddy 108 C4
Castlemartin 36 D6
Castlemilk 109 J5
Castlemorris 36 D2
Castlemorton 41 G2
Castleside 103 G3
Castlethorpe 44 B1
Castleton, Ang 138 C4
Castleton, Arg & Bt 126 C4
Castleton, Derby 79 F3
Castleton, N Yorks 105 F7
Castleton, Newp 26 B2
Castletown, Highl IV2 154 B4
Castletown, Highl KW14 169 F3
CASTLETOWN, I of M 90 B6
Castletown, T & W 104 C2
Castleweary 110 D2
Castlewigg 99 F5
Caston 72 C7
Castor 70 B7
Cat's Ash 26 C1
Catacol 116 D3
Catbrain 27 E2
Catcleugh 111 G2
Catcliffe 80 B3
Catcott 16 B2
CATERHAM 32 D5
Catesby 56 D6
Catfield 73 G4
Catfirth 175 F5
CATFORD 32 D3
Catforth 84 C3
Cathcart 118 C1
Cathedine 39 J3
Catherington 19 H4
Catherton 54 B4
Catlodge 143 J4
Catlowdy 110 D5
Catmore 29 G2
Caton, Devon 6 D3
Caton, Lancs 92 D5
Cator Court 6 C3
Catrine 118 C5
Catsfield 22 D4
Catshill 55 E4
Cattal 95 F6
Cattawade 48 E2
Catterall 84 D2
Catterick 94 D2
Catterick Bridge 94 D2
Catterick Garrison 94 C2
Catterlen 102 A4
Catterline 147 F6
Catterton 87 G2
Catthorpe 56 D4
Cattistock 8 D4
Catton, N Yorks 95 E4
Catton, Norf 73 F5
Catton, Northum 102 E2
Catwick 89 F2
Catworth 58 A4
Caudworthy Bridge 12 C6
Caulcott 43 H3
Cauldcots 139 F4
Cauldhame 128 D3
Cauldon 67 F2
Caulkerbush 100 D2
Caulside 110 D4
Caunsall 54 D3
Caunton 80 E5
Causeway End 99 F3
Causeway Foot 86 B3
Causewayhead, Cumbr 101 F2
Causewayhead, Stir 129 F3
Causewayhead Garden 128 C3
Causey Park Bridge 113 F3
Causeyend 147 G2
Causeyton 146 D2
Cautley 93 E2
Cavendish 60 B7
Cavenham 59 H5
Cavers 121 E6
Caversfield 43 H3
Caversham 30 B3
Caverswall 67 E2
Cawdor 154 C3
Cawkwell 83 E4
Cawood 87 G3
Cawsand 5 H5
Cawston 72 E4
Cawthorne 86 D6
Cawthorpe 70 A4
Cawton 96 B4
Caxton 58 D6
Caxton Gibbet 58 C5
Caynham 53 J4
Caythorpe, Lincs 69 H2
Caythorpe, Notts 69 E2
Cayton 97 F3
Ceann a Bhàigh, Na Eilean HS4 159 G3
Ceann a Bhàigh, Na Eilean HS6 149 C3
Ceann a Deas Loch Baghasdail 148 C3
Ceann a Tuath Loch Baghasdail 148 C2
Ceann Shiphoirt 161 F6
Ceann Tarabhaigh 161 F6
Ceann-na-Cleithe 159 F3
Cearsiadair 161 G5
Ceathramh Meadhanach 158 C5
Cedig 64 C4
Cefn Berain 76 B5
Cefn Coch 64 E4
Cefn Cribwr 25 F2
Cefn Cross 25 F2
Cefn Einion 53 F3
Cefn Hengoed 39 J6
Cefn-brith 76 B6
Cefn-coed-y-cymmer 39 H5
Cefn-ddwysarn 64 C3
Cefn-gorwydd 52 C7
Cefn-mawr 65 F2
Cefn-y-bedd 77 F6
Cefn-y-pant 37 F3
Cefneithin 38 C4
Cefnpennar 39 H5
Ceidio 74 D3
Ceint 74 D4
Cel-bach 50 E6
Cellan 51 G7
Cellarhead 67 E2
Cemaes 74 C2
Cemmaes 64 B6
Cemmaes Road 64 B6
Cenarth 37 G1
Cenin 63 E2
Ceol na Mara 134 B2
Ceòs 161 G5
Ceres 130 D1
Cerne Abbas 9 E3
Cerney Wick 42 C6
Cerrigceinwen 74 D4
Cerrigydrudion 64 C2
Cessford 121 G5
Ceunant 75 E5
Chaceley 41 H2
Chacewater 3 F3
Chackmore 44 A2
Chacombe 43 G1
Chad Valley 55 F3
CHADDERTON 85 G6
Chaddesden 68 B3
Chaddesley Corbett 54 D4
Chaddleworth 29 G3
Chadlington 43 F3
Chadshunt 56 B6
Chadwell 69 F4
Chadwell St Mary 33 G3
Chadwick End 55 H4
Chadwick Green 77 H2
Chaffcombe 16 B4
Chagford 6 D2
Chailey 21 G4
Chainhurst 33 H6
Chalbury Common 18 B5
Chaldon 32 D5
Chaldon Herring or East Chaldon 9 F5
Chale 11 F6
Chale Green 11 F6
Chalfont Common 30 E1
Chalfont St Giles 44 D6
Chalfont St Peter 30 E1
Chalford 41 H5
Chalgrove 43 J6
Chalk 33 G3
Chalk End 47 G4
Challacombe 24 D6
Challoch 99 E3
Challock 34 D5
Chalmington 8 D3
Chalton, Beds 45 E3
Chalton, Hants 19 J4
Chalvington 22 B5
Champany 129 H5
Chandler's Cross 45 E6
Chandler's Ford 19 F3
Chanlockfoot 109 E2
Channel Tunnel Terminal 23 H2
Channerwick 176 D5
Chantry, Somer 27 G6
Chantry, Suff 48 E1
Chapel 130 B3
Chapel Allerton, Somer 26 D5
Chapel Allerton, W Yorks 86 E3
Chapel Amble 4 C3
Chapel Brampton 57 F5
Chapel Chorlton 66 D3
Chapel Cross 22 C3
Chapel Green 55 H3
Chapel Haddlesey 87 G4
Chapel Hill, Aberd 157 H5
Chapel Hill, Lincs 82 E6
Chapel Hill, Monm 40 E5
Chapel Lawn 53 G4
Chapel of Garioch 156 E6
Chapel of Stoneywood 147 F2
Chapel Row 29 H4
Chapel St Leonards 83 H4
Chapel Stile 92 B1
Chapel Town 3 G2
Chapel-en-le-Frith 79 E3
Chapel-le-Dale 93 F4
Chapeldonan 106 D2
Chapelgate 70 E4
Chapelhall 128 E6
Chapelhill, Highl 165 E6
Chapelhill, Pth & Kin PH1 137 H5
Chapelhill, Pth & Kin PH2 138 B6
Chapelknowe 110 C5
Chapelton, Ang 139 F4
Chapelton, Devon 13 F3
Chapelton, S Lanak 118 D3
Chapeltown, Bburn & Da 85 F5
Chapeltown, Mor 155 G6
Chapeltown, S Yorks 79 H2
Chapmans Well 12 D6
Chapmanslade 27 H6
Chappel 48 B3
CHARD 16 B5
Chardstock 16 B5
Charfield 27 G1
Charing 34 C6
Charing Heath 34 C6
Charingworth 42 E2
CHARLBURY 43 F4
Charlcombe 27 G4
Charlecote 55 H6
Charles 14 C2
Charles Tye 60 D6
Charlesfield 121 E5
Charleston 138 C4
Charlestown, C of Aber 147 G3
Charlestown, Corn 4 D5
Charlestown, Dorset 9 E6
Charlestown, Fife 129 H4
Charlestown, Highl IV1 154 A4
Charlestown, Highl IV21 162 C6
CHARLESTOWN OF ABERLOUR 155 G4
Charlesworth 78 E2
Charlton, G Lon 32 E3
Charlton, Hants 29 F6
Charlton, Herts 45 F3
Charlton, Northnts 43 H2
Charlton, Somer 27 F5
Charlton, W Susx 20 B4

206 Charlton, Wilts SN16 Colworth

Charlton, Wilts SN16 28 B2
Charlton, Wilts SN9 28 D5
Charlton, Wilts SP7 17 H3
Charlton, Worces 55 F7
Charlton Abbots 42 C3
Charlton Adam 16 D3
Charlton Horethorne 17 E3
Charlton Kings 42 B3
Charlton Mackrell 16 D3
Charlton Marshall 17 G5
Charlton Musgrove 17 F2
Charlton- All-Saints 18 C3
Charlton-on-Otmoor 43 H4
Charlwood 32 C6
Charlynch 15 J2
Charminster 9 E4
Charmouth 8 B4
Charndon 44 A3
Charney Bassett 43 F6
Charnock Richard 84 D5
Charsfield 61 F6
Chart Sutton 33 H5
Charter Alley 29 H5
Charterhouse 26 D5
Chartershall 129 E3
Charterville Allotments 43 F5
Chartham 34 E5
Chartham Hatch 34 E5
Chartridge 44 D5
Charvil 30 B3
Charwelton 56 D6
Chase End Street 41 G2
Chase Terrace 67 F6
Chasetown 67 F6
Chastleton 42 E3
Chasty 12 D5
Chatburn 85 F2
Chatcull 66 C3
CHATHAM 33 H4
Chathill 123 G5
Chattenden 33 H3
CHATTERIS 58 D3
Chattisham 48 D1
Chatto 122 C6
Chatton 123 F5
Chawleigh 14 D4
Chawston 58 B6
Chawton 19 J2
CHEADLE, G Man 78 C3
Cheadle, Staffs 67 F2
CHEADLE HULME 78 C3
Cheam 32 C4
Chearsley 44 B4
Chebsey 66 D4
Checkendon 30 A2
Checkley, Ches 66 C2
Checkley, Staffs 67 F3
Chedburgh 59 H6
Cheddar 26 D5
Cheddington 44 D4
Cheddleton 78 D6
Cheddon Fitzpaine 15 J3
Chedglow 42 B6
Chedgrave 73 G7
Chedington 16 C5
Chediston 61 G4
Chedworth 42 C4
Chedzoy 16 B2
Cheesden 85 G5
Cheeseman's Green 23 G2
Cheetham Hill 85 G6
Cheldon 14 D4
Chelford 78 C4
Chellaston 68 B3
Chellington 57 H6
Chelmarsh 54 C3
Chelmondiston 49 F2
Chelmorton 79 F5
CHELMSFORD 47 H5
CHELSEA 32 C3
Chelsfield 33 E4
Chelsworth 60 C7
CHELTENHAM 42 B3
Chelveston 57 H5
Chelvey 26 D4
Chelwood 27 F4
Chelwood Gate 21 H3
Chelworth 42 B6
Cheney Longville 53 H3
Chenies 44 E6
CHEPSTOW 40 E6
Cherhill 28 C3
Cherington, Glos 41 J6
Cherington, Warw 43 E2
Cheriton, Devon EX14 15 H5
Cheriton, Devon EX35 24 E6
Cheriton, Hants 19 G3
Cheriton, Swan 38 B6
Cheriton Bishop 14 D6
Cheriton Fitzpaine 14 E5
Cheriton or Stackpole Elidor 36 D6
Cherrington 66 B5
Cherry Burton 88 D2
Cherry Green 47 F3
Cherry Hinton 59 E6
Cherry Willingham 82 C4
CHERTSEY 31 E4
Cheselbourne 9 F3
CHESHAM 44 D5
Chesham Bois 44 D6
CHESHUNT 46 D5
Cheslyn Hay 67 E6
Chessington 31 F4
CHESTER 77 G5
CHESTER-LE-STREET 104 B2
Chesterblade 27 F6
CHESTERFIELD, Derby 79 H4
Chesterfield, Staffs 67 G6
Chesterhill 130 C6
Chesters, Scot Bord TD8 121 F5
Chesters, Scot Bord TD9 111 F1
Chesterton, Cambs CB4 59 E5
Chesterton, Cambs PE7 58 B2
Chesterton, Oxon 43 H3
Chesterton, Shrops 66 C7
Chesterton, Staffs 78 C7
Chesterton, Warw 56 B6
Chestfield 34 E4
Cheswardine 66 C4
Cheswick 123 F3
Cheswick Green 55 G4
Chetnole 16 E5
Chettiscombe 15 F4
Chettisham 59 F3
Chettle 17 H4
Chetton 54 B2
Chetwode 43 J3
Chetwynd Aston 66 C5
Cheveley 59 G5
Chevening 33 E5
Chevington 59 H6
Chevithorne 15 F4
Chew Magna 27 E4
Chew Stoke 27 E4
Chewton Keynsham 27 F4
Chewton Mendip 27 E5
Chicheley 57 H7
CHICHESTER 20 B5
Chickerell 9 E5
Chicklade 17 H2
Chickney 47 F3
Chicksands 45 F2
Chicksgrove 17 H2
Chidden 19 H4
Chiddingfold 20 C2
Chiddingly 22 B4
Chiddingstone 33 E6
Chiddingstone Causeway 33 F6
Chideock 8 C4
Chidham 20 A5
Chieveley 29 G3
Chignall Smealy 47 G4
Chignall St James 47 G5
CHIGWELL 47 E6
Chigwell Row 47 E6
Chilbolton 19 E2
Chilcomb 19 G3
Chilcombe 8 D4
Chilcompton 27 F5
Chilcote 67 H5
Child Okeford 17 G4
Child's Ercall 66 B4
Childer Thornton 77 F4
Childerditch 33 G2
Childrey 29 F2
Childswickham 42 C2
Childwall 77 G3
Childwick Green 45 F4
Chilfrome 8 D4
Chilgrove 20 B4
Chilham 34 D5
Chillaton 5 H2
Chillenden 35 F5
Chillerton 11 F5
Chillesford 61 G6
Chillingham 123 F5
Chillington, Devon 6 D6
Chillington, Somer 16 B4
Chilmark 17 H2
Chilson 43 F4
Chilsworthy, Corn 5 H3
Chilsworthy, Devon 12 D5
Chilthorne Domer 16 D4
Chilton, Bucks 44 A4
Chilton, Durham 104 B5
Chilton, Oxon 29 G2
Chilton Candover 19 G2
Chilton Cantelo 16 D3
Chilton Foliat 29 F3
Chilton Lane 104 C4
Chilton Polden 16 B2
Chilton Street 59 H7
Chilton Trinity 16 A2
Chilworth, Hants 19 F4
Chilworth, Surrey 30 E6
Chimney 43 F5
Chineham 30 A5
CHINGFORD 46 D6
Chinley 79 E3
Chinley Head 79 E3
Chinnor 44 B5
Chipnall 66 C3
Chippenham, Cambs 59 G5
CHIPPENHAM, Wilts 28 B3
Chipperfield 45 E5
Chipping, Herts 46 D2
Chipping, Lancs 85 E2
Chipping Campden 42 D2
Chipping Hill 48 B4
CHIPPING NORTON 43 F3
CHIPPING ONGAR 47 F5
CHIPPING SODBURY 27 G2
Chipping Warden 56 C7
Chipstable 15 G3
Chipstead 32 C5
Chirbury 65 F7
Chirk 65 F3
Chirk Bank 65 F3
Chirmorrie 106 E5
Chirnside 122 D2
Chirnsidebridge 122 D2
Chirton 28 C5
Chisbridge Cross 30 C2
Chisbury 29 E4
Chiselborough 16 C4
Chiseldon 28 D3
Chiselhampton 43 H6
CHISLEHURST 33 E3
Chislet 35 F4
Chiswell Green 45 F5
CHISWICK 31 G3
Chisworth 78 D2
Chithurst 20 B3
Chittering 59 E4
Chitterne 28 B6
Chittlehamholt 14 C3
Chittlehampton 13 G3
Chittoe 28 B4
Chivenor 13 F2
Chobham 30 D4
Choicelee 122 C2
Cholderton 28 E6
Cholesbury 44 D5
Chollerton 112 D5
Cholsey 29 H2
Cholstrey 53 H6
Chop Gate 95 G2
Choppington, Northum
NE62 5PY 113 G4
Choppington, Northum
NE62 5SZ 113 G4
Chopwell 103 H2
Chorley, Ches 77 H6
CHORLEY, Lancs 84 D5
Chorley, Shrops 54 B3
Chorley, Staffs 67 F5
CHORLEYWOOD 44 E6
Chorlton 78 B6
Chorlton Lane 65 H2
Chorlton-cum-Hardy 78 C2
Chowley 77 G6
Chrishall 47 E2
Chrisswell 127 G5
Christchurch, Cambs 59 E2
CHRISTCHURCH, Dorset 10 C4
Christchurch, Glos 41 E4
Christchurch, Newp 26 C2
Christian Malford 28 B3
Christleton 77 G5
Christmas Common 44 B6
Christon 26 C5
Christon Bank 123 H5
Christow 6 E2
Chudleigh 6 E3
Chudleigh Knighton 6 E3
Chulmleigh 14 C4
Chunal 78 E2
CHURCH 85 F4
Church Aston 66 C5
Church Brampton 57 F5
Church Broughton 67 H3
Church Cove 3 F6
Church Crookham 30 C5
Church Eaton 66 D5
Church End, Beds LU6 1 44 D3
Church End, Beds LU6 3 45 E4
Church End, Beds SG15 45 F2
Church End, Cambs 70 D6
Church End, Essex CB10 47 F1
Church End, Essex CM7 47 H3
Church End, Glos 41 H2
Church End, Hants 30 A5
Church End, Lincs LN11 83 G2
Church End, Lincs PE11 70 C3
Church End, Oxon 43 F5
Church End, Warw B46 55 H2
Church End, Warw CV10 55 H2
Church End, Wilts 28 C3
Church Fenton 87 G3
Church Green 15 H6
Church Gresley 67 H5
Church Hanborough 43 G4
Church Houses 96 B2
Church Knowle 9 H5
Church Langton 57 F2
Church Lawford 56 C4
Church Lawton 78 C6
Church Leigh 67 F3
Church Lench 55 F6
Church Minshull 78 A5
Church Norton 20 B6
Church Preen 65 J7
Church Pulverbatch 65 H6
Church Stoke 53 F2
Church Stowe 56 E6
Church Street 33 H3
Church Stretton 53 H2
Church Village 25 H2
Church Warsop 80 C5
Churcham 41 G4
Churchdown 41 H4
Churchend, Essex CM6 47 G3
Churchend, Essex SS3 34 D1
Churchgate Street 47 E4
Churchill, Devon 8 A3
Churchill, N Som 26 D5
Churchill, Oxon 43 E3
Churchill, Worces DY10 54 D4
Churchill, Worces WR7 54 E6
Churchinford 15 J4
Churchover 56 D3
Churchstanton 15 H4
Churchstow 6 D6
Churchtown, Cumbr 101 H3
Churchtown, I of M 90 D3
Churchtown, Lancs 84 C2
Churchtown, Mers 84 B5
Churston Ferrers 7 F5
Churt 20 B2
Churton 77 G6
Churwell 86 D3
Chute Standen 29 F5
Chwilog 62 E3
Chyandour 2 C4
Chyanvounder 3 E5
Cilan Uchaf 62 C4
Cilcain 76 D5
Cilcennin 51 F5
Cilcewydd 65 F6
Cilfrew 38 E5
Cilfynydd 25 H1
Cilgerran 37 F1
Cilgwyn, Carm 38 E3
Cilgwyn, Pemb 37 E2
Ciliau- Aeron 51 F6
Cill Amhlaidh 149 C5
Cill Donnain 148 C2
Cille Bhrighde 148 C3
Cille Pheadair 148 C3
Cilmaengwyn 38 E5
Cilmery 52 D6
Cilrhedyn 37 G2
Ciltwrch 40 A1
Cilybebyll 38 E5
Cilycwm 38 E2
Cinderford 41 F4
Circebost 160 E4
CIRENCESTER 42 C5
Ciribhig 161 F3
City Dulas 74 D3
CITY OF LONDON 32 D2
Clabhach 132 D3
Clachaig 127 F4
Clachan, Arg & Bt PA26 8BL 127 F1
Clachan, Arg & Bt PA29 6YP 116 B2
Clachan, Arg & Bt PA34 4RH 134 B7
Clachan, Arg & Bt PA34 5UL 134 C4
Clachan, Highl IV23 163 F5
Clachan, Highl IV40 151 E5
Clachan, Na Eilean 149 C5
Clachan Mór 132 B4
Clachan na Luib 149 D3
Clachan of Campsie 128 D5
Clachan of Glendaruel 126 D4
Clachan- Seil 134 B7
Clachanmore 98 B5
Clachbreck 126 B5
Clachnabrain 138 C2
Clachtoll 166 B7
Clackmannan 129 G3
CLACTON-ON-SEA 49 E4
Cladach Chireboist 149 C3
Claddach 124 A5
Cladich 135 E6
Claggan 134 A4
Claigan 150 B3
Claines 54 D6
Clandown 27 F5
Clanfield, Hants 19 H4
Clanfield, Oxon 43 E5
Clannaborough Barton 14 D5
Clanville 29 F6
Clanyard 98 C6
Claonaig 116 C2
Claonel 164 B3
Clap Gate 86 E2
Clapgate 10 B3
Clapham, Beds 57 J6
CLAPHAM, G Lon 32 C3
Clapham, N Yorks 93 F5
Clapham, W Susx 20 D5
Clapham Hill 34 E4
Clappers 123 E2
Clappersgate 92 B1
Clapton 16 C5
Clapton in Gordano 26 D3
Clapton-on-the-Hill 42 D4
Clapworthy 14 C3
Clarbeston 37 E3
Clarbeston Road 36 E3
Clarborough 80 E3
Clardon 169 F3
Clare 59 H7
Clarebrand 108 E6
Clarencefield 109 H6
Clarilaw 120 E6
Clarkston 118 C2
Clashcoig 164 C4
Clashindarroch 156 B5
Clashmore, Highl IV25 164 D5
Clashmore, Highl IV27 166 B6
Clashnessie 166 B6
Clashnoir 155 G6
Clathy 137 G7
Clatt 156 C6
Clatter 52 C2
Clatterford End 47 F5
Clatterin' Brig 146 D6
Clatworthy 15 G2
Claughton, Lancs LA2 92 D5
Claughton, Lancs PR3 84 D2
Claverdon 55 G5
Claverham 26 D4
Clavering 47 E2
Claverley 54 C2
Claverton 27 G4
Clawdd Poncen 64 D2
Clawdd-newydd 76 C6
Clawfin 107 H2
Clawthorpe 92 D4
Clawton 12 D6
Claxby, Lincs LN13 83 G4
Claxby, Lincs LN8 82 D2
Claxton, N Yorks 96 B5
Claxton, Norf 73 G6
Clay Common 61 H3
Clay Coton 56 D4
CLAY CROSS 79 H5
Clay of Allan 165 E6
Claybokie 145 E4
Claybrooke Magna 56 C3
Claybrooke Parva 56 C3
Claydon, Oxon 56 C7
Claydon, Suff 60 E7
Claygate, Kent 33 H6
Claygate, Surrey 31 F4
Claygate Cross 33 G5
Clayhanger, Devon 15 G3
Clayhanger, W Mids 67 F6
Clayhidon 15 H4
Clayock 169 F4
Claypole 69 G2
Clayton, S Yorks 87 F6
Clayton, Staffs 66 D2
Clayton, W Susx 21 F4
Clayton, W Yorks 86 C3
Clayton Brook 84 D4
Clayton West 86 D5
CLAYTON-LE-MOORS 85 F3
Clayton-le-Woods 84 D4
Clayworth 80 E3
Cleadale 140 D5
Cleadon 113 H6
Clearbrook 6 B4
Clearwell 41 E5
Cleasby 104 B6
Cleat 171 E6
Cleatlam 103 H6
Cleatop 93 G5
Cleator 100 E6
CLEATOR MOOR 100 E6
Clebrig 167 G6
CLECKHEATON 86 C4
Clee St Margaret 54 A3
Cleedownton 54 A3
Cleehill 54 A4
CLEETHORPES 89 H6
Cleeton St Mary 54 B4
Cleeve 26 D4
Cleeve Hill 42 B3
Cleeve Prior 55 F7
Cleghorn 119 G3
Clehonger 40 D2
Cleigh 134 C6
Cleish 129 H3
Cleland 119 F2
Clench Common 28 D4
Clenchwarton 71 F4
Clent 54 E4
Cleobury Mortimer 54 B4
Cleobury North 54 B3
Cleongart 114 B3
Clephanton 154 C3
Clerklands 120 E5
Clestrain 170 D4
Cleuch Head 111 E1
Cleughbrae 109 H5
Clevancy 28 C3
CLEVEDON 26 D3
Cleveley 43 F3
CLEVELEYS 84 B2
Clevelode 54 D7
Cleverton 28 B2
Clewer 26 D5
Cley next the Sea 72 D2
Cliaid 148 B4
Cliasmaol 159 E2
Clibberswick 177 D2
Cliburn 102 B5
Click Mill 172 D4
Cliddesden 29 J6
Cliff End 23 E4
Cliffe, Med 33 H3
Cliffe, N Yorks 87 H3
Cliffe Woods 33 H3
Clifford, Co of H 53 F7
Clifford, W Yorks 87 F2
Clifford Chambers 55 G6
Clifford's Mesne 41 G3
Cliffs End 35 G4
Clifton, Beds 45 F2
Clifton, C of Bris 27 E3
Clifton, C of Notts 68 D3
Clifton, Cumbr 102 B5
Clifton, Derby 67 G2
Clifton, Devon 24 D6
Clifton, Lancs 84 C3
Clifton, Northum 113 G4
Clifton, Oxon 43 G2
Clifton, S Yorks 80 C2
Clifton, Stir 135 H5
Clifton, Worces 54 D7
Clifton Campville 67 H5
Clifton Hampden 43 H6
Clifton Reynes 57 H6
Clifton upon Dunsmore 56 D4
Clifton upon Teme 54 C5
Climping 20 C5
Climpy 119 G2
Clint 94 D6
Clint Green 72 D5
Clinterty 147 F2
Clintmains 121 F4
Cliobh 160 D4
Clippesby 73 H5
Clipsham 69 H5
Clipston, Northnts 57 F3
Clipston, Notts 68 E3
CLITHEROE 85 F2
Cliuthar 159 F3
Clive 65 J4
Clivocast 177 D3
Clocaenog 76 C6
Clochan 156 B2
Clock Face 77 H2
Cloddymoss 154 D3
Clodock 40 C3
Clola 157 H4
Cloncaird Castle 107 F2
Clonrae 109 F3
Clophill 45 E2
Clopton, Northnts 58 A3
Clopton, Suff 61 F6
Clopton Green 59 H6
Close Clark 90 B5
Closeburn 109 F3
Closworth 16 D4
Clothall 46 C2
Clothan 177 B5
Clotton 77 H5
Clouds 41 E2
Clough Foot 85 H4
Cloughton 97 F2
Cloughton Newlands 97 F2
Clousta 174 E5
Clouston 170 C3
Clova, Aberd 156 B6
Clova, Ang 145 H6
Clovelly 12 D3
Clovenfords 120 D4
Clovenstone 147 E2
Cloves 155 F2
Clovullin 134 E2
Clowne 80 B4
Clows Top 54 C4
Cloyntie 107 F2
Cluanach 124 C5
Clubworthy 12 C6
Clun 53 G3
Clunbury 53 G3
Clunderwen 37 F4
Clune 156 C2
Clunes 142 E5
Clungunford 53 G4
Clunie, Aberd 156 D3
Clunie, Pth & Kin 137 J4
Cluniter 127 F5
Clunton 53 G3
Cluny 130 B3
Clutton, Bth 27 F5
Clutton, Ches 77 G6
Clwt-y-bont 75 E5
Clydach, Monm 40 B4
Clydach, Swan 38 D5
Clydach Vale 39 G6
CLYDEBANK 128 B5
Clydey 37 G2
Clyffe Pypard 28 C3
Clynder 127 G4
Clynelish 165 E3
Clynnog-fawr 74 D6
Clyro 40 B1
Clyst Honiton 15 F6
Clyst Hydon 15 G5
Clyst St George 15 F7
Clyst St Lawrence 15 G5
Clyst St Mary 15 F6
Clyth 169 G6
Clyth Mains 169 G6
Cnip 160 D4
Cnoc Amhlaigh 161 J4
Cnoc an t-Solais 161 H3
Cnoc Dubh 169 F6
Cnwch Coch 51 G4
Coachford 156 B4
Coad's Green 5 F3
Coal Aston 79 H4
Coalbrookdale 66 B6
Coalburn 119 F4
Coalburns 113 F6
Coalcleugh 102 E3
Coaley 41 G5
Coalpit Heath 27 F2
Coalpits Grange 103 F2
Coalport 66 B6
Coalsnaughton 129 G3
Coaltown of Balgonie 130 B3
Coaltown of Burnturk 130 C2
Coaltown of Wemyss 130 C3
COALVILLE 68 C5
Coalway 41 E4
Coast 162 D4
Coat 16 C3
COATBRIDGE 128 E6
Coatdyke 128 E6
Coate 28 C4
Coates, Cambs 70 D7
Coates, Glos 42 B5
Coatham 105 F5
Coatham Mundeville 104 B5
Coatsgate 109 H2
Cobairdy 156 C4
Cobbaton 13 G3
Coberley 42 B4
Cobham, Kent 33 G4
Cobham, Surrey 31 F4
Cobleland 128 C3
Cobnash 53 H5
Coburty 157 G2
Cock Alley 80 B5
Cock Bridge 145 G3
Cock Clarks 48 B5
Cockayne 95 H2
Cockayne Hatley 58 C7
Cockburnspath 131 G5
COCKENZIE AND PORT SETON 130 D5
Cockerham 84 C1
Cockerington 83 F2
COCKERMOUTH 101 F4
Cockernhoe 45 F3
Cockfield, Durham 103 H5
Cockfield, Suff 60 C6
Cockfosters 46 C6
Cocking 20 B4
Cockington 7 E4
Cocklake 26 D6
Cockley Beck 91 D1
Cockley Cley 71 H6
Cockpole Green 30 B2
Cockshutt 65 H4
Cockthorpe 72 C2
Cockwood 7 F2
Cockyard 40 D2
Coddenham 60 E6
Coddington, Ches 77 G6
Coddington, Co of H 41 G1
Coddington, Notts 81 F6
Codford St Mary 17 H2
Codford St Peter 17 H1
Codicote 45 G4
Codmore Hill 20 D3
Codnor 80 B7
Codrington 27 G3
Codsall 66 D6
Codsall Wood 66 D6
Coed Morgan 40 C4
Coed Ystumgwern 63 F4
Coed-y-paen 40 C6
Coed-yr-ynys 39 J3
Coedely 25 H2
Coedkernew 26 B2
Coedpoeth 76 E6
Coelbren 39 F4
Coffinswell 7 E4
Cofton Hackett 55 F4
Cogenhoe 57 G5
Coggeshall 48 B3
Coggeshall Hamlet 48 B3
Coggins Mill 22 B3
Coig Peighinnean 161 J1
Coig Peighinnean Bhuirgh 161 H2
Coillacriech 145 H4
Coillantogle 128 C2
Coillaig 134 E6
Coille Mhorgil 142 D3
Coilleag 148 C3
Coillore 150 C5
Coity 25 G2
Col 161 H3
Col Uarach 161 H4
Colaboll 164 B2
Colan 3 G1
Colaton Raleigh 7 G2
Colbost 150 B4
Colburn 94 C2
Colby, Cumbr 102 C5
Colby, I of M 90 B5
Colby, Norf 73 F3
COLCHESTER 48 C3
Cold Ash 29 H4
Cold Ashby 56 E4
Cold Ashton 27 G3
Cold Aston 42 D4
Cold Blow 37 F4
Cold Brayfield 57 H6
Cold Hanworth 82 C3
Cold Hesledon 104 D3
Cold Higham 56 E6
Cold Kirby 95 G3
Cold Newton 69 F6
Cold Norton 48 B5
Cold Overton 69 G5
Coldbackie 167 H4
Coldblow 33 F3
Coldean 21 G5
Coldeast 6 E3
Colden Common 19 F3
Coldfair Green 61 H5
Coldham 71 E6
Coldharbour, Dorset 9 E5
Coldharbour, Surrey 31 F6
Coldingham 131 J6
Coldrain 129 H2
Coldred 35 F6
Coldridge 14 C5
Coldrife 112 E3
Coldstream, Ang 138 C5
COLDSTREAM, Scot Bord 122 D4
Coldwaltham 20 D4
Coldwells 157 J5
Coldwells Croft 156 C6
Cole 17 E2
Cole End 55 G3
Cole Green 46 C4
Colebatch 53 G3
Colebrook 15 G5
Colebrooke 14 D6
Coleby, Lincs 81 G5
Coleby, N Linc 88 C5
Coleford, Devon 14 D5
Coleford, Glos 41 E4
Coleford, Somer 27 F6
Colehill 10 B3
Coleman's Hatch 21 H2
Colemere 65 H3
Coleorton 68 C5
Colerne 27 H3
Colesbourne 42 B4
Colesden 58 B6
Coleshill, Bucks 44 D6
Coleshill, Oxon 42 E6
Coleshill, Warw 55 H3
Colfin 98 B4
Colgate 21 F2
Colgrain 127 H4
Colinsburgh 130 D2
Colinton 130 B6
Colintraive 126 E5
Colkirk 72 C4
Collace 138 B5
Collafirth, Shetld ZE2 9PZ 175 F4
Collafirth, Shetld ZE2 9RX 177 A5
Collaton St Mary 6 E4
Collessie 130 B1
Collets Green 54 D6
Collier Row 33 E1
Collier Street 33 H6
Colliers End 46 D3
Colliery Row 104 C3
Collieston 157 H6
Collin 109 H5
Collingbourne Ducis 28 E5
Collingbourne Kingston 28 E5
Collingham, Notts 81 F5
Collingham, W Yorks 87 E2
Collington 54 B5
Collingtree 57 F6
Colliston 139 F4
Collynie 157 F5
Collyweston 69 H6
Colmonell 106 D4
Colmworth 58 B6
Coln Rogers 42 C5
Coln St Aldwyns 42 D5
Coln St Dennis 42 C4
Colnabaichin 145 G3
Colnbrook 30 E3
Colne, Cambs 58 D4
COLNE, Lancs 85 G2
Colne Engaine 48 B2
Colney 73 E6
Colney Heath 45 G5
Colney Street 45 F5
Colp 156 E4
Colpy 156 D5
Colquhar 120 C3
Colscott 12 D4
Colsterdale 94 C3
Colsterworth 69 H4
Colston Bassett 69 E3
Coltfield 155 F2
Colthrop 29 H4
Coltishall 73 F5
Colton, Cumbr 92 B3
Colton, N Yorks 87 G2
Colton, Norf 72 E6
Colton, Staffs 67 F4
Colvend 100 C2
Colvister 177 C4
Colwall 41 G1
Colwall Green 41 G1
Colwall Stone 41 G1
Colwell 112 D5
Colwich 67 F4
Colwinston 25 G3
Colworth 20 C5

Place	Page	Grid
COLWYN BAY	75	H4
Colyford	15	J6
Colyton	15	J6
Comb	111	G3
Combe, Co of H	53	G5
Combe, Oxon	43	G4
Combe, W Berks	29	F4
Combe Florey	15	H2
Combe Hay	27	G4
Combe Martin	24	C6
Combe Moor	53	G5
Combe Raleigh	15	H5
Combe St Nicholas	16	B4
Combebow	5	H2
Combeinteignhead	7	J3
Comberbach	77	J4
Comberton, Cambs	58	D6
Comberton, Co of H	53	H5
Combpyne	8	A4
Combrook	55	J6
Combs, Derby	79	E4
Combs, Suff	60	D6
Combs Ford	60	D6
Combwich	26	B6
Comers	146	D3
Comins Coch	51	G3
Commercial End	59	F5
Commins Coch	64	B6
Common End	100	E5
Common Moor	5	H4
Common Side	79	H4
Commondale	105	F6
Commonside	67	H2
Commonwood	45	E5
Compstall	78	D2
Compton, Devon	6	E4
Compton, Hants	19	F3
Compton, Surrey	30	D6
Compton, W Berks	29	H3
Compton, W Susx	20	A4
Compton, Wilts	28	D5
Compton Abbas	17	G4
Compton Abdale	42	C4
Compton Bassett	28	C3
Compton Beauchamp	29	E2
Compton Bishop	26	C5
Compton Chamberlayne	18	B3
Compton Dando	27	H4
Compton Dundon	16	B3
Compton End	19	F3
Compton Martin	27	E5
Compton Pauncefoot	17	E3
Compton Valence	8	D4
Comrie	137	E6
Conchra, Arg & Bt	126	E4
Conchra, Highl	152	A6
Concraigie	137	J4
Conder Green	92	C6
Conderton	42	B2
Condicote	42	D3
Condorrat	128	E5
Condover	65	H6
Coney Weston	60	C4
Coneyhurst	20	D3
Coneysthorpe	96	C4
Coneythorpe	95	E6
Conford	20	B2
Congash	155	E6
Congerstone	68	B6
Congham	71	H4
Congl-y-wal	63	H2
CONGLETON	78	C5
Congresbury	26	D4
Conicavel	154	D4
Coningsby	82	E6
Conington, Cambs CB3	58	D5
Conington, Cambs PE7	58	B3
CONISBROUGH	80	C2
Conisby	124	B4
Conisholme	83	G2
Coniston, Cumbr	92	B2
Coniston, E Yorks	89	F3
Coniston Cold	93	H6
Conistone	94	A5
Conland	156	D4
CONNAH'S QUAY	77	F5
Connel	134	D5
Connel Park	118	D6
Connor Downs	2	D4
Conon Bridge	153	H3
Cononley	86	A2
Conordan	151	E5
Consall	67	E2
CONSETT	103	H4
Constable Burton	94	C2
Constantine	3	F5
Constantine Bay	4	B3
Contin	153	G3
Contlaw	147	F3
Contullich	154	A1
CONWY	75	G4
Conyer	34	C4
Cookbury	13	E5
Cookham	30	C2
Cookham Dean	30	C2
Cookham Rise	30	C2
Cookhill	55	F6
Cookley, Suff	61	G4
Cookley, Worcs	54	D3
Cookley Green	30	A1
Cookney	147	H4
Cooksbridge	21	H4
Cooksmill Green	47	G5
Coolham	20	E3
Cooling	33	H3
Coombe, Corn EX23	12	C4
Coombe, Corn PL26	4	C5
Coombe, Corn TR3	3	G3
Coombe, Devon EX6	6	E2
Coombe, Devon TQ9	6	D5
Coombe Bissett	18	C3
Coombe Hill	41	H3
Coombe Keynes	9	G5
Coombes	21	E5
Copdock	48	E1
Copford Green	48	C3
Copister	177	B6
Cople	44	E1
Copley	103	G5
Coplow Dale	79	F4
Copmanthorpe	87	G2
Coppathorne	12	C5
Coppenhall	66	E5
Copperhouse	2	D4
Coppingford	58	B3
Copplestone	14	D5
Coppull	84	D7
Copsale	21	E3
Copster Green	85	E3
Copston Magna	56	C3
Copt Heath	55	H6
Copt Hewick	94	E4
Copt Oak	68	C5
Copthorne	21	G2
Copy Lake	14	C1
Copythorne	18	E4

Place	Page	Grid
Corbridge	112	D6
CORBY	57	G3
Corby Glen	69	J4
Coreley	54	B4
Corfe	15	J4
Corfe Castle	9	H5
Corfe Mullen	9	H4
Corfton	53	H3
Corgarff	145	G3
Corhampton	19	H3
Corlae	108	D3
Corley	55	J3
Corley Ash	55	H3
Corley Moor	55	H3
Cornaa	90	D4
Cornabus	124	C6
Cornaigbeg	132	B4
Cornelly	25	F2
Corney	91	C2
Cornforth	104	C4
Cornhill	156	C3
Cornhill-on-Tweed	122	D4
Cornholme	85	H4
Cornish Hall End	47	G2
Cornquoy	171	F5
Cornriggs	103	E3
Cornsay	103	H3
Corntown	153	H3
Cornwell	42	E3
Cornwood	6	C5
Cornworthy	6	C5
Corpach	142	C6
Corpusty	72	E4
Corran, Highl IV40	141	H3
Corran, Highl PH33	134	E2
Corranbuie	126	C6
Corrany	90	D4
Corravachie	164	A6
Corrie	116	E3
Corrie Common	110	B4
Corriecravie	116	D5
Corriedoo	108	D4
Corriekinloch	167	E7
Corriemoillie	153	F2
Corrievorrie	154	B6
Corrigal	172	D5
Corrimony	153	F5
Corringham, Lincs	81	F2
Corringham, Thurk	33	H2
Corris	63	H6
Corris Uchaf	63	H6
Corrow	127	F2
Corry	151	F6
Corry of Ardnagrask	153	H4
Corrymuckloch	137	F5
Corrynachenchy	133	J4
Corscombe	16	D5
Corse, Aberd	156	D4
Corse, Glos	41	G3
Corse Lawn	41	H2
Corsebank	119	F6
Corsewall	98	B3
Corsham	27	H3
Corsindae	146	D3
Corsley	27	H6
Corsley Heath	27	H6
Corsock	108	E5
Corston, Bth	27	F4
Corston, Orkney	172	D5
Corston, Wilts	28	B2
Corstorphine	130	B5
Cortachy	138	C3
Corton, Suff	73	J7
Corton, Wilts	28	B6
Corton Denham	17	E3
Corunna	149	D3
Corwen	64	D2
Coryton, Devon	5	H2
Coryton, Thurk	33	H2
Cosby	56	D2
COSELEY	55	E2
Cosgrove	44	B1
Cosham	19	H5
Cosheston	36	E5
Cossall	68	C2
Cosses	106	D4
Cossington, Leic	68	E5
Cossington, Somer	16	B1
Costa	172	D4
Costessey	73	E5
Costock	68	D4
Coston	69	G4
Cote	43	F5
Cotebrook	77	H5
Cotegill	93	E1
Cotehill	102	A2
Cotes, Leic	68	D4
Cotes, Staffs	66	D3
Cotesbach	56	D3
Cotgrave	68	D3
Cothall, Aberd	147	F2
Cothall, Mor	155	F2
Cotham	69	F2
Cothelstone	15	H2
Cotherstone	103	G6
Cothill	15	J5
Cotleigh	15	J5
Coton, Cambs	58	E6
Coton, Northnts	56	E4
Coton, Staffs	67	E3
Coton Clanford	66	D4
Coton in the Elms	67	H5
Cott	6	D4
Cottam, Lancs	84	D3
Cottam, Notts	81	F4
Cottartown	155	E5
Cottenham	59	E5
Cotterdale	93	G2
Cottered	46	D3
Cotterstock	57	J2
Cottesbrooke	57	F4
Cottesmore	69	H5
COTTINGHAM, E Yorks	88	E3
Cottingham, Northnts	57	G2
Cottisford	43	H2
Cotton, Staffs	67	F2
Cotton, Suff	60	D5
Cotton End	58	A7
Cotton Stones	86	A4
Cottown, Aberd AB51	147	E2
Cottown, Aberd AB53	157	F4
Cottown, Pth & Kin	138	B6
Cottwalton	66	E3
Couch's Mill	5	E5
Coughton, Co of H	41	E3
Coughton, Warw	55	F5
Coulaghailtro	126	B6
Coulags	152	B4
Coulby Newham	104	E6
Coulderton	100	D7
Coulin Lodge	152	C3
Coull	146	C3
Coulport	127	G4
COULSDON	32	C5
Coulston	28	B5

Place	Page	Grid
Coulter	119	H4
Coultershaw Bridge	20	C4
Coultings	26	B6
Coulton	95	H4
Coultra	138	C6
Cound	65	J6
Coundon	104	B5
Coundon Grange	104	B5
Countersett	93	H3
Countess Wear	15	F7
Countesthorpe	56	D2
Countisbury	24	E6
COUPAR ANGUS	138	B4
Coupland	123	E4
Cour	116	C3
Court, Co of H	40	D1
Court, Powys	39	J2
Court Gardens	41	F2
Court Henry	38	C3
Court-at-Street	23	G2
Courteenhall	57	F6
Courtsend	48	D6
Courtway	15	J2
Cousland	130	C6
Cousley Wood	22	C2
Coustonn	127	E5
COVE, Arg & Bt	127	G4
Cove, Devon	15	F4
Cove, Hants	30	C5
Cove, Highl	162	C4
Cove Bay	147	G3
Covehithe	61	J3
Coven	66	E6
Coveney	59	E3
Covenham St Bartholomew	83	F2
Covenham St Mary	83	F2
COVENTRY	56	B4
Coverack	3	F6
Coverham	94	C3
Covesea	155	F1
Covington, Cambs	58	A4
Covington, S Lanak	119	G4
Cowan Bridge	93	E4
Cowbeech	22	C4
Cowbit	70	C5
COWBRIDGE	25	G3
Cowden	33	E6
COWDENBEATH	129	J3
Cowers Lane	67	J2
COWES	11	F4
Cowesby	95	F3
Cowfold	21	F3
Cowgill	93	F3
Cowgrove	9	H3
Cowick	87	H4
Cowie, Aberd	147	F5
Cowie, Stir	129	F4
Cowley, Devon	15	F6
Cowley, G Lon	31	E2
Cowley, Glos	42	B4
Cowley, Oxon	43	F4
Cowling, N Yorks BD22	85	H2
Cowling, N Yorks DL8	94	D3
Cowlinge	59	H6
Cowmes	86	C5
Cowpen Bewley	104	D5
Cowplain	19	H4
Cowshill	103	E3
Cowstrandburn	129	H3
Cowthorpe	87	F1
Cox Common	61	H3
Coxbank	66	B2
Coxbench	68	B2
Coxford	72	B4
Coxheath	33	H5
Coxhoe	104	C4
Coxley	27	E6
Coxtie Green	47	F6
Coxwold	95	G4
Coychurch	25	G3
Coylton	117	J6
Coylumbridge	144	D2
Coynach	146	B3
Coynachie	156	B5
Coytrahen	25	F2
Crabbet Park	21	G2
Crabbs Cross	55	F5
Crabtree	21	F3
Crabtree Green	65	G2
Crackenthorpe	102	C5
Crackington	12	B6
Crackington Haven	12	B6
Cracklebank	66	C5
Crackpot	93	H2
Cracoe	94	A5
Craddock	15	G4
Cradhlastadh	160	D4
Cradley	54	C7
Crafthole	5	D5
Cragabus	124	C6
Cragg Vale	86	B4
Craggan, Highl	155	E6
Craggan, Mor	155	F5
Craggie, Highl IV2	154	B5
Craggie, Highl KW8	165	E2
Craghead	104	B2
Crai	39	F3
Craibstone	156	B3
Craichie	138	C4
Craichie Mill	138	E4
Craig, Aberd	157	G6
Craig, D & G DG2	99	H3
Craig, D & G DG7 3	108	D5
Craig, Highl	152	C4
Craig, S Ayr	107	F2
Craig-cefn-parc	38	D5
Craig-y-nos	39	F4
Craigdallie	138	B6
Craigdam	157	F5
Craigdarroch, D & G	108	E3
Craigdarroch, E Ayr	108	D2
Craigearn	146	E2
Craigellachie	155	G4
Craigend	137	J6
Craigendive	127	F4
Craigendoran	127	H4
Craigends	127	J6
Craigenputtock	108	E4
Craigens, Arg & Bt	124	B4
Craigens, E Ayr	118	C6
Craigfad	107	F2
Craighall	138	A4
Craighat	128	B4
Craighead, Fife	131	F2
Craighead, Highl	154	B2
Craighlaw Mains	98	E3
Craighouse	125	C6
Craighu	153	G4
Craigie, Aberd	147	G2
Craigie, Pth & Kin	137	J4
Craigie, S Ayr	118	B4
Craigiefield	171	E3
Craigielaw	130	B5
Craiglockhart	130	B5
Craiglug	147	F4
Craigmalloch	107	G3
Craigmaud	157	F3

Place	Page	Grid
Craigmillar	130	B5
Craignant	65	F3
Craigneuk, N Lanak ML1	118	E2
Craigneuk, N Lanak ML6	128	E6
Craignure	134	B5
Craigo	139	F2
Craigow	129	H2
Craigrothie	130	C1
Craigroy	155	F3
Craigruie	136	B3
Craigsmithe	138	C6
Craigton, Ang DD5	138	C3
Craigton, Ang DD8	138	C3
Craigton, C of Aber	147	F3
Craigton, Highl	164	C4
Craigton, Stir	128	B3
Craigtown	168	C4
Craik, Aberd	156	B5
Craik, Scot Bord	110	C2
CRAIL	131	F2
Crailing	121	F5
Crailinghall	121	F5
Crakehall	94	D2
Crakehill	95	F4
Crambe	96	C5
Cramlington	113	G6
Cramond	130	A5
Cramond Bridge	130	A5
Cranage	78	B5
Cranberry	66	D3
Cranborne	18	B4
Cranbourne	30	D4
Cranbrook	22	D2
Cranbrook Common	22	D2
Cranfield	44	D1
Cranford, Devon	12	D3
Cranford, G Lon	31	F3
Cranford St Andrew	57	H4
Cranford St John	57	H4
Cranham, G Lon	33	F2
Cranham, Glos	41	H4
Crank	77	H2
Cranleigh	20	D2
Cranmore, I of W	11	B5
Cranmore, Somer	27	F6
Cranna	156	D3
Crannoch	156	B3
Cranoe	57	F2
Cransford	61	G5
Cranshaws	121	F1
Cranstal	90	D2
Crantock	3	F1
Cranwell	82	C7
Cranwich	59	H2
Cranworth	72	C6
Craobh Haven	126	B2
Crapstone	5	J4
Crarae	126	D3
Crask of Aigas	153	G4
Craskins	146	C3
Craster	123	H6
Craswall	40	B2
Cratfield	61	G4
Crathes	146	E4
Crathie, Aberd	145	G4
Crathie, Highl	143	H4
Crathorne	104	D7
Craven Arms	53	H3
Crawcrook	113	F6
Crawford, Lancs	84	C4
Crawford, S Lanak	119	G5
Crawfordjohn	119	F5
Crawick	118	E6
Crawley, Hants	19	F2
Crawley, Oxon	43	F4
CRAWLEY, W Susx	21	F2
Crawley Down	21	G2
Crawleyside	103	F3
Crawshawbooth	85	G4
Crawton	147	F5
Cray, N Yorks	93	H4
Cray, Pth & Kin	138	A2
Cray's Pond	29	J2
CRAYFORD	33	F3
Crayke	95	G4
Crays Hill	33	H1
Creacombe	14	E4
Creag Ghoraidh	149	C5
Creagan	134	D4
Creaganterve Mhòr	126	C2
Creaton	57	F4
Creca	110	B5
Credenhill	40	D1
CREDITON	14	E6
Creebank	107	F5
Creebridge	107	E5
Creech Heathfield	16	A3
Creech St Michael	16	A3
Creed	4	C6
Creekmoor	9	H4
Creekmouth	33	E2
Creeksea	48	C6
Creeting St Mary	60	D6
Creeton	69	J4
Creetown	99	F4
Creggans	127	E2
Cregneash	90	A6
Cregrina	52	E6
Creich	138	C6
Creigiau	25	H2
Cremyll	5	H5
Cressage	66	A6
Cressbrook	79	F4
Cresselly	37	E5
Cressing	47	H3
Cresswell, Northum	113	G3
Cresswell, Staffs	67	E3
Cresswell Quay	37	E5
Creswell	80	C4
Cretingham	61	F5
Cretshengan	126	B6
CREWE	78	B6
Crewe-by-Farndon	77	H6
Crewgreen	65	G3
CREWKERNE	16	C5
Crews Hill	46	D5
Crianlarich	135	H4
Cribyn	51	F6
CRICCIETH	63	E3
Crich	79	H6
Crichton	120	C1
Crick, Monm	26	D1
Crick, Northnts	56	D4
Crickadarn	39	H1
Cricket Malherbie	16	B4
Cricket St Thomas	16	B5
Crickheath	65	F4
Crickhowell	40	B4
CRICKLADE	42	D6
Cridling Stubbs	87	G4
CRIEFF	137	F6
Criggion	65	F3
Crigglestone	86	E5
Crimond	157	H3
Crimonmogate	157	H3
Crimplesham	71	G6

Place	Page	Grid
Crimscote	55	H7
Crinan	126	B3
Cringleford	73	E6
Crinow	37	F4
Cripp's Corner	22	D3
Cripplesease	2	D4
Crix	47	H4
Croasdale	101	E6
Crockenhill	33	F4
Crock Street	16	B4
Crockenhill	33	F4
Crockernwell	14	D6
Crockerton	27	H6
Crocketford	109	F5
Crockey Hill	87	H2
Crockham Hill	33	E5
Crockhurst Street	33	G6
Crockleford Heath	48	D3
Crockness	170	D5
Croes y pant	40	C5
Croes-an-wra	2	B5
Croes-goch	36	C2
Croes-lan	37	H1
Croes-y-mwyalch	26	C1
Croesau Bach	65	F4
Croeserw	39	F6
Croesor	63	G2
Croesyceiliog, Carm	37	J4
Croesyceiliog, Torf	40	C6
Croft, Co of H	53	H5
Croft, Leic	56	D2
Croft, Lincs	83	H5
Croft, Warr	77	J2
Croft-on-Tees	104	B7
Croftamie	128	B4
Croftgarbh	136	E4
Croftinloan	137	G3
Crofton, W Yorks	87	E5
Crofton, Wilts	28	E4
Crofts	108	E5
Crofts of Benachielt	169	F6
Crofts of Haddo	157	F5
Crofts of Inverthernie	156	E4
Crofty	38	C6
Croggan	134	B6
Croglin	100	B3
Crogo Mains	108	E5
Croick, Highl IV24	164	A4
Croick, Highl KW13	168	C4
Crois Dùghaill	148	C3
CROMARTY	154	B2
Crombie, Ang	139	E5
Crombie, Fife	129	H4
Cromblet	157	E5
Cromdale	155	E6
Cromer, Herts	46	C3
CROMER, Norf	73	F2
Cromer Hyde	45	G4
Cromford	79	G6
Cromhall	27	F1
Cromhall Common	27	F2
Cromor	161	G5
Cromwell	81	E5
Cronberry	118	D5
Crondall	30	B6
Cronk-y-Voddy	90	C4
Cronkedonney	90	B5
Cronton	77	G3
Crook, Cumbr	92	C2
CROOK, Durham	103	H4
Crook of Devon	129	H2
Crookedholm	118	B4
Crookgate Bank	103	H2
Crookham, Northum	122	E4
Crookham, W Berks	29	H4
Crookham Village	30	B6
Crookhouse	122	C5
Crooklands	92	D3
Crooks Marsh	27	E2
Cropredy	55	G7
Cropston	68	D5
Cropthorne	42	B1
Cropton	96	C3
Cropwell Bishop	69	E3
Cropwell Butler	69	E3
Cros	161	H1
Crosbie	117	G2
Crosbost	161	G5
Crosby, Cumbr	100	E4
Crosby, I of M	90	C5
CROSBY, Mers	77	F2
Crosby, N Linc	88	C5
Crosby Court	95	E2
Crosby Garrett	102	D7
Crosby Ravensworth	102	C6
Crosby-on-Eden	110	D7
Croscombe	27	E6
Cross	26	D5
Cross Ash	40	D4
Cross Green, Devon	12	D7
Cross Green, Suff	60	C6
Cross Hands	38	C4
Cross Head Lane	54	C2
Cross Hills	86	B2
Cross Houses	65	J6
Cross in Hand	22	B3
Cross Inn, Cered SA44	50	D6
Cross Inn, Cered SY23	51	F5
Cross Inn, Rho Cyn Taf	25	H2
Cross Lanes, Corn	3	E5
Cross Lanes, N Yorks	95	G5
Cross Lanes, Wrex	65	G2
Cross o th hands	67	H2
Cross of Jackston	156	E5
Cross Roads	86	B3
Cross-at-Hand	33	H6
Crossaig	116	C2
Crossapol	132	B4
Crosscanonby	100	E4
Crossdale Street	73	F3
Crossens	84	B5
Crossflatts	86	C2
Crossford, Fife	129	H4
Crossford, S Lanak	119	F3
Crossgate	70	C4
Crossgatehall	130	C6
Crossgates, Fife	129	J4
Crossgates, Powys	52	D5
Crossgill	92	D5
Crosshands, Carm	37	F3
Crosshands, E Ayr	118	B4
Crosshill, Fife	130	A3
Crosshill, S Ayr	107	F2
Crosshouse	117	H4
Crossings	110	C5
Crosskeys	26	B1
Crosskirk	168	E3
Crosslanes	65	G5
Crosslee, Renf	127	J6
Crosslee, Scot Bord	120	C6
Crossmichael	108	E6
Crossmoor	84	C3
Crossroads	146	E4
Crosston	139	E2

Place	Page	Grid
Crossway, Co of H	40	C3
Crossway, Monm	40	D4
Crossway, Powys	52	D6
Crossway Green	54	D5
Crossways	9	F5
Crosswell	37	F2
Crosthwaite	92	C2
Croston	84	C5
Crostwick	73	F5
Crostwight	73	G3
Crothair	160	E4
Crouch	33	G5
Croughly	155	F6
Croughton	43	H2
Crovie	157	F2
Crow Hill	41	F3
Crowan	2	E4
CROWBOROUGH	22	B2
Crowcombe	15	H2
Crowdecote	79	F5
Crowell	44	B6
Crowfield, Northnts	43	J1
Crowfield, Suff	60	E6
Crowhurst, E Susx	22	D4
Crowhurst, Surrey	32	D6
Crowland	70	C6
Crowle, N Linc	88	B5
Crowle, Worcs	54	E6
Crowmarsh Gifford	29	J2
Crown Corner	61	F4
Crownhill	5	H5
Crownland	60	D4
Crownthorpe	72	D6
Crowntown	2	E4
Crowthorne	30	C4
Crowton	77	H4
Croxall	67	G5
Croxby	82	D2
Croxdale	104	B4
Croxden	67	F3
Croxley Green	45	E6
Croxton, Cambs	58	C5
Croxton, N Linc	89	E5
Croxton, Norf	60	B3
Croxton, Staffs	66	C3
Croxton Kerrial	69	G4
Croy, Highl	154	B4
Croy, N Lanak	128	E5
Croyde	13	E2
Croydon, Cambs	58	D7
CROYDON, G Lon	32	D4
Cruckmeole	65	H6
Cruckton	65	H5
Cruden Bay	157	H5
Crudgington	66	B5
Crudwell	28	B1
Crug	52	D4
Crugmeer	4	C3
Crugybar	38	D2
Crulabhig	160	E4
Crumlin	40	B6
Crumplehorn	5	F5
Crundale, Kent	34	D6
Crundale, Pemb	36	D4
Cruwys Morchard	14	E4
Crux Easton	29	G5
Crwbin	38	B4
Crymlyn	75	F2
Crymych	37	F2
Crynant	39	E5
Cuaig	151	G3
Cuan	126	B1
Cubbington	56	B5
Cubert	3	F2
Cublington	44	C3
Cuckfield	21	G3
Cucklington	17	F3
Cuckney	80	C4
Cuddesdon	43	J5
Cuddington, Bucks	44	B4
Cuddington, Ches	77	J4
Cuddington Heath	65	H2
Cuddy Hill	84	C3
Cudham	33	E5
Cudliptown	6	B3
Cudworth, S Yorks	87	E6
Cudworth, Somer	16	B4
Cuffley	46	D5
Cuidhir	148	B4
Cuidhtinis	159	E4
Cuidrach	150	C3
Cùl Doirlinn	141	F6
Culbo	154	A2
Culbokie	153	J3
Culburnie	153	G4
Culcabock	154	A4
Culcairn	153	J2
Culcharry	154	C3
Culcheth	77	J2
Culdrain	156	C5
Culduie	151	G4
Culford	60	B5
Culfordheath	60	B5
Culgaith	102	C5
Culgower	165	F2
Culham	43	H6
Culkein	166	B6
Culkerton	42	B6
Cullachie	144	D1
CULLEN	156	C2
Cullercoats	113	H5
Cullicudden	154	A2
Cullingworth	86	B3
Cullipool	126	B1
Cullisse	165	E6
Culloch	137	E7
Culloden	154	B4
Cullompton	15	G5
Culmaily	165	E4
Culmington	53	H3
Culmstock	15	H4
Culnacraig	162	E3
Culnaknock	151	E3
Culrain	164	B4
CULROSS	129	G4
Culroy	117	H6
Culsh, Aberd AB34	146	C3
Culsh, Aberd AB53	157	F4
Culshabbin	98	E4
Culswick	176	B3
Cultercullen	157	G6
Cults, Aberd	156	C5
Cults, C of Aber	147	F3
Cults, D & G	99	F5
Culverstone Green	33	G4
Culverthorpe	69	J2
Culworth	56	D7
CUMBERNAULD	128	E5
Cumbernauld Village	128	E5
Cumberworth	83	H4

208 Cuminestown Dunlappie

Cuminestown 157 F3
Cumlewick 176 D5
Cumloden 99 F3
Cummersdale 101 H2
Cummertrees 109 J6
Cummingstown 155 F2
CUMNOCK 118 C5
Cumnor 43 G5
Cumrew 102 B2
Cumwhinton 101 J2
Cumwhitton 102 B2
Cundall 95 F4
Cunninghamhead 117 H3
Cunnister 177 C4
CUPAR 138 C7
Cupar Muir 130 C1
Curbar 79 G4
Curbridge, Hants 19 G4
Curbridge, Oxon 43 F5
Curdridge 19 G4
Curdworth 55 G2
Curland 16 A4
Curland Common 16 A4
Currarie 106 D3
Curridge 29 G3
Currie 130 A6
Curry Mallet 16 B3
Curry Rivel 16 B3
Curteis Corner 22 E2
Curtisden Green 33 H6
Curtisknowle 6 D5
Cury 3 E5
Cushnie 157 E2
Cushuish 15 H2
Cusop 40 B1
Cutcloy 99 F6
Cutcombe 15 F2
Cutiau 63 G5
Cutlers Green 47 F2
Cutnall Green 54 D5
Cutsdean 42 C2
Cutthorpe 79 H4
Cutts 176 D4
Cuxham 44 A6
Cuxton 33 H4
Cuxwold 82 D1
Cwm, Blae. Gw 40 A5
Cwm, Denb 76 C4
Cwm Ffrwd-oer 40 B5
Cwm Irfon 52 B7
Cwm Penmachno 63 H2
Cwm-Cewydd 64 B5
Cwm-Cou 37 G1
Cwm-Llinau 64 B6
Cwm-twrch Isaf 38 E4
Cwm-twrch Uchaf 38 E4
Cwm-y-glo 75 E5
Cwmafan 25 E1
Cwmaman 39 H6
Cwmann 51 F7
Cwmavon 40 B5
Cwmavon House 40 B5
Cwmbach, Carm 37 G3
Cwmbach, Powys 40 A2
Cwmbach, Rho Cyn Taf 39 H5
Cwmbelan 52 C3
CWMBRAN 40 B6
Cwmbrwyno 51 H3
Cwmcarn 40 B6
Cwmcarvan 40 D5
Cwmcrawnon 39 J4
Cwmdare 39 G5
Cwmdu, Carm 38 D2
Cwmdu, Powys 40 A3
Cwmduad 37 H2
Cwmerfyn 51 H3
Cwmfelin Boeth 37 F4
Cwmfelin Mynach 37 G3
Cwmfelinfach 26 A1
Cwmffrwd 38 B4
Cwmgledd 39 E4
Cwmgors 38 E5
Cwmgwrach 39 F5
Cwmifor 38 D3
Cwmisfael 38 B4
Cwmllynfell 38 E4
Cwmorgan 37 G2
Cwmparc 39 G6
Cwmpengraig 37 H2
Cwmsychbant 51 E7
Cwmsymlog 51 G3
Cwmtillery 40 B5
Cwmyoy 40 B3
Cwmystwyth 51 H4
Cwrt 63 G6
Cwrt-y-cadno 38 D1
Cwrt-y-gollen 40 B4
Cwrtnewydd 51 E7
Cyffylliog 76 C6
Cyfronydd 64 B6
Cymer 39 F6
Cymmer 25 H1
Cynghordy 39 F2
Cynheidre 38 B5
Cynwyd 64 D2
Cynwyl Elfed 37 H3

D

Daccombe 7 F4
Dacre, Cumbr 102 A5
Dacre, N Yorks 94 C5
Dacre Banks 94 C5
Daddry Shield 103 E4
Dadford 44 A2
Dadlington 68 C7
Dafen 38 C5
Daffy Green 72 C6
DAGENHAM 33 E2
Daglingworth 42 B5
Dagnall 44 D4
Dail Beag 161 F3
Dail Mòr 161 F3
Daill 125 A6
Dailly 106 E2
Dairsie or Osnaburgh 138 D7
Dalabrog 148 C2
Dalavich 126 D1
DALBEATTIE 109 F6
Dalbeg 144 A2
Dalblair 118 D6
Dalbog 146 C6
Dalbury 67 H3
Dalby, I of M 90 B5
Dalby, Lincs 83 G4
Dalcairnie 107 G2
Dalchalloch 136 E2
Dalchalm 165 F3
Dalchenna 127 E2
Dalchirach 155 F5
Dalchonzie 136 E6
Dalchork 164 B2
Dalchreichart 143 E2
Dalchruin 136 E7
Dalderby 83 E5
Dale 36 C5
Dale Abbey 68 C3
Dale Head 101 J6
Dale of Walls 174 C5
Dalelia 141 G7
Daless 154 C5
Dalfaber 144 D2
Dalgarven 117 G3
Dalgety Bay 129 J4
Dalgig 118 C6
Dalginross 137 E6
Dalguise 137 G4
Dalhalvaig 168 C4
Dalham 59 H5
Daligan 127 H4
Dalivaddy 116 A6
DALKEITH 130 C6
Dallam 77 H2
Dallas 155 F3
Dalleagles 108 C1
Dallinghoo 61 F6
Dallington 22 C4
Dalmadilly 146 E2
Dalmally 135 F6
Dalmarnock 137 G4
Dalmary 128 C3
Dalmellington 107 G2
Dalmeny 129 J5
Dalmigavie 144 B2
Dalmore 154 A2
Dalmorton 107 F2
Dalnabreck 141 F7
Dalnacreich 153 F3
Dalnahaitnach 144 C1
Dalnavie 164 C6
Dalness 135 F3
Dalnessie 164 C2
Dalqueich 129 H2
Dalquhairn 107 F3
Dalreavoch 164 D3
Dalroy 154 B4
Dalry 117 G3
Dalrymple 117 H6
Dalserf 119 F2
Dalston 101 H2
Dalswinton 109 G4
Dalton, D & G 109 J5
Dalton, Lancs 84 C6
Dalton, N Yorks DL11 103 H7
Dalton, N Yorks YO7 95 F4
Dalton, Northum NE18 113 F5
Dalton, Northum NE46 103 F2
Dalton, S Yorks 80 B2
Dalton Piercy 104 D4
DALTON-IN-FURNESS 91 D4
Dalton-le-Dale 104 D3
Dalton-on-Tees 104 B7
Dalveich 136 D6
Dalvennan 107 F1
Dalwhinnie 143 J5
Dalwood 15 J5
Damerham 18 C4
Damgate 73 H6
Damnaglaur 98 C6
Dams of Craigie 147 G2
Danbury 47 H5
Danby 105 G7
Danby Wiske 94 E2
Dandalieth 155 G4
Dandderwen 37 F3
Danderhall 130 C6
Dane End 46 D3
Danebridge 78 D5
Danehill 21 H3
Danesfield 30 C2
Danskine 131 E6
Darenth 33 F3
Daresbury 77 H3
Darfield 87 F6
Dargate 34 D4
Darite 5 F4
DARLASTON 55 E2
Darley 94 C6
Darley Bridge 79 G5
Darley Head 94 C6
Darlingscott 42 E1
DARLINGTON 104 B6
Darliston 66 A3
Darlochan 114 B4
Darlton 80 E4
Darnford 146 E4
Darnick 120 E4
Darowen 64 B6
Darra 156 E4
Darras Hall 113 F5
Darrington 87 F5
Darsham 61 H5
DARTFORD 33 F3
Dartford Crossing 33 F3
Dartington 6 D4
Dartmeet 6 C3
DARTMOUTH 6 E5
Darton 86 E5
DARVEL 118 C4
DARWEN 85 E4
Datchet 30 D3
Datchworth 46 C4
Daugh of Kinermony 155 G4
Dauntsey 28 B2
Dava 154 E5
Davenham 77 J4
DAVENTRY 56 D5
Davidston 154 B2
Davidstow 5 E2
Davington 110 B2
Daviot, Aberd 156 E6
Daviot, Highl 154 B5
Davoch of Grange 156 B3
Dawley 66 B6
DAWLISH 7 F3
Dawlish Warren 7 F3
Dawn 75 H4
Daws Heath 34 B2
Daws House 5 G2
Dawsmere 71 E3
Daylesford 42 E3
Ddôl Cownwy 64 D5
Deadwater 111 F3
DEAL 35 G5
Dean, Cumbr 100 E5
Dean, Devon 6 D4
Dean, Dorset 17 H4
Dean, Hants 19 G4
Dean, Oxon 43 F3
Dean, Somer 27 F6
Dean Prior 6 D4
Dean Row 78 C3
Deanburnhaugh 120 D6
Deane 29 H5
Deanland 17 H4
Deans 129 H6
Deanscales 101 E5
Deanshanger 44 B2
Deanston 128 E2
Dear Hill 104 C4
Dearham 100 E4
Debach 61 F6
Debden 47 F2
Debden Green 47 F2
Debenham 60 E5
Dechmont 129 H5
Deddington 43 G2
Dedham 48 D2
Dedham Heath 48 D2
Dedridge 129 H6
Deene 57 H2
Deenethorpe 57 H2
Deepcar 79 G2
Deepcut 30 D5
Deepdale 93 F3
Deeping Gate 70 B6
Deeping St James 70 B6
Deeping St Nicholas 70 C5
Deerhill 156 B3
Deerhurst 41 H3
Defford 42 B1
Defynnog 39 G3
Deganwy 75 G3
Deighton, N Yorks 95 E1
Deighton, Yk 87 H2
Deiniolen 75 E5
Delabole 4 D2
Delamere 77 H5
Delfrigs 157 G6
Delliefure 155 E5
Delly End 43 F4
Delnabo 145 F2
Delny 154 B1
Delph 86 A6
Delvine 137 J4
Dembleby 69 J3
Den of Lindores 138 B7
DENBIGH 76 C5
Denbury 6 E4
Denby 68 B2
Denby Dale 86 D6
Denchworth 29 F1
Dendron 91 D4
Denend 156 C5
Denford 57 H4
Dengie 48 C5
Denham, Bucks 31 E2
Denham, Suff IP21 61 E4
Denham, Suff IP29 59 H5
Denham Green 31 E2
Denham Street 61 E4
Denhead, Aberd 157 H3
Denhead, Fife 130 D1
Denhead of Arbirlot 139 E4
Denhead of Gray 138 C5
Denholm 121 E6
Denholme 86 B3
Denholme Clough 86 B3
Denmead 19 H4
Denmill 147 F2
Denmore 147 G2
Denmoss 156 D4
Dennington 61 F5
DENNY 129 F4
Dennyloanhead 129 F4
Denshaw 85 H5
Denside 147 F4
Densole 35 F6
Denston 59 H6
Denstone 67 F2
Dent 93 F3
Denton, Cambs 58 B3
Denton, Darl 104 B6
Denton, E Susx 21 H5
DENTON, G Man 78 D2
Denton, Kent 35 F6
Denton, Lincs 69 G3
Denton, N Yorks 86 C2
Denton, Norf 61 F3
Denton, Northnts 57 G6
Denton, Oxon 43 H5
Denver 71 G6
Denwick 123 H6
Deopham 72 D6
Deopham Green 72 D7
Depden 59 H6
Depden Green 59 H6
DEPTFORD, G Lon 32 D3
Deptford, Wilts 18 B2
DERBY 68 B3
Derbyhaven 90 B6
Dergoals 98 D4
Deri 39 J5
Derringstone 35 F6
Derrington 66 D4
Derry Hill 28 B3
Derryguaig 133 G5
Derrythorpe 88 C6
Dersingham 71 G3
Dervaig 133 G3
Derwen 76 C6
Derwenlas 63 H7
DESBOROUGH 57 G3
Desford 68 C6
Detchant 123 F4
Detling 33 H5
Deuddwr 65 F5
Deunant-isaf 76 B5
Devauden 40 D6
Devil's Bridge 51 H4
Devitts Green 55 H2
DEVIZES 28 B4
Devonport 5 H5
Devonside 129 G3
Devoran 3 F4
Dewar 120 C3
Dewartown 130 C6
Dewlish 9 F4
DEWSBURY 86 D4
Dhail bho Dheas 161 H1
Dhoon 90 D4
Dhoor 90 D3
Dhowin 90 D2
Dial Post 21 E4
Dibden 19 F5
Dibden Purlieu 19 F5
Dickens Heath 55 G4
Dickleburgh 60 E3
Didbrook 42 C2
DIDCOT 29 H2
Diddington 58 B5
Diddlebury 53 J3
Didley 40 D2
Didling 20 B4
Didmarton 27 H2
Didsbury 78 C2
Didworthy 6 C4
Digby 82 C6
Digg 150 D2
Diggle 86 B6
Digswell 46 C4
Dihewyd 51 E6
Dilham 73 G4
Dilhorne 67 E2
Dilston 112 D6
Dilton Marsh 27 H6
Dilwyn 53 H6
Dinas, Carm 37 G2
Dinas, Gwyn LL53 62 C3
Dinas, Gwyn LL54 74 D6
Dinas Cross 36 E2
Dinas Mawddwy 64 B5
Dinas Powys 26 A3
Dinchope 53 H3
Dinder 27 E6
Dinedor 41 E2
Dines Green 54 D6
Dingestow 40 D4
Dingley 57 F3
DINGWALL 153 H3
Dinlabyre 110 E3
Dinnet 146 B4
Dinnington, S Yorks 80 C3
Dinnington, Somer 16 C4
Dinnington, T & W 113 G5
Dinorwig 75 E5
Dinton, Bucks 44 B4
Dinton, Wilts 18 B2
Dinwoodie Mains 109 J3
Dinworthy 12 D4
Dippen 116 E5
Dippenhall 30 C6
Dipple, Mor 155 H3
Dipple, S Ayr 106 E2
Diptford 6 D5
Dipton 103 H2
Dirdhu 155 E6
Dirleton 130 E4
Discoed 53 F5
Diseworth 68 C4
Dishes 173 G4
Dishforth 95 E4
Disley 78 D3
DISS 60 E4
Disserth 52 D6
Distington 100 E5
Ditcheat 17 E2
Ditchingham 61 G2
Ditchling 21 G4
Ditteridge 27 H4
Dittisham 6 E5
Ditton, Halt 77 G3
Ditton, Kent 33 H5
Ditton Green 59 G6
Ditton Priors 54 B3
Dixonfield 169 F3
Dixton, Glos 42 B2
Dixton, Monm 40 E4
Dobwalls 5 F4
Doccombe 6 D2
Dochgarroch 153 J4
Docking 71 H3
Docklow 54 A6
Dockray 101 H5
Dodburn 110 D2
Doddinghurst 47 F6
Doddington, Cambs 58 D2
Doddington, Kent 34 C5
Doddington, Lincs 81 G5
Doddington, Northum 123 E4
Doddington, Shrops 54 B4
Doddiscombsleigh 6 E2
Dodford, Northnts 56 E5
Dodford, Worces 54 E4
Dodington 27 G2
Dodleston 77 F5
Dodworth 86 E6
Doe Lea 80 B5
Dog Village 15 F6
Dogdyke 82 E6
Dogmersfield 30 B5
Dol-fôr 64 B6
Dol-y-Bont 51 G3
Dol-y-cannau 53 F7
Dolanog 64 D5
Dolau 52 E5
Dolbenmaen 63 F2
Dolfach 52 C4
Dolfor 52 E3
Dolgarrog 75 G5
DOLGELLAU 63 H5
Dolgoch 63 G6
Dolgran 38 B2
Doll 165 E3
DOLLAR 129 G3
Dolley Green 53 F5
Dolphinholme 84 D1
Dolphinton 119 J3
Dolton 13 F4
Dolwen, Conwy 75 H4
Dolwen, Powys 64 C6
Dolwyddelan 75 G6
Dolyhir 53 F6
Domgay 65 F5
DONCASTER 87 G6
Donhead St Andrew 17 H3
Donhead St Mary 17 H3
Donibristle 129 J4
Donington 70 C3
Donington on Bain 82 E3
Donington South Ing 70 C3
Donisthorpe 68 B5
Donkey Town 30 D4
Donnington, Co of H 41 G2
Donnington, Glos 42 D3
Donnington, Shrops 66 A6
Donnington, Tel & Wrek 66 C5
Donnington, W Berks 29 G4
Donnington, W Susx 20 B5
Donvaston 65 G4
Donyatt 16 B4
Doonfoot 117 H6
Doonholm 117 H6
DORCHESTER, Dorset 9 E4
Dorchester, Oxon 43 H6
Dordon 67 H6
Dore 79 H3
Dores 153 H5
DORKING 31 F5
Dormans Park 32 D6
Dormansland 32 E6
Dormanstown 104 E5
Dormington 41 E1
Dorney 30 D3
Dornie 152 A6
DORNOCH 164 D5
Dornock 110 B6
Dorrery 168 E4
Dorridge 55 G4
Dorrington, Lincs 82 C6
Dorrington, Shrops CW3 66 C2
Dorrington, Shrops SY5 65 H6
Dorsell 146 C2
Dorsington 55 G7
Dorstone 40 C1
Dorton 44 A4
Dorusduain 152 B6
Dosthill 67 H6
Dothan 74 C4
Dottery 8 C4
Doublebois 5 E4
Doughton 27 H1
DOUGLAS, I of M 90 C5
Douglas, S Lanak 119 F4
Douglas and Angus 138 D5
Douglas Water 119 F4
Douglastown 138 D4
Doulting 27 F6
Dounby 172 C4
Doune, Highl IV27 164 A3
Doune, Highl PH22 144 C2
DOUNE, Stir 128 E2
Dounepark 156 E2
Douneside 146 B3
Dounie, Highl IV19 164 C5
Dounie, Highl IV24 164 B4
Dousland 6 B4
Dove Holes 79 E4
Dovecote 40 D3
Dovenby 101 E4
Dovendale 83 F3
DOVER 35 G6
Dovercourt 49 F2
Doverdale 54 D5
Doveridge 67 G3
Dowally 137 H4
Dowdeswell 42 C4
Dowhill 106 E2
Dowland 13 F4
Dowlands 8 A4
Dowlish Wake 16 B4
Down Ampney 42 D6
Down Hatherley 41 H3
Down St Mary 14 D5
Down Thomas 5 J5
Downderry 5 G5
Downe 33 E4
Downend, I of W 11 G5
Downend, W Berks 29 G3
Downfield 138 C5
Downgate 5 G3
Downham, Essex 47 H6
Downham, Lancs 85 F2
Downham, Northum 122 D4
DOWNHAM MARKET 71 G6
Downhead 27 F6
Downholland Cross 84 B6
Downholme 94 C2
Downies 147 G4
Downing 76 D4
Downley 44 C6
Downs 25 J3
Downside 26 D4
Downton, Hants 10 D4
Downton, Wilts 18 C3
Downton on the Rock 53 H4
Dowsby 70 B4
Dowsdale 70 C5
Dowthwaitehead 101 H5
Doxey 66 D4
Doxford Park 104 C2
Doynton 27 G3
Draethen 26 B2
Draffan 119 E3
Dragons Green 21 E3
Drakeland Corner 6 B5
Drakemyre 117 G2
Drakes Broughton 54 E7
Drakewalls 5 H3
Draughton, N Yorks 86 B1
Draughton, Northnts 57 F4
Drax 87 H4
Draycot Cerne 28 B3
Draycote 56 C4
Draycott, Derby 68 C3
Draycott, Glos 42 D2
Draycott, Somer 26 D5
Draycott in the Clay 67 G4
Draycott in the Moors 67 E2
Drayton, C of Port 19 H5
Drayton, Leic 57 G2
Drayton, Norf 73 E5
Drayton, Oxon OX14 43 G6
Drayton, Oxon OX15 43 G1
Drayton, Somer 16 C3
Drayton, Warw 55 G6
Drayton, Worces 54 E4
Drayton Bassett 67 G6
Drayton Parslow 44 C3
Drayton St Leonard 43 H6
Dre-fach, Carm 38 D4
Dre-fach, Cered 51 E7
Dreemskerry 90 D3
Dreenhill 36 D4
Drefach, Carm SA14 38 C4
Drefach, Carm SA44 37 H2
Drefelin 37 H2
Dreggie 155 E6
Dreghorn 117 H4
Drem 130 E5
Dreumasdal 149 C6
Drewsteignton 14 D6
Driby 83 F4
DRIFFIELD, E Yorks 97 F6
Driffield, Glos 42 C6
Drift 2 C5
Drigg 91 B2
Drighlington 86 D4
Drimnin 133 H3
Drimpton 16 C5
Drimsynie 127 F2
Drinisiadar 159 F3
Drinkstone 60 C5
Drinkstone Green 60 C5
Drochaid Lusa 151 F6
Drointon 67 F4
DROITWICH SPA 54 D5
Droman 166 C4
Dron 137 J7
DRONFIELD 79 H4
Dronfield Woodhouse 79 H4
Drongan 118 B6
Dronley 138 C5
Droop 17 F5
Droxford 19 H4
DROYLSDEN 78 C2
Druid 64 D2
Druidston 36 C4
Druimarbin 142 C6
Druimavuic 134 E4
Druimdrishaig 126 B5
Druimindarroch 141 F5
Druimkinnerras 153 G4
Drum, Arg & Bt 126 D5
Drum, Pth & Kin 129 H2
Drumaa Voulin 114 B6
Drumbeg 166 C6
Drumblade 156 C4
Drumblair 156 D4
Drumbuie, D & G 108 C4
Drumbuie, Highl 151 G5
Drumburgh 110 B7
Drumchapel 128 C5
Drumchardine 153 H4
Drumchork 162 C5
Drumclog 118 D4
Drumderfit 154 A3
Drumeldrie 130 D2
Drumelzier 119 J4
Drumfearn 141 F2
Drumgley 138 D3
Drumguish 144 B4
Drumin 155 F5
Drumlassie 146 D3
Drumlemble 114 B5
Drumligair 147 G2
Drumlithie 147 E5
Drummond 153 J2
Drummore 98 C6
Drumnadrochit 153 H5
Drumnagorrach 156 C3
Drumnahive 146 B2
Drumoak 147 E4
Drumore 116 B5
Drumphail 98 D3
Drumrack 131 E2
Drumrash 108 D5
Drumrunie 163 F3
Drums 157 G6
Drumsallie 142 B6
Drumshang 117 G6
Drumsturdy 138 D5
Drumtroddan 99 E5
Drumuie 150 D4
Drumuillie 144 D1
Drumvaich 128 D2
Drumwhindle 157 G5
Drunkendub 139 F4
Drury 77 E5
Dry Doddington 69 G2
Dry Drayton 58 D5
Dry Sandford 43 G5
Dry Street 33 G2
Drybeck 102 C6
Drybridge, Mor 156 B2
Drybridge, N Ayr 117 H4
Drybrook 41 F4
Dryhope 120 B5
Drymen 128 B4
Drymuir 157 G4
Drynoch 150 D5
Dryplaid 146 D7
Dryslwyn 38 C3
Dryton 66 A6
Dubford 157 E2
Dubton 139 E3
Dubwath 101 F4
Duchal Mains 127 H6
Duck End 47 G3
Duck's Cross 58 B6
Duckington 77 G6
Ducklington 43 F5
Duddenhoe End 47 E2
Duddingston 130 B5
Duddington 69 H6
Duddo 123 E3
Duddon 77 H5
Duddon Bridge 91 D3
Dudleston Heath 65 G3
Dudley, T & W 113 G5
DUDLEY, W Mids 55 E2
Duffield 68 B2
Duffryn, Newp 26 C2
Duffryn, Nth Pt Talb 39 F6
DUFFTOWN 155 H5
Duffus 155 F2
Dufton 102 C5
Duggleby 96 D5
Duirinish 151 G5
Duisdalemore 141 G2
Duisky 142 C6
Dukestown 39 J4
DUKINFIELD 78 D2
Dulas 74 D3
Dulcote 27 E6
Dulford 15 G5
Dull 137 F4
Dullatur 128 E5
Dullingham 59 G6
Dulnain Bridge 154 D6
Duloe, Beds 58 B5
Duloe, Corn 5 F5
Dulsie 154 D4
Dulverton 15 F3
Dulwich 32 D3
DUMBARTON 127 H5
Dumbleton 42 C2
Dumcrieff 109 J2
Dumeath 156 B5
Dumfin 127 H4
DUMFRIES 109 G5
Dumgoyne 128 C4
Dummer 29 H6
Dumpford 20 B3
Dun 139 F3
Dùn Chàrlabhaigh 160 E3
Dunalastair 136 E3
Dunan 151 E6
Dunans 126 E3
Dunball 26 C6
DUNBAR 131 F5
Dunbeath 169 F7
Dunbeg 134 C5
DUNBLANE 128 E2
Dunbog 138 B7
Duncanston 153 H3
Duncanstone 156 C6
Dunchideock 6 E2
Dunchurch 56 C4
Duncote 56 E6
Duncow 109 G4
Duncrievie 129 J2
Duncton 20 C4
DUNDEE 138 C5
Dundon 16 C2
Dundonald 117 H4
Dundonnell 163 E5
Dundraw 101 G3
Dundreggan 143 F2
Dundreggan Lodge 143 F2
Dundrennan 100 B3
Dundry 27 E4
Dunecht 146 E3
Dunfallandy 137 G3
DUNFERMLINE 129 J4
Dunfield 42 D6
Dunford Bridge 86 C6
Dungeness 23 G4
Dungworth 79 G2
Dunham on Trent 81 F4
Dunham Town 78 B3
Dunham-on-the-Hill 77 G4
Dunhampton 54 D5
Dunholme 82 C4
Dunino 131 E1
Dunipace 129 F4
Dunira 136 E6
Dunk's Green 33 G5
Dunkeld 137 H4
Dunkerton 27 G5
Dunkeswell 15 H5
Dunkirk 34 D5
Dunlappie 139 E2

Place	Page	Grid
Dunley	54	C5
Dunlop	117	J3
Dunmore, Arg & Bt	116	B1
Dunmore, Falk	129	F4
Dunnet	169	G2
Dunnichen	138	E4
Dunning	129	H1
Dunnington, E Yorks	89	F1
Dunnington, Warw	55	H6
Dunnington, Yk	87	H1
Dunnockshaw	85	G4
Dunollie	134	C5
Dunoon	98	C4
DUNOON	98	C4
Dunragit	127	F5
DUNS	122	C2
Duns Tew	43	G3
Dunsby	70	B4
Dunscore	109	F4
Dunscroft	87	H6
Dunsdale	105	F6
Dunsden Green	30	B3
Dunsfold	20	D2
Dunsford	14	E7
Dunshalt	130	B1
Dunsinnan	138	A5
Dunsley	105	H6
Dunsmore	44	C5
Dunsop Bridge	85	E1
DUNSTABLE	44	E3
Dunstall	67	G4
Dunstall Green	59	H5
Dunstan	123	H5
Dunster	25	G6
Dunston, Lincs	82	C5
Dunston, Norf	73	F6
Dunston, Staffs	66	E5
Dunston, T & W	113	G6
Dunstone, Devon PL8	6	B5
Dunstone, Devon TQ7	6	D6
Dunsville	87	H6
Dunswell	88	E3
Dunsyre	119	H3
Dunterton	5	G3
Dunthrop	43	F3
Duntisbourne Abbots	42	B5
Duntisbourne Leer	42	B5
Duntisbourne Rouse	42	B5
Duntish	17	E5
Duntocher	128	B5
Dunton, Beds	46	C1
Dunton, Bucks	44	C3
Dunton, Norf	72	B3
Dunton Bassett	56	D2
Dunton Green	33	F5
Dunton Wayletts	33	G1
Duntulm	159	J5
Dunure	117	G6
Dunvant	38	C6
Dunvegan	150	B4
Dunwich	61	H4
Durdar	101	J2
Durdie	138	B6
Durgates	22	C2
DURHAM	104	B3
Durisdeer	109	F2
Durisdeermill	109	F2
Durleigh	16	A2
Durley, Hants	19	G4
Durley, Wilts	28	E4
Durnamuck	162	E4
Durness	167	F3
Durno	156	E6
Duror	134	D3
Durran, Arg & Bt	126	D2
Durran, Highl	169	F3
Durrington, W Susx	20	E5
Durrington, Wilts	28	D6
Dursley	41	G6
Durston	16	A3
Durweston	17	G5
Dury	175	F4
Duston	57	F5
Duthil	154	D6
Dutlas	53	F4
Duton Hill	47	G3
Dutton	77	H4
Duxford	59	E7
Dwygyfylchi	75	G4
Dwyran	74	D5
DYCE	147	F2
Dyers Green	58	D7
Dyffryn, Brig	39	F6
Dyffryn, I of Angl	74	B4
Dyffryn Ardudwy	63	F4
Dyffryn Ceidrych	38	E3
Dyffryn Cellwen	39	F5
Dyke, Lincs	70	B4
Dyke, Mor	154	D3
Dykehead, Ang	138	C2
Dykehead, N Lanak	119	F2
Dykehead, Stir	128	C3
Dykelands	146	E7
Dykend	138	B3
Dylife	52	B2
Dymchurch	23	H3
Dymock	41	G2
Dyrham	27	G3
Dysart	130	C3
Dyserth	76	C4
E		
Eadar Dha Fhadhail	160	D4
Eagland Hill	84	C2
Eagle	81	F5
Eagle Moor	81	F5
Eaglescliffe	104	D6
Eaglesfield, Cumbr	101	F5
Eaglesfield, D & G	110	B5
Eaglesham	118	C3
Eairy	90	B5
Eakring	80	D5
Ealand	88	B5
EALING	31	F2
Eamont Bridge	102	B6
EARBY	85	H2
Earcroft	85	E4
Eardington	54	C2
Eardisland	53	H6
Eardisley	53	G7
Eardiston, Shrops	65	G4
Eardiston, Worcs	54	B5
Earith	58	D4
Earl Shilton	56	C2
Earl Soham	61	F5
Earl Sterndale	79	E5
Earl Stonham	60	E6
Earl's Croome	41	H1
Earl's Green	60	D5
Earle	123	E5
Earlestown	77	H2
Earlham	73	F6
Earlish	150	C2
Earls Barton	57	G5
Earls Colne	48	B3
Earls Common	55	E6
Earlsdon	56	B4
EARLSFERRY	130	D3
Earlsford	157	F5
Earlston, E Ayr	117	J4
Earlston, Scot Bord	121	E4
Earlstoun	108	D4
Earlswood, Monm	40	D6
Earlswood, Warw	55	G4
Earnley	20	B6
Earsairidh	148	C5
Earsdon	113	H5
Earshaig	109	H2
Earsham	61	G3
Earswick	95	H6
Eartham	20	C5
Easby	104	E7
Easebourne	20	B3
Easenhall	56	C4
Eashing	30	D6
Easington, Bucks	44	A4
Easington, Durham	104	D3
Easington, E Yorks	89	H5
Easington, Northum	123	G4
Easington, Oxon	44	A6
Easington, Red & Clev	105	G6
Easington Colliery	104	D3
Easington Lane	104	C3
Easingwold	95	G5
Easole Street	35	F5
Eassie	138	C4
East Aberthaw	25	H4
East Allington	6	D6
East Anstey	14	E3
East Ardsley	86	E4
East Ashling	20	B5
East Auchronie	147	F3
East Barkwith	82	D3
East Barming	33	H5
East Barnby	105	G5
EAST BARNET	46	C6
East Barsham	72	C3
East Beckham	72	E2
East Bedfont	31	E3
East Bennan	116	D5
East Bergholt	48	D2
East Bilney	72	C5
East Blatchington	21	H6
East Boldre	11	E3
East Brent	26	C5
East Bridgford	69	E2
East Buckland	14	C2
East Budleigh	7	G2
East Burrafirth	175	E5
East Burton	9	G5
East Butterwick	88	C6
East Cairnbeg	146	E6
East Calder	129	H6
East Carleton	72	E6
East Carlton	57	G3
East Challow	29	F2
East Charleton	6	D6
East Chiltington	21	G4
East Chinnock	16	C4
East Chisenbury	28	D5
East Cholderton	29	E6
East Clandon	31	E5
East Claydon	44	B3
East Coker	16	D4
East Combe	15	H2
East Compton	27	F6
East Cornworthy	6	E5
East Cottingwith	87	J2
East Cowes	11	G4
East Cowick	87	H4
East Cowton	94	E1
East Cramlington	113	G6
East Cranmore	27	F6
East Creech	9	H5
East Croachy	154	A6
East Croftmore	144	D2
East Davoch	146	B3
East Dean, E Susx	22	B6
East Dean, Hants	18	D3
East Dean, W Susx	20	C4
EAST DEREHAM	72	C5
East Down	14	D2
East Drayton	80	E4
East End, Dorset	9	H4
East End, Hants RG20	29	G4
East End, Hants SO41	10	E4
East End, Herts	47	E3
East End, Kent	22	E2
East End, N Som	26	D3
East End, Oxon	43	F4
East End, Suff	48	E2
East Farleigh	33	H5
East Farndon	57	F3
East Ferry	81	F2
East Fortune	131	E5
East Fulwood	128	B6
East Garston	29	F3
East Ginge	29	G2
East Goscote	68	E5
East Grafton	28	E4
EAST GRINSTEAD	21	G2
East Guldeford	23	F3
East Haddon	56	E5
East Hagbourne	29	H2
East Halton	89	F5
EAST HAM	32	E2
East Hanney	43	G6
East Hanningfield	47	H5
East Hardwick	87	F5
East Harling	60	C3
East Harlsey	95	F2
East Harptree	27	E5
East Hartford	113	G5
East Harting	20	A4
East Hatley	58	C6
East Hauxwell	94	C2
East Haven	139	E5
East Heckington	70	B2
East Hedleyhope	103	H3
East Hendred	29	G2
East Heslerton	96	E4
East Hoathly	22	B4
East Hogaland	177	A6
East Horrington	27	E6
East Horsley	31	E5
East Huntspill	26	C6
East Hyde	45	F4
East Ilkerton	24	E6
East Ilsley	29	G2
East Keal	83	F5
East Kennett	28	D4
East Keswick	87	E2
EAST KILBRIDE	118	D2
East Kirkby	83	F5
East Knapton	96	D4
East Knighton	9	G5
East Knoyle	17	G2
East Kyloe	123	F4
East Lambrook	16	C4
East Lamington	164	D6
East Langdon	35	G6
East Langton	57	F2
East Langwell	164	D3
East Lavington	20	C4
East Layton	103	H7
East Leake	68	D4
East Learmouth	122	D4
East Leigh	14	C5
East Lexham	72	B5
East Lilburn	123	F5
EAST LINTON	131	E5
East Liss	20	A3
East Looe	5	F5
East Lound	81	E2
East Lulworth	9	G5
East Lutton	97	E5
East Lydford	16	D2
East Lyng	16	B3
East Mains	146	D4
East Malling	33	H5
East March	138	D5
East Marden	20	B4
East Markham	80	E4
East Marton	85	H1
East Meon	19	H3
East Mere	15	F4
East Mersea	48	D4
East Mey	169	H2
East Midlands Airport	68	C4
East Molesey	31	F4
East Morden	9	H4
East Morton	86	B2
East Ness	96	B4
East Norton	69	F6
East Nynehead	15	H3
East Oakley	29	H6
East Ogwell	6	E3
East Orchard	17	G4
East Ord	123	E2
East Panson	12	D6
East Peckham	33	G6
East Pennard	16	D2
East Perry	58	B5
East Portlemouth	6	D7
East Prawle	6	D7
East Preston	20	D5
East Putford	12	D4
East Quantoxhead	25	J6
East Rainton	104	C3
East Ravendale	82	E2
East Raynham	72	B4
East Rudham	72	B4
East Runton	73	F2
East Ruston	73	G4
East Saltoun	130	D6
East Sleekburn	113	G4
East Somerton	73	H5
East Stockwith	81	E2
East Stoke, Dorset	9	G5
East Stoke, Notts	80	E7
East Stour	17	G3
East Stourmouth	35	F4
East Stratton	19	G2
East Studdal	35	G6
East Taphouse	5	E4
East Thirston	113	F3
East Tilbury	33	G3
East Tisted	19	J2
East Torrington	82	D3
East Tuddenham	72	D5
East Tullyfergus	138	B4
East Tytherley	18	D3
East Tytherton	28	B3
East Village	14	E5
East Wall	53	J2
East Walton	71	H5
East Wellow	18	E3
East Wemyss	130	C3
East Whitburn	129	G6
East Whitefield	138	A5
East Williamston	37	E5
East Winch	71	G5
East Winterslow	18	D2
East Wittering	20	A6
East Witton	94	C3
East Woodburn	112	D4
East Woodhay	29	G4
East Worldham	19	J2
East Worlington	14	D3
East-the-Water	13	E3
EASTBOURNE	22	C6
Eastbridge	61	H5
Eastburn	97	E6
Eastbury, Herts	31	E1
Eastbury, W Berks	29	F3
Eastby	94	B6
Eastchurch	34	C3
Eastcombe	41	H5
Eastcote, G Lon	31	F2
Eastcote, Northnts	56	E6
Eastcote, W Mids	55	G4
Eastcott, Corn	12	C4
Eastcott, Wilts	28	B1
Eastcourt	28	B1
Eastdam	171	E5
Easter Ardross	164	C6
Easter Balgedie	130	A2
Easter Balmoral	145	G4
Easter Boleskine	153	H6
Easter Compton	27	E2
Easter Culfosie	146	E3
Easter Elchies	155	G4
Easter Fearn	164	C5
Easter Galcantray	154	C4
Easter Howgate	130	B6
Easter Kinkell	153	H3
Easter Knox	139	E5
Easter Lednathie	138	C2
Easter Lochend	154	C3
Easter Moniack	153	H4
Easter Ord	147	F3
Easter Quarff	176	D4
Easter Skeld	176	C3
Easter Suddie	154	A3
Easter Whyntie	156	D2
Eastergate	20	C5
Eastern Green	55	H4
Easterton	28	C5
Eastertown	26	C5
Eastfield, N Lanak	129	F6
Eastfield, N Yorks	97	F3
Eastfield Hall	113	G2
Eastgate, Durham	103	F4
Eastgate, Norf	72	E4
Eastham, Mers	77	F4
Eastham, Worcs	54	B5
Easthampstead	30	C4
Easthope	54	A2
Easthorpe	48	C3
Eastington, Devon	14	D4
Eastington, Glos GL10	41	G5
Eastington, Glos GL54	42	D4
Eastleach Martin	42	E5
Eastleach Turville	42	D5
Eastleigh, Devon	13	E3
EASTLEIGH, Hants	19	F4
Eastling	34	C5
Eastney	11	H4
Eastnor	41	G2
Eastoft	88	C5
Easton, Cambs	58	B4
Easton, Cumbr	110	D5
Easton, Devon	14	D7
Easton, Dorset	9	E6
Easton, Hants	19	G2
Easton, Lincs	69	H4
Easton, Norf	72	D5
Easton, Somer	26	E6
Easton, Suff	61	F6
Easton, Wilts	27	H3
Easton Grey	27	H2
Easton Maudit	57	G6
Easton on the Hill	69	J6
Easton Royal	28	E4
Easton- in-Gordano	26	E3
Eastrea	70	C7
Eastriggs	110	B6
Eastrington	88	B4
Eastry	35	G5
Eastshore	176	C6
Eastside	171	E5
Eastville	83	G6
Eastwell	69	F4
Eastwick, Herts	47	E4
Eastwick, Shetld	177	A6
EASTWOOD, Notts	68	C2
Eastwood, S-on-Sea	34	B2
Eastwood, W Yorks	85	H4
Eathorpe	56	B5
Eaton, Ches CW12	78	C5
Eaton, Ches CW6	77	H5
Eaton, Leic	69	F4
Eaton, Norf	73	F6
Eaton, Notts	80	E4
Eaton, Oxon	43	G4
Eaton, Shrops SY6	53	J3
Eaton, Shrops SY9	53	G5
Eaton Bishop	40	D2
Eaton Bray	44	D3
Eaton Constantine	66	B6
Eaton Hall	77	E5
Eaton Hastings	42	E6
Eaton Socon	58	B6
Eaton upon Tern	66	B4
Eavestone	94	D5
Ebberston	96	D3
Ebbesbourne Wake	17	H3
EBBW VALE	40	A5
Ebchester	103	H2
Ebford	7	F2
Ebrington	42	D2
Ecchinswell	29	G5
Ecclaw	131	G6
Ecclefechan	110	A5
ECCLES, G Man	78	B2
Eccles, Kent	33	H4
Eccles, Scot Bord	122	C3
Eccles on Sea	73	H4
Eccles Road	60	D2
Ecclesfield	79	H2
Ecclesgreig	139	G2
Eccleshall	66	D4
Ecclesmachan	129	H5
Eccleston, Ches	77	E5
Eccleston, Lancs	84	D5
Eccleston, Mers	77	G2
Eccup	86	D2
Echt	146	E3
Eckford	121	G5
Eckington, Derby	80	B4
Eckington, Worces	42	B1
Ecton	57	G5
Edale	79	F3
Edburton	21	F4
Edderside	101	F3
Edderton	164	D5
Eddington	35	E4
Eddleston	120	B3
Eden Park	32	D4
Edenbridge	33	E6
Edenfield	85	F5
Edenhall	102	B4
Edenham	70	A4
Edensor	79	B4
Edentaggart	127	H3
Edenthorpe	87	H6
Ederline	126	C2
Edern	62	C3
Edgarley	16	D2
Edgbaston	55	F3
Edgcote	56	D7
Edgcott	44	A3
Edge, Glos	41	H5
Edge, Shrops	65	G6
Edge End	41	E4
Edgebolton	66	A4
Edgefield	72	E3
Edgefield Street	72	D3
Edgeley	65	G5
Edgeworth	42	B5
Edgmond	66	C4
Edgmond Marsh	66	C4
Edgton	53	G3
EDGWARE	31	G1
Edgworth	85	F5
Edinample	136	C6
Edinbane	150	C3
Edinbarnet	128	C5
EDINBURGH	130	B5
Edinburgh Airport	129	J5
Edingale	67	H5
Edingley	80	D6
Edingthorpe	73	G3
Edington, Somer	16	B2
Edington, Wilts	28	B5
Edistone	12	C3
Edith Weston	69	H6
Edithmead	26	C6
Edlesborough	44	D4
Edlingham	113	F2
Edlington	82	D4
Edmondsham	18	B4
Edmondsley	104	B3
Edmondthorpe	69	G5
Edmonstone	173	E4
Edmonton, Corn	4	C3
EDMONTON, G Lon	32	D1
Edmundbyers	103	G3
Ednam	122	C4
Ednaston	67	H2
Edney Common	47	G5
Edradynate	137	F3
Edrom	122	D2
Edstaston	65	J3
Edstone	55	G5
Edvin Loach	54	B6
Edwalton	68	D3
Edwardstone	48	C1
Edwinsford	38	D2
Edwinstowe	80	D5
Edworth	45	G1
Edwyn Ralph	54	B6
Edzell	139	F2
Efail Isaf	25	H2
Efail-rhyd	64	E4
Efailnewydd	62	D3
Efailwen	37	F3
Efenechtyd	76	D6
Effingham	31	F5
Effirth	174	E5
Efford	15	E5
Egerton, G Man	85	F5
Egerton, Kent	34	C6
Egerton Forstal	34	B6
Egerton Green	77	H6
Eggborough	87	G4
Eggesford	44	D3
Eggington	67	H4
Egginton	67	H4
Egglescliffe	104	D6
Eggleston	103	G5
EGHAM	30	E3
Egleton	69	G6
Eglingham	123	G6
Egloshayle	4	D3
Egloskerry	5	F2
Eglwys Cross	65	H2
Eglwys Fach	51	G2
Eglwys- Brewis	25	H4
Eglwysbach	75	H4
Eglwyswen	37	F2
Eglwyswrw	37	F2
Egmanton	80	E5
EGREMONT	100	E6
Egton	105	H7
Egton Bridge	96	D1
Egypt	30	D2
Eight Ash Green	48	C3
Eilanreach	141	H4
Eilean Darach	163	F5
Einacleit	160	E5
Eisgein	159	H1
Eisingrug	63	G3
Elan Village	52	C5
Elberton	27	F2
Elburton	6	B5
Elcho	138	A6
Elcombe	28	D2
Eldernell	70	D7
Eldersfield	41	H2
Elderslie	118	B1
Eldrick	106	E4
Eldroth	93	F5
Eldwick	86	C2
Elford, Northum	123	G4
Elford, Staffs	67	G5
ELGIN	155	G2
Elgol	140	E2
Elham	35	E6
ELIE	130	D2
Elim	74	C3
Eling	18	E4
Eliock	109	E2
Elishader	151	E2
Elishaw	112	C3
Elkesley	80	D4
Elkstone	42	B4
Ellan	154	C6
ELLAND	86	C4
Ellary	126	B5
Ellastone	67	G2
Ellemford	121	G1
Ellen's Green	20	D2
Ellenabeich	134	B7
Ellenhall	66	D4
Ellerbeck	95	F2
Ellerby	105	G6
Ellerdine Heath	66	B4
Elleric	135	E4
Ellerker	88	D4
Ellerton, E Yorks	87	J3
Ellerton, Shrops	66	C4
Ellesborough	44	C5
Ellesmere	65	H3
ELLESMERE PORT	77	F4
Ellingham, Hants	18	C5
Ellingham, Norf	61	G2
Ellingham, Northum	123	G5
Ellingstring	94	C3
Ellington, Cambs	58	B4
Ellington, Northum	113	G3
Ellisfield	29	J6
Ellistown	68	C5
ELLON	157	G5
Ellonby	101	J4
Elloughton	88	D4
Ellwood	41	E5
Elm	71	E6
Elm Park	33	F2
Elmbridge	54	E5
Elmdon, Essex	47	E2
Elmdon, W Mids	55	G3
Elmdon Heath	55	G3
Elmesthorpe	56	C2
Elmhurst	67	G5
Elmley Castle	42	B1
Elmley Lovett	54	D5
Elmore	41	G4
Elmore Back	41	G4
Elmscott	12	C3
Elmsett	60	D7
Elmstead Market	48	D3
Elmsted	34	E6
Elmstone	35	F4
Elmstone Hardwicke	42	B3
Elmswell, E Yorks	97	E6
Elmswell, Suff	60	C5
Elmton	80	C4
Elphin	163	G2
Elphinstone	130	C5
Elrick, Aberd	147	F3
Elrick, Mor	156	B6
Elrig	98	E7
Elrington	112	D3
Elsdon	112	D3
Elsecar	79	H1
Elsenham	47	F3
Elsfield	43	H4
Elsham	88	E5
Elsing	72	D5
Elslack	85	H2
Elstead	30	D6
Elsted	20	B4
Elsthorpe	70	A4
Elstob	104	C5
Elston, Lancs	84	D3
Elston, Notts	69	F2
Elstone	14	C4
Elstow	57	J7
Elstree	45	F6
Elstronwick	89	G3
Elswick	84	C3
Elsworth	58	D5
Elterwater	92	B1
ELTHAM	32	E3
Eltisley	58	C6
Elton, Cambs	58	A2
Elton, Ches	77	G4
Elton, Co of H	53	H4
Elton, Derby	79	G5
Elton, Glos	41	G4
Elton, Notts	69	F3
Elton, Stock on T	104	D6
Elvanfoot	119	G6
Elvaston	68	C3
Elveden	60	B4
Elvingston	130	D5
Elvington, Kent	35	F5
Elvington, Yk	87	J2
Elwick, Hartp	104	D4
Elwick, Northum	123	G4
Elworth	78	B5
Elworthy	15	G2
ELY, Cambs	59	F4
Ely, Card	25	J3
Emberton	57	G7
Embleton, Cumbr	101	F4
Embleton, Northum	123	H5
Embo	165	E4
Emborough	27	F5
Embsay	86	B1
Emeraconart	125	A6
Emery Down	18	D5
Emley	86	D5
Emley Moor	86	D5
Emmer Green	30	B3
Emmington	44	B5
Emneth	71	E6
Emneth Hungate	71	F6
Empingham	69	H6
Empshott	20	A2
EMSWORTH	19	J5
Enborne	29	G4
Enchmarsh	53	J2
Enderby	68	D7
Endmoor	92	D3
Endon	78	D6
ENFIELD	46	D6
Enford	28	D5
Engine Common	27	F2
Englefield	29	J3
Englefield Green	30	D3
English Bicknor	41	E4
English Frankton	65	H4
Englishcombe	27	G4
Engollan	4	B4
Enham- Alamein	29	F6
Enmore	15	J2
Ennerdale Bridge	100	E6
Enochdhu	137	H2
Ensay	133	F4
Ensbury	10	B4
Ensdon	65	H5
Ensis	13	F3
Enstone	43	F3
Enterkinfoot	109	F2
Enville	54	D3
Eòlaigearraidh	148	C4
Eòropaidh	161	J1
Epperstone	68	E2
EPPING	47	E5
Epping Green, Essex	47	E5
Epping Green, Herts	46	C5
Epping Upland	47	E5
Eppleby	103	H6
EPSOM	31	G4
Epwell	43	F1
Epworth	88	B6
Erbistock	65	G2
Erbusaig	151	G6
Erchless Castle	153	G4
Erdington	55	G2
Eredine	126	D2
Eriboll	167	F4
Ericstane	109	H1
Eridge Green	22	B2
Erines	126	C5
ERITH	33	F3
Erlestoke	28	B5
Ermington	6	C5
Erpingham	73	E3
Errogie	153	H6
Errol	138	B6
ERSKINE	128	B5
Erskine Br	128	B5
Ervadale	172	E3
Ervie	98	A3
Erwarton	49	F2
Erwood	39	H1
Eryholme	104	C7
Eryrys	76	E6
Escomb	103	H5
Escrick	87	H2
Esgair	37	H3
Esgairgeiliog	63	H6
Esh	103	H3
Esh Winning	103	H3
ESHER	31	F4
Esholt	86	C2
Eshott	113	G3
Eshton	93	H6
Eskadale	153	G5
Eskbank	130	C6
Eskdale Green	91	C1
Eskdalemuir	110	B3
Eskham	83	F2
Esknish	125	A6
Esprick	84	C3
Essendine	69	J5
Essendon	46	C5
Essich	154	A5
Essington	66	E6
Esslemont	157	G6
Eston	104	E6
Eswick	175	F5
Etal	122	E4
Etchilhampton	28	C4
Etchingham	22	D3
Etchinghill, Kent	23	H2
Etchinghill, Staffs	67	F5
Etherley	103	H5
Ethie Mains	139	F4
ETON	30	D3
Eton Wick	30	D3
Etteridge	144	A4
Ettersgill	103	E5
Ettington	55	H7
Etton, C of Peter	70	B6
Etton, E Yorks	88	D2
Ettrick	120	B6
Ettrickbridge	120	C5
Ettrickdale	127	E6
Ettrickhill	120	B6
Etwall	67	H3
Euston	60	B4
Euxton	84	D5
Evanton	153	J2
Evedon	70	A2

210 Evelix Fyvie

Evelix 164 D4
Evenjobb 53 F5
Evenley 43 H2
Evenlode 42 E3
Evenwood 103 H5
Everbay 173 G4
Evercreech 17 E2
Everdon 56 D6
Everingham 88 C2
Everleigh 28 E5
Everley 97 E3
Eversholt 44 D2
Evershot 16 D5
Eversley 30 B4
Eversley Centre 30 B4
Eversley Cross 30 B4
Everthorpe 88 D3
Everton, Beds 58 C6
Everton, Hants 10 D4
Everton, Notts 80 D2
Evertown 110 C5
Evesbatch 54 B7
EVESHAM 42 C1
Evington 68 E6
Ewart Newtown 123 E4
Ewden Village 79 G2
EWELL 31 G4
Ewell Minnis 35 F6
Ewelme 29 J1
Ewen 42 C6
Ewenny 25 G3
Ewerby 70 B2
Ewerby Thorpe 70 B2
Ewes 110 C3
Ewhurst 20 D1
Ewhurst Green 22 D3
Ewhurst Green 20 D2
Ewloe 77 F5
Eworthy 13 E6
Ewshot 30 C6
Ewyas Harold 40 C3
Exbourne 13 G5
Exbury 11 F3
Exebridge 15 F3
Exelby 94 D3
EXETER 15 F6
Exeter Airport 15 G6
Exeter Cross 6 E3
Exford 14 E2
Exhall, Warw B49 55 G6
Exhall, Warw CV7 56 B3
Exminster 7 F2
EXMOUTH 7 G2
Exnaboe 176 C6
Exning 59 G5
Exton, Devon 7 F2
Exton, Hants 19 H3
Exton, Rut 69 H5
Exton, Somer 15 F2
Eyam 79 G4
Eydon 56 D6
Eye, C of Peter 70 C6
Eye, Co of H 53 H5
EYE, Suff 60 E4
Eye Green 70 C6
EYEMOUTH 123 E1
Eyeworth 58 C7
Eyhorne Street 34 B5
Eyke 61 G6
Eynesbury 58 B6
Eynort 150 C6
Eynsford 33 F4
Eynsham 43 G5
Eype 8 C4
Eyre 150 D3
Eythorne 35 F6
Eyton, Co of H 53 H5
Eyton, Shrops 53 G3
Eyton, Wrex 65 G2
Eyton upon the Weald Moors 66 B5

F

Faccombe 29 F5
Faceby 95 F1
Faddiley 77 H6
Fadmoor 96 B3
Faebait 153 G3
Faerdre 38 D5
Faifley 128 C5
Failand 27 E3
Failford 118 B5
FAILSWORTH 78 D1
Fain 163 F6
Fair Green 71 G5
Fair Oak 19 F4
Fair Oak Green 30 A4
Fairbourne 63 G5
Fairburn 87 F4
Fairfield, Worces B61 55 E4
Fairfield, Worces DY11 54 D4
FAIRFORD 42 D5
Fairlands 30 D5
Fairlie 117 G2
Fairlight 22 E4
Fairlight Cove 23 E4
Fairmile 15 G6
Fairmilehead 130 B6
Fairnington 121 F5
Fairoak 66 C3
Fairseat 33 G4
Fairstead 47 H4
Fairwarp 21 H3
Fairy Cross 13 E3
FAKENHAM 72 C4
Fala 120 D1
Fala Dam 120 D1
Falahill 120 C2
Faldingworth 82 C3
Falfield, Fife 130 D2
Falfield, S Glos 41 F6
Falkenham 49 F2
FALKIRK 129 F4
FALKLAND 130 B2
Falla 121 G6
Fallgate 79 H5
Fallin 129 F3
Falmer 21 G5
FALMOUTH 3 G4
Falstone 111 G4
Fanagmore 166 C5
Fancott 44 E3
Fangdale Beck 95 G2
Fangfoss 88 B1
Fanmore 133 G4
Fans 121 F3
Far Cotton 57 F6
Far Forest 54 C4
Far Gearstones 93 F3
Farcet 58 C2
Farden 54 A4
FAREHAM 19 G5
Farewell 67 F5
Farforth 83 F4
FARINGDON 43 E6
Farington 84 D4
Farlam 111 E7
Farlary 164 D3
Farleigh, N Som 26 D4
Farleigh, Surrey 32 D4
Farleigh Hungerford 27 H5
Farleigh Wallop 29 J6
Farlesthorpe 83 G4
Farleton, Cumbr 92 D3
Farleton, Lancs 92 D5
Farley, Shrops 65 G6
Farley, Staffs 67 F2
Farley, Wilts 18 D3
Farley Green 31 E6
Farley Hill 30 B4
Farleys End 41 G4
Farlington 95 H5
Farlow 54 B3
Farmborough 27 F4
Farmcote 42 C3
Farmington 42 D4
Farmoor 43 G5
Farmtown 156 C3
Farnborough, G Lon 33 E4
FARNBOROUGH, Hants 30 C5
Farnborough, W Berks 29 G2
Farnborough, Warw 56 C7
Farncombe 30 D6
Farndish 57 H5
Farndon, Ches 77 G6
Farndon, Notts 80 E6
Farnell 139 F3
Farnham, Dorset 17 H4
Farnham, Essex 47 E3
Farnham, N Yorks 95 E5
Farnham, Suff 61 G5
FARNHAM, Surrey 30 C6
Farnham Common 30 D2
Farnham Green 47 E3
Farnham Royal 30 D2
Farningham 33 F4
Farnley 86 D2
Farnley Tyas 86 C5
Farnsfield 80 D6
FARNWORTH, G Man 85 F6
Farnworth, Halt 77 G3
Farr, Highl IV1 154 A5
Farr, Highl KW14 167 J3
Farr, Highl PH21 144 C3
Farringdon 15 G6
Farrington Gurney 27 F5
Farsley 86 D3
Farthinghoe 43 H2
Farthingloe 35 F6
Farthingstone 56 E6
Farway 15 H6
Fasach 150 A4
Fascadale 140 E6
Fasnacloich 134 E4
Fasque 146 D6
Fassfern 142 C6
Fatfield 104 B2
Fattahead 156 D3
Faugh 102 B2
Fauldhouse 119 G1
Faulkbourne 47 H4
Faulkland 27 G5
Fauls 66 A3
FAVERSHAM 34 D4
Favillar 155 G5
Fawfieldhead 79 E5
Fawkham Green 33 F4
Fawler 43 F4
Fawley, Bucks 30 B2
Fawley, Hants 11 F3
Fawley, W Berks 29 F2
Fawley Chapel 41 E3
Fawsyde 147 F6
Faxfleet 88 C4
Faygate 21 F2
Fazeley 67 H6
Fearby 94 C3
Fearn 165 E6
Fearn Station 165 E6
Fearnan 136 E4
Fearnbeg 151 G3
Fearnhead 77 J2
Fearnmore 151 G2
Featherstone, Staffs 67 E6
FEATHERSTONE, W Yorks 87 F4
Feaval 172 C4
Feckenham 55 F5
Fedderate 157 F3
Feering 48 B3
Feetham 94 A2
Feizor 93 F5
Felbridge 21 G2
Felbrigg 73 F3
Felcourt 32 D6
Felden 45 E5
Felindre, Carm SA19 38 E3
Felindre, Carm SA32 38 C3
Felindre, Carm SA44 37 H2
Felindre, Powys 52 E3
Felindre, Swan 38 D5
Felindre Farchog 37 F2
Felinfach, Cered 51 F6
Felinfach, Powys 39 H2
Felinfoel 38 C5
Felingwmuchaf 38 C3
Felixkirk 95 F3
Felixkirk Airfield 95 F3
FELIXSTOWE 49 G2
Felkington 123 E3
Fell End 93 F2
Fell Side 101 H4
Felldownhead 5 G2
Felling 113 G6
Felmersham 57 H6
Felmingham 73 F4
Felpham 20 C6
Felsham 60 C6
Felsted 47 G3
FELTHAM 31 F3
Felthorpe 72 E5
Felton, Co of H 54 A7
Felton, N Som 27 E4
Felton, Northum 113 F2
Felton Butler 65 G5
Feltwell 59 H2
Fen Ditton 59 E5
Fen Drayton 58 D5
Fen End 55 H4
Fenay Bridge 86 C5
Fence 85 G3
Fence Houses 104 C2
Fencote 94 D2
Fencott 43 H4
Fenhouses 70 C2
Feniscowles 85 E4
Feniton 15 G6
Feniton Court 15 H6
Fenny Bentley 79 F6
Fenny Bridges 15 H6
Fenny Compton 56 C6
Fenny Drayton 56 B2
Fenny Stratford 44 C2
Fenrother 113 F3
Fenstanton 58 D5
Fenton, C of Stoke 66 D2
Fenton, Cambs 58 D4
Fenton, Lincs LN1 81 F4
Fenton, Lincs NG23 81 F6
Fenton, Northum 123 E4
Fenton Barns 130 E4
Fenwick, E Ayr 118 B3
Fenwick, Northum NE18 112 E5
Fenwick, Northum TD15 123 F3
Fenwick, S Yorks 87 G5
Feochaig 116 B6
Feock 3 G4
Feolin Ferry 125 B6
Ferindonald 141 F3
Feriniquarrie 150 A4
Fern 138 D2
FERNDALE 39 G6
Ferndown 10 B4
Ferness 154 D4
Fernham 29 E1
Fernhill Heath 54 D6
Fernhurst 20 B3
Fernie 138 C7
Ferniegair 118 E2
Fernilea 150 C5
Fernilee 78 E4
Ferrensby 95 E5
Ferriby Sluice 88 D4
Ferring 20 D5
Ferrybridge 87 F4
Ferryden 139 G3
Ferryhill 104 B4
Ferryside 37 H4
Fersfield 60 D3
Fersit 143 F6
Ferwig 50 B6
Feshiebridge 144 C3
Fetcham 31 F5
Fetterangus 157 G3
Fettercairn 146 D6
Fewston 94 C6
Ffair-Rhos 51 H5
Ffairfach 38 D3
Ffaldybrenin 38 D1
Ffarmers 38 D1
Ffawyddog 40 B4
FFESTINIOG 63 H2
Ffordd-las 76 D5
Fforest 38 C5
Fforest-fach 38 D6
Ffoshelyg 51 G5
Ffostrasol 50 D7
Ffridd Uchaf 75 E6
Ffrith 76 E6
Ffynnon-ddrain 37 J3
Ffynnongroyw 76 D3
Fidden 133 F6
Fiddes 147 F5
Fiddington, Glos 42 B2
Fiddington, Somer 26 B6
Fiddleford 17 G4
Fiddlers Green 157 H3
Fiddlers Hamlet 47 E5
Field 67 F3
Field Broughton 92 B3
Field Dalling 72 D3
Field Head 68 C6
Fifehead Magdalen 17 F3
Fifehead Neville 17 F4
Fifield, Oxon 42 E4
Fifield, W&M 30 D3
Fifield Bavant 18 B3
Figheldean 28 D6
Filby 73 H5
FILEY 97 G3
Filgrave 57 G7
Filkins 42 E5
Filleigh, Devon EX17 14 D4
Filleigh, Devon EX32 14 C3
Fillingham 81 G3
Fillongley 55 H3
Filton 27 F3
Fimber 96 D5
Finavon 138 D3
Finchairn 126 D2
Fincham 71 G6
Finchampstead 30 B4
Finchdean 19 J4
Finchingfield 47 G2
FINCHLEY 32 C1
Findern 67 J3
Findhorn 155 E2
Findo Gask 137 H6
FINDOCHTY 156 B2
Findon, Aberd 147 G4
Findon, W Susx 20 E5
Findon Mains 153 J2
Findrassie 155 F2
Finedon 57 H4
Fingal Street 61 F4
Fingask 157 E6
Fingest 30 B1
Finghall 94 C3
Fingland, Cumbr 101 G2
Fingland, D & G 118 E6
Finglesham 35 G5
Fingringhoe 48 D3
Finlarig 136 C5
Finlaystone 127 H5
Finmere 43 J2
Finnart 136 C3
Finningham 60 D5
Finningley 80 D2
Finnygaud 156 D3
FINSBURY 32 D2
Finsthwaite 92 B3
Finstock 43 F4
Finstown 170 D3
Fintry, Aberd 156 E3
Fintry, Stir 128 D4
Finzean 146 D4
Fionnphort 133 F6
Fionsabhagh 159 E4
Fioscabhaig 150 C5
Fir Tree 103 H4
Firbank 93 E2
Firbeck 80 C3
Firgrove 85 H5
Firs Road 18 D2
Firsby 83 G5
First Coast 162 D4
Firth 175 F3
Fishbourne, I of W 11 G4
Fishbourne, W Susx 20 B5
Fishburn 104 C4
Fishcross 129 F3
Fisher's Pond 19 F3
Fisherford 156 D5
Fishermead 44 C2
Fisherstreet 20 C2
Fisherton, Highl 154 B3
Fisherton, S Ayr 117 G6
Fisherton de la Mere 18 B2
Fisherton Industrial Estate 154 B3
FISHGUARD 36 D2
Fishlake 87 H5
Fishleigh Barton 13 F3
Fishpond Bottom 8 B4
Fishpool 85 G6
Fishtoft 70 D2
Fishtoft Drove 70 D2
Fishwick 122 E2
Fiskerton, Lincs 82 C4
Fiskerton, Notts 80 E6
Fittleton 28 D6
Fittleworth 20 D4
Fitton End 71 E5
Fitz 65 H5
Fitzhead 15 H3
Fitzwilliam 87 F5
Fiunary 133 J4
Five Ashes 22 B3
Five Oak Green 33 G6
Five Oaks 20 D3
Five Roads 38 B5
Fivehead 16 B3
Fivelanes 5 F2
Flackwell Heath 30 C1
Fladbury 55 E7
Fladda 177 A5
Fladdabister 176 D4
Flagg 79 F5
Flamborough 97 H4
Flamstead 45 E4
Flansham 20 C5
Flasby 93 H6
Flash 78 E5
Flashader 150 C3
Flaunden 44 E5
Flawborough 69 F2
Flawith 95 F5
Flax Bourton 26 E4
Flaxby 95 E6
Flaxley 41 F4
Flaxpool 15 H2
Flaxton 96 B5
Fleckney 56 E2
Flecknoe 56 D5
Fleet, Dorset 9 E5
FLEET, Hants 30 C5
Fleet, Lincs 70 D4
Fleet Hargate 70 D4
FLEETWOOD 84 B2
Flemingston 25 H3
Flemington 118 D2
Flempton 60 B5
Fleoideabhagh 159 E4
Fletchertown 101 G3
Fletching 21 H3
Flexbury 12 C5
Flexford 30 D6
Flimby 100 E4
Flimwell 22 D2
FLINT 76 E4
Flint Cross 46 E1
Flint Mountain 76 E4
Flintham 69 F2
Flinton 89 G3
Flitcham 71 H4
Flitton 45 E2
Flitwick 45 E2
Flixborough 88 C5
Flixborough Stather 88 C5
Flixton, G Man 78 B2
Flixton, N Yorks 97 F4
Flixton, Suff 61 G3
Flockton 86 D5
Flodaigh 149 D4
Flodden 122 E4
Flodigarry 150 D1
Flookburgh 92 B4
Flordon 73 E7
Flore 56 E5
Flotterton 112 D2
Flowton 60 D7
Flugarth 175 F4
Flushing, Aberd 157 H4
Flushing, Corn TR11 3 G4
Flushing, Corn TR12 3 F5
Flyford Flavell 55 E6
Fobbing 33 H2
Fochabers 155 H3
Fochriw 39 J5
Fockerby 88 C5
Fodderletter 155 F6
Fodderty 153 H3
Foel 64 C5
Foffarty 138 D4
Foggathorpe 88 B3
Fogo 122 C3
Fogorig 122 C3
Fogwatt 155 G3
Foindle 166 C5
Fold Hill 83 G6
Folda 138 A2
Fole 67 F3
Foleshill 56 B3
Folke 17 E4
FOLKESTONE 23 J2
Folkingham 70 A3
Folkington 22 B5
Folksworth 58 B2
Folkton 97 F4
Folla Rule 156 E5
Follifoot 86 E1
Folly Gate 13 F6
Fonthill Bishop 17 H2
Fonthill Gifford 17 H2
Fontmell Magna 17 G4
Fontwell 20 C5
Foodieash 138 C7
Foolow 79 F4
Foots Cray 33 E3
Forbestown 145 H2
Force Forge 92 B2
Forcett 103 H6
Ford, Arg & Bt 126 C2
Ford, Bucks 44 B5
Ford, Devon EX39 13 E3
Ford, Devon TQ7 6 D6
Ford, Glos 42 C3
Ford, Mers 77 F2
Ford, Northum 123 E4
Ford, Shrops 65 H5
Ford, Staffs 79 E6
Ford, W Susx 20 D5
Ford, Wilts SN14 27 H3
Ford, Wilts SP4 18 C2
Ford End, Essex CB11 47 E2
Ford End, Essex CM3 47 G4
Ford Street 15 H4
Fordcombe 22 B1
Fordell 129 J4
Forden 65 F6
Forder Green 6 D4
Fordham, Cambs 59 G4
Fordham, Essex 48 C3
Fordham, Herts 45 G3
Fordham, Norf 71 G7
Fordingbridge 18 C4
Fordington 83 G4
Fordon 97 F4
Fordoun 146 E6
Fordstreet 48 C3
Fordton Mill 14 E6
Fordwells 43 F4
Fordwich 35 E5
Fordyce 156 C2
Foremark 68 B4
Forest Gate 32 E2
Forest Green 31 F6
Forest Head 102 B2
Forest Hill 43 H5
Forest Mill 129 G3
Forest Row 21 H2
Forest Town 80 C5
Forest- in-Teesdale 103 E5
Forestburn Gate 112 E3
Forestside 20 A4
FORFAR 138 D3
Forgandenny 137 H7
Forge 63 H6
Forge Side 40 B5
Forgie 155 H3
Forgue 156 D4
Formal 138 B3
FORMBY 84 B6
Forncett End 60 E2
Forncett St Mary 60 E2
Forncett St Peter 60 E2
Forneth 137 H4
Fornham All Saints 60 B5
Fornham St Martin 60 B5
Fornighty 154 D3
FORRES 155 E3
Forrestfield 129 F6
Forsbrook 67 E2
Forse 169 G6
Forsinard 168 C5
Forston 9 E4
Fort Augustus 143 F3
Fort George 154 B3
FORT WILLIAM 142 D6
Forter 138 A2
Forteviot 137 H7
Forth 119 G2
Forth Road Bridge 129 J5
Forthampton 41 H2
Fortingall 136 E4
Forton, Lancs 84 C1
Forton, Shrops 65 H5
Forton, Somer 16 B5
Forton, Staffs 66 C4
Fortrie, Aberd AB41 157 G4
Fortrie, Aberd AB53 156 D4
FORTROSE 154 B3
FORTUNESWELL 9 E6
Forty Green 44 B5
Forty Hill 46 D6
Forward Green 60 D6
Fosbury 29 F5
Foscot 42 E3
Fosdyke 70 D3
Foss 137 E3
Foss-y-ffin 51 E5
Fossebridge 42 C4
Foster Street 47 E5
Foston, Derby 67 G3
Foston, Lincs 69 G2
Foston, N Yorks 96 B5
Foston on the Wolds 97 F6
Fotherby 83 F2
Fotheringhay 58 A2
Foubister 171 F4
Foul Mile 22 C4
Foulden, Norf 71 H7
Foulden, Scot Bord 122 E2
Foulridge 85 G2
Foulsham 72 D4
Fountainhall 120 D3
Four Ashes 60 D4
Four Crosses, Powys SY21 64 D6
Four Crosses, Powys SY22 65 F5
Four Crosses, Staffs 67 E6
Four Elms 33 E6
Four Forks 15 J2
Four Gotes 71 E5
Four Lanes 3 E4
Four Marks 19 H2
Four Mile Bridge 74 B4
Four Oaks, E Susx 22 E3
Four Oaks, W Mids 67 G7
Four Oaks, W Mids 55 H3
Four Throws 22 D3
Fourlanes End 78 C6
Fourpenny 164 E4
Fourstones 112 C6
Fovant 18 B3
Foveran 157 G6
FOWEY 4 E5
Fowlis 138 C5
Fowlis Wester 137 G6
Fowlmere 58 E7
Fownhope 41 E2
Fox Corner 30 D5
Fox Lane 30 C5
Fox Street 48 D3
Foxcombe Hill 43 G5
Foxcote 42 C4
Foxdale 90 B5
Foxearth 48 B1
Foxfield 91 D3
Foxham 28 B3
Foxhole 4 C5
Foxholes 97 F4
Foxhunt Green 22 B4
Foxley, Norf 72 D4
Foxley, Wilts 27 H2
Foxt 67 F2
Foxton, Cambs 58 E7
Foxton, Durham 104 C5
Foxton, Leic 57 F2
Foxup 93 G4
Foxwist Green 77 J5
Foy 41 F3
Foyers 153 G6
Fraddon 4 C5
Fradley 67 G5
Fradswell 67 E3
Fraisthorpe 97 G5
Framfield 22 A3
Framingham Earl 73 F6
Framingham Pigot 73 F6
FRAMLINGHAM 61 F5
Frampton, Dorset 8 E4
Frampton, Lincs 70 D3
Frampton Cotterell 27 F2
Frampton Mansell 42 B5
Frampton on Severn 41 G5
Frampton West End 70 C2
Framsden 61 F6
Framwellgate Moor 104 B3
Franche 54 D4
Frankby 76 E3
Frankley 55 E3
Frankton 56 C4
Frant 22 B2
FRASERBURGH 157 G2
Frating Green 48 D3
Fratton 11 H3
Freathy 5 H5
Freckenham 59 G4
FRECKLETON 84 C4
Freeby 69 G4
Freeland 43 G4
Freester 175 F5
Freethorpe 73 H6
Freiston 70 D2
Freiston Shore 70 D2
Fremington, Devon 13 F2
Fremington, N Yorks 94 B2
Frenchbeer 6 C2
Frenich 127 J2
Frensham 30 C6
Fresgoe 168 D3
Freshfield 84 A6
Freshford 27 G4
Freshwater 10 E5
Freshwater East 36 E6
Fressingfield 61 F4
Freston 48 E2
Freswick 169 H3
Fretherne 41 G5
Frettenham 73 F5
Freuchie 130 B2
Freystrop 36 D4
Friar's Gate 21 H2
Friday Bridge 71 E6
Friday Street 22 C5
Fridaythorpe 96 D6
FRIERN BARNET 32 C1
Friesland 132 D3
Friesthorpe 82 C3
Frieth 30 B1
Frilford 43 G6
Frilsham 29 H3
FRIMLEY 30 C5
Frindsbury 33 H4
Fring 71 H3
Fringford 43 J3
Frinsted 34 B5
FRINTON-ON-SEA 49 F3
Friockheim 139 E4
Frisby on the Wreake 69 E5
Friskney 83 G6
Friskney Eaudyke 83 G6
Friskney Tofts 83 G6
Friston, E Susx 22 B6
Friston, Suff 61 H5
Fritchley 79 H6
Frith Bank 70 D2
Frith Common 54 B5
Fritham 18 D4
Frithelstock 13 E4
Frithelstock Stone 13 E4
Frithville 83 F6
Frittenden 34 B6
Fritton, Norf NR15 61 F2
Fritton, Norf NR31 73 H6
Fritwell 43 H3
Frizington 100 E6
Frocester 41 G5
Frodesley 65 J6
FRODSHAM 77 H4
Frog Pool 54 D5
Froggatt 79 G4
Froghall 67 F2
Frogham 18 C4
Frogmore, Devon 6 D6
Frogmore, Hants 30 C4
Frogmore, Herts 45 F5
Frogpool 3 F4
Frolesworth 56 D2
FROME 27 G6
Frome St Quintin 8 D3
Fromes Hill 54 B7
Fron, Gwyn 62 D2
Fron, Powys LD1 52 D5
Fron, Powys SY21 65 F6
Froncysyllte 65 F2
Frongoch 64 C3
Frostenden 61 H3
Frosterley 103 G4
Frotoft 172 E4
Froxfield 29 E4
Froxfield Green 19 J3
Fryerning 47 G5
Fryster 169 F3
Fryton 96 B4
Fulbeck 81 G6
Fulbourn 59 F6
Fulbrook 42 E4
Fulford, Somer 15 J3
Fulford, Staffs 67 E3
Fulford, Yk 87 H2
FULHAM 32 C3
Fulking 21 F4
Full Sutton 96 C6
Fuller Street 47 H4
Fuller's Moor 77 H6
Fullerton 19 E2
Fulletby 83 E4
Fullwood 118 B2
Fulmer 30 E2
Fulmodeston 72 C3
Fulnetby 82 C4
Fulready 55 H7
Fulstow 83 F2
Fulwell, Oxon 43 F3
Fulwell, T & W 113 H7
FULWOOD, Lancs 84 D3
Fulwood, S Yorks 79 H3
Fundenhall 60 E2
Funtington 20 A5
Funtley 19 G5
Funzie 177 D4
Furley 16 A5
Furnace, Arg & Bt 126 E3
Furnace, Cered 51 G2
Furness Vale 78 E3
Furneux Pelham 47 E3
Furzebrook 9 H5
Furzehill 24 E6
Furzey Lodge 10 E3
Fyfett 15 J4
Fyfield, Essex 47 F5
Fyfield, Glos 42 E5
Fyfield, Hants 29 E6
Fyfield, Oxon 43 G6
Fyfield, Wilts 28 D4
Fylingthorpe 97 E1
Fyvie 156 E5

G

Place	Page	Grid
Gabhsann bho Dheas	161	H2
Gabhsann bho Thuath	161	H2
Gablon	164	D4
Gabroc Hill	118	B2
Gaddesby	69	E5
Gadfa	74	D3
Gaer	40	A3
Gaer- fawr	40	D6
Gaerllwyd	74	D4
Gaerwen	43	G3
Gagingwell	66	E5
Gailey	103	H6
Gainford	81	F2
GAINSBOROUGH	47	H2
Gainsford End	110	B2
Gair	110	B2
Gairloch	162	D5
Gairlochy	142	D5
Gairney Bank	129	J3
Gaisgill	93	E1
Gaitsgill	101	H3
GALASHIELS	120	D4
Galby	69	E6
Galgate	92	C6
Galhampton	17	E3
Gallachoille	126	B4
Gallanach, Arg & Bt PA34	134	C6
Gallanach, Arg & Bt PA78	132	E2
Gallatown	130	B3
Galley Common	56	B2
Galleywood	47	H5
Gallowfauld	138	D4
Gallowstree Common	30	A2
Galltair	141	H1
Galmisdale	140	D6
Galmpton, Devon	6	C6
Galmpton, Tbay	7	E5
Galphay	94	D4
GALSTON	118	C4
Galtrigill	150	A3
Gamble's Green	47	H4
Gamblesby	102	C4
Gamesley	78	E2
Gamlingay	58	C6
Gammaton	13	E3
Gammersgill	94	B3
Gamston, Notts DN22	80	E4
Gamston, Notts NG2	68	E3
Ganarew	40	E4
Ganavan	134	C5
Ganllwyd	63	H4
Gannochy	146	C6
Gansclet	169	H5
Ganstead	89	F3
Ganthorpe	96	B4
Ganton	97	E4
Gaodhail	133	J5
Garbat	153	G2
Garbhallt	126	E3
Garboldisham	60	D3
Gardenstown	157	E2
Garderhouse	176	C3
Gare Hill	17	F1
Garelochhead	127	G3
Garford	43	G6
GARFORTH	87	F3
Gargrave	93	H6
Gargunnock	128	E3
Garlieston	99	F5
Garlogie	147	E3
Garmond	157	F3
Garmony	134	A4
Garmouth	155	H2
Garn	62	C3
Garn-yr-erw	40	B4
Garnant	38	D4
Garndolbenmaen	63	E2
Garnett Bridge	92	D2
Garnkirk	128	D5
Garpel	118	D5
Garra Eallabus	124	B3
Garrabost	161	J4
Garraburn	156	B3
Garrachra	127	E4
Garraron	126	C2
Garras	3	F5
Garreg	63	G2
Garreg Bank	65	F5
Garrick	129	F1
Garrigill	102	D3
Garroch	108	C4
Garros	150	D2
Garrow	137	F4
Garrygualach	142	D3
Garryhorn	108	C3
Garsdale	93	F3
Garsdale Head	93	F2
Garsdon	28	B2
Garshall Green	67	E3
Garsington	43	H5
Garstang	84	C2
GARSTON	77	G3
Garswood	77	H1
Gartachoil	128	C3
Gartbreck	124	B5
Gartcosh	128	D6
Garth, Brig	25	F1
Garth, I of M	90	C5
Garth, Powys	52	C7
Garth, Shetld	174	D5
Garth, Wrex	65	F2
Garthatra	124	C4
Garthbrengy	39	H2
Gartheli	51	F6
Garthmyl	65	E7
Garthorpe, Leic	69	G4
Garthorpe, N Linc	88	C5
Gartly	156	C5
Gartmore	128	C3
Gartnagrenach	116	C2
Gartness, N Lanak	128	E6
Gartness, Stir	128	C4
Gartocharn	128	B2
Garton	89	G3
Garton-on- the-Wolds	97	E6
Gartymore	165	G2
Garvald	131	E5
Garvard	125	A3
Garve	153	F2
Garvestone	72	D6
Garvock, Aberd	146	E6
Garvock, Inver	127	G5
Garwaldwaterfoot	110	B2
Garway	40	D3
Garway Hill	40	D3
Gask	157	H2
Gass	107	G2
Gastard	27	H4
Gasthorpe	60	C3
Gatcombe	11	F5
Gate Burton	81	F3
Gate Helmsley	96	B6
Gatebeck	92	D3
Gateford	80	C3
Gateforth	87	G4
Gatehead	117	H4
Gatehouse	111	G4
GATEHOUSE OF FLEET	99	G4
Gatelawbridge	109	G3
Gateley	72	C4
Gatenby	94	E3
GATESHEAD	113	G6
Gatesheath	77	G5
Gateside, Aberd	146	D2
Gateside, Ang	138	D4
Gateside, E Renf	118	B2
Gateside, Fife	130	A2
Gateside, N Ayr	117	H2
Gathurst	84	D6
GATLEY	78	C3
Gattonside	121	E4
Gaufron	52	D5
Gauldry	138	C6
Gauls	137	H5
Gaunt's Common	18	B5
Gauntons Bank	66	A2
Gautby	82	D4
Gavinton	122	C2
Gawber	86	E6
Gawcott	44	A2
Gawsworth	78	C5
Gawthrop	93	E3
Gawthwaite	92	A3
Gay Street	20	D3
Gaydon	56	B6
Gayfield	172	E1
Gayhurst	57	G7
Gayle	93	G3
Gayles	103	H7
Gayton, Mers	76	E3
Gayton, Norf	71	H5
Gayton, Northnts	57	F6
Gayton, Staffs	67	E4
Gayton le Marsh	83	G3
Gayton Thorpe	71	H5
Gaywood	71	G4
Gazeley	59	H5
Gearraidh Bhaird	161	G5
Geàrraidh ma Mònadh	148	C3
Gearraidh na h-Aibhne	161	F4
Geary	150	B2
Geddes	60	C6
Gedding	57	G3
Geddington	57	G3
Gedintailor	151	E5
Gedney	70	E4
Gedney Broadgate	70	E4
Gedney Drove End	71	E4
Gedney Dyke	70	E4
Gedney Hill	70	D5
Gee Cross	78	D2
Geilston	127	H5
Geirinis	149	C5
Geise	169	F3
Geisiader	160	E4
Geldeston	61	G2
Gell, Conwy	75	H5
Gell, Gwyn	63	E2
Gelli	37	E4
Gellifor	76	D5
Gelligaer	39	J6
Gellilydan	63	G3
Gellioedd	64	C2
Gellyburn	137	H5
Gellywen	37	G3
Gelston	108	E7
Genoch Mains	98	C4
Gentleshaw	67	F5
Geocrab	159	F3
George Nympton	14	D3
Georgeham	13	E2
Georgia	2	C4
Germansweek	13	E6
Germoe	2	D5
Gerrans	3	G4
GERRARDS CROSS	30	D2
Gestingthorpe	48	B2
Geuffordd	65	F5
Geufron	52	B3
Gibbieston	137	H5
Gibraltar, Bucks	44	B4
Gibraltar, Lincs	83	H6
Gidea Park	33	F2
Gidleigh	14	C7
Gifford	130	E6
Giffordland	117	G3
Giffordtown	130	B1
Giggleswick	93	G5
Gilberdyke	88	C4
Gilchriston	130	D6
Gilcrux	100	E4
Gildersome	86	D4
Gildingwells	80	C3
Gileston	25	H4
Gilfach Goch	25	G2
Gilfachreda	50	E6
Gilgarran	100	E5
Gill	117	G3
Gill of Garth	171	E4
Gill's Green, Kent TN17	22	D2
Gill's Green, Kent TN18	22	D2
Gillamoor	96	B2
Gillan	3	F5
Gillen	150	B3
Gilling East	95	H4
Gilling West	94	C1
GILLINGHAM, Dorset	17	G3
GILLINGHAM, Med	33	H4
Gillingham, Norf	61	H2
Gillow Heath	78	C6
Gills	169	H2
Gills Green	120	C5
Gilmanscleuch	119	H2
Gilmerton, C of Edin	130	B6
Gilmerton, Pth & Kin	137	F6
Gilmilnscroft	118	C5
Gilmonby	103	F6
Gilmorton	56	D3
Gilsland	111	H6
Gilsland Spa	111	H6
Gilson	56	D2
Gilston, Herts	47	E4
Gilston, Scot Bord	120	D2
Gilston Park	47	E4
Gilwern	40	B4
Gimingham	73	F3
Giosla	160	E5
Gipping	60	D5
Gipsey Bridge	83	E7
Girlsta	175	F5
Girsby	104	C7
Girthon	99	H4
Girton, Cambs	58	E6
Girton, Notts	81	F5
GIRVAN	106	D3
Gisburn	85	G2
Gisleham	61	J3
Gislingham	60	D4
Gissing	60	E3
Gittisham	15	H6
Gladestry	53	F6
Gladsmuir	130	D5
Glais	38	E5
Glaisdale	96	C1
Glame	151	E4
Glamis	138	C4
Glan Conwy	75	H6
Glan Denys	51	F6
Glan-y-don	76	D4
Glan-yr-afon, Gwyn LL21	64	C2
Glan-yr-afon, Gwyn LL23	64	C2
Glanaman	38	D4
Glandford	72	D2
Glandwr, Caer	40	B5
Glandwr, Pemb	37	F3
Glandy Cross	37	F3
Glangrwyney	40	B4
Glanmule	52	E2
Glanrhyd	37	F1
Glanton	123	F6
Glanton Pyke	123	F6
Glanvilles Wootton	17	E5
Glapthorn	57	J2
Glapwll	80	B5
Glas-allt-Shiel	145	G5
Glasbury	40	A2
Glaschoil	155	E5
Glascoed, Denb	76	B4
Glascoed, Monm	40	C5
Glascoed, Powys	64	E6
Glascorrie	146	B4
Glascote	67	H6
Glascwm	52	E6
Glasdrum	134	E4
Glasfryn	76	B6
GLASGOW	128	C6
Glasgow International Airport	128	B6
Glasgow Prestwick International Airport	117	H5
Glashvin	150	D2
Glasinfryn	75	E5
Glasnakille	141	E2
Glaspwll	63	H7
Glassburn	153	F5
Glasserton	99	F6
Glassford	118	E3
Glasshouse Hill	41	G3
Glasshouses	94	C5
Glasslaw	157	F3
Glasslie	130	B2
Glasson, Cumbr	110	B6
Glasson, Lancs	92	C6
Glassonby	102	B4
Glasterlaw	139	E3
Glaston	69	G6
GLASTONBURY	16	C2
Glatton	58	B3
Glazebury	78	A2
Glazeley	54	C3
Gleadless	79	H3
Gleadsmoss	78	C5
Gleann Dail bho Dheas	148	C3
Gleann dail bho Tuath	148	C3
Gleann Tholastaidh	161	J3
Gleaston	91	D4
Glecknabae	126	E6
Glemsford	60	B7
Glen, D & G DG2	109	F5
Glen, D & G DG7	99	G4
Glen Auldyn	90	D3
Glen Bernisdale	150	D4
Glen Mona	90	D4
Glen of Newmill	156	B3
Glen Parva	68	D7
Glen Rossal	164	A3
Glen Sluain	127	E3
Glen Village	129	F5
Glen Vine	90	C5
Glenancross	141	F4
Glenarm	138	C2
Glenastle	124	C6
Glenbarr	114	B3
Glenbeg, Highl PH26	154	E6
Glenbeg, Highl PH36	133	H2
Glenbervie	146	E5
Glenboig	128	E6
Glenborrodale	133	J2
Glenbranter	127	F3
Glenbreck	119	H5
Glenbuck	118	E5
Glenburn	118	B1
Glencaple	109	G6
Glencarse	138	A6
Glencat	146	C4
Glenceitlein	135	E4
Glencoe	135	E3
Glencraig	130	A3
Glencrosh	108	E4
Glendevon	129	G2
Glendoebeg	143	G3
Glendoick	138	B6
Glendoune	106	D3
Glenduckie	138	B7
Glenegedale	124	C5
Glenelg	141	H2
Glenfarg	129	J1
Glenfield	68	D6
Glenfinnan	142	B5
Glenfoot	138	A7
Glengarnock	117	H2
Glengennet	106	E3
Glengolly	169	F3
Glengorm Castle	133	G1
Glengrasco	150	D4
Glenhoul	108	D4
Glenkerry	120	B6
Glenkindie	146	B2
Glenlair	108	E5
Glenlatterach	155	G3
Glenlean	127	E4
Glenlee, Ang	146	B6
Glenlee, D & G	108	D4
Glenlichorn	129	E1
Glenlivet	155	F6
Glenlochar	108	E6
Glenluce	98	D4
Glenmallan	127	G3
Glenmavis	128	E6
Glenmaye	90	B5
Glenmidge	109	F4
Glenmooar	90	B4
Glenmore, Arg & Bt PA20	126	E6
Glenmore, Arg & Bt PA34	126	C1
Glenmore, Highl	150	D4
Glenmoy	138	D2
Glenochar	119	G6
Glenogil	138	D2
Glenprosen Village	138	C2
Glenquiech	138	D2
Glenralloch	126	C6
Glenrazie	99	E3
Glenreasdell Mains	116	C2
Glenridding	101	H6
GLENROTHES	130	B2
Glensaugh	146	D6
Glenstriven	127	E5
Glentham	81	H2
Glenton	146	D1
Glentress	120	B4
Glentrool Village	107	F5
Glentruan	90	D2
Glentworth	81	G3
Glenuig	141	F6
Glenurquhart	154	B2
Glespin	119	F5
Gletness	175	F5
Glewstone	41	E3
Glinton	70	B6
Glooston	57	F2
Glororum	123	G4
GLOSSOP	78	E2
Gloster Hill	113	G2
GLOUCESTER	41	H4
Gloucestershire Airport	41	H3
Gloup	177	C3
Glusburn	86	B2
Gluss	175	E3
Glutt	168	C6
Glympton	43	G3
Glyn - neath	39	F5
Glyn Ceiriog	65	F3
Glynarthen	50	D7
Glyncoch	25	H1
Glyncorrwg	39	F6
Glynde	21	H5
Glyndebourne	21	H4
Glyndyfrdwy	64	E2
Glynllan	25	G2
Glynogwr	25	G2
Glyntaff	25	H2
Glyntawe	39	F4
Glyntwymyn	64	B6
Gnosall	66	D4
Gnosall Heath	66	D4
Goadby	69	F7
Goadby Marwood	69	F4
Goatacre	28	C3
Goathill	17	E4
Goathland	96	D1
Goathurst	16	A2
Gobhaig	158	E2
Gobowen	65	G3
GODALMING	30	D6
Godington	43	J3
GODMANCHESTER	58	C4
Godmanstone	9	E4
Godmersham	34	D5
Godney	26	D6
Godolphin Cross	2	E4
Godolphin House	2	E4
Godshill, Hants	18	C4
Godshill, I of W	11	G5
Goff's Oak	46	D5
Gogar	130	A5
Gogarth	75	G3
Goginan	51	G3
Golan	63	F2
Golant	4	E5
Golberdon	5	G3
GOLBORNE	77	H2
Golcar	86	C5
Goldcliff	26	C2
Golden Cross	22	B4
Golden Green	33	G6
Golden Grove	38	C4
Golden Pot	30	B6
Golden Valley	41	J3
Goldenhill	78	C6
Golders Green	32	C2
Goldfinch Bottom	29	H4
Goldhanger	48	C5
Golding	65	J6
Goldsborough, N Yorks HG5	95	E6
Goldsborough, N Yorks YO21	105	H6
Goldsithney	2	D4
Goldthorpe	87	F6
Goldworthy	12	D3
Gollanfield	154	C3
Golspie	165	E4
Golval	168	C3
Gomeldon	18	C2
Gomersal	86	D4
Gomshall	31	E6
Gonalston	68	E2
Gonfirth	175	E4
Good Easter	47	G4
Gooderstone	71	H6
Goodleigh	13	G2
Goodmanham	88	C2
Goodnestone, Kent CT3	35	F5
Goodnestone, Kent ME13	34	D4
Goodrich	41	E4
Goodrington	7	E5
GOODWICK	36	D2
Goodworth Clatford	29	F6
Goodyers End	56	B3
GOOLE	88	B4
Goonbell	3	F3
Goonhavern	3	F4
Gooseham	12	C4
Goosey	29	F1
Goosnargh	84	D3
Goostrey	78	B5
Gordieston	109	F4
Gordon	121	F3
Gordonbush	165	E3
Gordonstown, Aberd AB45	156	C3
Gordonstown, Aberd AB51	156	E6
Gorebridge	120	C1
Gorefield	70	E5
Goring	29	J2
Goring-by-Sea	20	E5
Gorleston-on-Sea	73	J6
Gorrachie	156	E3
Gorran Churchtown	4	D6
Gorran Haven	4	D6
Gors	51	G4
Gorsedd	76	D4
GORSEINON	38	C6
Gorseness	172	E5
Gorsgoch	51	E6
Gorslas	38	C4
Gorsley	41	F3
Gorsley Common	41	F3
Gorstan	153	F3
Gortantaoid	125	A5
Gorton	78	C2
Gosbeck	60	E6
Gosberton	70	B4
Gosberton Clough	70	B4
Gosfield	47	H4
Gosforth, Cumbr	91	B1
Gosforth, T & W	113	G6
Gosmore	45	F3
GOSPORT	11	H4
Gossabrough	177	C5
Goswick	123	F3
Gotham	68	D3
Gotherington	42	B3
Gott	176	D3
Goudhurst	22	D2
Goulceby	83	E4
Gourdas	157	E3
Gourdon	147	F6
GOUROCK	127	G5
Govan	128	C6
Goveton	6	D6
Govilon	40	B4
Gowanhill	157	H2
Gowdall	87	H4
Gowerton	38	C6
Goxhill, E Yorks	89	F2
Goxhill, N Linc	89	E4
Goxhill Haven	89	F4
Grabhair	161	G6
Graby	70	B4
Graemeshall	171	E4
Graffham	20	C4
Grafham, Cambs	58	C5
Grafham, Surrey	30	D6
Grafton, Co of H	40	D2
Grafton, N Yorks	95	F5
Grafton, Oxon	42	E5
Grafton, Worcs	54	A5
Grafton Flyford	55	E6
Grafton Regis	57	F7
Grafton Underwood	57	H3
Grafty Green	34	B6
Graianrhyd	76	E6
Graig, Conwy	75	H4
Graig, Denb	76	C4
Graig Penllyn	25	G3
Graig-fechan	76	D6
Grain	34	B3
Grains o' th' Beck	103	E5
Grainsby	83	E2
Grainthorpe	83	F2
Graizelound	80	E2
Gramasdail	149	D4
Grampound	4	C6
Grampound Road	4	C5
Granby	69	F3
Granborough	44	B3
Grandborough	56	C5
Grandtully	137	G3
Grange, Cumbr	101	G6
Grange, Med	33	H4
Grange, Mers	76	E3
Grange, Pth & Kin	138	B6
Grange Crossroads	156	B3
Grange Hill	33	E1
Grange Moor	86	D5
Grange of Lindores	138	B7
GRANGE-OVER-SANDS	92	C4
Grangemill	79	G6
Grangepans	129	H4
Grangetown	104	E5
Granish	144	C2
Gransmoor	97	G6
Granston	36	C2
Grantchester	59	E6
GRANTHAM	69	H3
Grantlodge	146	E2
Granton	130	B5
GRANTOWN-ON-SPEY	155	E6
Grantshouse	131	H6
Grappenhall	77	J3
Grasby	89	E6
Grasmere	101	H7
Grasscroft	86	A6
Grassendale	77	G3
Grassholme	103	F5
Grassington	94	B5
Grassmoor	79	J5
Grassthorpe	81	E5
Grateley	29	E6
Gratwich	67	F3
Graveley, Cambs	58	C5
Graveley, Herts	46	C3
Gravelly Hill	55	F2
Gravels	65	G7
GRAVESEND	33	G3
Graven	175	F3
Graveney	34	D4
Grayingham	81	G2
Grayrigg	92	D2
GRAYS	33	G3
Grayshott	20	B2
Grayson Green	100	D5
Grayswood	20	C2
Graythorp	104	E5
Grazeley	30	A4
Greasbrough	80	B2
Greasby	76	E3
Great Abington	59	F7
Great Addington	57	H4
Great Alne	55	G6
Great Altcar	84	B6
Great Amwell	46	D4
Great Asby	102	C6
Great Ashfield	60	C5
Great Ayton	104	E6
Great Baddow	47	H5
Great Bardfield	47	G2
Great Barford	58	B6
Great Barr	55	F2
Great Barrington	42	E4
Great Barrow	77	G5
Great Barton	60	B5
Great Barugh	96	C4
Great Bavington	112	D4
Great Bealings	61	F7
Great Bedwyn	29	E4
Great Bentley	48	E3
Great Bircham	71	H3
Great Blakenham	60	E6
Great Bolas	66	B4
Great Bookham	31	F5
Great Bosullow	2	C4
Great Bourton	56	C7
Great Bowden	57	F3
Great Bradley	59	G6
Great Braxted	48	B4
Great Bricett	60	D6
Great Brickhill	44	D2
Great Bridgeford	66	D4
Great Brington	56	E5
Great Bromley	48	D3
Great Broughton, Cumbr	100	E4
Great Broughton, N Yorks	104	E7
Great Budworth	78	A4
Great Burdon	104	C6
Great Burstead	33	H1
Great Busby	95	G1
Great Canfield	47	F4
Great Canney	48	B5
Great Carlton	83	G3
Great Casterton	69	J6
Great Chart	34	C6
Great Chatwell	66	C5
Great Chesterford	47	F1
Great Cheverell	28	B5
Great Chishill	46	E1
Great Clacton	48	E4
Great Clifton	100	E5
Great Coates	89	E5
Great Comberton	42	B1
Great Corby	102	A2
Great Cornard	48	B1
Great Coxwell	42	E6
Great Cransley	57	G4
Great Cressingham	72	B6
Great Crosby	77	F2
Great Cubley	67	G3
Great Dalby	69	F5
Great Doddington	57	G5
Great Dunham	72	B5
GREAT DUNMOW	47	G3
Great Durnford	18	C2
Great Easton, Essex	47	G3
Great Easton, Leic	57	G2
Great Eccleston	84	C2
Great Edstone	96	C3
Great Ellingham	60	D2
Great Elm	27	G6
Great Eversden	58	D6
Great Fencote	94	D2
Great Finborough	60	D6
Great Fransham	72	B5
Great Gaddesden	44	E4
Great Gate	67	F2
Great Gidding	58	B3
Great Givendale	88	C1
Great Glemham	61	G5
Great Glen	68	E7
Great Gonerby	69	G3
Great Gransden	58	C6
Great Green	60	C6
Great Habton	96	C4
Great Hale	70	B2
Great Hallingbury	47	F4
Great Hampden	44	C5
Great Harrowden	57	G4
GREAT HARWOOD	85	F3
Great Haseley	43	J5
Great Hatfield	89	F2
Great Hautbois	73	F4
Great Haywood	67	F4
Great Heck	87	G4
Great Henny	48	B2
Great Hinton	28	B5
Great Hockham	60	C2
Great Holland	49	F4
Great Horkesley	48	C2
Great Hormead	46	E3
Great Horwood	44	B2
Great Houghton, Northnts	57	F6
Great Houghton, S Yorks	87	F6
Great Hucklow	79	F4
Great Kelk	97	G6
Great Kimble	44	C5
Great Kingshill	44	C6
Great Langton	94	D2
Great Leighs	47	H4
Great Limber	89	F6
Great Linford	44	C1
Great Livermere	60	B4
Great Longstone	79	G4
Great Lumley	104	B3
Great Lyth	65	H6
GREAT MALVERN	54	C7
Great Maplestead	48	B2
Great Marton	84	B3
Great Massingham	71	H4
Great Milton	43	J5
Great Missenden	44	C5
Great Mitton	85	F3
Great Mongeham	35	G5
Great Moulton	60	E2
Great Munden	46	D3
Great Musgrave	102	D6
Great Ness	65	G5
Great Notley	47	H3
Great Oakley, Essex	49	E3
Great Oakley, Northnts	57	G3
Great Offley	45	F3
Great Ormside	102	D6
Great Orton	101	H2
Great Ouseburn	95	F5
Great Oxendon	57	F3
Great Palgrave	72	B5
Great Parndon	47	E5
Great Paxton	58	C5
Great Plumstead	73	G5
Great Ponton	69	H3
Great Preston	87	F4
Great Raveley	58	C3
Great Rissington	42	D4
Great Rollright	43	F2
Great Ryburgh	72	C4
Great Ryle	123	F6
Great Ryton	65	H6
Great Saling	47	H3
Great Salkeld	102	B4
Great Sampford	47	G2
Great Sankey	77	H3
Great Saxham	59	H5
Great Shefford	29	F3
Great Shelford	59	E6
Great Smeaton	94	E1
Great Snoring	72	C3
Great Somerford	28	B2
Great Stainton	104	C5
Great Stambridge	34	B1
Great Staughton	58	B5
Great Steeping	83	G5
Great Stonar	35	G5
Great Strickland	102	B5
Great Stukeley	58	C4
Great Sturton	82	E4
Great Sutton	53	J3
Great Swinburne	112	D5
Great Tew	43	F3
Great Thirkleby	95	F4
Great Thurlow	59	G6
GREAT TORRINGTON	13	E4
Great Tosson	112	E2
Great Totham, Essex CM9 8BW	48	B4
Great Totham, Essex CM9 8DU	48	B4
Great Urswick	92	A4
Great Wakering	34	C2
Great Waldingfield	48	C1
Great Walsingham	72	C3
Great Waltham	47	G4
Great Warley	33	F1
Great Washbourne	42	B2
Great Welnetham	60	B6
Great Wenham	48	D2
Great Whittington	112	E5
Great Wigborough	48	C4
Great Wilbraham	59	F6
Great Wishford	18	B2
Great Witcombe	42	A4
Great Witley	54	C5
Great Wolford	42	E2
Great Wratting	59	G7
Great Wymondley	45	G3
Great Wyrley	66	E6
Great Wytheford	66	A5
GREAT YARMOUTH	73	J5
Great Yeldham	47	H2
Greatford	70	A5

212 Greatham, Hants Headon

Greatham, Hants 20 A2
Greatham, Hartp 104 D5
Greatham, W Susx 20 D4
Greatstone-on-Sea 23 G3
Greatworth 43 H1
Greeba 90 B4
Green 156 D3
Green End 46 D3
Green Hammerton 95 F6
Green Hill 28 C2
Green Lane, Co of H 54 B7
Green Lane, Powys 52 E2
Green Ore 27 E5
Green Street, Glos 41 H4
Green Street, Herts 45 F6
Green Street Green 33 E4
Green Tye 47 E4
Greenacres 120 B2
Greenan 117 H6
Greenbank 177 C3
Greenburn 119 G1
Greendykes 123 F5
Greenfield, Beds 45 E2
Greenfield, Flint 76 D4
Greenfield, G Man 86 A6
Greenfield, Highl 142 D3
Greenfield, Oxon 30 B1
GREENFORD 31 F2
Greengairs 128 E5
Greenham 29 G4
Greenhaugh 111 G4
Greenhead 111 F6
Greenhill, E Susx 22 B3
Greenhill, Falk 129 F5
Greenhill, G Lon 31 F2
Greenhill, Kent 34 E4
Greenhill, S Yorks 79 H3
Greenhithe 33 F3
GREENHOLM 118 C4
Greenholme 92 D1
Greenhouse 121 E5
Greenhow 94 C5
Greenigoe 170 E4
Greenland 169 G3
Greenlands 30 B2
Greenlaw 121 G3
Greenloaning 129 F2
Greenmeadow 40 C5
Greenmount 85 F5
Greenmow 176 D5
GREENOCK 127 G5
Greenodd 92 B3
Greens Norton 56 E7
Greens of Bogside 155 F3
Greenside 113 F6
Greensidehill 123 E6
Greenskares 157 E2
Greenspot 157 E5
Greenstead Green 48 B3
Greensted 47 F5
Greenway 15 H3
GREENWICH 32 D3
Greeny 172 C4
Greet 42 C2
Greete 54 A4
Greetham, Lincs 83 F4
Greetham, Rut 69 H5
Greetland 86 B4
Gregson Lane 84 D4
Gréin 148 B4
Greinetobht 158 C5
Greinton 16 C2
Gremista 176 D3
Grenaby 90 B5
Grendon, Northnts 57 G5
Grendon, Warw 67 H7
Grendon Common 67 H7
Grendon Green 54 A6
Grendon Underwood 44 A3
Grenofen 5 H3
Grenoside 79 H2
Greosabhagh 159 F3
Gresford 77 F6
Gresham 72 E3
Greshornish 150 C3
Greshornish Ho 150 C3
Gressenhall 72 C5
Gressingham 92 D5
Greta Bridge 103 G6
Gretna 110 C6
Gretna Green 110 C6
Gretton, Glos 42 C2
Gretton, Northnts 57 G2
Gretton, Shrops 53 J2
Grewelthorpe 94 D4
Greyfriars 31 E6
Greygarth 94 C4
Greynor 38 C5
Greys Green 30 B2
Greysouthen 100 E5
Greystoke 101 J4
Greystone, Aberd 146 B4
Greystone, Ang 139 E4
Greystone, Lancs 85 G2
Greywell 30 B5
Griais 161 H3
Grianan 161 H4
Gribthorpe 88 B3
Griff 56 B3
Griffithstown 40 B6
Grimbister 170 D3
Grimeford Village 85 E5
Grimethorpe 87 F6
Griminis 149 C4
Griminis 158 B5
Grimister 177 B4
Grimley 54 D5
Grimmet 107 F1
Grimness 171 E5
Grimoldby 83 F3
Grimpo 65 G4
Grimsargh 84 D3
GRIMSBY 89 G5
Grimscote 56 E6
Grimscott 12 C5
Grimsthorpe 69 J4
Grimston, Leic 69 E4
Grimston, Norf 71 H4
Grimstone 9 E4
Grindale 97 G4
Grindigar 171 F4
Grindiscol 176 D3
Grindle 66 C6
Grindleford 79 G4
Grindleton 85 F2
Grindley 67 F4
Grindley Brook 65 J2
Grindlow 79 F4
Grindon, Northum 122 E3
Grindon, Staffs 79 E6
Gringley on the Hill 80 E2
Grinsdale 101 H2
Grinshill 65 J4
Grinton 94 B2
Griomsidar 161 H5
Grisedale 93 F2
Grishipoll 132 D3
Gristhorpe 97 F3
Griston 72 C7
Gritley 171 F4
Grittenham 28 C2
Grittleton 27 H2
Grizebeck 91 D3
Grizedale 92 B2
Grobister 173 G4
Groby 68 D6
Groes, Conwy 76 C5
Groes, Nth Pt Talb 25 E2
Groes- faen 25 H2
Groesffordd 62 C3
Groeslon 74 D6
Grogport 116 C3
Gromford 61 G6
Gronant 76 C3
Groombridge 22 B2
Grosmont, Monm 40 D3
Grosmont, N Yorks 96 D1
Groton 48 C1
Grove, Dorset 9 F6
Grove, Kent 35 F4
Grove, Notts 80 E4
Grove, Oxon 29 G1
Grove End 55 G2
Grove Park 32 E3
Grovesend 38 C5
Grudgehouse 169 H5
Grudie 153 F2
Gruids 164 B3
Gruinart Flats 124 B4
Grula 150 C6
Gruline 133 H4
Grumbla 2 C5
Grunasound 176 C4
Grundisburgh 61 F6
Gruting 174 D6
Grutness 176 D6
Gualachulain 135 F4
Guardbridge 138 D7
Guarlford 54 D7
Guay 137 H4
Gubbergill 91 B2
Guestling Green 22 E4
Guestwick 72 D4
Guestwick Green 72 D4
Guide Post 113 G4
Guilden Morden 46 C1
Guilden Sutton 77 G5
GUILDFORD 30 E6
Guildtown 137 J5
Guilsborough 56 E4
Guilsfield 65 F5
Guineaford 13 F2
GUISBOROUGH 105 F6
GUISELEY 86 C2
Guist 72 C4
Guiting Power 42 C3
Gullane 130 D4
Gulval 2 C4
Gumfreston 37 F5
Gumley 56 E2
Gunby, E Yorks 87 J3
Gunby, Lincs NG33 69 H4
Gunby, Lincs PE23 83 G5
Gundleton 19 H2
Gunn 13 G2
Gunnerside 93 H2
Gunnerton 112 D5
Gunness 88 C5
Gunnislake 5 H3
Gunnista 176 E3
Gunthorpe, Norf 72 D3
Gunthorpe, Notts 68 E2
Gunwalloe 3 E5
Gunwalloe Fishing Cove 2 E5
Gurnard 11 F4
Gurney Slade 27 F6
Gurnos 38 E5
Gussage All Saints 18 B4
Gussage St Michael 17 H4
Guston 35 G6
Gutcher 177 C4
Guthram Gowt 70 B4
Guthrie 139 E3
Guy's Head 71 E4
Guy's Marsh 17 G3
Guyhirn 70 D6
Guyhirn Gull 70 D6
Guyzance 113 G2
Gwaelod- y-Garth 25 J2
Gwaenysgor 76 C3
Gwalchmai 74 C4
Gwarallt 38 B2
Gwardafolog 50 E7
Gwaun-Cae-Gurwen 38 E4
Gwbert 50 B7
Gweek 3 F5
Gwehelog 40 C5
Gwenddwr 39 H1
Gwennap 3 F4
Gwenter 3 F6
Gwernaffield 76 E5
Gwernafon 52 C2
Gwernesney 40 D5
Gwernogle 38 C2
Gwernymynydd 76 E5
Gwersyllt 77 F6
Gwespyr 76 D3
Gwinear 2 D4
Gwithian 2 D3
Gwndwn 38 B2
Gwyddelwern 64 D2
Gwyddgrug 38 B2
Gwystre 52 D5
Gwytherin 75 H5
Gyfelia 65 G2
Gyffin 75 G4

H

Habberley, Shrops 65 G6
Habberley, Worces 54 D4
Habrough 89 F5
Haccombe 7 E3
Haceby 69 J3
Hacheston 61 G6
Hackford 72 D6
Hackforth 94 D2
Hackland 172 D4
Hackleton 57 G6
Hackness, N Yorks 97 E2
Hackness, Orkney 170 D5
HACKNEY 32 D2
Hackthorn 81 G3
Hackthorpe 102 B5
Haconby 70 B4
Hadden 122 C4
Haddenham, Bucks 44 B5
Haddenham, Cambs 59 E4
HADDINGTON, E Loth 130 E5
Haddington, Lincs 81 G5
Haddiscoe 61 H2
Haddon 58 B2
Hademore 67 G6
Hadfield 78 E2
Hadham Cross 46 E4
Hadham Ford 47 E3
Hadleigh, Essex 34 B2
HADLEIGH, Suff 48 D1
Hadleigh Heath 48 C1
Hadley 66 B5
Hadley End 67 G4
Hadlow 33 G6
Hadlow Down 22 B3
Hadnall 65 J4
Hadstock 47 F1
Hadzor 54 E5
Haffenden Quarter 34 B6
Hafod-Dinbych 75 H6
Hafod-y-Green 76 C4
Haggbeck 110 D5
Haggrister 175 E3
Hagley, Co of H 41 E1
Hagley, Worces 54 E3
Hagworthingham 83 F5
Haigh 85 E6
Haighton Green 84 D3
Hail Weston 58 B5
Haile 100 E7
Hailes 42 C2
Hailey, Herts 46 D4
Hailey, Oxon 43 F4
HAILSHAM 22 B5
Haimer 169 F3
Hainault 47 E6
Hainford 73 F5
Hainton 82 D3
Haisthorpe 97 G5
Halam 80 D6
Halberton 15 G4
Halcro 169 G3
HALE, G Man 78 B3
Hale, Halt 77 G3
Hale, Hants 18 C4
Hale, Lincs 70 B2
Hale, Surrey 30 C6
Hale Bank 77 G3
Hale Street 33 G6
Halebarns 78 B3
Hales, Norf 73 G7
Hales, Staffs 66 C3
Hales Place 34 E5
HALESOWEN 55 E3
HALESWORTH 61 G4
Halewood 77 G3
Halford, Shrops 53 H3
Halford, Warw 55 H7
Halfpenny Green 54 D2
Halfway, Carm SA19 38 D2
Halfway, Carm SA20 39 F2
Halfway, W Berks 29 G4
Halfway House 65 G5
Halfway Houses 34 C3
HALIFAX 86 B4
Halistra 150 B3
Halket 117 J2
Halkirk 169 F4
Halkyn 76 E4
Hall Dunnerdale 91 D2
Hall Green 55 G3
Hall of Clestrain 170 C4
Hall of Tankerness 171 F4
Hall of the Forest 53 F3
Halland 22 B4
Hallaton 57 F2
Hallatrow 27 F5
Hallbankgate 111 E7
Hallen 27 E2
Halliburton 121 F3
Hallin 150 B3
Halling 33 H4
Hallington, Lincs 83 F3
Hallington, Northum 112 D5
Halloughton 80 D6
Hallow 54 D6
Hallrule 121 E6
Halls 131 F5
Hallsands 6 E7
Hallthwaites 91 C3
Hallworthy 5 E2
Hallyne 120 A3
Halmer End 66 D2
Halmore 41 G5
Halmyre Mains 120 A3
Halnaker 20 C5
Halsall 84 B5
Halse, Northnts 43 H1
Halse, Somer 15 H3
Halsetown 2 D4
Halsham 89 G4
Halsinger 13 F2
HALSTEAD, Essex 48 B2
Halstead, Kent 33 E4
Halstead, Leic 69 F6
Halstock 16 D5
Haltham 83 E5
Haltoft End 70 D2
Halton, Bucks 44 C4
Halton, Halt 77 H3
Halton, Lancs 92 D5
Halton, Northum 112 D6
Halton, Wrex 65 G3
Halton Camp 44 C5
Halton East 94 B6
Halton Gill 93 G4
Halton Holegate 83 G5
Halton Lea Gate 111 F7
Halton West 93 G6
Haltwhistle 111 G6
Halvergate 73 H6
Halvosso 3 F4
Halwell 6 D5
Halwill 13 E6
Halwill Junction 13 E6
Ham, G Lon 31 F3
Ham, Glos 41 F6
Ham, Highl 169 G2
Ham, Kent 35 G5
Ham, Shetld 174 A7
Ham, Somer 16 A3
Ham, Wilts 29 F4
Ham Green, N Som 27 E3
Ham Green, Worces 55 F5
Ham Street 16 D2
Hamble- le-Rice 19 F5
Hambleden 30 B2
Hambledon, Hants 19 H4
Hambledon, Surrey 20 C2
Hambleton, Lancs 84 B2
Hambleton, N Yorks 87 G3
Hambridge 16 B3
Hambrook, S Glos 27 F3
Hambrook, W Susx 20 A5
Hameringham 83 F5
Hamerton 58 B4
Hametoun 174 A7
HAMILTON 118 E2
HAMMERSMITH 32 C3
Hammerwich 67 F6
Hammond Street 46 D5
Hammoon 17 G4
Hamnavoe, Shetld ZE2 9BA 177 B5
Hamnavoe, Shetld ZE2 9JY 176 C4
Hamnavoe, Shetld ZE2 9QF 175 F3
Hamnavoe, Shetld ZE2 9RS 174 D2
Hampden Park 22 C5
Hampen 42 C4
Hamperden End 47 F2
Hampnett 42 D4
Hampole 87 G5
Hampreston 10 B4
HAMPSTEAD 32 C2
Hampstead Norreys 29 H3
Hampsthwaite 94 D6
Hampton, G Lon 31 F3
Hampton, Shrops 54 C3
Hampton, Worces 42 C1
Hampton Bishop 41 E2
Hampton Heath 65 J2
Hampton in Arden 55 H3
Hampton Lovett 54 D5
Hampton Lucy 55 H6
Hampton on the Hill 55 H5
Hampton Poyle 43 H4
Hamptworth 18 D4
Hamsey 21 H4
Hamstall Ridware 67 G5
Hamstead, I of W 11 F4
Hamstead, W Mids 55 F2
Hamstead Marshall 29 G4
Hamsterley, Durham DL13 103 H4
Hamsterley, Durham NE17 103 H2
Hamstreet 23 G2
Hamworthy 9 H4
Hanbury, Staffs 67 G4
Hanbury, Worces 55 E5
Hanbury Woodend 67 G4
Hanchet End 59 G7
Hanchurch 66 D2
Handbridge 77 G5
Handcross 21 F2
Handforth 78 C3
Handley 77 G6
Handsacre 67 F5
Handsworth, S Yorks 80 B3
Handsworth, W Mids 55 F2
Hanford 66 D2
Hangersley 18 C5
Hanging Houghton 57 F4
Hanging Langford 18 B2
Hanham 27 F3
Hankelow 66 B2
Hankerton 28 B1
Hankham 22 C5
Hanley 66 D2
Hanley Castle 41 H1
Hanley Child 54 B5
Hanley Swan 41 H1
Hanley William 54 B5
Hanlith 93 H5
Hanmer 65 H3
Hannah 83 H4
Hannington, Hants 29 H5
Hannington, Northnts 57 G4
Hannington, Swin 42 D6
Hannington Wick 42 D6
Hanslope 57 G7
Hanthorpe 70 A4
Hanwell 43 G1
Hanwood 65 H6
Hanworth, G Lon 31 F3
Hanworth, Norf 73 E3
Happendon 119 F4
Happisburgh 73 G3
Happisburgh Common 73 G4
Hapsford 77 G4
Hapton, Lancs 85 F3
Hapton, Norf 60 E2
Harberton 6 D5
Harbertonford 6 D5
Harbledown 34 E5
Harborne 55 F3
Harborough Magna 56 C4
Harbottle 112 D2
Harbourneford 6 D4
Harbridge 18 C5
Harbury 56 B5
Harby, Leic 69 F3
Harby, Notts 81 F4
Harcombe 15 H6
Harcourt 3 G4
Harden 86 B3
Hardendale 102 B6
Hardgate, Aberd 147 E3
Hardgate, D & G 109 F6
Hardham 20 D4
Hardhorn 84 B3
Hardingham 72 D6
Hardings Wood 78 C6
Hardingstone 57 F6
Hardington 27 G5
Hardington Mandeville 16 D4
Hardington Marsh 16 D5
Hardley 19 F5
Hardley Street 73 G6
Hardmead 57 H7
Hardraw 93 G2
Hardstoft 80 B5
Hardway, Hants 11 H3
Hardway, Somer 17 F2
Hardwick, Bucks 44 C4
Hardwick, Cambs 58 D6
Hardwick, Norf 61 F3
Hardwick, Northnts 57 G5
Hardwick, Oxon OX6 43 H3
Hardwick, Oxon OX8 43 F5
Hardwick Village 80 D4
Hardwicke, Co of H 40 B1
Hardwicke, Glos GL2 41 G4
Hardwicke, Glos GL51 42 B3
Hardys Green 48 C3
Hare Hatch 30 C3
Hare Street, Herts SG9 0 46 D3
Hare Street, Herts SG9 9 46 D3
Hareby 83 F5
Hareden 85 E1
Harefield 31 E1
Harehope 123 F5
Harelaw 119 G3
Harescombe 41 H4
Haresfield 41 H5
Hareshaw 118 D3
Harewood, Corn 5 H4
Harewood, W Yorks 86 E2
Harewood End 40 E3
Harford 6 C5
Hargrave, Beds 57 J4
Hargrave, Ches 77 G5
Hargrave, Suff 59 H6
Harker 110 C6
Harkstead 49 E2
Harlaston 67 H5
Harlaxton 69 G3
Harle Syke 85 G3
Harlech 63 F3
Harlesden 31 G2
Harleston, Devon 6 D6
HARLESTON, Norf 61 F3
Harleston, Suff 60 D5
Harlestone 57 F5
Harley 66 A6
Harlington, Beds 45 E2
Harlington, S Yorks 87 F6
Harlosh 150 B4
HARLOW 47 E4
Harlow Hill 112 E6
Harlthorpe 88 B3
Harlton 58 D6
Harlyn 4 B3
Harman's Cross 9 H5
Harmby 94 C3
Harmer Green 46 C4
Harmer Hill 65 H4
Harmondsworth 31 E3
Harmston 81 G5
Harnham 18 C3
Harnhill 42 C5
Harold Hill 33 F1
Harold Wood 33 F1
Haroldston West 36 C4
Haroldswick 177 D2
Harome 96 B3
HARPENDEN 45 F4
Harpford 15 G6
Harpham 97 F5
Harpley, Norf 71 H4
Harpley, Worces 54 B5
Harpole 57 E5
Harpsdale 169 F4
Harpsden 30 B2
Harpswell 81 G3
Harpur Hill 79 E4
Harpurhey 85 G6
Harrapool 141 F1
Harrier 174 A6
Harrietfield 137 G6
Harrietsham 34 B5
Harrington, Cumbr 100 D5
Harrington, Lincs 83 F4
Harrington, Northnts 57 F4
Harringworth 69 H7
Harris 140 C4
Harriseahead 78 C6
Harriston 101 F3
HARROGATE 94 E6
Harrold 57 H6
HARROW 31 F2
Harrow on the Hill 31 F2
Harrowbarrow 5 H3
Harrowden 58 A7
Harston, Cambs 58 E6
Harston, Leic 69 G3
Hart 104 D4
Hartburn 113 E4
Hartest 60 B6
Hartfield 21 H2
Hartford, Cambs 58 C4
Hartford, Ches 77 J4
Hartford End 47 G4
Hartfordbridge 30 B5
Hartforth 103 H7
Harthill, Ches 77 H6
Harthill, N Lanak 129 G6
Harthill, S Yorks 80 B3
Hartington 79 F5
Hartland 12 C3
Hartlebury 54 D4
HARTLEPOOL 104 E4
Hartley, Cumbr 102 D7
Hartley, Kent DA3 33 G4
Hartley, Kent TN17 22 D2
Hartley, Northum 113 H5
Hartley Wespall 30 A5
Hartley Wintney 30 B5
Hartlip 34 B4
Harton, N Yorks 96 C5
Harton, Shrops 53 H3
Harton, T & W 113 H6
Hartpury 41 G3
Hartshill 56 B2
Hartshorne 68 B4
Hartsop 101 J6
Hartwell 57 F6
Hartwood 119 F2
Harvel 33 G4
Harvington 55 F7
Harwell 29 G2
HARWICH 49 F2
Harwood, Durham 102 E4
Harwood, G Man 85 F5
Harwood Dale 97 E2
Harworth 80 D2
Hascombe 20 C1
Haselbech 57 F4
Haselbury Plucknett 16 C4
Haseley 55 H5
Haselor 55 G6
Hasfield 41 H3
Hasguard 36 C5
Haskayne 84 B6
Hasketon 61 F6
Hasland 79 H5
HASLEMERE 20 B2
HASLINGDEN 85 F4
Haslingden Grane 85 F4
Haslingfield 58 E6
Haslington 78 B6
Hass 111 F1
Hassall 78 B6
Hassall Green 78 B6
Hassell Street 34 D6
Hassendean 121 E5
Hassingham 73 G6
Hassocks 21 F4
Hassop 79 G4
Haster 169 H4
Hastigrow 169 G3
Hastingleigh 34 D6
HASTINGS 22 E5
Hastingwood 47 E5
Hastoe 44 D5
Haswell 104 C3
Haswell Plough 104 C3
Hatch, Beds 58 B7
Hatch, Hants 30 A5
Hatch, Wilts 17 H3
Hatch Beauchamp 16 B3
Hatch End 31 F1
Hatching Green 45 F4
Hatchmere 77 H4
Hatcliffe 82 E1
Hatfield, Co of H 54 A6
HATFIELD, Herts 45 G5
Hatfield, S Yorks 87 H6
Hatfield Broad Oak 47 F4
Hatfield Garden Village 45 G4
Hatfield Heath 47 F4
Hatfield Peverel 47 H4
Hatfield Woodhouse 87 H6
Hatford 43 F6
Hatherden 29 F5
Hatherleigh 13 F5
Hathern 68 C4
Hatherop 42 D5
Hathersage 79 G3
Hatherton, Ches 66 B2
Hatherton, Staffs 67 E5
Hatley St George 58 C6
Hatston 171 E3
Hatt 5 G4
Hattingley 19 H2
Hatton, Aberd 157 H5
Hatton, Derby 67 H4
Hatton, G Lon 31 E3
Hatton, Lincs 82 D4
Hatton, Shrops 53 H2
Hatton, Warr 77 J3
Hatton, Warw 55 H5
Hatton Heath 77 G5
Hatton of Fintray 147 F2
Hattoncrook 157 F6
Haugh Head 123 F5
Haugh of Glass 156 B5
Haugh of Urr 109 F6
Haugham 83 F3
Haughhead 128 D5
Haughley 60 D5
Haughley Green 60 D5
Haughley New Street 60 D5
Haughton, Notts 80 D4
Haughton, Shrops SY11 65 G4
Haughton, Shrops TF6 65 J5
Haughton, Shrops WV16 54 B2
Haughton, Staffs 66 D4
Haughton Green 78 D2
Haughton Moss 77 H6
Haultwick 46 D3
Haunn 133 F4
Haunton 67 H5
Hauxley 113 G2
Hauxton 59 E6
HAVANT 19 J5
Haven 53 H6
Havenstreet 11 G4
HAVERFORDWEST 36 D4
HAVERHILL 59 G7
Haverigg 91 C4
Havering-atte-Bower 47 F6
Haversham 44 C1
Haverthwaite 92 B3
Havington 54 D4
Hawarden 77 F5
Hawbridge 54 E7
Hawes 93 G3
Hawford 54 D5
HAWICK 120 E6
Hawkchurch 8 B3
Hawkedon 59 H6
Hawkenbury 34 B6
Hawkeridge 27 H5
Hawkerland 15 G7
Hawkes End 55 J3
Hawkesbury 27 G2
Hawkesbury Upton 27 G2
Hawkhill 123 H6
Hawkhurst 22 D2
Hawkinge 23 J2
Hawkley 19 J3
Hawkridge 14 E2
Hawkshead 92 B2
Hawksland 119 F4
Hawkswick 93 H4
Hawkswick Cote 93 H4
Hawksworth, Notts 69 F2
Hawksworth, W Yorks 86 C2
Hawkwell 34 B1
Hawley, Hants 30 C5
Hawley, Kent 33 F3
Hawling 42 C3
Hawn 172 E4
Hawnby 95 G3
Haworth 86 B3
Hawsker 105 J7
Hawstead 60 B6
Hawthorn 104 D3
Hawthorn Hill, B For 30 C3
Hawthorn Hill, Lincs 82 E6
Hawthorpe 69 J4
Hawton 81 E6
Haxby 95 H6
Haxey 80 E2
Hay Street 46 D3
HAY-ON-WYE 40 B1
HAYDOCK 77 H2
Haydon 17 E4
Haydon Bridge 112 C6
Haydon Wick 28 D2
Haye 5 G4
Hayes, G Lon 32 E4
HAYES, G Lon 31 F2
Hayfield 78 E3
Hayhillock 139 E4
Hayle 2 D4
Haynes 45 E1
Haynes Church End 45 E1
Hayscastle 36 C3
Hayscastle Cross 36 D3
Hayton, Cumbr CA4 102 B2
Hayton, Cumbr CA5 101 F3
Hayton, E Yorks 88 C2
Hayton, Notts 80 E3
Hayton's Bent 53 J3
Haytor Vale 6 D3
Haytown 12 D4
HAYWARDS HEATH 21 G3
Haywood Oaks 80 D6
Hazel End 47 E3
HAZEL GROVE 78 D3
Hazelbank 119 F3
Hazelbury Bryan 17 F5
Hazeleigh 48 B5
Hazeley 30 B5
Hazelrigg 123 F4
Hazelside 119 F5
Hazelslade 67 F5
Hazelton Walls 138 C6
Hazelwood 68 B2
Hazlemere 44 C6
Hazlerigg 113 G5
Hazleton 42 C4
Hazlewood 86 B1
Heacham 71 G3
Head of Muir 129 F4
Headbourne Worthy 19 F2
Headcorn 34 B6
Headingley 86 D3
Headington 43 H5
Headlam 103 H6
Headless Cross 55 F5
Headley, Hants GU35 20 B2
Headley, Hants RG19 29 H4
Headley, Surrey 31 G5
Headley Down 20 B2
Headon 80 E4

Heads Nook

Hoton

213

Heads Nook 102 A2
Heage 79 H6
Healaugh, N Yorks DL11 94 B2
Healaugh, N Yorks LS24 87 G2
Heald Green 78 C3
Heale 24 D6
Healey, G Man 85 G5
Healey, N Yorks 94 C3
Healey, Northum 103 G2
Healeyfield 103 G3
Healing 89 G5
Heamoor 2 C4
Heanish 132 C4
HEANOR 68 C2
Heanton Punchardon 13 F2
Heapham 81 F3
Hearthstane 119 J5
Heasley Mill 14 D2
Heaste 141 F2
Heath, Card 26 A3
Heath, Derby 80 B5
Heath and Reach 44 D3
Heath End, Hants 29 H4
Heath End, Surrey 30 C6
Heath Hayes 67 F5
Heath Hill 66 C5
Heath House 26 D6
Heathall 109 G5
Heathcot 147 F3
Heathcote 79 F5
Heather 68 B5
Heatherfield 150 D4
Heathfield, Devon 6 E3
HEATHFIELD, E Susx 22 B3
Heathfield, Renf 117 H1
Heathfield, Somer 15 H3
Heathton 54 D2
Heatley 78 B3
Heaton, Lancs 92 C5
Heaton, Staffs 78 D5
Heaton, T & W 113 G6
Heaton Moor 78 C2
Heaverham 33 F5
Heaviley 78 D3
HEBBURN 113 H6
Hebden 94 B5
HEBDEN BRIDGE 86 A4
Hebden Green 77 J5
Hebing End 46 D3
Hebron, Carm 37 F3
Hebron, Northum 113 F4
Heck 109 H4
Heckfield 30 B4
Heckfordbridge 48 C3
Heckington 70 B2
HECKMONDWIKE 86 D4
Heddington 28 C4
Heddle 170 D3
Heddon-on-the-Wall 113 F6
Hedenham 61 G2
Hedge End 19 G4
Hedgehog Bridge 70 C2
Hedgerley 30 D2
Hedging 16 B3
Hedley on the Hill 113 E7
Hednesford 67 F5
HEDON 89 F4
Hedsor 30 D2
Hegdon Hill 54 A6
Heggerscales 102 E6
Heglibister 175 E5
Heighington, Darl 104 B5
Heighington, Lincs 82 C5
Heights of Brae 153 H2
Heights of Kinlochewe 152 C2
Heilam 167 F3
Heiton 121 G4
Helbeck 102 E6
Hele, Devon EX34 24 C6
Hele, Devon EX5 15 F5
Hele Barton 14 D4
HELENSBURGH 127 G4
Helford 3 F5
Helford Passage 3 F5
Helhoughton 72 B4
Helions Bumpstead 47 G1
Hellaby 80 C2
Helland 4 D3
Hellesdon 73 F5
Hellidon 56 D6
Hellifield 93 G6
Hellingly 22 B4
Hellington 73 G6
Hellister 175 E6
Helmdon 43 H1
Helmingham 61 E6
Helmsdale 165 G2
Helmshore 85 F4
Helmsley 95 H3
Helperby 95 F5
Helperthorpe 97 E4
Helpringham 70 B2
Helpston 70 B6
Helsby 77 H4
HELSTON 3 E5
Helstone 4 D2
Helton 102 B5
Helwith Bridge 93 G5
Hemblington 73 G5
HEMEL HEMPSTEAD 45 E5
Hemingbrough 87 H3
Hemingby 82 E4
Hemingford Abbots 58 C4
Hemingford Grey 58 C4
Hemingstone 60 E6
Hemington, Northnts 58 A3
Hemington, Somer 27 G5
Hemley 49 F1
Hemlington 104 E6
Hempholme 88 E1
Hempnall 61 F2
Hempnall Green 61 F2
Hempriggs 155 F2
Hempstead, Essex 47 G2
Hempstead, Norf NR12 73 H4
Hempstead, Norf NR25 72 E3
Hempsted 41 H4
Hempton, Norf 72 C4
Hempton, Oxon 43 G2
Hemsby 73 H5
Hemswell 81 G2
Hemswell Cliff 81 G3
HEMSWORTH 87 F5
Hemyock 15 H4
Henbury, C of Bris 27 E3
Henbury, Ches 78 C4
Henderland 109 F5
Hendersyde Park 122 C4
HENDON, G Lon 31 G2
Hendon, T & W 104 D2
Hendra 3 F4
Hendre 76 D5
Hendreforgan 25 G2
Hendy 38 C5
Heneglwys 74 D4
Henfield 21 F4
Henford 12 D6
Henghurst 23 F2
Hengoed, Caer 39 J6
Hengoed, Powys 53 F6
Hengoed, Shrops 65 F3
Hengrave 60 B5
Henham 47 F3
Henlade 16 A3
Henley, Shrops 53 J4
Henley, Somer 16 C2
Henley, Suff 60 E6
Henley, W Susx 20 B3
HENLEY-ON-THAMES 30 B2
Henley Park 30 D5
Henley's Down 22 D4
Henley-in-Arden 55 G5
Henllan, Cered 37 H1
Henllan, Denb 76 C5
Henllan Amgoed 37 F4
Henllys 40 B6
Henlow 45 F2
Hennock 6 E2
Henny Street 48 B2
Henry's Moat 37 E3
Henryd 75 G4
Hensall 87 G4
Henshaw 111 G6
Henstead 61 H3
Henstridge 17 F4
Henstridge Marsh 17 F3
Henton, Oxon 44 B5
Henton, Somer 26 D6
Henwood 5 F3
Henwood and Lamborough Hill 43 G5
Heogan 176 D3
Heol Senni 39 G3
Heol-y- Cyw 25 G2
Hepburn 123 F5
Hepple 112 D2
Hepscott 113 G4
Heptonstall 86 A4
Hepworth, Suff 60 C4
Hepworth, W Yorks 86 C6
Herbrandston 36 C5
Herdicott 12 D6
HEREFORD 40 E1
Hergest 53 F6
Heriot 120 C2
Hermiston 130 A5
Hermitage, Dorset 17 E5
Hermitage, Scot Bord 110 E3
Hermitage, W Berks 29 H3
Hermitage, W Susx 20 A5
Hermon, Carm 37 H2
Hermon, I of Angl 74 C5
Hermon, Pemb 37 G2
Herne 35 E4
HERNE BAY 35 E4
Herne Common 35 E4
Herner 13 F3
Hernhill 34 D4
Herodsfoot 5 F4
Herongate 33 G1
Heronsford 106 D4
Heronsgate 45 E6
Herra 175 F4
Herriard 30 A6
Herringfleet 73 H7
Herrings Green 45 E1
Herringswell 59 H4
Herrington 104 C2
Hersden 35 F4
Hersham 31 F4
Herstmonceux 22 C4
Herston 171 E5
HERTFORD 46 D4
Hertford Heath 46 D4
Hertingfordbury 46 D4
Hesket Newmarket 101 H4
Hesketh Bank 84 C4
Hesketh Lane 85 E2
Heskin Green 84 D5
Hesleden 104 D4
Hesleyside 112 C4
Heslington 87 H1
Hessay 87 G1
Hessenford 5 G5
Hessett 60 C5
HESSLE 88 E4
Hest Bank 92 C5
Hestinsetter 176 B3
Heston 31 F3
Hestwall 170 C3
HESWALL 76 E3
Hethe 43 H3
Hethersett 72 E6
Hethersgill 110 D6
Hethpool 122 D5
Hett 104 B4
Hetton 93 H6
HETTON- LE-HOLE 104 C3
Heugh 113 E5
Heugh-head, Aberd AB34 146 C4
Heugh-head, Aberd AB36 145 H2
Heveningham 61 G4
Hever 33 E6
Heversham 92 C3
Hevingham 73 E4
Hewas Water 4 C6
Hewelsfield 41 E5
Hewelsfield Common 41 E5
Hewish, N Som 26 D4
Hewish, Somer 16 C5
HEXHAM 112 D6
Hextable 33 F3
Hexton 45 F2
Hexworthy 6 C3
Heybridge, Essex CM4 47 G6
Heybridge, Essex CM9 48 B5
Heybridge Basin 48 B5
Heybrook Bay 5 J6
Heydon, Cambs 47 E1
Heydon, Norf 72 E4
Heydour 69 J3
Heylipol 132 B4
Heylor 174 D2
HEYSHAM 92 C5
Heyshott 20 B4
Heytesbury 28 B6
Heythrop 43 F3
HEYWOOD, G Man 85 G5
Heywood, Wilts 27 H5
Hibaldstow 88 D6
Hickleton 87 F6
Hickling, Norf 73 H4
Hickling, Notts 69 E4
Hickling Green 73 H4
Hickling Heath 73 H4
Hickstead 21 F3
Hidcote Boyce 42 D1
High Ackworth 87 F5
High Bankhill 102 B3
High Banton 128 E5
High Beach 46 E6
High Beaumont Hill 104 B5
High Bentham 93 E5
High Bickington 13 G3
High Birkwith 93 F4
High Blantyre 118 D2
High Bonnybridge 129 F5
High Bradfield 79 G2
High Bray 14 C2
High Bullen 13 F3
High Buston 113 G2
High Callerton 113 F5
High Catton 87 J1
High Cogges 43 F5
High Coniscliffe 104 B6
High Cross, Hants 19 J3
High Cross, Herts 46 D4
High Dougarie 116 C4
High Easter 47 G4
High Ellington 94 C3
High Enoch 109 F2
High Ercall 66 A5
High Ferry 70 D2
High Garrett 47 H3
High Grange 103 H4
High Grantley 94 D5
High Green, Norf 72 E6
High Green, S Yorks 79 H2
High Green, Worces 54 D7
High Halden 23 E2
High Halstow 33 H3
High Ham 16 C2
High Harrington 100 E5
High Hatton 66 B4
High Heath 66 B4
High Hesket 102 A3
High Houses 93 G3
High Hoyland 86 D6
High Hunsley 88 D3
High Hurstwood 21 H3
High Hutton 96 C5
High Keil 114 B6
High Lane, Co of H 54 B5
High Lane, G Man 78 D3
High Laver 47 F5
High Legh 78 B3
High Littleton 27 F5
High Melton 87 G6
High Newton 92 C3
High Newton-by-the-Sea 123 H5
High Offley 66 C4
High Ongar 47 F5
High Onn 66 D5
High Risby 88 D5
High Roding 47 G4
High Salvington 20 E5
High Shaw 93 G2
High Shincliffe 104 B3
High Spen 113 F6
High Street, Corn 4 C5
High Street, Kent 22 D2
High Street, Suff IP12 61 H6
High Street, Suff NR34 61 G3
High Street Green 60 D6
High Toynton 83 E5
High Trewhitt 112 E2
High Wardses 93 E2
High Wray 92 B2
High Wych 47 E4
HIGH WYCOMBE 44 C6
Higham, Derby 79 H6
Higham, Kent 33 H3
Higham, Lancs 85 G3
Higham, Suff CO7 48 D2
Higham, Suff IP28 59 H5
Higham Dykes 113 F5
HIGHAM FERRERS 57 H5
Higham Gobion 45 F2
Higham on the Hill 56 B2
Higham Wood 33 G6
Highampton 13 E5
Highbridge, Highl 142 D5
Highbridge, Somer 26 C6
Highbrook 21 G2
Highburton 86 C5
Highclere 29 G4
Highcliffe 10 D4
Higher Ansty 9 F3
Higher Ashton 6 E2
Higher Ballam 84 B3
Higher Bockhampton 9 F4
Higher Cheriton 15 H5
Higher Clovelly 12 D3
Higher Crackington 12 B6
Higher Downs 2 D4
Higher End 84 D6
Higher Folds 78 A1
Higher Kingcombe 8 D4
Higher Kinnerton 77 F5
Higher Northcott 12 D6
Higher Penwortham 84 D4
Higher Poynton 78 D3
Higher Prestacott 12 D6
Higher Tale 15 G5
Higher Town 2 N9
Higher Walreddon 5 H3
Higher Walton, Lancs 84 D4
Higher Walton, Warr 77 H3
Higher Whitley 77 J3
Higher Wincham 78 A4
Higher Wych 65 J2
Highfield, E Yorks 88 B3
Highfield, N Ayr 117 H2
Highfield, T & W 113 F7
Highfields, Cambs 58 D6
Highfields, S Yorks 87 G6
Highlane, Ches 78 C5
Highlane, Derby 79 J3
Highlaws 101 F3
Highleadon 41 G3
Highleigh 20 B6
Highley 54 C3
Highmoor Cross 30 B2
Highmoor Hill 26 D2
Highnam 41 G3
Highsted 34 C4
Hightae 109 H5
Hightown, Ches 78 C5
Hightown, Mers 84 A6
Hightown Green 60 C6
Highway, Corn 5 E5
Highway, Wilts 28 C3
HIGHWORTH 28 E1
Hilborough 72 B6
Hilcote 80 B6
Hildenborough 33 F6
Hildersham 59 F7
Hilderstone 67 E3
Hilderthorpe 97 G5
Hilfield 17 E5
Hilgay 71 G7
Hill, S Glos 41 F6
Hill, Warw 56 C5
Hill Brow 20 A3
Hill End, Durham 103 G4
Hill End, Fife 129 H3
Hill Head 11 G3
Hill Mountain 36 D5
Hill of Beath 129 J3
Hill of Fearn 165 E6
Hill Ridware 67 F5
Hill Top 11 F3
Hill Wootton 55 J5
Hillam 87 G4
Hillberry 90 C5
Hillborough 35 F4
Hillbrae, Aberd AB51 0 157 E6
Hillbrae, Aberd AB51 8 157 F5
Hillbrae, Aberd AB54 156 D4
Hilldyke 70 D2
Hillend, Fife 129 J4
Hillend, Midlo 130 B6
Hillerton 14 D6
Hillesden 44 A3
Hillesden Hamlet 44 A2
Hillesley 27 G2
Hillfarrance 15 H3
Hillhead, Aberd 156 C5
Hillhead, Devon 7 F5
Hillhead, S Ayr 118 B6
Hillhead of Auchentumb 157 G3
Hillhead of Cocklaw 157 H4
Hilliard's Cross 67 G5
Hilliclay 169 F3
HILLINGDON 31 E2
Hillington 71 H4
Hillmorton 56 D4
Hillockhead 145 H3
Hillside, Aberd 147 G4
Hillside, Ang 139 G2
Hillside, Orkney 171 E5
Hillside, Shetld 175 F4
Hillswick 174 D3
Hillway 11 H5
Hillwell 176 C6
Hilmarton 28 C3
Hilperton 27 H5
Hilsea 11 H3
Hilton, Aberd 157 G5
Hilton, Cambs 58 C5
Hilton, Cumbr 102 D5
Hilton, Derby 67 H3
Hilton, Dorset 9 F3
Hilton, Durham 103 H5
Hilton, Highl 165 F5
Hilton, Shrops 54 C2
Hilton, Stock on T 104 D6
Hilton of Cadboll 165 E6
Himbleton 55 E6
Himley 54 D2
Hincaster 92 D3
HINCKLEY 56 C2
Hinderclay 60 D4
Hinderwell 105 G6
Hindford 65 G3
Hindhead 20 B2
Hindhope 111 G1
HINDLEY 85 E6
Hindley Green 85 E6
Hindlip 54 D6
Hindolveston 72 D4
Hindon 17 H2
Hindringham 72 C3
Hingham 72 D6
Hinstock 66 B4
Hintlesham 48 D1
Hinton, Co of H 40 C2
Hinton, Hants 10 D4
Hinton, Northnts 56 D6
Hinton, S Glos 27 G3
Hinton, Shrops 65 H6
Hinton Ampner 19 G3
Hinton Blewett 27 E5
Hinton Charterhouse 27 G5
Hinton Martell 18 B5
Hinton on the Green 42 C1
Hinton Parva 28 E2
Hinton St George 16 C4
Hinton St Mary 17 F4
Hinton Waldrist 43 F6
Hinton-in-the-Hedges 43 H2
Hints, Shrops 54 B4
Hints, Staffs 67 G6
Hinwick 57 H5
Hinxhill 34 D6
Hinxton 59 E7
Hinxworth 46 C1
Hipperholme 86 C4
Hiraeth 37 F3
Hirn 146 E3
Hirnant 64 D4
Hirst 113 G4
Hirst Courtney 87 H4
Hirwaen 76 D5
Hirwaun 39 G5
Hiscott 13 F3
Histon 59 E5
Hitcham 60 C6
HITCHIN 45 F3
Hither Green 32 E3
Hittisleigh 14 D6
Hixon 67 F4
Hoaden 35 F5
Hoaldalbert 40 C3
Hoar Cross 67 G4
Hoarwithy 41 E3
Hoath 35 F4
Hobarris 53 G4
Hobbister 170 D4
Hobkirk 121 E6
Hobson 103 H2
Hoby 68 E5
Hockering 72 D5
Hockerton 80 E6
Hockley 34 B1
Hockley Heath 55 G4
Hockliffe 44 D3
Hockwold cum Wilton 59 H3
Hockworthy 15 G4
HODDESDON 46 D5
Hoddlesden 85 F4
Hodgeston 36 E6
Hodnet 66 B4
Hodsock 80 D3
Hodthorpe 80 C4
Hoe 72 C5
Hoe Gate 19 H4
Hoff 102 C6
Hoffleet Stow 70 C3
Hoggeston 44 C3
Hoggrills End 55 H2
Hogha Gearraidh 149 C2
Hoghton 85 E4
Hognaston 79 G6
Hogsthorpe 83 H4
HOLBEACH 70 D4
Holbeach Bank 70 D4
Holbeach Clough 70 D4
Holbeach Drove 70 D5
Holbeach Hurn 70 D4
Holbeach St Johns 70 D5
Holbeach St Marks 70 D3
Holbeach St Matthew 70 E3
Holbeck 80 C4
Holberrow Green 55 F6
Holbeton 6 C5
Holborn 32 D2
Holborough 33 H4
Holbrook, Derby 68 B2
Holbrook, Suff 48 E2
Holburn 123 F4
Holbury 11 F3
Holcombe, Devon 7 F3
Holcombe, Somer 27 F6
Holcombe Rogus 15 G4
Holcot 57 F5
Holden 85 F2
Holdenby 57 E5
Holder's Green 47 G3
Holdgate 54 A3
Holdingham 70 A2
Holditch 8 B3
Hole in the Wall 41 F3
Holemoor 13 E5
Holestane 109 F3
Holford 26 A6
Holker 92 B4
Holkham 72 B2
Holl's Green 46 C3
Hollacombe 12 D5
Holland, Orkney KW17 2AJ 173 G4
Holland, Orkney KW17 2BU 172 E1
Holland-on-Sea 49 F4
Hollandstoun 173 H1
Hollee 110 B6
Hollesley 49 G1
Hollinfare 78 A2
Hollingbourne 34 B5
Hollingbury 21 G5
Hollington, Derby 67 H3
Hollington, E Susx 22 D4
Hollington, Staffs 67 F3
Hollingworth 78 E2
Hollins 85 G6
Hollinsclough 79 E5
Hollinwood 65 J3
Hollocombe 13 G4
Holloway 79 H6
Hollowell 57 E4
Holly End 71 E6
Hollybush, Caer 40 A5
Hollybush, E Ayr 117 H6
Hollybush, Worces 41 G2
Hollym 89 H4
Hollywood 55 F4
Holmbury St Mary 31 F6
Holme, Cambs 58 B3
Holme, Cumbr 92 D4
Holme, Notts 81 F6
Holme, W Yorks 86 C6
Holme Chapel 85 G4
Holme Green 87 G2
Holme Hale 72 B6
Holme Lacy 41 E2
Holme Marsh 53 G6
Holme next the Sea 71 H2
Holme on the Wolds 88 D2
Holme Pierrepoint 68 E3
Holme-on- Spalding-Moor 88 C3
Holmehead 108 E4
Holmer 40 E1
Holmer Green 44 C6
Holmes Chapel 78 B5
Holmesfield 79 H4
Holmeswood 84 C5
Holmewood 80 B5
HOLMFIRTH 86 C6
HOLMHEAD 118 C5
Holmpton 89 H4
Holmrook 91 B2
Holmsgarth 176 D3
Holmside 104 B3
Holne 6 D4
Holnest 17 E4
HOLSWORTHY 12 D5
Holsworthy Beacon 12 D5
Holt, Dorset 10 B3
HOLT, Norf 72 D3
Holt, Wilts 27 H4
Holt, Worces 54 D5
Holt, Wrex 77 G6
Holt End 55 F5
Holt Fleet 54 D5
Holt Heath, Dorset 18 B5
Holt Heath, Worces 54 D5
Holtby 96 B6
Holton, Oxon 43 J5
Holton, Somer 17 E3
Holton, Suff 61 G4
Holton cum Beckering 82 D3
Holton Heath 9 H4
Holton le Clay 89 G6
Holton le Moor 82 C2
Holton St Mary 48 D2
Holway 76 D4
Holwell, Dorset 17 F4
Holwell, Herts 45 F2
Holwell, Leic 69 F4
Holwell, Oxon 42 E5
Holwick 103 F5
Holworth 9 F5
Holy Cross 54 E4
Holy Island 123 G3
Holybourne 30 B6
HOLYHEAD 74 B3
Holymoorside 79 H5
Holyport 30 C3
Holystone 112 D2
Holytown 118 E1
Holywell, Beds 44 E4
Holywell, Cambs 58 D4
Holywell, Corn 3 F2
Holywell, Dorset 16 D5
HOLYWELL, Flint 76 D4
Holywell, Warw 55 G5
Holywell Green 86 B5
Holywell Lake 15 H3
Holywell Row 59 H4
Holywood 109 G4
Hom Green 41 E3
Homer 66 B6
Homersfield 61 F3
Homington 18 C3
Honey Hill 34 E4
Honeybourne 42 D1
Honeychurch 13 G5
Honiley 55 H4
Honing 73 G4
Honingham 72 E5
Honington, Lincs 69 H2
Honington, Suff 60 C4
Honington, Warw 42 E1
HONITON 15 H6
Honley 86 C5
Hoo 61 F6
Hoo St Werburgh 33 H3
Hooe, C of Ply 5 J5
Hooe, E Susx 22 C5
Hooe Common 22 C4
Hook, E Yorks 88 B4
Hook, G Lon 31 F4
Hook, Hants 30 B5
Hook, Pemb 36 D4
Hook, Wilts 28 C2
Hook Green 33 G3
Hook Norton 43 F2
Hooke 8 D4
Hooker Gate 113 F7
Hookgate 66 C3
Hookway 14 E6
Hookwood 32 C6
Hoole 77 G5
Hooley 32 C5
Hooton 77 F4
Hooton Levitt 80 C2
Hooton Pagnell 87 F6
Hooton Roberts 80 B2
Hop Pole 70 B5
Hope, Derby 79 F3
Hope, Devon 6 C6
Hope, Durham 103 G7
Hope, Flint 77 F6
Hope, Highl 167 F3
Hope, Powys 65 F6
Hope, Shrops SY5 0JB 65 G6
Hope Bagot 54 A4
Hope Bowdler 53 H2
Hope End Green 47 F3
Hope Mansell 41 F4
Hope under Dinmore 53 J6
Hopeman 155 F2
Hopesay 53 G3
Hopton, Derby 79 G6
Hopton, Staffs 67 E4
Hopton, Suff 60 C4
Hopton Cangeford 53 J3
Hopton Castle 53 G4
Hopton on Sea 73 J6
Hopton Wafers 54 B4
Hoptonheath 53 G4
Hopwas 67 G6
Hopwood 55 F4
Horam 22 B4
Horbling 70 B3
HORBURY 86 D5
Horcott 42 D5
Horden 104 D3
Horderley 53 H3
Hordle 10 D4
Hordley 65 G3
Horeb, Carm 38 C3
Horeb, Cered 37 H1
Horgabost 158 E3
Horham 61 F4
Horkstow 88 D5
Horley, Oxon 43 G1
HORLEY, Surrey 32 C6
Horn Hill 30 E1
Hornblotton Green 16 D2
Hornby, Lancs 92 D5
Hornby, N Yorks DL6 95 E1
Hornby, N Yorks DL8 94 D2
HORNCASTLE 83 E5
HORNCHURCH 33 F2
Horncliffe 122 E3
HORNDEAN, Hants 19 J4
Horndean, Scot Bord 122 D3
Horndon 6 B2
Horndon on the Hill 33 G2
Horne 32 D6
Hornick 4 C5
Horniehaugh 138 D2
Horning 73 G5
Horninghold 57 G2
Horninglow 67 H4
Horningsea, Cambs 59 E5
Horningsea, Herts 45 F3
Horningsham 27 H6
Horningtoft 72 C4
Horningtops 5 F4
Horns Cross 12 D3
Horns Green 33 E5
Hornsby 102 B2
HORNSEA 89 F2
HORNSEY 32 D2
Hornton 56 B7
Horrabridge 6 B4
Horringer 60 B5
Horse Bridge 78 D6
Horsebridge, Devon 5 H3
Horsebridge, E Susx 22 B4
Horsebridge, Hants 18 E2
Horsebrook 66 D5
Horsehay 66 B6
Horseheath 59 G7
Horsehouse 94 B3
Horsell 30 D5
Horseman's Green 65 H2
Horsendon 44 B5
Horseway 58 E3
Horsey 73 H4
Horsford 73 E5
HORSFORTH 86 D3
HORSHAM, W Susx 21 E2
Horsham, Worces 54 C6
Horsham St Faith 73 F5
Horsington, Lincs 82 D5
Horsington, Somer 17 F3
Horsley, Derby 68 B2
Horsley, Glos 41 H6
Horsley, Northum NE15 113 E6
Horsley, Northum NE19 112 C3
Horsley Cross 48 E3
Horsley Woodhouse 68 B2
Horsleycross Street 48 E3
Horsleyhill 120 E6
Horsmonden 33 G6
Horspath 43 H5
Horstead 73 F5
Horsted Keynes 21 G3
Horton, Bucks 44 D4
Horton, Dorset 18 B5
Horton, Lancs 85 G1
Horton, Northnts 57 G6
Horton, Northum 123 F4
Horton, S Glos 27 G2
Horton, Somer 16 B4
Horton, Staffs 78 D6
Horton, Swan 24 B2
Horton, W&M 30 E3
Horton, Wilts 28 C4
Horton Grange 113 G5
Horton Green 77 G7
Horton Heath 19 F4
Horton in Ribblesdale 93 G4
Horton Kirby 33 F4
Horton-cum-Studley 43 J4
HORWICH 85 E5
Horwood 13 F3
Hose 69 F4
Hoses 91 D2
Hosh 137 F6
Hosta 149 C2
Hoswick 176 D5
Hotham 88 C3
Hothfield 34 C6
Hoton 68 D4

Place	Page	Grid
Houbie	177	D4
Hough	78	B6
Hough Green	77	G3
Hough-on-the-Hill	69	H2
Hougham	69	G2
Houghton, Cambs	58	C4
Houghton, Cumbr	110	D7
Houghton, Hants	18	E2
Houghton, Pemb	36	D5
Houghton, W Susx	20	D4
Houghton Conquest	45	E1
Houghton on the Hill	68	E6
HOUGHTON REGIS	44	E3
Houghton St Giles	72	C3
HOUGHTON-LE-SPRING	104	C3
Houghton-le-Side	104	B5
Houlland	175	E5
Houlskye	105	G7
Hound Green	30	B5
Houndscroft	41	H5
Houndslow	121	F3
Houndwood	131	H6
HOUNSLOW	31	F3
Housay	175	H3
Househill	154	C3
Housetter	177	A5
Houss	176	C4
Houston	127	J6
Houstry, Highl KW1	169	G4
Houstry, Highl KW5	169	F6
Houstry of Dunn	169	G4
Houton	170	D4
HOVE	21	F5
Hoveringham	69	F2
Hoveton	73	G5
Hovingham	96	B4
How	102	B2
How Caple	41	F2
How End	45	E1
Howden	88	B4
Howden- le-Wear	103	H4
Howe, Highl	169	H3
Howe, Norf	73	F6
Howe Green	47	H5
Howe of Teuchar	157	F4
Howe Street, Essex CM3	47	G4
Howe Street, Essex CM7	47	G2
Howell	70	B2
Howey	52	D6
Howgate, Midlo	120	B2
Howgate, Scot Bord	122	C5
Howick	123	H6
Howle	66	B4
Howlett End	47	F2
Howley	14	A5
Hownam	122	C6
Howpasley	110	C2
Howsham, N Linc	88	E6
Howsham, N Yorks	96	C5
Howtel	122	D4
Howton	40	D3
Howtown	101	J6
Howwood	117	H1
Hoxa	171	E5
Hoxne	60	E4
Hoy	170	C4
HOYLAKE	76	E3
HOYLAND	79	H1
Hoylandswaine	86	D6
Hubberholme	93	H4
Hubbert's Bridge	70	C2
Huby, N Yorks LS17	86	D2
Huby, N Yorks YO61	95	G5
Hucclecote	41	H4
Hucking	34	B5
HUCKNALL	68	D2
HUDDERSFIELD	86	C5
Huddington	55	E6
Hudswell	94	C1
Huggate	96	D6
HUGH TOWN	2	N9
Hughenden Valley	44	C6
Hughley	66	A7
Huish, Devon	13	F4
Huish, Wilts	28	D4
Huish Champflower	15	G3
Huish Episcopi	16	C3
Huisinis	158	D1
Hulcote	57	F6
Hulcott	44	C4
Hulland	67	H2
Hulland Ward	67	H2
Hullavington	27	H2
Hullbridge	48	B6
Hulme End	79	F6
Hulme Walfield	78	C5
Hulver Street	61	H3
Humber Bridge	88	E4
Humberside International Airport	89	G4
Humberston	89	H6
Humbie	120	D1
Humbleton, E Yorks	89	G3
Humbleton, Northum	123	H3
Humby	69	J3
Hume	121	G3
Humehall	121	G3
Humshaugh	112	D5
Huna	169	H2
Huncoat	85	F3
Huncote	68	D7
Hundalee	121	F6
Hunderthwaite	103	F5
Hundleby	83	F5
Hundleton	36	D5
Hundon	59	H7
Hundred Acres	19	G4
Hundred End	84	C4
Hundred House	52	E6
Hungarton	69	E6
Hungerford	29	F4
Hungerford Newtown	29	F3
Hungladder	150	C1
Hunmanby	97	F4
Hunningham	56	B5
Hunsdon	46	E4
Hunsdonbury	46	E4
Hunsingore	87	F1
Hunsonby	102	B4
Hunspow	169	G2
HUNSTANTON	71	G2
Hunstanworth	103	F3
Hunston, Suff	60	C5
Hunston, W Susx	20	B5
Hunstrete	27	F4
Hunt End	55	F5
Hunt's Cross	77	G3
Hunter's Quay	127	F5
Hunters Forstal	35	E4
Huntford	111	F2
HUNTINGDON	58	C4
Huntingfield	61	G4
Huntingford	17	G2
Huntington, Co of H	53	F6
Huntington, E Loth	130	D5
Huntington, Staffs	67	E5
Huntington, Yk	95	H6
Huntingtower	137	H6
Huntley	41	G4
HUNTLY	156	C5
Huntlywood	121	F3
Hunton, Kent	33	H6
Hunton, N Yorks	94	C2
Hunton Bridge	45	E5
Huntsham	15	G3
Huntshaw	13	F3
Huntspill	26	C6
Huntworth	16	B2
Hunwick	103	H4
Hunworth	72	D3
Hurdsfield	78	D4
Hurley, W&M	30	C2
Hurley, Warw	55	H2
Hurlford	118	B4
Hurliness	170	C6
Hurn	10	C4
Hursley	19	F3
Hurst, G Man	78	D1
Hurst, N Yorks	94	B1
Hurst, Wokham	30	B3
Hurst Green, E Susx	22	D3
Hurst Green, Lancs	85	E3
Hurst Green, Surrey	32	C5
Hurstbourne Priors	29	G6
Hurstbourne Tarrant	29	F5
Hurstpierpoint	21	F4
Hurworth-on-Tees	104	C6
Hury	103	F5
Husbands Bosworth	56	E3
Husborne Crawley	44	D2
Husthwaite	95	G4
Hustwood	85	G3
Hutcherleigh	6	D5
Huthwaite	80	B6
Huttoft	83	H4
Hutton, Cumbr	101	J5
Hutton, Essex	47	G6
Hutton, Lancs	84	D4
Hutton, N Som	26	C5
Hutton, Scot Bord	122	E2
Hutton Bonville	94	E1
Hutton Buscel	97	E3
Hutton Conyers	94	E4
Hutton Cranswick	88	E1
Hutton End	101	J4
Hutton Henry	104	D4
Hutton Magna	103	H6
Hutton Roof, Cumbr CA11	101	H4
Hutton Roof, Cumbr LA6	92	D4
Hutton Rudby	95	F1
Hutton Sessay	87	G1
Hutton-le-Hole	96	C3
Huttons Ambo	96	C5
Huxley	77	H5
Huxter, Shetld ZE2 9AH	175	G4
Huxter, Shetld ZE2 9LN	175	E5
Hycemoor	91	B3
HYDE, G Man	78	D2
Hyde, Glos	41	H5
Hyde, Hants	18	C4
Hyde Heath	44	D5
Hydestile	30	D6
Hyndlee	111	E2
Hynford Bridge	119	G3
Hynish	132	B5
Hyssington	53	G2
Hythe, Hants	19	F5
HYTHE, Kent	23	H2
Hythe End	30	E3
Hythie	157	H3

I

Place	Page	Grid
Ibberton	17	F5
Ible	79	G6
Ibsley	18	C5
Ibstock	68	C5
Ibstone	44	B6
Ibthorpe	29	F5
Ibworth	29	H5
Ickburgh	60	B2
Ickenham	31	E2
Ickford	43	J5
Ickham	35	F5
Ickleford	45	F2
Icklesham	23	E4
Ickleton	47	E1
Icklingham	59	H4
Ickwell	58	B7
Icomb	42	E3
Idbury	42	E4
Iddesleigh	13	F5
Ide	15	E6
Ide Hill	33	E5
Ideford	7	E3
Iden	23	F3
Iden Green, Kent TN17 2	22	D2
Iden Green, Kent TN17 4	22	E2
Idlicote	43	E1
Idmiston	18	C2
Idridgehay	67	H2
Idrigill	150	C2
Idstone	28	E2
Idvies	139	E4
Ifield	21	F2
Ifold	20	D2
Iford	21	H5
Ifton Heath	65	G3
Ightfield	66	A3
Ightham	33	F5
Iken	61	H6
Ilam	79	F6
Ilchester	16	D3
Ilderton	123	F5
ILFORD	33	E2
ILFRACOMBE	24	C6
ILKESTON	68	C2
Ilketshall St Andrew	61	G3
Ilketshall St Lawrence	61	G3
Ilketshall St Margaret	61	G3
ILKLEY	86	C2
Illey	55	E3
Illington	60	C2
Illingworth	86	B4
Illogan	3	E3
Illston on the Hill	69	F7
Ilmer	44	B5
Ilmington	42	E1
ILMINSTER	16	B4
Ilsington	6	D3
Ilston	24	C1
Ilton, N Yorks	94	C4
Ilton, Somer	16	B4
Imachar	116	C3
Immingham	89	F5
Impington	59	E5
Ince	77	G4
Ince Blundell	84	B6
INCE-IN-MAKERFIELD	84	D6
Inch of Arnhall	146	D6
Inchbare	139	F2
Inchberry	155	H3
Incheril	152	C2
Inchgrundle	146	B6
Inchina	162	D4
Inchindown	164	C6
Inchinnan	128	B6
Inchlaggan	142	D3
Inchlumpie	164	B6
Inchmore	153	F4
Inchnadamph	163	G1
Inchree	135	E2
Inchture	138	B6
Inchyra	138	A6
Indian Queens	4	C5
Inerval	124	C6
Ingatestone	47	G6
Ingbirchworth	86	D6
Ingestre	67	E4
Ingham, Lincs	81	G3
Ingham, Norf	73	G4
Ingham, Suff	60	B4
Ingleborough	71	E5
Ingleby	68	B4
Ingleby Arncliffe	95	F1
Ingleby Greenhow	104	E7
Inglesbatch	27	G4
Inglesham	42	E6
Ingleton, Durham	103	H5
Ingleton, N Yorks	93	E4
Inglewhite	84	D2
Ingliston	129	J5
Ingoe	112	E5
Ingoldisthorpe	71	G3
Ingoldmells	83	H5
Ingoldsby	69	J3
Ingon	55	H6
Ingram	123	F6
Ingrave	33	G1
Ings	92	C2
Ingst	27	E2
Ingworth	73	E4
Injebreck	90	C4
Inkberrow	55	F6
Inkhorn	157	G5
Inkpen	29	F4
Inkstack	169	G2
Innellan	127	F5
Inner Hope	6	C7
Innerhadden	136	D3
INNERLEITHEN	120	C4
Innerleven	130	B4
Innermessan	98	B3
Innerwick, E Loth	131	G5
Innerwick, Pth & Kin	136	C4
Innsworth	41	H3
Insch	156	D6
Insh	144	C3
Inshegra	166	D4
Inshore	166	E3
Inskip	84	C3
Instow	13	E2
Intake	84	A3
Inver, Aberd	145	G4
Inver, Highl IV20	165	E5
Inver, Highl KW6	169	F6
Inver, Pth & Kin	137	H4
Inverailort	141	G5
Inveralligin	151	H3
Inverallochy	157	H2
Inveran	156	E6
Inveraray	164	B4
INVERARAY	127	E2
Inverardran	135	H6
Inverarish	151	E5
Inverarity	138	D4
Inverarnan	135	H7
Inverasdale	162	C5
INVERBERVIE	147	F6
Inverbrough	154	C5
Invercassley	164	A3
Invercharnan	135	F4
Invercharron	153	E3
Inverchoran	134	E4
Inverdruie	144	C2
Inverebrie	157	G5
Invereshie	130	C5
Inverey	145	E5
Inverfarigaig	153	H6
Invergarry	143	F3
Invergelder	145	G4
Invergeldie	136	E6
INVERGORDON	154	B2
Invergowrie	138	C5
Inverguseran	141	G3
Inverharroch	155	H5
Inverie	141	G3
Inverinan	134	D7
Inverinate	152	B6
Inverkeilor	139	F4
INVERKEITHING	129	J4
Inverkeithny	156	D4
Inverkip	127	G5
Inverkirkaig	163	E1
Inverlael	163	F5
Inverlaidnan	154	C6
Inverlauren	127	H4
Inverlochlarig	136	B7
Inverlochy	135	F6
Invermoidart	141	F6
Invermoriston	143	G2
Invernaver	167	J3
Inverneill	126	C4
INVERNESS	154	A4
Invernoaden	127	F3
Inverquharity	138	D3
Inverquhomery	157	H4
Inverroy	142	E5
Invershiel	142	B2
Invershin	164	B4
Inversnaid	127	H2
Inveruglas	127	H2
Inverugie	157	H4
INVERURIE	157	E6
Invervar	136	D4
Inverythan	156	E4
Inwardleigh	13	F6
Inworth	48	B4
Iochdar	149	C5
Iping	20	B3
Ipplepen	6	E4
Ipsden	29	J2
Ipstones	78	E7
IPSWICH	48	E1
Irby	76	E3
Irby in the Marsh	83	G5
Irby Upon Humber	89	F6
Irchester	57	H5
Ireby, Cumbr	101	G4
Ireby, Lancs	93	E4
Ireland, Orkney	170	D4
Ireland, Shetld	176	D5
Ireleth	91	D4
Ireshopeburn	103	E4
IRLAM	78	B2
Irnham	69	J4
Iron Acton	27	F2
Iron Cross	55	F6
Ironbridge	66	B6
Ironmacannie	108	D5
Ironside	157	F3
Ironville	80	B6
Irstead	73	G4
irthington	110	E6
IRTHLINGBOROUGH	57	H4
Irton	97	F3
IRVINE	117	H4
Isauld	168	D3
Isbister, Orkney KW17 2EX	172	D5
Isbister, Orkney KW17 2JH	172	C4
Isbister, Shetld ZE2 9AJ	175	G4
Isbister, Shetld ZE2 9RY	177	A4
Isfield	21	H4
Isham	57	G4
Isle Abbotts	16	B3
Isle Brewers	16	B3
Isle of Dogs	32	D3
Isle of Man (Ronaldsway) Airport	90	B6
Isle of Whithorn	99	F6
Isleham	59	G4
Isleham Marina	59	G4
Isleornsay or Eilean Iarmain	141	F2
Islesburgh	175	E4
Islesteps	109	G5
ISLEWORTH	31	F3
Isley Walton	68	C4
Islibhig	160	C5
ISLINGTON	32	D2
Islip, Northnts	57	H4
Islip, Oxon	43	H4
Istead Rise	33	G4
Isycoed	77	G6
Itchen Abbas	19	G2
Itchen Stoke	19	G2
Itchingfield	21	E3
Itchington	27	F2
Itteringham	72	E3
Itton	14	C6
Itton Common	40	D6
Ivegill	101	J3
Ivelet	93	H2
Iver	31	E2
Iver Heath	30	E2
Iveston	103	H2
Ivinghoe	44	D4
Ivinghoe Aston	44	D4
Ivington	53	H6
Ivington Green	53	H6
Ivy Hatch	33	F5
Ivy Todd	72	B6
IVYBRIDGE	6	C5
Ivychurch	23	G3
Iwade	34	C4
Iwerne Courtney or Shroton	17	G4
Iwerne Minster	17	G4
Ixworth	60	C4
Ixworth Thorpe	60	C4

J

Place	Page	Grid
Jack Hill	86	D1
Jackstown	156	E5
Jackton	118	C2
Jacobs Well	30	E5
Jacobstow	12	B6
Jacobstowe	13	F5
Jameston	37	E6
Jamestown, D & G	110	C3
Jamestown, Highl	153	G3
Jamestown, W Dunb	127	H4
Janefield	154	B3
JARROW	113	H6
Jarvis Brook	22	B3
Jawcraig	129	F5
Jayes Park	31	F6
Jaywick	48	E4
JEDBURGH	121	F5
Jeffreyston	37	E5
Jemimaville	154	B2
Jersay	119	F1
Jevington	22	B5
Jewells Cross	12	C5
Jocks Lodge	88	E3
Jodrell Bank	78	B4
John o' Groats	169	H2
John's Cross	22	D3
Johnby	101	J4
Johnshaven	139	G2
Johnston	36	D4
JOHNSTONE	128	B6
Johnstonebridge	109	H3
Jordans	30	D1
Jordanston	36	D2
Jump	79	H1
Juniper	112	D7
Juniper Green	130	B6
Juniper Hill	43	H2
Jurby East	90	C3
Jurby West	90	C3

K

Place	Page	Grid
Kaber	102	D6
Kaimes	130	B6
Kames, Arg & Bt	126	D5
Kames, E Ayr	118	D5
Kea	3	G3
Keadby	88	C5
Keal Cotes	83	F5
KEARSLEY	85	F6
Kearstwick	93	E3
Kearton	94	A2
Kearvaig	166	D2
Kebholes	156	D3
Keddington	83	F3
Kedington	59	H7
Kedleston	67	J2
Keelby	89	F5
Keele	66	D2
Keeley Green	57	J7
Keeres Green	47	F4
Keeston	36	D4
Keevil	28	B5
Kegworth	68	C4
Kehelland	2	E5
Keig	146	D2
KEIGHLEY	86	B2
Keilarsbrae	129	F3
Keilhill	156	E3
Keillmore	126	A4
Keillor	138	B4
Keillour	137	G6
Keills	125	B6
Keills	125	C6
Keinton Mandeville	16	D2
Keir Mill	109	F3
Keisby	69	J4
Keiss	169	H3
KEITH	156	B3
Keithock	139	F2
Kelbrook	85	H2
Kelby	69	J2
Keld, Cumbr	102	B6
Keld, N Yorks	93	G1
Keldholme	96	C3
Kelfield	87	G3
Kelham	80	E6
Kellan	133	H4
Kellas, Ang	138	D5
Kellas, Mor	155	F3
Kelleth	93	E1
Kelleythorpe	97	F6
Kelling	72	D2
Kellington	87	G4
Kelloe	104	C4
Kelly	5	G2
Kelly Bray	5	G3
Kelmarsh	57	F4
Kelmscott	42	E6
Kelsale	61	G5
Kelsall	77	H5
Kelsay	46	D2
Kelsick	101	F2
KELSO	121	G4
Kelstedge	79	H5
Kelstern	83	E2
Kelston	27	G4
Keltneyburn	136	C4
Kelton, D & G	109	G5
Kelton, Durham	103	F5
Kelty	129	J3
Kelvedon	48	B4
Kelvedon Hatch	47	F6
Kelynack	2	B5
Kemacott	24	D6
Kemback	138	D7
Kemberton	66	C6
Kemble	42	B6
Kemerton	42	B2
Kemeys Commander	40	C5
Kemnay	146	E2
Kemp Town	21	G5
Kempley	41	F3
Kempley Green	41	F3
Kempsey	54	D7
Kempsford	42	D6
KEMPSTON	57	J7
Kempston Hardwick	45	E1
Kempton	53	G3
Kemsing	33	F5
Kemsley	34	C4
Kenardington	23	F2
Kenchester	40	D1
Kencott	42	E5
KENDAL	92	D2
Kendram	159	J5
Kenfig	25	F2
Kenfig Hill	25	F2
KENILWORTH	55	H4
Kenknock	136	B5
Kenley, Shrops	65	J6
Kenley, Surrey	32	C5
Kenmore, Highl	151	G3
Kenmore, Pth & Kin	137	E4
Kenn, Devon	7	F2
Kenn, N Som	26	D4
Kennacraig	116	C1
Kennerleigh	14	E5
Kennet	129	G3
Kennethmont	156	C6
Kennett	59	G5
Kennford	7	F2
Kenninghall	60	D3
Kennington, Kent	34	D6
Kennington, Oxon	43	H5
Kennoway	130	C2
Kenny Hill	59	G4
Kennythorpe	96	C5
Kenovay	132	B4
Kensaleyre	150	D3
KENSINGTON	32	C3
Kensworth	44	E4
Kent International Airport/ RAF Manston	35	G4
Kent's Green	41	G3
Kent's Oak	18	E3
Kentallen	134	E3
Kentchurch	40	D3
Kentford	59	H5
Kentisbeare	15	G5
Kentisbury	24	D6
Kentisbury Ford	24	D6
Kentmere	92	C1
Kenton, Devon	7	F2
KENTON, G Lon	31	F2
Kenton, Suff	61	E5
Kentra	141	F7
Kents Bank	92	B4
Kenwick	65	H3
Kenwyn	3	G3
Kenyon	77	J2
Keoldale	167	E3
Keppanach	135	E2
Keppoch	152	A6
Keprigan	114	B5
Kepwick	95	F2
Keresley	56	B3
Kerne Bridge	41	E4
Kerridge	78	D4
Kerris	2	C5
Kerry	52	E3
Kerry's Gate	40	C2
Kerrycroy	117	F1
Kerrymenoch	117	F2
Kerrysdale	162	C6
Kersall	80	E5
Kersey	48	D1
Kershopefoot	110	D4
Kersoe	42	B1
Kerswell	15	G5
Kerswell Green	54	D7
Kesgrave	61	F2
Kessingland	61	J3
Kestle Mill	3	G2
KESWICK, Cumbr	101	G5
Keswick, Norf NR12	73	G3
Keswick, Norf NR4	73	H6
Ketsby	83	G4
KETTERING	2	E5
Ketteringham	72	E6
Kettins	138	B5
Kettlebaston	60	C6
Kettlebridge	130	C2
Kettlebrook	67	H6
Kettleburgh	61	F5
Kettlehill	130	C2
Kettleholm	109	J5
Kettleness	105	H6
Kettleshulme	78	D4
Kettlesing Bottom	94	D6
Kettlestone	72	C3
Kettlethorpe	81	F4
Kettlewell	93	H4
Ketton	69	H6
Kew	31	F3
Kew Bridge	31	F3
Kewstoke	26	C4
Kexbrough	86	E6
Kexby, Lincs	81	F3
Kexby, Yk	87	J1
Key Green	78	C5
Keycol	34	B4
Keyham	68	E6
Keyhaven	10	E4
Keyingham	89	G4
Keymer	21	G4
KEYNSHAM	27	F4
Keysoe	58	A5
Keysoe Row	58	A5
Keyston	57	J4
Keyworth	68	E3
Kibblesworth	104	B2
Kibworth Beauchamp	56	E2
Kibworth Harcourt	57	E2
Kidbrooke	32	E3
Kiddal Lane End	87	F3
Kiddemore Green	66	D6
KIDDERMINSTER	54	D4
Kiddington	43	G3
KIDLINGTON	43	G4
Kidmore End	30	A3
KIDSGROVE	78	C6
Kidstones	93	H3
KIDWELLY	37	J5
Kielder	111	F3
Kilbarchan	127	J6
Kilbeg	141	F3
Kilberry	126	B6
Kilberry Castle	126	B6
Kilbirnie	117	H2
Kilbride, Arg & Bt PA20	126	E6
Kilbride, Arg & Bt PA34	134	C6
Kilbride, Highl	141	E1
Kilburn, Derby	68	B2
Kilburn, N Yorks	95	G4
Kilby	56	E2
Kilchamaig	116	C1
Kilchattan	125	A3
Kilchattan Bay	116	E2
Kilchenzie	116	A5
Kilcheran	134	C5
Kilchiaran	124	B4
Kilchoan	133	G2
Kilchoman	124	B4
Kilchrenan	135	E6
Kilconquhar	130	D2
Kilcot	41	F3
Kilcoy	153	H3
Kilcreggan	127	G5
Kildale	105	F7
Kildalloig	116	B6
Kildary	164	D6
Kildavanan	126	E6
Kildonan	116	E5
Kildonan	140	D5
Kildrummy	146	B2
Kildwick	86	B2
Kilfinan	126	D5
Kilfinnan	143	E4
Kilgetty	37	F5
Kilgwrrwg Common	40	D6
Kilham, E Yorks	97	F5
Kilham, Northum	122	D4
Kilkenneth	132	B4
Kilkerran	107	F2
Kilkhampton	12	C4
Killamarsh	80	B3
Killay	38	D6
Killbeg	133	J4
Killean	116	A3
Killearn	128	C4
Killellan Park	116	A6
Killen	154	A3
Killerby	103	H6
Killichonate	142	E5
Killichonan	133	H4
Killiecrankie	137	G2
Killiemor	133	G5
Killilan	152	B5
Killimster	169	H4
Killin	136	C5
Killinallan	125	A5
Killinghall	94	D1
Killingholme	93	E3
Killochyett	120	D3
Killocraw	114	B3
Killundine	133	H4
Kilmacolm	127	H6
Kilmahog	128	D1
Kilmahumaig	126	B3
Kilmalieu	134	C3
Kilmaluag	159	J5
Kilmany	138	C6
KILMARNOCK	118	B4
Kilmartin	126	C3
Kilmaurs	117	J3
Kilmelford	126	C1
Kilmeny	125	A6
Kilmersdon	27	F5
Kilmeston	19	G3
Kilmichael	116	A5
Kilmichael Glassary	126	C3
Kilmichael of Inverlussa	126	B4
Kilmington, Devon	8	A4
Kilmington, Wilts	17	F2
Kilmington Common	17	F2
Kilmoluaig	132	B4
Kilmorack	153	G4
Kilmore, Arg & Bt	134	C6
Kilmore, Highl	141	F3
Kilmory, Arg & Bt	126	B5
Kilmory, Highl PH36	140	E6
Kilmory, Highl PH43	140	C3
Kilmory, N Ayr	116	D5
Kilmuir, Highl IV1	154	A4
Kilmuir, Highl IV18	164	D6
Kilmuir, Highl IV51	150	C1
Kilmuir, Highl IV55	150	B4
Kilmun	127	F4
Kiln Pit Hill	103	G2
Kilnave	124	B3
Kilncadzow	119	F3
Kilndown	22	D2
Kilnhurst	80	B2
Kilninian	133	F4
Kilninver	134	C6
Kilnsea	89	J5

Name	Page	Grid
Kilnsey	93	H5
Kilnwick	88	E2
Kiloran	125	A3
Kilpatrick, Arg & Bt	134	B5
Kilpatrick, N Ayr	116	D5
Kilpeck	40	D2
Kilphedir	165	F2
Kilpin	88	B4
KILRENNY	131	E2
Kilsby	56	D4
Kilspindie	138	B6
KILSYTH	128	E5
Kiltarlity	153	H4
Kilton	26	A6
Kiltyrie	136	D5
Kilvaxter	150	C2
Kilve	26	A6
Kilvington	69	F2
KILWINNING	117	H3
Kimberley, Norf	72	D6
Kimberley, Notts	68	C2
Kimble	44	C5
Kimble Wick	44	C5
Kimblesworth	104	B3
Kimbolton, Cambs	58	A5
Kimbolton, Co of H	53	J5
Kimcote	56	D3
Kimmeridge	9	H6
Kimmerston	123	E4
Kimpton, Hants	29	E6
Kimpton, Herts	45	F4
Kinbrace	168	C6
Kinbuck	128	C2
Kincaple	138	D7
Kincardine, Fife	129	G4
Kincardine, Highl	164	C5
Kincardine Br	129	G4
Kincardine O'Neil	146	C4
Kinclaven	138	A5
Kincorth	147	G3
Kincraig	144	C3
Kincraigie	137	G4
Kindallachan	137	G3
Kinerras	153	G4
Kineton, Glos	42	C3
Kineton, Warw	56	B6
Kinfauns	138	A6
King Edward	156	E3
King Sterndale	79	E4
King's Acre	40	D1
King's Bromley	67	G5
King's Caple	41	E3
King's Cliffe	57	J2
King's Coughton	55	F6
King's Heath	55	F3
King's Hill	33	G5
KING'S LYNN	71	G4
King's Meaburn	102	C5
King's Norton, Leic	69	E6
King's Norton, W Mids	55	F4
King's Nympton	14	C4
King's Pyon	53	H6
King's Somborne	18	E2
King's Stag	17	F4
King's Stanley	41	H5
King's Thorn	40	D2
King's Walden	45	F3
Kingarth	117	E2
Kingcoed	40	D5
Kingerby	82	C2
Kingham	42	E3
Kingholm Quay	109	G5
KINGHORN	130	B4
Kinglassie	130	B3
Kingoodie	138	C6
Kings Green	41	G2
Kings Langley	45	E5
Kings Muir	120	B4
Kings Ripton	58	C4
Kings Sutton	43	G2
Kings Worthy	19	F2
Kingsand	5	H5
Kingsbarns	131	E1
Kingsbourne Green	45	F4
KINGSBRIDGE, Devon	6	D6
Kingsbridge, Somer	15	F2
Kingsburgh	150	C3
Kingsbury, G Lon	31	F2
Kingsbury, Warw	55	H2
Kingsbury Episcopi	16	C3
Kingscavil	129	H5
Kingsclere	29	H5
Kingscote	41	H6
Kingscott	13	F4
Kingscross	117	E5
Kingsdon	16	D3
Kingsdown	35	G6
Kingseat	129	J3
Kingsey	44	B5
Kingsfold	21	E2
Kingsford, Aberd	146	C2
Kingsford, E Ayr	118	B3
Kingsford, Worces	54	D3
Kingsforth	88	E5
Kingshall Street	60	C5
Kingsheanton	13	F2
Kingshouse	136	C6
Kingside Hill	101	F2
Kingskerswell	7	E4
Kingskettle	130	C2
Kingsland	53	H5
Kingsley, Ches	77	H4
Kingsley, Hants	20	A2
Kingsley, Staffs	67	F2
Kingsley Green	20	B2
Kingsmuir	138	D2
Kingsnorth, Kent	23	G2
Kingsnorth, Med	34	B3
Kingstanding	55	F2
Kingsteignton	6	E3
Kingsteps	154	D3
Kingston, Cambs	58	D6
Kingston, Devon	9	H6
Kingston, Dorset BH20	9	H6
Kingston, Dorset DT10	17	F5
Kingston, E Loth	131	E4
Kingston, Hants	10	C3
Kingston, I of W	11	F5
Kingston, Kent	35	E5
Kingston, Mor	155	H2
Kingston Bagpuize	43	G6
Kingston Blount	44	B6
Kingston by Sea	21	F5
Kingston Deverill	17	G2
Kingston Gorse	20	D5
Kingston Lisle	29	F2
Kingston near Lewes	21	G5
Kingston on Soar	68	D4
Kingston Seymour	26	D4
Kingston St Mary	15	J3
KINGSTON UPON HULL	89	E4
KINGSTON UPON THAMES	31	F4
Kingstone, Co of H	40	D2
Kingstone, Somer	16	B4
Kingstone, Staffs	67	F4
Kingstown	101	H2
Kingswear	7	E5
Kingswell	118	C3
Kingswells	147	F3
Kingswinford	54	D3
Kingswood, Bucks	44	A4
Kingswood, Co of H	53	F6
Kingswood, Glos	27	G1
Kingswood, Kent	34	B5
Kingswood, Powys	65	F6
KINGSWOOD, S Glos	27	F3
Kingswood, Surrey	32	C5
Kingswood, Warw	55	G4
Kingthorpe	82	D4
KINGTON, Co of H	53	G6
Kington, Worces	55	E6
Kington Langley	28	B3
Kington Magna	17	F3
Kington St Michael	28	B3
KINGUSSIE	144	B3
Kingweston	16	D2
Kinharrachie	157	G5
Kinkell Bridge	137	G2
Kinknockie	157	H4
Kinlet	54	C3
Kinloch, Fife	130	B1
Kinloch, Highl IV27	166	E6
Kinloch, Highl IV43	141	F2
Kinloch, Highl PH43	140	D4
Kinloch, Pth & Kin PH10	138	A4
Kinloch, Pth & Kin PH12	138	B4
Kinloch Hourn	142	B3
Kinloch Laggan	143	H5
Kinloch Rannoch	136	D3
Kinlochard	128	B2
Kinlochbervie	166	D4
Kinlochell	142	B6
Kinlochewe	152	C2
Kinlochleven	135	F2
Kinlochmoidart	141	G6
Kinlochmore	135	F2
Kinlochspelve	134	A6
Kinloss	155	E2
Kinmel Bay	76	B3
Kinmuck	147	F2
Kinmundy	147	F2
Kinnadie	157	G4
Kinnaird	138	B6
Kinneff	147	H6
Kinnelhead	109	H2
Kinnell	139	F3
Kinnerley	65	G4
Kinnersley, Co of H	53	G7
Kinnersley, Worces	41	H1
Kinnerton, Ches	77	F5
Kinnerton, Powys	53	F5
Kinnesswood	130	A2
Kinninvie	103	G5
Kinnordy	138	C3
Kinoulton	68	E3
KINROSS	129	J2
Kinrossie	138	A5
Kinsey Heath	66	B2
Kinsham	53	G5
Kinsley	87	F5
Kintbury	29	F4
Kintessack	154	E3
Kintillo	137	J7
Kintocher	146	C3
Kinton, Co of H	53	H4
Kinton, Shrops	65	G5
KINTORE	147	E2
Kintour	124	D5
Kintra	124	C6
Kintraw	126	C2
Kinuachdrachd	126	B3
Kinveachy	144	D2
Kinver	54	D3
Kippax	87	F3
Kippen	128	D3
Kippford	100	C2
Kipping's Cross	22	C1
Kirbister	101	D4
Kirbuster, Orkney KW17 2AG	173	G4
Kirbuster, Orkney KW17 2LW	172	C4
Kirby Bedon	73	F6
Kirby Bellars	69	F5
Kirby Cane	61	G2
Kirby Cross	49	F3
Kirby Grindalythe	96	C5
Kirby Hill, N Yorks DL11	103	H7
Kirby Hill, N Yorks YO51	95	E5
Kirby Knowle	95	F3
Kirby Misperton	96	C4
Kirby Muxloe	68	D6
Kirby Row	61	G2
Kirby Sigston	95	F2
Kirby Underdale	96	D6
Kirby Wharfe	87	G2
Kirby Wiske	95	E3
Kirby- le-Soken	49	F3
Kirdford	20	D3
Kirk	169	G4
Kirk Bramwith	87	H5
Kirk Deighton	87	E1
Kirk Ella	88	E4
Kirk Hammerton	95	F6
Kirk Ireton	79	G6
Kirk Langley	67	H3
Kirk Merrington	104	B4
Kirk Michael	90	C3
Kirk of Shotts	119	F1
Kirk Sandall	87	H6
Kirk Smeaton	87	G5
Kirk Yetholm	122	D5
Kirkabister	176	D4
Kirkandrews	99	H5
Kirkandrews on-Eden	101	H2
Kirkbampton	101	H2
Kirkbean	109	G7
Kirkbride	101	G2
Kirkbuddo	138	E4
Kirkburn, E Yorks	97	E6
Kirkburn, Scot Bord	120	B4
Kirkburton	86	C5
Kirkby, Lincs	82	C2
Kirkby, Mers	77	G2
Kirkby, N Yorks	95	G1
Kirkby Fleetham	94	D2
Kirkby Green	82	C6
KIRKBY IN ASHFIELD	80	B6
Kirkby la Thorpe	70	A2
KIRKBY LONSDALE	93	E4
Kirkby Malham	93	G5
Kirkby Mallory	68	C6
Kirkby Malzeard	94	D4
Kirkby Mills	96	C3
Kirkby on Bain	83	E5
Kirkby Overblow	86	E2
KIRKBY STEPHEN	102	D7
Kirkby Thore	102	C5
Kirkby Underwood	70	A4
Kirkby-in-Furness	91	D3
Kirkbymoorside	96	B3
KIRKCALDY	130	B3
Kirkcambeck	110	E6
Kirkcarswell	100	B3
Kirkcolm	98	B3
Kirkconnel	118	E6
Kirkconnell	109	G6
Kirkcowan	98	C3
KIRKCUDBRIGHT	99	H4
Kirkfieldbank	119	F3
Kirkgunzeon	109	F6
KIRKHAM, Lancs	84	C3
Kirkham, N Yorks	96	C5
Kirkhamgate	86	D4
Kirkheaton, Northum	112	E5
Kirkheaton, W Yorks	86	C5
Kirkhill, Ang	139	F2
Kirkhill, Highl	153	H4
Kirkhill, Mor	155	G5
Kirkhill Pendicle	157	G4
Kirkhope	120	C5
Kirkhouse	120	C4
Kirkibost	141	E2
Kirkinch	138	C4
Kirkinner	99	F4
KIRKINTILLOCH	128	D5
Kirkland, Cumbr CA10	102	C4
Kirkland, Cumbr CA26	100	E6
Kirkland, D & G DG3	109	F3
Kirkland, D & G DG4	118	E6
Kirklands	131	F2
Kirkleatham	105	E5
Kirklevington	104	D6
Kirkley	61	J2
Kirklington, N Yorks	94	E3
Kirklington, Notts	80	D6
Kirklinton	110	D6
Kirkliston	129	J5
Kirkmaiden	98	C6
Kirkmichael, Pth & Kin	137	H3
Kirkmichael, S Ayr	107	F2
Kirkmichael Mains	109	H4
Kirkmuirhill	119	E3
Kirknewton, Northum	122	E4
Kirknewton, W Loth	129	J6
Kirkney	156	C5
Kirkoswald, Cumbr	102	B3
Kirkoswald, S Ayr	106	E2
Kirkpatrick Durham	108	E5
Kirkpatrick- Fleming	110	B5
Kirksanton	91	C3
Kirkstile	156	C5
Kirkstyle	169	H2
Kirkton, Aberd AB42	157	J3
Kirkton, Aberd AB52	156	D6
Kirkton, Aberd AB53	156	D3
Kirkton, Ang DD4	138	D5
Kirkton, Ang DD8	138	D4
Kirkton, D & G	109	G4
Kirkton, Fife	138	C6
Kirkton, Highl IV2	154	B3
Kirkton, Highl IV40	151	H6
Kirkton, Highl IV54	152	B4
Kirkton, Highl KW10	164	E4
Kirkton, Pth & Kin	137	G7
Kirkton, S Lanak	119	G5
Kirkton, Scot Bord	121	E6
Kirkton, Stir	128	C2
Kirkton Manor	120	B4
Kirkton of Airlie	138	C3
Kirkton of Auchterhouse	138	C5
Kirkton of Auchterless	156	E4
Kirkton of Barevan	154	C4
Kirkton of Bourtie	157	F6
Kirkton of Collace	138	A5
Kirkton of Craig	139	G3
Kirkton of Culsalmond	156	D5
Kirkton of Durris	147	E4
Kirkton of Glenbuchat	145	H2
Kirkton of Glenisla	138	B2
Kirkton of Kingoldrum	138	C3
Kirkton of Lethendy	137	J4
Kirkton of Logie Buchan	157	G6
Kirkton of Maryculter	147	F4
Kirkton of Menmuir	139	E2
Kirkton of Monikie	139	E5
Kirkton of Rayne	156	D5
Kirkton of Skene	147	F3
Kirkton of Tough	146	D2
Kirktown	157	H3
Kirktown of Alvah	156	D2
Kirktown of Deskford	156	C2
Kirktown of Fetteresso	147	F5
KIRKWALL	171	E4
Kirkwhelpington	112	D4
Kirmington	89	F5
Kirminnoch	98	B3
Kirmond le Mire	82	D2
Kirn	127	F5
KIRRIEMUIR	138	C3
Kirstead Green	73	F7
Kirtlebridge	110	B5
Kirtling	59	G6
Kirtling Green	59	G6
Kirtlington	43	G4
Kirtomy	168	B3
Kirton, Lincs	70	D3
Kirton, Notts	80	D5
Kirton, Suff	49	F2
Kirton End	70	C2
Kirton Holme	70	C2
Kirton in Lindsey	81	G2
Kislingbury	57	E6
Kites Hardwick	56	C5
Kittle	24	C2
Kittybrewster	147	G3
Kitwood	19	H2
Kiveton Park	80	B3
Knaith	81	F3
Knaphill	30	D5
Knapp, Pth & Kin	138	B5
Knapp, Somer	16	A3
Knapton, N Yorks	96	D4
Knapton, Norf	73	G3
Knapton, Yk	87	G1
Knapton Green	53	H6
Knapwell	58	D5
KNARESBOROUGH	94	E6
Knarsdale	102	C2
Knaven	157	F4
Knayton	95	F3
Knebworth	46	C4
Knedlington	88	B4
Kneesall	80	E5
Kneesworth	46	D1
Kneeton	69	F2
Knelston	24	B2
Knettishall	60	C3
Knightacott	14	C2
Knightcote	56	B6
Knighton, C of Leic	68	E6
Knighton, Devon	6	B6
KNIGHTON, Powys	53	F4
Knighton, Staffs ST20	66	C4
Knighton, Staffs TF9	66	C2
Knightwick	54	C6
Knill	53	F5
Knipton	69	G3
Knitsley	103	H3
Kniveton	79	G6
Knochenkelly	117	E5
Knock, Arg & Bt	133	H5
Knock, Cumbr	102	C5
Knock, Mor	156	C3
Knockandhu	155	G6
Knockando	155	F4
Knockbain	153	J3
Knockbreck	164	D5
Knockbrex	99	G5
Knockdee	169	F3
Knockdolian	106	D4
Knockdow	127	F5
Knockdown	27	H2
Knockenstob	118	E6
Knockentiber	117	H4
Knockholt	33	E5
Knockholt Pound	33	E5
Knockin	65	G4
Knockin Heath	65	G4
Knocknaha	116	A6
Knocknain	98	A3
Knocknalling	108	C4
Knockrome	125	C5
Knocksharry	90	B4
Knodishall	61	H5
Knolls Green	78	C5
Knolton	65	G3
Knook	28	B6
Knossington	69	G6
Knott End-on-Sea	84	B2
Knotting	57	J5
Knotting Green	57	J5
KNOTTINGLEY	87	F4
Knotty Green	30	D1
Knowbury	54	A4
Knowe	107	F5
Knowehead	108	D3
Knowes of Elrick	156	D3
Knowesgate	112	D4
Knowesside	117	G6
Knowetownhead	121	E6
Knowhead, Aberd	157	G3
Knowhead, E Ayr	118	C5
Knowl Green	47	H1
Knowl Hill	30	C3
Knowl Wall	66	D3
Knowle, C of Bris	27	F3
Knowle, Devon EX17	14	D5
Knowle, Devon EX33	13	E2
Knowle, Devon EX9	7	G2
Knowle, Shrops	54	A4
Knowle, W Mids	55	G4
Knowle Green	85	E3
Knowlton	35	F5
Knowsley	77	G2
Knowstone	14	E3
Knucklas	53	F4
KNUTSFORD	78	B4
Knypersley	78	C6
Kuggar	3	H6
Kyle of Lochalsh	151	G6
Kyleakin	151	G6
Kylerhea	141	G1
Kyles Scalpay	166	D6
Kylesku	166	D6
Kyloe	123	F3
Kynnersley	66	B5
Kyre	54	B5

L

Name	Page	Grid
Labost	161	F3
Lacasaidh	161	G5
Lacasdail	161	H4
Laceby	89	G6
Lacey Green	44	C6
Lach Dennis	78	B4
Lache	77	F5
Lackford	59	H4
Lacock	28	B4
Ladbroke	56	C6
Laddingford	33	G6
Lade Bank	83	F6
Ladock	3	G2
Lady	173	G2
Lady's Green	59	H6
LADYBANK, Fife	130	C1
Ladybank, S Ayr	106	E2
Ladycross	5	G2
Ladykirk	122	D3
Ladysford	157	G2
Laga	133	J2
Lagavulin	124	D6
Lagg, Arg & Bt	125	C5
Lagg, N Ayr	116	D5
Lagg, S Ayr	117	G6
Laggan, Arg & Bt	124	B5
Laggan, Highl PH20	143	J4
Laggan, Highl PH34	143	E4
Laggan, S Ayr	106	E4
Lagganulva	133	G4
Lagrae	118	E6
Laide	162	C4
Laindon	33	G2
Lair, Highl	152	C4
Lair, Pth & Kin	138	A2
Lairg	164	B3
Lairgmore	153	H5
Laithes	102	A4
Lake, Devon	13	F2
Lake, Wilts	18	C2
Lakenham	73	F6
Lakenheath	59	H3
Lakesend	92	B3
Lakeside	31	E4
Laleham	31	E4
Laleston	25	F3
Lamancha	120	B2
Lamarsh	48	B2
Lamas	73	F4
Lamb Corner	48	D2
Lambden	122	C3
Lamberhurst	22	C2
Lamberton	123	E2
LAMBETH	32	D3
Lambfell Moar	90	B4
Lambley, Northum	102	C2
Lambley, Notts	68	E2
Lambourn	29	F3
Lambourn Woodlands	29	F3
Lambourne End	47	E6
Lambs Green	21	F2
Lambston	36	D4
Lamerton	5	H3
Lamesley	104	B2
Lamington, Highl	164	D6
Lamington, S Lanak	119	G4
Lamlash	116	E4
Lamloch	107	H3
Lamonby	101	A4
Lamorna	2	C5
Lamorran	3	G3
LAMPETER	51	F2
Lampeter Velfrey	37	F4
Lamphey	36	E5
Lamplugh	101	E5
Lamport	57	F4
Lamyatt	17	E2
Lana, Devon EX22 6	12	D6
Lana, Devon EX22 7	12	C5
LANARK	119	F3
LANCASTER	92	C5
Lanchester	103	H3
Lancing	21	E5
Landbeach	59	E5
Landcross	13	E3
Landerberry	146	E3
Landford	18	D4
Landhallow	169	F6
Landimore	38	B6
Landkey	13	F2
Landmoor	38	D6
Landrake	5	G4
Landscove	6	D4
Landshipping	36	E4
Landulph	5	H4
Landwade	59	G5
Landywood	67	E6
Lane End, Bucks	30	C1
Lane End, Cumbr	91	C2
Lane End, Devon	6	B2
Lane End, Dorset	9	G4
Lane End, Kent	33	F3
Lane Green	66	D6
Lane Head, Durham	103	H6
Lane Head, W Yorks	86	C6
Laneast	5	F2
Laneham	81	F4
Lanehead	111	G4
Lanercost	111	E6
Laneshaw Bridge	85	H2
Langar	69	F3
Langbank	127	H5
Langbar	86	B1
Langcliffe	93	G5
Langdale End	97	E2
Langdon Beck	103	E4
Langdon Cross	12	D7
Langdon Hills	33	G2
Langdyke	130	C2
Langenhoe	48	D4
Langford, Beds	45	F1
Langford, Devon	15	G5
Langford, Essex	48	B5
Langford, Notts	81	F6
Langford, Oxon	42	E5
Langford Budville	15	H3
Langham, Essex	48	D2
Langham, Norf	72	D2
Langham, Rut	69	G5
Langham, Suff	60	C5
Langho	85	F3
LANGHOLM	110	C4
Langleeford	123	E5
Langley, Ches	78	D4
Langley, Essex	47	E2
Langley, Hants	11	F3
Langley, Herts	45	G3
Langley, Kent	23	J5
Langley, Slou	30	D3
Langley, W Susx	20	B3
Langley, Warw	55	G6
Langley Burrell	28	B3
Langley Green	34	B5
Langley Heath	34	B5
Langley Marsh	15	G3
Langley Mill	68	C2
Langley Park	104	B3
Langley Street	73	G6
Langney	22	C5
Langold	80	C3
Langore	5	F2
Langport	16	C3
Langrick	70	C2
Langridge	27	G4
Langridgeford	13	F3
Langrigg	101	F3
Langrish	19	J3
Langsett	79	G1
Langshaw	120	E4
Langside	128	E1
Langskaill	172	E2
Langstone, Hants	19	J5
Langstone, Newp	26	C1
Langthorne	94	D2
Langthorpe	95	E5
Langthwaite	94	B1
Langtoft, E Yorks	97	F5
Langtoft, Lincs	70	B5
Langton, Durham	103	H6
Langton, Lincs LN9	82	E5
Langton, Lincs PE23	83	F4
Langton, N Yorks	96	C5
Langton by Wragby	82	D4
Langton Green	22	B2
Langton Herring	8	E4
Langton Long Blandford	17	H5
Langton Matravers	10	B6
Langtree	13	E4
Langwathby	102	B4
Langwith	80	C5
Langwith Junction	80	C5
Langworth	82	C4
Lanivet	4	D4
Lanjeth	4	D5
Lanlivery	4	D5
Lanner	3	F4
Lanreath	5	F4
Lanrick	128	D2
Lansallos	5	E5
Lansdown	27	G4
Lanteglos	4	D2
Lanton, Northum	122	E4
Lanton, Scot Bord	121	F5
Lapford	14	D5
Lapford Cross	14	D5
Laphroaig	124	D6
Lapley	66	D5
Larachbeg	134	A4
Larbert	129	F4
Larches	84	D3
Larden Green	77	H6
Largie	156	D5
Largiemore	126	D4
Largoward	130	D2
LARGS	117	G2
Largybeg	117	E5
Largymore	117	E5
Larkfield	127	G5
Larkhall	118	E2
Larkhill	28	D6
Larling	60	C2
Larrick	5	G3
Larriston	111	E3
Lartington	103	G6
Lary	145	H3
Lasham	30	A6
Lassington	41	G3
Lastingham	96	C2
Latchford	46	D3
Latchingdon	48	B5
Latchley	5	H3
Lately Common	78	A2
Lathallan Mill	130	D2
Lathbury	57	G7
Latheron	169	F6
Latheronwheel	169	F6
Lathones	130	D2
Latimer	44	E6
Latteridge	27	F2
Lattiford	17	E3
Latton	42	C6
Lauchintilly	146	E2
LAUDER	120	E3
Laugharne	37	H4
Laughterton	81	F4
Laughton, E Susx	22	B4
Laughton, Leic	56	E3
Laughton, Lincs	81	F2
Laughton Common	80	C3
Laughton-en-le-Morthen	80	C3
Launcells	12	C5
LAUNCESTON	5	G2
Launde Abbey	69	F6
Launton	43	J3
LAURENCEKIRK	146	E6
Laurieston	99	H3
Lavant	20	B5
Lavendon	57	H6
Laverham	60	C7
Laverhay	109	J3
Lavernock	26	A4
Laversdale	110	D6
Laverstock	18	C2
Laverstoke	29	G6
Laverton, Glos	42	C2
Laverton, N Yorks	94	D4
Laverton, Somer	27	G5
Law	119	F2
Lawers, Pth & Kin PH15	136	D5
Lawers, Pth & Kin PH7	137	F6
Lawford	48	D2
Lawhitton	5	G2
Lawkland	93	F5
Lawley	66	B6
Lawnhead	66	D4
Lawrenny	36	E5
Lawshall	60	B6
Lawton	53	H6
Laxey	90	D4
Laxfield	61	F4
Laxfirth, Shetld ZE2 9PR	175	F5
Laxfirth, Shetld ZE2 9SG	176	D3
Laxford Bridge	166	D5
Laxo	175	F4
Laxton, E Yorks	88	B4
Laxton, Northnts	57	H2
Laxton, Notts	80	E5
Laycock	86	B2
Layer Breton	48	C4
Layer de la Haye	48	C4
Layer Marney	48	C4
Layham	48	D1
Laytham	88	B3
Lazenby	104	E6
Lazonby	102	B4
Lea, Co of H	41	F3
Lea, Derby	79	H6
Lea, Lincs	81	F3
Lea, Shrops SY5	65	H6
Lea, Shrops SY9	53	G3
Lea, Wilts	28	B2
Lea Line	41	F3
Lea Marston	55	H2
Lea Town	84	C3
Lea Valley	45	F4
Leac a` Li	159	F3
Leachkin	154	A4
Leadburn	120	B2
Leaden Roding	47	F4
Leadenham	81	G6
Leadgate, Cumbr	102	D3
Leadgate, Durham	103	H2
Leadhills	119	F6
Leafield	43	F4
Leagrave	45	E3
Leake	95	F2
Leake Commonside	83	F6
Leake Hurn's End	70	E2
Lealands	22	B4
Lealholm	105	G7
Lealt, Arg & Bt	125	D3
Lealt, Highl	151	E2
Leamington Hastings	56	C5
Leanach	127	E3
Leanaig	153	H3
Leargybreck	125	C5
Learmouth	122	D4
Leasgill	92	C3
Leasingham	70	A2
Leask	157	H5
Leaston	130	D6
LEATHERHEAD	31	F5
Leathley	86	D2
Leaton	65	H5
Leaveland	34	D5
Leavenheath	48	C2
Leavening	96	C5
Leaves Green	32	E4
Lebberston	97	F3
LECHLADE	42	E6
Leck	93	E4
Leckford	18	E2
Leckfurin	167	J4
Leckgruinart Cottages	124	B4
Leckhampstead, Bucks	44	B2
Leckhampstead, W Berks	42	B3
Leckhampton	42	B3
Leckie	152	C2
Leckmelm	163	F4
Leckwith	26	A3
Leconfield	88	D3
Ledaig	134	D5
Ledburn	44	D3
LEDBURY	41	G2
Ledcharrie	136	C6
Ledgemoor	53	H6
Ledicot	53	H5
Ledmore	163	G4
Lednagullin	168	C3
Ledsham, Ches	77	F4
Ledsham, W Yorks	87	F4
Ledston	87	F4
Ledwell	43	G3
Lee, Arg & Bt	133	G6
Lee, Devon	24	B6
Lee, Hants	18	E4
Lee, Lancs	92	D6
Lee, Shrops	65	H3
Lee Brockhurst	65	J4

216
Lee Clump
Llanwnda, Gwyn

Lee Clump 44 D5
Lee Mill 6 C5
Lee Moor 6 B4
Lee-on-the-Solent 11 G4
Leeans 176 C3
Leebotten 176 D5
Leebotwood 65 H7
Leece 91 D5
Leeds, Kent 34 B5
LEEDS, W Yorks 86 E3
Leeds Bradford
International Airport 86 D2
Leedstown 2 E4
LEEK 78 D6
Leek Wootton 55 H5
Leeming, N Yorks 94 D3
Leeming, W Yorks 86 B3
Leeming Bar 94 D2
Lees, Derby 67 H3
Lees, G Man 85 H6
Leeswood 76 E6
Leetown 138 B6
Leftwich 77 J4
Legars 121 G3
Legbourne 83 F3
Legburthwaite 101 H6
Legerwood 121 E3
Legsby 82 D3
LEICESTER 68 D6
Leicester Forest East 68 D6
Leigh, Dorset 16 E5
LEIGH, G Man 78 A1
Leigh, Kent 33 F6
Leigh, Shrops 65 G6
Leigh, Surrey 31 G6
Leigh, Wilts 28 C1
Leigh, Worces 54 C6
Leigh Beck 34 B2
Leigh Common 17 F3
Leigh Delamere 27 H3
Leigh Green 23 F2
Leigh Sinton 54 C6
Leigh upon Mendip 27 F6
Leigh Woods 27 E3
Leigh-on-Sea 34 B2
Leighterton 27 H1
Leighton, Powys 65 F6
Leighton, Shrops 66 B6
Leighton, Somer 27 G6
Leighton Bromswold 58 B4
LEIGHTON BUZZARD 44 D3
Leim 114 B2
Leinthall Earls 53 H5
Leinthall Starkes 53 H5
Leintwardine 53 H4
Leire 56 D2
Leirinmore 167 F3
LEISTON 61 H5
Leitfie 138 B4
Leith 130 B5
Leitholm 122 C3
Lelant 2 D4
Lelley 89 G3
Lem Hill 54 C4
Lempitlaw 122 C4
Lenchwick 55 F7
Lendalfoot 106 D4
Lendrick Lodge 128 C2
Lenham 34 B5
Lenham Heath 34 C6
Lenie 153 H6
Lennel 122 D3
Lennoxtown 128 D5
Lenton, C of Notts 68 D3
Lenton, Lincs 69 J3
Lenwade 72 D5
Lenzie 128 D5
Leoch 138 C5
Leochel Cushnie 146 C2
LEOMINSTER 53 H6
Leonard Stanley 41 H5
Leorin 124 C6
Lepe 11 F4
Lephin 150 A4
Lephinmore 126 D3
Leppington 96 C5
Lepton 86 D5
Lerryn 5 E5
LERWICK 176 D3
Lesbury 123 H6
Leschangie 146 E2
Lescrow 4 E5
Leslie, Aberd 156 C6
LESLIE, Fife 130 B2
Lesmahagow 119 F4
Lesnewth 12 B6
Lessendrum 156 C4
Lessingham 73 G4
Lessonhall 101 G2
Leswalt 98 B3
Letchmore Heath 45 F6
LETCHWORTH 45 G2
Letcombe Bassett 29 F2
Letcombe Regis 29 F2
Letham, Ang 139 E4
Letham, Fife 130 C1
Letham Grange 139 F4
Lethenty 157 F4
Letheringham 61 F6
Letheringsett 72 D3
Lettaford 6 D2
Lettan 173 H2
Letterewe 152 B1
Letterfearn 152 A6
Letterfinlay 142 E4
Lettermore 133 G4
Letters 163 F5
Letterston 36 D3
Lettoch, Highl PH25 145 E2
Lettoch, Highl PH26 155 F5
Letton, Co of H HR3 53 G7
Letton, Co of H SY7 53 G4
Letty Green 46 C4
Letwell 80 C3
Leuchars 138 D6
Leumrabhagh 159 H1
Levaneap 175 F4
Levedale 66 D5
Leven, E Yorks 89 F2
LEVEN, Fife 130 C2
Levens 92 C3
Levenshulme 78 C2
Levenwick 176 D5
Leverburgh (An t-Ob) 158 E4
Leverington 71 E5
Leverton 70 E2
Leverton Lucasgate 70 E2
Leverton Outgate 70 E2
Levington 49 F2
Levisham 96 D2
Levishie 143 G2
Lew 43 F5
Lewaigue 90 D3
Lewannick 5 F2
Lewdown 5 H2
LEWES 21 H4
Leweston 36 D3
LEWISHAM 32 D3
Lewiston 153 H6
Lewistown 25 G2
Lewknor 44 B6
Leworthy 14 C2
Lewtrenchard 5 H2
Ley, Aberd 146 C2
Ley, Corn 5 E4
Ley Green 45 F3
Leybourne 33 G5
Leyburn 94 C2
Leycett 66 C2
LEYLAND 84 D4
Leylodge 147 E2
Leys, Aberd AB34 146 B3
Leys, Aberd AB42 157 H3
Leys, Pth & Kin 138 B5
Leys of Cossans 138 C4
Leysdown-on-Sea 34 D3
Leysmill 139 F4
Leysters 53 J5
LEYTON 32 D2
Lezant 5 G3
Lhanbryde 155 G2
Liatrie 152 E5
Libanus 39 G3
Libberton 119 G3
Liberton 130 B6
Liceasto 159 F3
LICHFIELD 67 G6
Lickey 55 E4
Lickey End 55 E4
Lickfold 20 C3
Liddel 171 E6
Liddesdale 134 B3
Liddington 28 E2
Lidgate, Derby 79 H4
Lidgate, Suff 59 H6
Lidlington 44 D2
Lieurary 168 E3
Liff 138 C5
Lifton 5 G2
Liftondown 5 G2
Lighthorne 56 B6
Lightwater 30 D4
Lightwood 66 D2
Lightwood Green, Ches 66 B2
Lightwood Green, Wrex 65 G2
Lilbourne 56 D4
Lilleshall 66 C5
Lilley 45 F3
Lilliesleaf 120 E5
Lillingstone Dayrell 44 B2
Lillingstone Lovell 44 B1
Lillington 17 E4
Lilstock 26 A6
Lilyhurst 66 C5
Limbrick 84 E5
Limefield 85 G5
Limekilnburn 118 E2
Limekilns 129 H4
Limerigg 129 F5
Limington 16 D3
Limmerhaugh Muir 118 D5
Limpenhoe 73 G6
Limpley Stoke 27 G4
Limpsfield 32 D5
Linby 80 C6
Linchmere 20 B2
Lincluden 109 G5
LINCOLN 81 G4
Lincomb 54 D5
Lincombe, Devon EX34 24 B6
Lincombe, Devon TQ9 6 D5
Lindal in Furness 91 D4
Lindale 92 C3
Lindean 120 D4
Lindfield 21 G3
Lindford 20 B2
Lindifferon 138 C7
Lindores 138 B7
Lindridge 54 B5
Lindsell 47 G3
Lindsey 48 C1
Lindsey Tye 60 C7
Linfairn 107 F2
Linford, Hants 18 C5
Linford, Thurk 33 G3
Lingague 90 B5
Lingdale 105 F6
Lingen 53 G5
Lingfield 32 D6
Lingreabhagh 159 E4
Lingwood 73 G6
Linhope 123 E6
Linicro 150 C2
Linkenholt 29 F5
Linkhill 22 E3
Linkinhorne 5 G3
Linklater 171 E6
Linksness, Orkney KW16 170 C4
Linksness, Orkney KW17 171 F3
Linktown 130 B3
Linley 53 G2
Linley Green 54 B6
LINLITHGOW 129 H5
Linlithgow Bridge 129 G5
Linshiels 112 C2
Linsiadar 161 F4
Linsidecroy 164 B4
Linsidemore 164 B4
Linslade 44 D3
Linstead Parva 61 G4
Linstock 101 J2
Linthwaite 86 C5
Lintlaw 122 D2
Lintmill 156 C2
Linton, Cambs 59 F7
Linton, Co of H 41 F3
Linton, Derby 67 H5
Linton, Kent 33 H6
Linton, N Yorks 94 A5
Linton, Northum 113 G3
Linton, Scot Bord 122 C5
Linton, W Yorks 87 E2
Linton-on-Ouse 95 F5
Linwood, Hants 18 C5
Linwood, Lincs 82 D3
Linwood, Renf 128 B6
Lionacleit 149 C5
Lional 161 J1
Liphook 20 B2
Liscombe 14 E2
LISKEARD 5 F4
Liss 20 A3
Liss Forest 20 A3
Lissett 97 G6
Lissington 82 D3
Liston 48 B1
Lisvane 26 A2
Litcham 72 B5
Litchborough 56 E6
Litchfield 29 G5
LITHERLAND 77 F2
Litlington, Cambs 46 D1
Litlington, E Susx 22 B5
Little Abington 59 F7
Little Addington 57 H4
Little Alne 55 G5
Little Asby 102 C7
Little Aston 67 F6
Little Atherfield 11 F6
Little Ayre 170 D5
Little Ayton 104 E6
Little Baddow 47 H5
Little Badminton 27 H2
Little Ballinluig 137 G3
Little Bampton 101 G2
Little Bardfield 47 G2
Little Barford 58 B6
Little Barningham 72 E3
Little Barrington 42 E4
Little Barugh 96 C4
Little Bealings 61 F7
Little Bedwyn 29 E4
Little Bentley 48 E3
Little Berkhamsted 46 C5
Little Birch 40 E2
Little Blakenham 60 E7
Little-Bollington 78 B3
Little Bowden 57 F3
Little Bradley 59 G6
Little Brampton 53 G3
Little Braxted 48 B4
Little Brechin 139 E2
Little Brickhill 44 D2
Little Brington 56 E5
Little Bromley 48 D3
Little Budworth 77 H5
Little Burstead 33 G1
Little Bytham 69 J5
Little Carlton 83 F3
Little Casterton 69 J6
Little Cawthorpe 83 F3
Little Chalfont 44 D6
Little Chart 34 C6
Little Chesterford 47 F1
Little Cheverell 28 B5
Little Chishill 46 E2
Little Clacton 48 E4
Little Comberton 42 B1
Little Common 22 D5
Little Compton 42 E2
Little Cornard 48 C2
Little Cowarne 54 B6
Little Coxwell 43 E6
Little Creich 164 C5
Little Cressingham 72 B6
Little Cubley 67 G3
Little Dalby 69 F5
Little Dens 157 H4
Little Dewchurch 41 E2
Little Downham 59 F3
Little Driffield 97 F6
Little Duchrea 99 H3
Little Dunham 72 B5
Little Dunkeld 137 H4
Little Dunmow 47 G3
Little Easton 47 G3
Little Eaton 68 B2
Little Eccleston 84 C2
Little Ellingham 72 D7
Little End 47 F5
Little Eversden 58 D6
Little Fakenham 60 C4
Little Faringdon 42 E5
Little Fencote 94 D2
Little Fenton 87 G3
Little Finborough 60 D6
Little Fransham 72 C5
Little Gaddesden 44 D4
Little Gidding 58 B3
Little Glemham 61 G6
Little Glenshee 137 G5
Little Gransden 58 C6
Little Gruinard 162 D5
Little Habton 96 C4
Little Hadham 47 E3
Little Hale 70 B2
Little Hallingbury 47 E4
Little Hampden 44 C5
Little Harrowden 57 G4
Little Haseley 43 J5
Little Hautbois 73 F4
Little Haven 36 C4
Little Hay 67 G6
Little Hayfield 78 E3
Little Haywood 67 F4
Little Hereford 53 J5
Little Horkesley 48 C2
Little Hormead 46 D3
Little Horsted 21 H4
Little Horwood 44 B2
Little Houghton 57 G6
Little Hucklow 79 F4
Little Hulton 85 F6
Little Kineton 56 B6
Little Kingshill 44 C6
Little Langdale 92 B1
Little Langford 18 B2
Little Laver 47 F5
Little Leigh 77 J4
Little Leighs 47 H4
LITTLE LEVER 85 F6
Little Linford 44 C1
Little London, E Susx 22 B4
Little London, Hants RG26 29 J5
Little London, Hants SP11 29 F6
Little London, Lincs 70 C4
Little Longstone 79 F4
Little Lynturk 146 C2
Little Malvern 41 G1
Little Maplestead 48 B2
Little Marcle 41 F2
Little Marlow 30 C2
Little Massingham 71 H4
Little Melton 72 E6
Little Mill 40 C5
Little Milton 43 J5
Little Missenden 44 D6
Little Musgrave 102 D6
Little Ness 65 H5
Little Newcastle 36 D3
Little Newsham 103 H6
Little Oakley, Essex 49 F3
Little Oakley, Northnts 57 G3
Little Orton 101 H2
Little Ouse 59 G3
Little Ouseburn 95 F5
Little Paxton 58 B5
Little Petherick 4 C3
Little Pill 13 F2
Little Pitlurg 156 B4
Little Plumstead 73 G5
Little Ponton 69 H3
Little Rahane 127 G4
Little Raveley 58 C4
Little Ribston 87 E1
Little Rissington 42 D4
Little Ryburgh 72 C4
Little Ryle 123 F6
Little Ryton 65 H6
Little Salkeld 102 B4
Little Sampford 47 G2
Little Saxham 59 H5
Little Scatwell 153 F3
Little Shelford 59 E6
Little Shrewley 55 H5
Little Silver 14 E5
Little Smeaton 87 G5
Little Snoring 72 C3
Little Sodbury 27 G2
Little Somerford 28 B2
Little Stainton 104 C6
Little Stanney 77 G4
Little Staughton 58 B5
Little Steeping 83 G5
Little Stonham 60 E6
Little Stretton, Leic 68 E6
Little Stretton, Shrops 53 H2
Little Strickland 102 B6
Little Stukeley 58 C4
Little Swinburne 112 D5
Little Tew 43 F3
Little Tey 48 B3
Little Thetford 59 F4
Little Thirkleby 95 F4
Little Thurlow 59 G6
Little Thurrock 33 G3
Little Torboll 164 D4
Little Torrington 13 E4
Little Totham 48 B4
Little Town 101 G6
Little Wakering 34 C2
Little Walden 47 F1
Little Waldingfield 60 C7
Little Walsingham 72 C3
Little Waltham 47 H4
Little Warley 33 G1
Little Weighton 88 D3
Little Welnetham 60 B6
Little Wenlock 66 B6
Little Whittingham Green 61 F4
Little Wilbraham 59 F6
Little Witcombe 42 B4
Little Witley 54 C5
Little Wittenham 43 H6
Little Wolford 42 E2
Little Wratting 59 G7
Little Wymondley 45 G3
Little Wyrley 67 F6
Little Yeldham 47 H2
Little-ayre 175 E4
Littlebeck 96 D1
LITTLEBOROUGH, G Man 85 H5
Littleborough, Notts 81 F3
Littlebourne 35 F5
Littlebredy 8 D5
Littlebury 47 F2
Littlebury Green 47 E2
Littledean 41 F4
Littleferry 164 E4
Littleham, Devon EX39 13 E3
Littleham, Devon EX8 7 G2
LITTLEHAMPTON 20 D5
Littlehempston 6 E4
Littlehoughton 123 H6
Littlemark 108 C1
Littlemill, Aberd 145 H4
Littlemill, E Ayr 118 B6
Littlemill, Highl 154 D3
Littlemore 43 H5
Littleover 68 B3
Littleport 59 F3
Littlester 177 C6
Littlestone-on-Sea 23 G3
Littlethorpe, Leic 56 D2
Littlethorpe, N Yorks 94 E5
Littleton, Ches 77 G5
Littleton, Hants 19 F2
Littleton, Pth & Kin 138 B5
Littleton, Somer 16 C2
Littleton, Surrey 31 E4
Littleton Drew 27 H2
Littleton Panell 28 C5
Littleton-upon- Severn 27 E1
Littletown 104 C3
Littlewick Green 30 C2
Littleworth, Oxon 43 F6
Littleworth, Staffs 67 F5
Littleworth, W Susx 21 E3
Littleworth, Worces 54 D7
Littley Green, Essex 47 G4
Littley Green, Suff 60 B7
Litton, Derby 79 F4
Litton, N Yorks 93 H4
Litton, Somer 27 E5
Litton Cheney 8 D4
Liurbost 161 G5
LIVERPOOL 77 F2
Liverpool Airport 77 G3
LIVERSEDGE 86 D4
Liverton, Devon 6 E3
Liverton, Red & Clev 105 G6
Liverton Street 34 B5
LIVINGSTON 129 H6
Livingston Village 129 H6
Lixwm 76 D4
Lizard 3 F6
Llaethdy 52 D3
Llaingarreglwyd 50 E6
Llan-non 51 F5
Llan-y-pwll 77 F6
Llanaber 63 G5
Llanaelhaearn 62 D2
Llanafan 51 G4
Llanafan-fawr 52 C6
Llanallgo 74 D3
Llanarmon 62 E3
Llanarmon Dyffryn Ceiriog 64 E3
Llanarmon-yn-Ial 76 D6
Llanarth, Cered 50 E6
Llanarth, Monm 40 C4
Llanarthne 38 C3
Llanasa 76 D3
Llanbabo 74 C3
Llanbadarn Fawr 51 G3
Llanbadarn Fynydd 52 E4
Llanbadarn-y-garreg 52 E7
Llanbadrig 74 C2
Llanbedr, Gwyn 63 F4
Llanbedr, Powys LD2 52 E7
Llanbedr, Powys NP8 40 B3
Llanbedr-Dyffryn-Clwyd 76 D6
Llanbedr-y-cennin 75 G5
Llanbedrgoch 74 E3
Llanbedrog 62 D3
Llanberis 75 E5
Llanbethery 25 H4
Llanbister 52 E4
Llanblethian 25 G3
Llanboidy 37 G3
Llanbradach 25 J1
Llanbrynmair 64 B6
Llancarfan 25 H3
Llancayo 40 C5
Llancynfelyn 51 G2
Llandaff 26 A3
Llandanwg 63 F4
Llandarcy 38 E6
Llandawke 37 G4
Llanddaniel Fab 74 D4
Llanddarog 38 C4
Llanddeiniol 51 F4
Llanddeiniolen 75 E5
Llandderfel 64 C3
Llanddeusant, Carm 38 E3
Llanddeusant, I of Angl 74 C3
Llanddew 39 H2
Llanddewi 24 B2
Llanddewi Brefi 51 G6
Llanddewi Rhydderch 40 C4
Llanddewi Velfrey 37 F4
Llanddewi Ystradenni 52 E5
Llanddewi'r Cwm 52 D7
Llanddoged 75 H5
Llanddona 75 E4
Llanddowror 37 G4
Llanddulas 75 J4
Llanddwywe 63 F4
Llanddyfnan 74 E4
Llandefaelog, Carm 38 B4
Llandefaelog, Powys 39 H2
Llandefaelog tre'r-graig 39 J2
Llandefalle 39 J2
Llandegai 75 E4
Llandegfan 75 E4
Llandegla 76 D6
Llandegley 52 E5
Llandegveth 40 C6
Llandegwning 62 C3
LLANDEILO 38 D3
Llandeilo Graban 39 H1
Llandeilo'r-Fan 39 F2
Llandeloy 36 C3
Llandenny 40 D5
Llandevaud 26 D1
Llandevenny 26 D2
Llandinabo 40 E3
Llandinam 52 D3
Llandissilio 37 F3
Llandogo 40 E5
Llandough, V of Glam CF64 26 A3
Llandough, V of Glam CF71 25 G3
LLANDOVERY 38 E2
Llandow 25 G3
Llandre, Carm 38 D1
Llandre, Cered 51 G3
Llandrillo 64 D3
Llandrillo-yn-Rhos 75 H3
LLANDRINDOD WELLS 52 D5
Llandrinio 65 F5
LLANDUDNO 75 G3
Llandudno Junction 75 G4
Llandudwen 62 C3
Llandwrog 74 D6
Llandybie 38 D4
Llandyfan 38 D4
Llandyfriog 37 H1
Llandyfrydog 74 D3
Llandygwydd 37 G1
Llandyrnog 76 D5
Llandyssil 53 E2
Llandysul 38 B1
Llaneglwys 39 H2
Llanegryn 63 F6
Llanegwad 38 C3
Llanelian-yn-Rhôs 75 H4
Llanelidan 76 D6
Llanelieu 40 A2
Llanellen 40 C4
LLANELLI 38 C5
Llanelltyd 63 H5
Llanelly 40 B4
Llanelly Hill 40 B4
Llanelwedd 52 D6
Llanenddwyn 63 F4
Llanengan 62 C4
Llanerchymedd 74 D3
Llanerfyl 64 D6
Llanfabon 39 J6
Llanfachraeth 74 C3
Llanfachreth 63 H4
Llanfaelog 74 C4
Llanfaelrhys 62 C4
Llanfaes 75 F4
Llanfaethlu 74 C3
Llanfaglan 74 D5
Llanfair 63 F4
Llanfair Caereinion 64 E6
Llanfair Clydogau 51 G6
Llanfair Dyffryn Clwyd 76 D6
Llanfair Kilgeddin 40 C5
Llanfair Pwllgwyngyll 74 E4
Llanfair Talhaiarn 76 B4
Llanfair Waterdine 53 F4
Llanfair- Nant-Gwyn 37 F2
LLANFAIRFECHAN 75 F4
Llanfairyneubwll 74 C4
Llanfairynghornwy 74 C2
Llanfallteg 37 F4
Llanfaredd 52 D6
Llanfarian 51 F4
Llanfechain 65 E4
Llanfechan 52 C6
Llanfechell 74 C2
Llanfendigaid 63 F6
Llanferres 76 D5
Llanfflewyn 74 C3
Llanfigael 74 C3
Llanfihangel Glyn Myfyr 64 C2
Llanfihangel Nant Bran 39 G2
Llanfihangel Rhydithon 52 E5
Llanfihangel Rogiet 26 D2
Llanfihangel Tal-y-llyn 39 J3
Llanfihangel uwch-Gwili 38 B3
Llanfihangel yn Nhowyn 74 C4
Llanfihangel- ar-arth 38 B2
Llanfihangel- y-Creuddyn 51 G4
Llanfihangel-Nant-Melan 52 E6
Llanfihangel-y-pennant, Gwyn
LL36 63 G6
Llanfihangel-y-pennant, Gwyn
LL51 63 F2
Llanfihangel-y-Traethau 63 F3
Llanfihangel-yng-Ngwynfa 64 D5
Llanfilo 39 J2
Llanfoist 40 B4
Llanfor 64 C3
Llanfrechfa 40 C6
Llanfrothen 63 G2
Llanfrynach 39 H3
Llanfwrog, Denb 76 D6
Llanfwrog, I of Angl 74 C3
Llanfyllin 64 E5
Llanfynydd, Carm 38 C3
Llanfynydd, Flint 76 E6
Llanfyrnach 37 G2
Llangadfan 64 D5
Llangadog 38 E3
Llangadwaladr, I of Angl 74 C5
Llangadwaladr, Powys 64 E3
Llangaffo 74 D5
Llangain 37 H4
Llangammarch Wells 52 C7
Llangan 25 G3
Llangarron 40 E3
Llangasty- Talyllyn 39 J3
Llangathen 38 C3
Llangattock 40 B4
Llangattock Lingoed 40 C3
Llangattock-Vibon-Avel 40 D4
Llangedwyn 64 E4
LLANGEFNI 74 D4
Llangeinor 25 G2
Llangeitho 51 G6
Llangeler 37 H2
Llangelynnin 63 F6
Llangennech 38 C5
Llangennith 24 B1
Llangenny 40 B4
Llangernyw 75 H5
Llangian 62 C4
Llangiwg 38 E5
Llangloffan 36 D2
Llanglydwen 37 F3
Llangoed 75 F4
Llangoedmor 50 B7
LLANGOLLEN 65 F2
Llangolman 37 F3
Llangolman Common 37 F3
Llangorse 39 J3
Llangorwen 51 G3
Llangovan 40 D5
Llangower 64 C3
Llangranog 50 D6
Llangristiolus 74 D4
Llangrove 40 E4
Llangua 40 C3
Llangunllo 53 F4
Llangunnor 38 B4
Llangurig 52 C4
Llangwm, Conwy 64 C2
Llangwm, Monm 40 D5
Llangwm, Pemb 36 D5
Llangwnnadl 62 C3
Llangwyfan 76 D5
Llangwyllog 74 D4
Llangwyryfon 51 F4
Llangybi, Cered 51 G6
Llangybi, Gwyn 62 E2
Llangybi, Monm 40 C6
Llangyfelach 38 D6
Llangyndeyrn 38 B4
Llangynhafal 76 D5
Llangynidr 39 J4
Llangynin 37 G4
Llangynog, Carm 37 H4
Llangynog, Powys 64 D4
Llangynwyd 25 F2
Llanhamlach 39 H3
Llanharan 25 H2
Llanharry 25 H2
Llanhennock 26 C1
Llanhilleth 40 B5
LLANIDLOES 52 C3
Llaniestyn 62 C3
Llanigon 40 B1
Llanilar 51 G4
Llanilid 25 G2
Llanishen, Card 26 A2
Llanishen, Monm 40 D5
Llanllawddog 38 B3
Llanllechid 75 F5
Llanllowell 40 C6
Llanllugan 64 D6
Llanllwch 37 H4
Llanllwchaiarn 52 E2
Llanllwni 38 B2
Llanllyfni 74 D6
Llanmadoc 38 B6
Llanmaes 25 G4
Llanmartin 26 C2
Llanmerewig 52 E2
Llanmihangel 25 G3
Llanmiloe 37 G5
Llanmorlais 38 C6
Llannefydd 76 B4
Llannerch-y-mor 76 D4
Llannon 38 C5
Llannor 62 D3
Llanover 40 C5
Llanpumsaint 38 B3
Llanrhaeadr 76 C5
Llanrhaeadr-ym-Mochnant 64 E4
Llanrhian 36 C2
Llanrhidian 24 B1
Llanrhos 75 G3
Llanrhyddlad 74 C3
Llanrhystud 51 F5
Llanrothal 40 D4
Llanrug 74 E5
LLANRWST 75 H5
Llansadurnen 37 G4
Llansadwrn, Carm 38 D2
Llansadwrn, I of Angl 75 E4
Llansaint 37 H5
Llansamlet 38 D6
Llansanffraid Glan Conwy 75 H4
Llansannan 76 B5
Llansannor 25 G3
Llansantffraed, Cered 51 F5
Llansantffraed, Powys 39 J3
Llansantffraed- Cwmdeuddwr 52 C5
Llansantffraed-in-Elwel 52 D6
Llansantffraid-ym-Mechain 65 F4
Llansawel 38 D2
Llansilin 65 F4
Llansoy 40 D5
Llanspyddid 39 H3
Llanstadwell 36 D5
Llansteffan 37 H4
Llanstephan 39 J1
Llanteg 37 F4
Llanthony 40 B3
Llantilio Crossenny 40 C4
Llantilio Pertholey 40 C4
Llantood 37 F1
Llantrisant, I of Angl 74 C3
Llantrisant, Monm 40 C6
Llantrisant, Rho Cyn Taf 25 H2
Llantrithyd 25 H3
Llantwit Fardre 25 H2
Llantwit Major 25 G4
Llanuwchllyn 64 B3
Llanvaches 26 D1
Llanvair Discoed 26 D1
Llanvapley 40 C4
Llanvetherine 40 C4
Llanveynoe 40 C2
Llanvihangel Crucorney 40 C3
Llanvihangel Gobion 40 C5
Llanvihangel- Ystern-Llewern 40 D4
Llanwarne 40 E3
Llanwddyn 64 D5
Llanwenog 51 E7
Llanwern 26 C2
Llanwinio 37 G3
Llanwnda, Gwyn 74 D6

Llanwnda, Pemb
Marley Hill
217

Llanwnda, Pemb 36 D2
Llanwnnen 51 F7
Llanwnog 52 D2
Llanwonno 39 H6
Llanwrda 38 E2
Llanwrin 63 H6
Llanwrthwl 52 C5
Llanwrtyd 52 B7
LLANWRTYD WELLS 52 B7
Llanwyddelan 64 D6
Llanyblodwel 65 F4
Llanybri 37 H4
Llanybydder 38 C1
Llanycefn 37 E3
Llanychaer 36 D2
Llanycil 64 C3
Llanycrwys 51 G7
Llanymawddwy 64 C5
Llanymynech 65 F4
Llanynghenedl 74 C3
Llanynys 76 D5
Llanyre 52 D5
Llanystumdwy 63 E3
Llanywern 39 J3
Llawhaden 37 E4
Llawnt 65 F3
Llawr Dref 62 C4
Llawryglyn 52 C2
Llay 77 F6
Llechcynfarwy 74 C3
Llechfaen 39 H3
Llechrhyd 39 J5
Llechryd 37 G1
Llechrydau 65 F3
Lledrod 51 G4
Llidiad-Nenog 38 C2
Llithfaen 62 D2
Llong 76 E5
Llowes 40 A1
Lloyney 53 F4
Llundain-fach 51 F6
Llwydcoed 39 G5
Llwyn 53 F3
Llwyn -y-groes 51 F6
Llwyn-y-brain 37 F4
Llwyncelyn 50 E6
Llwyndafydd 50 D6
Llwynderw 65 F6
Llwyndyrys 62 D2
Llwyngwril 63 F6
Llwynhendy 38 C6
Llwynmawr 65 F3
Llwynypia 39 G6
Llynclys 65 F4
Llynfaes 74 D4
Llys-y-fran 37 E3
Llysfaen 75 H4
Llyswen 39 J2
Llysworney 25 G3
Llywel 39 F2
Loan 129 G5
Loandhu 165 E6
Loanend 123 E2
LOANHEAD 130 B6
Loans 117 H4
Loans of Tullich 165 E6
Lobb 13 E2
Loch a' Charnain 149 D5
Loch a' Ghainmhich 161 F5
Loch Euphort 149 D3
Loch Head 98 E5
Loch Sgioport 149 D6
Lochailort 141 G5
Lochaline 134 A4
Lochanhully 154 D6
Lochans 98 B4
Locharbriggs 109 G4
Lochawe 135 F6
Lochboisdale
(Loch Baghasdail) 148 C2
Lochbuie 133 J6
Lochcarron 152 A5
Lochdon 134 B5
Lochdrum 163 G6
Lochead 126 B5
Lochearnhead 136 C6
Lochee 138 C5
Lochend, Highl IV3 153 H5
Lochend, Highl KW14 169 G3
Locherben 109 G3
Lochfoot 109 F5
Lochgair 126 D3
Lochgarthside 143 H2
LOCHGELLY 130 A3
LOCHGILPHEAD 126 C4
Lochgoilhead 127 G2
Lochhill 155 G2
Lochinver 163 E1
Lochlane 137 F6
Lochluichart 153 F2
LOCHMABEN 109 H4
Lochmaddy
(Loch nam Madadh) 149 E3
Lochore 130 A3
Lochportain 149 E2
Lochranza 116 D2
Lochside, Aberd 139 G2
Lochside, Highl IV2 154 C3
Lochside, Highl IV27 167 F4
Lochside, Highl KW1 169 G3
Lochside, Highl KW11 168 C6
Lochslin 165 E5
Lochton 146 E4
Lochty, Ang 139 E2
Lochty, Fife 130 E2
Lochuisge 134 B3
Lochurr 108 E4
Lochwinnoch 117 H2
Lochwood, C of Glas 128 D6
Lochwood, D & G 109 H3
Lockengate 4 D4
LOCKERBIE 109 J4
Lockeridge 28 D4
Lockerley 18 D3
Locking 26 C5
Lockinge 29 G2
Lockington, E Yorks 88 D2
Lockington, Leic 68 C4
Lockleywood 66 B4
Locks Heath 19 F5
Lockton 96 D3
Loddington, Leic 69 F6
Loddington, Northnts 57 G4
Loddiswell 6 D6
Loddon 73 G7
Lode 59 F5
Loders 8 C4
Lodsworth 20 C3
Lofthouse 94 C4
Lofthouse Gate 86 E4
LOFTUS 105 G6
Logan, D & G 98 B5
Logan, E Ayr 118 C5
Logan Mains 98 B5
Loganlee 119 G1
Loggerheads 66 C3
Loggie 163 F4
Logie, Ang 139 F2
Logie, Fife 138 D6
Logie, Mor 155 E3
Logie, Pth & Kin 137 J4
Logie Coldstone 146 B3
Logie Hill 164 D6
Logie Newton 156 D5
Logie Pert 139 F2
Logierait 137 G3
Login 37 F3
Lolworth 58 D5
Lonbain 151 F3
Londesborough 88 C2
LONDON 32 D2
London (City Airport) 32 E2
London (Gatwick)
Airport RH6 0NT 32 C6
London Apprentice 4 D5
London Colney 45 F5
London Heathrow Airport 31 E3
London Luton Airport 45 F3
London Stansted Airport 47 F3
Londonderry 94 E3
Londonthorpe 69 H3
Lòndubh 162 C5
Lonemore, Highl IV21 162 B6
Lonemore, Highl IV25 164 D5
Long Ashton 27 E3
Long Bennington 69 G2
Long Bredy 8 D4
Long Buckby 56 E5
Long Clawson 69 F4
Long Common 19 G4
Long Compton, Staffs 66 D4
Long Compton, Warw 43 E2
Long Crendon 44 A5
Long Crichel 17 H4
Long Ditton 31 F4
Long Drax 87 H4
Long Duckmanton 80 B4
LONG EATON 68 D3
Long Gill 93 F6
Long Hanborough 43 G4
Long Itchington 56 C5
Long Lawford 56 C4
Long Load 16 C3
Long Marston, Herts 44 C4
Long Marston, N Yorks 87 G1
Long Marston, Warw 55 G7
Long Marton 102 C5
Long Melford 60 B7
Long Newton 28 B1
Long Preston 93 G6
Long Riston 89 F2
Long Stratton 61 E2
Long Street 57 F7
Long Sutton, Hants 30 B6
Long Sutton, Lincs 71 E4
Long Sutton, Somer 16 C3
Long Thurlow 60 D5
Long Whatton 68 C4
Long Wittenham 43 H6
Longbar 117 H2
LONGBENTON 113 G6
Longborough 42 D3
Longbridge, W Mids 55 F4
Longbridge, Warw 55 H5
Longbridge Deverill 27 H6
Longburgh 110 C7
Longburton 17 E4
Longcliffe 79 G6
Longcot 28 E1
Longcroft 129 E5
Longcross, Devon 5 H3
Longcross, Surrey 30 D4
Longden 65 H6
Longdon, Staffs 67 F5
Longdon, Worces 41 H2
Longdon on Tern 66 B5
Longdown 14 E6
Longdowns 3 F4
Longdrum, Aberd 147 G2
Longdrum, Ang 138 B2
Longfield, Kent 33 G4
Longfield, Shetld 176 C6
Longford, Derby 67 H3
Longford, G Lon 31 E3
Longford, Glos 41 H3
Longford, Shrops 66 B3
Longford, Tel & Wrek 66 C5
Longford, W Mids 56 B3
Longforgan 138 C5
Longformacus 121 F2
Longframlington 113 F2
Longham, Dorset 10 B4
Longham, Norf 72 C5
Longhirst 113 G4
Longhope, Glos 41 F4
Longhope, Orkney 170 D5
Longhorsley 113 F3
Longhoughton 123 H6
Longlane, Derby 67 H3
Longlane, W Berks 29 H3
Longley Green 54 C6
Longmanhill 156 E2
Longmoor Camp 20 A2
Longmorn 155 G3
Longnewton, Scot Bord 121 E5
Longnewton, Stock on T 104 C6
Longney 41 G4
Longniddry 130 D5
Longnor, Shrops 65 H6
Longnor, Staffs 79 E5
Longparish 29 G6
LONGRIDGE, Lancs 84 E3
Longridge, W Loth 119 G1
Longriggend 129 F5
Longrock 2 D4
Longsdon 78 D6
Longside 157 H4
Longslow 66 B3
Longstanton 58 D5
Longstock 18 E2
Longstone 2 D4
Longstowe 58 D6
Longstreet 28 D5
Longthorpe 70 B7
Longthwaite 101 J5
Longton, C of Stoke 66 E2
Longton, Lancs 84 C4
Longtown, Co of H 40 C3
Longtown, Cumbr 110 C6
Longville in the Dale 53 J2
Longwick 44 B5
Longwitton 112 E4
Longworth 43 F6
Longyester 131 E6
Lonmay 157 H3
Lonmore 150 B4
LOOE 5 F5
Loose 33 H5
Loosegate 70 D4
Loosley Row 44 C5
Lopcombe Corner 18 D2
Lopen 16 C4
Loppington 65 H4
Lopwell 5 H4
Lorbottle 112 E2
Lornty 138 A4
Lorton 101 F5
Loscoe 68 C2
Losgaintir 159 E3
LOSSIEMOUTH 155 G1
Lossit 124 A5
Lostock Gralam 78 A4
Lostock Junction 85 E6
LOSTWITHIEL 4 E5
Lothbeg 165 F2
Lothersdale 85 H2
Lothmore 165 F2
Loudwater 30 D1
LOUGHBOROUGH 68 D5
Loughor 38 C6
LOUGHTON, Essex 47 E6
Loughton, Mil Key 44 C2
Loughton, Shrops 54 B3
Lound, Lincs 70 A5
Lound, Notts 80 D3
Lound, Suff 73 J7
Lount 68 B5
Lour 138 D4
LOUTH 83 F3
Love Clough 85 G4
Lover 18 D4
Loversall 80 C2
Loves Green 47 G5
Lovesome Hill 95 E2
Loveston 37 E5
Lovington 16 D2
Low Ackworth 87 F5
Low Ballevain 114 B4
Low Bentham 93 E5
Low Bradfield 79 G2
Low Bradley 86 B2
Low Braithwaite 101 J3
Low Brunton 112 D6
Low Burnham 88 B6
Low Burton 94 D3
Low Catton 87 J1
Low Coniscliffe 104 B6
Low Dinsdale 104 C6
Low Dovengill 93 F2
Low Ellington 94 D3
Low Gate 112 D6
Low Green 94 D6
Low Ham 16 C3
Low Harker 110 C6
Low Haygarth 93 E2
Low Hesket 102 A3
Low Hesleyhurst 113 E3
Low Laithe 94 C5
Low Leighton 78 E3
Low Marishes 96 D4
Low Mill 96 B2
Low Moor 85 F2
Low Newton-by-the-Sea 123 H5
Low Risby 88 D5
Low Row, Cumbr 111 E6
Low Row, N Yorks 94 A2
Low Thornley 113 F7
Low Torry 129 H4
Low Toynton 83 E4
Low Wood 92 B3
Low Worsall 104 C7
Lowca 100 D5
Lowdham 68 E2
Lower Aisholt 15 J2
Lower Ansty 9 F3
Lower Apperley 41 H3
Lower Ashton 6 E2
Lower Assendon 30 B2
Lower Badcall 166 C5
Lower Basildon 29 J3
Lower Beeding 21 F3
Lower Benefield 57 H3
Lower Bockhampton 9 F4
Lower Boddington 56 C6
Lower Boscaswell 2 B4
Lower Brailes 43 F2
Lower Breinton 40 D2
Lower Broadheath 54 D6
Lower Buckenhill 41 F2
Lower Bullingham 40 E2
Lower Bullington 29 G6
Lower Cam 41 G5
Lower Chapel 39 H2
Lower Cheriton 15 H5
Lower Chute 29 F5
Lower Cragabus 124 C6
Lower Darwen 85 E4
Lower Dean 57 J5
Lower Diabaig 151 G2
Lower Dicker 22 B4
Lower Dinchope 53 H3
Lower Down 53 G3
Lower Dunsforth 95 F5
Lower End 57 G5
Lower Farringdon 19 J2
Lower Foxdale 90 B5
Lower Frankton 65 G3
Lower Freystrop 36 D4
Lower Froyle 30 B6
Lower Gledfield 164 B4
Lower Godney 26 D6
Lower Green, Essex 47 E2
Lower Green, Norf 72 C3
Lower Green, W Berks 29 F4
Lower Green Bank 92 D6
Lower Halstow 34 B4
Lower Hardres 34 E5
Lower Hawthwaite 91 D3
Lower Heyford 43 G3
Lower Higham 33 H3
Lower Holbrook 49 E2
Lower Hordley 65 G4
Lower Horsebridge 22 B4
Lower Killeyan 124 B6
Lower Kingcombe 8 D4
Lower Kinnerton 77 F5
Lower Kinsham 53 G5
Lower Langford 26 D4
Lower Largo 130 D2
Lower Lemington 42 E2
Lower Lye 53 H5
Lower Machen 26 B2
Lower Maes-coed 40 C2
Lower Milovaig 150 A4
Lower Moor 55 E7
Lower Nazeing 46 D5
Lower Oddington 42 E3
Lower Ollach 151 E5
Lower Penarth 26 A3
Lower Penn 54 D2
Lower Pennington 10 E4
Lower Peover 78 B4
Lower Quinton 55 G7
Lower Raydon 48 D2
Lower Seagry 28 B2
Lower Sheering 47 E4
Lower Shelton 44 D1
Lower Shiplake 30 B3
Lower Shuckburgh 56 C5
Lower Slaughter 42 D3
Lower Stanton St Quintin 28 B2
Lower Stoke 34 B3
Lower Stondon 45 F2
Lower Stow Bedon 60 C2
Lower Street, Dorset 9 G4
Lower Street, E Susx 22 D4
Lower Street, Norf 73 F3
Lower Sundon 45 E3
Lower Swanwick 19 F5
Lower Swell 42 D3
Lower Tadmarton 43 G2
Lower Tean 67 F3
Lower Thurlton 73 H7
Lower Thurnham 92 C6
Lower Tote 151 E2
Lower Tysoe 56 B7
Lower Upham 19 G4
Lower Vexford 15 H2
Lower Weare 26 D5
Lower Welson 53 F7
Lower Wield 19 H1
Lower Withington 78 C5
Lower Woodend 30 C2
Lower Woodford 18 C2
Lower Wraxall 27 H4
Lowesby 69 F6
LOWESTOFT 61 J2
Loweswater 101 F5
Lowgill, Cumbr 93 E2
Lowgill, Lancs 93 E5
Lowick, Cumbr 92 A3
Lowick, Northnts 57 H3
Lowick, Northum 123 F4
Lownie Moor 138 D4
Lowood 120 E4
Lowsonford 55 G5
Lowther 102 B5
Lowthorpe 97 F5
Lowton 77 J2
Lowton Common 77 J2
Loxbeare 15 F4
Loxhill 20 D2
Loxhore 13 G2
Loxley 55 H6
Loxton 26 C5
Loxwood 20 D2
Lubcroy 163 H3
Lubenham 57 F3
Lubfearn 153 F1
Luccombe 25 G6
Luccombe Village 11 G5
Lucker 123 G4
Luckett 5 G3
Luckington 27 H2
Lucklawhill 138 D6
Luckwell Bridge 15 F2
Lucton 53 H5
Ludag 148 C3
Ludborough 83 E2
Ludchurch 37 F4
Luddenden 86 B4
Luddesdown 33 G4
Luddington, N Linc 88 C5
Luddington, Warw 55 G6
Luddington in the Brook 58 B3
Ludford 82 D3
Ludgershall, Bucks 44 A4
Ludgershall, Wilts 28 E5
Ludgvan 2 D4
Ludham 73 G5
LUDLOW 53 J4
Ludney 83 F2
Ludwell 17 H3
Ludworth 104 C3
Luffincott 12 D6
Lugar 118 C5
Luggate Burn 131 F5
Luggiebank 128 E5
Lugton 118 B2
Lugwardine 41 E1
Luib 151 E6
Lulham 40 D1
Lullington, Derby 67 H5
Lullington, Somer 27 G5
Lulsgate Bottom 26 E4
Lulsley 54 C6
Lulworth Camp 9 G5
Lumby 87 F3
Lumloch 128 D6
Lumphanan 146 C3
Lumphinnans 130 A3
Lumsdaine 131 H6
Lumsden 156 B6
Lunan 139 F3
Lunanhead 138 D3
Luncarty 137 H6
Lund, E Yorks 88 D2
Lund, N Yorks 87 H3
Lund, Shetld 177 C3
Lunderton 157 J4
Lundie 138 B5
Lundin Links 130 D2
Lundy 12 M9
Lunga 126 B2
Lunna 175 F4
Lunning 175 G4
Lunnister 175 E3
Lunsford's Cross 22 D4
Lunt 77 F1
Luntley 53 G6
Luppitt 15 H5
Lupton 92 D3
Lurgashall 20 C3
Lusby 83 F5
Luss 127 H3
Lussagiven 125 D4
Lusta 150 B3
Lustleigh 6 D2
Luston 53 H5
Luthermuir 139 F2
Luthrie 138 C7
Luton, Devon 7 F3
LUTON, Luton 45 E3
Luton, Med 33 H4
LUTTERWORTH 56 D3
Lutton, Devon 6 B5
Lutton, Lincs 71 E4
Lutton, Northnts 58 B3
Lutworthy 14 D4
Luxborough 15 F2
Luxulyan 4 D5
Lybster 169 G6
Lydbrook 41 F4
Lydbury North 53 G3
Lydcott 14 C2
LYDD 23 G3
Lydd Airport 23 G3
Lydd-on-Sea 23 G4
Lydden 35 F6
Lyddington 57 G2
Lydeard St Lawrence 15 H2
Lydford, Devon 6 B2
Lydford, Somer 16 D2
Lydgate 85 H4
Lydham 53 G2
Lydiard Millicent 28 C2
Lydiate 84 B6
Lydlinch 17 F4
Lydney 41 F5
Lydstep 37 E6
Lye 54 E3
Lye Green 44 D5
Lyford 43 F6
Lymbridge Green 34 E6
Lyme Green 78 D4
LYME REGIS 8 B4
Lyminge 34 E6
LYMINGTON 10 E4
Lyminster 20 D5
LYMM 78 A3
Lymore 10 D4
Lympne 23 H2
Lympsham 26 C5
Lympstone 7 G2
Lynchat 144 B3
Lyndhurst 18 D5
Lyndon 69 H6
Lyne 30 E4
Lyne of Gorthleck 143 H1
Lyne of Skene 146 E2
Lyneal 65 H3
Lyneham, Oxon 43 E3
Lyneham, Wilts 28 C3
Lyneholmeford 110 E5
Lynemore 155 E6
Lynemouth 113 G3
Lyness 170 D5
Lynford 60 B2
Lyng, Norf 72 D5
Lyng, Somer 16 B3
Lynmore 155 E5
Lynmouth 24 E6
Lynsted 34 C4
LYNTON 24 E6
Lyon's Gate 17 E5
Lyonshall 53 G6
Lytchett Matravers 9 H4
Lytchett Minster 9 H4
Lyth 169 G3
Lytham 84 B4
LYTHAM ST ANNE'S 84 B4
Lythe 105 H6
Lythes 171 E6

M

Mabe Burnthouse 3 F4
MABLETHORPE 83 H3
MACCLESFIELD 78 D4
Macclesfield Forest 78 D4
MACDUFF 156 E2
Macharioch 114 C6
MACHEN 26 B2
Machrihanish 114 B4
MACHYNLLETH 63 H6
Mackworth 68 B3
Macmerry 130 D5
Madderty 137 G6
Maddiston 129 G5
Madehurst 20 C4
Madeley 66 C2
Madeley Heath 66 C2
Madingley 58 D5
Madley 40 D2
Madresfield 54 D7
Madron 2 C4
Maenaddwyn 74 D3
Maenclochog 37 E3
Maendy 25 H3
Maentwrog 63 G2
Maer 66 C3
Maerdy, Conwy 64 D2
Maerdy, Rho Cyn Taf 39 G6
Maes Pennant 76 D4
Maes- glas 26 C2
Maesbrook 65 G4
Maesbury Marsh 65 G4
Maeshafn 76 E5
Maesllyn 37 H1
Maesmynis 52 D7
MAESTEG 25 F1
Maesybont 38 C4
Maesycrugiau 38 B1
Maesycwmmer 39 J6
Magdalen Laver 47 F5
Maggieknockater 155 H4
Magham Down 22 C4
MAGHULL 84 B6
Magor 26 D2
Maiden Bradley 17 G2
Maiden Law 103 H3
Maiden Newton 8 E4
Maiden Wells 36 D6
Maiden's Green 30 C3
Maidencombe 7 F4
MAIDENHEAD 30 C2
Maidens 106 E2
Maidensgrove 30 B2
Maidenwell 5 E3
Maidford 56 E6
Maids Moreton 44 B2
MAIDSTONE 33 H5
Maidwell 57 F4
Mail 176 D5
Main 153 G5
Mains of Abergeldie 145 G4
Mains of Arboll 165 E5
Mains of Ardestie 138 E5
Mains of Balhall 139 E2
Mains of Ballindarg 138 D3
Mains of Balnakettle 146 D6
Mains of Balthayock 138 A6
Mains of Burgie 155 E3
Mains of Clunas 154 C4
Mains of Craigmill 155 E3
Mains of Crichie 157 G4
Mains of Dalvey 155 F5
Mains of Dellavaird 146 E5
Mains of Drum 147 F4
Mains of Kildrummy 146 B2
Mains of Kirktonhill 139 F2
Mains of Laithers 156 D4
Mains of Mayen 156 C4
Mains of Melgund 139 E3
Mains of Thornton 146 D6
Mains of Throsk 129 F3
Mains of Watten 169 G4
Mainstone 53 F3
Maisemore 41 H3
Majors Green 55 F4
Makerstoun 121 F4
Malacleit 158 C5
Malborough 6 D7
MALDON 48 B5
Malham 93 H5
Maligar 150 D2
Mallaig 141 F4
Mallaig Bheag 141 F4
Malling 128 C2
Malltraeth 74 D5
Mallwyd 64 B5
MALMESBURY 28 B2
Malmsmead 25 E6
MALPAS, Ches 65 H2
Malpas, Corn 3 G3
Malpas, Newp 26 C1
Maltby, Lincs 83 F3
MALTBY, S Yorks 80 C2
Maltby, Stock on T 104 D6
Maltby le Marsh 83 G3
Maltman's Hill 34 C6
MALTON 96 C4
Malvern Link 54 C7
Malvern Wells 41 G1
Mamble 54 B4
Manaccan 3 F5
Manafon 64 E6
Manais 159 F4
Manaton 6 D2
Manby 83 F3
Mancetter 56 B2
MANCHESTER 78 C2
Manchester International
Airport 78 C3
Mancot 77 F5
Mandally 143 E3
Manea 59 E3
Maneight 107 H2
Manfield 104 B6
Mangaster 175 E3
Mangotsfield 27 F3
Mangurstadh 160 D4
Mankinholes 85 H4
Manley 77 H4
Manmoel 40 A5
Mannal 132 B4
Manningford Bohune 28 D5
Manningford Bruce 28 D5
Mannings Heath 21 F3
Mannington 18 B5
Manningtree 48 E2
Mannofield 147 G3
Manorbier 37 E6
Manorbier Newton 37 E5
Manordeilo 38 D3
Manorowen 36 D2
Manquhill 108 D3
Mansell Gamage 40 C1
Mansell Lacy 53 H7
Mansergh 92 E3
Mansfield, E Ayr 118 D6
MANSFIELD, Notts 80 C5
MANSFIELD WOODHOUSE 80 C5
Mansriggs 92 A3
Manston, Dorset 17 G4
Manston, Kent 35 G4
Manswood 17 H5
Manthorpe 70 A5
Manton, N Linc 88 D6
Manton, Rut 69 G6
Manton, Wilts 28 D4
Manuden 47 E3
Maple Cross 45 E6
Maplebeck 80 E5
Mapledurham 30 A3
Mapledurwell 30 A5
Maplehurst 21 E3
Mapleton 67 G2
Mapperley 68 C2
Mapperton 8 D4
Mappleborough Green 55 F5
Mappleton 89 G2
Mappowder 17 F5
Màraig 159 G2
Marazion 2 D4
Marbhig 161 H6
Marbury 66 A2
MARCH 58 E2
Marcham 43 G6
Marchamley 66 A4
Marchington 67 G3
Marchington Woodlands 67 G4
Marchlands 119 G4
Marchwiel 65 G2
Marchwood 19 E4
Marcross 25 G4
Marden, Co of H 53 J7
Marden, Kent 33 H6
Marden, Wilts 28 C5
Marden Thorn 33 H6
Mardu 53 F3
Mardy 40 C4
Marefield 69 F6
Mareham le Fen 83 E5
Mareham on the Hill 83 E5
Marehill 20 D4
Maresfield 21 H3
Marfleet 89 F4
Margam 25 E2
Margaret Marsh 17 G4
Margaret Roding 47 F4
Margaretting 47 G5
MARGATE 35 G3
Margnaheglish 116 E4
Margreig 109 F5
Marham 71 H6
Marhamchurch 12 C5
Marholm 70 B6
Marian-glas 74 E3
Mariansleigh 14 D3
Marishader 150 D2
Mark 26 C6
Mark Causeway 26 C6
Mark Cross 22 B2
Markbeech 33 E6
Markby 83 G4
Market Bosworth 68 C6
MARKET DEEPING 70 B5
MARKET DRAYTON 66 B3
MARKET HARBOROUGH 57 F3
Market Lavington 28 C5
Market Overton 69 G5
MARKET RASEN 82 D3
Market Stainton 82 E4
MARKET WARSOP 80 C5
Market Weighton 88 C2
Market Weston 60 C4
Markethill 138 B5
Markfield 68 C5
Markham 40 A5
Markham Moor 80 E4
MARKINCH 130 B2
Markington 94 D5
Marks Tey 48 C3
Marksbury 27 F4
Markwell 5 G5
Markyate 45 E4
MARLBOROUGH 28 D4
Marlcliff 55 F6
Marldon 6 E4
Marlesford 61 G6
Marley Green 66 A2
Marley Hill 103 J2

Marlingford 72 E6
Marloes 36 B5
MARLOW 30 C2
Marlow Bottom 30 C2
Marlpit Hill 33 E6
Marnhull 17 F4
Marnock 156 E3
Marnock 128 E6
MARPLE 78 D3
Marr 87 G6
Marrick 94 B2
Marrister 175 G4
Marros 37 G5
Marsden 86 B5
Marsett 93 H3
Marsh 16 A4
Marsh Baldon 43 H6
Marsh Gibbon 43 J3
Marsh Green, Devon 15 G6
Marsh Green, Kent 33 E6
Marsh Green, Tel & Wrek 66 B5
Marsh Lane, Derby 79 J4
Marsh Lane, Glos 41 E5
Marshalls Heath 45 F4
Marshalsea 8 B3
Marsham 73 E4
Marshaw 84 D1
Marshborough 35 G5
Marshbrook 53 H3
Marshchapel 83 F2
Marshfield, Newp 26 B2
Marshfield, S Glos 27 G3
Marshgate 12 B6
Marshland St James 71 F6
Marshside, Kent 35 F4
Marshside, Mers 84 B5
Marshwood 8 B4
Marske 94 C1
MARSKE-BY-THE-SEA 105 F5
Marston, Ches 78 A4
Marston, Co of H 53 G6
Marston, Lincs 69 G2
Marston, Oxon 43 H5
Marston, Staffs ST18 66 E4
Marston, Staffs ST20 66 D5
Marston, Warw 55 H2
Marston, Wilts 28 B5
Marston Doles 56 C6
Marston Green 55 G3
Marston Magna 16 D3
Marston Meysey 42 D6
Marston Montgomery 67 G3
Marston Moretaine 44 D1
Marston on Dove 67 H4
Marston St Lawrence 43 H1
Marston Stannett 54 A6
Marston Trussell 57 E3
Marstow 41 E4
Marsworth 44 D4
Marten 29 E5
Marthall 78 C4
Martham 73 H5
Martin, Hants 18 B4
Martin, Kent 35 G6
Martin, Lincs 82 D6
Martin Dales 82 D5
Martin Drove End 18 B3
Martin Hussingtree 54 D5
Martin Mill 35 G6
Martindale 101 J6
Martinhoe 24 D6
Martinscroft 77 J3
Martinstown 9 E5
Martlesham 61 F7
Martlesham Heath 61 F7
Martletwy 36 E4
Martley 54 C5
Martock 16 C4
Marton, Ches 78 C5
Marton, Lincs 81 F3
Marton, Midlb 104 E6
Marton, N Yorks YO51 95 F5
Marton, N Yorks YO62 96 C3
Marton, Shrops 65 F6
Marton, Warw 56 C5
Marton Abbey 95 G5
Marton-le-Moor 95 E4
Marwick 172 C4
Marwood 13 F2
Mary Tavy 5 J3
Marybank 153 G3
Maryburgh 153 H3
Marygold 122 D1
Marykirk 139 F2
MARYLEBONE, G Lon 32 C2
Marylebone, G Man 84 D6
Marypark 155 F5
MARYPORT, Cumbr 100 C6
Maryport, D & G 98 C6
Marystow 5 H2
Maryton, Ang DD10 139 F3
Maryton, Ang DD8 138 C3
Marywell, Aberd AB12 147 G4
Marywell, Aberd AB34 146 C4
Marywell, Ang 139 F4
Masham 94 D3
Mashbury 47 G4
Masongill 93 E4
Mastrick 147 G3
Matching 47 F4
Matching Green 47 F4
Matching Tye 47 F4
Matfen 112 E5
Matfield 33 G6
Mathern 26 E1
Mathon 54 C7
Mathry 36 C2
Matlaske 72 E3
MATLOCK 79 G5
Matlock Bath 79 G6
Matson 41 H4
Matterdale End 101 H5
Mattersey 80 D3
Mattingley 30 B5
Mattishall 72 D5
Mattishall Burgh 72 D5
Mauchline 118 B5
Maud 157 G4
Maugersbury 42 D3
Maughold 90 D3
Mauld 153 G5
Maulden 45 E2
Maulds Meaburn 102 C6
Maunby 95 E3
Maund Bryan 53 J6
Maundown 15 G3
Mautby 73 H5
Mavesyn Ridware 67 F5
Mavis Enderby 83 F5
Mawbray 101 E3
Mawdesley 84 C5
Mawdlam 25 F2
Mawgan 3 F5
Mawgan Porth 4 B4
Mawla 3 F5
Mawnan 3 F5

Mawnan Smith 3 F5
Mawthorpe 83 G4
Maxey 70 B6
Maxstoke 55 H3
Maxton 121 F4
Maxwellheugh 121 G4
Maxwelston 106 E2
Maxworthy 12 C6
MAYBOLE 107 F2
Mayfield, E Susx 22 B3
Mayfield, Midlo 130 C6
Mayfield, Staffs 67 G2
Mayfield, Surrey 30 C5
Mayford 30 D5
Mayland 48 C5
Maylandsea 48 C5
Maynard's Green 22 B4
Maypole 2 N9
Maypole, Kent 35 E4
Maypole, Monm 40 D4
Maypole Green 61 H2
Maywick 176 C5
Mead End 18 B3
Meadle 44 C5
Meadowtown 65 G6
Meal Bank 92 D2
Mealabost 161 H4
Mealabost Bhuirgh 161 H2
Mealasta 160 C5
Mealsgate 101 G3
Mearbeck 93 G5
Meare 26 D6
Meare Green 16 B3
Mears Ashby 57 G5
Measham 68 B5
Meathop 92 C3
Meaux 89 E3
Meavy 6 B4
Medbourne 57 F2
Medburn 113 F5
Meddon 12 C4
Meden Vale 80 C5
Medlam 83 F6
Medmenham 30 C2
Medomsley 103 H2
Medstead 19 H2
Meer End 55 H4
Meerbrook 78 D5
Meesden 47 E2
Meeth 13 F5
Meggethead 120 A5
Meidrim 37 G3
Meifod 64 E5
Meigle 138 B4
Meikle Earnock 118 E2
Meikle Grenach 117 E1
Meikle Obney 137 H5
Meikle Rahane 127 G4
Meikle Strath 146 D6
Meikle Tarty 157 G6
Meikle Wartle 156 E5
Meikle Whitefield 138 A5
Meikleour 138 A5
Meikleyard 118 C4
Meinciau 38 B4
Meir 66 E2
Meir Heath 66 E3
Melbourn 46 D1
Melbourne, Derby 68 B4
Melbourne, E Yorks 88 B2
Melbury Abbas 17 G4
Melbury Bubb 16 D5
Melbury Osmond 16 D5
Melbury Sampford 16 D5
Melchbourne 57 J5
Meldon, Devon 13 F6
Meldon, Northum 113 F4
Meldreth 58 D7
Melfort 126 C1
Melgarve 143 G4
Meliden 76 C3
Melin-y-coed 75 H5
Melin-y-ddol 64 D6
Melin-y-Wig 64 D2
Melinbyrhedyn 39 F5
Melinthorpe 102 B5
Melkridge 111 G6
MELKSHAM 28 B4
Melldalloch 126 D5
Melling, Lancs 92 D4
Melling, Mers 77 F1
Mellis 60 E4
Mellon Charles 162 C4
Mellon Udrigle 162 C3
Mellor, G Man 78 D3
Mellor, Lancs 85 E3
Mellor Brook 85 E3
Mells, Somer 27 G6
Mells, Suff 61 H4
Melmerby, Cumbr 102 C4
Melmerby, N Yorks DL8 94 B3
Melmerby, N Yorks HG4 94 E4
Melplash 8 C4
MELROSE 121 E4
Melsetter 170 C6
Melsonby 103 H7
Meltham 86 B5
Melton 61 F7
Melton Constable 72 D3
MELTON MOWBRAY 69 F5
Melton Ross 88 E5
Meltonby 88 B1
Melvaig 162 B5
Melverley 65 G6
Melverley Green 65 G5
Melvich 168 C3
Membury 8 A3
Memsie 157 G2
Memus 138 D3
Menabilly 4 D5
MENAI BRIDGE 75 E4
Mendham 61 F3
Mendlesham 60 E5
Mendlesham Green 60 D5
Menheniot 5 F4
Menna 4 C5
Mennock 109 F2
Menston 86 C2
Menstrie 129 F3
Mentmore 44 D4
Meole Brace 65 H6
Meonstoke 19 H4
Meopham 33 G4
Meopham Station 33 G4
Mepal 59 E3
Meppershall 45 F2
Merbach 53 G7
Mercaston 67 H2
Mere, Ches 78 B3
MERE, Wilts 17 F3
Mere Brow 84 C5
Mere Green 55 G3
Mereclough 85 G3
Mereworth 33 G5
Mergie 147 E5
Meriden 55 H3

Merkadale 150 C5
Merkland, D & G 108 C5
Merkland, S Ayr KA26 0 106 C3
Merkland, S Ayr KA26 9 106 E2
Merley 10 B4
Merlin's Bridge 36 D4
Merrington 65 H4
Merriott 36 D6
Merriott 16 C4
Merrivale 6 B3
Merry Hill 45 F6
Merrymeet 5 F4
Mersham 23 G2
Merstham 32 C5
Merston 20 B5
Merstone 11 G5
Merther 3 G3
Merthyr 37 H3
Merthyr Cynog 39 G2
Merthyr Dyfan 25 J3
Merthyr Mawr 25 F3
MERTHYR TYDFIL 39 H5
Merthyr Vale 39 H6
Merton, Devon 13 F4
MERTON, G Lon 32 C4
Merton, Norf 72 C7
Merton, Oxon 43 H4
Mervinslaw 121 F6
Meshaw 14 D4
Messing 48 B4
Messingham 88 C6
Metcombe 15 G6
Metfield 61 F3
Metheringham 82 C5
METHIL 130 C3
Methlem 62 B3
Methley 87 E4
Methlick 157 F5
Methven 137 H6
Methwold 59 H3
Methwold Hythe 59 H2
Mettingham 61 G3
Metton 73 F3
Mevagissey 4 D6
MEXBOROUGH 80 B2
Mey 169 G2
Meysey Hampton 42 D5
Miabhaig, Na Eilean HS2 160 D4
Miabhaig, Na Eilean HS3 3AW 159 F3
Miabhaig, Na Eilean HS3 3DZ 159 F3
Michaelchurch 40 E3
Michaelchurch Escley 40 C3
Michaelchurch-on-Arrow 53 F6
Michaelston-le-Pit 26 A3
Michaelston-y-Fedw 26 B2
Michaelstow 4 D3
Micheldever 19 G2
Michelmersh 18 E3
Mickfield 60 E5
Mickle Trafford 77 G5
Micklebring 80 C2
Mickleby 105 H6
Micklefield 87 F3
Mickleham 31 F5
Mickleover 68 B3
Mickleton, Durham 103 F5
Mickleton, Glos 42 D1
Mickletown 87 F4
Mickley 94 D4
Mickley Square 112 E6
Mid Ardlaw 157 G2
Mid Beltie 146 D3
Mid Calder 129 H6
Mid Clyth 169 G6
Mid Culbeuchly 156 D2
Mid Garrary 107 H5
Mid Garth 173 G4
Mid Letter 127 E2
Mid Main 153 G5
Mid Urchany 154 C4
Mid Walls 175 D5
Mid Yell 177 C4
Midbea 172 E2
Middle Assendon 30 B2
Middle Aston 43 G3
Middle Barton 43 G3
Middle Claydon 44 B3
Middle Crackington 12 B6
Middle Cragabus 124 C6
Middle Drums 139 E3
Middle Handley 79 J4
Middle Harling 60 D3
Middle Kames 126 D4
Middle Littleton 55 F7
Middle Maes-coed 40 C2
Middle Mill 36 C3
Middle Rasen 82 C3
Middle Rigg 129 H2
Middle Tysoe 43 F1
Middle Wallop 18 D2
Middle Winterslow 18 C2
Middle Woodford 18 C2
Middlebie 110 B5
Middleham 94 C3
Middlehill, Aberd 157 F4
Middlehill, Corn 5 F4
Middlehope 53 H3
Middlemarsh 17 E5
Middlemuir 157 G6
MIDDLESBROUGH 104 E6
Middleshaw 92 D3
Middlesmoor 94 B4
Middlestone Moor 104 B4
Middlestown 86 D5
Middleton, Aberd 147 F2
Middleton, Arg & Bt 132 B4
Middleton, Co of H 53 J5
Middleton, Cumbr 93 E3
Middleton, Derby DE4 79 G6
Middleton, Derby DE45 79 F5
Middleton, Essex 48 B2
MIDDLETON, G Man 85 G6
Middleton, Hants 29 G6
Middleton, Lancs 92 C6
Middleton, Midlo 120 C2
Middleton, N Ayr 117 G1
Middleton, N Yorks LS29 86 C2
Middleton, N Yorks YO18 96 C3
Middleton, Norf 71 G5
Middleton, Northnts 57 G3
Middleton, Northum NE61 112 E4
Middleton, Northum NE70 123 G4
Middleton, Northum NE71 123 F5
Middleton, Pth & Kin KY13 129 J2
Middleton, Pth & Kin PH10 138 A4
Middleton, Shrops SY11 65 G4
Middleton, Shrops SY15 65 F7
Middleton, Shrops SY8 53 J4
Middleton, Suff 61 H5
Middleton, Swan 24 B2
Middleton, W Yorks 86 E4
Middleton, Warw 67 G7
Middleton Bank Top 112 E4
Middleton Cheney 43 G1
Middleton Green 67 E3
Middleton Hall 123 E5

Middleton on the Hill 53 J5
Middleton Priors 54 B2
Middleton Scriven 54 B3
Middleton St George 104 C6
Middleton Stoney 43 H3
Middleton Tyas 94 D1
Middleton-in-Teesdale 103 F5
Middleton-on-the-Wolds 88 D2
Middleton-on-Leven 104 D7
Middleton-on-Sea 20 C5
Middletown, Cumbr 100 D7
Middletown, Powys 65 G6
MIDDLEWICH 78 B5
Middlewood Green 60 D5
Middlezoy 16 B2
Middridge 104 B5
Midfield 167 G3
Midge Hall 84 D4
Midgeholme 111 F7
Midgham 29 H4
Midgley 86 B4
Midhopestones 79 G2
Midhurst 20 B3
Midlem 120 E5
Midpark 116 E2
MIDSOMER NORTON 27 F5
Midtown 162 C5
Midtown of Buchromb 155 H4
Midville 83 F6
Migdale 164 C4
Migvie 146 B3
Milarrochy 127 J3
Milborne Port 17 E4
Milborne St Andrew 9 G4
Milborne Wick 17 E3
Milbourne, Northum 113 F5
Milbourne, Wilts 28 B2
Milburn 102 C5
Milbury Heath 27 F1
Milcombe 43 G2
Milden 60 C7
Mildenhall, Suff 59 H4
Mildenhall, Wilts 28 E4
Mile Elm 28 B4
Mile End, Essex 48 C3
Mile End, Glos 41 E4
Mile Oak 21 F5
Mile-end 99 H5
Milebush 33 H6
Mileham 72 C5
Milesmark 129 H4
Milfield 122 E4
Milford, Derby 68 B2
Milford, Devon 12 C3
Milford, Staffs 67 E4
Milford, Surrey 30 D6
MILFORD HAVEN 36 D5
Milford on Sea 10 D4
Milkwall 41 E5
Mill Bank 86 B4
Mill Common 61 H3
Mill Corner 22 E3
Mill End, Bucks 30 B2
Mill End, Herts 46 D2
Mill Green, Essex 47 G5
Mill Green, Shrops 66 B4
Mill Hill 45 G6
Mill Houses 93 E5
Mill of Balrownie 139 E2
Mill of Kingoodie 157 F6
Mill of Uras 147 F5
Mill Park 114 C6
Mill Side 92 C3
Mill Street 72 D5
Milland 20 B3
Millbeck 101 G5
Millbounds 173 F3
Millbreck 157 H4
Millbrex 157 F4
Millbridge 30 C6
Millbrook, Beds 44 E2
Millbrook, C of Soton 19 E4
Millbrook, Corn 5 H5
Millbrook, G Man 78 D1
Millburn 118 B5
Millcombe 6 E6
Milldale 79 F6
Millden 147 G2
Mildens 139 E3
Millerhill 130 C6
Millhouse, Arg & Bt 126 D5
Millhouse, Cumbr 101 H4
Millhousebridge 109 J4
Millikenpark 117 J1
Millington 88 C1
Millmeece 66 D3
Millness 153 F5
MILLOM 91 G3
Millpool 4 E3
Millthorpe, Derby 79 H4
Millthorpe, Lincs 70 B3
Millthrop 93 E2
Milltimber 147 F3
Milltown, D & G 110 C5
Milltown, Derby 79 H5
Milltown, Devon 13 F2
Milltown, Highl IV12 154 D4
Milltown, Highl KW1 169 H3
Milltown of Aberdalgie 137 H6
Milltown of Auchindoun 155 H4
Milltown of Craigston 157 E3
Milltown of Edinville 155 G4
Milltown of Kildrummy 146 B2
Milltown of Rothiemay 156 C4
Milltown of Towie 146 B2
Milnathort 129 J2
MILNGAVIE 128 C5
Milnquarter 129 F5
MILNROW 85 H5
Milnthorpe 92 C3
Milo 38 C4
Milovaig 150 A4
Milrig 118 C4
Milson 54 B4
Milstead 34 C5
Milston 28 D6
Milton, Ang 138 C4
Milton, C of Stoke 78 D6
Milton, Cambs 59 E5
Milton, Cumbr 111 E6
Milton, D & G DG2 109 F5
Milton, D & G DG8 98 D4
Milton, Derby 68 B4
Milton, Highl IV12 154 D3
Milton, Highl IV16 164 D6
Milton, Highl IV3 153 G6
Milton, Highl IV6 7QQ 153 F3
Milton, Highl IV6 7SH 153 H4
Milton, Highl KW1 169 H4
Milton, Mor AB37 145 G2
Milton, Mor AB56 156 C2

Milton, Notts 80 E4
Milton, Oxon OX14 29 G1
Milton, Oxon OX15 43 G2
Milton, Pemb 36 E5
Milton, Pth & Kin 137 G5
Milton, Stir 128 C2
Milton, W Dunb 128 B5
Milton Abbas 9 G3
Milton Abbot 13 F5
Milton Bridge 120 B1
Milton Bryan 44 D2
Milton Clevedon 17 E2
Milton Coldwells 157 G5
Milton Combe 5 H4
Milton Common 44 A5
Milton Damerel 12 D4
Milton Ernest 57 J6
Milton Green 77 G6
Milton Hill 29 G1
MILTON KEYNES 44 C2
Milton Keynes Village 44 C2
Milton Lilbourne 28 D4
Milton Malsor 57 F6
Milton Morenish 136 D5
Milton of Auchinhove 146 C3
Milton of Balgonie 130 C2
Milton of Buchanan 128 B3
Milton of Campfield 146 D3
Milton of Campsie 128 D5
Milton of Corsindae 146 D3
Milton of Cushnie 146 C2
Milton of Dalcapon 137 G3
Milton of Edradour 137 G3
Milton of Gollanfield 154 B3
Milton of Lesmore 156 B6
Milton of Machany 137 G7
Milton of Murtle 147 F3
Milton of Noth 156 C6
Milton of Tullich 145 H4
Milton on Stour 17 F3
Milton Regis 34 B4
Milton-under-Wychwood 42 E4
Miltonduff 155 F2
Miltonhill 155 E2
Miltonise 106 D5
Milverton 15 H3
Milwich 67 E3
Mimbridge 30 D4
Minard 126 D3
Minard Castle 126 D3
Minchington 17 H4
Minchinhampton 41 H5
Mindrum 122 D4
MINEHEAD 15 G6
Minera 76 E6
Minety 28 C1
Minffordd, Gwyn LL36 63 H5
Minffordd, Gwyn LL48 63 F3
Mingarrypark 141 F7
Mingary 133 H2
Mingearraidh 148 C2
Miningsby 83 F5
Minions 5 F3
Minishant 117 H6
Minley Manor 30 C5
Minllyn 64 B5
Minnes 157 G6
Minngaff 99 F3
Minskip 95 E5
Minstead 19 E4
Minsted 20 B3
Minster, Kent CT124AQ 35 G4
Minster, Kent ME12 34 C3
Minster Lovell 43 F4
Minsteracres 103 G2
Minsterley 65 G6
Minsterworth 41 G4
Minterne Magna 17 E5
Minting 82 D4
Mintlaw 157 H4
Mintlaw Station 157 G4
Minto 121 E5
Minton 53 H2
Minwear 36 E4
Minworth 55 G2
Mirbister 172 D5
Mireland 169 H3
MIRFIELD 86 C5
Miserden 42 B5
Miskin 25 H2
Misson 80 D2
Misterton, Leic 56 D3
Misterton, Notts 80 E2
Misterton, Somer 16 C5
Mistley 48 E2
MITCHAM 32 C4
Mitchel Troy 40 D4
Mitcheldean 41 G4
Mitchell 3 G2
Mitchelland 92 C2
Mitford 113 F4
Mithian 3 F2
Mitton 41 G3
Mixbury 43 J2
Mixon 79 E6
Moat 110 D5
Mobberley 78 B4
Moccas 53 H7
Mochdre, Conwy 75 H4
Mochdre, Powys 52 D3
Mochrum 99 E5
Mockbeggar 18 C5
Mockerkin 101 E5
Modbury 6 C5
Moddershall 66 E3
Moelfre, I of Angl 74 E3
Moelfre, Powys 64 E4
MOFFAT 109 H2
Moggerhanger 58 B7
Moira 68 B5
Molash 34 D5
MOLD 76 E5
Molehill Green 47 F3
Molescroft 88 E2
Molesworth 58 A4
Molland 14 E3
Mollington, Ches 77 F5
Mollington, Oxon 43 G1
Mollinsburn 128 E5
Monachyle 136 B7
Monaughty 53 F5
Monboddo 146 E6
Mondynes 147 E6
Monevechadan 127 F2
Monewden 61 F6
Moneydie 137 H6
Moniaive 108 E3
MONIFIETH 138 E5
Monikie 138 E5
Monimail 130 B1
Monington 37 F1
Monk Fryston 87 F4
Monk Sherborne 29 J5
Monk Soham 61 F5

Monk Street 47 G3
Monk's Heath 78 C4
Monken Hadley 46 C6
Monkhopton 54 B2
Monkland 53 H6
Monkleigh 13 E3
Monknash 25 G3
Monkokehampton 13 F5
Monks Eleigh 60 C7
Monks Kirby 56 C3
Monks Risborough 44 C5
Monkshill 157 E4
Monksilver 15 G2
Monkswood 40 C5
Monkton, Devon 15 H5
Monkton, Kent 35 F4
Monkton, S Ayr 117 H5
Monkton, T & W 113 H6
Monkton Combe 27 G4
Monkton Deverill 17 G2
Monkton Farleigh 27 H4
Monkton Heathfield 15 J3
Monkton Up Wimborne 18 B4
Monkwood 19 H2
MONMOUTH 40 E4
Monnington on Wye 40 C1
Monreith 99 E5
Monreith Mains 99 E5
Montacute 16 C4
Montford 65 H5
Montford Bridge 65 H5
Montgarrie 146 C2
MONTGOMERY 53 F2
Montgreenan 117 H3
Montrave 130 C2
MONTROSE 139 G3
Montsale 48 D6
Monxton 29 F6
Monyash 79 F5
Monymusk 146 D2
Monzie 137 F6
Moodiesburn 128 D5
Moonzie 138 C7
Moor End 88 C3
Moor Monkton 95 G6
Moor of Balvack 146 D2
Moorby 83 E5
Moorcot 53 G6
Moordown 10 C4
Moore 77 H3
Moorend 41 G5
Moorends 87 H5
Moorfea 170 C5
Moorhall 79 H4
Moorhampton 53 G7
Moorhouse, Cumbr 101 H4
Moorhouse, Notts 80 E5
Moorlinch 16 B2
Moorsholm 105 F6
Moorside 85 H6
Moortown, I of W 11 F5
Moortown, Lincs 82 C2
Morangie 164 D5
Morar 141 F4
Morborne 58 B2
Morchard Bishop 14 D5
Morcombelake 8 C4
Morcott 69 H6
Morda 65 F4
Morden, Dorset 9 H4
MORDEN, G Lon 32 C4
Mordiford 41 E2
Mordon 104 C5
More 53 G2
More Crichel 17 H5
Morebath 15 F3
Morebattle 122 C5
MORECAMBE 92 C5
Morefield 163 F4
Moreleigh 6 E6
Morenish 136 D5
Moresby 100 D5
Moresby Parks 100 D6
Morestead 19 G3
Moreton, Co of H 53 J5
Moreton, Dorset 9 G5
Moreton, Essex 47 F5
Moreton, Mers 76 E2
Moreton, Oxon 44 A5
Moreton, Staffs 66 C5
Moreton Corbet 65 J4
Moreton Jeffries 54 B7
Moreton Morrell 56 B6
Moreton on Lugg 53 J7
Moreton Pinkney 56 D7
Moreton Say 66 B3
Moreton Valence 41 G5
Moreton-in-Marsh 42 E2
Moretonhampstead 6 D2
Morfa 62 B3
Morfa Bach 37 H4
Morfa Bychan 63 F3
Morfa Glas 39 F5
Morfa Nefyn 62 C2
Morgan's Vale 18 C3
Mork 41 E5
Morland 102 B5
Morley, Derby 68 B2
Morley, Durham 103 H5
MORLEY, W Yorks 86 D4
Morley Green 78 C3
Morley St Botolph 72 D7
Morningside, C of Edin 130 B5
Morningside, N Lanak 119 F2
Morningthorpe 61 F2
MORPETH 113 F4
Morphie 139 G2
Morrey 67 G5
Morriston 38 D6
Morston 72 D2
Mortehoe 24 B6
Mortimer 29 J4
Mortimer West End 29 J4
Mortimer's Cross 53 H5
Mortlake 31 G3
Morton, Derby 79 J5
Morton, Lincs DN21 81 F2
Morton, Lincs PE10 70 A4
Morton, Norf 72 E5
Morton, Notts 80 E6
Morton, S Glos 27 F1
Morton, Shrops 65 F4
Morton Bagot 55 H6
Morton-on-Swale 94 E2
Morvah 2 C4
Morval 5 F5
Morvich, Highl IV28 164 D3
Morvich, Highl IV40 152 B6
Morville 54 B2
Morwellham 5 H4
Morwenstow 12 C4
Mosborough 80 B3
Moscow 118 B3
Mosedale 101 H4
Moselden Height 86 B5

Place	Pg	Grid
Moseley, W Mids	55	F3
Moseley, Worces	54	D6
Moss, Arg & Bt	132	B4
Moss, Highl	134	A2
Moss, S Yorks	87	G5
Moss, Wrex	77	F6
Moss Bank	77	H2
Moss of Barmuckity	155	G2
Moss of Tain	169	G3
Moss Side	84	B3
Moss-side	154	C3
Mossat	146	B2
Mossbank	175	F3
Mossblown	117	J5
Mossburnford	121	F6
Mossdale	108	D5
Mossend	118	E1
Mosser	171	E6
Mossgiel	118	B5
Mosside, Ang	138	D3
Mosside, S Ayr	118	B4
MOSSLEY	85	H6
Mosstodloch	155	H2
Mosston	139	E4
Mosterton	16	C5
Mostyn	76	D3
Motcombe	17	G3
Motherby	101	J5
MOTHERWELL	118	E2
Mottingham	32	E3
Mottisfont	18	E3
Mottistone	11	F5
Mottram in Longdendale	78	D2
Mottram St Andrew	78	C4
Mouldsworth	77	H4
Moulin	137	G3
Moulsecoomb	21	G5
Moulsford	29	H2
Moulsoe	44	D1
Moulton, Ches	77	J5
Moulton, Lincs	70	D4
Moulton, N Yorks	94	D1
Moulton, Northnts	57	F5
Moulton, Suff	59	G5
Moulton Chapel	70	C5
Moulton Seas End	70	D4
Moulton St Mary	73	G6
Mount, Corn PL30	5	E4
Mount, Corn TR4	3	F2
Mount Ambrose	3	F3
Mount Bures	48	C2
Mount Hawke	3	F3
Mount Tabot	86	B4
MOUNTAIN ASH	39	H6
Mountain Cross	119	J3
Mountbenger	120	C5
Mountfield	22	D3
Mountgerald	153	H2
Mountjoy	3	G1
Mountnessing	47	G6
Mounton	40	E6
Mountsorrel	68	D5
Mountstuart	117	F2
Mousehole	2	C5
Mousen	123	G4
Mouswald	109	H5
Mow Cop	78	C6
Mowhaugh	122	D5
Mowsley	56	E3
Moy, Highl IV13	154	B5
Moy, Highl PH31	143	G5
Moy Hall	154	B5
Moylgrove	37	F1
Muasdale	116	A3
Much Birch	40	E2
Much Cowarne	54	B7
Much Dewchurch	40	D2
Much Hadham	46	E4
Much Hoole	84	C4
Much Marcle	41	F2
MUCH WENLOCK	66	B7
Muchalls	147	F4
Muchelney	16	C3
Muchlarnick	5	F5
Muchrachd	153	E5
Mucking	33	G2
Mucklestone	66	C3
Muckleton	66	A4
Muckletown	156	C6
Muckton	83	F3
Mudale	167	G6
Muddiford	13	F2
Muddles Green	22	B4
Mudeford	10	C4
Mudford	16	D4
Mudgley	26	D6
Mugdock	128	C5
Mugeary	150	D5
Mugginton	67	H2
Muggleswick	103	G3
Muie	164	C3
Muir	145	E5
Muir Cottage	145	E5
Muir of Fairburn	153	G4
Muir of Fowlis	146	C2
Muir of Kinellar	147	F2
Muir of Lochs	155	H2
Muir of Ord	153	H3
Muirden	156	E3
Muirdrum	139	E5
Muirhead, Ang	138	C5
Muirhead, Fife	130	B2
Muirhead, Mor	155	E2
Muirhead, N Lanak	128	D6
Muirhouses	129	H4
Muirkirk	118	D5
Muirshearlich	142	D5
Muirskie	147	F4
Muirtack, Aberd AB41	157	H5
Muirtack, Aberd AB53	157	H4
Muirton, Highl	154	B2
Muirton, Pth & Kin	129	G1
Muirton Mains	153	G3
Muirton of Ardblair	138	A4
Muirton of Ballochy	139	F2
Muiryfold	156	E3
Muker	93	H2
Mulbarton	73	E6
Mulben	155	H3
Mulindry	124	C5
Mullbuie	169	F6
Mullion	3	E6
Mullion Cove	3	E6
Mumby	83	H4
Mundam	20	B5
Munderfield Row	54	B6
Munderfield Stocks	54	B6
Mundesley	73	G3
Mundford	59	J2
Mundham	73	G7
Mundon	48	B5
Mundurno	147	G2
Munerigie	142	E3
Mungasdale	162	D4
Mungoswells	130	D5
Mungrisdale	101	H4

Place	Pg	Grid
Munlochy	154	A3
Munsley	41	F1
Munslow	53	J3
Murch	26	A3
Murchington	14	C7
Murcott	43	H4
Murieston	129	H6
Murkle	169	F3
Murlaggan, Highl PH31	143	F5
Murlaggan, Highl PH34	142	C4
Murra	170	C4
Murrow	70	D6
Mursley	44	C3
Murthill	138	D3
Murthly	137	H5
Murton, Cumbr	102	D5
Murton, Durham	104	C3
Murton, Northum	123	F3
Murton, Yk	87	H1
Musbury	8	A4
Muscoates	96	B3
Musdale	134	D6
MUSSELBURGH	130	C5
Muston, Leic	69	G3
Muston, N Yorks	97	G4
Mustow Green	54	D4
Mutford	61	H3
Muthill	137	F7
Mutterton	15	G5
Mybster	169	F4
Myddfai	38	E2
Myddle	65	H4
Mydroilyn	51	E6
Mylor Bridge	3	G4
Mylor Churchtown	3	G4
Mynachlog-ddu	37	F2
Myndtown	53	G3
Mynydd Bodafon	74	D3
Mynydd Isa	76	E5
Mynydd Llandegai	75	F5
Mynydd Marian	75	H4
Mynydd Mechell	74	C3
Mynydd-bach	40	D6
Mynyddygarreg	38	B5
Mynytho	62	D3
Myrebird	146	E4
Myrelandhorn	169	G4
Mytchett	30	C5
Mytholm	86	A4
Mytholmroyd	86	B4
Myton-on-Swale	95	F5

N

Place	Pg	Grid
Na Buirgh	158	E3
Na Gearrannan	160	E3
Naast	162	C5
Naburn	87	G2
Nackington	34	E5
Nacton	49	F1
Nafferton	97	F6
Nailbridge	41	F4
Nailsea	26	D3
Nailstone	68	C6
NAILSWORTH	41	H5
NAIRN	154	C3
Nancegollan	2	E4
Nancledra	2	C4
Nanhoron	62	C3
Nannerch	76	D5
Nanpantan	68	D5
Nanpean	4	C5
Nanstallon	4	D4
Nant Glas	52	C5
Nant Peris	75	F6
Nant-ddu	39	H4
Nant-y-derry	40	C5
Nant-y-moel	39	G6
Nanternis	50	D6
Nantgaredig	38	B3
Nantgarw	25	J2
Nantglyn	76	C5
Nantlle	74	E6
Nantmawr	65	F4
Nantmel	52	D5
Nantmor	63	F2
NANTWICH	77	J6
Nantycaws	38	B4
Nantyffyllon	39	F6
NANTYGLO	40	A5
Naphill	44	C6
Nappa	85	G1
Napton on the Hill	56	C5
NARBERTH	37	F4
Narborough, Leic	68	D7
Narborough, Norf	71	H5
Nasareth	74	D7
Naseby	57	E4
Nash, Bucks	44	B2
Nash, Co of H	53	G5
Nash, Newp	26	C2
Nash, Shrops	54	A5
Nash Lee	44	C5
Nassington	58	A2
Nasty	46	D3
Nateby, Cumbr	102	D7
Nateby, Lancs	84	C2
Nately Scures	30	B5
Natland	92	D3
Naughton	60	D7
Naunton, Glos	42	D3
Naunton, Worces	41	H2
Naunton Beauchamp	55	E6
Navenby	81	G6
Navestock Heath	47	F6
Navestock Side	47	F6
Navidale	165	G2
Navity	154	B2
Nawton	96	B3
Nayland	48	C2
Nazeing	46	E5
Neacroft	10	C4
Neal's Green	56	B3
Neap	175	G5
Neasham	104	C6
NEATH	38	E6
Neatishead	73	G4
Nebo, Cered	51	F5
Nebo, Conwy	75	H6
Nebo, Gwyn	74	D6
Necton	72	B6
Nedd	166	C6
Nedderton	113	G4
Nedging Tye	60	D7
Needham	61	F3
Needham Market	60	D6
Needingworth	58	D4
Neen Savage	54	B4
Neen Sollars	54	B4
Neenton	54	B3
Nefyn	74	C6
Neilston	118	B2
Nelson, Caer	39	J6

Place	Pg	Grid
NELSON, Lancs	85	G3
Nelson Village	113	G5
Nemphlar	119	F3
Nempnett Thrubwell	27	E4
Nenthall	102	D3
Nenthead	102	D3
Nenthorn	121	F4
Nerabus	124	B5
Nercwys	76	E5
Nerston	118	D2
Nesbit	123	E4
Ness	77	E4
Nesscliffe	65	G5
NESTON, Ches	77	E4
Neston, Wilts	27	H4
Nether Alderley	78	C4
Nether Blainslie	121	E3
Nether Broughton	69	E4
Nether Burrow	93	E4
Nether Cassock	110	B2
Nether Cerne	9	E4
Nether Compton	16	D4
Nether Crimond	157	F6
Nether Dallachy	155	H2
Nether Exe	15	F5
Nether Handwick	138	C4
Nether Haugh	80	B2
Nether Heyford	56	E6
Nether Hindhope	111	G1
Nether Howcleuch	119	H6
Nether Kellet	92	D5
Nether Kinmundy	157	H4
Nether Kinnell	129	G5
Nether Kirkton	118	B2
Nether Lenshie	156	D4
Nether Obney	137	H5
Nether Padley	79	G4
Nether Poppleton	95	G6
Nether Ringorm	155	G4
Nether Row	101	H4
Nether Silton	95	F2
Nether Stowey	15	H2
Nether Thainston	146	D6
Nether Urquhart	130	A2
Nether Wallop	18	E2
Nether Wasdale	91	C1
Nether Wellwood	118	D5
Nether Whitacre	55	H2
Nether Winchendon or Lower Winchendon	44	B4
Nether Worton	43	G2
Netheravon	28	D6
Netherbrae	157	E3
Netherbrough	172	D5
Netherburn	119	F3
Netherbury	8	C4
Netherby, Cumbr	110	C5
Netherby, N Yorks	86	E2
Nethercote	56	D5
Netherend	41	E6
Netherfield	22	D4
Netherhampton	18	C3
Netherlaw	100	B3
Netherley	147	F4
Nethermill	109	H4
Nethermuir	157	G4
Netherplace	118	C2
Netherseal	67	H5
Nethershield	118	C5
Netherthird	118	C6
Netherthong	86	C5
Netherthorpe	80	C3
Netherton, Ang	139	E3
Netherton, Devon	7	E3
Netherton, Mers L23	77	F1
Netherton, Mers L30	77	F1
Netherton, Northum	112	D2
Netherton, Pth & Kin	138	A3
Netherton, S Lanak	119	G2
Netherton, Stir	128	C5
Netherton, W Yorks	86	D5
Netherton, Worces	42	B1
Nethertown, Cumbr	100	D7
Nethertown, Highl	170	D7
Nethertown, Lancs	85	F3
Netherwitton	113	F3
Netherwood	118	D5
Nethy Bridge	155	E6
Netley	19	F5
Netley Marsh	18	E4
Nettlebed	30	B2
Nettlebridge	27	F6
Nettlecombe	8	D4
Nettleden	44	E4
Nettleham	81	H4
Nettlestead	33	G5
Nettlestead Green	33	G5
Nettlestone	11	H4
Nettleton, Lincs	82	D1
Nettleton, Wilts	27	H3
Nevendon	33	H1
Nevern	37	E2
Nevill Holt	57	G2
New Abbey	109	G6
New Aberdour	157	F2
New Addington	32	D4
New Alresford	21	G3
New Alyth	138	B4
New Arley	55	H3
New Ash Green	33	G4
New Barn	33	G4
New Belses	121	E5
New Bewick	123	F5
New Bolingbroke	83	F6
New Brancepeth	104	B3
New Brighton, Flint	76	E5
New Brighton, Mers	77	E2
New Brinsley	80	B6
New Broughton	77	F6
New Buckenham	60	D2
New Byth	157	F3
New Cheriton	19	G3
New Clipstone	80	C5
New Costessey	73	E6
New Cross	51	E4
New Cumnock	118	D6
New Deer	157	F4
New Duston	57	F5
New Earswick	95	H6
New Edlington	80	C2
New Ellerby	89	F3
New Eltham	33	E3
New End	55	F6
New Farnley	86	D3
New Ferry, Mers L43	76	E3
New Ferry, Mers L62	77	F3
New Fryston	87	F4
NEW GALLOWAY	108	D5
New Gilston	130	D2
New Grimsby	2	M9
New Hartley	113	H4
New Hedges	37	F5
New Herrington	104	C2
New Holland	88	E4
New Horndean	122	D3
New Houghton, Derby	80	C5

Place	Pg	Grid
New Houghton, Norf	71	H4
New Houses	93	G4
New Hutton	92	D2
New Hythe	33	H5
New Inn, Carm	38	B2
New Inn, Monm NP4	40	C6
New Inn, Monm NP6	40	D5
New Invention	53	F4
New Kelso	152	B4
New Lanark	119	F3
New Lane	84	C5
New Leake	83	G6
New Leeds	157	G3
New Longton	84	D4
New Luce	98	C3
NEW MALDEN	31	G4
New Marske	105	F5
New Marton	65	G3
New Mickfield	87	F3
New Mill, Corn	2	C5
New Mill, Herts	44	D4
New Mill, W Yorks	86	C6
New Mill End	45	F4
New Mills, Ches	78	B3
New Mills, Monm	40	E5
New Mills, Powys	64	D6
New Milton	10	D4
New Moat	37	E3
New Ollerton	80	D5
New Park	36	E4
New Pitsligo	157	F3
New Polzeath	4	C3
NEW QUAY	50	D6
New Rackheath	73	F5
New Radnor	53	F5
New Ridley	112	E7
NEW ROMNEY	23	G3
New Rossington	80	D2
New Row	85	E3
New Sauchie	129	G3
New Scone	137	J6
New Silksworth	104	C2
New Skelton	105	F6
New Stanton	68	C3
New Town, E Loth	130	D5
New Town, E Susx	21	H3
New Town, Glos	42	C2
New Tredegar	39	J5
New Ulva	126	B4
New Waltham	89	G6
New Wimpole	58	D7
New Winton	130	D5
New Yatt	43	F4
New York, Lincs	83	E6
New York, T & W	113	H5
Newark, C of Peter	70	C6
Newark, Orkney	173	H2
Newark, S Ayr	117	H6
NEWARK ON TRENT	81	E6
Newarthill	118	E2
Newbarn	23	H2
Newbie	109	H6
Newbiggin, Cumbr CA10	102	C5
Newbiggin, Cumbr CA11	102	A5
Newbiggin, Cumbr CA4	102	B3
Newbiggin, Cumbr LA12	92	A5
Newbiggin, Durham	103	F5
Newbiggin, N Yorks DL8 3JA	93	H2
Newbiggin, N Yorks DL8 3TB	94	B3
NEWBIGGIN-BY-THE-SEA	113	H4
Newbiggin-on-Lune	93	F1
Newbigging, Ang DD4	138	D5
Newbigging, Ang DD5	138	D5
Newbigging, Ang PH12	138	B5
Newbigging, S Lanak	119	H3
Newbold, Derby	79	H4
Newbold, Leic	68	C5
Newbold on Avon	56	C4
Newbold Pacey	55	H6
Newbold Verdon	68	C6
Newbold-on-Stour	55	H7
Newborough, C of Peter	70	C6
Newborough, Staffs	67	G4
Newbottle	43	H2
Newbourne	49	F1
Newbridge, C of Edin	129	J5
NEWBRIDGE, Caer	40	B6
Newbridge, Corn PL17	5	G4
Newbridge, Corn TR20	2	C4
Newbridge, D & G	109	G5
Newbridge, Hants	18	D4
Newbridge, I of W	11	F5
Newbridge, Wrex	65	F2
Newbridge-on-Wye	52	D6
Newbridge-on-Usk	40	C6
Newbuildings	14	D5
Newburgh, Aberd AB41	157	H5
Newburgh, Aberd AB43	157	G3
NEWBURGH, Fife	138	B7
Newburgh, Lancs	84	C5
Newburgh, Scot Bord	120	C5
Newburn	113	F6
NEWBURY	29	G4
Newby, Cumbr	102	B5
Newby, Lancs	85	G2
Newby, N Yorks LA2	93	F5
Newby, N Yorks TS8	104	E6
Newby Bridge	92	B3
Newby East	102	A2
Newby West	101	H2
Newby Wiske	95	E3
Newcastle, Monm	40	D4
Newcastle, Shrops	53	F3
NEWCASTLE EMLYN	37	H1
Newcastle International Airport	113	F5
NEWCASTLE UPON TYNE	113	G6
NEWCASTLE-UNDER-LYME	66	D2
Newcastleton	110	D4
Newchapel, Pemb	37	G2
Newchapel, Staffs	78	C6
Newchapel, Surrey	32	C6
Newchurch, Carm	37	H3
Newchurch, I of W	11	G5
Newchurch, Kent	23	G3
Newchurch, Monm	40	D6
Newchurch, Powys	53	F6
Newchurch in Pendle	85	G3
Newcott	15	J5
Newcraighall	130	C5
Newdigate	31	F6
Newell Green	30	C3
Newenden	22	E3
Newent	41	G3
Newerne	41	F4
Newfield, Durham	103	J4
Newfield, Highl	164	D6
Newgale	36	C3
Newgate	72	D2
Newgate Street	46	D5
Newhall, Ches	66	B2
Newhall, Derby	67	H4
Newhall, Midlo	120	A2
Newham	123	G5

Place	Pg	Grid
NEWHAVEN	21	H5
Newhey	85	H5
Newholm	105	H6
Newhouse	119	E1
Newick	21	H3
Newington, Kent	34	B4
Newington, Oxon	43	J6
Newland, Glos	41	E5
Newland, N Yorks	87	H4
Newland, Worces	54	C7
Newlandrig	120	C1
Newlands, Highl	154	B4
Newlands, Mor	155	H3
Newlands, Northum	103	G2
Newlands, Scot Bord	110	E3
Newlands of Geise	168	E3
Newlands Park	74	B3
Newlot	171	F3
NEWLYN	2	C5
Newmachar	147	F2
Newmains	119	F2
Newmans Place	53	G7
Newmarket, Na Eilean	161	H4
NEWMARKET, Suff	59	G5
Newmill, Aberd AB39	147	E5
Newmill, Aberd AB51	157	F6
Newmill, Mor	156	B3
Newmill, Scot Bord	110	D1
Newmill of Inshewan	138	D2
Newmiln	137	J5
NEWMILNS	118	C4
Newnham, Glos	41	F4
Newnham, Hants	30	B5
Newnham, Herts	46	C2
Newnham, Kent	34	C5
Newnham, Northnts	56	D6
Newnham, Warw	55	G5
Newnham, Worces	54	B5
Newnoth	156	C5
Newport, Devon	13	F2
Newport, E Yorks	88	C3
Newport, Essex	47	F2
Newport, Glos	41	G6
Newport, Highl	169	F7
NEWPORT, I of W	11	G5
Newport, Norf	73	J5
Newport, Pemb	37	E2
NEWPORT, Newp	26	C2
NEWPORT, Tel & Wrek	66	C5
NEWPORT-ON-TAY	138	D6
NEWPORT PAGNELL	44	C1
Newpound Common	20	D3
NEWQUAY	3	G1
Newseat, Aberd AB42	157	H4
Newseat, Aberd AB51	156	E5
Newsells	46	D2
Newsham, N Yorks	103	H6
Newsham, Northum	113	H5
Newsholme, E Yorks	88	B4
Newsholme, Lancs	85	G1
Newstead, Northum	123	G5
Newstead, Notts	80	C6
Newstead, Scot Bord	121	E4
Newthorpe	87	F3
Newtoft	82	C3
Newton, Aberd	156	B4
Newton, Arg & Bt	126	E3
Newton, Brig	25	F3
Newton, Cambs CB2	59	E7
Newton, Cambs PE13	71	E5
Newton, Card	26	B3
Newton, Ches CH3	77	H6
Newton, Ches WA6	77	H4
Newton, Co of H HR2	40	C2
Newton, Co of H HR6	53	J6
Newton, Cumbr	91	D4
Newton, D & G	109	J3
Newton, Dorset	17	F4
Newton, Highl IV1	154	B4
Newton, Highl IV11	154	B2
Newton, Highl IV27	166	D6
Newton, Highl IV6	153	H3
Newton, Highl KW1	169	H5
Newton, Lancs BB7	85	E1
Newton, Lancs LA6	92	D4
Newton, Lincs	69	J3
Newton, N Ayr	116	D2
Newton, Norf	72	B5
Newton, Northnts	57	G3
Newton, Northum	112	E6
Newton, Notts	69	E2
Newton, Pth & Kin	137	F5
Newton, S Lanak G72	118	D1
Newton, S Lanak ML12	119	G4
Newton, Scot Bord	121	F5
Newton, Staffs	67	F4
Newton, Suff	48	C1
Newton, Swan	25	F3
Newton, W Loth	129	H5
Newton, Warw	56	D4
Newton, Wilts	18	D3
NEWTON ABBOT	6	E3
Newton Arlosh	101	G2
NEWTON AYCLIFFE	104	B5
Newton Bewley	104	D5
Newton Blossomville	57	H6
Newton Bromswold	57	H5
Newton Burgoland	68	B6
Newton by Toft	82	C3
Newton Ferrers	6	B6
Newton Flotman	73	F7
Newton Harcourt	56	E2
Newton Kyme	87	F2
Newton Linford	68	D6
Newton Longville	44	C2
Newton Mearns	118	C2
Newton Morrell	104	B7
Newton of Ardtoe	141	F6
Newton of Balcanquhal	129	J1
Newton of Falkland	130	B2
Newton on the Moor	113	F2
Newton on Trent	81	F4
Newton Poppleford	15	G7
Newton Purcell	43	J2
Newton Regis	67	H6
Newton Solney	67	H4
Newton St Cyres	14	E6
Newton St Faith	73	F5
Newton St Loe	27	G4
Newton St Petrock	13	E4
Newton Stacey	19	F1
NEWTON STEWART	99	F3
Newton Tony	18	D2
Newton Tracey	13	F3
Newton under Roseberry	104	E6
Newton upon Derwent	88	B2
Newton Valence	19	J2
Newton with Scales	84	C3
NEWTON-LE-WILLOWS, Mers	77	H2
Newton-le-Willows, N Yorks	94	D3
Newton-on-Ouse	95	G5
Newton-on-Rawcliffe	96	D2
Newtonairds	109	F4
Newtongrange	130	C6
Newtonhill	147	G4

Place	Pg	Grid
Newtonmill	139	F2
Newtonmore	144	B4
Newtown, Arg & Bt	127	E2
Newtown, Co of H	41	F1
Newtown, Cumbr	110	E6
Newtown, Derby	78	D3
Newtown, Glos	41	F5
Newtown, Hants PO17	19	H4
Newtown, Hants RG20	29	G4
Newtown, Hants SO43	18	D4
Newtown, Hants SO51	18	E3
Newtown, Highl	143	F3
Newtown, I of M	90	C5
Newtown, I of W	11	H4
Newtown, Northum NE65	112	E2
Newtown, Northum NE66	123	F5
Newtown, Poole	10	B4
NEWTOWN, Powys	52	E2
Newtown, Shrops	65	H3
Newtown, Staffs SK17	79	E5
Newtown, Staffs ST8	78	D5
Newtown, Wilts	17	H3
Newtown St Boswells	121	E4
Newtown Unthank	68	C6
Newtown- in-St Martin	3	F6
Newtyle	138	B4
NEYLAND	36	D5
Nibley	27	F2
Nicholashayne	15	H4
Nicholaston	24	C2
Nidd	94	E5
Nigg, C of Aber	147	G3
Nigg, Highl	154	C1
Nigg Ferry	154	B2
Niggards	174	A7
Nilig	76	C6
Nine Ashes	47	F5
Nine Mile Burn	120	A2
Ninebanks	102	D2
Ninfield	22	D4
Ningwood	11	F5
Nipster	169	G4
Nisbet	121	F5
Nisthouse	170	D3
Niton	11	G6
Nitshill	118	C1
Niwbwrch	74	D5
No Man's Heath, Ches	65	J2
No Man's Heath, Warw	67	H6
Noak Bridge	33	G1
Noak Hill	47	F6
Nobold	65	H5
Nobottle	56	E5
Nocton	82	C5
Noke	43	H4
Nolton	36	C4
Nolton Haven	36	C4
Nomansland, Devon	14	E4
Nomansland, Hants	18	D4
Noneley	65	H4
Nonington	35	F5
Nook, Cumbr CA6	110	D5
Nook, Cumbr LA6	92	D3
Noonsbrough	174	C5
Noranside	138	D2
Norbury, Derby	67	G2
Norbury, Shrops	53	G2
Norbury, Staffs	66	C4
Norbury Common	65	J2
Norby	174	D5
Norchard	54	D5
Nordelph	71	F6
Norden, Dorset	9	H5
Norden, G Man	85	G5
Nordley	54	B2
Norham	122	E3
Norley	77	H4
Norleywood	10	E4
Norman Cross	58	B2
Norman's Green	15	G5
Normanby, N Linc	88	C5
Normanby, N Yorks	96	C3
Normanby le Wold	82	D2
Normanby-by-Spital	81	H3
Normandy	30	D5
Normanton, C of Derb	68	B3
Normanton, Leic	69	G2
Normanton, Lincs	69	H2
Normanton, Notts	80	E6
Normanton, Rut	69	H6
NORMANTON, W Yorks	87	E4
Normanton le Heath	68	B5
Normanton on Soar	68	D4
Normanton on Trent	81	E5
Normanton-on-the-Wolds	68	E3
Normoss	84	B3
Norrington Common	27	H4
Norris Hill	68	B5
North Ascot	30	D3
North Aston	43	G3
North Ballachulish	135	E2
North Balloch	107	F3
North Barrow	16	E3
North Barsham	72	C3
North Benfleet	33	H2
NORTH BERWICK	131	E4
North Boarhunt	19	H4
North Bovey	6	D2
North Bradley	27	H5
North Brentor	17	F2
North Brewham	17	F2
North Brora Muir	165	E3
North Buckland	13	E1
North Burlingham	73	G5
North Cadbury	17	E3
North Cairn	98	A2
North Carlton	81	G4
North Cave	88	C3
North Cerney	42	C5
North Charford	18	C4
North Chariton	123	G5
North Cheriton	17	E3
North Chideock	8	C4
North Cliffe	88	C3
North Cockerington	83	F2
North Coker	16	D4
North Connel	134	D5
North Cornelly	25	F2
North Cotes	83	F1
North Cove	61	H3
North Cowton	94	D1
North Cranna	156	D3
North Crawley	44	D1
North Cray	33	E3
North Creake	72	B3
North Curry	16	B3
North Dalton	88	D1
North Dawn	171	E4
North Deighton	87	E1
North Duffield	87	H3
North Dykes	102	B4
North Elkington	83	E2
North Elmham	72	C4
North Elmsall	87	F5

North End, C of Port ... 11 H3
North End, Essex CB11 ... 47 F2
North End, Essex CM6 ... 47 G4
North End, Hants ... 29 G4
North End, N Som ... 26 D4
North End, W Susx ... 20 E5
North Erradale ... 162 B5
North Fambridge ... 48 B6
North Fearns ... 151 E5
North Ferriby ... 88 D4
North Flobbets ... 157 E5
North Frodingham ... 89 F1
North Gluss ... 175 E3
North Gorley ... 18 C4
North Green ... 61 F3
North Greetwell ... 82 C4
North Grimston ... 96 D5
North Halley ... 171 F4
North Hayling ... 11 J3
North Hazelrigg ... 123 F4
North Heasley ... 14 D2
North Heath ... 20 D3
North Hill, Cambs ... 59 E4
North Hill, Corn ... 5 F3
North Hinksey Village ... 43 G5
North Holmwood ... 31 F6
North Huish ... 6 D5
North Hykeham ... 81 G5
North Kelsey ... 82 C1
North Kessock ... 154 A4
North Killimster ... 169 H4
North Killingholme ... 89 F5
North Kilvington ... 95 F3
North Kilworth ... 56 E3
North Kyme ... 82 D6
North Lancing ... 21 E5
North Lee ... 44 C5
North Leigh ... 43 F4
North Leverton
  with Habblesthorpe ... 81 E3
North Littleton ... 55 F7
North Lopham ... 60 D3
North Luffenham ... 69 H6
North Marden ... 20 B4
North Marston ... 44 B3
North Middleton, Midlo ... 120 C2
North Middleton, Northum ... 123 F5
North Molton ... 14 D3
North Moreton ... 29 H2
North Mundham ... 20 B5
North Muskham ... 81 E6
North Newbald ... 88 D3
North Newington ... 43 G2
North Newnton ... 28 D5
North Newton ... 16 A2
North Nibley ... 41 G6
North Oakley ... 29 H5
North Ockendon ... 33 F2
North Ormsby ... 83 E2
North Otterington ... 95 E3
North Owersby ... 82 C2
North Perrott ... 16 C5
North Petherton ... 16 A2
North Petherwin ... 12 C7
North Pickenham ... 72 B6
North Piddle ... 55 E6
North Queensferry ... 129 J4
North Radworthy ... 14 D2
North Rauceby ... 69 J2
North Reston ... 83 F3
North Rigton ... 86 D2
North Rode ... 78 C5
North Roe ... 177 A5
North Runcton ... 71 G5
North Sandwick ... 177 C4
North Scale ... 91 C5
North Scarle ... 81 F5
North Seaton ... 113 G4
North Shian ... 134 D4
North Shields ... 113 H6
North Shoebury ... 34 C2
North Shore ... 84 B3
North Side ... 70 C7
North Skelton ... 105 F6
North Somercotes ... 83 G2
North Stainley ... 94 D4
North Stainmore ... 102 E6
North Stifford ... 33 F2
North Stoke, Bth ... 27 G4
North Stoke, Oxon ... 29 J2
North Stoke, W Susx ... 20 D4
North Street, Hants ... 19 H2
North Street, Kent ... 34 D5
North Sunderland ... 123 H4
North Tamerton ... 12 D6
North Tawton ... 14 C5
North Thoresby ... 83 E2
North Tidworth ... 28 E6
North Tuddenham ... 72 D5
NORTH WALSHAM ... 73 F3
North Waltham ... 29 H6
North Warnborough ... 30 B5
North Water Bridge ... 139 F2
North Watten ... 169 G4
North Weald Bassett ... 47 E5
North Wheatley ... 80 E3
North Whilborough ... 6 E4
North Wick ... 27 E4
North Widcombe ... 27 E5
North Willingham ... 82 D3
North Wingfield ... 80 B5
North Witham ... 69 H4
North Wootton, Dorset ... 17 E4
North Wootton, Norf ... 71 G4
North Wootton, Somer ... 27 E6
North Wraxall ... 27 G3
NORTHALLERTON ... 95 E2
Northam, C of Soton ... 19 F4
NORTHAM, Devon ... 13 E3
NORTHAMPTON ... 57 F5
Northaw ... 46 C5
Northborough ... 70 B6
Northbourne ... 35 G5
Northbrook ... 43 G3
Northchapel ... 20 C3
Northchurch ... 44 D5
Northcote Manor ... 13 G4
Northcott ... 12 D6
Northcott Hamlet ... 12 D6
Northdyke ... 172 C4
Northend, Bth ... 27 G4
Northend, Bucks ... 30 B1
Northend, Warw ... 56 B6
Northfield, C of Aber ... 147 G3
Northfield, Scot Bord ... 131 J6
Northfield, W Mids ... 55 F4
NORTHFLEET ... 33 G3
Northgate ... 70 B4
Northiam ... 22 E3
Northill ... 58 B7
Northington ... 19 G2
Northlands ... 83 F6
Northleach ... 42 D4
Northleigh ... 15 H6
Northlew ... 13 F6
Northmoor ... 43 G5

Northmoor Green or Moorland . 16 B2
Northmuir ... 138 C3
NORTHOLT ... 31 F2
Northop ... 76 E5
Northop Hall ... 76 E5
Northorpe, Lincs DN21 ... 81 F2
Northorpe, Lincs PE10 ... 70 A5
Northorpe, Lincs PE11 ... 70 C3
Northowram ... 86 D4
Northpunds ... 176 D5
Northrepps ... 73 F3
Northtown ... 171 E5
Northwall ... 173 H2
Northway, Devon ... 12 D3
Northway, Glos ... 42 B2
NORTHWICH ... 77 J4
Northwick ... 27 E2
Northwold ... 59 H2
Northwood, Derby ... 79 G5
NORTHWOOD, G Lon ... 31 E1
Northwood, I of W ... 11 F4
Northwood, Wrex ... 65 H3
Northwood Green ... 41 G4
Norton, Derby ... 79 H3
Norton, Glos ... 41 H3
Norton, Halt ... 77 H3
Norton, Herts ... 46 C2
Norton, I of W ... 10 E5
Norton, Northnts ... 56 C4
Norton, Notts ... 80 C4
Norton, Powys ... 53 G5
Norton, S Yorks ... 87 G5
Norton, Shrops SY4 ... 66 A6
Norton, Shrops SY7 ... 53 H3
Norton, Shrops TF11 ... 66 C6
Norton, Stock on T ... 104 D5
Norton, Suff ... 60 C5
Norton, W Susx ... 20 C5
Norton, Wilts ... 27 H2
Norton, Worces WR11 ... 55 F7
Norton, Worces WR5 ... 54 D6
Norton Bavant ... 28 B6
Norton Bridge ... 66 D3
Norton Canes ... 67 F6
Norton Canon ... 53 G7
Norton Disney ... 81 F6
Norton East ... 67 F6
Norton Ferris ... 17 F2
Norton Fitzwarren ... 15 H3
Norton Green ... 10 E5
Norton Hawkfield ... 27 E4
Norton Heath ... 47 F5
Norton in Hales ... 66 C3
Norton Lindsey ... 55 H5
Norton Malreward ... 27 F4
Norton Mandeville ... 47 F5
Norton St Philip ... 27 G5
Norton sub Hamdon ... 16 C4
Norton Subcourse ... 73 H7
Norton-in-the-Moors ... 78 C6
Norton-Juxta-Twycross ... 68 B6
Norton-le-Clay ... 95 F4
NORTON-ON-DERWENT ... 96 C4
Norwell ... 80 E5
Norwell Woodhouse ... 80 E5
NORWICH ... 73 F6
Norwich Airport ... 73 F5
Norwick ... 177 D2
Norwood ... 80 B3
Norwood Green ... 31 F3
Norwood Hill ... 32 C6
Noseley ... 69 F7
Noss ... 176 C6
Noss Mayo ... 6 B6
Nosterfield ... 94 D3
Nostie ... 151 H6
Notgrove ... 42 D3
Nottage ... 25 F3
NOTTINGHAM ... 68 D3
Nottington ... 9 E5
Notton, N Yorks ... 86 E5
Notton, Wilts ... 28 B4
Nounsley ... 47 H4
Noutard's Green ... 54 C5
Nowton ... 60 B5
Nox ... 65 H5
Nuffield ... 30 A2
Nun Monkton ... 95 G6
Nunburnholme ... 88 C2
NUNEATON ... 56 B2
Nuneham Courtenay ... 43 H6
Nunney ... 27 G6
Nunnington ... 96 B4
Nunnykirk ... 113 E3
Nunthorpe ... 104 E6
Nunton ... 18 C3
Nunwick ... 112 C5
Nursling ... 19 E4
Nursted ... 20 A2
Nutbourne, W Susx PO18 ... 20 A5
Nutbourne, W Susx RH20 ... 20 D4
Nutfield ... 32 D5
Nuthall ... 68 D2
Nuthampstead ... 46 E2
Nuthurst, W Susx ... 21 E3
Nuthurst, Warw ... 55 G4
Nutley ... 21 H3
Nutwell ... 87 H6
Nyadd ... 128 E3
Nybster ... 169 H3
Nyetimber ... 20 B6
Nyewood ... 20 A3
Nymet Rowland ... 14 D5
Nymet Tracey ... 14 D5
Nympsfield ... 41 H5
Nynehead ... 15 H3
Nyton ... 20 C5

O

Oad Street ... 34 B4
Oadby ... 68 E6
Oak Cross ... 13 F6
Oakamoor ... 67 F2
Oakbank ... 129 H6
Oakdale ... 40 A6
Oake ... 15 H3
Oaken ... 66 D6
Oakenclough ... 84 D2
Oakengates ... 66 C5
Oakenshaw, Durham ... 103 J4
Oakenshaw, W Yorks ... 86 C4
Oakerthorpe ... 79 H6
Oakford, Cered ... 51 E6
Oakford, Devon ... 15 F3
Oakfordbridge ... 15 F3
Oakgrove ... 78 D5
OAKHAM ... 69 G6
Oakhanger ... 20 A2
Oakhill ... 27 F6
Oakington ... 59 E5
Oaklands, Conwy ... 75 H6
Oaklands, Herts ... 46 C4

Oakle Street ... 41 G4
Oakley, Beds ... 57 H6
Oakley, Bucks ... 43 J4
Oakley, Fife ... 129 H4
Oakley, Hants ... 29 H5
Oakley, Poole ... 10 B4
Oakley, Suff ... 60 E4
Oakley Green ... 30 D3
Oakridge ... 42 B5
Oaks ... 65 H6
Oaksey ... 42 B6
Oakthorpe ... 68 B5
Oakwood ... 112 D6
Oakwoodhill ... 21 E2
Oakworth ... 86 B3
Oare, Kent ... 34 D4
Oare, Somer ... 25 F6
Oare, Wilts ... 28 D4
Oasby ... 69 J3
Oatfield ... 116 A6
Oatlaw ... 138 D3
OBAN ... 134 C6
Obney ... 137 H5
Oborne ... 17 E4
Occlestone Green ... 78 A5
Occold ... 60 E4
Occumster ... 169 G6
Ochiltree ... 118 C5
Ochtermuthill ... 137 F7
Ochtertyre ... 137 F6
Ockbrook ... 68 C3
Ockham ... 31 E5
Ockle ... 141 E6
Ockley ... 31 F6
Ocle Pychard ... 54 A7
Ocraquoy ... 176 D4
Odcombe ... 16 D4
Oddendale ... 102 B6
Oddingley ... 54 E6
Oddington, Glos ... 42 E3
Oddington, Oxon ... 43 H4
Odell ... 57 H6
Odie ... 173 G4
Odiham ... 30 B5
Odstock ... 18 C3
Odstone ... 68 B6
Offchurch ... 56 B5
Offenham ... 55 F7
Offerton Green ... 78 D3
Offham, E Susx ... 21 G4
Offham, Kent ... 33 G5
Offord Cluny ... 58 C5
Offord D'Arcy ... 58 C5
Offton ... 60 D7
Offwell ... 15 H6
Ogbourne Maizey ... 28 D3
Ogbourne St Andrew ... 28 D3
Ogbourne St George ... 28 D3
Ogil ... 138 D2
Ogle ... 113 F5
Ogmore ... 25 F3
Ogmore Vale ... 25 G3
Ogmore- by-Sea ... 25 F3
Okeford Fitzpaine ... 17 G4
OKEHAMPTON ... 13 F6
Okehampton Camp ... 13 F6
Olantigh ... 34 D6
Old ... 57 F4
Old Aberdeen ... 147 G3
Old Alresford ... 19 G2
Old Arley ... 55 H2
Old Basing ... 30 A5
Old Beetley ... 72 C5
Old Belses ... 121 E5
Old Bewick ... 123 F5
Old Bolingbroke ... 83 F5
Old Brampton ... 79 H4
Old Bridge of Urr ... 108 E6
Old Buckenham ... 60 D2
Old Burghclere ... 29 G5
Old Byland ... 95 G3
Old Castleton ... 110 E3
Old Cleeve ... 25 H6
Old Clipstone ... 80 D5
Old Colwyn ... 75 H4
Old Court ... 40 C1
Old Craighall ... 130 C5
Old Crombie ... 156 C3
Old Dailly ... 106 E3
Old Dalby ... 68 E4
Old Deer ... 157 G4
Old Denaby ... 80 B2
Old Down ... 27 F2
Old Duffus ... 155 F2
Old Ellerby ... 89 F3
Old Felixstowe ... 49 G2
Old Gore ... 41 F3
Old Heath ... 48 D3
Old Hunstanton ... 71 G2
Old Hurst ... 58 C4
Old Hutton ... 92 D3
Old Kea ... 3 G3
Old Kilpatrick ... 128 B5
Old Kinnernie ... 146 E3
Old Knebworth ... 46 C3
Old Leake ... 83 G6
Old Malton ... 96 C4
Old Micklefield ... 87 F3
Old Milverton ... 55 H5
Old Monkland ... 128 E6
Old Newton ... 60 D5
Old Park ... 66 B6
Old Philpstoun ... 129 H5
Old Radnor ... 53 F6
Old Rattray ... 157 H3
Old Rayne ... 156 D6
Old Romney ... 23 G3
Old Scone ... 137 J6
Old Shields ... 129 F5
Old Sodbury ... 27 G2
Old Somerby ... 69 H3
Old Stratford ... 44 B1
Old Swarland ... 113 F2
Old Town ... 2 N9
Old Town, Cumbr ... 92 D3
Old Warden ... 45 F1
Old Weston ... 30 D3
Old Windsor ... 30 D3
Old Wives Lees ... 34 D5
Olderfleet ... 55 G5
Oldborough ... 14 D5
Oldbury, Shrops ... 54 C2
OLDBURY, W Mids ... 55 E3
Oldbury, Warw ... 56 B2
Oldbury on the Hill ... 27 H2
Oldbury-on- Severn ... 27 F1
Oldcastle ... 40 C3
Oldcastle Heath ... 65 H4
Oldcotes ... 80 C3
Oldcroft ... 41 F5
Oldfield, W Yorks ... 86 B3
Oldfield, Worces ... 54 D5
Oldford ... 27 G5
OLDHAM ... 85 H6
Oldhamstocks ... 131 G5
Oldland ... 27 F3

OLDMELDRUM ... 157 F6
Oldshore Beg ... 166 C4
Oldshoremore ... 166 D4
Oldstead ... 95 G4
Oldtown ... 156 C6
Oldtown of Ord ... 156 D3
Oldwalls ... 24 B1
Oldways End ... 14 D3
Oldwhat ... 157 F3
Oldwood ... 54 A5
Olgrinmore ... 169 E4
Oliver ... 119 J5
Oliver's Battery ... 19 F3
Ollaberry ... 177 A5
Ollach ... 151 E5
Ollerton, Ches ... 78 B4
Ollerton, Notts ... 80 D5
Ollerton, Shrops ... 66 B4
Olney ... 57 G6
Olton ... 55 G3
Olveston ... 27 F2
Ombersley ... 54 D5
Ompton ... 80 D5
Onchan ... 90 C5
Onecote ... 79 E6
Onehouse ... 60 D6
Ongar Hill ... 71 F4
Ongar Street ... 53 G5
Onibury ... 53 H4
Onich ... 135 E2
Onllwyn ... 39 F4
Onneley ... 66 C2
Onslow Green ... 47 G4
Onslow Village ... 30 D6
Onziebust ... 172 E4
Opinan, Highl IV21 ... 151 G1
Opinan, Highl IV22 ... 162 C4
Orange Lane ... 122 C3
Orasaigh ... 159 H1
Orbliston ... 155 H3
Orbost ... 150 B4
Orby ... 83 G5
Orchard ... 17 G4
Orchard Leigh ... 44 D5
Orchard Portman ... 15 J3
Orcheston ... 28 C6
Orcop ... 40 D3
Orcop Hill ... 40 D3
Ord ... 141 F2
Ord Muir ... 153 H3
Ordhead ... 146 D2
Ordie ... 146 B3
Ordiquish ... 155 H3
Ordley ... 156 E4
Ore ... 22 E4
Oreton ... 54 B3
Orford, Suff ... 61 H7
Orford, Warr ... 77 H2
Orgreave ... 67 G5
Orlestone ... 23 F2
Orleton, Co of H ... 53 H5
Orleton, Worces ... 54 B5
Orlingbury ... 57 G4
Ormesby ... 104 E6
Ormesby St Margaret ... 73 H5
Ormesby St Michael ... 73 H5
Ormidale ... 126 E4
Ormiscaig ... 162 C4
Ormiston ... 130 D6
Ormsaigmore ... 133 G2
Ormsary ... 126 B5
ORMSKIRK ... 84 C6
Orphir ... 170 D4
ORPINGTON ... 33 E4
ORRELL ... 84 D6
Orrock ... 147 G2
Orroland ... 100 B3
Orsett ... 33 G2
Orslow ... 66 D5
Orston ... 69 F2
Orton, Cumbr ... 102 C7
Orton, Mor ... 155 H3
Orton, Northnts ... 57 G4
Orton, Scot Bord ... 120 D2
Orton Longueville ... 58 B2
Orton-on-the-Hill ... 67 J6
Orwell ... 58 D6
Osbaldeston ... 85 E3
Osbaston ... 68 C6
Osbournby ... 70 A3
Oscroft ... 77 H5
Ose ... 150 C4
Osgathorpe ... 68 C5
Osgodby, Lincs ... 82 C2
Osgodby, N Yorks YO11 ... 97 F3
Osgodby, N Yorks YO8 ... 87 H3
Oskaig ... 151 E5
Oskamull ... 133 G5
Osmaston ... 67 G2
Osmington ... 9 F5
Osmington Mills ... 9 F5
Osmotherley ... 95 F2
Ospisdale ... 164 D5
Ospringe ... 34 D4
OSSETT ... 86 D5
Ossington ... 80 E5
Ostend, Essex ... 48 C6
Ostend, Norf ... 73 G3
Oswaldkirk ... 95 H4
OSWALDTWISTLE ... 85 F4
OSWESTRY ... 65 F4
Otford ... 33 F5
Otham ... 33 H5
Othery ... 16 B2
Otley, Suff ... 61 F6
OTLEY, W Yorks ... 86 D2
Otter Ferry ... 126 D4
Otterbourne ... 19 F3
Otterburn, N Yorks ... 93 G6
Otterburn, Northum ... 112 C3
Otterburn Camp ... 112 C3
Otterham ... 12 B6
Ottershaw ... 30 E4
Otterswick ... 177 C5
Otterton ... 7 G2
OTTERY ST MARY ... 15 H6
Ottinge ... 89 G4
Oughterby ... 101 G2
Oughtershaw ... 93 G3
Oughtibridge ... 79 H2
Oulston ... 95 G4
Oulton, Cumbr ... 101 G2
Oulton, Norf ... 72 E4
Oulton, Staffs ... 66 E3
Oulton, Suff ... 61 J2
Oulton, W Yorks ... 87 F4
Oulton Broad ... 61 J2
Oulton Street ... 72 E4
OUNDLE ... 57 J3
Ousby ... 102 C4
Ousdale ... 165 G1
Ousden ... 59 H6
Ouseburn ... 95 F5
Ousefleet ... 88 C4
Ouston ... 104 D3
Out Newton ... 89 H4

Out Rawcliffe ... 84 C2
Outer Hope ... 6 C6
Outertown ... 170 C3
Outgate ... 92 B2
Outhgill ... 93 F1
Outlands ... 66 C3
Outlane ... 86 B5
Outwell ... 71 F6
Outwood, Surrey ... 32 D6
Outwood, W Yorks ... 86 E4
Outwoods ... 66 C5
Ovenden ... 86 B4
Ovenden ... 119 J5
Over, Cambs ... 58 D4
Over, S Glos ... 27 E2
Over Compton ... 16 D4
Over Green ... 55 G2
Over Haddon ... 79 G5
Over Kellet ... 92 C4
Over Kiddington ... 43 G3
Over Norton ... 43 F3
Over Peover ... 78 B4
Over Silton ... 95 F2
Over Stratton ... 16 C4
Over Wallop ... 18 D2
Over Whitacre ... 55 H2
Over Worton ... 43 G3
Overbister ... 173 G2
Overbury ... 42 B2
Overcombe ... 9 E5
Overseal ... 67 H5
Oversland ... 34 D5
Oversley Green ... 55 F6
Overstone ... 57 G5
Overstrand ... 73 F2
Overthorpe ... 43 G1
Overton, Aberd ... 146 E2
Overton, C of Aber ... 147 F2
Overton, D & G ... 109 G6
Overton, Hants ... 29 H6
Overton, Lancs ... 92 C6
Overton, Shrops ... 53 J4
Overton, Swan ... 24 B2
Overton, Wrex ... 65 G2
Overtown, N Lanak ... 119 F2
Overtown, Swin ... 28 D3
Oving, Bucks ... 44 B3
Oving, W Susx ... 20 C5
Ovingdean ... 21 G5
Ovingham ... 113 E6
Ovington, Durham ... 103 H6
Ovington, Essex ... 47 H1
Ovington, Hants ... 19 G2
Ovington, Norf ... 72 C6
Ovington, Northum ... 112 E6
Ower ... 18 E4
Owermoigne ... 9 F5
Owler Bar ... 79 G4
Owlswick ... 44 B5
Owmby-by-Spital ... 81 H3
Owslebury ... 19 G3
Owston ... 69 F6
Owston Ferry ... 81 F1
Owstwick ... 89 G3
Owthorpe ... 68 E3
Owton Manor ... 104 D5
Oxborough ... 71 H6
Oxcombe ... 83 F4
Oxen End ... 47 G3
Oxen Park ... 92 B3
Oxenholme ... 92 D3
Oxenhope ... 86 B3
Oxenton ... 42 B2
Oxenwood ... 29 F5
OXFORD ... 43 H5
Oxhill ... 56 B7
Oxley ... 66 E6
Oxley's Green ... 22 C3
Oxnam ... 121 G6
Oxshott ... 31 F4
Oxspring ... 86 D6
Oxted ... 32 D5
Oxton, Notts ... 80 D6
Oxton, Scot Bord ... 120 D2
Oxwell Mains ... 131 G5
Oxwich ... 24 B2
Oxwich Green ... 24 B2
Oxwick ... 72 C4
Oykel Bridge ... 163 H3
Oyne ... 156 D6

P

Pabail Iarach ... 161 J4
Packington ... 68 B5
Padanaram ... 138 C3
Padbury ... 44 B2
PADDINGTON ... 32 C2
Paddlesworth ... 23 H2
Paddock Wood ... 33 G6
Paddockhaugh ... 155 G3
Paddolgreen ... 65 J3
Padeswood ... 76 E5
Padiham ... 85 G3
PADSTOW ... 4 C4
Padworth ... 29 J4
Pagham ... 20 B6
Paglesham Churchend ... 48 C6
Paglesham Eastend ... 34 C1
Paibeil ... 149 C3
PAIGNTON ... 7 E4
Pailton ... 56 C3
Painscastle ... 52 E7
Painshawfield ... 112 E6
Painswick ... 41 H5
Painter's Forstal ... 34 C5
PAISLEY ... 118 B1
Pakefield ... 61 J2
Pakenham ... 60 C5
Pale ... 64 C3
Palestine ... 28 E6
Paley Street ... 30 C3
Palgowan ... 107 F4
Palgrave ... 60 E4
Palmerston ... 25 J3
Palnackie ... 100 C2
Palnure ... 99 F3
Palterton ... 80 B5
Pamber End ... 29 J5
Pamber Green ... 29 J5
Pamber Heath ... 29 J4
Pamington ... 42 B2
Pamphill ... 10 B3
Pampisford ... 59 E7
Panbride ... 139 E5
Pancrasweek ... 12 C5
Pandy, Monm ... 40 C3
Pandy, Powys ... 64 C6
Pandy, Wrex ... 65 E3
Pandy Tudur ... 75 H5
Panfield ... 47 H3
Pangbourne ... 29 J3
Pannal ... 86 E1

Pant ... 65 F4
Pant Glâs ... 63 E2
Pant Mawr ... 52 B3
Pant-glas ... 63 H7
Pant-lasau ... 38 D5
Pant-Meredith ... 38 D3
Pant-y-dwr ... 52 C4
Pant-y-ffridd ... 64 E6
Panteg ... 36 D2
Pantgwyn ... 50 C7
Panton ... 82 D4
Pantperthog ... 63 H6
Pantyffynnon ... 38 D4
Panxworth ... 73 G5
Papcastle ... 101 F4
Papil ... 176 C4
Papple ... 131 E5
Papplewick ... 80 C6
Papworth Everard ... 58 C5
Papworth St Agnes ... 58 C5
Par ... 4 —
Parbold ... 84 C5
Parbrook ... 16 D2
Parc Seymour ... 26 D1
Parc-Henri ... 38 C3
Parcllyn ... 50 C6
Pardshaw ... 101 E5
Parham ... 61 G5
Parish Holm ... 118 E5
Park ... 109 G3
Park Bernisdale ... 150 D3
Park Corner ... 30 A2
Park End ... 112 C5
Park Gate ... 19 G5
Parkend ... 41 F5
Parkeston ... 49 F2
Parkgate, Ches ... 76 E4
Parkgate, D & G ... 109 H4
Parkgate, Surrey ... 31 G6
Parkham ... 12 D3
Parkham Ash ... 12 D3
Parkhill ... 138 A4
Parkhouse ... 40 E5
Parkhurst ... 11 F4
Parkmill ... 24 C2
Parkside ... 156 B6
Parkstone ... 10 B4
Parley Cross ... 10 B4
Parracombe ... 24 D6
Parrog ... 37 E2
Parson Cross ... 79 H2
Parson Drove ... 70 D6
Parsonby ... 101 F4
Partick ... 128 C6
Partington ... 78 B2
Partney ... 83 G5
Parton, Cumbr ... 100 D5
Parton, D & G ... 99 H2
Partridge Green ... 21 E4
Partrishow ... 40 B3
Parwich ... 79 F6
Passenham ... 44 B2
Passingford Bridge ... 47 F6
Paston ... 73 G3
Patcham ... 21 G5
Patching ... 20 D5
Patchole ... 24 D6
Patchway ... 27 F2
Pateley Bridge ... 94 C5
Path of Condie ... 129 H1
Pathe ... 16 B2
Pathfinder Village ... 14 E6
Pathhead, E Ayr ... 118 D6
Pathhead, Fife ... 130 B3
Pathhead, Midlo ... 130 C6
Pathlow ... 55 G6
Patmore Heath ... 47 E3
Patna ... 107 G1
Patney ... 28 C5
Patrick ... 90 B4
Patrick Brompton ... 94 D2
Patrington ... 89 H4
Patrixbourne ... 35 E5
Patterdale ... 101 H4
Pattingham ... 66 D7
Pattishall ... 56 E6
Pattiswick ... 48 B3
Patton Bridge ... 92 D2
Paul ... 2 C5
Paulerspury ... 57 F7
Paull ... 89 F4
Paulsgrove ... 19 H5
Paulton ... 27 F5
Pauperhaugh ... 113 F3
Pavenham ... 57 H6
Pawlett ... 26 B6
Pawston ... 122 D4
Paxford ... 42 D2
Paxton ... 122 E2
Payhembury ... 15 G5
Paythorne ... 85 G1
Peacehaven ... 21 H5
Peak Dale ... 79 F4
Peak Forest ... 79 F4
Peakirk ... 70 B6
Pean Hill ... 34 E4
Pearsie ... 138 C3
Pease Pottage ... 21 F2
Peasedown St John ... 27 G5
Peasemore ... 29 G3
Peasenhall ... 61 G5
Peaslake ... 31 E6
Peasmarsh ... 23 E3
Peaston ... 130 D6
Peastonbank ... 130 D6
Peat Inn ... 130 D2
Peathill ... 157 G2
Peatling Magna ... 56 D2
Peatling Parva ... 56 D3
Peaton ... 53 J3
Pebmarsh ... 48 B2
Pebworth ... 55 G7
Pecket Well ... 86 A4
Peckforton ... 77 H6
Peckleton ... 68 C6
Pedmore ... 54 E3
Pedwell ... 16 C2
PEEBLES ... 120 B3
Peel ... 90 B4
Pegswood ... 113 G4
Peinchorran ... 151 E5
Peinlich ... 150 D3
Pelaw ... 113 G6
Pelcomb Cross ... 36 C4
Peldon ... 48 C4
Pelsall ... 67 F6
Pelton ... 104 B2
Pelutho ... 101 F3
Pelynt ... 5 —
Pembrey ... 38 B5
Pembridge ... 53 G6
PEMBROKE ... 36 D5
Pembroke Dock ... 36 D5
Pembury ... 33 G6
Pen-y-coedcae ... 26 H3
Pen-allt ... 41 E3

Pen-bont Rhydybeddau 51 G3
Pen-clawdd 38 C6
Pen-llyn 74 C3
Pen-sarn, Gwyn LL45 63 F4
Pen-sarn, Gwyn LL53 62 E2
Pen-y-banc 38 D3
Pen-y-bont, Carm 37 H3
Pen-y-bont, Powys 65 F4
Pen-y-bont Llanerch Emrys 65 F4
Pen-y-bryn, Gwyn 63 G5
Pen-y-bryn, Pemb 37 F1
Pen-y-cae 39 F4
Pen-y-cae-mawr 40 D6
Pen-y-cefn 39 G5
Pen-y-clawdd 40 D5
Pen-y-fai 25 F2
Pen-y-ffordd 76 D3
Pen-y-garn 38 C2
Pen-y-garnedd 74 E4
Pen-y-graig 62 C3
Pen-y-groes 38 C4
Pen-y-lan 25 G3
Pen-y-Park 40 B1
Pen-y-stryt 76 D6
Pen-yr-heol 40 D4
Penallt 40 E5
Penally 37 F6
Penare 4 D6
PENARTH 26 A3
Penbryn 50 C6
Pencader 38 B2
Pencaitland 130 D6
Pencarreg 51 F7
Pencelli 39 H3
Pencoed 25 G2
Pencombe 54 A6
Pencoyd 40 E3
Pencraig, Co of H 41 E3
Pencraig, Powys 64 D4
Pencroesoped 40 C5
Pendas Fields 87 E3
Pendeen 2 B4
Penderyn 39 G5
Pendine 37 G5
Pendlebury 78 B1
Pendleton 85 F3
Pendock 41 G2
Pendoggett 4 D3
Pendomer 16 D4
Pendoylan 25 H3
Penegoes 63 H6
Penelewey 3 G3
Penffordd 37 E3
Penffridd 74 E6
PENGE 32 D3
Pengenffordd 40 A2
Pengorffwysfa 74 D2
Pengover Green 5 F4
Pengwern 76 C4
Penhale 4 C5
Penhallow 3 F2
Penhalurick 3 F4
Penhow 26 D1
Penhurst 22 C4
PENICUIK 120 B1
Peniel 150 D4
Penifiler 116 B5
Penisa'r Waun 75 E5
PENISTONE 86 D6
Penjerrick 3 F4
Penketh 77 H3
Penkill 106 E3
Penkridge 66 E5
Penley 65 H3
Penllech 62 C3
Penllergaer 38 D6
Penllyn 25 G3
Penmachno 75 G6
Penmaen, Caer 40 A6
Penmaen, Swan 24 C2
PENMAENMAWR 75 G4
Penmaenpool 63 G5
Penmark 25 H4
Penmon 75 F3
Penmorfa 63 F2
Penmynydd 74 E4
Penn 44 D6
Penn Street 44 D6
Pennal 63 H6
Pennan 157 F2
Pennant, Cered 51 F5
Pennant, Conwy 75 H6
Pennant, Powys 64 D2
Pennant Melangell 64 D4
Pennard 24 C2
Pennerley 65 G7
Pennington 91 D4
Penny Bridge 92 B3
Pennycross 133 H6
Pennygate 73 G4
Pennygown 133 H4
Pennymoor 14 E4
Pennyvenie 107 G2
Penparc 50 C7
Penparcau 51 F3
Penperlleni 40 C5
Penpillick 4 D5
Penpol 3 G4
Penpoll 5 E5
Penponds 2 D5
Penpont 109 F4
Penre-bach 51 F7
Penrherber 37 G2
Penrhiw-llan 37 H1
Penrhiwceiber 39 H6
Penrhiwpal 50 D7
Penrhos, Gwyn 62 D3
Penrhos, I of Angl 74 B3
Penrhos, Monm 40 D4
Penrhos, Powys 39 F4
Penrhyn Bay 75 H3
Penrhyn-coch 51 G3
Penrhyn-side 75 H3
Penrhyndeudraeth 63 G3
Penrhys 39 H6
PENRITH 102 B5
Penrose 4 B3
Penruddock 101 J5
PENRYN 3 F4
Pensarn 76 B4
Pensax 54 C5
Pensby 76 E3
Penselwood 17 F2
Pensford 27 F4
Pensham 42 B1
Penshaw 104 C2
Penshurst 33 F6
Pensilva 5 F4
Penston 130 D5
Pentewan 4 D6
Pentir 75 E5
Pentire 3 F1
Pentney 71 H6
Penton Mewsey 29 F6

Pentraeth 74 E4
Pentre, Powys 52 D3
Pentre, Shrops 65 G5
Pentre, Wrex LL14 65 F2
Pentre, Wrex LL20 64 E3
Pentre Berw 74 D4
Pentre Dolau Honddu 39 G1
Pentre Galar 37 F2
Pentre Gwynfryn 63 F4
Pentre Halkyn 76 E4
Pentre Isaf 75 H5
Pentre'r beirdd 65 E5
Pentre'r-felin 39 G2
Pentre- Morgan 37 J3
Pentre-bach 39 G2
Pentre-celyn, Denb 76 D6
Pentre-celyn, Powys 64 B6
Pentre-cwrt 37 H2
Pentre-dwr 38 D6
Pentre-Gwenlais 38 D4
Pentre-Llanrhaeadr 76 C5
Pentre-llwyn-llwyd 52 C6
Pentre-llyn 51 G4
Pentre-llyn-cymmer 76 B6
Pentre-mawr 76 C4
Pentre-tafarn-y-fedw 75 H5
Pentre-ty-gwyn 39 F2
Pentrebach, Merth Tyd 39 H5
Pentrebach, Swan 38 D5
Pentrecagal 37 H1
Pentreclwydau 39 F5
Pentredwr 65 F2
Pentrefelin, Carm 38 C3
Pentrefelin, Conwy 75 H4
Pentrefelin, Gwyn 63 F3
Pentrefelin, Powys 64 E4
Pentrefoelas 75 H6
Pentregat 50 D6
Pentreheyling 53 F2
Pentrich 79 H6
Pentridge 18 B4
Pentwyn 26 B2
Pentyrch 25 J2
Penuwch 51 F5
Penwithick 4 D5
Penwyllt 39 F4
Penybont 52 E5
Penybontfawr 64 D4
Penybryn 39 J6
Penycae 65 F2
Penycwm 36 C3
Penyffordd 77 F5
Penygarnedd 64 E4
Penygraig 74 D6
Penygroes 74 D2
Penysarn 39 G5
Penywaun 2 C5
PENZANCE 2 E6
Peopleton 46 B3
Peover Heath 78 D6
Peper Harow 30 D6
Peplow 66 B4
Perceton 117 H3
Percie 146 C4
Percyhorner 157 G2
Perham Down 28 E6
Perivale 31 F2
Perkhill 146 C3
Perlethorpe 80 D4
Perran Downs 2 D4
Perranarworthal 3 F4
Perranporth 3 F2
Perranuthnoe 2 D5
Perranwell 3 F4
Perranzabuloe 3 F2
Perry Barr 55 F2
Perry Green 47 E4
Perrystone Hill 41 F3
Pershall 66 D1
Pershore 46 B3
Pert 143 E4
Pertenhall 58 A5
PERTH 130 B7
Perthy 65 F3
Perton 50 B1
Peter Tavy 6 B3
Peter's Green 45 F4
PETERBOROUGH 70 B6
Peterburn 162 B5
Peterchurch 40 C2
Peterculter 147 F3
PETERHEAD 157 J4
PETERLEE 104 D4
Peters Marland 13 E4
PETERSFIELD 19 J3
Peterston- super-Ely 25 H3
Peterstone Wentlooge 26 B2
Peterstow 41 E3
Petertown 170 D4
Petham 34 E5
Petrockstowe 13 F5
Pett 23 E4
Pettaugh 60 E6
Pettinain 119 G3
Pettistree 61 F6
Petton, Devon 15 G3
Petton, Shrops 65 H4
Petts Wood 33 E4
Petty 156 E5
Pettycur 130 B4
Pettymuick 157 G6
Petworth 20 C3
Pevensey 22 C5
Pevensey Bay 22 C5
Pewsey 28 D5
Philham 12 C3
Philiphaugh 120 D5
Phillack 2 D4
Philleigh 3 G4
Philpstoun 129 H5
Phocle Green 41 F3
Phoenix Green 30 B5
Phorp 155 E5
Pica 100 E5
Piccadilly Corner 61 F3
Piccotts End 45 F5
Pickerells 47 F5
PICKERING 96 C3
Picket Piece 29 F6
Picket Post 18 C5
Pickford Green 55 H5
Pickhill 94 E3
Picklescott 65 H7
Pickletillem 138 D6
Pickmere 78 A4
Pickney 15 H3
Pickstock 66 C4
Pickwell, Devon 24 B6
Pickwell, Leic 69 F5
Pickworth, Lincs 69 H5
Pickworth, Rut 77 G4
Picton, Ches 77 F4
Picton, N Yorks 104 D7
Piddinghoe 21 H5
Piddington, Bucks 44 C6
Piddington, Northnts 57 G6

Piddington, Oxon 43 J4
Piddlehinton 9 F4
Piddletrenthide 9 F3
Pidley 58 D4
Piercebridge 104 B6
Pierowall 172 E2
Pigdon 113 F4
Pikehall 79 F6
Pilgrims Hatch 47 F6
Pilham 81 F2
Pill 26 E3
Pillaton 5 G4
Pillerton Hersey 55 J7
Pillerton Priors 55 H7
Pilleth 53 F5
Pilley, Hants 10 E4
Pilley, S Yorks 79 H1
Pilling 84 C2
Pilling Lane 84 B2
Pillowell 27 E2
Pilsbury 79 F5
Pilsdon 8 C4
Pilsgate 70 A6
Pilsley, Derby DE45 79 G4
Pilsley, Derby S45 80 B5
Pilton, Northnts 57 J3
Pilton, Rut 69 H6
Pilton, Somer 27 E6
Pilton Green 24 B2
Pimperne 17 H5
Pinchbeck 70 C4
Pinchbeck West 70 C4
Pinfold 84 B5
Pinhay 8 B4
Pinhoe 15 F6
Pinley Green 55 H5
Pinminnoch 106 D3
Pinmore 106 E3
Pinn 7 H2
PINNER 31 F2
Pinvin 55 E7
Pinwherry 106 D4
Pinxton 80 E1
Pipe and Lyde 40 E1
Pipe Gate 66 C2
Pipe Ridware 67 F5
Piperhall 117 F2
Pipers Pool 5 F2
Pipewell 57 G3
Pippacott 13 F2
Pipton 40 A2
Pirbright 30 D5
Pirbright Camp 30 D5
Pirnmill 116 C3
Pirton, Herts 45 F2
Pirton, Worces 54 D7
Pishill 30 B2
Pistyll 62 D2
Pitagowan 137 F2
Pitblae 157 G2
Pitcairngreen 137 H6
Pitcalnie 154 C1
Pitcaple 156 E6
Pitch Green 44 B5
Pitch Place 30 D5
Pitchaish 155 F4
Pitchcombe 41 H5
Pitchcott 44 B3
Pitchford 65 J6
Pitcombe 17 E2
Pitcox 131 F5
Pitcur 138 B5
Pitfichie 146 D2
Pitforthie 147 F6
Pitgrudy 164 D4
Pitkennedy 139 E3
Pitkevy 130 B2
Pitlessie 130 C2
PITLOCHRY 137 G3
Pitmachie 156 D6
Pitmedden 157 F6
Pitminster 15 J4
Pitmuies 139 E4
Pitmunie 146 D2
Pitney 16 C3
Pitscottie 130 D1
Pitsea 33 H2
Pitsford 57 F5
Pitsford Hill 15 H2
Pitstone Green 44 D4
Pittendreich 155 F2
Pittentrail 164 D3
PITTENWEEM 131 E2
Pittington 104 C3
Pitton, Swan 24 B2
Pitton, Wilts 18 D2
Pittulie 157 G2
Pityme 4 C3
Pixey Green 61 F4
Place Newton 96 D4
Plaidy 156 E4
Plains 129 E6
Plaish 53 J2
Plaistow 20 D2
Plaitford 18 D4
Plas 38 B3
Plas Brondanw 63 G2
Plas Esgair 64 B6
Plas Gogerddan 51 G3
Plas Gwynant 75 F6
Plas Llysyn 63 H6
Plas Nantyr 64 E3
Plas-rhiw-Saeson 64 C6
Plastow Green 29 H4
Platt 33 G5
Plawsworth 104 B3
Plaxtol 23 F3
Play Hatch 30 B3
Playden 21 F3
Playford 61 F7
Playing Place 3 G3
Plealey 65 H6
Plean 129 F4
Pleasington 85 E4
Pleasley 80 B5
Plenderleith 122 C6
Plenmeller 111 G6
Pleshey 47 G4
Plockton 151 H5
Plocrapol 159 F3
Plowden 53 G3
Ploxgreen 65 G6
Pluckley 34 C6
Pluckley Thorne 34 C6
Plumbland 101 H4
Plumley 78 B4
Plumpton, Cumbr 102 A4
Plumpton, E Susx 21 G4
Plumpton, Lancs 84 B3
Plumpton Green 21 G4
Plumpton Head 102 B4
Plumpton Rocks 87 E1
Plumstead, G Lon 33 E2
Plumstead, Norf 72 E3

Plumtree 68 E3
Plungar 69 F3
Plush 9 F3
Plwmp 50 D6
PLYMOUTH 5 H5
Plymouth City Airport 5 J4
Plympton 6 B5
Plymstock 6 B5
Plymtree 15 G5
Pockley 96 B3
Pocklington 88 C2
Pockthorpe 72 B4
Pode Hole 70 C4
Podimore 16 D3
Podington 57 H5
Podmore 66 C3
Point Clear 48 D4
Pointon 70 B3
Pokesdown 10 C4
Pol a' Charra 148 C3
Polapit Tamar 12 D7
Polbae 106 E5
Polbain 162 E3
Polbathic 5 G5
Polbeth 129 H6
Poldean 109 J2
Polebrook 58 A3
Polegate 22 B5
Poles 164 D4
Polesworth 67 H6
Polglass 162 E3
Polgooth 4 C5
Poling 20 D5
Polkerris 4 D4
Polla 167 E4
Pollington 87 H5
Polloch 134 B2
Pollokshaws 118 C1
Pollokshields 128 C6
Polmassick 4 C6
Polmont 129 G5
Polnessan 118 B6
Polperro 5 F5
Polruan 4 E5
Polsham 26 E6
Polskeoch 108 D2
Polstead 48 C2
Polstead Heath 48 C1
Poltalloch 126 C3
Poltimore 15 F6
Polton 130 C6
Polwarth 122 C2
Polyphant 5 F2
Polzeath 4 C3
Pond Street 47 E2
Ponde 39 J2
Ponders End 46 D6
Pondersbridge 58 C2
Ponsanooth 3 F4
Ponsonby 100 D7
Pont Aberglaslyn 63 F2
Pont Creuddyn 51 F6
Pont Crugnant 52 B2
Pont Cyfyng 75 G6
Pont Henri 38 B5
Pont Llanio 51 G6
Pont Llogel 64 D5
Pont Pen-y-benglog 75 F5
Pont Rhyd-y-cyff 25 F2
Pont-faen 39 G2
Pont-rhyd-y-groes 51 H4
Pont-rug 74 E5
Pont-Sian 51 E7
Pont-y-pant 75 G6
Pont-yr-hafod 36 D3
Pontamman 38 D4
Pontantwn 38 B4
Pontardawe 38 E5
Pontarddulais 38 C5
Pontarsais 38 B3
Pontdolgoch 52 D2
PONTEFRACT 87 F4
PONTELAND 113 F6
Ponterwyd 51 H3
Pontesbury 65 G6
Pontesford 65 H6
Pontfadog 65 F3
Pontfaen 36 E2
Pontgarreg 50 D6
Ponthir 40 C6
Ponthirwaun 50 C7
PONTLLANFRAITH 40 A4
Pontlliw 38 D5
Pontllyfni 74 D6
Pontlottyn 39 J5
Pontneddfechan 39 G5
Pontrhydfendigaid 51 H6
Pontrhydyfen 39 E6
Pontrilas 40 C3
Pontrobert 64 E5
Ponts Green 22 C4
Pontshill 41 F3
Pontsticill 39 H4
Pontyates 38 B5
Pontyberem 38 C4
Pontybodkin 76 E6
Pontyclun 25 H2
PONTYCYMER 25 G1
Pontymister 26 B2
PONTYPOOL 40 B6
PONTYPRIDD 25 H1
Pontywaun 40 B6
Pooksgreen 18 E4
Pool, Corn 3 E5
Pool, W Yorks 86 D2
Pool of Muckhart 129 G6
Pool Quay 65 F5
POOLE 10 B4
Poole Keynes 42 C6
Poolewe 162 C5
Pooley Bridge 102 A5
Poolhill 41 G3
Poorton 8 D4
Pope Hill 36 D4
Popeswood 29 H6
Popham 32 D2
POPLAR 11 F4
Porchfield 73 F6
Poringland 4 E4
Porkellis 3 F5
Porlock 25 F6
Porlock Weir 25 F6
Port Ann 126 D4
Port Appin 134 D4
Port Askaig 125 B6
Port Bannatyne 127 E6
Port Carlisle 110 B6
Port Charlotte 124 B5
Port Driseach 126 D5
Port e Vullen 90 D3
Port Ellen 124 C6
Port Elphinstone 147 E2
Port Erin 90 A6
Port Gaverne 4 D3
PORT GLASGOW 127 H5

Port Henderson 162 B6
Port Isaac 4 D2
Port Logan 98 B5
Port Mholair 161 J4
Port Mór 140 D6
Port Mulgrave 105 G6
Port nan Giuran 161 J4
Port nan Long 158 C5
Port Nis 161 J1
Port of Menteith 128 C2
Port Quin 4 C2
Port St Mary 90 B6
Port Sunlight 77 F3
PORT TALBOT 24 E1
Port Tennant 38 E6
Port Wemyss 124 A5
Port William 99 E5
Port-an-eorna 151 G5
Port-Eynon 24 B2
Portachoillan 116 B2
Portavadie 126 D6
Portbury 26 E3
Portchester 19 H5
Portclair 143 G2
Portencross 117 F3
Portesham 8 E5
Portfield Gate 36 D4
Portgate 5 H2
Portgordon 156 A2
Portgower 165 G2
PORTH 25 H1
Porth Navas 3 F5
Porth-y-waen 65 F4
Porthallow 3 F5
PORTHCAWL 25 F3
Porthcothan 4 B3
Porthcurno 2 B5
Porthgain 36 C2
Porthkerry 25 H4
Porthleven 2 E5
Porthllechog 74 D2
PORTHMADOG 63 F3
Porthmeor 2 C4
Porthoustock 3 G5
Porthpean 4 D5
Porthtowan 3 E4
Portincaple 127 G3
Portington 88 B3
Portinnisherrich 126 D1
Portinscale 101 G5
PORTISHEAD 26 D3
PORTKNOCKIE 156 B2
Portlethen 147 G4
Portlethen Village 147 G4
Portloe 4 C7
Portmahomack 165 H5
Portmeirion 63 F3
Portmellon 4 D6
Portmore 10 E4
Portnacroish 134 C4
Portnahaven 124 A5
Portnalong 150 D5
Portnaluchaig 141 F5
Portnancon 167 F3
Portobello 130 C5
Porton 18 C2
Portpatrick 98 B4
Portreath 3 E4
Portree 150 D4
Portrye 117 F2
Portscatho 3 G4
Portsea 11 H3
Portskerra 168 C3
Portskewett 26 D2
PORTSLADE-BY-SEA 21 F5
Portslogan 98 A4
PORTSMOUTH 11 H4
PORTSOY 156 C2
Portswood 19 F4
Portuairk 133 G2
Portway 55 F4
Portwrinkle 5 G5
Poslingford 59 H7
Postbridge 6 C3
Postcombe 44 B6
Postling 23 H2
Postwick 73 F6
Pott Row 71 H4
Pott Shrigley 78 D4
Potten End 44 E5
Potter Heigham 73 H5
Potter Street 47 E5
Potterhanworth 82 C5
Potterhanworth Booths 82 C5
Potterne 28 B5
Potterne Wick 28 B5
POTTERS BAR 46 C5
Potters Corner 34 C6
Potters Crouch 45 F5
Potters Forstal 34 B6
Potterspury 44 B1
Potterton 147 G2
Potto 95 F1
Potton 58 C7
Poughill, Corn 12 C5
Poughill, Devon 14 E5
Poulshot 28 B5
Poulton 42 D5
POULTON-LE-FYLDE 84 B3
Pound Bank 54 C4
Pound Hill 21 H3
Poundgate 21 H3
Poundland 106 D4
Poundon 43 J3
Poundsgate 6 D3
Poundstock 12 C6
Powburn 123 F6
Powderham 7 F2
Powerstock 8 D4
Powfoot 109 J6
Powick 54 D6
Powmill 129 H3
Poxwell 9 F5
Poyle 31 F3
Poynings 21 F4
Poyntington 17 E4
Poynton 78 D3
Poynton Green 66 A5
Poyntzfield 154 B2
Poystreet Green 60 C6
Praa Sands 2 D5
Pratt's Bottom 33 E4
Praze-an- Beeble 2 E4
Predannack Wollas 3 E6
Prees 65 J3
Prees Green 65 J3
Prees Heath 65 J3
Prees Higher Heath 66 A3
Preesall 84 B2

Preesgweene 65 F3
Pren- gwyn 38 B1
Prendwick 123 F6
Prenteg 63 F2
Prenton 77 E3
PRESCOT 77 G2
Prescott 65 H4
Pressen 122 D4
PRESTATYN 76 C3
Prestbury, Ches 78 D4
Prestbury, Glos 42 B3
PRESTEIGNE 53 G5
Presthope 66 A7
Prestleigh 17 E1
Preston, Bri & Ho 21 G5
Preston, Devon 6 E3
Preston, Dorset 9 E5
Preston, E Loth 131 E5
Preston, E Yorks 89 F3
Preston, Glos GL7 42 C5
Preston, Glos HR8 41 F2
Preston, Herts 45 F3
Preston, Kent 35 H4
PRESTON, Lancs 84 D4
Preston, Northum 123 G5
Preston, Rut 69 G6
Preston, Scot Bord 122 C2
Preston, Wilts 28 C3
Preston Bagot 55 G5
Preston Bissett 44 A3
Preston Bowyer 15 H3
Preston Brockhurst 65 J4
Preston Brook 77 H3
Preston Candover 29 J6
Preston Capes 56 D6
Preston Green 55 G5
Preston Gubbals 65 H5
Preston on Stour 55 H7
Preston on the Hill 77 H3
Preston on Wye 40 C1
Preston St Mary 60 C6
Preston upon the Weald Moors 66 B5
Preston Wynne 53 J7
Preston-under-Scar 94 B2
Prestonmill 100 D2
PRESTONPANS 130 C5
PRESTWICH 85 G6
Prestwick, Northum 113 F5
PRESTWICK, S Ayr 117 H5
Prestwood 44 C5
Price Town 25 G1
Prickwillow 59 F3
Priddy 27 E5
Priest Hutton 92 D4
Priest Weston 53 F2
Priestland 118 C4
Primethorpe 56 D2
Primrose Green 72 D5
Princes Gate 37 F4
PRINCES RISBOROUGH 44 C5
Princethorpe 56 C4
Princetown 6 B3
Prion 76 C5
Prior Muir 130 E1
Priors Frome 41 E2
Priors Hardwick 56 C6
Priors Marston 56 C6
Priory Wood 53 F7
Priston 27 F4
Prittlewell 34 B2
Privett 19 H3
Prixford 13 F2
Probus 4 B6
Proncy 164 D4
Prospect 101 F3
PRUDHOE 113 E6
Pubil 136 B4
Puckeridge 46 D3
Puckington 16 B4
Pucklechurch 27 F4
Puddington, Ches 77 F4
Puddington, Devon 14 E4
Puddledock 60 D2
Puddletown 9 F4
Pudleston 54 A6
PUDSEY 86 D3
Pulborough 20 D4
Puleston 66 C4
Pulford 77 F6
Pulham 17 F5
Pulham Market 61 E3
Pulham St Mary 61 F3
Pulley 65 H6
Pulloxhill 45 E2
Pulp Mill 117 H4
Pulrossie 164 D5
Pulverbatch 65 H6
Pumsaint 38 D1
Puncheston 36 E3
Puncknowle 8 D5
Punnett's Town 22 C3
Purbrook 19 H5
Purfleet 33 F3
Puriton 16 B6
Purleigh 48 B5
PURLEY 32 D4
Purley on Thames 30 A3
Purlogue 53 F4
Purls Bridge 59 E3
Purse Caundle 17 E4
Purslow 53 G3
Purston Jaglin 87 F5
Purton, Glos GL13 41 F5
Purton, Glos GL15 41 F5
Purton, Wilts 28 C2
Purton Stoke 28 C1
Pury End 57 F7
Pusey 43 F6
Putley 41 F2
Putley Green 41 F2
PUTNEY 32 C3
Puttenham, Herts 44 C4
Puttenham, Surrey 30 D6
Puttock End 48 B1
Puxton 26 D4
Pwll 38 B5
Pwll-glâs 76 D6
Pwll-trap 37 G4
Pwllcrochan 36 D5
Pwllgloyw 39 H2
PWLLHELI 62 D3
Pwllmeyric 26 E1
Pye Corner 26 C2
Pyecombe 21 F4
Pyle, Brig 25 F2
Pyle, I of W 11 F6
Pylle 16 E2
Pymore (Pymoor) 59 E3
Pyrford 31 E5
Pyrford Village 31 E5
Pyrton 44 A6
Pytchley 57 G4
Pyworthy 12 D5

Q

Quabbs 53 F3
Quadring 70 C3
Quadring Eaudike 70 C3
Quainton 44 B4
Quarley 28 E6
Quarndon 68 B2
Quarrier's Village 127 H6
Quarrington 69 J2
Quarrington Hill 104 C4
Quarry Bank, Ches 77 H5
Quarry Bank, W Mids 54 E3
Quarryhill 164 D5
Quarrywood 155 F2
Quarter 118 E2
Quatford 54 C2
Quatt 54 C3
Quebec 103 H3
Quedgeley 41 H4
Queen Adelaide 59 F3
Queen Camel 16 D3
Queen Charlton 27 F4
Queen Street 33 G6
Queenborough 34 C3
Queens Head 65 G4
QUEENSBURY 86 C4
QUEENSFERRY, C of Edin 129 J5
Queensferry, Flint 77 F5
Queenzieburn 128 D5
Quemerford 28 C4
Quendale 176 C6
Quendon 47 F3
Queniborough 68 E5
Quenington 42 D5
Quernmore 92 D5
Quethiock 5 G4
Quholm 170 C3
Quidenham 60 D3
Quidhampton, Hants 29 H5
Quidhampton, Wilts 18 C2
Quilquox 157 G5
Quina Brook 65 J3
Quindry 171 E5
Quine's Hill 90 C5
Quinton 57 F6
Quintrell Downs 3 G1
Quoditch 13 E6
Quoig 137 F6
Quorn (Quorndon) 68 D5
Quothquan 119 G4
Quoyburray 171 F4
Quoyloo 172 C4
Quoyness 170 C4
Quoys, Shetld ZE2 9EQ 177 D2
Quoys, Shetld ZE2 9PR 175 F5
Quoyscottie 172 D4
Quzlewell Green 86 E4

R

Raby 77 F5
Rachub 75 F5
Rackenford 14 E4
Rackham 20 D4
Rackheath 73 F5
Racks 109 H5
Rackwick, Orkney KW16 170 C5
Rackwick, Orkney KW17 172 E1
Radbourne 67 H3
RADCLIFFE, G Man 85 F6
Radcliffe, Northum 113 G2
Radcliffe on Trent 68 E3
Radclive 44 A2
Radcot 43 E6
Raddery 154 B3
Radernie 130 D2
Radford 43 G3
Radford Semele 56 B5
RADLETT 45 F6
Radley 43 H6
Radnage 44 B6
RADSTOCK 27 F5
Radstone 43 H1
Radway 56 B7
Radway Green 78 B6
Radwell, Beds 57 J6
Radwell, Herts 46 C2
Radwinter 47 G2
Radyr 25 J2
Raera 134 C6
Rafford 155 E3
Ragdale 68 E5
Raglan 40 D5
Ragnall 81 F4
RAINFORD 77 G1
RAINHAM, G Lon 33 F2
Rainham, Med 34 B4
Rainhill 77 G2
Rainow 78 D4
Rainton 95 E4
Rainworth 80 C6
Raisbeck 102 C7
Raise 102 D3
Rait 138 B6
Raithby 83 F3
Raithby by Spilsby 83 F5
Rake 20 B3
Ram Lane 34 C6
Ramasaig 150 A4
Rame, Corn PL10 5 H6
Rame, Corn TR10 3 F4
Ramnageo 177 D3
Rampisham 8 D3
Rampside 91 D5
Rampton, Cambs 58 E5
Rampton, Notts 81 E4
RAMSBOTTOM 85 F5
Ramsbury 29 E3
Ramscraigs 169 F7
Ramsdean 19 J3
Ramsdell 29 H5
Ramsden 43 F4
Ramsden Bellhouse 47 H6
Ramsden Heath 47 H6
RAMSEY, Cambs 58 C3
Ramsey, Essex 49 F2
RAMSEY, I of M 90 D3
Ramsey Forty Foot 58 D3
Ramsey Heights 58 C3
Ramsey Island 48 C5
Ramsey Mereside 58 C3
Ramsey St Mary's 58 C3
Ramseycleuch 120 B6
RAMSGATE 35 G4
Ramsgill 94 C4
Ramshorn 67 F2
Ramsnest Common 20 C2
Ranais 161 H5
Ranby, Lincs 82 E4

Ranby, Notts 80 D3
Rand 82 D4
Randwick 41 H5
Ranfurly 127 H6
Rangemore 67 G4
Rangeworthy 27 F2
Rank's Green 47 H4
Rankinston 118 B6
Ranmore 141 H5
Ranskill 80 D3
Ranton 66 D4
Ranworth 73 G5
Rapness 173 F2
Rascarrel 100 B3
Raskelf 95 F4
Rassau 39 J4
Rastrick 86 C4
Ratagan 142 B1
Ratby 68 D6
Ratcliffe Culey 68 B7
Ratcliffe on Soar 68 C4
Ratcliffe on the Wreake 68 E5
Rathen 157 H2
Rathillet 138 C6
Rathmell 93 G5
Ratho 129 J5
Ratho Station 129 J5
Rathven 156 B2
Ratley 56 B7
Ratlinghope 53 H2
Rattar 169 G2
Ratten Row 84 C2
Rattery 6 D4
Rattlesden 60 C6
RATTRAY 138 A4
Rauceby 69 J2
Raughton Head 101 H3
RAUNDS 57 H4
Ravenfield 80 B2
Ravenglass 91 B2
Raveningham 61 G2
Ravenscar 97 E1
Ravensdale 90 C3
Ravensden 58 A6
Ravenseat 93 G1
Ravenshaw 86 A2
Ravenshead 80 C6
Ravensmoor 51 F4
Ravensthorpe, Northnts 56 E4
Ravensthorpe, W Yorks 86 D4
Ravenstone, Leic 68 C5
Ravenstone, Mil Key 57 G6
Ravenstonedale 93 F1
Ravenstown 92 B4
Ravenstruther 119 G3
Ravensworth 103 H7
Raw 97 E1
Rawcliffe, E Yorks 87 H4
Rawcliffe, Yk 95 G6
Rawcliffe Bridge 87 J4
Rawdon 86 D3
RAWMARSH 80 B2
Rawreth 47 H6
Rawridge 15 J5
RAWTENSTALL 85 G4
Raxton 157 F5
Raydon 48 D2
Raylees 112 D3
RAYLEIGH 34 B1
Rayne 47 H3
Reach 59 F5
Read 85 F3
READING 30 B3
Reading Street 23 F2
Reagill 102 C6
Rearquhar 164 D4
Rearsby 68 E5
Rease Heath 77 A6
Reaster 169 G3
Reawick 176 C3
Reawla 2 E4
Reay 168 D3
Rechullin 151 H3
Reculver 35 F4
Red Barns 123 G4
Red Dial 101 G3
Red Lodge 59 G5
Red Oaks Hill 47 G2
Red Rock 84 D6
Red Roses 37 G4
Red Row 113 G3
Red Street 78 C6
Red Wharf Bay 74 E3
Redberth 37 E5
Redbourn 45 F4
Redbourne 81 G1
Redbrook 41 E4
Redburn, Highl IV12 154 D4
Redburn, Highl IV16 153 H2
REDCAR 105 F5
Redcastle, Ang 139 F3
Redcastle, Highl 153 H4
Redcliff Bay 26 D3
Redcloak 147 F5
Reddicap Heath 55 G2
Redding 129 G5
Reddingmuirhead 129 G5
Reddish 78 C2
REDDITCH 55 F5
Rede 60 B6
Redenhall 61 F3
Redesdale Camp 112 C3
Redesmouth 112 C4
Redford, Ang 139 E4
Redford, Durham 103 G4
Redfordgreen 120 C6
Redgorton 137 H6
Redgrave 60 D4
Redheugh 138 D2
Redhill, Aberd AB32 147 E3
Redhill, Aberd AB51 156 D5
Redhill, N Som 26 E4
REDHILL, Surrey 32 C5
Redhouses 125 A6
Redisham 61 H3
Redland, C of Bris 27 E3
Redland, Orkney 172 D4
Redlingfield 61 E4
Redlynch, Wilts 10 D3
Redlynch, Somer 17 F2
Redmain 130 D6
Redmarley D'Abitot 41 G2
Redmarshall 104 C5
Redmile 69 F3
Redmire 94 B2
Rednour 4 D4
Rednal 65 G4
Redpath 121 E4
Redpoint 151 G2
REDRUTH 3 E3
Redwick, Newp 26 D2
Redwick, S Glos 27 E2
Redworth 104 B5
Reed 46 D2
Reedham 73 H5

Reedness 88 B4
Reepham, Lincs 82 C4
Reepham, Norf 72 D4
Reeth 94 B2
Regaby 90 D3
Regil 27 E4
Regoul 154 C3
Reiff 162 D2
REIGATE 32 C5
Reighton 97 G4
Reinigeadal 159 G2
Reiss 169 H4
Reiss Lodge 169 H4
Rejerrah 3 G2
Relubbus 2 D4
Relugas 154 D4
Remenham 30 B2
Remenham Hill 30 B2
Remony 136 E4
Rempstone 68 D4
Rendcomb 42 C5
Rendham 61 G5
Rendlesham 61 G6
RENFREW 128 C6
Renhold 58 A6
Renishaw 80 B4
Rennington 123 H6
Renton 127 H5
Renwick 102 B3
Repps 73 H5
Repton 67 J4
Rescobie 138 E3
Resipole 134 B2
Resolis 154 A2
Resolven 39 F5
Reston 122 D1
Reswallie 138 E3
Retew 4 C5
RETFORD 80 E3
Rettendon 47 H6
Rettendon Place 47 H6
Revesby 83 E5
Rewe 15 F6
Reydon 61 H4
Reymerston 72 D6
Reynalton 37 E5
Reynoldston 24 B1
Rezare 5 G3
Rhadmad 51 F4
Rhandirmwyn 38 E1
Rhayader 52 C5
Rhedyn 62 C3
Rheindown 153 H4
Rhemore 133 H3
Rhes-y-cae 76 D4
Rhes-y-coed 77 J6
Rhes-goch 53 E7
Rhes-Hill 37 F1
Rhôs-on-Sea 75 H3
Rhos-y-brithdir 64 E4
Rhos-y-gwaliau 64 C3
Rhos-y-llan 62 C3
Rhos-y-mawn 75 H5
Rhos-y-meirch 53 F5
Rhoscefnhir 74 E4
Rhoscolyn 74 B4
Rhoscrowther 36 D5
Rhosdylluan 64 B3
Rhosesmor 76 E5
Rhosgadfan 74 D3
Rhosgoch 74 D3
Rhoshirwaun 62 B4
Rhoslan 63 E2
Rhoslefain 63 F6
Rhosllanerchrugog 65 G2
Rhosmaen 38 D3
Rhosmeirch 74 D4
Rhosneigr 74 C4
Rhosnesni 77 F6
Rhossili 24 B2
Rhosson 36 B3
Rhostryfan 74 D6
Rhostyllen 65 G2
Rhosybol 74 D3
Rhu, Arg & Bt G84 127 G4
Rhu, Arg & Bt PA29 126 C6
Rhuallt 76 C4
Rhuddlan 76 C4
Rhue 163 E4
Rhugarbh 134 D4
Rhulen 52 E7
Rhunahaorine 116 B3
Rhuvoult 166 D4
Rhyd, Gwyn 63 G2
Rhyd, Powys 64 C6
Rhyd-Ddu 75 E6
Rhyd-Rosser 51 F5
Rhyd-uchaf 64 C3
Rhyd-y-clafdy 62 D3
Rhyd-y-foel 75 J4
Rhyd-y-fro 38 E5
Rhyd-y-meudwy 76 D6
Rhyd-yr-onen 63 G6
Rhydargaeau 38 B3
Rhydcymerau 38 C2
Rhydd 54 D7
Rhydding 38 E6
Rhydlewis 50 D7
Rhydlios 62 B3
Rhydlydan 75 H6
Rhydowen 51 E7
Rhydspence 53 F7
Rhydtalog 76 E6
Rhydwyn 74 C3
Rhydycroesau 65 F3
Rhydyfelin, Cered 51 F4
Rhydyfelin, Rho Cyn Taf 25 H2
Rhydymain 63 J4
Rhydymwyn 76 E5
Rhydywrach 37 F4
RHYL 76 B3

RHYMNEY 39 J5
Rhynd 138 A6
Rhynie, Aberd 156 B6
Rhynie, Highl 165 E6
Ribbesford 54 C4
Ribble Head 93 F4
Ribbleton 84 D3
Ribchester 85 E3
Riber 79 H6
Ribigill 167 G4
Riby 89 F6
Riccall 87 H3
Riccarton 118 B4
Richards Castle 53 H5
Richborough Port 35 G4
Richings Park 31 E3
RICHMOND, G Lon 31 F3
RICHMOND, N Yorks 94 C1
Rickarton 147 F5
Rickinghall 60 D4
Rickling 47 E2
RICKMANSWORTH 45 E6
Riddell 120 E5
Riddlecombe 13 G4
Riddlesden 86 B2
Ridge, Dorset 9 H5
Ridge, Herts 45 G5
Ridge, Wilts 17 H2
Ridge Lane 55 H2
Ridgemarsh 48 D6
Ridgeway 79 J3
Ridgeway Cross 54 C7
Ridgewell 47 H1
Ridgewood 21 H4
Ridgmont 44 D2
Ridgway 53 G3
Riding Mill 112 E6
Ridley 33 G4
Ridleywood 77 F6
Ridlington, Norf 73 G3
Ridlington, Rut 69 G6
Ridsdale 112 D4
Riechip 137 H4
Rienachait 166 B7
Rievaulx 95 G3
Rigg 110 B6
Riggend 128 E5
Rigside 119 F4
Rileyhill 67 G5
Rilla Mill 5 F3
Rillington 96 D4
Rimington 85 G2
Rimpton 16 E3
Rimswell 89 H4
Rinaston 36 D3
Ring's End 70 D6
Ringasta 176 C6
Ringford 99 H4
Ringland 72 E5
Ringles Cross 21 H3
Ringmer 21 H4
Ringmore 6 C3
Ringorm 61 H3
Ringsfield 61 H3
Ringsfield Corner 61 H3
Ringshall, Bucks 44 D4
Ringshall, Suff 60 D6
Ringshall Stocks 60 D6
Ringstead, Norf 71 H2
Ringstead, Northnts 57 H4
Ringwood 18 C5
Ringwould 35 G6
Rinmore 146 B2
Rinnigill 170 D5
Rinsey 2 D5
Riof 160 E4
Ripe 22 B4
RIPLEY, Derby 79 H6
Ripley, Hants 10 C4
Ripley, N Yorks 94 D5
Ripley, Surrey 31 E5
Riplingham 88 D3
RIPON 94 E4
Rippingale 70 A4
Ripple, Kent 35 G6
Ripple, Worces 41 H2
Ripponden 86 B5
Rireavach 162 E4
Risabus 124 C6
Risbury 53 J6
Risby, N Linc 88 D5
Risby, Suff 59 H5
RISCA 26 B1
Rise 89 F2
Risegate 70 C4
Riseley, Beds 57 J5
Riseley, Hants 30 B4
Rishangles 60 E5
RISHTON 85 F3
Rishworth 86 B5
Rising Bridge 85 F4
Risley, Derby 68 C3
Risley, Warr 77 J2
Risplith 94 D5
Rispond 167 F3
Rivar 29 F4
Rivenhall, Cambs 47 E1
Rivenhall, Essex 48 B4
Rivenhall End 48 B4
River Bank 59 F5
Riverhead 33 F5
Rivington 85 E5
Roa Island 91 D5
Roachill 14 E3
Roade 57 H6
Roadhead 110 E5
Roadmeetings 119 F3
Roadside 169 F3
Roadside of Catterline 147 F6
Roadside of Kinneff 147 F6
Roadwater 15 G2
Roag 150 B4
Roath 26 B3
Roberton, S Lanak 119 G5
Roberton, Scot Bord 120 D6
Robertsbridge 22 D3
Robertstown 155 G4
Roberttown 86 C4
Robeston Cross 36 C5
Robeston Wathen 37 E4
Robeston West 36 C5
Robin Hood, Derby 79 G4
Robin Hood, W Yorks 86 E4
Robin Hood's Bay 97 E1
Robinhood End 47 H2
Roborough, C of Ply 5 J4
Roborough, Devon 13 F4
Robroyston 128 D6
Roby Mill 84 D6
Rocester 67 G3
Roch 36 C3
Rochallie 138 A3
ROCHDALE 85 G5
Roche 4 C4
ROCHESTER, Med 33 H4
Rochester, Northum 112 C3
Rochford, Essex 34 B1

Rochford, Worces 54 B5
Rock, Corn 4 C3
Rock, Northum 123 H5
Rock, Worces 54 C4
Rock Ferry 77 F3
Rockbeare 15 G6
Rockbourne 18 C4
Rockcliffe, Cumbr 110 C6
Rockcliffe, D & G 100 C2
Rockfield, Highl 165 F5
Rockfield, Monm 40 D4
Rockhampton 41 F6
Rockhill 53 F4
Rockingham 57 G2
Rockland All Saints 60 C2
Rockland St Mary 73 G6
Rockland St Peter 72 C7
Rockley 28 D3
Rockwell End 30 B2
Rockwell Green 15 H4
Rodbourne 28 B2
Rodd 53 G5
Roddam 123 F5
Rodden 8 E5
Roddymoor 103 H4
Rode 27 H5
Rode Heath 78 C6
Rodeheath 78 C5
Roden 66 A5
Rodhuish 15 G2
Rodington 66 A5
Rodley 41 G4
Rodmarton 42 B6
Rodmell 21 H5
Rodmersham 34 C4
Rodney Stoke 26 D5
Rodsley 67 H2
Rodway 95 E5
Roecliffe 95 E5
Roehampton 31 G3
Roesound 175 E4
Roffey 21 E2
Rogart 164 D3
Rogate 20 B3
Rogerstone 26 B2
Rogerton 118 D2
Roghadal 158 E4
Rogiet 26 D2
Rogue 43 J6
Roker 113 J7
Rollesby 73 H5
Rolleston, Leic 69 F6
Rolleston, Notts 80 E6
Rolleston, Staffs 67 H4
Rolston 89 G2
Rolstone 26 C4
Rolvenden 22 E2
Rolvenden Layne 22 E2
Romaldkirk 103 F5
Romanby 95 E2
Romannobridge 119 J3
Romansleigh 14 D3
ROMFORD 33 F2
ROMILEY 78 D2
ROMSEY 18 E3
Romsley, Shrops 54 C3
Romsley, Worces 55 E4
Ronague 90 B5
Rookby 102 E6
Rookhey Hill 21 H5
Rookhope 103 F3
Rookley 11 G5
Rooks Bridge 26 C5
Roos 89 G3
Roosebeck 91 D5
Roosecote 91 D5
Rootpark 119 G2
Ropley 19 H2
Ruan Lanihorne 4 B6
Ripley Dean 19 H2
Ropsley 69 H3
Rora 157 H3
Rorandle 146 D2
Rorrington 65 F6
Rosarie 155 H4
Rose 3 F2
Rose Ash 14 D3
Roseacre 84 C3
Rosebank 119 F3
Rosebrough 123 G5
Rosebush 37 E3
Rosedale Abbey 96 C2
Roseden 123 F5
Rosefield 154 C3
Rosehall 164 A3
ROSEHEARTY 157 G2
Rosehill, Aberd 146 C4
Rosehill, Shrops 66 B3
Roseisle 155 F2
Rosemarket 36 D5
Rosemarkie 154 B3
Rosemary Lane 15 H4
Rosemount, Pth & Kin 138 A4
Rosemount, S Ayr 117 H5
Rosenannon 4 C4
Rosepool 36 C4
Rosewell 120 B1
Roseworthy 2 E4
Rosgill 102 B6
Roshven 141 G6
Roskhill 150 B4
Rosley 101 H3
Roslin 130 B6
Rosliston 67 H5
Rosneath 127 G4
Ross, D & G 99 H5
Ross, Northum 123 G4
Ross, Pth & Kin 136 E6
ROSS-ON-WYE 41 F3
Rossett 77 F6
Rossie Ochill 129 H1
Rossington 80 D2
Rosskeen 154 A2
Rossland 128 B5
Roster 169 G6
Rostherne 78 B3
Rosthwaite 101 G6
Roston 67 G2
Rosudgeon 2 D5
Rosyth 129 J4
Rothbury 112 E2
Rotherby 68 E5
Rotherfield 22 B3
Rotherfield Greys 30 B2
Rotherfield Peppard 30 B2
ROTHERHAM 80 B2
Rotherthorpe 57 F6
Rotherwas 41 E2
Rotherwick 30 B5
ROTHES 155 G4
ROTHESAY 127 E6
Rothiebrisbane 156 E5
Rothienorman 156 E5
Rothiesholm 173 G4
Rothley, Leic 68 D5
Rothley, Northum 112 E4
Rothmaise 156 D5
Rothwell, Lincs 82 D2

ROTHWELL, Northnts 57 G3
ROTHWELL, W Yorks 87 E4
Rotsea 88 E1
Rottal 145 H7
Rottingdean 21 G5
Rottington 100 D6
Roud 11 G5
Rough Close 66 E3
Rough Common 34 E5
Rough Haugh 167 J5
Rougham 72 B4
Rougham Green 60 C5
Roughburn 143 F5
Roughlee 85 G2
Roughley 67 G7
Roughsike 110 E5
Roughton, Lincs 82 E5
Roughton, Norf 73 F3
Roughton, Shrops 54 C2
Roundbush Green 47 F4
Roundhay 86 E3
Roundstreet Common 20 D3
Roundway 28 C4
Rounton 95 F1
Rous Lench 55 F6
Rousdon 8 A4
Rousham 43 G3
Routdenburn 117 G2
Routenburn 117 F1
Routh 89 E2
Row, Corn 4 D3
Row, Cumbr 92 C3
Rowanburn 110 D5
Rowberrow 26 D5
Rowde 28 B4
Rowen 75 G4
Rowfoot 111 F6
Rowhedge 48 D3
Rowhook 20 E2
Rowington 55 H5
Rowington Green 55 H5
Rowland 79 G4
Rowland's Castle 19 J4
ROWLANDS GILL 103 H2
Rowledge 30 C6
Rowlestone 40 C3
Rowley, Durham 103 G3
Rowley, Shrops 65 G6
Rowley Regis 55 E3
Rowly 31 E6
Rowney Green 55 F4
Rownhams 19 E4
Rowsham 44 C4
Rowsley 79 G5
Rowston 82 C6
Rowton, Ches 77 G5
Rowton, Shrops 65 G5
Rowton, Tel & Wrek 66 B5
Roxburgh 121 G4
Roxby, N Linc 88 D5
Roxby, N Yorks 105 G6
Roxton 58 B6
Roxwell 33 F2
Royal British Legion Village 33 H5
ROYAL LEAMINGTON SPA 56 B5
ROYAL TUNBRIDGE WELLS 22 B2
Royals Green 65 J2
Roybridge 142 E5
Roydon, Essex 46 E5
Roydon, Norf IP22 60 D3
Roydon, Norf PE32 71 H4
ROYSTON, Herts 46 D1
ROYSTON, S Yorks 87 E5
ROYTON 85 H6
Ruabon 65 G2
Ruaig 132 C4
Ruan Major 3 F6
Ruan Minor 3 F6
Ruardean 41 F4
Ruardean Woodside 41 F4
Rubery 55 E4
Ruabha Ghaisinis 149 D5
Ruckcroft 102 B3
Ruckhall 40 D2
Ruckinge 23 G2
Ruckland 83 F4
Ruckley 65 J6
Ruddington 68 C3
Rudford 41 G3
Rudge 27 H5
Rudgeway 27 F2
Rudgwick 20 D2
Rudhall 41 F3
Rudheath Woods 78 B4
Rudley Green 48 B5
Rudloe 27 H4
Rudry 26 A2
Rudston 97 F5
Rudyard 78 D6
Rufford 84 C5
Rufforth 87 G1
RUGBY 56 D4
RUGELEY 67 F5
Ruilick 153 H4
Ruishton 16 A3
Ruisigearraidh 158 D4
RUISLIP 31 E2
Ruislip Common 31 E2
Rumbling Bridge 129 H3
Rumburgh 61 G3
Rumford 4 B3
Rumney 26 B3
Rumwell 15 H3
RUNCORN 77 H3
Runcton 20 B5
Runcton Holme 71 G6
Runfold 30 C6
Runhall 72 D6
Runham 73 H5
Runnington 15 H3
Runsell Green 47 H5
Runswick Bay 105 H6
Runtaleave 138 B2
Runwell 47 H6
Ruscombe 30 B3
Rush Green 33 F2
Rushall, Co of H 41 F2
Rushall, Norf 61 E3
Rushall, W Mids 67 F6
Rushall, Wilts 28 D5
Rushbrooke 60 B5
Rushbury 53 J2
Rushden, Herts 46 D2
RUSHDEN, Northnts 57 H5
Rushford 60 C3
Rushlake Green 22 C4
Rushmere 61 H3
Rushmere St Andrew 61 F7
Rushmoor 30 C6
Rushock 54 D4
Rusholme 78 C2
Rushton, Ches 77 H5
Rushton, Northnts 57 G3
Rushton, Shrops 66 B6
Rushton Spencer 78 D5
Rushwick 54 D6

Place	Pg	Grid
Rushyford	104	B5
Ruskie	128	D2
Ruskington	82	C6
Rusland	92	B3
Rusper	21	F2
Ruspidge	41	F4
Russell's Water	30	B2
Rustington	20	D5
Ruston Parva	97	F5
Ruswarp	105	H7
Rutherend	118	D2
Rutherford	121	F4
RUTHERGLEN	118	C1
Ruthernbridge	4	D4
Ruthers of Howe	169	G3
RUTHIN	76	D6
Ruthrieston	147	G3
Ruthven, Aberd	156	C4
Ruthven, Ang	138	B4
Ruthven, Highl IV13	154	C5
Ruthven, Highl PH21	144	B4
Ruthvenfield	137	H6
Ruthvoes	4	C4
Ruthwell	109	H6
Ruyton-XI-Towns	65	G4
Ryal	112	E5
Ryal Fold	85	E4
Ryall, Dorset	8	C4
Ryall, Worces	41	H1
Ryarsh	33	G5
Rydal	101	H7
RYDE	11	G4
Rye	23	F3
Rye Foreign	23	E3
Rye Harbour	23	F4
Ryefield	153	H3
Ryhall	69	J5
Ryhill	87	E5
Ryhope	104	D2
Ryhope Colliery	104	D2
Rylstone	93	H6
Ryme Intrinseca	16	D4
Ryther	87	G3
Ryton, Glos	41	G2
Ryton, N Yorks	96	C4
Ryton, Shrops	66	C6
RYTON, T & W	113	F6
Ryton-on-Dunsmore	56	B4

S

Place	Pg	Grid
Saasaig	141	F3
Sabden	85	F3
Sackers Green	48	C2
Sacombe	46	D4
Sacriston	104	B3
Sadberge	104	C6
Saddell	116	B4
Saddington	56	E2
Saddle Bow	71	G5
Sadgill	92	C1
SAFFRON WALDEN	37	F5
Sageston	72	C6
Saham Toney	149	D3
Saighdinis	77	G5
St Abbs	131	J6
St Agnes	2	M10
St Agnes, Corn	3	F2
ST ALBANS	45	F5
St Allen	3	G2
ST ANDREWS	138	E7
St Andrews Major	25	J3
St Ann's	109	H3
St Ann's Chapel, Corn	5	H3
St Ann's Chapel, Devon	6	C6
St Annes	84	B4
St Anthony-in-Meneage	3	F5
St Arvans	40	E6
St Asaph / Llanelwy	76	C4
St Athan	25	H4
ST AUSTELL	4	D5
St Bees	100	D6
St Blazey	4	D5
St Blazey Gate	4	D5
St Boswells	121	E4
St Breock	4	C3
St Breward	4	D3
St Briavels	41	E5
St Bride's Major	25	F3
St Bride's-super-Ely	25	H3
St Brides	26	B4
St Brides Wentlooge	26	B2
St Budeaux	5	H5
St Buryan	2	C5
St Catherine	27	G3
St Catherines	127	F2
St Clears	37	G4
St Cleer	5	F4
St Clement	3	G3
St Clether	5	F2
St Colmac	127	E6
St Columb Major	4	C4
St Columb Minor	3	G1
St Columb Road	4	C5
St Combs	157	H2
St Cross South Elmham	61	F3
St Cyrus	139	G2
ST DAVID'S, Pemb	36	B3
St David's, Pth & Kin	137	G7
St Day	3	F3
St Dennis	4	C5
St Dogmaels	50	B7
St Dominick	5	H5
St Donat's	25	G4
St Endellion	4	C3
St Enoder	3	G2
St Erme	3	G2
St Erth	2	D4
St Erth Praze	2	D4
St Ervan	4	B3
St Eval	4	C3
St Ewe	4	C6
St Fagans	25	J3
St Fergus	157	J2
St Fillans	136	E6
St Florence	37	E3
St Gennys	12	B6
St George	76	B4
St George's	25	J3
St Georges	26	C4
St Germans	5	G5
St Giles in the Wood	13	H4
St Giles on the Heath	12	D7
St Harmon	52	C4
St Helen Auckland	103	H5
St Helens, I of W	11	H5
ST HELENS, Mers	77	H2
St Hilary, Corn	2	D4
St Hilary, V of Glam	25	H3
St Illtyd	40	B5
St Ippollitts	45	F3
St Ishmael	37	H5
St Ishmael's	36	C5
St Issey	4	C3
St Ive	5	G4
ST IVES, Cambs	58	D4
ST IVES, Corn	2	D3
St Ives, Dorset	10	C3
St James South Elmham	61	G3
St John	5	H5
St John's	90	B4
St John's Chapel	103	E4
St John's Fen End	71	F5
St John's Highway	71	F5
St John's Town of Dalry	108	D4
St Johns	54	D6
St Johns Chapel	13	F3
St Judes	90	C3
St Just in Roseland	3	G4
St Just	2	B4
St Katherines	157	E5
St Keverne	3	F5
St Kew	4	D3
St Kew Highway	4	D3
St Keyne	5	F4
St Kilda	158	M9
St Lawrence, Corn	4	D4
St Lawrence, Essex	48	C5
St Lawrence, I of W	11	G6
St Leonards, Bucks	44	D5
St Leonards, Dorset	10	C3
St Leonards, E Susx	22	E5
St Levan	2	B5
St Lythans	25	J3
St Mabyn	4	D3
St Madoes	138	A6
St Margaret South Elmham	61	G3
St Margaret's at Cliffe	35	G6
St Margaret's Hope	171	E5
St Margarets	40	C2
St Mark's	90	B5
St Martin, Corn PL13	5	F5
St Martin, Corn TR12	3	F5
St Martin's	65	G3
St Martins	138	A5
St Mary Bourne	29	G5
St Mary Church	25	G3
St Mary Cray	33	E4
St Mary Hill	25	G3
St Mary Hoo	34	B3
St Mary in the Marsh	23	G3
St Mary's	171	E4
St Mary's Bay	23	G3
St Marys Croft	98	B3
St Mawes	3	G4
St Mawgan	3	G1
St Mellion	5	H5
St Mellons	26	B2
St Merryn	4	B3
St Mewan	4	C5
St Michael Caerhays	4	C6
St Michael Penkevil	3	G3
St Michael South Elmham	61	G3
St Michael's on Wyre	84	C2
St Michaels, Kent	23	E2
St Michaels, Worces	54	A5
St Minver	4	D3
ST MONANS	130	E2
St Neot	5	E4
ST NEOTS	58	B5
St Newlyn East	3	G2
St Nicholas, Pemb	36	C2
St Nicholas, V of Glam	25	H3
St Nicholas at Wade	35	F4
St Ninians	129	E3
St Olaves	73	H7
St Osyth	48	E4
St Owen's Cross	41	E3
St Paul's Cray	33	E4
St Paul's Walden	45	F3
St Peter's	35	G4
St Petrox	36	D6
St Pinnock	5	F4
St Quivox	117	H5
St Stephen	4	C5
St Stephens, Corn PL12	5	H5
St Stephens, Corn PL15	5	G2
St Teath	4	D3
St Tudy	4	D3
St Twynnells	36	C3
St Veep	5	E5
St Vigeans	139	F4
St Wenn	4	C4
St Weonards	40	D3
St Winnow	4	E5
Saint Hill	21	G2
Saintbury	42	D2
SALCOMBE	6	D7
Salcombe Regis	15	H7
Salcott	48	C4
Salcott-cum-Virley	48	C4
SALE	78	C2
Sale Green	54	E6
Saleby	83	G4
Salehurst	22	D3
Salem, Carm	38	D3
Salem, Cered	51	G3
Salen, Arg & Bt	133	H4
Salen, Highl	134	A2
Salesbury	85	E3
Salford, Beds	44	D2
SALFORD, G Man	78	B2
Salford, Oxon	43	E3
Salford Priors	55	F6
Salfords	32	C6
Salhouse	73	G5
Saline	129	H3
SALISBURY	18	C3
Salkeld Dykes	102	B4
Sallachy, Highl IV27	164	B3
Sallachy, Highl IV40	152	B5
Salle	72	E4
Salmonby	83	F4
Salmond's Muir	139	E5
Salperton	42	C3
Salph End	58	A6
Salsburgh	119	F1
Salt	67	E4
Saltaire	86	C3
SALTASH	5	H5
Saltburn	154	B2
SALTBURN-BY-THE-SEA	105	F4
Saltby	69	G4
SALTCOATS	117	G3
Saltdean	21	G5
Salter	93	E5
Salter Street	55	G4
Salterforth	85	G2
Salterhill	155	G2
Salterswall	77	H3
Saltfleet	83	G2
Saltfleetby All Saints	83	G2
Saltfleetby St Clement	83	G2
Saltfleetby St Peter	83	G3
Saltford	27	F4
Salthouse	72	D2
Saltmarshe	88	B4
Salton	96	C3
Saltwick	113	F4
Saltwood	23	H2
Salum	132	C4
Salwarpe	54	D5
Salwayash	8	C4
Sambourne	55	F5
Sambrook	66	C4
Samhla	149	C3
Samlesbury	84	D3
Samlesbury Bottoms	85	E4
Sampford Arundel	15	H4
Sampford Brett	15	G1
Sampford Courtenay	13	G5
Sampford Peverell	15	G4
Sampford Spiney	6	B3
Samuelston	130	D5
Sanaigmore	124	B3
Sancreed	2	C5
Sancton	88	D3
Sand, Highl	162	D4
Sand, Shetld	176	C3
Sand Hole	88	C3
Sand Hutton	96	B6
Sandaig, Arg & Bt	132	B4
Sandaig, Highl	141	G3
SANDBACH	78	B5
Sandbank	127	F4
Sandbanks	10	B5
Sandend	156	C2
Sanderstead	32	D4
Sandford, Cumbr	102	D6
Sandford, Devon	14	E5
Sandford, Dorset	9	H5
Sandford, I of W	11	G5
Sandford, N Som	26	D5
Sandford, S Lanak	118	E3
Sandford Orcas	16	E3
Sandford St Martin	43	G3
Sandford-on-Thames	43	H5
Sandfordhill	157	J4
Sandgate	23	J2
Sandgreen	99	G4
Sandhaven	157	G2
Sandhead	98	B4
Sandhoe	112	D6
Sandhole	126	E3
Sandholme, E Yorks	88	C3
Sandholme, Lincs	70	D3
Sandhurst, B For	30	C4
Sandhurst, Glos	41	H3
Sandhurst, Kent	22	D3
Sandhutton	95	E3
Sandiacre	68	C3
Sandilands	83	H3
Sandiway	77	J4
Sandleheath	18	C4
Sandling	33	H5
Sandness	174	C5
Sandon, Essex	47	H5
Sandon, Herts	46	D2
Sandon, Staffs	67	E4
SANDOWN	11	G5
Sandplace	5	F5
Sandridge	45	F4
Sandringham	71	G4
Sandsend	105	H6
Sandside	36	D3
Sandsound	176	C3
Sandtoft	88	B6
Sandvoe	177	A4
Sandway	34	B5
Sandwell	82	C6
SANDWICH	35	G5
Sandwick, Cumbr	101	J6
Sandwick, Orkney	171	E6
Sandwick, Shetld	176	D5
Sandwith	100	D6
SANDY	58	B7
Sandy Haven	36	C5
Sandy Lane	28	B4
Sandycroft	77	F5
Sandygate, Devon	6	E3
Sandygate, I of M	90	C3
Sandyhills	100	C2
Sandylands	167	F3
Sangobeg	167	F2
Sanna	140	D7
Sanndabhaig, Na Eilean HS1	161	H4
Sanndabhaig, Na Eilean HS8	149	D5
Sannox	116	E3
SANQUHAR	108	E2
Santon	88	D5
Santon Bridge	91	C1
Santon Downham	60	B3
Sapcote	56	C2
Sapey Common	54	C5
Sapperton, Glos	42	B5
Sapperton, Lincs	69	J3
Saracen's Head	70	D4
Sarclet	169	H5
Sarisbury	19	G5
Sarn, Brig	25	G2
Sarn, Powys	53	F2
Sarn Bach	62	C3
Sarn Meyllteyrn	62	C3
Sarnau, Carm	37	H4
Sarnau, Cered	50	D6
Sarnau, Gwyn	64	C3
Sarnau, Powys LD3	39	H2
Sarnau, Powys SY22	65	F5
Sarnesfield	53	G6
Saron, Carm SA18	38	D4
Saron, Carm SA44	37	H2
Saron, Denb	76	C6
Sarratt	45	E6
Sarre	35	F4
Sarsden	43	E3
Sarsgrum	167	E3
Satley	103	H3
Satron	93	H3
Satterleigh	14	C3
Satterthwaite	92	B2
Sauchen	146	E2
Saucher	138	A5
Sauchieburn	146	D7
Sauchrie	117	H6
Saughall	77	F4
Saughtree	111	F3
Saul	41	G5
Saundby	81	E3
Saunderton	44	B5
Saundersfoot	37	F5
Saunton	13	E2
Sausthorpe	83	F5
Saval	164	B3
Savary	133	J4
Saverley Green	67	E3
Sawbridge	56	D5
SAWBRIDGEWORTH	47	E4
Sawdon	97	E3
Sawley, Derby	68	C3
Sawley, Lancs	85	F2
Sawley, N Yorks	94	D5
Sawrey	92	B2
Sawston	58	E7
Sawtry	58	B3
Saxby, Leic	69	G4
Saxby, Lincs	81	H3
Saxby All Saints	88	D5
Saxelbye	69	F4
Saxilby	81	F4
Saxlingham	72	D3
Saxlingham Green	61	F2
Saxlingham Nethergate	61	G2
Saxlingham Thorpe	73	F7
SAXMUNDHAM	61	G5
Saxon Street	59	G6
Saxtead	61	F5
Saxtead Green	61	F5
Saxthorpe	72	E3
Saxton	87	F3
Sayers Common	21	F4
Scackleton	96	B4
Scadabhagh	159	F3
Scaftworth	80	D2
Scagglethorpe	96	D4
Scalasaig	125	A3
Scalby	97	F2
Scalby Mills	97	F2
Scaldwell	57	F4
Scale Houses	102	B3
Scaleby	110	D6
Scaleby Hill	110	D6
Scales, Cumbr CA12	101	H5
Scales, Cumbr LA12	92	A4
Scalford	69	F4
Scaling	105	G6
Scallastle	134	A5
Scalloway	176	D4
Scambesby	83	E4
Scamodale	141	H6
Scampston	96	D4
Scampton	81	G4
Scapa	171	E4
Scar	173	G2
SCARBOROUGH	97	F3
Scarcewater	4	C5
Scarcliffe	80	B5
Scarcroft	87	E2
Scardroy	152	E3
Scardroy Lodge	152	E3
Scarff	174	D2
Scarfskerry	169	G2
Scargill	103	G6
Scarinish	132	C4
Scarisbrick	84	B5
Scarning	72	C5
Scarrington	69	F2
Scarth Hill	84	C6
Scartho	89	G6
Scatraig	154	B5
Scawby	88	D6
Scawton	95	G3
Scayne's Hill	21	G3
Scethrog	39	J3
Scholar Green	78	C6
Scholes, W Yorks	86	C6
Scholes, W Yorks	87	E3
Schoolhill, Aberd AB12	147	G4
Schoolhill, Aberd AB32	146	E3
Scleddau	36	D2
Sco Ruston	73	F4
Scofton	80	D3
Scole	60	E3
Scolpaig	158	B5
Scolton	36	D3
Sconser	151	E5
Scoor	133	G7
Scopwick	82	C6
Scopwick Heath	82	C6
Scoraig	162	E4
Scorborough	88	E2
Scorrier	3	F3
Scorriton	6	D4
Scorton, Lancs	84	D2
Scorton, N Yorks	94	D1
Scotbheinn	149	D4
Scotby	101	J2
Scotch Corner	94	D1
Scotforth	92	C6
Scothern	82	C4
Scotland Gate	113	G4
Scotlandwell	130	A2
Scots' Gap	112	E4
Scotsburn	164	D6
Scotscraig	138	D6
Scotston, Aberd	146	E6
Scotston, Pth & Kin	137	G3
Scotstown	134	C2
Scottas	141	G4
Scotter	81	F1
Scotterthorpe	81	F1
Scotton, Lincs	81	F2
Scotton, N Yorks DL9	94	C2
Scotton, N Yorks HG5	94	E6
Scottow	73	F4
Scoughall	131	F4
Scoulag	117	F2
Scoulton	72	C6
Scourie	166	C5
Scourie More	166	C5
Scousburgh	176	C6
Scrabster	169	E2
Scrainwood	112	D2
Scrane End	70	D2
Scraptoft	68	E6
Scratby	73	J5
Scrayingham	96	C5
Scredington	70	A2
Scremby	83	G5
Scremerston	123	F3
Screveton	69	F2
Scriven	94	E6
Scronkey	84	C2
Scrooby	80	D2
Scropton	67	G3
Scrub Hill	82	C6
Scruton	94	D2
Scuggate	110	D5
Sculcoates	89	E3
Sculthorpe	72	B3
SCUNTHORPE	88	C5
Scurlage	24	B2
Sea Palling	73	H4
Seaborough	8	D3
Seabridge	66	D2
Seabrook	16	C5
Seaburn	104	D2
Seacombe	77	F2
Seacroft	87	E3
Seafield, Shetld	177	C4
Seafield, W Loth	129	H6
Seaford, E Susx BN20	22	B6
SEAFORD, E Susx BN25	21	H6
Seaforth	77	F2
Seagrave	68	E5
SEAHAM	104	D2
Seahouses	123	H4
Seal	33	F5
Sealand	77	F5
Seale	30	C6
Seamer, N Yorks TS9	104	D6
Seamer, N Yorks YO12	97	F3
Searby	88	E6
Seasalter	34	D4
Seascale	91	B1
Seathorne	83	H5
Seathwaite, Cumbr CA12	101	G6
Seathwaite, Cumbr LA20	91	D2
Seatoller	101	G6
Seaton, Ang	139	F4
Seaton, Corn	5	G5
Seaton, Cumbr	100	E4
SEATON, Devon	15	J6
Seaton, Durham	104	C2
Seaton, E Yorks	89	F2
Seaton, Northum	113	H5
Seaton, Rut	69	H7
Seaton Burn	113	G5
Seaton Carew	104	E5
Seaton Delaval	113	H5
Seaton Junction	15	J6
Seaton Ross	88	B2
Seaton Sluice	113	H5
Seatown	8	C4
Seave Green	95	G1
Seaview	11	H4
Seaville	101	E2
Seavington St Mary	16	C4
Seavington St Michael	16	C4
Seawick	48	E4
Sebastopol	40	B6
Sebergham	101	H3
Seckington	67	H6
Second Coast	162	D4
SEDBERGH	93	E2
Sedbury	41	E6
Sedbusk	93	G2
Sedgeberrow	42	C2
Sedgebrook	69	G3
Sedgefield	104	C5
Sedgeford	71	H3
Sedgehill	17	G3
SEDGLEY	54	E2
Sedgwick	92	D3
Sedlescombe	22	D4
Seend	28	B4
Seend Cleeve	28	B4
Seer Green	30	D1
Seething	73	G7
Sefton	77	F1
Seghill	113	G5
Seifton	53	H3
Seighford	66	D4
Seilebost	159	E3
Seion	75	E5
Seisdon	54	D2
Seisiadar	161	J4
Selattyn	65	F3
Selborne	19	J2
SELBY	87	H3
Selham	20	C3
SELKIRK	120	D5
Sellack	41	E3
Sellafirth	177	C4
Sellibister	173	H2
Sellindge	23	G2
Selling	34	D5
Sells Green	28	B4
Selly Oak	55	F3
Selmeston	22	B5
Selsdon	32	D4
Selsey	20	B6
Selsfield Common	21	G2
Selside, Cumbr	92	D2
Selside, N Yorks	93	F4
Selston	80	B6
Selworthy	25	G6
Semblister	175	D5
Semer	60	D7
Semington	27	H4
Semley	17	G3
Send	30	E1
Senghenydd	25	J1
Sennen	2	B5
Sennen Cove	2	B5
Sennybridge	39	G3
Sessay	95	F4
Setchey	71	G5
Setley	10	E3
Setter, Shetld ZE2 9BG	177	B5
Setter, Shetld ZE2 9ES	176	E3
Setter, Shetld ZE2 9LW	175	E5
Settiscarth	172	D5
Settle	93	G5
Settrington	96	D4
Seven Kings	33	E2
Seven Sisters	39	F5
Sevenhampton, Glos	42	C3
Sevenhampton, Swin	28	E1
SEVENOAKS	33	F5
Sevenoaks Weald	33	F5
Severn Beach	27	E2
Severn Stoke	41	H1
Sevington	34	D6
Sewards End	47	F2
Sewardstone	46	D6
Sewerby	97	H5
Seworgan	3	F4
Sewstern	69	G4
Sezincote	42	D2
Sgarasta Bheag	158	E3
Sgarasta Mhor	158	E3
Sgiogarstaigh	161	J1
Shabbington	44	A5
Shackerley	66	D6
Shackerstone	68	B6
Shackleford	30	D6
Shadforth	104	C3
Shadingfield	61	H3
Shadoxhurst	23	F2
Shadwell	86	E3
Shaftenhoe End	46	E2
SHAFTESBURY	17	G3
Shafton	87	F5
Shalbourne	29	F4
Shalcombe	11	E5
Shalden	30	A6
Shaldon	7	F3
Shalfleet	11	F5
Shalford, Essex	47	H3
Shalford, Surrey	30	E6
Shalford Green	47	H3
Shallowford	34	D5
Shalmsford Street	34	D5
Shalstone	43	H2
Shamley Green	31	E6
Shandon	127	G4
Shandwick	165	E6
Shangton	56	E2
SHANKLIN	11	G5
Shannochie	116	D5
Shanquhar	156	C5
Shantron	127	H4
Shanzie	138	B3
Shap	102	B6
Shapwick, Dorset	9	H3
Shapwick, Somer	16	C2
Shardlow	68	C3
Shareshill	66	D6
Sharlston	87	E5
Sharnbrook	57	H6
Sharnford	56	C2
Sharoe Green	84	D3
Sharow	94	E4
Sharpenhoe	45	E2
Sharperton	112	D2
Sharpness	41	F5
Sharpthorne	21	G2
Sharrington	72	D3
Shatterford	54	C3
Shattering	35	F5
Shaugh Prior	6	B4
Shavington	78	B6
SHAW, G Man	85	H6
Shaw, W Berks	29	G4
Shaw, Wilts	27	H4
Shaw Mills	94	D5
Shawbury	65	J4
Shawdon Hall	123	F6
Shawell	56	D3
Shawford	19	F3
Shawforth	85	G4
Shawhead	109	F5
Sheandow	155	G5
Shearsby	56	E2
Shebbear	13	E5
Shebdon	66	C4
Shebster	168	E3
Shedfield	19	G4
Sheen	79	F5
Sheepscombe	41	H4
Sheepstor	6	B4
Sheepwash	13	E5
Sheepway	26	D3
Sheepy Magna	68	B6
Sheepy Parva	68	B6
Sheering	47	F4
SHEERNESS	34	C3
SHEFFIELD	79	H3
Sheffield Bottom	29	J4
Sheffield City Airport	79	J3
Shefford	45	F2
Sheigra	166	C3
Sheinton	66	B6
Shelderton	53	H4
Sheldon, Derby	79	F5
Sheldon, Devon	15	H5
Sheldon, W Mids	55	G3
Sheldwich	34	D5
Shelf	86	C4
Shelfanger	60	E3
Shelfield	67	F6
Shelford	68	E2
Shelley	86	D5
Shellingford	43	F6
Shellow Bowells	47	G5
Shelly Green	55	G4
Shelsley Beauchamp	54	C5
Shelsley Walsh	54	C5
Shelton, Beds	57	J5
Shelton, Norf	61	F2
Shelton, Notts	69	F2
Shelton, Shrops	65	H5
Shelton Green	61	F2
Shelve	65	G7
Shelwick	40	E1
Shenfield	47	G6
Shenington	43	F1
Shenley	45	F5
Shenley Brook End	44	C2
Shenley Church End	44	C2
Shenleybury	45	F5
Shenmore	40	C2
Shennanton	99	E3
Shenstone, Staffs	67	G6
Shenstone, Worces	54	D4
Shenton	68	B6
Shenval, Highl	153	G6
Shenval, Mor	155	G6
Shepeau Stow	70	D5
Shepherd's Green	30	B3
Shepherdswell or Sibertswold	35	F6
Shepley	86	C5
Shepperdine	41	F6
Shepperton	31	E4
Shepreth	58	D7
SHEPSHED	68	C5
Shepton Beauchamp	16	C4
SHEPTON MALLET	27	F6
Shepton Montague	17	E2
Sheraton	104	D4
SHERBORNE, Dorset	17	E4
Sherborne, Glos	42	D4
Sherborne St John	29	J5
Sherbourne	55	H5
Sherburn, Durham	104	C3
Sherburn, N Yorks	97	E4
Sherburn in Elmet	87	F3
Shere	31	E6
Shereford	72	B4
Sherfield English	18	D3
Sherfield on Loddon	30	A5
Sherford	6	D6
Sheriff Hutton	96	B5
Sheriffhales	66	C5
SHERINGHAM	72	E2
Sherington	57	G7
Shernborne	71	H3
Sherrington	17	H2
Sherston	27	H2
Sherwood Green	13	F3
SHETLAND SUMBURGH	176	C6
Shettleston	128	D6
Shevington	84	D6
Shevington Moor	84	D5
Shevington Vale	84	D6
Sheviock	5	G5
Shiel Bridge	142	B2
Shielbrae	128	E4
Shieldaig, Highl IV21	151	H1
Shieldaig, Highl IV54	151	H1
Shieldhill, Falk	129	F5
Shieldhill, S Lanak	119	H3
Shielfoot	141	F7
Shielhill	138	D3
Shifnal	66	C6
Shilbottle	113	G2
SHILDON	104	B5
Shillingford, Devon	15	H3
Shillingford, Oxon	29	H1
Shillingford St George	7	F2
Shillingstone	17	G4
Shillington	45	F2
Shillmoor	112	C2
Shilton, Oxon	42	E4
Shilton, Warw	56	C3
Shimpling, Norf	60	E3
Shimpling, Suff	59	H6
Shimpling Street	60	B6
Shincliffe	104	B3
Shiney Row	104	C2
Shinfield	30	B4
Shingay	58	D7
Shingle Street	49	G1
Shinness	168	C4
Shipbourne	33	F5

Place	Page	Grid
Shipdham	72	C6
Shipham	26	D5
Shiphay	7	E4
Shiplake	30	B3
Shipley, Shrops	54	D2
Shipley, W Susx	21	E3
SHIPLEY, W Yorks	86	C3
Shipley Bridge	21	G1
Shipmeadow	61	G3
Shippon	43	G6
Shipston-on-Stour	42	E1
Shipton, Glos	42	C4
Shipton, N Yorks	95	G6
Shipton, Shrops	54	A2
Shipton Bellinger	28	E6
Shipton Gorge	8	C4
Shipton Green	20	B6
Shipton Moyne	27	H2
Shipton-on-Cherwell	43	G4
Shipton-under-Wychwood	42	E4
Shiptonthorpe	88	C2
Shirburn	44	A6
Shirdley Hill	84	B5
Shire Oak	67	F6
SHIREBROOK	80	C5
Shirehampton	27	E3
Shiremoor	113	H5
Shirenewton	40	D6
Shireoaks	80	C3
Shirkoak	23	F2
Shirl Heath	53	H6
Shirland	79	H6
Shirley, C of Soton	19	E4
Shirley, Derby	67	H2
Shirley, W Mids	55	G4
Shirrell Heath	19	G4
Shirwell	13	F2
Shiskine	116	D5
Shobdon	53	H5
Shobrooke	14	E5
Shocklach	65	H2
Shoeburyness	34	C2
Sholden	35	G5
Sholing	19	F4
Sholver	85	H6
Shoot Hill	65	H5
Shop, Corn EX23	12	C4
Shop, Corn PL28	4	B3
Shore Mill	154	B2
SHOREDITCH	32	D2
Shoreham	33	F4
Shoreham Airport	21	F5
Shoreham Beach	21	F5
SHOREHAM-BY-SEA	21	F5
Shoresdean	123	E3
Shoreswood	123	E3
Shoreton	153	J2
Shorncote	42	C6
Shorne	33	G3
Short Green	60	D3
Short Heath, Derby	67	J5
Short Heath, W Mids	55	G2
Shortacombe	6	B2
Shortgate	21	H4
Shortgrove	47	F2
Shorthampton	43	F3
Shortlanesend	3	G3
Shortlees	118	B4
Shortstown	58	A7
Shorwell	11	F5
Shoscombe	27	G5
Shotesham	73	F2
Shotgate	47	H6
Shotley	49	F2
Shotley Bridge	103	G2
Shotley Gate	49	F2
Shotleyfield	103	G2
Shottenden	34	D5
Shottermill	20	B2
Shottery	55	G6
Shotteswell	56	C7
Shottisham	49	G1
Shottle	79	H7
Shottlegate	68	B2
Shotton, Durham	104	D4
Shotton, Flint	77	F5
Shotton, Northum	122	D4
Shotton Colliery	104	C3
Shotts	119	F1
Shotwick	77	F4
Shoughlaige- e-Caine	90	C4
Shouldham	71	G6
Shouldham Thorpe	71	G6
Shoulton	54	D6
Shrawardine	65	H5
Shrawley	54	D5
Shrewley	55	H5
SHREWSBURY	65	J5
Shrewton	28	C6
Shripney	20	C5
Shrivenham	28	E2
Shropham	60	C2
Shrub End	48	C3
Shucknall	41	E1
Shudy Camps	47	G1
Shurdington	42	B4
Shurlock Row	30	C3
Shurrery	168	B6
Shurton	26	B6
Shustoke	55	H2
Shute	15	J6
Shutford	43	F1
Shuthonger	41	H2
Shutlanger	57	F7
Shuttington	67	H6
Shuttlewood	80	B4
Siabost	161	G3
Siadar	161	G2
Sibbertoft	56	E3
Sibdon Carwood	53	H3
Sibford Ferris	43	F2
Sibford Gower	43	F2
Sible Hedingham	47	H2
Sibsey	83	F6
Sibsey Fen Side	83	F6
Sibson, Cambs	70	A7
Sibson, Leic	68	B6
Sibster	169	H4
Sibthorpe	69	F2
Sibton	61	G5
Sicklesmere	60	B5
Sicklinghall	87	E2
Sidbury, Devon	15	H6
Sidbury, Shrops	54	B3
SIDCUP	33	E3
Siddick	100	E4
Siddington, Ches	78	C4
Siddington, Glos	42	C6
Sidestrand	73	F3
Sidford	15	H6
Sidlesham	20	B6
Sidley	22	D5
Sidlow	32	C6
SIDMOUTH	7	H2
Sigford	6	D3
Sigglesthorne	89	F2
Sigingstone	25	G3
Silchester	29	J4
Sildinis	161	F6
Sileby	68	C5
Silecroft	91	C3
Silfield	72	E7
Silian	51	F6
Silk Willoughby	69	J2
Silkstone	86	D6
Silkstone Common	86	D6
Silloth	101	F2
Sillyearn	156	C3
Siloh	38	E2
Silpho	97	E2
Silsden	86	B2
Silsoe	45	E2
Silton	17	F3
Silver End	48	B4
Silver Hill	22	D3
Silverburn	120	B1
Silverdale, Lancs	92	C4
Silverdale, Staffs	66	D2
Silverford	157	E2
Silverley's Green	61	F4
Silverstone	44	A1
Silverton	15	F5
Silvington	54	B4
Silwick	176	B3
Simister	85	G6
Simonburn	112	C5
Simonsbath	14	D2
Simonstone	85	F3
Simprim	122	D3
Simpson	44	C2
Simpson Cross	36	C4
Sinclairston	118	B6
Sinderby	94	E3
Sinderhope	103	E2
Sindlesham	30	B4
Singdean	111	E2
Singleton, Lancs	84	B3
Singleton, W Susx	20	B4
Singlewell	33	G3
Sinnahard	146	B2
Sinnington	96	C3
Sinton Green	54	D5
Sipson	31	E3
Sirhowy	39	J4
Sisland	73	G7
Sissinghurst	22	D2
Siston	27	F3
Sithney	2	E5
SITTINGBOURNE	34	C4
Six Ashes	54	C3
Six Mile Bottom	59	F6
Sixhills	82	D3
Sixmile	34	E6
Sixpenny Handley	17	J4
Sizewell	61	H5
Skail	167	J5
Skaill, Orkney KW16	172	C5
Skaill, Orkney KW17 2DN	172	E1
Skaill, Orkney KW17 2QD	172	E3
Skaill, Orkney KW17 2QJ	171	F4
Skares, Aberd	156	D5
Skares, E Ayr	118	C6
Skateraw	131	G5
Skaw	175	G4
Skeabost	150	D4
Skeabrae	172	C4
Skeeby	94	D1
Skeffington	69	F6
Skeffling	89	H5
Skegby	80	B5
SKEGNESS	83	H5
Skelberry	176	C6
Skelbo	164	D4
Skeldyke	70	D3
Skellingthorpe	81	G4
Skellister	175	F5
Skellow	87	G5
Skelmanthorpe	86	D5
SKELMERSDALE	84	C6
Skelmonae	157	F5
Skelmorlie	127	F6
Skelmuir	157	G4
Skelpick	168	B4
Skelton, Cumbr	101	J4
Skelton, E Yorks	88	B4
Skelton, N Yorks	94	B1
SKELTON, Red & Clev	105	F6
Skelton, Yk	95	G6
Skelton on Ure	95	E5
Skelwick	172	C4
Skelwith Bridge	92	B1
Skendleby	83	G5
Skenfrith	40	D3
Skerne	97	F6
Skeroblingarry	116	B5
Skerray	167	H3
Skerricha	166	D4
Sketty	38	D6
Skewen	38	E6
Skewsby	95	H4
Skeyton	73	F4
Skidbrooke	83	G2
Skidby	88	E3
Skilgate	15	F3
Skillington	69	G4
Skinburness	101	F2
Skinflats	129	G4
Skinidin	150	B4
Skinningrove	105	G6
Skipness	116	C2
Skipsea	97	G6
SKIPTON	86	A1
Skipton-on-Swale	95	E4
Skipwith	87	H3
Skirlaugh	89	F3
Skirling	119	H4
Skirmett	30	B1
Skirpenbeck	96	C6
Skirwith	102	C4
Skirza	169	H3
Skittle Green	44	B5
Skinkle	37	E6
Skulamus	141	F1
Skullomie	167	H2
Skye of Curr	154	D6
Slack	85	H3
Slackhall	79	E3
Slackhead	156	B2
Slacks of Cairnbanno	157	F4
Slade	41	H5
Slade Green	33	F3
Slade Hooton	80	C3
Slaggyford	102	C2
Slaidburn	85	F1
Slaithwaite	86	B5
Slaley	103	F2
Slamannan	129	F5
Slapton, Bucks	44	D3
Slapton, Devon	6	E6
Slapton, Northnts	56	E7
Slate Haugh	156	B2
Slaugham	21	F3
Slaughterford	27	H3
Slawston	57	F2
Sleaford, Hants	20	B2
SLEAFORD, Lincs	70	A2
Sleagill	102	B6
Sleapford	66	B3
Sledge Green	41	H2
Sledmere	97	E5
Sleightholme	103	F6
Sleights	105	H7
Slepe	9	H4
Slickly	169	G3
Sliddery	116	D5
Sliemore	145	E1
Sligachan	150	D6
Sligrachan	127	F3
Slimbridge	41	G5
Slindon, Staffs	66	D3
Slindon, W Susx	20	C5
Slinfold	20	E2
Slingsby	96	B4
Slioch	156	C5
Slip End	45	E4
Slipton	57	H4
Slochd	154	C6
Slockavullin	126	C3
Sloley	73	F4
Sloothby	83	G4
Slough, Hants	40	D5
Slough, Powys	53	G5
SLOUGH, Slou	30	D3
Slyne	92	C5
Smailholm	121	F4
Small Dole	21	F4
Small Hythe	23	E2
Smallbridge	85	H5
Smallburgh	73	G4
Smallburn, Aberd	157	H4
Smallburn, E Ayr	118	D5
Smalley	68	C2
Smallfield	32	D6
Smallridge	8	B3
Smardale	102	D7
Smarden	34	D4
Smeatharpe	15	J4
Smeeth	23	G2
Smeeton Westerby	56	E2
Smeircleit	148	C3
Smerral	169	F6
SMETHWICK	55	F3
Smisby	68	B5
Smith End Green	54	C6
Smithfield	110	D6
Smithincott	15	G5
Smithton	154	B4
Smithy Green	48	C4
Smythe's Green	48	C4
Snailbeach	65	G6
Snailwell	59	G5
Snainton	96	D4
Snaith	87	H4
Snape, N Yorks	94	D3
Snape, Suff	61	G6
Snape Green	84	B5
Snarestone	68	B6
Snarford	82	C3
Snargate	23	F3
Snatchwood	40	B5
Snave	23	G3
Sneachill	54	E6
Snead	53	G2
Sneath Common	60	E3
Sneaton	105	H7
Sneatonthorpe	96	E1
Snelland	82	C3
Snelston	67	H2
Snetterton	60	C2
Snettisham	71	G3
Snevlabreck	177	C4
Snippigar	171	F4
Sniseabhal	149	C6
Snitter	112	E2
Snitterby	81	G2
Snitterfield	55	H6
Snitton	53	J4
Snodhill	40	C1
Snodland	33	H4
Snowden	35	F5
Snowshill	42	C2
Soar	124	C6
Soberton	19	H4
Soberton Heath	19	H4
Sockburn	104	C7
Sodylt Bank	65	G3
Soham	59	F4
Solas	158	C5
Solas Airfield	158	C5
Soldon Cross	12	D4
Soldridge	20	A2
Sole Street, Kent CT4	34	D6
Sole Street, Kent DA12	33	G4
SOLIHULL	55	G4
Solitote	159	J5
Sollers Dilwyn	53	H6
Sollers Hope	41	F2
Sollom	84	C5
Solva	36	B3
Somerby	69	F5
Somercotes	80	B6
Somerford Keynes	42	C6
Somerley	20	B6
Somerleyton	61	H2
Somersal Herbert	67	G3
Somersby	83	F4
Somersham, Cambs	58	D4
Somersham, Suff	60	D7
Somerton, Oxon OX6 4LJ	43	G3
SOMERTON, Somer	16	C3
Somerton, Suff	60	B6
Sompting	21	E5
Sonning	30	B3
Sonning Common	30	B2
Sopley	10	C4
Sopworth	27	H2
Sorbie	99	F5
Sordale	169	F3
Sorisdale	132	E2
Sorn	118	C5
Sornhill	118	C4
Sortat	169	G3
Sotby	82	E4
Sots Hole	82	B5
Sotterley	61	H3
Soudley	66	C4
Soughton / Sychdyn	76	E5
Soulbury	44	C3
Soulby	102	D6
Souldern	43	H2
Souldrop	57	H5
Sound, Ches	66	B2
Sound, Shetld ZE1	176	D3
Sound, Shetld ZE2	175	E5
Soundwell	27	F3
Sourhope	122	D5
Sourin	172	E3
Sourton	13	F6
Soutergate	91	D3
South Acre	72	B5
South Allington	6	D7
South Alloa	129	F3
South Ambersham	20	C3
South Ballachulish	135	E3
South Balloch	107	F3
South Balquhindachy	157	F4
South Bank	104	E5
South Barrow	16	E3
SOUTH BENFLEET	33	H2
South Bowood	8	C4
South Brent	6	D5
South Brewham	17	F2
South Burlingham	73	G6
South Cadbury	17	E3
South Cairn	98	A3
South Carlton	81	G4
South Cave	88	D3
South Cerney	42	C6
South Chard	16	B5
South Charlton	123	G5
South Cheriton	17	E3
South Cliffe	88	C3
South Clifton	81	F4
South Cockerington	83	F3
South Cornelly	25	F2
South Corriegills	116	E4
South Cove	61	H3
South Creake	72	B3
South Croxton	69	E5
South Dalton	88	D2
South Darenth	33	F4
South Duffield	87	H3
South Elkington	83	E3
South Elmsall	87	F5
South End, Cumbr	91	D5
South End, N Linc	89	F4
South Erradale	151	G1
South Fambridge	48	B6
South Fawley	29	F2
South Ferriby	88	D4
South Garvan	142	B6
South Gluss	175	C3
South Godstone	32	D6
South Gorley	18	C4
South Green	47	G6
South Hanningfield	47	H6
South Harting	20	A4
South Hayling	11	J4
South Heath	44	D5
South Heighton	21	H5
South Hetton	104	C3
South Hiendley	87	E5
South Hill	5	G3
South Hinksey	43	H5
South Hole	12	C4
South Holmwood	31	F6
South Hornchurch	33	F2
South Horrington	27	E6
South Hourat	117	G2
South Hykeham	81	G5
South Hylton	104	C2
South Kelsey	82	C2
South Killingholme	89	F5
South Kilvington	95	F3
South Kilworth	56	E3
South Kirkby	87	F5
South Kirkton	146	E3
South Kyme	70	B2
South Lancing	21	E5
South Leigh	43	F5
South Leverton	81	E3
South Littleton	55	F7
South Lopham	60	D3
South Luffenham	69	H6
South Mains	106	E2
South Malling	21	H4
South Marston	28	D2
South Middleton	123	E5
South Milford	87	F3
South Milton	6	D6
South Mimms	45	G5
SOUTH MOLTON	14	D3
South Moor	103	H2
South Moreton	29	H2
South Mundham	20	B5
South Muskham	81	E6
South Newbald	88	D3
South Newington	43	G2
South Newton	18	B2
South Normanton	80	B6
South Norwood	32	D4
South Nutfield	32	D6
South Ockendon	33	F2
South Ormsby	83	F4
South Otterington	95	F3
South Oxhey	31	F1
South Perrott	16	C5
South Petherton	16	C4
South Petherwin	5	G2
South Pickenham	72	B6
South Pool	6	D6
South Radworthy	14	D2
South Rauceby	69	J2
South Raynham	72	B4
South Redbriggs	157	E4
South Reston	83	G3
South Runcton	71	G6
South Scarle	81	F5
South Shian	134	D4
SOUTH SHIELDS	113	H6
South Shore	84	B3
South Somercotes	83	G2
South Stainley	94	E5
South Stainmore	103	E6
South Stoke, Oxon	29	J2
South Stoke, W Susx	20	D5
South Straiton	138	D6
South Street, E Susx	21	G4
South Street, Kent	33	G4
South Tawton	14	C6
South Thoresby	83	G4
South Tidworth	28	E6
South Town	19	H2
South View	176	C3
South Walsham	73	G5
South Warnborough	30	B6
South Weald	47	F6
South Weston	44	A6
South Wheatley	12	C6
South Widcombe	27	E5
South Wigston	68	D7
South Willingham	82	D3
South Wingfield	79	H6
South Witham	69	H5
South Wonston	19	F2
South Woodham Ferrers	48	B6
South Wootton	71	G4
South Wraxall	27	H4
South Zeal	14	C6
SOUTHALL	31	F2
Southam, Glos	42	B3
Southam, Warw	56	C6
SOUTHAMPTON	19	F4
Southampton International (Eastleigh) Airport	19	F4
Southbar	128	B6
SOUTHBOROUGH	33	F6
Southbourne, Bourne	10	C4
Southbourne, W Susx	20	A5
Southburgh	72	C6
Southburn	97	E6
Southchurch	34	C2
Southdean	111	F2
Southease	21	H5
Southend, Arg & Bt	114	B6
Southend, W Berks	29	H3
Southend Municipal Airport	34	B2
SOUTHEND-ON-SEA	34	B2
Southerndown	25	F3
Southerness	100	D2
Southerton	15	G6
Southery	59	G2
Southey Green	47	H2
Southfields	33	G2
Southgate, G Lon	46	C6
Southgate, Norf NR10	72	E4
Southgate, Norf PE31	71	G3
Southgate, Swan	24	C2
Southill	45	F1
Southleigh	15	J6
Southminster	48	C6
Southmoor	43	F6
Southoe	58	B5
Southolt	61	E5
Southorpe	70	A6
Southowram	86	C4
SOUTHPORT	84	B5
Southpunds	176	D5
Southrepps	73	F3
Southrey	82	D5
Southrop	42	D5
Southrope	30	A6
Southsea	11	H4
Southstoke	27	G4
Southtown	171	E5
SOUTHWOLD	61	J4
Southwood, Norf	73	G6
Southwood, Somer	16	D2
Southwaite	101	J3
Southwater	21	E3
Southway	26	E6
SOUTHWELL, Notts	80	D6
Southwick, Hants	19	H5
Southwick, Northnts	57	J2
Southwick, T & W	104	C2
SOUTHWICK, W Susx	21	F5
Southwick, Wilts	27	H5
Southwell, Dorset	9	E6
Soval	164	B4
Sowerby, N Yorks	95	F3
SOWERBY BRIDGE	86	B4
Sowerby Row	101	H3
Sowton	15	F6
Soyal	164	B4
Spa Common	73	F3
SPALDING	70	C4
Spaldwick	58	B4
Spalford	81	F5
Spanby	70	A3
Sparham	72	D5
Spark Bridge	92	B3
Sparkford	16	E3
Sparkwell	6	B5
Sparrowpit	79	E3
Sparsholt, Hants	19	F2
Sparsholt, Oxon	29	F2
Spaunton	96	C2
Spaxton	15	J2
Spean Bridge	142	E5
Speen, Bucks	44	C6
Speen, W Berks	29	G4
Speeton	97	G4
SPEKE	77	G3
Speldhurst	33	F6
Spellbrook	47	E4
Spelsbury	43	F3
Spen Green	78	C5
Spencers Wood	30	B4
Spennithorne	94	C3
SPENNYMOOR	104	B4
Spetchley	54	D6
Spetisbury	9	H3
Spexhall	61	G3
Spey Bay	155	H2
Speybank	144	C3
Speybridge	155	E6
SPILSBY	83	F5
Spindlestone	123	G4
Spinkhill	80	B4
Spinningdale	164	C5
Spirthill	28	B3
Spitewinter	79	H5
Spithurst	21	H4
Spittal, D & G	99	E4
Spittal, E Loth	130	D5
Spittal, Highl	169	F4
Spittal, Northum	123	F2
Spittal, Pemb	36	D3
Spittal of Glenmuick	145	H5
Spittal of Glenshee	145	E4
Spittalfield	137	J4
Spixworth	73	F5
Splatt	4	C3
Spofforth	87	E1
Spondon	68	C3
Spooner Row	72	D7
Sporle	72	B5
Spott	131	F5
Spratton	57	F4
Spreakley	30	C6
Spreyton	14	D6
Spridlington	81	H3
Springburn	128	D6
Springfield, Arg & Bt	126	C3
Springfield, D & G	110	C6
Springfield, Fife	130	C1
Springfield, Mor	155	E3
Springfield, W Mids	55	F3
Springholm	109	F6
Springkell	110	B6
Springthorpe	81	F3
Sproatley	89	F3
Sproston Green	78	B5
Sprotbrough	87	G6
Sproughton	48	E1
Sprouston	122	C4
Sproxton, Leic	69	G4
Sproxton, N Yorks	96	B3
Spurstow	77	H6
Square and Compass	36	B3
Sranda	158	E4
Srondubh	162	C5
Ssuddabdp	150	C2
Stackhouse	93	G5
Stackpole	36	D6
Stacksteads	85	G4
Staddiscombe	6	B5
Staddlethorpe	88	C4
Staddon	12	D5
Stadhampton	43	J6
Stadhlaigearraidh	149	C6
Staffield	102	B3
Staffin	150	D2
STAFFORD	66	E4
Stagsden	57	H7
Stainburn, Cumbr	100	E5
Stainburn, N Yorks	86	D2
Stainby	69	H4
Staincross	86	E6
Staindrop	103	H5
STAINES	31	E3
Stainfield, Lincs LN8	82	D4
Stainfield, Lincs PE10	70	A4
Stainforth, N Yorks	93	G5
Stainforth, S Yorks	87	H5
Staining	84	B3
Stainland	86	B5
Stainsacre	105	J7
Stainton, Cumbr CA11	102	A5
Stainton, Cumbr LA8	92	D3
Stainton, Durham	103	G6
Stainton, Midlb	104	D6
Stainton, N Yorks	94	C3
Stainton, S Yorks	80	C2
Stainton by Langworth	82	C4
Stainton le Vale	82	D2
Stainton with Adgarley	91	D4
Staintondale	97	E2
Stair, Cumbr	101	G5
Stair, S Ayr	118	B5
Stairhaven	98	C4
Staithes	105	G6
Stake Pool	84	C2
Stakeford	113	G4
Stalbridge	17	F4
Stalbridge Weston	17	F4
Stalham	73	G4
Stalham Green	73	G4
Stalisfield Green	34	C5
Stalling Busk	93	H3
Stallingborough	89	F5
Stalmine	84	B2
STALYBRIDGE	78	D2
Stambourne	47	H2
Stambourne Green	47	H2
STAMFORD	69	J6
Stamford Bridge	96	C6
Stamfordham	113	E5
Stanborough	45	G4
Stanbridge, Beds	44	D3
Stanbridge, Dorset	10	B3
Stanbury	86	B3
Stand	128	E6
Standburn	129	G5
Standeford	66	E6
Standen	22	E1
Standford	20	B2
STANDISH	84	D5
Standlake	43	F5
Standon, Hants	19	F3
Standon, Herts	46	D3
Standon, Staffs	66	D3
Stane	119	F2
Stanfield	72	C4
Stanford, Beds	45	F1
Stanford, Kent	23	H2
Stanford Bishop	54	C5
Stanford Bridge	54	C5
Stanford Dingley	29	H3
Stanford in the Vale	43	F6
Stanford on Avon	56	D4
Stanford on Soar	68	D4
Stanford on Teme	54	C5
Stanford Rivers	47	F5
Stanford-le-Hope	33	G2
Stanghow	105	F6
Stanhoe	72	B3
Stanhope, Durham	103	G4
Stanhope, Scot Bord	119	J5
Stanion	57	H3
Stanley, Derby	68	C2
STANLEY, Durham	103	J2
Stanley, Pth & Kin	137	J3
Stanley, Staffs	78	D6
Stanley, W Yorks	86	E4
Stanley Common	68	C2
Stanley Crook	103	H4
Stanley Ferry	87	E4
Stanmer	21	G5
STANMORE, G Lon	31	F1
Stanmore, W Berks	29	G3
Stanningfield	60	B6
Stannington, Northum	113	G5
Stannington, S Yorks	79	H3
Stansbatch	53	G5
Stansfield	59	H6
Stanstead	60	B7
Stanstead Abbots	46	D4
Stansted	33	G4
STANSTED MOUNTFITCHET	47	F3
Stanton, Derby	67	H5
Stanton, Glos	42	C2
Stanton, Monm	40	C3
Stanton, Northum	113	F4
Stanton, Staffs	67	G2
Stanton, Suff	60	C4
Stanton by Bridge	68	B4
Stanton Drew	27	E4
Stanton Fitzwarren	28	D1
Stanton Harcourt	43	G5
Stanton Hill	80	B5
Stanton in Peak	79	G5
Stanton Lacy	53	H4
Stanton Long	54	A2
Stanton Prior	27	F4
Stanton St Bernard	28	C4
Stanton St John	43	H5
Stanton St Quintin	28	B3
Stanton Street	60	C5
Stanton under Bardon	68	C5
Stanton upon Hine Heath	66	A4
Stanton Wick	27	F4
Stanton-by-Dale	68	C3
Stanton-on-the-Wolds	68	E3
Stanwardine in the Fields	65	H4
Stanway, Essex	48	C3
Stanway, Glos	42	C2
Stanwell	31	E3
Stanwick	57	H4
Stanwick-St-John	103	H6
Staoinebrig	149	C6
Stape	96	C2
Stapehill	10	B3
Stapeley	78	A7
Stapenhill	67	H4
Staple	35	F5
Staple Fitzpaine	16	A4
Staplecross	22	D3
Staplefield	21	F3

Stapleford, Cambs 59 E6
Stapleford, Herts 46 D4
Stapleford, Leic 69 G5
Stapleford, Lincs 81 F6
STAPLEFORD, Notts 68 C3
Stapleford, Wilts 18 B2
Stapleford Abbotts 47 F6
Stapleford Tawney 47 F6
Staplegrove 15 J3
Staplehay 15 J3
Staplehurst 33 H6
Staplers 11 G5
Stapleton, C of Bris 27 F3
Stapleton, Co of H 53 G5
Stapleton, Cumbr 110 E5
Stapleton, Leic 68 C7
Stapleton, N Yorks 104 B6
Stapleton, Shrops 65 H6
Stapleton, Somer 16 C3
Stapley 15 H4
Staploe 58 B5
Staplow 41 F1
Star, Fife 130 C2
Star, Pemb 37 G2
Star, Somer 26 D5
Starbotton 93 H4
Starcross 7 F2
Stareton 56 B4
Starlings Green 47 E2
Starston 61 F3
Startforth 103 G6
Startley 28 B2
Stathe 16 B3
Stathern 69 F3
Station Town 104 D4
Staughton Highway 58 B5
Staunton, Glos GL16 41 E4
Staunton, Glos GL19 41 G3
Staunton in the Vale 69 G2
Staunton on Arrow 53 G5
Staunton on Wye 53 G7
Staupes 94 D6
Staveley, Cumbr 92 C2
STAVELEY, Derby 80 B4
Staveley, N Yorks 95 E5
Staveley-in-Cartmel 6 D4
Staverton, Devon 6 D4
Staverton, Glos 41 H3
Staverton, Northnts 56 D5
Staverton, Wilts 27 H4
Stawell 16 B2
Staxigoe 169 H4
Staxton 97 H4
Staylittle 52 B2
Staynall 84 B2
Staythorpe 80 E6
Stean 94 B4
Steane 43 H2
Stearsby 95 H4
Steart 26 B6
Stebb Hill 173 G4
Stebbing 47 G3
Stebbing Green 47 G3
Stedham 20 B3
Steel Cross 22 B2
Steele Road 110 E3
Steen's Bridge 53 J6
Steep 19 J3
Steeple, Dorset 9 H5
Steeple, Essex 48 C5
Steeple Ashton 28 B5
Steeple Aston 43 G3
Steeple Barton 43 G3
Steeple Bumpstead 47 G1
Steeple Claydon 44 A3
Steeple Gidding 58 B3
Steeple Langford 18 B2
Steeple Morden 46 C1
Steeton 86 B2
Stein 150 B3
Steinis 161 H4
Steinmanhill 157 E4
Stelling Minnis 34 E6
Stembridge 16 C3
Stemster 169 F3
Stenalees 4 D5
Stenhousemuir 129 F4
Stenigot 83 E3
Stenness 174 D3
Stenscholl 150 D2
Stenso 172 D4
Stenton 131 F5
Stepaside, Corn 4 C5
Stepaside, Pemb 37 F5
STEPNEY 32 D2
Steppingley 44 E2
Stepps 128 D6
Sternfield 61 G5
Stert 28 C5
Stetchworth 59 G6
STEVENAGE 46 C3
STEVENSTON 117 G3
Steventon, Hants 29 H6
Steventon, Oxon 29 G1
Stevington 57 H6
Stewartby 44 E1
Stewarton, Arg & Bt 116 A6
STEWARTON, E Ayr 118 B3
Stewkley 44 C3
Stewton 83 F3
Steyning 21 E4
Steynton 36 D5
Stibb 12 C4
Stibb Cross 13 E4
Stibb Green 28 E4
Stibbard 72 C4
Stibbington 70 A7
Stichill 121 G4
Sticker 4 C5
Stickford 83 F5
Sticklepath, Devon EX20 13 G6
Sticklepath, Devon EX31 13 F2
Stickney 83 F6
Stiffkey 72 C2
Stifford's Bridge 87 G2
Stillingfleet 84 C7
Stillington, N Yorks 95 G5
Stillington, Stock on T 104 C5
Stinchcombe 58 B3
Stinsford 9 F4
Stirchley 66 C6
Stirling, Aberd 157 J4
STIRLING, Stir 129 F3
Stisted 47 H3
Stithians 3 F4
Stittenham 164 C6
Stivichall 56 B4
Stixwould 82 D5
Stoak 77 G4
Stobieside 118 D4
Stobo 120 A4
Stoborough 9 H5
Stoborough Green 9 H5
Stobshiel 130 D6
Stobswood 113 G3

Stobwood 119 G2
Stock 47 G8
Stock Green 55 E6
Stock Wood 55 F6
Stockbridge, Hants 18 E2
Stockbridge, W Yorks 86 B2
Stockbriggs 119 E4
Stockbury 34 B4
Stockcross 29 G4
Stockdalewath 101 H3
Stockerston 69 G7
Stocking Pelham 47 E3
Stockingford 56 B2
Stockland 15 H5
Stockland Bristol 26 B6
Stockleigh English 14 E5
Stockleigh Pomeroy 14 E5
Stockley 28 C4
Stocklinch 16 B4
Stockport 78 C3
STOCKSBRIDGE 79 G2
Stocksfield 112 E6
Stockton, Co of H 53 J5
Stockton, Norf 61 G2
Stockton, Shrops 66 C7
Stockton, Warw 56 C5
Stockton, Wilts 77 J3
Stockton Heath 77 J3
Stockton on Teme 54 C5
Stockton on the Forest 96 B6
STOCKTON-ON-TEES 104 D6
Stodday 92 C6
Stodmarsh 35 H4
Stody 72 D3
Stoer 166 B7
Stoford, Dorset 16 D4
Stoford, Wilts 18 B2
Stogumber 15 G2
Stogursey 26 B6
Stoke, Devon 12 C3
Stoke, Hants PO10 11 J3
Stoke, Hants SP11 29 G5
Stoke, Med 34 B3
Stoke Abbott 8 C3
Stoke Albany 57 G3
Stoke Ash 60 E4
Stoke Bardolph 68 E2
Stoke Bliss 54 B5
Stoke Bruerne 57 F7
Stoke by Clare 47 H1
Stoke Canon 15 F6
Stoke Charity 19 F2
Stoke Climsland 5 G3
Stoke D'Abernon 31 F5
Stoke Doyle 57 J3
Stoke Dry 57 G2
Stoke Ferry 71 H6
Stoke Fleming 6 E6
Stoke Gabriel 6 E5
Stoke Gifford 27 F3
Stoke Golding 56 B2
Stoke Goldington 57 G7
Stoke Hammond 44 C3
Stoke Heath, Shrops 66 B4
Stoke Heath, Worces 55 E5
Stoke Holy Cross 73 F6
Stoke Lacy 54 B7
Stoke Lyne 43 H3
Stoke Mandeville 44 C4
STOKE NEWINGTON 32 D2
Stoke on Tern 66 B4
Stoke Orchard 42 B3
Stoke Poges 30 D2
Stoke Prior, Co of H 53 J6
Stoke Prior, Worces 55 E5
Stoke Rivers 13 G2
Stoke Rochford 69 H4
Stoke Row 30 A2
Stoke St Gregory 16 B3
Stoke St Mary 16 A3
Stoke St Michael 27 F6
Stoke St Milborough 54 A3
Stoke sub Hamdon 16 C4
Stoke Talmage 44 A6
Stoke Trister 17 F3
Stoke-by-Nayland 48 C2
STOKE-ON-TRENT 66 D2
Stokeford 9 G5
Stokeham 81 E4
Stokeinteignhead 7 F3
Stokenchurch 44 B6
Stokenham 6 E6
Stokesay 53 H3
Stokesby 73 H5
Stokesley 104 E7
Stolford 26 B6
Ston Easton 27 F5
Stondon Massey 47 F5
Stone, Bucks 44 B4
Stone, Glos 41 F6
Stone, Kent 33 F3
STONE, Staffs 66 E3
Stone, Worces 54 D4
Stone Allerton 26 D5
Stone Cross 22 C5
Stone House 93 F3
Stone in Oxney 23 F3
Stone Street, Kent 33 F5
Stone Street, Suff 61 G3
Stone-edge Batch 26 D3
Stonebroom 79 J6
Stonegate 22 C3
Stonegrave 96 B4
Stonehaugh 111 G5
STONEHAVEN 147 F5
Stonehouse, Glos 41 H5
Stonehouse, Northum 111 F7
Stonehouse, S Lanak 118 E3
Stoneleigh 56 B4
Stonely 58 B5
Stoner Hill 19 J3
Stones Green 48 E3
Stonesby 69 G4
Stonesfield 43 F4
Stonethwaite 101 G6
Stoney Cross 18 D4
Stoney Middleton 79 G4
Stoney Stanton 56 C2
Stoney Stoke 17 F2
Stoney Stratton 17 E2
Stoney Stretton 65 G6
Stonybreck 176 M8
Stoneyburn 119 G1

Stonyfield 164 C6
Stoodleigh 15 F4
Stopham 20 D4
Stopsley 45 F3
Storeton 77 F3
Stormontfield 137 J6
STORNOWAY (STEORNABHAGH) 161 H4
Storridge 54 C7
Storrington 20 D4
Storrs 92 C2
Storth 92 G2
Stotfold 45 G2
Stottesdon 54 B3
Stoughton, Leic 68 E6
Stoughton, Surrey 30 D5
Stoughton, W Susx 20 B4
Stoulton 54 E7
Stour Provost 17 F3
Stour Row 17 G3
STOURBRIDGE 54 E3
Stourpaine 17 G5
STOURPORT-ON-SEVERN 54 D3
Stourton, Staffs 54 D3
Stourton, Warw 43 E2
Stourton, Wilts 17 F4
Stourton Caundle 17 F4
Stove, Orkney 173 G3
Stove, Shetld 176 D5
Stoven 61 H3
Stow, Lincs 81 F3
Stow, Scot Bord 120 D3
Stow Bardolph 71 G6
Stow Bedon 60 C2
Stow cum Quy 59 F5
Stow Longa 58 B4
Stow Maries 48 B6
STOW-ON-THE-WOLD 42 D3
Stowbridge 71 G6
Stowe, Glos 41 E5
Stowe, Shrops 53 G4
Stowe-by-Chartley 66 D3
Stowell 17 E3
Stowey 27 E5
Stowford 5 H2
Stowlangtoft 60 C5
STOWMARKET 60 D6
Stowting 34 E6
Stowupland 60 D6
Straad 116 E1
Strachan 146 D4
Strachur 127 E2
Stradbroke 61 F4
Stradishall 59 H6
Stradsett 71 G6
Stragglethorpe 81 G6
Straith 109 F4
Straiton, Midlo 120 B6
Straiton, S Ayr 107 F2
Straloch, Aberd 157 F6
Straloch, Pth & Kin 137 H2
Stramshall 67 F3
Strang 90 C5
STRANRAER 98 B3
Stratfield Mortimer 30 A4
Stratfield Saye 30 A4
Stratfield Turgis 30 A5
STRATFORD, G Lon 32 D2
Stratford, Worces 41 H4
Stratford St Andrew 61 G5
Stratford St Mary 48 D2
Stratford Tony 18 B3
STRATFORD-UPON-AVON 55 G6
Strath 166 B6
Strathallan Cas 137 G7
Strathan, Highl IV27 163 E1
Strathan, Highl PH33 142 B4
Strathaven 118 E3
Strathblane 128 C5
Strathcanaird 163 F3
Strathcarron 152 B4
Strathcoil 134 A5
Strathdon 145 H2
Strathkinness 138 D7
Strathmiglo 130 B1
Strathpeffer 153 G3
Strathrannoch 163 H6
Strathtay 137 G3
Strathwhillan 116 E4
Strathy 168 C3
Strathyre 136 C7
STRATTON, Corn 12 C5
Stratton, Dorset 9 E4
Stratton, Glos 42 C5
Stratton Audley 43 J3
Stratton St Margaret 28 D2
Stratton St Michael 61 F2
Stratton Strawless 73 F4
Stratton-on-the-Fosse 27 F5
Stravithie 130 E1
Streat 21 G4
STREATHAM 32 D3
Streatley, Beds 45 E3
Streatley, W Berks 29 H2
Street, Lancs 84 D1
Street, N Yorks 96 C1
STREET, Somer 16 C2
Street Dinas 65 G3
Street End, Kent 34 E5
Street End, W Susx 20 B6
Street on the Fosse 16 E2
Streethay 67 G5
Streetlam 94 E2
Streetly 67 F7
Strefford 53 H3
Strensall 95 H5
Strensham 41 J1
Stretcholt 26 B6
Strete 6 E6
Stretford, Co of H 53 H6
STRETFORD, G Man 78 B2
Strethall 47 E2
Stretham 59 F4
Strettington 20 B5
Stretton, Ches 77 G6
Stretton, Derby 79 H5
Stretton, Rut 69 H5
Stretton, Staffs DE13 67 H4
Stretton, Staffs ST19 66 D5
Stretton, Warr 77 J3
Stretton en le Field 67 J5
Stretton Grandison 41 F1
Stretton Heath 65 G5
Stretton Sugwas 40 D1
Stretton under Fosse 56 C3
Stretton Westwood 66 A4
Stretton-on-Dunsmore 56 C4
Stretton-on-Fosse 42 E2
Strichen 157 G3
Stringston 26 A6
Strixton 57 H5
Stroat 41 E6
Stromeferry 151 H5
Stromemore 151 H5
STROMNESS 170 C4
Stronaba 142 E5

Stronachie 129 H2
Stronachlachar 127 J1
Stronchreggan 142 C6
Stronchrubie 163 G2
Strone, Arg & Bt 127 F4
Strone, Highl IV3 153 H6
Strone, Highl PH33 142 D5
Stronmilchan 135 F6
Stronord 99 F3
Strontian 134 C2
Strood 33 H4
STROUD, Glos 41 H5
Stroud, Hants 19 J3
Stroud Green 69 H3
Stroxton 69 H3
Struan, Highl 150 C5
Struan, Pth & Kin 137 F2
Strubby 83 G3
Strumpshaw 73 G6
Strutherhill 118 E3
Struthers 130 C2
Struy 153 G5
Stuartfield 157 G4
Stubbington 11 G3
Stubbins 85 F5
Stubhampton 17 H4
Stubshaw Cross 77 H1
Stubton 69 G2
Stuckgowan 127 H2
Stuckton 18 C4
Studfold 93 G4
Studham 44 E4
Studland 10 B5
Studley, Warw 55 F5
Studley, Wilts 28 B3
Studley Roger 94 D4
Stuntney 59 F4
Stunts Green 22 C4
Sturbridge 66 D3
Sturgate 81 F3
Sturmer 47 G1
Sturminster Marshall 9 H4
Sturminster Newton 17 F4
Sturry 34 E4
Sturton by Stow 81 F3
Sturton le Steeple 81 E3
Stutton, N Yorks 87 F2
Stutton, Suff 48 E2
Styal 78 C3
Styrrup 80 D2
Suainebost 161 J1
Succoth, Aberd 156 B5
Succoth, Arg & Bt 127 G2
Suckley 54 C6
Suckquoy 171 E6
Sudborough 57 H3
Sudbourne 61 H6
Sudbrook, Lincs 69 H2
Sudbrook, Monm 26 E2
Sudbrooke 82 C4
Sudbury, Derby 67 G3
SUDBURY, Suff 48 B1
Sudgrove 42 B5
Suffield, N Yorks 97 E2
Suffield, Norf 73 F3
Sugnall 66 C3
Suladale 150 C3
Sulaisiadar 161 J4
Sulby 90 C3
Sulgrave 56 D7
Sulham 29 J3
Sulhamstead 29 J4
Sulland 173 F2
Sullington 20 D4
Sullom 175 E3
Sully 26 A4
Sultagic 170 D3
Sumburgh 176 D7
Summerbridge 94 D5
Summercourt 3 G2
Summerfield 71 H3
Summerhill 66 C5
Summerleaze 26 D2
Summerscales 94 C6
Summerseat 85 F5
Summit 85 H5
Sunadale 173 F2
Sunbiggin 102 C7
SUNBURY 31 F4
Sundaywell 109 F4
Sunderland, Cumbr 101 F4
Sunderland, Scot Bord 120 D4
SUNDERLAND, T & W 104 C2
Sunderland Bridge 104 B4
Sundhope 120 C5
Sundon Park 45 E3
Sundridge 33 E5
Sunhill 28 D5
Sunipol 139 E6
Sunk Island 89 G5
Sunningdale 30 D4
Sunninghill 30 D4
Sunningwell 43 G5
Sunniside, Durham 103 H4
Sunniside, T & W 113 G2
Sunny Bank 92 A2
Sunnylaw 129 E3
Sunnymead 21 G2
Sunnyside 130 A5
SURBITON 31 F4
Surfleet 70 C4
Surfleet Seas End 70 C4
Surlingham 73 G6
Sustead 73 E3
Susworth 88 C6
Sutcombe 12 D4
Suton 72 D7
Sutors of Cromarty 154 C2
Sutterby 83 G5
Sutterton 70 C3
Sutterton Dowdyke 70 C3
Sutton, Beds 58 C7
Sutton, C of Peter 70 A7
Sutton, Cambs 59 E4
SUTTON, G Lon 32 C4
Sutton, Kent 35 G6
Sutton, Lincs 81 F6
Sutton, Norf 73 G4
Sutton, Notts NG13 69 G2
Sutton, Oxon 43 G5
Sutton, S Yorks 87 G5
Sutton, Shrops TF9 66 B3
Sutton, Shrops WV16 54 C2
Sutton, Somer 16 E2
Sutton, Staffs 66 C4
Sutton, Suff 61 G7
Sutton, W Susx 20 C4
Sutton -on-Hull 89 F3
Sutton Abinger 31 F6
Sutton at Hone 33 F3
Sutton Bassett 57 E2
Sutton Benger 28 B3
Sutton Bonington 68 D4
Sutton Bridge 71 E4
Sutton Cheney 68 C6
SUTTON COLDFIELD 55 G2
Sutton Courtenay 43 H6
Sutton Crosses 71 E4
Sutton cum Lound 80 D3

Sutton Grange 94 D4
Sutton Green 30 E5
Sutton Hill 66 C6
Sutton Howgrave 94 E4
SUTTON IN ASHFIELD 80 C6
Sutton Lane Ends 78 D4
Sutton Leach 77 H2
Sutton Maddock 66 C6
Sutton Mallet 16 B2
Sutton Mandeville 17 H3
Sutton Montis 16 E3
Sutton on Sea 83 H3
Sutton on Trent 81 E5
Sutton on the Hill 67 J3
Sutton St Edmund 70 D5
Sutton St James 70 D5
Sutton St Nicholas 53 J7
Sutton Scarsdale 80 B5
Sutton Scotney 19 F2
Sutton upon Derwent 87 J2
Sutton Valence 34 B6
Sutton Veny 27 H6
Sutton Waldron 17 G4
Sutton Weaver 77 H4
Sutton-in-Craven 86 B2
Sutton-on-the-Forest 95 G5
Sutton-under-Brailes 43 F2
Sutton-under-Whitestonecliffe 95 F3
Swaby 83 F4
SWADLINCOTE 67 J5
SWAFFHAM 72 B6
Swaffham Bulbeck 59 F5
Swaffham Prior 59 F5
Swafield 73 F3
Swainby 95 F1
Swainshill 40 D1
Swainsthorpe 73 F6
Swalcliffe 43 F2
Swalecliffe 34 E4
Swallow 89 F6
Swallowcliffe 17 H3
Swallowfield 30 B4
Swallownest 79 J3
Swan Green 78 B4
Swan Street 48 B3
SWANAGE 10 B6
Swanbourne 44 C3
Swanbridge 26 A4
Swancote 54 C2
Swanland 88 E4
Swanley 33 F4
Swanmore 19 G4
Swannington, Leic 68 C5
Swannington, Norf 72 E5
SWANSCOMBE 33 G3
Swansea 38 D6
Swanton Abbot 73 F4
Swanton Morley 72 D5
Swanton Novers 72 D3
Swanwick, Derby 79 J6
Swanwick, Hants 19 G5
Swarby 69 J2
Swardeston 73 F6
Swarister 177 C5
Swarkestone 68 B4
Swarland 113 F2
Swarthmoor 92 A4
Swartland 172 C4
Swaton 70 B3
Swavesey 58 D5
Sway 10 D4
Swayfield 69 H4
Swaythling 19 F4
Sweffling 61 G5
Swell 16 B3
Swepstone 68 B5
Swerford 43 F2
Swettenham 78 C5
Swffryd 40 B6
Swilland 61 E6
Swillbrook 84 C3
Swillington 87 F3
Swimbridge 13 G3
Swinbrook 42 D5
Swinderby 81 F5
Swindon, Glos 42 B3
Swindon, Staffs 54 D2
SWINDON, Swin 28 D2
Swine 89 F3
Swinefleet 88 B4
Swineshead, Beds 58 A5
Swineshead, Lincs 70 C2
Swineshead Bridge 70 C2
Swineside 94 B3
Swiney 169 G6
Swinford, Leic 56 D4
Swinford, Oxon 43 F5
Swingfield Minnis 35 F6
Swingfield Street 35 F6
Swinhill 118 E3
Swinhoe 123 H5
Swinhope 82 E2
Swining 175 F4
Swinister 176 C6
Swinithwaite 94 B3
Swinscoe 67 G2
Swinside Hall 121 G6
Swinstead 69 J4
SWINTON, G Man 78 B1
Swinton, N Yorks HG4 94 D4
Swinton, N Yorks YO17 96 C4
SWINTON, S Yorks 80 B2
Swinton, Scot Bord 122 D3
Swintonmill 122 D3
Swithland 68 D5
Swordale 153 H2
Swordland 141 G4
Swordly 168 B3
Sworton Heath 78 A3
Swydduffynnon 51 G5
Swynnerton 66 D3
Swyre 8 D5
Syde 42 B4
Sydenham, G Lon 32 D3
Sydenham, Oxon 44 B5
Sydenham Damerel 5 H3
Syderstone 72 B3
Sydling St Nicholas 29 G5
Sydmonton 29 G5
Syerston 69 G2
Syke 85 H5
Sykehouse 87 G5
Sykes 85 E1
Syleham 61 F4
Sylen 38 C5
Symbister 175 G4
Symington, S Ayr 117 H4
Symington, S Lanak 119 H4
Symonds Yat 41 E4
Symondsbury 8 C5
Synod Inn 50 E6
Syre 167 H5
Syreford 42 C3
Syresham 43 J1
Syston, Leic 68 E5
Syston, Lincs 69 H2
Sytchampton 54 D5
Sywell 57 G5

T

Taagan 152 C2
Tabost, Na Eilean HS2 0 161 J1
Tabost, Na Eilean HS2 9 161 G6
Tackley 43 G3
Taclet 160 E4
Tacolneston 60 E2
Tadcaster 87 F2
Tadden 9 H3
Taddington 79 F4
Tadley 29 J4
Tadlow 58 C7
Tadmarton 43 F2
Tadworth 32 C5
Tafarn-y-Gelyn 76 B5
Tafarnaubach 39 J4
Taff's Well 25 J2
Tafolwern 64 B6
Tai'n Lon 74 D6
Tai'n Lôn 74 D7
Tai-bach 64 E4
Tai-bach 25 E2
TAIN, Highl IV19 164 D5
Tain, Highl KW14 169 G3
Tairgwaith 38 E4
Tairlaw 107 G2
Takeley 47 F3
Takeley Street 47 F3
Tal-sarn 51 F6
Tal-y-bont, Cered 51 G3
Tal-y-Bont, Conwy 75 G5
Tal-y-bont, Gwyn LL43 63 F4
Tal-y-bont, Gwyn LL57 75 F4
Tal-y-cafn 75 G5
Tal-y-llyn 63 H6
Tal-y-Wern 64 B6
Talachddu 39 H2
Talacre 76 D3
Talaton 15 G6
Talbenny 36 C4
Talbot Green 25 J2
Talerddig 64 C6
Talgarreg 50 E6
Talgarth 39 J2
Talisker 150 C5
Talke 78 C6
Talkin 102 B2
Talla Linnfoots 119 J5
Talladale 152 B1
Tallarn Green 65 H2
Tallentire 101 F4
Talley 38 D2
Tallington 70 A6
Talmine 167 G3
Talog 37 H3
Talsarnau 63 G3
Talskiddy 4 C4
Talwrn 74 D4
Talybont-on-Usk 39 J3
Talyllyn 39 J3
Talysarn 74 D6
Tamavoid 128 C3
Tamerton Foliot 5 H4
TAMWORTH 67 H6
Tan-y-fron 76 B5
Tan-y-groes 50 C7
Tandridge 32 D5
Tanfield 103 H2
Tanfield Moor 103 H2
Tangasdal 148 B4
Tangiers 36 D4
Tanglandford 157 F5
Tangley 29 F5
Tangmere 20 C5
Tangwick 174 D3
Tankerness 171 H4
Tankersley 79 H5
Tannach 169 H5
Tannachie 147 E5
Tannadice 138 D3
Tannington 61 F5
Tansley 79 H5
Tansor 57 J2
Tantobie 103 H2
Tanton 104 E6
Tanworth-in-Arden 55 G4
Tanygrisiau 63 G2
Taobh a Deas Loch Aineort 148 C2
Taobh a Tuath Loch Aineort 148 C2
Taobh a' Ghlinne 161 G6
Taobh Tuath 158 D3
Tappoch 129 F4
Tarbert, Arg & Bt PA29 126 C6
Tarbert, Arg & Bt PA41 114 B1
Tarbert, Arg & Bt PA60 125 D4
Tarbert (Tairbeart) 159 F2
Tarbet, Arg & Bt 127 H2
Tarbet, Highl IV27 166 C5
Tarbet, Highl PH41 141 G4
Tarbock Green 77 G3
Tarbolton 118 B5
Tarbrax 119 H2
Tarfside 146 B6
Tarland 146 B3
Tarleton 84 C4
Tarlogie 164 D5
Tarlscough 84 C5
Tarlton 42 B6
Tarnbrook 92 D6
Tarporley 77 H5
Tarr 15 H2
Tarrant Crawford 9 H3
Tarrant Gunville 17 H4
Tarrant Hinton 17 H4
Tarrant Keyneston 17 H5
Tarrant Launceston 17 H5
Tarrant Monkton 17 H5
Tarrant Rawston 17 H5
Tarrant Rushton 17 H5
Tarrel 165 E5
Tarring Neville 21 H1
Tarrington 41 F1
Tarsappie 137 J6
Tarskavaig 141 E3
Tarves 157 F5
Tarvie, Highl 153 G3
Tarvie, Pth & Kin 137 H2
Tarvin 77 G5
Tasburgh 61 F2
Tasley 54 B2
Taston 43 F3
Tatenhill 67 H4
Tatham 93 E3
Tathwell 83 F3
Tatsfield 32 E5
Tattenhall 77 G6
Tatterford 72 B4
Tattersett 72 B3
Tattershall 82 D6
Tattershall Bridge 82 D6

226
Tattershall Thorpe
TREORCHY/TREORCI

Tattershall Thorpe 82 E6
Tattingstone 48 E2
Tatworth 16 B5
TAUNTON 15 J3
Tavantaggart 116 B3
Taverham 72 E5
Tavernspite 37 F4
TAVISTOCK 5 H3
Taw Green 14 C6
Tawstock 13 F3
Taxal 78 E4
Tay Road Bridge 138 D6
Tayinloan 116 A3
Taymouth Castle 137 E4
Taynish 126 B4
Taynton, Glos 41 G3
Taynton, Oxon 42 E4
Taynuilt 134 D5
TAYPORT 138 D6
Tayvallich 126 B4
Tealby 82 D2
Tealing 138 D5
Teangue 141 F3
Teanna Mhachair 149 C3
Tebay 93 E1
Tebworth 44 D3
Tedburn St Mary 14 E6
TEDDINGTON, G Lon 31 F3
Teddington, Glos 42 B2
Tedstone Delamere 54 B6
Tedstone Wafre 54 B6
Teesport 104 E5
Teesside International Airport 104 C6
Teeton 57 E4
Teffont Evias 17 H2
Teffont Magna 17 H2
Tegryn 37 G2
Teigh 69 G5
Teigngrace 6 E3
TEIGNMOUTH 7 F3
TELFORD 66 B5
Telham 22 D4
Tellisford 27 H5
Telscombe 21 H5
Telscombe Cliffs 21 H5
Templand 109 H4
Temple, C of Glas 128 C6
Temple, Corn 5 E3
Temple, Midlo 120 C2
Temple Bar 51 F6
Temple Cloud 27 F5
Temple Ewell 35 F6
Temple Grafton 55 G6
Temple Guiting 42 C3
Temple Herdewyke 56 B6
Temple Hirst 87 H4
Temple Normanton 80 B5
Temple Sowerby 102 C5
Templebar 37 F5
Templecombe 17 F3
Templeton, Devon 15 E4
Templeton, Pemb 37 F4
Templeton Bridge 14 E4
Tempsford 58 B6
Ten Mile Bank 59 F2
Tenbury Wells 54 A5
TENBY 37 F5
Tendring 48 E3
Tenston 170 C3
TENTERDEN 23 E2
Terling 47 H4
Ternhill 66 B3
Terregles 109 G5
Terrington 96 B4
Terrington St Clement 71 F5
Terrington St John 71 F5
Terwick Common 20 B3
Teston 33 H5
Testwood 18 E4
TETBURY 41 H6
Tetbury Upton 41 H6
Tetchill 65 G3
Tetcott 12 D6
Tetford 83 F4
Tetney 83 F1
Tetney Lock 89 H6
Tetsworth 44 A5
Tettenhall 66 D6
Teuchan 157 H5
Teversal 80 B5
Teversham 59 E6
Teviothead 110 D2
Tewel 147 F5
Tewin 46 C4
TEWKESBURY 41 H2
Teynham 34 C4
Thainston 146 D6
Thakeham 20 E4
THAME 44 B5
Thames Ditton 31 F4
Thames Haven 33 H2
Thamesmead 33 E3
Thanington 34 E5
Thankerton 119 G4
Tharston 61 E2
THATCHAM 29 H4
Thatto Heath 77 G2
Thaxted 47 G2
The Aird 150 D3
The Bage 40 B1
The Balloch 137 F7
The Barony 172 C4
The Birks 146 E3
The Bog 65 G7
The Braes 151 E5
The Bratch 54 D2
The Bryn 40 C5
The Burf 54 D5
The Burn 146 C6
The Camp 42 B5
The Chequer 65 H2
The City 44 B6
The Common, Bucks 44 B2
The Common, Wilts 18 D2
The Craigs 164 A4
The Cronk 90 C3
The Den 117 H2
The Down 22 C2
The Drums 145 H7
The Fence 41 E5
The Flatt 111 E5
The Grange 95 G2
The Green, Cumbr 91 C3
The Green, Wilts 17 G2
The Grove 72 E4
The Hall 177 D4
The Haughs 156 C4
The Heath 73 E4
The Herberts 25 G3
The Hermitage 31 G5
The Hill 91 C3
The Howe, Cumbr 92 C3
The Howe, I of M 90 A6
The Hundred 53 J5
The Lee 44 D5
The Leigh 41 H3
The Lhen 90 C2
The Marsh 65 G7
The Middles 103 J2
The Moor 22 D3
The Mumbles 24 D2
The Mythe 41 H2
The North 40 E5
The Neuk 146 E4
The Old Byre 133 G3
The Polchar 144 C3
The Pole of Itlaw 156 D3
The Quarry 41 G6
The Rhos 36 E4
The Stocks 23 F3
The Towans 2 D4
The Town 2 M9
The Vauld 53 J7
The Village 54 D2
The Wyke 66 C6
Theakston 94 E3
Thealby 88 C5
Theale, Somer 26 D6
Theale, W Berks 29 J3
Thearne 88 E3
Theberton 61 H5
Thedden Grange 19 H2
Theddingworth 56 E3
Theddlethorpe All Saints 83 G3
Theddlethorpe St Helen 83 G3
Thelbridge Barton 14 D4
Thelnetham 60 D4
Thelveton 60 E3
Thelwall 77 J3
Themelthorpe 72 D4
Thenford 43 H1
Therfield 46 D2
THETFORD 60 B3
Theydon Bois 47 E6
Thick Hollins 86 C5
Thickwood 27 H3
Thimbleby, Lincs 83 E5
Thimbleby, N Yorks 95 F2
Thirkleby 95 F4
Thirlby 95 F3
Thirlestane 121 E3
Thirn 94 D3
Thirsk 95 F3
Thistleton 69 H5
Thistley Green 59 G4
Thixendale 96 D5
Thockrington 112 D5
Tholmair 149 D5
Tholomas Drove 70 E6
Tholthorpe 95 F5
Thomas Chapel 37 F5
Thomastown 156 C5
Thompson 60 C2
Thomshill 155 G3
Thong 33 G3
Thoralby 94 B3
Thoresthorpe 83 G4
Thoresway 82 D2
Thorganby, Lincs 82 E2
Thorganby, N Yorks 87 H2
Thorgill 96 C2
Thorington 61 H4
Thorington Street 48 D2
Thorlby 85 H1
Thorley Street 11 E5
Thormanby 95 F4
Thornaby-on-Tees 104 D6
Thornage 72 D3
Thornborough, Bucks 44 B2
Thornborough, N Yorks 94 D4
Thornbury, C of H 54 B6
Thornbury, Devon 13 E5
THORNBURY, S Glos 27 F1
Thornby 56 E4
Thorncliffe 78 E6
Thorncombe 8 B3
Thorncombe Street 30 D6
Thorncote Green 58 B7
Thorndon 60 E5
Thorndon Cross 13 F6
Thorne 87 H5
Thorne St Margaret 15 G3
Thorner 87 E2
Thorney, C of Peter 70 C6
Thorney, Notts 81 F4
Thorney Hill 10 C4
Thorney Toll 70 D6
Thornfalcon 16 A3
Thornford 16 E4
Thorngumbald 89 G4
Thornham 71 H2
Thornham Magna 60 E4
Thornham Parva 60 E4
Thornhaugh 70 A6
Thornhill, C of Soton 19 F4
Thornhill, Caer 26 A2
Thornhill, Cumbr 100 E7
Thornhill, D & G 109 F3
Thornhill, Derby 79 F3
Thornhill, Stir 128 D3
Thornhill Edge 86 D5
Thornholme 97 G5
Thornhurst 87 E2
Thornicombe 9 G3
Thornley, Durham DH6 104 C4
Thornley, Durham DL13 103 H4
Thornliebank 118 C2
Thorns 59 H6
Thornthwaite, Cumbr 101 G5
Thornthwaite, N Yorks 94 C6
Thornton, Ang 138 C4
Thornton, Bucks 44 B2
Thornton, E Yorks 88 B2
Thornton, Fife 130 B3
THORNTON, Lancs 84 B2
Thornton, Leic 68 C6
Thornton, Lincs 83 E5
Thornton, Mers 84 B6
Thornton, Northum 123 E3
Thornton, W Yorks 86 B3
Thornton Curtis 88 E5
Thornton Hough 77 F3
Thornton le Moor 82 C2
Thornton Park 123 E3
Thornton Rust 93 H3
Thornton Steward 94 C3
Thornton Watlass 94 D3
Thornton-in-Craven 85 H2
Thornton-le-Beans 95 E2
Thornton-le-Clay 96 B5
Thornton-le-Dale 96 D3
Thornton-le-Moor 95 E3
Thornton-le-Moors 77 G4
Thornton-le-Street 95 F3
Thorntonhall 118 C2
Thorntonloch 131 G5
Thornwood Common 47 E5
Thoroton 69 F2
Thorp Arch 87 F2
Thorp St Peter 83 G5
Thorpe, Cumbr 102 B5
Thorpe, Derby 79 F6
Thorpe, Lincs 83 H3
Thorpe, N Yorks 94 B5
Thorpe, Norf 73 H7
Thorpe, Notts 80 E7
Thorpe, Surrey 30 E4
Thorpe Abbotts 61 E4
Thorpe Acre 68 D4
Thorpe Arnold 69 F4
Thorpe Audlin 87 F5
Thorpe Bassett 96 D4
Thorpe Bay 34 C2
Thorpe by Water 57 G2
Thorpe Constantine 67 H6
Thorpe Culvert 83 G5
Thorpe End 73 F5
Thorpe Fendykes 83 G5
Thorpe Green 60 C6
Thorpe Hesley 79 H2
Thorpe in Balne 87 G5
Thorpe Langton 57 F2
Thorpe Larches 104 C5
Thorpe le Fallows 81 G3
Thorpe le Street 88 C2
Thorpe Malsor 57 G4
Thorpe Mandeville 43 H1
Thorpe Market 73 F3
Thorpe Morieux 60 C6
Thorpe on the Hill, Lincs 81 G5
Thorpe on the Hill, W Yorks 86 E4
Thorpe St Andrew 73 F6
Thorpe Salvin 80 C3
Thorpe Satchville 69 F5
Thorpe Thewles 104 D5
Thorpe Underwood 95 F6
Thorpe Waterville 57 J3
Thorpe Willoughby 87 G3
Thorpe- le-Soken 49 E3
Thorpeness 61 H6
Thorrington 48 D3
Thorverton 15 F5
Thrandeston 60 E4
THRAPSTON 57 H4
Threapland, Cumbr 101 F4
Threapland, N Yorks 94 A5
Threapwood 65 H2
Three Bridges, Lincs 83 G3
Three Bridges, W Susx 21 F2
Three Chimneys 22 E2
Three Cocks 40 A2
Three Crosses 38 C6
Three Cups Corner 22 C3
Three Holes 71 F6
Three Leg Cross 22 C2
Three Legged Cross 18 B5
Three Mile Cross 30 B4
Threekingham 70 A3
Threemilestone 3 F3
Threlkeld 101 H5
Threshers Bush 47 E5
Threshfield 94 A5
Threxton Hill 72 B7
Thrigby 73 H5
Thringarth 103 F5
Thringstone 68 C5
Thrintoft 94 E2
Thriplow 59 E7
Throckenholt 70 D6
Throcking 46 D2
Throckley 113 F6
Throckmorton 55 E7
Throphill 113 F4
Thropton 112 E2
Throsk 129 F3
Througham 42 B5
Throwleigh 14 C6
Throwley 34 C5
Thrumpton 68 D3
Thrumster 169 H5
Thrunton 113 E1
Thrupp, Glos 41 H5
Thrupp, Oxon 43 G4
Thrushelton 5 H2
Thrushgill 93 E5
Thrussington 68 E5
Thruxton, Co of H 40 D2
Thruxton, Hants 29 E6
Thrybergh 80 B2
Thulston 68 C3
Thundergay 116 C3
Thundridge 46 D4
Thurcaston 68 D5
Thurcroft 80 B3
Thurdon 12 C4
Thurgarton, Norf 73 E3
Thurgarton, Notts 69 E2
Thurgoland 79 G1
Thurlaston, Leic 68 D7
Thurlaston, Warw 56 C4
Thurlbear 16 A3
Thurlby, Lincs LN13 83 G4
Thurlby, Lincs LN5 81 G5
Thurlby, Lincs PE10 70 A5
Thurleigh 58 A6
Thurlestone 6 C6
Thurloxton 16 A2
Thurlstone 86 D6
Thurlton 73 H7
Thurmaston 68 E6
Thurnby 68 E6
Thurne 73 H5
Thurnham, Kent 34 B5
Thurnham, Lancs 92 C6
Thurning, Norf 72 D4
Thurning, Northnts 58 A3
Thurnscoe 87 F6
Thurnscoe East 87 F6
Thursby 101 H2
Thursford 72 C3
Thursford Green 72 C3
Thursley 20 C2
THURSO 169 F3
Thurstaston 76 E3
Thurston 60 C5
Thurston End 59 H6
Thurstonfield 101 H2
Thurstonland 86 C5
Thurton 73 G6
Thurvaston 67 H3
Thuxton 72 D6
Thwaite, N Yorks 93 G2
Thwaite, Suff 60 E5
Thwaite Head 92 B2
Thwaite St Mary 61 G2
Thwing 97 F4
Tibbermore 137 H6
Tibberton, Glos 41 G3
Tibberton, Tel & Wrek 66 B4
Tibberton, Worces 54 E6
Tibenham 60 E3
Tibshelf 80 B5
Tibthorpe 97 E6
Ticehurst 22 C2
Tichborne 19 G2
Tickencote 69 H6
Tickenham 26 D3
Tickhill 80 C2
Ticklerton 53 H2
Ticknall 68 B4
Tickton 88 E2
Tidcombe 29 E5
Tiddington, Oxon 43 J5
Tiddington, Warw 55 H6
Tidebrook 22 C3
Tideford 5 G5
Tidenham 41 E6
Tideswell 79 F4
Tidmarsh 29 J3
Tidmington 42 E2
Tidpit 18 B4
Tiers Cross 36 D4
Tiffield 57 E6
Tifty 157 E4
Tigerton 139 E2
Tigh a' Ghearraidh 149 C2
Tigh-na-Blair 137 E7
Tighnabruaich 126 D5
Tighnafiline 162 C5
Tigley 6 D4
Tilbrook 58 A5
TILBURY 33 G3
Tilbury Juxta Clare 47 H1
Tile Cross 55 G3
Tile Hill 55 H4
Tilehurst 30 A3
Tilford 30 C6
Tillathrowie 156 B5
Tillers Green 41 F2
TILLICOULTRY 129 G3
Tillingham 48 C5
Tillington, Co of H 53 H7
Tillington, W Susx 20 C3
Tillington Common 53 H7
Tillyarblet 139 E2
Tillybirloch 146 D3
Tillycorthie 157 G6
Tillydrine 146 D4
Tillyfour 146 C2
Tillyfourie 146 D2
Tillygarmond 146 D4
Tillygreig 157 F6
Tillykerrie 157 F6
Tillylodge 146 C3
Tilmanstone 35 G5
Tilney All Saints 71 F5
Tilney High End 71 F5
Tilney St Lawrence 71 F5
Tilshead 28 C6
Tilstock 65 J3
Tilston 77 G6
Tilstone Fearnall 77 H5
Tilsworth 44 D3
Tilton on the Hill 69 F6
Timberland 82 D6
Timbersbrook 78 C5
Timberscombe 25 G6
Timble 86 C1
Timperley 78 B3
Timsbury, Bth 27 F5
Timsbury, Hants 18 E3
Timsgearraidh 160 D4
Timworth Green 60 B5
Tincleton 9 F4
Tindale 111 F7
Tingewick 43 J2
Tingley 86 D4
Tingrith 44 E2
Tingwall 172 E4
Tinhay 5 G2
Tinshill 86 D3
Tinsley 79 H2
Tintagel 12 A7
Tintern Parva 40 E5
Tintinhull 16 D4
Tintwistle 78 E2
Tinwald 109 H4
Tinwell 69 J6
Tipperty 157 G6
Tipps End 59 F2
Tiptoe 10 D4
TIPTON 55 E2
Tipton St John 15 G6
Tiptree 48 B4
Tiptree Heath 48 B4
Tirabad 39 F1
Tirley 41 H3
Tirphil 39 J5
Tirril 102 B5
Tisbury 17 H3
Tisley Green 21 F2
Tisman's Common 20 D2
Tissington 79 F6
Titchberry 12 C3
Titchfield 19 G5
Titchmarsh 57 J4
Titchwell 71 H2
Titley 53 G5
Titlington 123 F6
Titson 12 C5
Tittensor 66 D3
Tittleshall 72 B4
Tiverton, Ches 77 H5
TIVERTON, Devon 15 F4
Tivetshall St Margaret 60 E3
Tivetshall St Mary 60 E3
Tixall 67 E4
Tixover 69 H6
Toab, Orkney 171 F4
Toab, Shetld 176 C6
TOBERMORY 133 H3
Toberonochy 126 B2
Tobha Beag 149 C6
Tobha Mòr 149 C6
Tobhtaral 160 E4
Tobson 160 E4
Tocher 156 D5
Tockenham 28 C3
Tockenham Wick 28 C2
Tockholes 85 E4
Tockington 27 F2
Tockwith 87 F1
Todber 17 G3
Toddington, Beds 44 E3
Toddington, Glos 42 C2
Toddington, W Susx 20 D5
Todenham 42 E2
Todhills, Ang 138 D5
Todhills, Cumbr 110 C6
Todlachie 146 D2
TODMORDEN 85 H4
Todwick 80 B3
Toft, Cambs 58 D6
Toft, Lincs 70 A5
Toft Hill 103 H5
Toft Monks 61 H2
Toft next Newton 82 C3
Toftrees 72 C4
Tofts 169 H3
Toftwood 72 C5
Togston 113 G2
Tokavaig 141 F2
Tokers Green 30 B3
Tolastadh a' Chaolais 160 E4
Toldish 4 C5
Toll Bar 87 G6
Toll of Birness 157 H5
Tolland 15 H2
Tollard Royal 17 H4
Tollbar End 56 B4
Toller Fratrum 8 D4
Toller Porcorum 8 D4
Toller Whelme 8 D3
Tollerton, N Yorks 95 G5
Tollerton, Notts 68 E3
Tollesbury 48 C4
Tolleshunt D'Arcy 48 C4
Tolleshunt Knights 48 C4
Tolleshunt Major 48 C4
Tolm 161 H4
Tolpuddle 9 F4
Tolstadh bho Thuath 161 J3
Tolworth 31 F4
Tom nan Ragh 127 F4
Tomatin 154 C6
Tomatin Distillery 154 B6
Tombreck 154 A5
Tomchrasky 142 E2
Tomdoun 142 D3
Tomdow 154 E4
Tomich, Highl IV18 154 B1
Tomich, Highl IV4 153 F6
Tomintoul, Aberd 145 F4
Tomintoul, Mor 145 F2
Tomnamoon 155 E3
Tomnaven 156 B5
Tomnavoulin 155 G6
Tomslèibhe 133 J5
Tomvaich 155 E5
Ton-teg 25 H2
TONBRIDGE 33 F6
Tonderghie 99 F6
Tondu 25 F2
Tonfanau 63 F6
Tong 66 C6
Tonge 68 C4
Tongham 30 C6
Tongland 99 H4
Tongue 167 G4
Tongue End 70 B5
Tongwynlais 25 J2
Tonmawr 39 F6
Tonna 38 E6
Tonwell 46 D4
TONYPANDY 25 G1
Tonyrefail 25 H2
Toot Baldon 43 H5
Toot Hill 47 F5
Toothill 19 E4
Topcliffe 95 F4
Topcroft 61 F2
Topcroft Street 61 F2
Toppesfield 47 H2
Toppings 85 F5
Topsham 15 F7
Torbeg 116 D4
Torbryan 6 E4
Torcastle 142 D6
Torcross 6 E6
Tore 153 J3
Torinturk 126 C6
Torksey 81 F4
Torlum 149 C4
Torlundy 142 D6
Tormarton 27 G3
Tormisdale 124 A5
Tormitchell 106 E3
Tormore, Highl 155 F5
Tormore, N Ayr 116 C4
Tornagrain 154 B4
Tornahaish 145 G3
Tornameal 168 E4
Tornapress 151 H4
Tornaveen 146 D3
Torness 153 H6
Torpenhow 101 G4
Torphichen 129 G5
Torphins 146 D3
TORPOINT 5 H5
TORQUAY 7 F4
Torquhan 120 D3
Torran, Arg & Bt 126 C2
Torran, Highl 164 D6
Torrance 128 D5
Torrans 133 G6
Torridon 152 B3
Torrie 100 D2
Torrin 141 E1
Torrisdale 167 H3
Torrish 165 F2
Torrisholme 92 C5
Torrlaoighseach 142 B2
Torroble 164 B3
Torry, Aberd 156 B4
Torry, C of Aber 147 G3
Torryburn 129 H4
Torrylinn 116 D5
Torsonce 120 D3
Torterston 157 H4
Torthorwald 109 H5
Tortington 20 D5
Tortworth 41 G6
Torvaig 150 D4
Torver 92 A2
Torwood 129 F4
Torworth 80 D3
Tosberry 12 C3
Toscaig 151 G5
Toseland 58 C5
Tosside 93 F6
Tostock 60 C5
Totaig, Highl IV40 151 H6
Totaig, Highl IV55 150 A3
Tote, Highl IV51 9JW 151 E3
Tote, Highl IV51 9PG 150 D4
Totegan 168 C3
Tothill 83 G3
Totland 10 E5
Totley 79 H4
TOTNES 6 E4
Toton 68 C3
Totronald 132 D3
Totscore 150 C2
TOTTENHAM 32 D1
Tottenhill 71 G5
Totteridge, Bucks 44 C6
Totteridge, G Lon 46 C6
Totternhoe 44 D3
Totterton 53 G3
Tottington 85 F5
TOTTON 18 E4
Tournaig 162 C5
Toux, Aberd AB42 157 G3
Toux, Aberd AB45 156 C3
Tovil 33 H5
TOW LAW 103 H4
Toward 127 F6
Toward Taynuilt 127 F6
Towcester 57 E7
Towednack 2 C4
Tower Hill 77 G1
Tower-of-Sark 110 C5
Towersey 44 B5
Towie, Aberd AB33 146 B2
Towie, Aberd AB43 157 F2
Towiemore 156 A4
Town End, Cambs 58 E2
Town End, Cumbr 92 C3
Town Row 22 B2
Town Yetholm 122 D5
Townfield 103 F3
Townhead, Cumbr 102 C4
Townhead, D & G 99 H5
Townhead of Greenlaw 108 E6
Townhill 129 J4
Townshend 2 D4
Towthorpe 95 H6
Towton 87 F3
Towyn, Conwy 76 B4
Towyn, Gwyn 62 C4
Toy's Hill 33 E5
Toynton All Saints 83 F5
Toynton Fen Side 83 F5
Toynton St Peter 83 G5
Trabboch 118 B5
Trabbochburn 118 B5
Traboe 3 F5
Tradespark, Highl 154 C3
Tradespark, Orkney 171 E4
Trafford Park 78 B2
Trallong 39 G3
Tranch 40 B5
TRANENT 130 D5
Trantlebeg 168 C4
Trantlemore 168 C4
Tranwell 113 F4
Trapp 38 D4
Traprain 131 E5
Traquair 120 C4
TRAWDEN 85 H3
Trawsfynydd 63 H3
Tre Taliesin 51 G2
Tre'r-ddol 51 G2
Tre-groes 37 J1
Trealaw 25 H1
Treales 84 C3
Trearddur 74 B4
Treaslane 150 C3
Trebarrow 12 C6
Trebartha 5 F3
Trebarwith 4 D2
Trebetherick 4 C3
Treblary 5 E2
Treborough 15 G2
Trebudannon 4 B4
Trebullett 5 G3
Treburley 5 G3
Trebyan 4 D4
Trecastle 39 F3
Trecwn 36 D2
Trecynon 39 G5
Tredavoe 2 C5
TREDEGAR 39 J5
Tredington, Glos 41 J3
Tredington, Warw 42 E1
Tredinnick, Corn PL14 5 F5
Tredinnick, Corn PL27 4 C3
Tredomen 39 J2
Tredrizzick 4 C3
Tredunnock 40 C6
Treen 2 B5
Treeton 80 B3
Trefdraeth 74 D4
Trefeca 39 J2
Trefeglwys 52 C2
Trefenter 51 G5
Treffgarne 36 D3
Treffynnon 36 C3
Trefil 39 J4
Trefilan 51 F6
Trefin 36 C2
Treflach 65 F4
Trefnanney 65 F5
Trefnant 76 C4
Trefonen 65 F4
Trefor, Gwyn 62 D2
Trefor, I of Angl 74 C3
Treforest 25 H2
Trefriw 75 G5
Tregadillett 5 F2
Tregaian 74 D4
Tregare 40 D4
Tregaron 51 G6
Tregarth 75 F5
Tregeare 5 F2
Tregeiriog 64 E3
Tregele 74 C2
Tregeseal 2 B4
Tregidden 3 F5
Treglemais 36 C3
Tregole 12 B6
Tregonetha 4 C4
Tregony 4 C6
Tregoyd 40 A2
Tregurrian 3 G1
Tregynon 64 D7
Trehafod 25 H1
Treharris 39 J6
TREHERBERT 39 G6
Treknow 4 D2
Trelan 3 F6
Trelash 12 B6
Trelawnyd 76 C4
Trelech 37 G2
Treleddyd- fawr 36 B3
Trelew 3 G4
Trelewis 39 J6
Treligga 4 D2
Trelights 4 C3
Trelill 4 D3
Trelissick 3 G4
Trellech 40 E5
Trelleck Grange 40 D5
Trelogan 76 D3
Trelowth 4 C5
Trelystan 65 F6
Tremadog 63 F2
Tremail 5 E2
Tremain 50 C7
Tremaine 12 C7
Tremar 5 F4
Trematon 5 G5
Tremeirchion 76 C4
Tremethick Cross 2 C4
Trenance 4 B4
Trenarren 4 D6
Trench 66 B5
Trenear 3 E4
Treneglos 5 F2
Trenewan 5 E5
Trent 16 D4
Trentham 66 D2
Trentishoe 24 D6
Treoes 25 G3
TREORCHY / TREORCI 39 G6

Trerice
Waterhill of Bruxie
227

Trerice 3 G2
Trerulefoot 5 G5
Tresaith 50 C6
Trescott 54 D2
Trescowe 2 D4
Tresham 27 G1
Tresillian 3 G3
Tresinney 4 E2
Tresinwen 36 D1
Treskinnick Cross 12 C6
Tresmeer 5 F2
Tresparrett 12 B6
Tressait 137 F2
Tresta, Shetld ZE2 9DJ 177 D4
Tresta, Shetld ZE2 9LT 175 E5
Treswell 81 E4
Trethewey 2 B5
Trethomas 26 A2
Trethowel 4 D5
Trethurgy 4 D5
Tretio 36 B3
Tretire 40 E3
Tretower 40 A3
Treuddyn 76 E6
Trevalga 12 A7
Trevanson 4 C3
Trevarren 4 C4
Trevarrian 3 G1
Trevarrick 4 C6
Trevaughan 37 F4
Trevellas 3 F2
Treverva 3 F4
Trevethin 40 B5
Trevigro 5 G4
Treviscoe 4 C5
Trevone 4 B3
Trewalder 4 D2
Trewarmett 4 D2
Trewarthenick 4 C6
Trewassa 5 E2
Trewellard 2 B4
Trewen 5 F2
Trewidland 5 F5
Trewint 12 B6
Trewithian 3 G4
Trewoon 4 C5
Treyarnon 4 B3
Treyford 20 B4
Triangle 86 B4
Trickett's Cross 10 B3
Trimdon 104 C4
Trimdon Colliery 104 C4
Trimdon Grange 104 C4
Trimingham 73 F3
Trimley St Martin 49 F2
Trimley St Mary 49 F2
Trimpley 54 C4
Trimsaran 38 B5
Trimstone 24 B6
Trinafour 136 E2
Trinant 40 B5
TRING 44 D4
Trinity 139 F2
Trislaig 142 C6
Trispen 3 G2
Tritlington 113 G3
Trochry 137 G4
Troedyraur 50 D7
Troedyrhiw 39 H5
Trofarth 75 H4
Trondavoe 175 E3
Troon, Corn 3 E4
TROON, S Ayr 117 H4
Troston 60 B4
Troswell 12 C6
Trottiscliffe 33 G4
Trotton 20 B3
Troutbeck, Cumbr CA11 101 H5
Troutbeck, Cumbr LA23 92 C1
Troutbeck Bridge 92 C1
Trow Green 41 E5
TROWBRIDGE 27 H5
Trowell 68 C3
Trowle Common 27 H5
Trowley Bottom 45 E4
Trows 121 F4
Trowse Newton 73 F6
Trudoxhill 27 G6
Trull 15 J3
Trumaisgearraidh 158 C5
Trumpan 150 B2
Trumpet 41 F2
Trumpington 59 E6
Trunch 73 F3
TRURO 3 G3
Trusham 6 E2
Trusley 67 H3
Trusthorpe 83 H3
Truthan 3 G2
Trysull 54 D2
Tubney 43 G6
Tuckenhay 6 E5
Tuckhill 54 C3
Tuddenham IP28 59 H4
Tuddenham St Martin 61 E7
Tudeley 33 G6
Tudhoe 104 B4
Tudweiliog 62 C3
Tuffley 41 H4
Tufton 37 E3
Tugby 69 F6
Tugford 53 J3
Tullibody 129 F3
Tullich, Arg & Bt 135 E7
Tullich, Highl 154 A6
Tullich Muir 164 D6
Tulliemet 137 H3
Tulloch, Aberd 147 E6
Tulloch, Mor AB56 155 H2
Tulloch, Mor IV36 155 E3
Tullochgorm 126 D3
Tulloes 138 E4
Tullybannocher 136 E6
Tullyfergus 138 B4
Tullymurdoch 138 A3
Tullynessle 146 C2
Tumble 38 C4
Tumby 82 E6
Tumby Woodside 83 E6
Tummel Bridge 136 E3
Tunga 161 H4
Tunnel Hill 41 H2
Tunstall, C of Stoke 78 C6
Tunstall, E Yorks 89 H3
Tunstall, Kent 34 B4
Tunstall, Lancs 93 E4
Tunstall, N Yorks 94 D2
Tunstall, Norf 73 H6
Tunstall, Suff 61 G6
Tunstead 73 G4
Tunworth 30 A6
Tupsley 40 E1
Tupton 79 H5
Tur Langton 57 F2
Turbiskill 126 B4
Turgis Green 30 A5
Turin 139 E3
Turkdean 42 D4
Turnastone 40 C2
Turnberry 106 E2
Turnchapel 5 H5
Turnditch 67 H2
Turners Green 55 G5
Turners Hill 21 G2
Turners Puddle 9 G4
Turnhouse 129 J5
Turnworth 17 G5
TURRIFF 156 E4
Turton Bottoms 85 F5
Turves 58 D2
Turvey 57 H6
Turville 30 B1
Turville Heath 30 B1
Turweston 43 J2
Tutbury 67 H4
Tutnall 55 E5
Tutshill 41 E6
Tuttington 73 F4
Tuxford 80 E4
Twatt, Orkney 172 C4
Twatt, Shetld 175 E5
Twechar 128 D5
Tweedmouth 123 E2
Tweedsmuir 119 H5
Twelveheads 3 F3
Twemloe Green 78 B5
Twenty 70 B4
Twerton 27 G4
TWICKENHAM 31 F3
Twigworth 41 H3
Twineham 21 F4
Twinhoe 27 G5
Twinstead 48 B2
Twitchen, Devon 14 D2
Twitchen, Shrops 53 G4
Two Bridges 6 C3
Two Dales 79 G5
Two Gates 67 H6
Twycross 68 B6
Twyford, Bucks 44 A3
Twyford, Derby 68 B4
Twyford, Dorset 17 G4
Twyford, Hants 19 F3
Twyford, Leic 69 F5
Twyford, Norf 72 D4
Twyford, Wokham 30 B3
Twyford Common 40 E2
Twyn-y-Sheriff 40 D5
Twyn-yr-odyn 25 J3
Twynholm 99 H4
Twyning 41 H2
Twyning Green 41 J2
Twynllanan 38 E3
Twywell 57 H4
Ty Mawr Cwm 64 C2
Ty Rhiw 25 J2
Ty'n-y-groes 75 G4
Ty-hen 62 B3
Ty-nant, Cered 51 F6
Ty-nant, Conwy 64 C2
Ty-nant, Gwyn 64 C4
Tyberton 40 C2
Tyburn 55 G2
Tycroes 38 D4
Tycrwyn 64 E5
Tydd Gote 71 E5
Tydd St Giles 70 E5
Tydd St Mary 71 E5
TYLDESLEY 85 E6
Tyler Hill 34 E4
Tyler's Green 47 F5
Tylers Green 44 D6
Tylorstown 39 H6
Tylwch 52 C3
Tyn-y-ffridd 64 E3
Tyn-y-graig 52 D6
Tyndrum 135 H5
Tyne Tunnel 113 H6
Tyneham 9 G5
Tynehead 120 C2
TYNEMOUTH 113 H6
Tynewydd 39 G6
Tyninghame 131 F5
Tynron 109 F3
Tynygongl 74 E3
Tynygraig 51 G5
Tyrie 157 G2
Tyringham 57 G7
Tythby 69 E3
Tythegston 25 F3
Tytherington, Ches 78 D4
Tytherington, S Glos 27 F2
Tytherington, Somer 27 G6
Tytherington, Wilts 28 B6
Tytherleigh 8 B3
Tytherton Lucas 28 B3
Tywardreath 4 D5
Tywyn, Conwy 75 G4
TYWYN, Gwyn 63 F6

U

Uachdar 149 C4
Ubbeston Green 61 G4
Ubley 27 E5
Uckerby 94 D1
UCKFIELD 21 H3
Uckington 42 B3
Uddingston 118 D1
Uddington 119 F4
Udimore 23 E4
Udny Green 157 F6
Udny Station 157 G6
Udstonhead 118 E3
Uffcott 28 D3
Uffculme 15 G4
Uffington, Lincs 70 A6
Uffington, Oxon 29 F2
Uffington, Shrops 65 J5
Ufford, C of Peter 70 A6
Ufford, Suff 61 F6
Ufton 56 B5
Ufton Nervet 29 J4
Ugadale 116 B5
Ugborough 6 C5
Uggeshall 61 H4
Ugglebarnby 105 H7
Ugley 47 F3
Ugley Green 47 F3
Ugthorpe 105 G6
Uig, Arg & Bt PA23 127 F4
Uig, Arg & Bt PA78 132 D3
UIG, Highl IV51 150 C2
Uig, Highl IV55 150 A3
Uiginish 150 B4
Uigshader 150 D4
Uisken 133 F7
Ulbster 169 H5
Ulceby, Lincs 83 G4
Ulceby, N Linc 89 F5
Ulceby Cross 83 G4
Ulcombe 34 B6
Uldale 101 G4
Uley 41 G6
Ulgham 113 G3
Ullapool 163 F4
Ullenhall 55 G5
Ullenwood 42 B4
Ulleskelf 87 G3
Ullesthorpe 56 D3
Ulley 80 B3
Ullingswick 54 A7
Ullinish 150 C5
Ullock 100 E5
Ulpha 91 C2
Ulrome 97 G6
Ulsta 177 B5
Ulting 48 B5
ULVERSTON 92 A4
Ulzieside 108 E2
Umberleigh 13 G3
Unapool 166 D6
Underbarrow 92 C2
Underhoull 177 C3
Underriver 33 F5
Underwood, Newp 26 C2
Underwood, Notts 80 B6
Undy 26 D2
Unifirth 174 D5
Union Mills 90 C5
Unstone 79 H4
Unstone Green 79 H4
Unthank 101 J4
Unthank End 102 A4
Up Cerne 9 E3
Up Exe 15 F5
Up Hatherley 42 B3
Up Holland 84 D6
Up Nately 30 B5
Up Somborne 19 E2
Up Sydling 8 E3
Upavon, Oxon 29 G1
Upavon, Wilts 28 D5
Upchurch 34 B4
Upcott 53 G6
Upend 59 G6
Uphall 129 H5
Upham, Devon 15 E5
Upham, Hants 19 G3
Uphampton 54 D5
Uphill 26 C5
Uplawmoor 118 B2
Upleadon 41 G3
Upleatham 105 F6
Uplees 34 C4
Uploders 8 D4
Uplowman 15 G4
Uplyme 8 B4
UPMINSTER 33 F2
Upnor 33 H3
Upottery 15 J5
Upper Affcot 53 H3
Upper Ardchronie 164 C5
Upper Ardoscadale 126 E6
Upper Arley 54 C3
Upper Aston 54 D2
Upper Astrop 43 H2
Upper Badcall 166 C5
Upper Basildon 29 H3
Upper Beeding 21 E4
Upper Benefield 57 H3
Upper Bentley 55 E5
Upper Bighouse 168 C4
Upper Boddington 56 C6
Upper Borth 51 G3
Upper Brailes 43 F2
Upper Breinton 40 D1
Upper Broadheath 54 D6
Upper Broughton 68 E4
Upper Bucklebury 29 H4
Upper Bullington 29 G6
Upper Burnhaugh 147 F4
Upper Caldecote 58 B7
Upper Camster 169 G5
Upper Catesby 56 D6
Upper Chapel 39 H1
Upper Chute 29 E5
Upper Clatford 29 F6
Upper Coberley 42 B4
Upper Cokeham 21 E5
Upper Cragabus 124 C6
Upper Dallachy 155 H2
Upper Dean 57 J5
Upper Denby 86 D6
Upper Derraid 155 E5
Upper Dicker 22 B5
Upper Dinchope 53 H3
Upper Dunsforth 95 F5
Upper Eathie 154 B2
Upper Elkstone 79 E6
Upper End 79 E4
Upper Farringdon 19 J2
Upper Framilode 41 G4
Upper Froyle 30 B6
Upper Gillock 169 H4
Upper Gills 169 H2
Upper Glenfintaig 142 E5
Upper Godney 26 D6
Upper Gravenhurst 45 F2
Upper Green 29 F4
Upper Hackney 79 G5
Upper Hale 30 C6
Upper Halling 33 G4
Upper Hambleton 69 H6
Upper Hardres Court 34 E5
Upper Hartfield 21 H2
Upper Haugh 80 B2
Upper Heath 54 A3
Upper Helmsley 96 B6
Upper Hergest 53 F6
Upper Heyford, Northnts 56 E6
Upper Heyford, Oxon 43 G3
Upper Hill 53 H6
Upper Hindhope 111 G2
Upper Hopton 86 C5
Upper Hulme 78 E5
Upper Inglesham 42 E6
Upper Killay 24 C1
Upper Kinsham 53 G5
Upper Knockando 155 F4
Upper Lambourn 29 F2
Upper Largo 130 D2
Upper Lochton 146 D4
Upper Longdon 67 F5
Upper Longwood 66 B6
Upper Ludstone 54 D2
Upper Maes-coed 40 C2
Upper Midhope 79 G2
Upper Milovaig 150 A4
Upper Minety 28 C1
Upper North Dean 44 C6
Upper Obney 137 H5
Upper Oddington 42 E3
Upper Olach 151 E5
Upper Poppleton 87 G1
Upper Quinton 55 G7
Upper Rochford 54 B5
Upper Sanday 171 F4
Upper Sapey 54 B5
Upper Seagry 28 B2
Upper Shelton 44 D1
Upper Sheringham 72 E2
Upper Skelmorlie 127 F6
Upper Slaughter 42 D3
Upper Soudley 41 F4
Upper Stoke 73 F6
Upper Stondon 45 F2
Upper Stowe 56 E6
Upper Street, Hants 18 C4
Upper Street, Norf NR11 73 F3
Upper Street, Norf NR12 73 G5
Upper Sundon 45 E3
Upper Swainswick 27 G4
Upper Swell 42 D3
Upper Tean 67 F3
Upper Tillyrie 129 J2
Upper Tooting 32 C3
Upper Tote 151 E3
Upper Tysoe 43 F1
Upper Upham 28 E3
Upper Wardington 56 C7
Upper Weald 44 B2
Upper Weedon 56 E6
Upper Wield 19 H2
Upper Winchendon 44 B4
Upper Woodford 18 C2
Upper Woolhampton 29 H4
Upper Wootton 29 H5
Uppermill 86 A6
Upperthong 86 C6
Upperton 20 C3
Uppertown 169 H2
UPPINGHAM 69 G7
Uppington 66 B6
Upsall 95 F3
Upsettlington 122 D3
Upsher Green 48 C1
Upshire 46 E5
Upstreet 35 F4
Upthorpe 60 C4
Upton, Bucks 44 B4
Upton, C of Peter 70 B6
Upton, Cambs 58 B4
Upton, Ches 77 G5
Upton, Corn 5 F3
Upton, Dorset 9 H4
Upton, Hants SO16 18 E4
Upton, Hants SP11 29 F5
Upton, Leic 68 B7
Upton, Lincs 81 F3
Upton, Mers 76 E3
Upton, Norf 73 G5
Upton, Northnts 57 F5
Upton, Notts DN22 80 E4
Upton, Notts NG23 80 E6
Upton, Oxon 29 H2
Upton, Slou 30 D3
Upton, Somer 15 F3
Upton, W Yorks 87 F5
Upton Bishop 41 F3
Upton Cheyney 27 F4
Upton Cressett 54 B2
Upton Cross 5 F3
Upton Grey 30 A6
Upton Hellions 14 E5
Upton Lovell 28 B6
Upton Magna 65 J5
Upton Noble 17 F2
Upton Pyne 15 F6
Upton St Leonards 41 H4
Upton Scudamore 27 H6
Upton Snodsbury 55 E6
Upton upon Severn 41 H1
Upton Warren 54 E5
Upwaltham 20 C4
Upware 59 F5
Upwell 71 F6
Upwey 9 E5
Upwood 58 C3
Uradale 176 D4
Urafirth 174 E3
Uragaig 125 A3
Urchfont 28 C5
Urdimarsh 53 J7
Ure 174 D3
Urgha 159 F3
Urlay Nook 104 D6
URMSTON 78 B2
Urquhart, Highl 153 H3
Urquhart, Mor 155 G2
Urra 95 G1
Urray 153 H3
Urswick 92 A4
Usan 139 G3
Ushaw Moor 104 B3
USK 40 C5
Uskmouth 26 C2
Usselby 82 C2
Utkinton 77 H5
Utley 86 B2
Uton 14 E6
Utterby 83 F2
UTTOXETER 67 F3
Uwchmynydd 62 B4
UXBRIDGE 31 E2
Uyeasound 177 C3
Uzmaston 36 D4

V

Vaila Hall 176 B3
Valley Truckle 4 E2
Valleyfield 129 H4
Valsgarth 177 D2
Valtos 151 E2
Vange 33 H2
Varteg 40 B5
Vatten 150 B4
Vaul 132 C4
Vaynol Hall 74 E5
Vaynor 39 H4
Veensgarth 176 D3
Velindre 40 A2
Vellow 15 G2
Veness 173 F4
Venn 6 D6
Venn Ottery 15 G6
Vennington 65 G6
Venny Tedburn 14 E6
VENTNOR 11 G6
Vernham Dean 29 F5
Vernham Street 29 F5
Vernolds Common 53 H3
Verwood 18 B5
Veryan 4 C7
Veryan Green 4 C6
Vicarage 15 J7
Vicarscross 77 G5
Vickerstown 91 C5
Victoria 4 C4
Vidlin 175 F4
Viewfield 121 G3
Viewpark 118 E1
Vigo Village 33 G4
Vinehall Street 22 D3
Vines Cross 22 B4
Virginia Water 30 E4
Virginstow 12 D6
Vobster 27 G6
Voe, Shetld ZE2 9PX 175 F4
Voe, Shetld ZE2 9RX 177 A5
Vowchurch 40 C2
Voxter 175 E3
Voy 170 C3

W

Waberthwaite 91 C2
Wackerfield 103 H5
Wacton 60 E2
Wadbister 175 F6
Wadborough 54 E7
Wadcrag 101 F5
Waddesdon 44 B4
Waddingham 81 G2
Waddington, Lancs 85 F2
Waddington, Lincs 81 G5
Waddington Aerodrome 81 G5
WADEBRIDGE 4 C3
Wadeford 16 B4
Wadenhoe 57 J3
Wadesmill 46 D4
Wadhurst 22 C2
Wadshelf 79 H4
Wadworth 80 C2
Waen 76 D5
Waen-fâch 65 F5
Wag 168 E7
Wagbeach 65 G6
Wainfleet All Saints 83 G6
Wainfleet Bank 83 G6
Wainfleet St Mary 83 H6
Wainfleet Tofts 83 G6
Wainhouse Corner 12 B6
Wainscott 33 H3
Wainstalls 86 B4
Waitby 102 D7
WAKEFIELD 86 E4
Wakerley 69 H7
Wakes Colne 48 B3
Walberswick 61 H4
Walberton 20 C5
Walcot, Lincs 70 A3
Walcot, Shrops 53 G3
Walcot, Tel & Wrek 66 A5
Walcot, Warw 55 G6
Walcote 56 D3
Walcott, Lincs 82 D6
Walcott, Norf 73 G3
Walden 94 B3
Walden Head 94 A3
Walden Stubbs 87 G5
Walderslade 33 H4
Walderton 20 A4
Walditch 8 C4
Waldley 67 G3
Waldridge 104 B2
Waldringfield 49 F1
Waldron 22 B4
Wales 80 B3
Walesby, Lincs 82 D2
Walesby, Notts 80 D4
Walford, Co of H HR9 41 E3
Walford, Co of H SY7 53 G4
Walford, Shrops 65 H4
Walgherton 66 B2
Walgrave 57 G4
Walk Mill 85 G3
Walkden 85 F6
Walker 113 G6
Walker Fold 85 E2
Walker's Green 53 J7
Walkerburn 120 C4
Walkeringham 80 E2
Walkerith 81 E2
Walkern 46 C3
Walkerville 94 D2
Walkhampton 6 B4
Walkington 88 E3
Wall, Northum 112 D6
Wall, Staffs 67 G6
Wall Bank 53 J2
Wall under Heywood 53 J2
Wallaceton 109 F4
Wallacetown, S Ayr KA26 106 E2
Wallacetown, S Ayr KA8 117 H5
WALLASEY 77 E2
WALLINGFORD 29 J2
WALLINGTON, G Lon 32 C4
Wallington, Hants 19 G5
Wallington, Herts 46 C2
Wallis 36 E3
Walliswood 20 E2
Wallridge 112 E5
Walls 174 D6
WALLSEND 113 G6
Wallyford 130 C5
Walmer 35 G5
Walmer Bridge 84 C4
Walmersley 85 G5
Walmley 55 G2
Walpole 61 G4
Walpole Cross Keys 71 F5
Walpole Highway 71 F5
Walpole St Andrew 71 F5
Walpole St Peter 71 E5
WALSALL 67 F7
Walsall Wood 67 F6
Walsden 85 H4
Walsgrave on Sowe 56 B3
Walsham Le Willows 60 D4
Walshford 87 F1
Walsoken 71 E6
Walston 119 H3
Walter's Ash 44 C6
Walterstone 40 C3
Waltham, Kent 34 E6
Waltham, NE Linc 89 G6
WALTHAM ABBEY 46 D5
Waltham Chase 19 G4
Waltham Cross 46 D5
Waltham on the Wolds 69 G4
Waltham St Lawrence 30 C3
WALTHAMSTOW 32 D2
Walton, Cumbr 110 E6
Walton, Derby 79 H5
Walton, Leic 56 D3
Walton, Mil Key 44 C2
Walton, Powys 53 F6
Walton, Somer 16 C2
Walton, Suff 49 G2
Walton, Tel & Wrek 66 A5
Walton, W Yorks 87 E5
Walton, W Yorks 87 F2
Walton, Warw 55 H6
WALTON -ON- THAMES 31 F4
Walton Cardiff 42 B2
Walton East 36 E3
Walton Highway 71 E5
Walton in Gordano 26 D3
Walton on the Hill 31 G5
Walton on the Wolds 68 D5
Walton West 36 C4
Walton-le-Dale 84 D4
WALTON-ON- THE-NAZE 49 F3
Walton-on-the-Hill 67 E4
Walton-on-Trent 67 H5
Walwen 76 E4
Walwick 112 D5
Walworth 104 B6
Walwyn's Castle 36 C4
Wambrook 16 A5
Wanborough 28 E2
WANDSWORTH 32 C3
Wangford, Suff IP27 59 H3
Wangford, Suff NR34 61 H4
Wanlip 68 D5
Wanlockhead 119 F6
Wannock 22 B5
Wansford, C of Peter 70 A7
Wansford, E Yorks 97 F6
WANSTEAD 32 E2
Wanstrow 27 G6
Wanswell 41 F5
WANTAGE 29 F2
Wapley 27 G3
Wappenbury 56 B5
Wappenham 56 E7
Warbleton 22 C4
Warborough 43 H6
Warboys 58 D4
Warbstow 12 C6
Warburton 78 B3
Warcop 102 D6
Ward Green 60 D5
Warden, Kent 34 D3
Warden, Northum 112 D6
Wardington 56 C7
Wardlaw 120 B6
Wardle, Ches 77 J6
Wardle, G Man 85 H5
Wardley 69 G6
Wardlow 79 F4
Wardy Hill 59 E3
WARE, Herts 46 D4
Ware, Kent 35 F4
WAREHAM 9 H5
Warehorne 23 F2
Waren Mill 123 G4
Warenford 123 G5
Warenton 123 G4
Wareside 46 D4
Waresley 58 C6
Warfield 30 C3
Wargrave 30 B3
Warham 72 C2
Wark, Northum NE48 112 C5
Wark, Northum TD12 122 D4
Warkleigh 14 C3
Warkton 57 G4
Warkworth 113 G2
Warlaby 94 E2
Warland 85 H4
Warleggan 5 E4
WARLINGHAM 32 D5
Warmfield 87 E4
Warmingham 78 B5
Warmington, Northnts 58 A2
Warmington, Warw 56 C7
WARMINSTER 27 H6
Warmlake 34 B5
Warmsworth 80 C1
Warmwell 9 F5
Warndon 54 D6
Warnford 19 H3
Warnham 21 E2
Warningcamp 20 D5
Warninglid 21 F3
Warren, Ches 78 C4
Warren, Pemb 36 D6
Warren Row 30 C2
Warren Street 34 C5
Warrington, Mil Key 57 G6
WARRINGTON, Warr 77 J3
Warsash 19 F5
Warse 169 H2
Warslow 79 E6
Warter 88 C1
Warthill 96 B6
Wartle 146 C3
Wartling 22 C5
Wartnaby 69 F4
Warton, Lancs LA5 92 C4
Warton, Lancs PR4 84 C4
Warton, Northum 112 E2
Warton, Warw 67 H6
WARWICK 55 H5
Warwick Bridge 102 A2
Warwick- on-Eden 102 A2
Wasbister 172 D3
Wasdale Head 101 F7
Washaway 4 D4
Washbourne 6 D5
Washbrook 48 E1
Washfield 15 F4
Washford 25 H6
Washford Pyne 14 E4
Washingborough 82 C4
WASHINGTON, T & W 104 C2
Washington, W Susx 20 E4
Wasing 29 H4
Waskerley 103 G3
Wasperton 55 H6
Wass 95 G4
WATCHET 25 H6
Watchfield, Oxon 28 E2
Watchfield, Somer 26 C6
Watchgate 92 D2
Watendlath 101 G6
Water 85 G4
Water End, Herts AL9 46 C5
Water End, Herts HP1 45 E4
Water Newton 58 B2
Water Orton 55 G2
Water Stratford 43 J2
Water Yeat 92 A3
Waterbeach 59 E5
Waterden 72 B3
Waterfall 79 E6
Waterfoot, Lancs 85 G4
Waterfoot, S Lanak 118 C2
Waterford 46 D4
Waterhead, Cumbr 92 B1
Waterhead, E Ayr 118 C6
Waterheads 120 B2
Waterhill of Bruxie 157 G4

Waterhouses, Durham 103 H3
Waterhouses, Staffs 79 E6
Wateringbury 33 G5
Waterlip 27 F6
Waterloo, Corn 4 E3
Waterloo, Mers 77 F2
Waterloo, N Lanak 119 F2
Waterloo, Norf 73 F5
Waterloo, Poole 10 B4
Waterloo, Pth & Kin 137 H5
Waterlooville 19 H5
Watermeetings 119 G6
Watermillock 101 J5
Waterperry 43 J5
Waterrow 15 G3
Waters Upton 66 B5
Watersfield 20 D4
Waterside, Aberd AB36 145 H2
Waterside, Aberd AB41 157 H6
Waterside, E Ayr KA3 118 B3
Waterside, E Ayr KA6 107 G2
Waterside, E Dunb 128 D5
Waterside, E Renf 118 C1
Waterstock 43 J5
Waterston 36 D5
Waterthorpe 80 B3
Waterybutts 138 B6
WATFORD, Herts 45 F6
Watford, Northnts 56 E5
Watford Gap 67 G6
Wath, N Yorks HG3 94 C5
Wath, N Yorks HG4 94 E4
WATH UPON DEARNE 80 B2
Watlington, Norf 71 G5
Watlington, Oxon 44 A6
Watnall 68 D2
Watten 169 G4
Wattisfield 60 D4
Wattisham 60 D6
Watton, E Yorks 88 E1
WATTON, Norf 72 C6
Watton at Stone 46 D4
Wattston 128 E5
Wattstown 39 H6
Wattsville 26 B1
Waunarlwydd 38 D6
Waunfawr 74 E6
Wavendon 44 D2
Waverbridge 101 G3
Waverton, Ches 77 G5
Waverton, Cumbr 101 G3
Wawne 89 E3
Waxham 73 H4
Waxholme 89 H4
Way Village 15 E4
Wayford 16 C5
Waytown 8 C4
Weachyburn 156 D3
Weald 43 F5
Wealdstone 31 F2
Weare 26 D5
Weare Giffard 13 E3
Wearhead 103 E4
Wearne 16 C3
Weasdale 93 E1
Weasenham All Saints 72 B4
Weasenham St Peter 72 B4
Weatheroak Hill 55 F4
Weaverham 77 J4
Weavering Street 33 H5
Weaverthorpe 97 E4
Webheath 55 F5
Webton Court 40 D2
Wedderlairs 157 F5
Weddington 56 B2
Wedges Mill 67 E6
Wedhampton 28 C5
Wedmore 26 D6
WEDNESBURY 55 E2
WEDNESFIELD 67 E6
Weecar 81 F5
Weedon 44 C4
Weedon Bec 56 E6
Weedon Lois 56 E7
Weeford 67 G6
Week 14 D4
Week St Mary 12 C6
Weekley 57 G3
Weel 88 E3
Weeley 48 E3
Weeley Heath 48 E3
Weem 137 F4
Weeping Cross 67 F4
Weeting 59 H3
Weeton, E Yorks 89 H4
Weeton, Lancs 84 B3
Weeton, N Yorks 86 D2
Weir 85 G4
Weirbrook 65 G4
Welbeck Abbey 80 C4
Welborne 72 D6
Welbourn 81 G6
Welburn 96 C5
Welbury 95 E1
Welby 69 H3
Welches Dam 59 E3
Welcombe 12 C4
Weldon 57 H3
Welford, Northnts 56 E3
Welford, W Berks 29 G3
Welford-on-Avon 55 G6
Welham, Leic 57 F2
Welham, Notts 80 E3
Welham Green 46 C5
Well, Hants 30 B6
Well, Lincs 83 G4
Well, N Yorks 94 D3
Well Hill 33 E4
Well Town 15 F5
Welland 41 G1
Wellbank 138 D5
Wellesbourne 55 H6
Welling 33 E3
WELLINGBOROUGH 57 G5
Wellingham 72 B4
Wellingore 81 G6
Wellington, Co of H 53 H7
WELLINGTON, Somer 15 H3
Wellington, Tel & Wrekr 66 B5
Wellington Heath 41 G1
Wellow, Bth 27 G5
Wellow, I of W 11 G6
Wellow, Notts 80 D5
Wellpond Green 46 B3
WELLS 27 E6
WELLS-NEXT-THE-SEA 72 C2
Wellsborough 68 B6
Wellwood 129 H4
Welney 59 F2
Welsh Bicknor 41 E4
Welsh End 65 J3
Welsh Frankton 65 G3
Welsh Hook 36 D3
Welsh Newton 40 D4
Welsh Newton Common 40 E4
Welsh St Donats 25 H3

Welshampton 65 H3
WELSHPOOL / TRALLWNG 65 F6
Welton, Cumbr 101 H3
Welton, E Yorks 88 D4
Welton, Lincs 82 C3
Welton, Northnts 56 D5
Welton le Marsh 83 G5
Welton le Wold 83 E3
Welwick 89 H4
Welwyn 46 C4
WELWYN GARDEN CITY 46 C4
Wem 65 J4
Wembdon 16 A2
WEMBLEY 31 F2
Wembury 6 B6
Wembworthy 14 C5
Wemyss Bay 127 F6
Wenallt 64 C2
Wendens Ambo 47 F2
Wendlebury 43 H4
Wendling 72 C5
WENDOVER 44 C5
Wendover Dean 44 C5
Wendron 3 E4
Wendy 58 D7
Wenhaston 61 H4
Wenlli 75 H5
Wennington, Cambs 58 C4
Wennington, G Lon 33 F2
Wennington, Lancs 93 E4
Wensley, Derby 79 G5
Wensley, N Yorks 94 B3
Wentbridge 87 F5
Wentnor 53 G2
Wentworth, Cambs 59 E4
Wentworth, S Yorks 79 H2
Wentworth, Surrey 30 D4
Wenvoe 25 J3
Weobley 53 H6
Weobley Marsh 53 H6
Wereham 71 G6
Wergs 66 D6
Wernheolydd 40 C4
Werrington, C of Peter 70 B6
Werrington, Corn 5 G2
Werrington, Staffs 67 E2
Wervin 77 G4
West Aberthaw 25 H4
West Acre 71 H5
West Allerdean 123 E3
West Alvington 6 D6
West Anstey 14 E3
West Ashby 83 E4
West Ashling 20 B5
West Ashton 27 H5
West Auckland 103 H5
West Bagborough 15 H2
West Barkwith 82 D3
West Barnby 105 H6
West Barns 131 F5
West Barsham 72 C3
West Bay 8 C4
West Beckham 72 E3
West Bennan 116 D5
West Bergholt 48 C3
West Bexington 8 D5
West Bilney 71 H5
West Blatchington 21 F5
West Bradford 85 F2
West Bradley 16 D2
West Bretton 86 D5
WEST BRIDGFORD 68 D3
WEST BROMWICH 55 F2
West Buckland, Devon 14 C2
West Buckland, Somer 15 H3
West Burrafirth 174 D5
West Burton, N Yorks 94 B3
West Burton, W Susx 20 C4
West Butterwick 88 C6
West Caister 73 J5
West Calder 119 H1
West Caldhame 138 D4
West Camel 16 D3
West Challow 29 F2
West Charleton 6 D6
West Chelborough 16 D5
West Chevington 113 G3
West Chiltington 20 D4
West Chiltington Common 20 D4
West Chinnock 16 C4
West Clandon 31 E5
West Cliffe 35 G6
West Clyne 165 E3
West Coker 16 D4
West Compton, Dorset 8 D4
West Compton, Somer 27 E6
West Cross 24 D2
West Curry 12 C6
West Curthwaite 101 H3
West Dean, Hants 18 D3
West Dean, W Susx 20 B6
West Deeping 70 B6
West Derby 77 G2
West Dereham 71 G6
West Ditchburn 123 G5
West Down 24 C6
WEST DRAYTON, G Lon 31 E3
West Drayton, Notts 80 E4
West Edington 113 F4
West End, Beds 57 H6
West End, E Yorks 88 D3
West End, Hants 19 F4
West End, N Som 26 D4
West End, Norf 73 J5
West End, Oxon 43 G5
West End, S Lanak 119 G3
West End, Surrey 30 D4
West End, Wilts 17 H3
West End Green 30 A4
West Farleigh 33 H5
West Felton 65 G4
West Firle 21 H5
West Fleetham 123 G5
West Ginge 29 G2
West Grafton 28 E4
West Green 30 B5
West Grinstead 21 E3
West Haddlesey 87 G4
West Haddon 56 E4
West Hagbourne 29 H2
West Hagley 54 E4
West Hall 111 G6
West Hallam 68 C2
West Halton 88 D4
WEST HAM 32 E2
West Handley 79 H4
West Hanney 43 G6
West Hanningfield 47 H6
West Hardwick 87 F3
West Harptree 27 E5
West Hatch 16 A3
West Heath, Hants GU14 30 C5
West Heath, Hants RG26 29 H5
West Helmsdale 165 G2

West Hendred 29 G2
West Heslerton 96 E4
West Hill 15 G6
West Hoathly 21 G2
West Holme 9 G5
West Horndon 33 G2
West Horrington 27 E6
West Horsley 31 E5
West Hougham 23 J1
West Houlland 174 D5
West Hyde 31 E1
West Hythe 23 H2
West Ilsley 29 G2
West Itchenor 20 A5
West Keal 83 F5
West Kennett 28 D4
West Kilbride 117 G3
West Kingsdown 33 F4
West Kington 27 H3
West Kirby 76 E3
West Knighton 9 F5
West Knoyle 17 G2
West Kyloe 123 F3
West Lambrook 16 C4
West Langdon 35 G6
West Langwell 164 C3
West Lavington, W Susx 20 B3
West Lavington, Wilts 28 C5
West Layton 103 H7
West Leake 68 D4
West Learmouth 122 D4
West Lexham 72 B5
West Lilling 96 B5
West Linton 119 J2
West Littleton 27 G3
West Looe 5 F5
West Luccombe 25 F6
West Lulworth 9 G5
West Lydford 16 D2
West Lyn 24 E6
West Lyng 16 B3
West Lynn 71 G5
West Mains, Northum 123 F3
West Mains, S Lanak 119 G3
West Malling 33 G5
West Malvern 54 C7
West Marden 20 A4
West Markham 80 E4
West Marton 85 G1
West Meon 19 H3
WEST MERSEA 48 D4
West Milton 8 D4
West Monkton 16 A3
West Moors 10 B3
West Mostard 93 F2
West Muir 139 E2
West Ness 96 B4
West Newton, E Yorks 89 F3
West Newton, Norf 71 G4
West Newton, Somer 16 A3
West Norwood 32 D3
West Ogwell 6 E4
West Orchard 17 G4
West Overton 28 D4
West Park 146 E4
West Parley 10 B4
West Peckham 33 G5
West Pennard 16 D2
West Pentire 3 F1
West Perry 58 B5
West Porlock 24 E6
West Putford 12 D4
West Quantoxhead 25 J6
West Rainton 104 C3
West Rasen 82 C3
West Raynham 72 B4
West Raynham Airfield 72 B4
West Rounton 95 F1
West Row 59 G4
West Rudham 72 B4
West Runton 73 E2
West Saltoun 130 D6
West Sandwick 177 B5
West Scrafton 94 B3
West Side, Blae. Gw 40 A5
West Side, Ork 173 F3
West Somerton 73 H5
West Stafford 9 F5
West Stockwith 81 E2
West Stoke 20 B5
West Stonesdale 93 G1
West Stoughton 26 D6
West Stour 17 F3
West Stourmouth 35 F4
West Stow 60 B4
West Stowell 28 D4
West Street 34 C5
West Tanfield 94 D4
West Tarbert 126 C6
West Thorney 20 A5
West Thurrock 33 F3
West Tilbury 33 G3
West Tisted 19 H3
West Tofts, Norf 60 B2
West Tofts, Pth & Kin 137 J5
West Torrington 82 D3
West Town 26 D4
West Tullyfergus 138 B4
West Tytherley 18 D3
West Walton 71 E5
West Wellow 19 E4
West Wemyss 130 C3
West Wick 26 C4
West Wickham, Cambs 59 G7
West Wickham, G Lon 32 D4
West Williamston 36 E5
West Winch 71 G5
West Winterslow 18 D2
West Wittering 20 A6
West Witton 94 B3
West Woodburn 112 C4
West Woodhay 29 F4
West Woodlands 27 G6
West Worldham 19 J2
West Worlington 14 D4
West Worthing 59 G4
West Wratting 59 G6
West Wycombe 44 C6
West Yell 177 B5
Westbere 35 E4
Westborough 69 G2
Westbourne, Bourne 10 B4
Westbourne, W Susx 20 A5
Westbrook 29 F4
Westbury, Bucks 43 J2
Westbury, Lincs 69 H4
Westbury, Shrops 65 G5
WESTBURY, Wilts 27 H5
Westbury Leigh 27 H5
Westbury-on-Severn 41 G4
Westbury-on-Trym 27 E3
Westbury-sub-Mendip 26 E5
Westby 84 B3
Westcliff-on-Sea 34 B2
Westcombe 17 E2

Westcote 42 E3
Westcott, Bucks 44 B4
Westcott, Devon 15 G5
Westcott, Surrey 31 F6
Westcott Barton 43 G3
Westdean 22 B6
Westdown Camp 28 C6
Wester Aberchalder 143 H1
Wester Balgedie 129 J2
Wester Dechmont 129 H5
Wester Denoon 138 C4
Wester Ellister 124 A5
Wester Fintray 147 F2
Wester Gruinards 164 B4
Wester Lealty 153 J1
Wester Main 153 G4
Wester Newburn 130 D2
Wester Ord 147 F3
Wester Quarff 176 D4
Wester Skeld 176 B3
Wester Watten 169 G4
Westerdale, Highl 169 F4
Westerdale, N Yorks 96 B1
Westerfield, Shetld 175 E5
Westerfield, Suff 60 E7
Westergate 20 C5
Westerham 33 E5
Westerleigh 27 G3
Westerton 139 F3
Westerwick 176 B3
Westfield, Co of H 54 C7
Westfield, E Susx 22 E4
Westfield, Highl 168 E3
Westfield, Norf 72 C6
Westfield, W Loth 129 G5
Westford 15 H3
Westgate, Durham 103 F4
Westgate, N Linc 88 B6
Westgate, Norf 72 C2
Westgate on Sea 35 G3
Westhall, Aberd 156 D6
Westhall, Suff 61 H3
Westham, E Susx 22 C5
Westham, Somer 26 D6
Westhampnett 20 B5
Westhay 26 D6
Westhead 84 C6
Westhide 41 E1
Westhill, Aberd 147 F3
Westhill, Highl 154 B4
Westhope, Co of H 53 H6
Westhope, Shrops 53 H3
Westhorpe, Lincs 70 C3
Westhorpe, Suff 60 D5
WESTHOUGHTON 85 E6
Westhouse 93 E4
Westhouses 80 B6
Westhumble 31 F5
Westing 177 C3
Westlake 6 C5
Westleigh, Devon EX16 15 G4
Westleigh, Devon EX39 13 E3
Westleton 61 H5
Westley, Shrops 65 G6
Westley, Suff 60 B5
Westley Waterless 59 G6
Westlinton 110 C6
Westmarsh 35 F4
Westmeston 21 G4
Westmill 46 D3
WESTMINSTER 32 D3
Westmuir 138 C3
Westness 172 D4
Westnewton, Cumbr 101 F3
Westnewton, Northum 122 E4
Weston, Bth 27 G4
Weston, Ches 78 B6
Weston, Dorset 9 E6
Weston, Halt 77 H3
Weston, Hants 19 J3
Weston, Herts 46 C2
Weston, Lincs 70 C4
Weston, N Yorks 86 C2
Weston, Northnts 56 D7
Weston, Notts 80 E5
Weston, S Lanak 119 H3
Weston, Shrops SY4 66 A4
Weston, Shrops TF13 54 A2
Weston, Staffs 67 F2
Weston, W Berks 29 F3
Weston Bampfylde 16 E3
Weston Beggard 41 E1
Weston by Welland 57 G2
Weston Colville 59 G6
Weston Green, Cambs 59 G6
Weston Green, Norf 72 E5
Weston Heath 66 C5
Weston Hills 70 C4
Weston in Gordano 26 D3
Weston Jones 66 C4
Weston Longville 72 E5
Weston Lullingfields 65 H4
Weston Patrick 30 A6
Weston Rhyn 65 F3
Weston Turville 44 C4
Weston under Penyard 41 F3
Weston under Wetherley 56 B5
Weston Underwood, Derby 67 H2
Weston Underwood, Mil Key 57 G6
Weston-on-the-Green 43 H4
Weston-on-Trent 68 C4
Weston-Sub-Edge 42 D7
WESTON-SUPER-MARE 26 C4
Weston-under-Lizard 66 D5
Westonbirt 27 H2
Westoning 45 E2
Westonzoyland 16 B2
Westow 96 C5
Westport, Arg & Bt 114 B4
Westport, Somer 83 F4
Westrigg 129 G6
Westruther 121 F3
Westry 70 D7
Westward 101 G3
Westward Ho! 13 E3
Westwell, Kent 34 C6
Westwell, Oxon 42 E5
Westwick, Cambs 58 E5
Westwick, Norf 73 F4
Westwood, Devon 15 G6
Westwood, Wilts 27 H5
Westwood Heath 55 H4
Westwoodside 80 E2
Wetheral 102 A2
WETHERBY 87 F2
Wetherden 60 D5
Wetheringsett 60 E5
Wethersfield 47 H2
Wetherup Street 60 E5
Wetherta 175 E4
Wetley Rocks 67 E2
Wettenhall 77 J5
Wetton 79 F6
Wetwang 96 E3
Wetwood 66 C3

Wexcombe 28 E5
Weybourne 72 E2
Weybread 61 F3
WEYBRIDGE 31 E4
Weydale 169 F3
Weyhill 29 F6
WEYMOUTH 9 E6
Whaddon, Bucks 44 C2
Whaddon, Cambs 58 D7
Whaddon, Glos 41 H4
Whaddon, Wilts 18 C3
Whale 102 B5
Whaley 80 C4
Whaley Bridge 78 E3
Whaley Thorns 80 C4
Whaligoe 169 H5
Whalley 85 F3
Whalton 113 F4
Wham 93 F5
Whaplode 70 D4
Whaplode Drove 70 D5
Whaplode St Catherine 70 D4
Wharfe 93 F5
Wharles 84 C3
Wharley End 44 D1
Wharncliffe Side 79 G2
Wharram le Street 96 D5
Wharton, Ches 78 A5
Wharton, Co of H 53 J6
Whashton 94 C1
Whatcombe 9 G3
Whatcote 43 F1
Whatfield 60 D7
Whatley 27 G6
Whatlington 22 D4
Whatstandwell 79 H6
Whatton 69 F3
Whauphill 99 F5
Whaw 94 A1
Wheatacre 61 H2
Wheathampstead 45 F4
Wheathill 54 B3
Wheatley, Hants 20 A2
Wheatley, Oxon 43 H5
Wheatley Hill 104 C4
Wheatley Lane 85 G3
Wheaton Aston 66 D5
Wheddon Cross 15 F2
Wheedlemont 156 B6
Wheelerstreet 30 D6
Wheelock 78 B6
Wheelock Heath 78 B6
Wheelton 84 E4
Wheen 145 H6
Wheldrake 87 H2
Whelford 42 D6
Whelpley Hill 44 D5
Whelston 76 E4
Whenby 95 H5
Whepstead 60 B6
Wherstead 48 E1
Wherwell 29 F6
Wheston 79 F4
Whetsted 33 G6
Whetstone 56 D2
Whicham 91 C3
Whichford 43 F2
WHICKHAM 113 G6
Whiddon Down 14 C6
Whigstreet 138 D4
Whilton 56 E5
Whimble 12 D5
Whimple 15 G6
Whimpwell Green 73 G4
Whin Lane End 84 B2
Whinburgh 72 D6
Whinnieliggate 100 B2
Whinnyfold 157 H5
Whippingham 11 G4
Whipsnade 44 E4
Whipton 15 F6
Whissendine 69 G5
Whissonsett 72 C4
Whistley Green 30 B3
Whiston, Mers 77 G2
Whiston, Northnts 57 G5
Whiston, S Yorks 80 B2
Whiston, Staffs ST10 67 F2
Whiston, Staffs ST19 66 D5
Whitacre Heath 55 H2
Whitbeck 91 C3
Whitbourne 54 C6
Whitburn, T & W 113 J6
WHITBURN, W Loth 129 G6
Whitby, Ches 77 F4
WHITBY, N Yorks 105 J6
Whitchurch, Bth 27 F4
Whitchurch, Bucks 44 C3
Whitchurch, Card 26 A3
Whitchurch, Co of H 41 E4
Whitchurch, Devon 5 H3
Whitchurch, Hants 29 G6
Whitchurch, Pemb 36 B3
WHITCHURCH, Shrops 65 J2
Whitchurch Canonicorum 8 B4
Whitchurch Hill 29 J3
Whitchurch-on-Thames 29 J3
Whitcombe 9 F5
Whitcott Keysett 53 F3
White Colne 48 B3
White Coppice 85 E5
White Cross 3 G2
White Kirkley 103 G4
White Lackington 9 F4
White Ladies Aston 54 E6
White Ness 176 C3
White Notley 47 H4
White Pit 83 F4
White Rocks 40 D3
White Roothing or White Roding 47 F4
White Waltham 30 C3
Whiteacen 155 G4
Whitebridge 143 G2
Whitebrook 41 E5
Whitecairn 98 D5
Whitecairns 147 G2
Whitecastle 119 H3
Whitechapel 84 D2
Whitecraig 130 C5
Whitecroft 41 F5
Whitecross, Falk 129 G5
Whitecross, Staffs 66 D4
Whiteface 164 C5
Whitefield, Aberd 157 E6
WHITEFIELD, G Man 85 G6
Whitefield, Highl 153 H6
Whitefield, Pth & Kin 138 A5
Whiteford 156 E6
Whitegate 77 J5
Whitehall 173 G4
Whitehall Village 173 G4
WHITEHAVEN 100 B6
Whitehill, Hants 20 A2
Whitehill, Kent 34 D5

Whitehill, Pemb 37 E5
Whitehills 156 D2
Whitehouse, Aberd 146 D3
Whitehouse, Arg & Bt 116 C1
Whitekirk 131 E4
Whitelackington 16 B4
Whiteleaf 44 C5
Whiteley Bank 11 G5
Whiteley Village 31 E4
Whiteleys 98 B4
Whitemans Green 21 G3
Whitemire 154 D3
Whitemoor 4 C5
Whiteparish 18 D3
Whiterashes 157 F5
Whiterow 169 H5
Whiteshill 41 H5
Whiteside, Northum 111 G6
Whiteside, W Loth 129 G6
Whitesmith 22 B4
Whitestaunton 16 A4
Whitestone 14 E6
Whiteway 42 B4
Whitewell, Aberd 157 G2
Whitewell, Lancs 85 E2
Whiteworks 6 C3
Whitewreath 155 G3
Whitfield, Kent 35 G6
Whitfield, Northnts 43 J2
Whitfield, Northum 102 D2
Whitfield, S Glos 27 F1
Whitford, Devon 8 A4
Whitford, Flint 76 D4
Whitgift 88 C4
Whitgreave 66 E4
WHITHORN 99 F5
Whiting Bay 117 E5
Whitland 37 F4
Whitletts 117 H5
Whitley, Ches 77 J4
Whitley, N Yorks 87 G4
Whitley, Rding 30 B3
Whitley, Wilts 27 H4
WHITLEY BAY 113 H5
Whitley Chapel 103 F2
Whitley Lower 86 D5
Whitley Row 33 E5
Whitlock's End 55 G4
Whitminster 41 H5
Whitmore 66 D2
Whitnage 15 G4
Whitnash 56 B5
Whitney-on-Wye 53 F7
Whitrigg, Cumbr CA5 1 101 G4
Whitrigg, Cumbr CA5 5 101 G3
Whitsbury 18 C4
Whitson 26 C2
WHITSTABLE 34 E4
Whitstone 12 C6
Whittingham 123 F6
Whittingslow 53 H3
Whittington, Derby 79 H4
Whittington, Glos 42 C3
Whittington, Lancs 92 E4
Whittington, Norf 71 H7
Whittington, Shrops 54 A4
Whittington, Staffs DY7 54 D3
Whittington, Staffs WS14 67 G6
Whittington, Worces 54 D6
Whittle-le-Woods 84 D4
Whittlebury 44 A1
WHITTLESEY 70 C7
Whittlesford 59 E7
Whitton, N Linc 88 D4
Whitton, Northum 112 E4
Whitton, Powys 53 F5
Whitton, Scot Bord 122 C5
Whitton, Shrops 54 A4
Whitton, Stock on T 104 C5
Whitton, Suff 60 E7
Whittonditch 29 E3
Whittonstall 103 G2
Whitway 29 G5
Whitwell, Derby 80 C4
Whitwell, Herts 45 F3
Whitwell, I of W 11 G6
Whitwell, N Yorks 94 D2
Whitwell, Rut 69 H6
Whitwell Street 72 E4
Whitwell-on-the-Hill 96 C5
Whitwick 68 C5
Whitwood 87 F4
WHITWORTH 85 G5
Whixall 65 J3
Whixley 95 F6
Whome 170 D5
Whorlton, Durham 103 H6
Whorlton, N Yorks 95 F1
Whygate 111 G5
Whyle 53 J5
Whyteleafe 32 D5
Wibdon 41 E6
Wibtoft 56 C3
Wichenford 54 C5
Wichling 34 C5
Wick, Bourne 10 C4
WICK, Highl 169 H4
Wick, S Glos 27 G3
Wick, Shetld 176 D4
Wick, V of Glam 25 G3
Wick, W Susx 20 D5
Wick, Worces 55 E7
Wick St Lawrence 26 C4
Wickam Street 59 H6
Wicken, Cambs 59 F4
Wicken, Northnts 44 B2
Wicken Bonhunt 47 E2
Wickenby 82 C3
Wickersley 80 B2
WICKFORD 47 H6
Wickham, Hants 19 G4
Wickham, W Berks 29 F3
Wickham Bishops 48 B4
Wickham Heath 29 G4
WICKHAM MARKET 61 G6
Wickham St Paul 48 B2
Wickham Skeith 60 D5
Wickham Street 60 D5
Wickhambreaux 35 F5
Wickhambrook 59 H6
Wickhamford 42 C1
Wickhampton 73 H6
Wicklewood 72 D6
Wickmere 72 E3
Wickwar 27 G2
Widdington 47 F2
Widdrington 113 G3
Widdrington Station 113 G3
Widecombe in the Moor 6 D3
Widegates 5 F5
Widemouth Bay 12 C5
Widewall 171 E5
Widford, Essex 47 G5
Widford, Herts 46 E4

Widmerpool Zennor

Widmerpool 68 E4
WIDNES 77 H3
Widworthy 15 J6
WIGAN 84 D6
Wiggaton 15 H6
Wiggenhall St Germans 71 F5
Wiggenhall St Mary Magdalen 71 F5
Wiggenhall St Mary the Virgin 71 F5
Wiggenhall St Peter 71 G5
Wigginton, Herts 44 D4
Wigginton, Oxon 43 F2
Wigginton, Staffs 67 H6
Wigginton, Yk 95 G6
Wigglesworth 93 G6
Wiggonby 101 G2
Wiggonholt 20 D4
Wighill 87 F2
Wighton 72 C3
Wigmore, Co of H 53 H5
Wigmore, Med 34 B4
Wigsley 81 F4
Wigsthorpe 57 J3
WIGSTON 68 E7
Wigthorpe 80 C3
Wigtoft 70 C3
Wigton 101 G3
WIGTOWN 99 F4
Wigtwizzle 79 G2
Wilbarston 57 G3
Wilberfoss 88 B1
Wilburton 59 E4
Wilby, Norf 60 D3
Wilby, Northnts 57 G5
Wilby, Suff 61 F4
Wilcot 28 D4
Wilcott 65 G5
Wilcove 5 H5
Wilcrick 26 D2
Wildboarclough 78 D5
Wilden, Beds 58 A6
Wilden, Worces 54 D4
Wildhern 29 F5
Wildhill 46 C5
Wildsworth 81 F2
Wildwood 67 E4
Wilford 68 D3
Wilkesley 66 B2
Wilkhaven 165 F5
Wilkieston 129 J6
Willand 15 G4
Willaston, Ches CW5 78 A6
Willaston, Ches L64 77 F4
Willen 44 C1
WILLENHALL, W Mids 67 E7
Willenhall, W Mids 56 B4
Willerby, E Yorks 88 E3
Willerby, N Yorks 97 F4
Willersey 42 D2
Willersley 53 G7
Willesborough Lees 34 D6
WILLESDEN 31 G2
Willett 15 H2
Willey, Shrops 66 B7
Willey, Warw 56 C3
Williamscot 56 C7
Willian 45 G2
Willimontswick 111 G6
Willingale 47 F5
Willingdon 22 B5
Willingham 58 E4
Willingham by Stow 81 F3
Willington, Beds 58 B7
Willington, Derby 67 H4
WILLINGTON, Durham 103 H4
Willington, T & W 113 H6
Willington, Warw 42 E2
Willington Corner 77 H5
Willisham Tye 60 D6
Willitoft 88 B3
Williton 25 H6
Willoughby, Lincs 83 G4
Willoughby, Warw 56 D5
Willoughby Waterleys 56 D2
Willoughby-on-the-Wolds 68 E4
Willoughton 81 G2
Wilmcote 55 G6
Wilmington, Devon 15 J6
Wilmington, E Susx 22 B5
Wilmington, Kent 33 F3
WILMSLOW 78 C3
Wilnecote 67 H6
Wilpshire 85 E3
Wilsden 86 B3
Wilsford, Lincs 69 J2
Wilsford, Wilts SN9 28 D5
Wilsford, Wilts SP4 18 C2
Wilsill 94 C5
Wilson 68 C4
Wilsontown 119 G2
Wilstead 45 E1
Wilsthorpe 70 A5
Wilstone 44 D4
Wilton, N Yorks 96 D3
Wilton, Red & Clev 104 E6
Wilton, Wilts SN8 28 E4
WILTON, Wilts SP2 18 B2
Wilton Dean 120 E6
Wimbish 47 F2
Wimbish Green 47 G2
Wimblebury 67 F5
WIMBLEDON 32 C3
Wimblington 58 E2
WIMBORNE MINSTER 10 B4
Wimborne St Giles 18 B4
Wimbotsham 71 G6
Wimpstone 55 H7
WINCANTON 17 F3
Wincham 78 A4
Winchburgh 129 H5
Winchcombe 42 C3
Winchelsea 23 F4
Winchelsea Beach 23 F4
WINCHESTER 19 F3
Winchet Hill 33 H6
Winchfield 30 B5
Winchmore Hill, Bucks 44 D6
Winchmore Hill, G Lon 46 D6
Wincle 78 D5
WINDERMERE 92 C2
Winderton 43 F1
Windhill 153 H4
Windhouse 177 B4
Windlesham 30 D4
Windley 67 J2
Windmill Hill, E Susx 22 C4
Windmill Hill, Somer 16 B4
Windrush 42 D4
WINDSOR 30 D3
Windy-Yett 118 B2
Windygates 130 C2
Windyridge 68 E4
Windywalls 172 E1
Wineham 21 F3
Winestead 89 H4
Winfarthing 60 E3
Winford, I of W 11 G5
Winford, N Som 27 E4
Winforton 53 G7
Winfrith Newburgh 9 G5
Wing, Bucks 44 C3
Wing, Rut 69 G6
Wingate 104 D4
Wingates, G Man 85 E6
Wingates, Northum 113 E3
Wingerworth 79 H5
Wingfield, Beds 44 E3
Wingfield, Suff 61 F4
Wingfield, Wilts 27 H5
Wingham 35 F5
Wingmore 35 E6
Wingrave 44 C4
Winkburn 80 E6
Winkfield 30 D3
Winkfield Row 30 C3
Winkhill 79 E6
Winkleigh 13 G5
Winksley 94 D4
Winkton 10 C4
Winless 169 H4
Winmarleigh 84 C2
Winnersh 30 B3
Winscales 100 E5
Winscombe 26 D5
WINSFORD, Ches 77 J5
Winsford, Somer 15 F2
Winsham 16 B5
Winshill 67 H4
Winskill 102 B4
Winslade 30 A6
Winsley 27 H4
Winslow 44 B3
Winson 42 C5
Winsor 18 E4
Winster, Cumbr 92 C2
Winster, Derby 79 G5
Winston, Durham 103 H6
Winston, Suff 61 E5
Winstone 42 B5
Winswell 13 E4
Winterborne Came 9 F5
Winterborne Clenston 9 G3
Winterborne Herringston 9 E5
Winterborne Houghton 17 G5
Winterborne Kingston 9 G4
Winterborne Monkton 9 E5
Winterborne Stickland 17 G5
Winterborne Whitechurch 9 G3
Winterborne Zelston 9 G4
Winterbourne, S Glos 27 F2
Winterbourne, W Berks 29 G3
Winterbourne Abbas 8 E4
Winterbourne Bassett 28 D3
Winterbourne Dauntsey 18 C2
Winterbourne Earls 18 C2
Winterbourne Gunner 18 C2
Winterbourne Monkton 28 D3
Winterbourne Steepleton 8 E5
Winterbourne Stoke 28 C6
Winterburn 93 H6
Winteringham 88 D4
Winterley 78 B6
Wintersett 87 E5
Wintershill 19 G4
Winterton 88 D5
Winterton-on-Sea 73 H5
Winthorpe, Lincs 83 H5
Winthorpe, Notts 81 F6
Winton, Bourne 10 B4
Winton, Cumbr 102 D6
Wintringham 96 D4
Winwick, Cambs 58 B3
Winwick, Northnts 56 E4
Winyates 55 F5
WIRKSWORTH 79 G6
Wirswall 65 J2
WISBECH 71 E6
Wisbech St Mary 70 E6
Wisborough Green 20 D3
Wiseton 80 E3
WISHAW, N Lanak 119 E2
Wishaw, Warw 55 G2
Wisley 31 E5
Wispington 82 E4
Wissett 61 G4
Wissington 48 C2
Wistanstow 53 H3
Wistanswick 66 B4
Wistaston 78 A6
Wistaston Green 78 A6
Wiston, Pemb 36 E4
Wiston, S Lanak 119 G4
Wiston, W Susx 21 E4
Wistow, Cambs 58 C3
Wistow, N Yorks 87 G3
Wiswell 85 F3
Witcham 59 E4
Witchampton 17 H5
Witchford 59 F4
Witcombe 16 C3
WITHAM 48 B4
Witham Friary 27 G6
Witham on the Hill 69 J5
Withcall 83 E3
Witherenden Hill 22 C3
Witheridge 14 E4
Witherley 68 B7
Withern 83 G3
WITHERNSEA 89 H4
Withernwick 89 F2
Withersdale Street 61 F3
Withersfield 59 G7
Witherslack 92 C3
Withiel 4 C4
Withiel Florey 15 F2
Withington, Co of H 41 E1
Withington, G Man 78 C2
Withington, Glos 42 C4
Withington, Shrops 66 A5
Withington, Staffs 67 F3
Withington Green 78 C4
Withleigh 15 F4
Withnell 85 E4
Withybrook 56 C3
Withycombe 25 H6
Withyham 21 H2
Withypool 14 E2
Witley 20 C2
Witnesham 61 E6
WITNEY 43 F4
Wittering 70 A6
Wittersham 23 E3
Witton 146 C6
Witton Bridge 73 G3
Witton Gilbert 104 B3
Witton Park 103 H4
Witton- le-Wear 103 H4
Wiveliscombe 15 G3
Wivelsfield 21 G3
Wivelsfield Green 21 G4
WIVENHOE 48 D3
Wiveton 72 D2
Wix 48 E3
Wixford 55 F6
Wixoe 47 H1
Woburn 44 D2
Woburn Sands 44 D2
WOKING 30 E5
WOKINGHAM 30 C4
Wold Newton, E Yorks 97 F4
Wold Newton, NE Linc 83 E2
Woldingham 32 D5
Woldingham Garden Village 32 D5
Wolf's Castle 36 D3
Wolfclyde 119 H4
Wolferlow 54 B5
Wolferton 71 G4
Wolfhill 138 A5
Wolfsdale 36 D3
Woll 120 D5
Wollaston, Northnts 57 H5
Wollaston, Shrops 65 G5
Wollerton 66 B3
Wolsingham 103 G4
Wolston 56 C4
Wolvercote 43 G5
WOLVERHAMPTON 66 E7
Wolverley, Shrops 65 H3
Wolverley, Worces 54 D4
Wolverton, Hants 29 H5
Wolverton, Mil Key 44 C1
Wolverton, Warw 55 H5
Wolvesnewton 40 D6
Wolvey 56 C3
Wolvey Heath 56 C3
Wolviston 104 D5
Wombleton 96 B3
Wombourne 54 D2
Wombwell 87 F6
Womenswold 35 F5
Womersley 87 G5
Wonastow 40 D4
Wonersh 30 E6
Wonson 14 C7
Wonston, Dorset 17 F5
Wonston, Hants 19 F2
Wooburn 30 D2
Wooburn Green 30 D2
Wood Burcote 57 E7
Wood Dalling 72 D4
Wood End, Beds 57 J7
Wood End, Herts 46 D3
Wood End, Warw B94 55 G4
Wood End, Warw CV9 67 H7
Wood Enderby 83 E5
WOOD GREEN 32 D1
Wood Lanes 78 D3
Wood Norton 72 D4
Wood Street 30 D5
Wood Street Village 30 D5
Woodale 94 B4
Woodbastwick 73 G5
Woodbeck 80 E4
Woodborough, Notts 68 E2
Woodborough, Wilts 28 D5
WOODBRIDGE 61 F7
Woodbury 7 G2
Woodbury Salterton 15 G7
Woodchester 41 H5
Woodchurch 23 F2
Woodcote, Oxon 29 J2
Woodcote, Tel & Wrek 66 C5
Woodcroft 41 E6
Woodcutts 17 H4
Woodditton 59 G6
Woodeaton 43 H4
Woodend, Aberd 146 D2
Woodend, Cumbr 91 C2
Woodend, Fife 130 B3
Woodend, Northnts 56 E7
Woodend, W Susx 20 B5
Woodfalls 18 C3
Woodford, Corn 12 C4
Woodford, Devon 6 D5
WOODFORD, G Lon 32 D1
Woodford, G Man 78 C3
Woodford, Glos 41 F6
Woodford, Northnts 57 H4
Woodford Bridge 32 E1
Woodford Green 32 E1
Woodford Halse 56 D6
Woodgate, Norf 72 D5
Woodgate, W Mids 55 E3
Woodgate, W Susx 20 C5
Woodgate, Worces 55 E5
Woodgate Valley 55 F3
Woodgreen 18 C4
Woodhall 93 H2
WOODHALL SPA 82 D5
Woodham 31 E4
Woodham Ferrers 47 H6
Woodham Mortimer 48 B5
Woodham Walter 48 B5
Woodhaven 138 D6
Woodhead 157 E5
Woodhill 54 C3
Woodhorn 113 G4
Woodhouse, Cumbr 92 D3
Woodhouse, Leic 68 D5
Woodhouse, S Yorks 80 B3
Woodhouse Eaves 68 D5
Woodhouselee 130 B6
Woodhouses, Cumbr 101 H2
Woodhouses, Staffs 67 G5
Woodhurst 58 D4
Woodingdean 21 G5
Woodland, Devon 6 D4
Woodland, Durham 103 G5
Woodlands, Aberd 147 E4
Woodlands, Dorset 18 B5
Woodlands, G Lon 33 E4
Woodlands, Hants 18 F4
Woodlands Park 30 C3
Woodlands St Mary 29 F3
Woodleigh 6 D6
Woodlesford 87 E4
Woodley 30 B3
Woodmancote, Glos GL52 42 B3
Woodmancote, Glos GL7 42 C5
Woodmancote, W Susx BN5 21 F4
Woodmancote, W Susx PO10 20 A5
Woodmancott 29 H6
Woodmansey 88 E3
Woodmansterne 32 C5
Woodminton 18 B3
Woodnesborough 35 G5
Woodnewton 57 J2
Woodplumpton 84 D3
Woodrising 72 C6
Woodseaves, Shrops 66 B3
Woodseaves, Staffs 66 C4
Woodsend 28 E3
Woodsetts 80 C3
Woodsford 9 F4
Woodside, B For 30 D3
Woodside, Fife 130 D2
Woodside, Herts 46 C5
Woodside, Pth & Kin 138 B5
WOODSTOCK 43 G4
Woodthorpe, Derby 80 B4
Woodthorpe, Leic 68 D5
Woodton 61 F2
Woodtown, Devon EX39 4 13 E3
Woodtown, Devon EX39 5 13 E3
Woodville, Ang 139 F4
Woodville, Derby 68 B5
Woodwalton 58 C3
Woodyates 18 B4
Woofferton 53 J5
Wookey 26 E6
Wookey Hole 27 E6
Wool 9 G5
Woolacombe 24 B6
Woolage Green 35 F6
Woolaston 41 E6
Woolavington 26 C6
Woolbeding 20 B3
Wooler 123 E5
Woolfardisworthy 14 E5
Woolfardisworthy or Woolsery 12 D3
Woolfords Cottages 119 H2
Woolhampton 29 H4
Woolhope 41 F2
Woolland 17 F5
Woollaton 13 E4
Woolley, Bth 27 G4
Woolley, Cambs 58 B4
Woolley, W Yorks 86 E5
Woolmer Green 46 C4
Woolmere Green 55 E5
Woolpit 60 C5
Woolscott 56 C5
Woolsington 113 F5
Woolstaston 65 H7
Woolsthorpe by Belvoir 69 G3
Woolsthorpe-by-Colsterworth 69 H4
Woolston, C of Soton 19 F4
Woolston, Devon 6 D6
Woolston, Shrops SY10 65 G4
Woolston, Shrops SY6 53 H3
Woolston, Warr 77 J3
Woolston Green 6 D4
Woolstone, Mil Key 44 C2
Woolstone, Oxon 29 E2
Woolton 77 G3
Woolton Hill 29 G4
Woolverstone 49 E2
Woolverton 27 G5
WOOLWICH 33 E3
Woolwich Ferry 33 E3
Woonton 53 G6
Wooperton 123 F5
Woore 66 C2
Wootton, Beds 57 J7
Wootton, Dorset 8 B4
Wootton, Hants 10 D4
Wootton, Kent 35 F6
Wootton, N Linc 89 E5
Wootton, Northnts 57 F6
Wootton, Oxon OX1 43 G5
Wootton, Oxon OX20 43 G4
Wootton, Shrops 53 H4
Wootton, Staffs DE6 67 G2
Wootton, Staffs ST21 66 D4
WOOTTON BASSETT 28 C2
Wootton Bridge 11 G4
Wootton Common 11 G4
Wootton Courtenay 25 G6
Wootton Fitzpaine 8 B4
Wootton Rivers 28 D4
Wootton St Lawrence 29 H5
Wootton Wawen 55 G5
WORCESTER 54 D6
Worcester Park 32 C4
Wordsley 54 D3
Wordwell 60 B4
Worfield 54 C2
Work 171 E3
WORKINGTON 100 E5
WORKSOP 80 C4
Worlaby 88 E5
World's End 29 G3
Worlds End 19 H4
Worle 26 C4
Worleston 77 J6
Worlingham 61 H3
Worlington, Devon 14 D4
Worlington, Suff 59 G4
Worlingworth 61 F5
Wormbridge 40 D2
Wormegay 71 G5
Wormelow Tump 40 D2
Wormhill 79 F4
Wormiehills 139 F5
Wormingford 48 C2
Worminghall 43 J5
Wormington 42 C2
Worminster 27 E6
Wormit 138 C6
Wormleighton 56 C6
Wormley, Herts 46 D5
Wormley, Surrey 20 C2
Wormley West End 46 D5
Wormshill 34 B5
Wormsley 53 H7
Worplesdon 30 D5
Worrall 79 H2
WORSBROUGH 87 E6
Worsley 78 B1
Worstead 73 G4
Worsthorne 85 G3
Worston 85 F2
Worth, Kent 35 G5
Worth, W Susx 21 F2
Worth Abbey 21 G2
Worth Matravers 9 H6
Wortham 60 D4
Worthen 65 G6
Worthenbury 65 H2
Worthing, Norf 72 D5
WORTHING, W Susx 21 E5
Worthington 68 C4
Wortley, Glos 27 G1
Wortley, S Yorks 79 H2
Worton 28 B5
Wortwell 61 F3
Wotherton 65 F6
Wotter 6 B4
Wotton 31 F6
Wotton Underwood 44 A4
Wotton-under- Edge 41 G6
Woughton on the Green 44 C2
Wouldham 33 H4
Wrabness 48 E2
Wrafton 13 E2
Wragby, Lincs 82 D4
Wragby, W Yorks 87 F5
Wramplingham 72 E6
Wrangham 156 D5
Wrangle 83 G6
Wrangle Bank 83 G6
Wrangle Lowgate 83 G6
Wrangway 15 H4
Wrantage 16 B3
Wrawby 88 E6
Wraxall, Dorset 8 D3
Wraxall, N Som 26 D3
Wraxall, Somer 16 E2
Wray 93 E5
Wraysbury 30 E3
Wrea Green 84 B3
Wreay, Cumbr CA11 101 J5
Wreay, Cumbr CA4 101 J3
Wrekenton 113 G7
Wrelton 96 C3
Wrenbury 66 A2
Wrenbury Heath 66 B2
Wreningham 72 E7
Wrentham 61 H3
Wressle, E Yorks 87 J3
Wressle, N Linc 88 D6
Wrestlingworth 58 C7
Wretham 60 C2
Wretton 71 G7
WREXHAM 77 F6
Wrexham Street 30 D2
Wribbenhall 54 C4
Wrightington Bar 84 D5
Wrinehill 66 C2
Wrington 26 D4
Writtle 47 G5
Wrockwardine 66 B5
Wroot 87 J6
Wrotham 33 G5
Wrotham Heath 33 G5
Wrotham Park 46 C6
Wroughton 28 D2
Wroxall, I of W 11 G6
Wroxall, Warw 55 H4
Wroxeter 66 A6
Wroxham 73 F5
Wroxton 43 G1
Wyaston 67 G2
Wyatt's Green 47 F6
Wyberton 70 D2
Wyboston 58 B6
Wybunbury 78 B7
Wych Cross 21 H2
Wychbold 54 E5
Wyche 41 G1
Wyck 20 A2
Wyck Rissington 42 D3
Wycliffe 103 H6
Wycoller 85 H3
Wycombe Marsh 30 C1
Wyddial 46 D2
Wye 34 D6
Wyke, Dorset 17 F3
Wyke, Shrops 66 B6
Wyke, W Yorks 86 C4
Wyke Regis 9 E6
Wykeham, N Yorks YO13 97 E3
Wykeham, N Yorks YO17 96 D4
Wyken 54 C2
Wykey 65 G4
Wylam 113 F6
Wylde Green 55 G2
Wyllie 40 A6
Wylye 18 B2
Wymering 19 H5
Wymeswold 68 E4
Wymington 57 H5
Wymondham, Leic 69 G5
WYMONDHAM, Norf 72 E6
Wyndham 25 G1
Wynford Eagle 8 D4
Wyng 170 D5
Wynyard Village 104 D5
Wyre Piddle 55 E7
Wysall 68 E4
Wythall 55 F4
Wytham 43 G5
Wyverstone 60 D5
Wyverstone Street 60 D5
Wyville 69 G4

Y

Y BALA 64 C3
Y Fan 52 C3
Y Felinheli 74 E5
Y Ferwig 50 B7
Y Ffôr 62 D3
Yaddlethorpe 88 C6
Yafford 11 F5
Yafforth 94 E2
Yalding 33 G5
Yanworth 42 C4
Yapham 88 B1
Yapton 20 C5
Yarburgh 83 F2
Yarcombe 15 J5
Yardley 55 G3
Yardley Gobion 44 B1
Yardley Hastings 57 G6
Yardro 53 F6
Yarkhill 41 F1
Yarlet 66 E4
Yarley 26 E6
Yarlington 17 E3
Yarm 104 D6
Yarmouth 10 E5
Yarnbrook 27 H5
Yarnfield 66 D3
Yarnscombe 13 F3
Yarnton 43 G4
Yarpole 53 H5
Yarrow 120 C5
Yarrow Feus 120 C5
Yarrowford 120 D4
Yarsop 53 H7
Yarwell 70 A7
YATE 27 G2
Yateley 30 C4
Yatesbury 28 C3
Yattendon 29 H3
Yatton, Co of H 53 H5
Yatton, N Som 26 D4
Yatton Keynell 27 H3
Yaverland 11 H5
Yaxham 72 D5
Yaxley, Cambs 58 B2
Yaxley, Suff 60 E4
Yazor 53 H7
Yeading 31 F2
YEADON 86 D2
Yealand Conyers 92 D4
Yealand Redmayne 92 C4
Yealmpton 6 B5
Yearby 105 F5
Yearsley 95 G4
Yeaton 65 H5
Yeaveley 67 G2
Yedingham 96 D4
Yelden 57 J5
Yelford 43 F5
Yelland 13 E2
Yelling 58 C5
Yelvertoft 56 D4
Yelverton, Devon 6 B4
Yelverton, Norf 73 F6
Yenston 17 F3
Yeo Mill 14 E3
Yeoford 14 D6
Yeolmbridge 5 G2
YEOVIL 16 D4
Yeovil Marsh 16 D4
Yeovilton 16 D3
Yerbeston 37 E5
Yesnaby 170 C3
Yetlington 112 E2
Yetminster 16 D4
Yettington 7 G2
Yetts o' Muckhart 129 H2
Yieldshields 119 F2
YIEWSLEY 31 E2
Yinstay 171 F3
Ynysboeth 39 H6
Ynysddu 26 A1
Ynyshir 25 H1
Ynyslas 51 G2
Ynyswen 39 F4
Ynysybwl 39 H6
Yockenthwaite 93 H4
Yockleton 65 G5
Yokefleet 88 C4
Yoker 128 C6
Yonder Bognie 156 C4
YORK 87 H1
Yorkletts 34 D4
Yorkley 41 F5
Yorton 65 J4
Youlgreave 79 G5
Youlstone 12 C4
Youlthorpe 96 C6
Youlton 95 F5
Young's End 47 H4
Yoxall 67 G5
Yoxford 61 G5
Ysbyty Cynfyn 51 H4
Ysbyty Ifan 64 B2
Ysbyty Ystwyth 51 H4
Ysceifiog 76 D4
Ystalyfera 38 E5
Ystrad 39 G6
Ystrad Aeron 51 F6
YSTRAD MYNACH 39 J6
Ystradfellte 39 G4
Ystradffin 51 H7
Ystradgynlais 39 E4
Ystradmeurig 51 H5
Ystradowen, Carm 38 E4
Ystradowen, V of Glam 25 H3
Ystumtuen 51 H4
Ythanbank 157 G5
Ythanwells 156 D5
Ythsie 157 F5

Z

Zeal Monachorum 14 D5
Zeals 17 F2
Zelah 3 G2
Zennor 2 C4

English Heritage and National Trust properties

English Heritage

London

1 Albert Memorial 23 H5
2 Chapter House, Pyx Chamber and Abbey Museum 23 F5
3 Chiswick House 23 G5
4 Coombe Conduit 23 G6
5 Eltham Palace 23 K5
6 Jewel Tower 23 H5
7 Kenwood 23 H4
8 London Wall 23 J4
9 Marble Hill House 23 G5
10 Ranger's House 23 J5
11 Winchester Palace 23 J5

South East

12 Abingdon County Hall 21 J3
13 Appuldurcombe House 7 K7
14 Battle Abbey and Battlefield 16 E4
15 Bayham Old Abbey 16 D2
16 Bishop's Waltham Palace 13 H4
17 Boxgrove Priory 14 C5
18 Bramber Castle 15 F4
19 Calshot Castle 13 G5
20 Camber Castle 17 G4
21 Carisbrooke Castle 7 J6
22 Conduit House 25 H7
23 Deal Castle 25 K7
24 Deddington Castle 33 G6
25 Donnington Castle 21 J6
26 Dover Castle 17 L1
27 Down House 23 K6
28 Dymchurch Martello Tower 17 J3
29 Eynsford Castle 23 L6
30 Farnham Castle Keep 14 B1
31 Faversham: Stone Chapel 25 F6
32 Flowerdown Barrows 13 G2
33 Fort Brockhurst 13 J5
34 Fort Cumberland 13 J6
35 Horne's Place Chapel 17 G2
36 Hurst Castle 13 F7
37 King James's and Landport Gates 13 J6
38 Kit's Coty House and Little Kit's Coty House 24 D7
39 Knights Templar Church 17 L1
40 Lullingstone Roman Villa 23 L6
41 Maison Dieu 25 F6
42 Medieval Merchant's House 13 G4
43 Milton Chantry 24 C6
44 Minster Lovell Hall and Dovecote 21 H1
45 Netley Abbey 13 G5
46 North Hinksey Conduit House 21 J2
47 North Leigh Roman Villa 21 J1
48 Northington Grange 13 H2
49 Old Soar Manor 24 C7
50 Osborne House 7 K5
51 Pevensey Castle 16 D5
52 Portchester Castle 13 J5
53 Reculver Towers and Roman Fort 25 J6
54 Richborough Roman Amphitheatre 25 K7
55 Richborough Castle, Roman Fort 25 K6
56 Rochester Castle 24 D6
57 Rollright Stones 32 E6
58 Royal Garrison Church 13 J6
59 Rycote Chapel 22 B2
60 St Augustine's Abbey 25 H7
61 St Augustine's Cross 25 K6
62 St Catherine's Oratory 7 J7
63 St John's Commandery 17 K1
64 St Leonard's Tower 24 C7
65 Silchester Roman City Walls and Amphitheatre 22 B6
66 Stone Chapel Sutton Valence Castle 16 F1
67 Temple Manor 24 D6
68 Titchfield Abbey 13 H5
69 Uffington Castle, White Horse and Dragon Hill 21 G4
70 Upnor Castle 24 D5
71 Walmer Castle and Gardens 25 K7
72 Waverley Abbey 14 B1
73 Wayland's Smithy 21 G4
74 Western Heights 17 L1
75 Wolvesey Castle (Old Bishop's Palace) 13 G3
76 Yarmouth Castle 13 F7

South West

77 Abbotsbury Abbey Remains 11 G7
78 Alexander Keiller Museum, Avebury 20 E6
79 Avebury Avebury Stone Circles 20 F5
80 Ballowall Barrow 2 B6
81 Bant's Carn Burial Chamber and Halangy Down Ancient Village 2 P2
82 Bayard's Cove Fort 5 J4
83 Belas Knap Long Barrow 32 C7
84 Berry Pomeroy Castle 5 J3
85 Blackbury Camp 10 C6
86 Blackfriars 20 C1
87 Bowhill 73 K2
88 Bradford-on-Avon Tithe Barn 20 C6
89 Bratton Camp and White Horse 20 D7
90 Butter Cross 10 A1
91 Carn Euny Ancient Village 2 C7
92 Chisbury Chapel 21 G6
93 Christchurch Castle and Norman House 12 D6
94 Chysauster Ancient Village 2 C6
95 Cirencester 20 E2
96 Cleeve Abbey 10 B1
97 Cromwell's Castle 2 N2
98 Dartmouth Castle 5 J4
99 Daws Castle 10 B1
100 Dupath Well 4 D3
101 Farleigh Hungerford Castle 20 B7
102 Fiddleford Manor 11 K4
103 Gallox Bridge 10 A1
104 Garrison Walls 2 P2
105 Glastonbury Tribunal 11 F2
106 Great Witcombe Roman Villa 20 D1
107 Greyfriars 20 C1
108 Grimspound 9 H7
109 Hailes Abbey 32 C7
110 Halliggye Fogou 2 F7
111 Harry's Walls 2 F2
112 Hatfield Earthworks 20 F7
113 Hound Tor Deserted Medieval Village 5 H1
114 Hurlers Stone Circles 4 C2
115 Innisidgen Lower and Upper Burial Chambers 2 P2
116 Jordan Hill Roman Temple 11 H7
117 King Charles's Castle 2 N2
118 King Doniert's Stone 4 C3
119 Kingston Russell Stone Circle 11 G7
120 Kingswood Abbey Gatehouse 20 B3
121 Kirkham House 5 J3
122 Knowlton Church and Earthworks 12 C4
123 Launceston Castle 8 D7
124 Leigh Barton 5 H5
125 Ludgershall Castle and Cross 12 E1
126 Lulworth Castle 11 K7
127 Lydford Castles and Saxon Town 8 F7
128 Maiden Castle 11 H7
129 Meare Fish House 11 F1
130 Merrivale Prehistoric Settlement 4 F2
131 Muchelney Abbey 11 F3
132 Netheravon Dovecote 12 D1
133 The Nine Stones 11 H6
134 Notgrove Long Barrow 32 C7
135 Nunney Castle 11 J1
136 Nympsfield Long Barrow 20 B2
137 Odda's Chapel 32 A7
138 Offa's Dyke 19 K3
139 Okehampton Castle 9 F6
140 Old Blockhouse 2 P2
141 Old Sarum 12 D2
142 Old Wardour Castle 12 B3
143 Over Bridge 20 C1
144 Pendennis Castle 3 G6
145 Penhallam 8 C6
146 Porth Hellick Down Burial Chamber 2 P2
147 Portland Castle 6 A7
148 Ratfyn Barrows 12 D1
149 Restormel Castle 7 K3
150 Royal Citadel 4 E4
151 St Breock Downs Monolith 3 H2
152 St Briavel's Castle 19 K2
153 St Catherine's Castle 3 K4
154 St Catherine's Chapel 11 G7
155 St Mary's Church 31 H6
156 St Mawes Castle 3 G6
157 The Sanctuary 20 F6
158 Sherborne Old Castle 11 H4
159 Silbury Hill 20 F6
160 Sir Bevil Grenville's Monument 20 B5
161 Stanton Drew Circles and Cove 19 L6
162 Stonehenge 12 D1
163 Stoney Littleton Long Barrow 20 B7
164 Temple Church 19 K5
165 Tintagel Castle 8 A7
166 Totnes Castle 5 H3
167 Tregiffian Burial Chamber 2 C7
168 Trethevy Quoit 4 C3
169 Uley Long Barrow (Hetty Pegler's Tump) 20 B2
170 Upper Plym Valley 4 F3
171 West Kennet Avenue 20 F5
172 West Kennet Long Barrow 20 F6
173 Windmill Hill 20 E6
174 Winterbourne Poor Lot Barrows 11 G6
175 Woodhenge 12 D1
176 Yarn Market 10 A1

Eastern Region

177 Audley End House and Park 35 J6
178 Baconsthorpe Castle 47 G3
179 Berkhamsted Castle 22 E2
180 Berney Arms Windmill 47 K6
181 Binham Priory 46 E3
182 Binham Wayside Cross 46 E3
183 Blakeney Guildhall 46 F2
184 Burgh Castle 47 K6
185 Bury St Edmunds Abbey 36 D3
186 Bushmead Priory 34 E3
187 Caister Roman Site 47 L5
188 Castle Acre Castle 46 D5
189 Castle Acre Priory 46 D5
190 Castle Acre: Bailey Gate 46 D5
191 Castle Rising Castle 46 B4
192 Church of the Holy Sepulchre 36 D1
193 Cow Tower 47 H6
194 Creake Abbey 46 D3
195 De Grey Mausoleum 34 D6
196 Denny Abbey 35 H3
197 Duxford Chapel 35 H5
198 Framlingham Castle 37 H3
199 Grime's Graves 36 D1
200 Hadleigh Castle 24 E4
201 Hill Hall 23 K3
202 Houghton House 34 D6
203 Isleham Priory Church 35 J3
204 Landguard Fort 37 H6
205 Leiston Abbey 37 K3
206 Lexden Earthworks and Bluebottle Grove 36 E7
207 Longthorpe Tower 44 E7
208 Mistley Towers 37 G6
209 Moulton Packhorse Bridge 36 B3
210 North Elmham Chapel 46 E4
211 Old Gorhambury House 23 G2
212 Orford Castle 37 K5
213 Prior's Hall Barn 35 J6
214 Row 111 House, Old Merchant's House and Greyfriars' Cloisters 47 L6
215 St Albans Roman Wall 23 G2
216 St Botolph's Priory 36 F7
217 St James's Chapel 36 E5
218 St John's Abbey Gate 36 F7
219 St Olave's Priory 47 K7
220 Saxtead Green Post Mill 37 H3
221 Thetford Priory 36 D1
222 Thetford Warren Lodge 36 D1
223 Tilbury Fort 24 C5
224 Waltham Abbey Gatehouse and Bridge 23 J2
225 Weeting Castle 36 C1
226 Wrest Park Gardens 34 D6

East Midlands

227 Arbor Low Stone Circle and Gib Hill Barrow 52 D7
228 Ashby de la Zouch Castle 43 F5
229 Bolingbroke Castle 55 H7
230 Bolsover Castle 53 G6
231 Chichele College 34 C3
232 Eleanor Cross 34 B1
233 Gainsborough Old Hall 54 C5
234 Geddington, Eleanor Cross Hardwick Old Hall 53 G7
235 Hob Hurst's House 52 E7
236 Jewry Wall 43 H6
237 Kirby Hall 44 C7
238 Kirby Muxloe Castle 43 H6
239 Leicester Jewry Wall Lincoln Bishop's Old Palace 54 D6
240 Lyddington Bede House 44 B7
241 Mattersey Priory 53 K5
242 Nine Ladies Stone Circle 52 E7
243 Peveril Castle 52 D5
244 Rufford Abbey 53 J7
245 Rushton Triangular Lodge 34 B1
246 Sibsey Trader Windmill 45 G1
247 Sutton Scarsdale Hall 53 G7
248 Tattershall College 45 F1
249 Wingfield Manor 43 F1

West Midlands

250 Acton Burnell Castle 41 G6
251 Arthur's Stone 30 E5
252 Boscobel House and the Royal Oak 42 A6
253 Buildwas Abbey 41 H6
254 Cantlop Bridge 41 G6
255 Clun Castle 30 D1
256 Croxden Abbey 42 C3
257 Edvin Loach Old Church 31 H4
258 Goodrich Castle 31 G7
259 Halesowen Abbey 32 B1
260 Haughmond Abbey 41 G5
261 Iron Bridge 41 H6
262 Kenilworth Castle 32 E2
263 Langley Chapel 41 G6
264 Leigh Court Barn 31 J4
265 Lilleshall Abbey 41 J5
266 Longtown Castle 30 E7
267 Mitchell's Fold Stone Circle 30 E1
268 Moreton Corbet Castle 41 G4
269 Mortimer's Cross Water Mill 31 F3
270 Old Oswestry Hill Fort 40 D3
271 Rotherwas Chapel 31 G6
272 Stokesay Castle 31 F1
273 Wall Roman Site (Letocetum) 42 D6
274 Wenlock Priory 41 H6
275 White Ladies Priory 42 A6
276 Wigmore Castle 31 F3
277 Witley Court 31 J3
278 Wroxeter Roman City 41 G6

Yorkshire and The Humber

279 Aldborough Roman Town 59 K4
280 Brodsworth Hall 53 H3
281 Burton Agnes Manor House 61 H4
282 Byland Abbey 59 L3
283 Clifford's Tower 60 D5
284 Conisbrough Castle 53 H4
285 Easby Abbey 66 B7
286 Gainsthorpe Medieval Village 54 D3
287 Helmsley Castle 60 D2
288 Howden Minster 60 E8
289 Kirkham Priory 60 E4
290 Marmion Tower 59 H3
291 Middleham Castle 59 G2
292 Monk Bretton Priory 53 F3
293 Mount Grace Priory 66 E8
294 Pickering Castle 60 F2
295 Piercebridge Roman Bridge 66 C6
296 Richmond Castle 66 B7
297 Rievaulx Abbey 60 C2
298 Roche Abbey 53 H5
299 St Mary's Church 59 H4
300 St Peter's Church 54 E1
301 Scarborough Castle 61 H2
302 Skipsea Castle 61 J5
303 Spofforth Castle 59 J5
304 Stanwick Iron Age Fortifications 66 B6
305 Steeton Hall Gateway 60 B7
306 Thornton Abbey and Gatehouse 54 F2
307 Wharram Percy Deserted Medieval Village 60 F4
308 Wheeldale Roman Road 67 J8
309 Whitby Abbey 67 K6

North West

310 Ambleside Roman Fort 63 J7
311 Arthur's Round Table 64 C5
312 Baguley Hall 51 H4
313 Beeston Castle 50 E8
314 Bow Bridge 57 F3
315 Brough Castle 64 E6
316 Brougham Castle 64 C5
317 Carlisle Castle 63 J2
318 Castlerigg Stone Circle 63 J5
319 Chester Castle: Agricola Tower and Castle Walls 50 D7
320 Chester Roman Amphitheatre 50 D7
321 Clifton Hall 64 C5
322 Countess Pillar 63 L5
323 Furness Abbey 57 F3
324 Goodshaw Chapel 51 H1
325 Hadrian's Wall 64 E1
326 Banks East Turret
327 Benwell Roman Temple
328 Benwell Vallum Crossing
329 Birdoswald Fort
330 Black Carts Turret
331 Brunton Turret
332 Cawfields Roman Wall
333 Chesters Bridge
334 Chesters Roman Fort
335 Corbridge Roman Site
336 Denton Hall Turret
337 Hare Hill
338 Harrow's Scar Milecastle
339 Heddon-on-the-Wall
340 Housesteads Roman Fort
341 Leahill Turret and Piper Sike Turret
342 Pike Hill Signal Tower
343 Planetrees Roman Wall
344 Poltross Burn Milecastle
345 Sewingshields Wall
346 Temple of Mithras, Carrawburgh
347 Vindolanda Fort
348 Walltown Crags
349 Willowford Wall, Turrets and Bridge
350 Winshields Wall
351 Hardknott Roman Fort 63 H7
352 Lanercost Priory 64 C1
353 Mayburgh Earthwork 64 C5
354 Penrith Castle 64 C5
355 Piel Castle 57 F4
356 Ravenglass Roman Bath 56 D1
357 Salley Abbey 58 C6
358 Sandbach Crosses 51 G7
359 Shap Abbey 64 C6
360 Stott Park Bobbin Mill 57 G2
361 Warton Old Rectory 57 H3
362 Wetheral Priory Gatehouse 63 K2
363 Whalley Abbey Gatehouse 58 C7

North East

364 Auckland Castle Deer House 66 C4
365 Aydon Castle 65 H1
366 Barnard Castle 65 H6
367 Belsay Hall, Castle and Gardens 75 G7
368 Berwick-upon-Tweed Barracks 83 H6
369 Berwick-upon-Tweed Castle 83 J6
370 Berwick-upon-Tweed Main Guard 83 H6
371 Berwick-upon-Tweed Ramparts 83 H6
372 Bessie Surtees House 66 C1
373 Bishop Auckland Deer House Black Middens Bastle House 74 D6
374 Bowes Castle 65 G6
375 Brinkburn Priory 75 H5
376 Derwentcote Steel Furnace 66 B2
377 Dunstanburgh Castle 75 J2
378 Edlingham Castle 75 H4
379 Egglestone Abbey 65 H6
380 Etal Castle 83 H8
381 Finchale Priory 66 C3
382 Gisborough Priory 67 G6
383 Hylton Castle 66 D2
384 Lindisfarne Priory 83 K7
385 Norham Castle 83 H7
386 Prudhoe Castle 65 H1
387 St Paul's Monastery and Bede's World Museum 66 D1
388 Tynemouth Priory and Castle 75 K8
389 Warkworth Castle and Hermitage 75 J4

National Trust

South West

SW1 A la Ronde 5 L1
SW2 Antony 4 E4
SW3 Arlington Court 9 G1
SW4 Avebury 20 E6
SW5 Avebury Manor and Garden 20 E6
SW6 Barrington Court 10 E4
SW7 Bradley 5 J2
SW8 Brownsea Island 12 C7
SW9 Buckland Abbey 4 E3
SW10 Castle Drogo 9 H6
SW11 Clevedon Court 19 J5
SW12 Clouds Hill 12 A6
SW13 Coleridge Cottage 10 C2
SW14 Coleton Fishacre House and Garden 5 K4
SW15 Compton Castle 5 J3
SW16 Corfe Castle 6 D6
SW17 Cornish Mines and Engines 2 E5
SW18 Cotehele 4 E3
SW19 The Courts Garden 20 C6
SW20 Dunster Castle 10 A1
SW21 Dunster Working Water-Mill 10 A1
SW22 Dyrham Park 20 B5
SW23 Finch Foundry 9 G6
SW24 Glendurgan Garden 2 F7
SW25 Great Chalfield Manor 20 C6
SW26 Hardy's Cottage 11 J6
SW27 Killerton 10 A6
SW28 Kingston Lacy 12 B5
SW29 Knightshayes Court 9 K4
SW30 Lacock Abbey 20 D6
SW31 Lanhydrock 3 J3
SW32 The Levant Steam Engine 2 B6
SW33 Lundy Island 8 B1
SW34 Lydford Gorge 8 F7
SW35 Lytes Cary Manor 11 G3
SW36 Max Gate 11 H6
SW37 Mompesson House 12 D3
SW38 Montacute House 11 F4
SW39 Newhall Equestrian Centre 9 K5
SW40 Overbecks 5 H6
SW41 Prior Park Landscape 20 B6
SW42 St Michael's Mount 2 D6
SW43 Saltram 4 F4
SW44 Shute Barton 10 D6
SW45 Stembridge Tower Mill 11 F2
SW46 Stourhead 11 J2
SW47 Tintagel Old Post Office 8 A7
SW48 Tintinhull Garden 11 G4
SW49 Treasurer's House 11 F4
SW50 Trelissick Garden 3 G6
SW51 Trengwainton 2 C6
SW52 Trerice 3 G4
SW53 Watersmeet House 9 H1
SW54 Westbury Court Garden 20 B1
SW55 Westwood Manor 20 C7

South East

SE1 Alfriston Clergy House 15 J5
SE2 Ascott 34 B7
SE3 Ashridge Estate 22 E1
SE4 Basildon Park 22 B5
SE5 Bateman's 16 D3
SE6 Bembridge Windmill 7 L6
SE7 Bodiam Castle 16 E3
SE8 Chartwell 23 K7
SE9 Clandon Park 22 F7
SE10 Claremont Landscape Garden 23 G6
SE11 Claydon House 33 K7
SE12 Cliveden 22 E4
SE13 Dapdune Wharf 14 C1
SE14 Emmetts Garden 23 K7
SE15 Gateway to the White Cliffs 17 L1
SE16 Hatchlands Park 22 F7
SE17 Hinton Ampner Garden 13 H3
SE18 Hughenden Manor 22 D3
SE19 Ightham Mote 24 B7
SE20 Knole 23 L7
SE21 Lamb House 17 G3
SE22 Monk's House 15 H5
SE23 Mottisfont Abbey Garden, House and Estate 13 F3
SE24 The Needles Old Battery 7 H6
SE25 Nymans Garden 15 F3
SE26 Oakhurst Cottage 14 C2
SE27 Old Town Hall, Newtown 7 J5
SE28 Owletts 24 C6
SE29 Petworth House and Park 14 C3
SE30 Polesden Lacey 23 G7
SE31 Princes Risborough Manor House 22 D2
SE32 Quebec House 23 K7
SE33 Runnymede 22 F5
SE34 St John's Jerusalem 23 L5
SE35 Sandham Memorial Chapel 21 J6
SE36 Scotney Castle Garden 16 D2
SE37 Shaw's Corner 23 G1
SE38 Sheffield Park Garden 15 H3
SE39 Sissinghurst Castle Garden 16 F2
SE40 Smallhythe Place 17 F2
SE41 Sprivers Garden 16 D2
SE42 Standen 15 G2
SE43 Stoneacre 24 D7
SE44 Stowe Landscape Garden 33 J6
SE45 Uppark 14 A4
SE46 The Vyne 22 B7
SE47 Waddesdon Manor 22 C1
SE48 Wakehurst Place 15 G2
SE49 West Wycombe Park 22 D3
SE50 West Wycombe Village and Hill 22 D3
SE51 Winkworth Arboretum 14 C1

London

L1 Blewcoat School Gift Shop 23 H5
L2 Carlyle's House 23 H5
L3 Fenton House 23 H4
L4 George Inn 23 J5
L5 Ham House 23 G5
L6 Morden Hall Park 23 H6
L7 Osterley Park 23 G5
L8 Rainham Hall 23 L4
L9 Sutton House 23 J4

East

E1 Anglesey Abbey 35 J3
E2 Belton House 44 C3
E3 Blickling Hall 47 G4
E4 Bourne Mill 36 F7
E5 Coggeshall Grange Barn 36 D7
E6 Felbrigg Hall Garden and Park 47 H3
E7 Flatford: Bridge Cottage 36 F6
E8 Gunby Hall 55 J7
E9 Houghton Mill 35 F2
E10 Ickworth House, Park 36 D3
E11 Lavenham: The Guildhall of Corpus Christi 36 E5
E12 Melford Hall 36 D5
E13 Oxburgh Hall 46 C6
E14 Paycocke's 36 D7
E15 Peckover House 45 H6
E16 Sheringham Park 47 G2
E17 Tattershall Castle 45 F1
E18 Theatre Royal 36 D3
E19 Wicken Fen National Nature Reserve 35 J2
E20 Wimpole Hall and Wimpole Home Farm 35 G4
E21 Woolsthorpe Manor 44 C4

Central

C1 Ashdown House 21 G4
C2 Attingham Park 41 G5
C3 Baddesley Clinton 32 D2
C4 Benthall Hall 41 H6
C5 Berrington Hall 31 G3
C6 Biddulph Grange Garden 42 A1
C7 Bredon Barn 32 B6
C8 Buscot Park 21 G3
C9 Calke Abbey 43 F4
C10 Canons Ashby House 33 H4
C11 Charlecote House 32 E4
C12 Chedworth Roman Villa 20 E1
C13 Clumber Park 53 J6
C14 Coughton Court 32 C3
C15 Croft Castle 31 F3
C16 Croome Landscape Park 32 A5
C17 Dudmaston 31 J1
C18 Farnborough Hall 33 G5
C19 The Fleece Inn 32 C5
C20 Great Coxwell Barn 21 G3
C21 The Greyfriars 32 A4
C22 Greys Court 22 C4
C23 Hanbury Hall 32 B3
C24 Hardwick Hall 53 G7
C25 Hidcote Manor Garden 32 D5
C26 Kedleston Hall 43 F3
C27 Lower Brockhampton 31 H4
C28 Lyveden New Bield 34 C1
C29 Moseley Old Hall 42 B6
C30 Mr Straw's House 53 H6
C31 Packwood House 32 D2
C32 Shugborough Estate 42 B4
C33 Snowshill Manor 32 C6
C34 Staunton Harold Church 43 F4
C35 Sudbury Hall 42 D3
C36 Upton House 33 F5
C37 The Weir 31 F5
C38 Wightwick Manor 42 A7
C39 Woodchester Park 20 C2

North West

NW1 Acorn Bank Garden and Water-Mill 64 D5
NW2 Beatrix Potter Gallery 63 A8
NW3 Dunham Massey 51 G5
NW4 Fell Foot Park 57 G2
NW5 Gawthorpe Hall 58 D7
NW6 Gondola 57 G1
NW7 Hill Top 57 G1
NW8 Little Moreton Hall 51 H8
NW9 Lyme Park 51 J5
NW10 Quarry Bank Mill 51 H5
NW11 Rufford Old Hall 50 D2
NW12 Sizergh Castle 57 H2
NW13 Speke Hall 50 D5
NW14 Tatton Park 51 G5
NW15 Townend 63 K7
NW16 Wordsworth House 63 G4

North East

NE1 Beningbrough Hall 60 C5
NE2 Cherryburn 65 H1
NE3 Cragside House, Gardens and Estate 75 G4
NE4 East Riddlesden Hall 59 F6
NE5 Farne Islands 83 L8
NE6 Fountains Abbey and Studley Royal Water Garden 59 H4
NE7 George Stephenson's Birthplace 65 J1
NE8 Gibside 66 B2
NE9 Lindisfarne Castle 83 K7
NE10 Nostell Priory 53 F2
NE11 Nunnington Hall 60 D3
NE12 Ormesby Hall 67 F6
NE13 Rievaulx Terrace and Temples 60 C2
NE14 Souter Lighthouse 66 E1
NE15 Treasurer's House 60 D5
NE16 Wallington 75 G6
NE17 Washington Old Hall 66 D2

Wales

W1 Aberconwy House 49 G3
W2 Aberdulais Falls 18 B3
W3 Bodnant Garden 49 H3
W4 Chirk Castle 40 D3
W5 Colby Woodland Garden 26 F6
W6 Conwy Suspension Bridge 49 G3
W7 Dinefwr Park 27 L4
W8 Dolaucothi Gold Mines 27 L2
W9 Erddig 40 E2
W10 Llanerchaeron 28 B3
W11 Penrhyn Castle 48 F3
W12 Plas Newydd 48 E4
W13 Plas Yn Rhiw 38 B4
W14 Powis Castle 40 D6
W15 Tudor Merchant's House 26 F6
W16 Ty Mawr Wybrnant 39 G1
W17 Ty'n-y-coed uchaf 39 G1

Boundary information

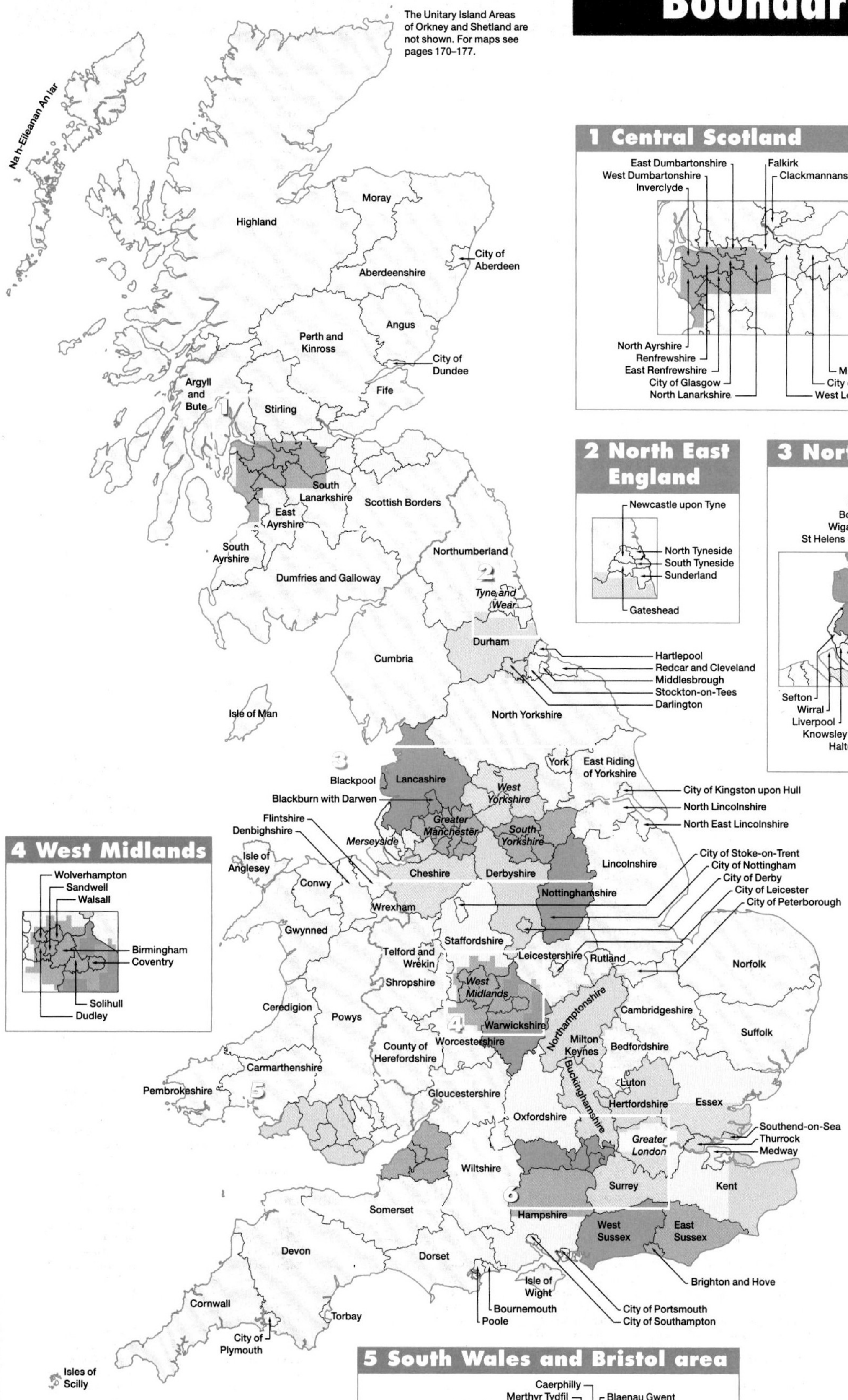

The Unitary Island Areas of Orkney and Shetland are not shown. For maps see pages 170–177.

Key

Thurrock County, Unitary Authority or Unitary Island Area name

Merseyside metropolitan area name

The coloured areas on the map correspond to the coverage of Ordnance Survey Street Atlases.

Main map labels

Na h-Eileanan An Iar
Highland
Moray
Aberdeenshire
City of Aberdeen
Angus
Perth and Kinross
City of Dundee
Fife
Argyll and Bute
Stirling
South Lanarkshire
East Ayrshire
Scottish Borders
South Ayrshire
Dumfries and Galloway
Northumberland
Tyne and Wear
Durham
Cumbria
Isle of Man
North Yorkshire
York
East Riding of Yorkshire
Blackpool
Lancashire
West Yorkshire
Blackburn with Darwen
Greater Manchester
South Yorkshire
Flintshire
Denbighshire
Merseyside
Isle of Anglesey
Conwy
Cheshire
Derbyshire
Lincolnshire
City of Kingston upon Hull
North Lincolnshire
North East Lincolnshire
Gwynned
Wrexham
Nottinghamshire
City of Stoke-on-Trent
City of Nottingham
City of Derby
City of Leicester
City of Peterborough
Ceredigion
Powys
Telford and Wrekin
Shropshire
Staffordshire
West Midlands
Leicestershire
Rutland
Norfolk
Warwickshire
Northamptonshire
Cambridgeshire
Carmarthenshire
County of Herefordshire
Worcestershire
Milton Keynes
Bedfordshire
Suffolk
Pembrokeshire
Gloucestershire
Oxfordshire
Buckinghamshire
Luton
Hertfordshire
Essex
Greater London
Southend-on-Sea
Thurrock
Medway
Wiltshire
Surrey
Kent
Somerset
Hampshire
West Sussex
East Sussex
Devon
Dorset
Isle of Wight
Brighton and Hove
Cornwall
Torbay
City of Portsmouth
City of Southampton
Bournemouth
Poole
City of Plymouth
Isles of Scilly

1 Central Scotland

East Dumbartonshire
West Dumbartonshire
Inverclyde
Falkirk
Clackmannanshire
North Ayrshire
Renfrewshire
East Renfrewshire
City of Glasgow
North Lanarkshire
East Lothian
Midlothian
City of Edinburgh
West Lothian

2 North East England

Newcastle upon Tyne
North Tyneside
South Tyneside
Sunderland
Gateshead
Hartlepool
Redcar and Cleveland
Middlesbrough
Stockton-on-Tees
Darlington

3 Northern England

Rochdale
Bury
Salford
Bolton
Wigan
St Helens
Calderdale
Bradford
Kirklees
Leeds
Wakefield
Doncaster
Barnsley
Rotherham
Sheffield
Sefton
Wirral
Liverpool
Knowsley
Halton
Oldham
Tameside
Stockport
Manchester
Trafford
Warrington

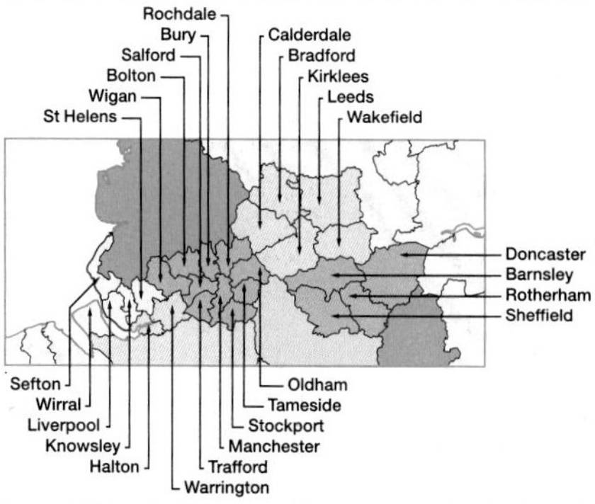

4 West Midlands

Wolverhampton
Sandwell
Walsall
Birmingham
Coventry
Solihull
Dudley

5 South Wales and Bristol area

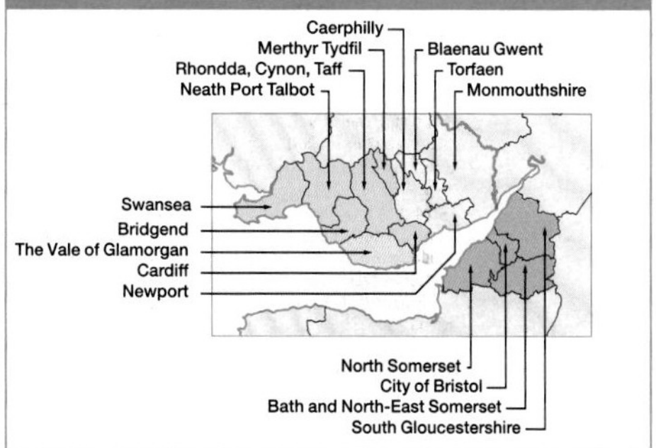

Caerphilly
Merthyr Tydfil
Rhondda, Cynon, Taff
Neath Port Talbot
Blaenau Gwent
Torfaen
Monmouthshire
Swansea
Bridgend
The Vale of Glamorgan
Cardiff
Newport
North Somerset
City of Bristol
Bath and North-East Somerset
South Gloucestershire

6 Thames Valley

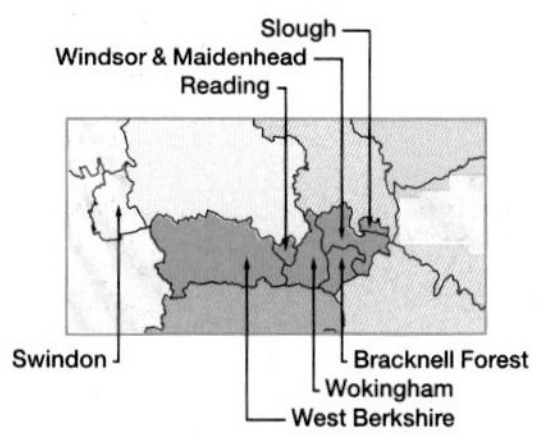

Slough
Windsor & Maidenhead
Reading
Swindon
Bracknell Forest
Wokingham
West Berkshire

Greater London

Hertfordshire
Essex
Surrey
Kent

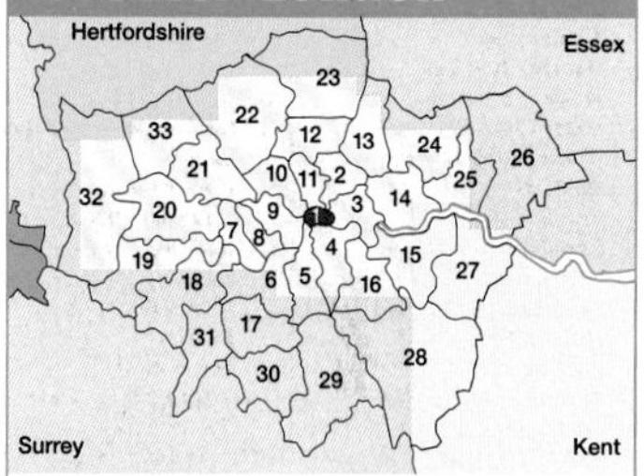

1 City and County of the City of London
2 Hackney
3 Tower Hamlets
4 Southwark
5 Lambeth
6 Wandsworth
7 Hammersmith and Fulham
8 Royal Borough of Kensington and Chelsea
9 City of Westminster
10 Camden
11 Islington
12 Haringey
13 Waltham Forest
14 Newham
15 Greenwich
16 Lewisham
17 Merton
18 Richmond upon Thames
19 Hounslow
20 Ealing
21 Brent
22 Barnet
23 Enfield
24 Redbridge
25 Barking and Dagenham
26 Havering
27 Bexley
28 Bromley
29 Croydon
30 Sutton
31 Kingston upon Thames
32 Hillingdon
33 Harrow

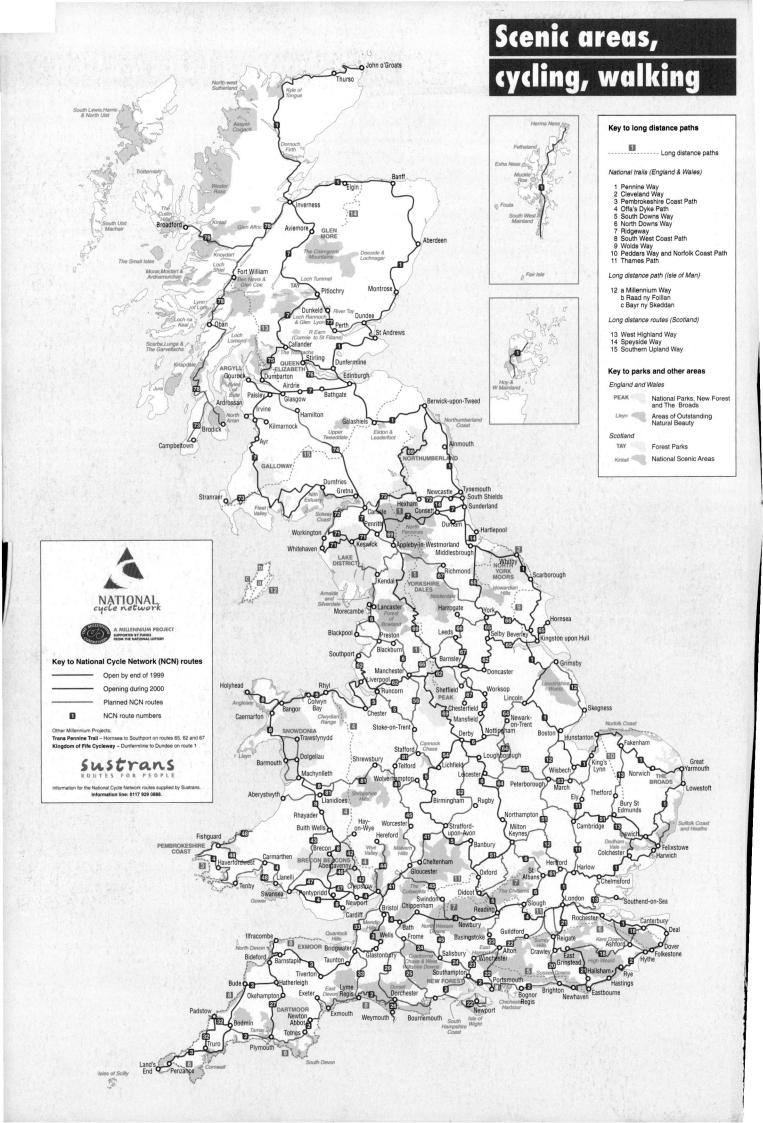